Hopewell Friends History

1734-1934

Frederick County, Virginia

RECORDS OF HOPEWELL MONTHLY MEETINGS
AND
MEETINGS REPORTING TO HOPEWELL

Two Hundred Years of
History and Genealogy

Compiled from Official Records by a
Joint Committee of Hopewell Friends

Assisted by
John W. Wayland

HERITAGE BOOKS
2007

HERITAGE BOOKS

AN IMPRINT OF HERITAGE BOOKS, INC.

Books, CDs, and more—Worldwide

For our listing of thousands of titles see our website
at
www.HeritageBooks.com

A Facsimile Reprint
Published 2007 by
HERITAGE BOOKS, INC.
Publishing Division
65 East Main Street
Westminster, Maryland 21157-5026

International Standard Book Number: 978-0-7884-0858-8

Hopewell Meeting House
1934
Looking Northeast

DEDICATION

TO THE EARLY FRIENDS, OUR
PIONEER ANCESTORS, STAUNCH STAND-
ARD-BEARERS OF TRUTH, WHO CON-
SCIENTIOUSLY HELD TO THEIR HIGH
IDEALS OF RIGHT LIVING, SETTING
BEFORE US EXAMPLES OF INTEGRITY
OF CHARACTER AND LOVE OF HUMAN-
ITY WHICH WE HUMBLY HOPE TO
EMULATE, THAT THEIR STANDARDS
MAY CONTINUE TO BE UPHELD AND
PASSED ON TO POSTERITY, THIS BOOK
IS DEDICATED WITH PROFOUND REV-
ERENCE BY THOSE OF US WHOSE PRIVI-
LEGE IT HAS BEEN TO DELVE INTO
THE RECORDS AND GLIMPSE THE
ACTIVITIES OF THOSE PAST GENERA-
TIONS.

CONTENTS

PART ONE

HISTORICAL

PART TWO

DOCUMENTARY

(Items from the records of Burlington, Haddonfield, and Chesterfield, relating to Hopewell, are incorporated in the Index.)

PART THREE

INDEX

MAPS AND ILLUSTRATIONS

PART ONE

HISTORICAL

The Quaker of the Olden Time

The Quaker of the olden time!—
　How calm and firm and true!
Unspotted by its wrong and crime
　He walked the dark earth through!
The lust of power, the love of gain,
　The thousand lures of sin
Around him, had no power to stain
　The purity within.

With that deep insight, which detects
　All great things in the small,
And knows how each man's life affects
　The spiritual life of all,
He walked by faith and not by sight,
　By love and not by law;—
The presence of the wrong or right,
　He rather felt than saw.

He felt that wrong with wrong partakes,
　That nothing stands alone,
That whoso gives the motive, makes
　His brother's sin his own.
And pausing not for doubtful choice
　Of evils great or small,
He listened to that inward voice
　Which called away from all.

Oh, spirit of that early day!
　So pure and strong and true,
Be with us in the narrow way
　Our faithful fathers knew.
Give strength the evil to forsake,
　The cross of Truth to bear,
And love and reverent fear to make
　Our daily lives a prayer!

J. G. Whittier

CHAPTER I

INTRODUCTION

As the date of the 200th anniversary of the "setting up" of Hopewell Friends' Meeting approached, Friends generally felt that the occasion was of sufficient historical interest to justify commemorative exercises as well as a printed record of the outstanding facts relating to the founding of the meeting and the individual men and women composing the same.

As early as 1930 preliminary steps were taken to procure a bronze tablet inscribed with a brief statement of facts and dates. This tablet, placed on a large limestone boulder taken from the meeting-house lot at Hopewell and erected at Clearbrook on U. S. Highway No. 11, makes an appropriate memorial monument. The spot occupied by this monument is at the entrance to Hopewell from the main highway between Winchester and Martinsburg, and the inscription is as follows:

HOPEWELL

FRIENDS MEETING HOUSE

ONE MILE WEST

MEETING ESTABLISHED 1734

SINCE WHICH TIME

REGULAR RELIGIOUS SERVICES

HAVE BEEN HELD

ERECTED 1934

Early in 1933 the Hicksite and the Orthodox Monthly Meetings of Hopewell Friends each appointed a committee, making a joint committee of eighteen, to commemorate the 200th anniversary by erecting the marker just described, by arranging suitable exercises, and by publishing in permanent form a record of our history. It was expected at first to have the anniversary celebration in the autumn of 1934, but that was soon found impossible. Another full year was necessary to complete the work of research and compilation and to publish the historical volume which is herewith presented.

A wealth of materials was found. All available Hopewell records have been gone over with painstaking care, with the result that countless items of historical significance and genealogical value have been assembled. The records of Hopewell Meeting have been supplemented from many other reliable sources in Virginia, North Carolina, Maryland, and Pennsylvania. From the archives in Richmond, Baltimore, and Philadelphia have been reproduced several rare documents and records. In the Handley Library in Winchester have been found various publications of service. Numerous individuals, Friends and others, have generously loaned important books and documents. Old letters and diaries in certain cases have proved useful in rounding out other sources of information.

The committee has been confronted with an abundance of sources of positive record. The most difficult task has been one of selection. From first to last every effort has been exerted to avoid errors and to present the matter of this volume in accurate and usable form. All quotations follow the spelling, capitals or lack of capitals, wording, and punctuation as they appear in the originals.

Inasmuch as certain words and terms may not be familiar to persons unaccustomed to the usage in Friends' literature, especially that of several generations past, a number of words and phrases that frequently appear are explained in this connection.

"In the room of"—in the place of, instead of.

"They appeared"—the appointed representatives were present.

"Under dealings"—members who have violated the rules of discipline to the extent that the meeting desires an investigation of the offense and appoints a committee to have an opportunity with the said members (or member), are thus designated.

"Opportunity with"—a personal interview with a purpose to ascertain facts or give wholesome admonition.

"Out going"—going out, for example, in marriage— marrying a person not a member of Friends. This was usually deemed sufficient ground for disownment unless the offender gave satisfaction.

"Satisfaction"—persons offending or failing to live up to the rules of discipline were under dealings by the monthly or business meeting, but might give satisfaction by signing a written statement that they had come to a "sight" and "sense" of their offenses and had experienced a true repentance. That the individual might do this was in all cases the desire of the meeting.

"Testimony against"—persons under dealings of the meeting who would not give the committee appointed to interview them satisfaction were testified against; that is, the committee would make a written statement concerning the matter. This report, after receiving the approval of the business meeting, was read at the close of a First-Day meeting.

"Laid down"—discontinued; used especially in reference to a meeting which was discontinued by permission (authority) of the superior meeting.

"Solid"—a term that was often used in Friends' records, signifying that the subject under consideration has been deliberated upon earnestly, prayerfully, and at length.

"Close season"—used in expressing an occasion or meeting in which a spiritual unity prevails.

MEETINGS

Meeting for worship—the term is self-explanatory. Such a meeting was not authorized to transact business.

Preparative meeting—a business meeting to digest information and prepare matters of business, as occasion may require, which may be proper to lay before the monthly meeting.

Monthly meeting—primarily a business meeting, invested with the care and oversight of the membership within its verge. A monthly meeting has a clerk and keeps records.

Quarterly meeting—a business meeting of higher rank, including several monthly meetings, meeting every three months, sometimes at the same place from time to time, sometimes alternating or circulating between two or more places.

Yearly meeting—an annual meeting of business and oversight which receives reports of the activities of all the monthly meetings under its authority, through the several quarterly meetings, summarizes, tabulates, and annually prints its proceedings. These are distributed to all the families of the Yearly Meeting.

Particular meeting—another term for a preparative meeting.

Select meeting—a meeting of ministers and elders (counselors), held under the authority of a monthly meeting.

Indulged meeting—a meeting, usually for worship only, granted by a monthly meeting to a group of Friends within its verge who were unable because of distance, bad weather, or bad roads to attend the regular meetings, to hold religious services in their own neighborhood, in a home or some other place.

Preparative meetings are accountable to the monthly meeting, monthly meetings to the quarterly meeting, and quarterly meetings to the yearly meeting. The monthly meeting is the typical or standard meeting for business and discipline.

Circular meetings are religious gatherings requested by a monthly meeting and approved by the quarterly meeting, held at one place in the forenoon and at another place in the afternoon of the same day. Sometimes a circular meeting was a monthly meeting which was held one month in one location and the next month at another place.

The Orthodox branch of Friends are united under the Five Years Meeting. The several yearly meetings of the Hicksite branch are brought together biennially in a group known as the Friends' General Conference.

There are also other meetings of considerable size and importance which do not report to any of the larger groups and are known as *independent meetings.*

Meeting for Sufferings. In 1778 the Baltimore Yearly Meeting provided a general committee, composed of representatives from the several subordinate meetings, to act for the Yearly Meeting when the latter was not in session. Accordingly, the powers of this committee were large and its duties comprehensive. In 1780 it was changed to the "Representative Committee," and again in 1913 to the "Executive Committee."

OFFICERS

Ministers and *elders* are charged with preaching and the spiritual life of the meeting. The elders especially are to help those who exercise profitably in the ministry, and restrain those who are inclined to speak without edification, running into words without life and power; and to endeavor always to show forth the fruits of the doctrine which they deliver to others, being examples to their brethren in word and deed. They may be men or women.

Overseers have care and direction of the temporal interests and business affairs of the meeting, preparing answers to queries, giving advice to those members who may be under dealing, and preventing the introduction of unnecessary matters and premature complaints into meetings for business and discipline.

Trustees are persons appointed by the meeting and confirmed by the court to hold title to properties.

The *clerk* presides at a meeting for business or discipline, formulates conclusions and decisions, and after the same are read by him and approved by the meeting writes them down as minutes in the record.

Epistles, or letters of good will and encouragement, are exchanged annually between nearly all of the yearly meetings of Friends in the world.

"Priest." This term is occasionally found in references to marriages outside of Friends' meetings, but it is not to be understood as referring necessarily to a member of the Catholic clergy. More frequently, perhaps, the "priest" referred to was an Anglican clergyman, and sometimes, it may be, a minister of some other Protestant denomination. As a matter of fact, there were very few Catholic priests in the Shenandoah Valley in early times.

Hopewell Friends' Meeting, having its beginnings in 1734, antedated the courts and records of Frederick County, Virginia, by nine years, all public business in the interval being transacted at Orange Court House, east of the Blue Ridge; and after 1743, when courts for Frederick County were established at Winchester, very few marriages of Friends or others were entered upon the county records for many years. Friends' marriages, as a rule, were not regularly reported to the county clerks or recorded by them until 1825 or thereabouts. Accordingly, early marriages at Hopewell and other

Friends' meetings in the lower Shenandoah Valley and adjacent regions are usually to be found only in Friends' records.

A special feature of this volume which was not at first contemplated, but which has justified itself as a natural and almost necessary development, is the geographical and historical directory—the extended list, with amplifications, of the many Friends' meetings in various quarters with which Hopewell had relations. Some of these meetings are not now in existence, and their locations in some cases are not known to the present generation.

The fact, moreover, that in a number of instances several different meetings, often widely separated by distance, bore the same name, presents difficulties to the casual reader and calls for explanation. The presentation of these names of meetings, both those that are now extinct and those that are still active, in alphabetical order, with various facts of interest concerning them, will, it is believed, prove of great convenience to the reader as well as of considerable value to the student of Friends' history.

The committee feels justified in calling special attention to the index at the end of the book. In a work such as this, in which occur thousands of names, a complete index is essential. Much time and labor have been expended upon this one, and it is, we believe, complete. We trust that it will be found reliable and that it will enable our readers to use this work with pleasure and increasing interest.

HOPEWELL ANNIVERSARY COMMITTEE

Walker McClun Bond, *Chairman*	Caroline Damon Lupton, *Secretary*
John William Jolliffe, *Treasurer*	Lewis Pidgeon
Susan Talbot Pidgeon	David Arthur Robinson
Annie Jackson Rees	Grace Edgerton Clevenger
Edith Maria Jolliffe	Sallie Gertrude Robinson
Joseph Lupton Jolliffe	Mary Anna Whitmore
Gladys Virginia Cochran	Albert Garrigues Robinson
Rebecca Russell Pidgeon	Virginia Noel Lupton
Daniel Walker Lupton	Howell McPherson Bond

[Daniel W. Lupton died June 19, 1935.]

The Anniversary Committee wish to take this opportunity to make special mention of the most valuable assistance rendered by Richard E. Griffith, Sr., who has been a constant attender at the meetings of the committee, has assisted in gathering materials from distant places, has been ever helpful in obtaining historical facts and assembling the same, and has written several of the chapters comprising this history.

We make grateful acknowledgment to all of the following:

Allen, Anna, Winchester, Virginia
and
Allen, Florence, Winchester, Virginia.
(Many days of searching records and securing notes which contribute to the chapters and statistical records throughout this book)

Atwell, Ruth, Winchester, Virginia
(Typing)

Baker, Julian Wright, Winchester, Virginia
(Helpful encouragement and numerous favors)

Chiles, C. M., Strasburg, Virginia
(Gave stone for base of monument erected at Clearbrook)

Crawford, Frank B., Winchester, Virginia
(Personal assistance in many ways)

Eddy, C. Vernon, Librarian, Handley Library, Winchester, Virginia
(Cordial interest and assistance)

Engle, James G., Clarksboro, New Jersey
(Loaned several helpful books)

Fawcett, Thomas H., Cheyney, Pennsylvania
(Supplied valuable materials)

Fothergill, Augusta B. Middleton, 1011 Grace Street, Richmond, Virginia
(Offered access to her files and gave information in correspondence)

Haworth, J. R., Huntington, West Virginia
(Supplied materials of family record)

Haworth, Lindley Murray, Clackamas, Oregon
(Offered help—gave information by correspondence)

Hayes, Dr. J. Russell, Librarian, Historical Section, Swarthmore College Library, Pennsylvania
(Searching meeting records)

Henkel, Dr. A. D., Winchester, Virginia
(Encouragement and personal information)

Hinshaw, William Wade, Mayflower Hotel, Washington, D. C.
(Supplied data during period for which Hopewell's minute books are missing)

Hull, Dr. William I., Swarthmore College, Swarthmore, Pennsylvania
(Important aid in locating book of reference)

Kelley, Dr. John A., Haverford College, Haverford, Pennsylvania
(Collecting data)

Lewis, Herbert S., 86 Eastern Avenue, Takoma Park, Maryland
  (Supplied data regarding meeting locations)

Library, Friends' Historical, Swarthmore College, Pennsylvania
  (Loaned book)

Library, The Handley, Winchester, Virginia
  (Storing Friends' Record Books when not in use—Access to old records)

Longshore, Marian, Langhorne, Pennsylvania
  (Searched records of Middletown Monthly Meeting, Pa.)

Louthan, Henry T., Duane, King William County, Virginia
  (Gave information and also offered pictures of Carters and Neills)

Lupton, Dorothy T., Winchester, Virginia
  (Typing)

Marine, Harriet P. (Genealogist), Druid Station, Box 40, Baltimore, Maryland
  (Much research work concerning the early history of Hopewell and Friends in Virginia—personal interview)

Marshall, Thomas W., 1341 Connecticut Avenue, Washington, D. C.
  (Supplied some missing data during period Hopewell's minute books are missing)

Musser, C. S., Shepherdstown, West Virginia
  (Collecting data)

Milbourne, Mrs. V. S., Charles Town, West Virginia
  (Information and data pertaining to Berkeley Meeting and Graveyard)

Nottingham Monthly Meeting (Melvin E. Reynolds, Clerk), Oxford, Pennsylvania
  (Gave permission to remove their record books from the vault to have photostatic copies made of the minutes, "setting up" Hopewell Meeting)

Oaks, Phylis, Winchester, Virginia
  (Typing)

O'Rear, Mrs. Silver, Clearbrook, Virginia
  (Many days securing records of importance and work upon this data)

Orndorff, Pearl J., Clearbrook, Virginia
  (Typing and other valuable work)

Palmer, Elizabeth, Newtown, Pennsylvania
  (Searched records of Wrightstown Meeting)

Pennsylvania Railroad
  (Land for Monument on Route 11 at Clearbrook, Virginia)

Ruebush, Joseph K., Dayton, Virginia
  (Loaned valuable books)

Scarborough, Henry W., 650 Real Estate Trust Bldg., Philadelphia, Pa.
  (Sent a great deal of information regarding families)

Sencindiver, Lucille, Winchester, Virginia
  (Typing)

Shaw, M. Emma, 140 S. Main Street, Quakertown, Pennsylvania
(List of removals from old records of Richland Monthly Meeting, Bucks County, Pa.)

Shoemaker, Cornelia, Lincoln, Virginia
(Loaned a valuable map and gave information about meetings in Loudoun County, Va.)

Smith, Anna W., 448 Washington Avenue, Newtown, Pennsylvania
(Searched records of Buckingham Meeting)

Smith, C. Arthur, Wycomb, Pennsylvania
(Certificates of removal from Wrightstown Meeting to "opecan in vergeny")

Star, Ella (Librarian), Friends' Historical Library, Park Avenue and Laurens Street, Baltimore, Md.
(Gave much time in assisting the committee to obtain minute books)

Virginia Historical Society, Richmond, Virginia
(Photostat copies of order in Council to Ross & Bryan—access to record books)

Virginia Land Office, Richmond, Virginia
(Aid in finding old land grants)

Whitmore, Phylis, Bunker Hill, West Virginia
(Typing)

Sincere thanks and grateful appreciation are hereby tendered also to the press, to the men and women who have accepted places on the anniversary programs, to the sponsors of this volume, and to all others who have in any way contributed to this publication, including the many far and near who have given cordial encouragement to the undertaking.

CHAPTER II

THE FATHERS OF THE COLONY

In the State Land Office at Richmond are to be found recorded in Book 16, pages 315-415, inclusive, the patents issued to the settlers who came to the Shenandoah Valley under authority of the Orders in Council made to Alexander Ross and Morgan Bryan. All bear date of November 12, 1735, and recite that the grantee is one of the seventy families brought in by them, and excepting location and acreage, are alike in wording and conditions, and are signed by William Gooch, Lieutenant-Governor of the Colony at that time. As an example, the patent issued to Isaac Perkins, or Parkins, is cited:

George the Second, by the Grace of God, of Great Britain, France and Ireland, King, Defender of the Faith, etc.,

To All Whom these Presents may come: GREETING,

Know Ye, that for divers good Causes and Considerations but more especially for the consideration mentioned in an Order of Our Lieut-Governor and Council of our Colony and Dominion of Virginia, bearing date the three and twentieth day of April One Thousand Seven Hundred and thirty-five, Granting leave to Alexander Ross and Morgan Bryan to survey in such manner as they should think fit, one thousand acres of land for each family of seventy families by them brought in to Our said Colony and settled upon the lands in the said Order mentioned and to sue out patents for the same; We have given Granted and confirmed and by the Presents do give Grant and confirm unto Isaac Perkins one certain tract or parcel of Land containing Seven Hundred and twenty-five acres and bounded as followeth: To wit: BEGINNING at a red oak on the West side of a Branch that runs into Opeckon next below the Branch which John Calvert lives on, and running thence with [*sic*] eighty West one hundred and three poles to a red oak, thence North twenty five degrees West one hundred and twenty poles to a white oak, thence North twenty eight degrees West one hundred and forty two poles to a red oak, thence north thirty eight degrees West sixty two poles to a red oak, thence north-west one hundred and twenty poles to a hickory, thence North forty degrees West eighty three poles to a hickory, thence North fifty degrees East eighty three poles crossing a small meadow to a red oak, thence south thirty six degrees East eighty poles, thence South sixty two degrees East one hundred poles to a hickory and red oak, thence South seventy five degrees East thirty seven poles, thence North fifteen degrees East one hundred poles, thence south seventy five degrees East forty four poles, thence South fifteen degrees East one hundred poles, thence South-east one hundred poles to a small hickory, thence South nine degrees East sixty seven poles to a Spanish oak, thence South twenty five degrees East thirty one poles to a hickory, thence South thirty degrees East seventy four poles to a white oak, thence South sixty six degrees East sixty six poles to a crooked red oak, thence North eleven degrees East one hundred and nine poles to a hickory, thence, South forty degrees East one hundred and twenty two poles to a red oak, thence South twenty degrees West sixty two poles to a red oak thense South fifty five degrees East sixty one poles to a red oak, thence south East fifty four poles to a white oak by a meadow, thence south west crossing the same forty poles to a hickory, thence north sixty eight degrees West one hundred and sixty poles to the Beginning; with all woods, underwood, swamps, marshes, low grounds, meadows, feedings, and his due shsare of all veins, mines and quarries, as well discovered as not discovered, within the bounds aforesaid and being part of the said quantity of seven hundred and twenty five acres of Land, and the rivers, waters, and water courses therein contained, together with the privilege of Hunting, Hawking, Fishing, Fowling, and all other profits, commodities and Hereditaments whatsoever to the same or any part thereof belonging or anywise appertaining. To Have and To Hold, possess and enjoy the said tract or parcel of Land and all other the before Granted premises and every part thereof, with their and every of their appurtenances, unto the said Isaac Perkins his heirs and assigns forever, to the only use and behoof of him, the said Isaac Perkins his heirs and assign forever. To be held for Us Our Heirs and Successors as of our Manor of East Greenwich in the County of Kent, in fee and Common Soccage, and not in Capite or by Knight Service; Yielding and paying unto Us, our Heirs and Successors, for every fifty acres of Land, the fee rent of one shilling yearly, to be paid upon the Feast of Saint Michael the Archangel, and also cultivating and improving three acres part of fifty of the tract above mentioned, within three years after the date of these presents. Provided always, that if three years of the said fee rent shall at any time be in arrears and unpaid, or if the said Isaac Perkins, his heirs or assigns do not within the speace of three years next coming, after the date of these presents Cultivate and improve three acres part of every fifty of the tract above mentioned, then the estate, cease and be utterly determined, and thereafter it shall, and may be, lawful to and for Us, Our Heirs, and Successors, to Grant the same Lands and appurtenances unto such other person or persons, as We, Our Heirs and Successors, shall think fit. In Witness whereof, We have caused, these Our letters patent to be made. Witness Our trusty and well beloved William Gooch, Esq., Our Lieut. Governor & Commander in Chief of Our said Colony and Dominion at Williamsburg, under the Seal of said Colony, the twelfth day of Novr. one thousand seven hundred and thirty five, in the ninth year of Our Reign.

WILLIAM GOOCH.

It will be noted that the land is held under the ancient English tenure of free soccage, and not in capite or by knight service, and was considered a part of the Manor of East Greenwich, in the County of Kent. These patents were issued under the seal of the colony and were grants from the Crown, free of any obligation of feudal services to the Fairfax family, who claimed the land as lords proprietors of the Northern Neck of Virginia. The sixth Lord Fairfax, who later established his home at Greenway Court near Winchester, instituted many suits against early settlers in the Shenandoah Valley, but it does not appear that any Friend who claimed under Ross and Bryan was ever ejected from his land.

Although it is specifically stated that seventy families have been "by them brought in to our said Colony and settled upon the Lands in the said Order mentioned," only thirty-six patents issued to thirty-four grantees have been found. The names of these grantees are here given, together with sundry information gathered from the minutes of various Friends' meetings, from the records of the counties of Orange and Frederick in Virginia, and Chester County, Pennsylvania.

Alexander Ross, 2373 acres in what is now Frederick County, lying six miles north of Winchester. On this tract Hopewell Meeting House stands, on land set aside by Ross for that purpose, and near by he established his home, where he was living at the time of his death in 1748. Of the ancestry and early life of Alexander Ross much has been written, based upon tradition and unsupported by recorded evidence, but the recent investigations of Thomas Hays Fawcett of the court records of Chester County, Pennsylvania, supply the most authentic record of his life, so far discovered. Mr. Fawcett says:

"Alexander Ross of Pennsylvania and Virginia was probably of Scotch-Irish descent and was born about 1682. He was brought to Pennsylvania as an indentured servant when about eleven years old. The following is from the record of the Court of Common Pleas, Chester County, Pennsylvania, 1681-1697:

The boys that Mauris Trent brought in to this country were called to be judged by the Court. Caleb Puseys boy, Alexander Ross, adjudged by the Court to be eleven years of age and to serve to the age of one and twenty and to have the custom of the country and be discharged from his servitude by the said Caleb Pusye.

"Caleb Pusey of Chester, a last-maker by trade, had a mill and was a prominent member of the community. Alexander Ross acquired the trade of a joiner. His term of service would have been up in 1703. Early in 1706 he married Katherine Chambers of Chichester. About the year 1709 he bought a lot in Chester and built a house on it, which he sold to George Simcock of Chester for 112 pounds. (Chester Co. Deeds, Book C P 126.) In 1713 he removed to Radnor and bought a tract of 150 acres in Whitland Township. He secured a warrant dated 9th month 5th, 1714, from the Commissioners of Property for the survey of 500 acres of land, for which he agreed to pay 50 pounds and a quit rent of one shilling per 100 acres. This was surveyed in the neighborhood of Nottingham Township on Conowingo Creek, April 20, 1716. He moved his certificate to Newark Monthly Meeting 9th month 8th, 1716. When New Garden Monthly Meeting was set off from Newark Monthly Meeting in 1718, he fell within the limits of that meeting. New Garden Monthly Meeting was divided and the first monthly meeting was held at Nottingham 4th month 20th, 1730. Almost at once he appears in the Nottingham Minute Book:

6th month 15th, 1730, Alexander Ross and others appointed to labor with Samuel White,

and very frequently thereafter, until the establishment of Hopewell Monthly Meeting in 1735."

Tracings of the signatures of this Alexander Ross of Nottingham, and Alexander Ross of Virginia, are apparently identical, and evidently were written by the same man.

The records of Orange County, Va., show that during the period Ross's land lay within its bounds, 1734-1743, he sold but two tracts from his original 2373 acres. The first one, recorded in Deed Book 2, page 465, is from Alexander Ross and Catherine his wife of Orange County, Colony of Virginia, to John Nickline of the same place, for 396 acres, being part of his patent of November 12, 1735. This deed bears date of August 21, 1738, and is witnessed by James Wright and Arthur Barrett. The second conveyance, recorded in Deed

Book 5, page 149, is from Alexander Ross of Orange County, Colony of Virginia, Yeoman, to John Ross of the same place, Yeoman, and is for 220 acres, part of the same tract. The deed is witnessed by James Wood, William Glover, and Isaac Parkins. The Frederick County records show but one conveyance &, (Deed Book 1, page 75), and that is to Joseph Bryan, son of his partner Morgan Bryan, to whom he sells 214 acres on April 13, 1744. No other sales appear in the records, and as he bought no additional land, he could hardly be considered a speculator in land, as some have claimed.

The will of Alexander Ross is recorded in Frederick County Will Book 1, page 226, is dated the "24th of ye 8th month, 1748," and was probated December 7, 1748. He therefore died some time after August 24, and before December 7, 1748, aged about 66 years. His will was witnessed by James Wright Senr., Robert Hutchings, and Lydia Barrett, and makes bequests to his wife Catherine, his sons David, John, and George, and his daughters Mary Litler, Albena Thomas, Lydia Day, and Catherine Ross, and requests that his slaves not be sold, but retained in the family.

Some epidemic was doubtless raging in the community at that time, as his sons David and John, his son-in-law John Littler, his wife Catherine, and several of his neighbors died within a few weeks.

His home plantation came into the possession of the heirs of his daughter Mary Littler, and from them by marriage to the Stribling family, who sold it to Maj. Burwell B. Washington. Maj. Washington's descendants held the property until a few years ago, when it was sold to a member of Hopewell Meeting, Mr. William Robinson, and it is now owned by his heirs.

Morgan Bryan, 2134 acres in four separate tracts. The tract on which he made his home lies in what is now Berkeley County, West Virginia, northwest of the village of Bunker Hill, along Mills' Creek.

Morgan Bryan is said to have been born in Ireland, and to have married in Chester County, Pa., Margaret Strode about 1725, but of these statements there seems to be no definite proof, other than family tradition. He was taxed in Chester

ALEXANDER ROSS HOMESTEAD, NEAR HOPEWELL.
Later Washington, now Robinson Home

County, Birmingham Township, in 1719, and in Marlborough Township in 1720, 1721, 1722, and 1726. He does not appear to have been a Friend, and his association with Alexander Ross before their venture in Virginia is unknown. On July 26, 27, 1738, as shown in the Orange County records, he sold to Daniel Chancey 264 acres of land known as Flat Springs, near the head of Tuscarora, a branch of Opeckon. The witnesses were George Taylor, Edward Herndon Jr., and Wm. McDonaugh.

Morgan Bryan's wife died in Virginia in 1748, after which date he sold the remainder of his land and moved southward, stopping for a period in what is now Rockingham County, and then proceeding to the Forks of the Yadkin River in North Carolina. At this place his granddaughter, Rebecca, daughter of his son Joseph, married Daniel Boone. The father of Daniel Boone had removed from the verge of Exeter Monthly Meeting, where the birth of Daniel Boone was recorded, to the Shenandoah Valley, sojourning there for several years. Squire Boone and Sarah Morgan, father and mother of Daniel Boone, were married at Gwynned Monthly Meeting in 1725, and during their stay in Virginia were probably members of Hopewell Monthly Meeting, but as the minutes covering this period were burned there is no record of their membership.

Morgan Bryan was quite active in the county affairs of Orange and Frederick, and appears frequently in the records of both, as overseer of various roads, serving on juries, appraising estates, etc., and is said to have been the first man to take a wagon through Cumberland Gap in southwest Virginia. He was prominent in his new home in the Yadkin Valley. He died on the Yadkin in 1793 at his home, which was called "The Point," and was buried there. His wife Margaret and son Joseph had died before he left Virginia. The Frederick County records show that on August 4, 1747, William Jolliffe was appointed administrator of Joseph Bryan's estate, and gave bond with Alexander Ross, James Wood, and John Littler as sureties.

Morgan Bryan and his wife had altogether ten children, most of whom were living in 1749 with their father on the

Yadkin River. One son had settled in Rockingham County, Va.

John Willson, 286 acres, lying in what is now Berkeley County, West Virginia.

Thomas Curtis, 418 acres, probably in what is now Berkeley County, W. Va. The Orange County (Va.) records show that Mary Curtiss was appointed administratrix of the estate of Thomas Curtiss July 23, 1741, with Morgan Bryan and Joseph Bryan as bondsmen. The will of Mary Curtiss was probated in Orange County, February 25, 1742. She makes bequests to her daughter Mary Curtiss, and mentions her father Morgan Bryan and her mother Martha [sic] Bryan. Her brother Joseph Bryan is named as executor.

The tax lists of Orange County for the year 1739 contain the name of Thomas Curtis.

Nathaniel Thomas, 850 acres. This land is described as being "at the head of the South Branch of Opeckon," and lies along the eastern foot of Little North Mountain. In 1747 Nathaniel Thomas sold 200 acres of this land to Nathaniel Cartmell, "Beginning at Joist Hite's corner," and "adjoining Cartmell's other land." Martin Cartmell, Wm. Glover, and Joseph Lupton were the witnesses.

The will of Nathaniel Thomas was probated March 1, 1763. He makes bequests to Ann, daughter of Morgan ap Morgan, to his sons Isaac and Jonathan, and to his daughters Catherine Emery, Rachel, Elizabeth, and Mary Thomas. The executors named are Robert Harper and Thomas Hart. Witnesses, Mary Magnus, Perrygren MackNess, William McKee, and John Smith.

Isaac Parkins, 1425 acres, in three separate tracts. His home plantation of 725 acres lay just south of, and partly within, the present corporate limits of the City of Winchester. The remaining two tracts lie about five miles northwest of Winchester. The records of Orange County, Va., show that in 1739 he sold part of this last-mentioned land to "William Hogg, the Younger," who settled thereon, and gave his name to the stream now known as Hogue Creek. When the new county of Frederick was erected in 1743 Isaac Parkins became very prominent in the conduct of its affairs. He served many years as a justice, a captain of militia, and a vestryman. He was elected to the House of Burgesses, representing Frederick County in the sessions of 1754 and 1755. He used his influence to ameliorate the sufferings of Friends caused by the laws governing those dissenting in religious opinions from the Established Church, and the court orders of Frederick County show that he repeatedly secured the release of persons "imprisoned for conscience sake," and was active in their defence. In 1751 he presented to the Frederick County Court a petition asking that the vestry for Frederick Parish be dissolved, charging misappropriation of funds. In the following February, 1752, the General Assembly passed an act charging the vestry for Frederick Parish with oppressive and corrupt practices, and ordering its dissolution and the election of a new vestry. Along with two other Friends, James Cromley and Lewis Neill, Isaac Parkins was elected to this new vestry, and served for many years.

After the settlement in 1749 in the Shenandoah Valley of Lord Fairfax, with whom Isaac Parkins was on very friendly terms, he secured from Fairfax several additional grants for lands in the Northern Neck, lying in the counties of Frederick and Hampshire. He maintained on his plantation a sawmill and two flour mills, probably the first erected in Frederick County. The journals and diaries of travelling Friends, ministers, and others, frequently mention visiting his home. At his house took place the first marriage in the Shenandoah Valley of Friends. On "Ye 19th day of December in ye Year of Our Lord 1734, Appeared in a Public Assembly of ye said People and others mett at ye house of Isaac Parkins of ye afsd. Place in Virginia, and ye sd. George Hollingsworth taking ye sd. Hannah McKoy by the hand," etc. Meetings for worship were frequently held in his house, and were continued there after his death by his son Isaac Parkins Jr. These meetings resulted in the setting up of Center Meeting, for which Isaac Parkins Jr. provided a lot of land, on which was a meeting house used until Center Meeting was moved about 1819 into Winchester. The graveyard adjoining Center Meeting was deeded to Hopewell Monthly Meeting as a gift from Isaac Parkins Jr. It may be seen to-day at the southwest border of the city, on the west side of the Valley Pike.

The home of Isaac Parkins Sr. passed through marriage and purchase to Isaac Hollingsworth who married his granddaughter, Hannah Parkins, and who erected in 1836, on the site of the old home, the present brick mansion. Isaac Hollingsworth also built near by a four-story stone flour mill, for many years regarded as the finest in the Shenandoah Valley, which survived the Civil War only to be destroyed by an incendiary some twenty-odd years ago. This ancient plantation was called "Milltown" and remained in the possession of the descendants of Isaac Parkins until 1881, when, after passing rapidly through several hands, it was purchased by Mr. Andrew Hack of Baltimore, whose descendants now own it.

On this same tract, about one-half mile east of the mansion-house, is the burying-ground of the Parkins and Hollingsworth families, which was devised to Hopewell Monthly Meeting in 1815 by will of John Parkins, for the use of Friends as a burying-ground.

John Hiatt Jr., 300 acres. No further information of certain character concerning this man appears, though various persons by the name of Hiatt (Hiett) were in the Shenandoah Valley and adjacent sections at later periods. At Hopewell, February 4, 1748, Ja. MaGrew and Jno. Hiatt were appointed to enquire into Richd. Merchant's claims to a certificate of removal to North Carolina or elsewhere. This John Hiatt was probably the John Hiatt Jr. of 1735. On February 28, 1782, Samuel Brockman Jr., Richard C. Webb, and William Thomas returned to the Orange County court an appraisement of the personal estate of John Hiatt, deceased. In 1795 Jonathan Hiatt and wife Mary, with others, of Fayette County, Ky., sold land on Terry's Run in Orange County, Va. It is not known that these Hiatts of later Orange were connected with the Hiatts of the Valley.

Thomas Anderson, 542 acres. This land lies on Mills' Creek, and on it Thomas Anderson made his home and built a mill. In his will, probated March 2, 1747, he leaves this home and mill to his son James Anderson. He provides for his wife Jane and his son Calvert Anderson. He makes bequests to Patrick Rily and William Mitchell, and his daughter Mary Yeats, who he states is a widow. His wife Jane and son James are to execute the will. The witnesses were Murty Hanty, John Cunningham, and Denish Sullivance.

John Mills Jr., 408 acres, in Berkeley County, now West Virginia, adjoining, or near to, his father's patent on Mills' Creek. In the Frederick County records may be found a deed, recorded March 9, 1743/4, from John Mills Jr., of Opekon in Frederick County, Colony of Virginia, Cordwainer, to John Beals of the same place, Farmer, for 165 acres, being a part of this patent of 408 acres.

John Peteate and George Robinson, 1650 acres lying "on both sides of Tuscarorror Branch" in Berkeley County, West Virginia, being about two miles west of Martinsburg. This property passed in 1737 into the hands of the Beeson family. On the 27th of the 1st month, 1736, Richard Beeson Sr. and his wife Charity requested a certificate of removal from New Garden Monthly Meeting to Hopewell. At that time they were living in Leacock Township, Chester County, Pa., and their son Richard Beeson Jr., with his wife, formerly Ann Brown, was living in West Nottingham, Chester County. They must have immediately removed to the Shenandoah Valley, as John Fothergill states in his journal that he had a meeting at Richard Beeson's 9th month 18th, 1736. Upon the property of Richard Beeson Sr. was Providence Meeting, which was perhaps nearly as old as Hopewell. Some writers have said that it was organized in 1733 at Richard Beeson's house in that year. This is probably incorrect, as he did not remove to Virginia until the winter of 1735-1736.

The will of Richard Beeson Jr. was probated November 1, 1748, and provides for his wife Ann, his sons Messer and Richard, and his daughters Charity Thornbrough and Hannah Beeson. In disposing of his land he excepts nine acres "adjoining the Meeting-house for the use of the sd. Meeting-house." This land remained in the Beeson family until 1776, when it was sold by Richard Beeson to William Patterson, and in this sale the meeting-house tract was likewise reserved.

In addition to the aforementioned patent for 1650 acres, John Peteate on the same day secured another patent for an additional 500 acres of land, on Middle Creek, in what is now Berkeley County, W. Va. He sold this land October 4, 1748, to Peter Sechan.

Robert Luna, 294 acres, on the south bank of the Potomac River.   On June 13, 1766, Robert Looney signed a power of attorney empowering James Jack of Frederick County to sell for him a certain tract of 294 acres described as patent land granted him November 12, 1735, by authority of an order in council made to Alexander Ross and Morgan Bryan.   It is stated in this instrument that Robert Looney was then a resident of Augusta County, Virginia.   Witnesses, Wm. Thompson, David Looney, Thomas Jefferson, Peter Hogg, G. Jones. On November 4, 1766, Robert Looney of Augusta County, by his attorney James Jack, sold to Jeremiah Jack of Frederick County this same 294 acres.   The property is described as being on the Potomac River and adjoining Samuel Owens.

John Richards, 500 acres.   This land lies on the south side of Cedar Creek, "beginning at John Branson's corner," etc.   John Richards was born at Budleigh, Devonshire, England, and probably came to this country about 1718.   He was taxed, 1720-26, in Tredyffrin Township, Chester County, Pa. His will was probated in Frederick County, Va., August 2, 1757, and refers to his brothers Peter and Henry and his sister Hannah as residents of England, and devises his property under certain conditions to his nieces and nephews, provided they would come to America.   His nephew Henry, son of his brother Peter, came to this country and possessed the property, under the will.   John's wife Ann waived any claim against the estate.   Joseph Lupton Sr. and Joseph Lupton Jr. were named executors.   The witnesses were Charles Parkins, Richard Hiland, and John Lupton.   From John Richards' nephew Henry Richards is descended the Richards family of southwest Frederick County, Va.

Giles Chapman, 400 acres joining John Littler and "Beginning near the head of Yorkshireman's Branch."   On August 31, 1744, Giles Chapman sold 150 acres of this land to Ulrich Ruble, and on June 3, 1744, Giles Chapman and Sarah his wife sold the remaining 250 acres of this tract to James Cromley.   Witnesses to this last-mentioned deed were John Littler, James Carter, John Frost, and W. Rannells.

James Brown, 121 acres.   The metes and bounds of this patent show it to have been on the Potomac River, and that it adjoined the lands of one Williams.   The will of James

Brown, probated September 2, 1767, mentions his brother Hugh, his sister Eleanor, and her daughter Agnes. He leaves to the four sons (not named) of his brother Samuel a certain bond due him from William Neivill; makes a bequest to Agnes, daughter of his brother Samuel; makes bequest to his sister Agnes and her three children (not named). Hugh Brown and David Vance Jr. were to be executors. They entered into bond with John Allen and Robert Beckett as sureties.

Luke Emlen, 125 acres. Nothing further has been certainly learned of this grantee.

Francis Tencher, 150 acres on Middle Creek in Berkeley County, now West Virginia. In Orange County, Va., deed book 1, pages 384, 386, appear lease and release of November 18 and 19, 1736:

"ffrancis Pincher of Orange County and Sarah his wife to John Van Metre of same in con. of twenty pounds for tract lying on Opecken Creek on the West Side of Sharundo river containing one hundred acres granted by patent to said ffrancis Pincher November 12, 1735, beginning at a white oak on the West side of Opeck Creek and running thence up the several courses of the same 346 poles agt. an island in the said run," . . . Signed with his mark. Witnesses: James Porteus, Charles Stevens, Thos Postgate, John Bramham. Proved November 25, 1736, on oaths of James Porteus, Charles Stephens, and John Braham.

Cornelius Cockerine, 172 acres in what is now Berkeley County, W. Va., near the mouth of Opequon Creek. The records of Orange County, Va., show that Elisha Parkins purchased this land from Cockerine in 1737. Part of the tract lay upon the Potomac River.

Cornelius Cockerine lived in Chester County, Pa., before coming to Virginia, owned property in Fallowfield and Sadsbury townships in that county, and was taxed there, where some of the name still reside. In Virginia the name is now spelled Cochran.

Josiah Ballinger, 500 acres. This land lies on Apple Pie Ridge, north of Winchester, and remained in the Ballinger family until about 1800, when it was purchased by Lt.-Col.

Meredith Helm. After Colonel Helm's death in 1811 his widow Frances and son Strother Helm sold it to Robert Gray of Winchester, and it was the residence of Gray's son, Dr. Joseph Glass Gray, for many years. A few years before the Civil War it was purchased by William Hiatt, a member of Hopewell Monthly Meeting, and is now in the possession of his descendants.

Josiah Ballinger died sometime prior to December 7, 1748, when his will was probated. He leaves 100 acres adjoining Thomas Babb to his son James upon his coming of age, being part of his home plantation. To James Wright Sr., whom he calls his father-in-law, he leaves half of his plantation. To his son Josiah, named as eldest son, he leaves the remainder of his plantation with the house, after the decease of his wife, Mary. He makes a bequest to his daughter Sarah, and names his wife Mary executrix. Witnesses, James Wright Sr., John Williams, and Rachell Clifton. Sureties on the bond of the executrix were James Wright Sr. and Evan Thomas Jr.

Josiah Ballinger was born in Burlington County, New Jersey, son of Henry Ballinger, and married Mary, daughter of James Wright Sr., of Nottingham, Chester County, Pa., 6th mo., 31st, 1727. His brother Henry Ballinger had married Hannah Wright, sister of Mary, the preceding year. In 1725 the Ballingers were living in the Monocacy Valley in what is now Frederick County, Md., and Josiah and his father and brother were prominent in the affairs of the Friends' meeting there. Josiah appears to have been intimately associated with Alexander Ross in promoting the Friends' settlement in the Shenandoah Valley, and later became possessed of large tracts of land other than the one above mentioned.

The column of Braddock's army commanded by Colonel Dunbar reached the "Widow Ballinger's" on May 3, 1755, at 3 p. m. "The Seaman's Journal," in the entry for this day, says in part, "this day was so excessively hot that several Officers and many men could not get on till the evening, but the body got to their ground at 3 o'clock. This is 5 miles from Winchester, a fine station if properly cleared." The column commanded by Sir Peter Halkett also passed this way, and the nurse, Mrs. Brown, following in a few weeks, spent the day with the Widow Ballinger, and speaks gratefully of the entertainment and care given her.

William Hogg, 411 acres. This land lies just southwest of the village of Kernstown and about four miles from Winchester. William Hogg, Hoge, or Hogue, as the name was variously spelled, was living in Chester County, Pa., where he was taxed in East Nottingham Township from 1718 to 1730, after which year he removed to Virginia. His first wife was Barbara Hume, who was the mother of all his children. William Hoge died before August 8, 1749. On that day his will was filed and recorded in the Frederick County clerk's office, but was not probated. His widow, Mary Hoge, declined accepting the provisions thereof, and claimed her dower. The land came into the possession of the Rev. John Hoge, the heir-at-law, he being the eldest son of his father John, who in turn was the eldest son of William. On this land stands the old Opequon Presbyterian Church, organized by the Rev. James Anderson in 1737, and which, except for one or two short periods, has served that denomination to this day. In 1745 William Hoge conveyed to the trustees of this church two acres for a burying ground, but did not as frequently stated, donate the church lot, which was purchased in 1795 by the trustees from Adam Kern and Christina, his wife, who at that time owned most of this old patent.

On the site of the original home of William Hoge stands the large mansion house, now the home of Mrs. Hardy Grim, and which was built about 1850 by Stephen Pritchard, whose family owned the tract for many years. In the graveyard west of this house are buried many of the Hoges and Pritchards.

William and Barbara Hoge left many descendants, among whom may be found ministers, college presidents, statesmen, and teachers, many of whom became nationally known. The minute books of Hopewell Monthly Meeting and the Frederick County records make frequent reference to his sons John, William Jr., Alexander, James, and George.

Benjamin Borden, 850 acres. This land lies upon the western slope of Apple Pie Ridge in Frederick County, and 750 acres of the tract were sold by his executors, Benjamin Borden Jr., his son, and Zeruiah Borden, his widow, on February 7, 1744. In this deed the grantee is referred to as

"Benjamin Borden, Gent., late of Orange County, Colony of Virginia, Deceased." Neither Benjamin Borden nor his family ever resided on this tract, which appears to have been one of his many speculations in land. His home plantation, known as "Borden's Great Spring Tract," of 3143 acres, granted him October 3, 1734, joined Greenway Court, the home of Lord Fairfax, on the southeast. Borden's house stood at, or near, the present residence of Thompson Sowers Esq., in Clarke County. He also had a tract of 1122 acres on the Bullskin Marsh near Summit Point, now W. Va., and a large tract on Smith's Creek, near New Market, Shenandoah County, Va. On November 6, 1739, he secured a patent for 92,100 acres on the headwaters of the James River, which became known as Borden's Manor, and lay mostly within the bounds of present Rockbridge County, Va. He appears to have been on intimate terms with Lord Fairfax, and by persistent tradition is generally believed to have acted in some way as Fairfax's agent. That Lord Fairfax purchased from his son John Borden, in 1756, 608 acres of the "Great Spring" tract at the very time he was waging a violent controversy with some settlers who claimed under Crown patents, certainly indicates some friendly arrangement with the Borden family.

Benjamin Borden was born in 1692, a son of Benjamin Borden and —— Grover, near Freehold, N. J., and died in Frederick County, Va., in 1743. He married Zeruiah Winter of West New Jersey, and came to Virginia sometime in 1732. He was prominent in the affairs of the county and was appointed to the first bench of justices on the organization of Orange County in 1734, and of Frederick County, when it was set off from Orange in 1743. He with others was the subject of religious persecution by the Orange court in October and November, 1737. His will, dated April 3, 1742, and probated October 9, 1743, in Frederick County, mentions his wife Zeruiah, his sons Benjamin Jr., John, and Joseph, and his daughters Abigail, wife of Jacob Worthington, Hannah, wife of Capt. Edward Rogers, Mercy, wife of William Fearnley, Rebeckah, wife of Thomas Branson, Elizabeth, wife of —— Branson, and Deborah and Lidy, still single. Witnesses: Thomas Sharp, Lancelot Westcott, Edward O. Borden, Thomas Hankins, and Thomas Rogers.

The religious persecution of his family continued after his death, and the Frederick County records show that on May 7, 1746, the grand jury for that county presented Zeruiah Borden, Deborah Borden, and Mercy Fearnley "for speaking several prophane, scandalous and contemptable words against the Holy Order of Baptism."

John Littler and James Wright, 438 acres, lying on the eastern slope of Apple Pie Ridge, about 5 miles north of Winchester. This tract has latterly been known as "Osceola."

James Wright was taxed in East Nottingham, Chester County, Pa., from 1718 to 1726 inclusive, after which time he probably removed to the Monocacy Valley in what is now Frederick County, Md. He was a distinguished minister of Friends, and with certificates from Hopewell Monthly Meeting travelled widely in the exercise of his ministry. He sustained much loss at the time of the French and Indian War, and with his wife Mary was the object of much concern of the Meeting for Sufferings in Philadelphia, which issued instructions that one-fifth of the money sent at that time for the relief of Friends in the ravaged district "be lay'd out for the Use of our aged Friends James Wright & his Wife." At the same time the clerk of Hopewell Monthly Meeting refers to them as follows: "Also our Antient Friends James Wright and his Wife Are Much Reduced Being driven from their Habitation and are unable to Labour for a Livelyhood."

The will of James Wright was probated March 4, 1764. He leaves to his son Thomas "the Home plantation, being 194 acres of my patent Land." He makes bequests to his sons John, James Jr., and Isaac, and to his daughters Lydia Wright, Mary Ballinger, Hannah Ballinger, Martha Mendenhall, Elizabeth Matthews, Ann McCool, and Sarah Pickering. His wife Mary is named executrix, who entered into bond with Evan Rogers and James Ballinger as bondsmen. The will was witnessed by Evan Rogers, James Ballinger, and Sarah Rogers.

The will of his wife Mary Wright was probated March 6, 1764, and made bequests to her children, leaving the home plantation to her grandson Thomas, his father being dead. Witnesses, Elinor Rogers, Sussannah Bevan, and Elizabeth Pennell. The executors were Jesse Pugh and William Pickering, who entered into bond with James McGin and Joseph Babb as sureties.

John Frost, 380 acres, described as "being above the path that leads from John Littler's to Abraham Hollingworth's." On September 20, 1743, John Frost sold this land to John Millbourne, and to the former description is added "the sd. 380 acres being betwixt John Littler & Hugh Parrell, and being the plantation where John Frost formerly lived." Witnesses to this deed were Alexander Ross, Thomas Wilson, John Littler, and William Jolliffe. It would appear from the records of Frederick County that John Frost owned other lands on Long Marsh in what is now Clarke County, Va., and also lands on Back Creek in Frederick County.

It is not known when John Frost died, but the records of Frederick County show that administration upon the estate of John Chambers was granted to John Frost, with Robert Worthington and Richard Morgan as sureties, on June 18, 1748.

Thomas Dawson, 295 acres, described in the patent as "near William Hogg." This places it near the village of Kernstown and on the southwestern edge of the said village.

On November 25, 26, 1739, Thomas Dawson "of the county of Kent upon Delaware," for £20 5sh., conveyed to Robert Smith of Orange County, Va., 295 acres adjoining the lands of William Hogg; witnesses, Thomas Baylis, George Agger, and Robert Willson. Accordingly, it seems probable that Thomas Dawson did not long reside in Virginia.

Thomas Branson, 850 acres in Frederick County "Beginning at Joist Hite's corner, at the head of a small stream or branch of the Opeckon River."

Thomas Branson was the son of Thomas Branson and Elizabeth his wife, daughter of John Day. Thomas Branson Sr. also had land in the Shenandoah Valley, and by his will, probated Nov. 21, 1744, in Springfield Township, Burlington County, New Jersey, devised it to his sons Thomas and Jacob, and describes it as "my lands on Shannandow River in Virginia which I laid out for Thomas Alexander and one called 'Scotch Robin'." This will was probated in Frederick County, Virginia, March 5, 1744, John and Thomas Branson qualifying as executors with Thomas Hankins and Thomas Sharp sureties. This land was near White Post, but now in Warren County; and near it Thomas Branson Jr. secured a patent in his own name for 1370 acres on both sides of Crooked Run. Near it Jacob Branson, his brother, received by patent in his own name 1000 acres. The will of Thomas Branson Sr. mentions his wife Elizabeth, sons David, Joseph, Jonathan, Lionel, William, Thomas, and John; his daughters Sarah Owin, Mary wife of Zachariah Robins, Elizabeth wife of William Rogers; his granddaughter Abigail Rogers; his grandson Thomas, son of John. Thomas Branson Jr. married Rebecca, daughter of Benjamin Borden, and John married Martha, widow of John Osmond and daughter of Thomas Antrim. William Branson, son of Thomas Sr., removed for a while to Stafford County, Va., and from him are descended the well known Branson family living until recent years near Clearbrook in Frederick County, Va. Lionel, son of Thomas Sr., settled on Lost River in what is now Hardy County, West Va., where some of his descendants reside at this time.

George Hobson, 937 acres on Middle Creek, in what is now Berkeley County, W. Va. On November 2, 1743, George Hobson and Elizabeth his wife made a deed of gift to George Hobson Jr. for 600 acres of this land, surveyed the day before by Alexander Ross. It is stated that the tract joined David Logan and John Mills and lay upon the "drains of Middle Creek," and was then in the possession of Thomas Brown. The witnesses to this deed were Alexander Ross, Morgan ap Morgan, and John Littler. On March 5, 1744, George Hobson Jr. and Hannah his wife conveyed to George Hobson Sr. a certain other part of this patent land, which had been conveyed to them previously.

The will of George Hobson Sr., probated December 6, 1748, leaves his home plantation to his grandsons George and William. He also makes bequests to his son George Jr., grandsons Stephen and Charles, and provides for his wife Elizabeth. She and their son George are made executors. The witnesses were William Geddis, Thomas Byard, and William Jolliffe. The executors gave bond with James Wood and John Chenowith as sureties.

Evan Thomas, 1014 acres. This land joined the plantation of Alexander Ross on the northeast. Evan Thomas came from Wales about the year 1719 and settled in Philadelphia County, Pa., within the verge of Gwynedd Monthly Meeting. In 1726 Evan Thomas and his wife Catherine removed to Goshen Monthly Meeting, and his certificate states that he was a minister. His son, Evan Thomas Jr., married Albenah, daughter of Alexander Ross and Catherine his wife, and was one of the early trustees of Hopewell Monthly Meeting. The will of Evan Thomas was dated "the 18th of the 6th month, called June, 1753," and was probated April 1, 1755. He mentions in his will his sons Evan Jr., John, Thomas, and Enos, and his daughter Martha, and appoints his son John Thomas executor. The witnesses were John Gore, John Bailey, and John Smith.

Evan Thomas was, perhaps, the first minister residing within the verge of Hopewell Monthly Meeting, and his family continued prominent among Friends for many years. The following memorial of Evan Thomas appears in the minute book of Hopewell Monthly Meeting:

He was born in Wales and educated in profession with the Church of England; but in tender years joined in society with friends; and proving faithful to the gift and measure of grace bestowed upon him, by the great giver of every good and perfect gift, he came to be early engaged in the work of the ministry, and was a serviceable instrument; being also a preacher in life and conversation, remarkably meek, humble and grave in his deportment. He was zealous of the honor of God and promotion of his blessed truth, and serviceable among friends, being one of the first settlers in these parts, and a constant attender of our meetings whilst in health. He died in a very serene frame of spirit, on the 4th day of the second month 1755, aged about seventy years.

John Calvert, 850 acres "near Abraham Hollingsworth," being the description in the patent. This land lies east of the village of Kernstown.

The will of John Calvert was probated in Orange County, Va., June 28, 1739, and mentions his wife Jane, his sons Robert, Isaiah, and Richard, his daughter Margaret, and names Rebecca and Ann as his two youngest daughters. He also makes a bequest to his niece Elizabeth Carey. The home plantation fell to his son Isaiah, and his sons Robert and Richard secured grants from Lord Fairfax in their own name, upon Red Bud Creek, in Frederick County.

John Littler, 1332 acres in his own name, and 438 acres in partnership with James Wright. The first-named tract lies five miles north of Winchester, and here John Littler first established his home, on the stream first called Yorkshireman's Branch, and then Littler's Run. In 1728 he married at Nottingham, Chester County, Pa., Mary, daughter of Alexander and Catherine Ross. In 1729/30 John Littler was living in Nottingham, and kept a public house in his dwelling, Alexander Ross being his bondsman. The Chester County Tavern License Papers, Vol. II, No. 60, contain the following petition indicative of John Littler's removal to Virginia:

To the Onerable Cort of qurtersessions to be heald at Chester ye Last tuesday in August for ye sd County 1731.

Your Peticioner humbly Shueth, Whereas John Littler having had a Lisens from this Coart to keep Publick house he now is going Away and your Peticioner Living upon ye same Road Joyning to ye sd Littler having a Mind to Keep Publick house for ye Entertainment of travellers or all Such as Stands in Need your Peticioner humbly Desires yt this Onerable Coart would Greant Me A Lisenes for ye Same which I hope Shall be Preformed with as Good Rule and Order as ye Law derects in Shuch a Case.

And your humbel Peticioner will be very Much ablidgs to this Onorable Coart.

The humbel Peticion of Thomas Hughes.

It is gratifying to know that this labored effort on the part of Thomas Hughes was successful, the petition being granted by the court. John Littler also kept tavern at his new home in Virginia, on the plantation which he named "Rocktown," and also operated thereon a grist mill and sawmill. About 1740 he moved to a tract of land about four miles northeast and established a new home, leaving the old home in the possession of his sons. The new home, where he operated grist mills, sawmills, and carding and fulling mills, he named "New Design." This place eventually became the village of Brucetown, and after his death Mary, his widow, continued to operate his various enterprises until her death in 17—.

John Littler was a man of great energy and enterprise, and amassed what was in his day a very considerable fortune. He frequently appears in the Frederick County records, in various business transactions, and as being by the court intrusted with laying out new roads and altering and improving old ones. His will is dated August 30, 1748, and was probated

December 6, 1748; so he must have died between these dates. He mentions his sons Samuel, John, and Nathan, and also provides for an expected child; makes a bequest to his niece Rachel, daughter of his brother Samuel, and appoints his wife executrix and Joseph Lupton, John Milbourn, and Evan Thomas Junr. executors. Only his wife qualified, with George Ross and Evan Thomas as sureties.

Mary Littler seems to have been a successful business woman, and among other activities operated a tavern, which entertained the officers of General Braddock's army on May 3, 1755. The diary of Mrs. Brown, a nurse with the detachment of sick following Braddock's army, has the following entries for June 7 and 8, 1755:

At 4 we began to march. Left Mr. Falkner behind, who did not choose to March with an empty stomach. Great Gusts of Rain. My Wagon and every thing in it wet, and all the Sick almost drown'd. At 4 we halted at my Friend Laittler's who bid me Wellcome, but had no whiskey which was the Soldier's first enquiry; for they were still in the Opinion that they could not live without it. We now live high, had for Dinner a Qr. of Lamb and a pye, to drink, my Friend's temperate Liquor—Spring Water. I spent the Evening very agreeable; Mr. Falkner favored me with several Tunes on his Flute. Chatted till 10 and then retired.

June 8th—

I slept but poorly, laying on a *deal* Feather Bed. Having had no sleep for 2 Nights did not hear the Drum. We march'd at 4. At 9 we halted at my Friend Bellinger's who bid me wellcome. My Brother set off for Winchester, 8 m off, But Mr. Falkner said he would do himself the Pleasure of staying with Me. We spent the Day very agreeably; had for Dinner some Veal and Greens, to drink french Wine, and for Supper Milk Punch.

Mary Littler left no will, but the appraisement of her personal estate, amounting to 505 pounds, 16 shillings, and 10 pence, a large sum for that time, was made by an order of Frederick County court, November term, 1771. The appraisers were John Rees, Thomas McClunn, and Richard Carter.

The lands of John Littler remained in the possession of his descendants for over 100 years, but passed to other hands when the owners joined the migration to the West. The large stone mansion-house built on the "Rocktown" plantation by Nathan, grandson of John Littler, is one of the show places of Frederick County. Some years ago the name was changed to "Kenilworth" when it was acquired by the Stephenson family. The last home of John Littler, "New Design," with its mills and tavern, has become the village of Brucetown. Nearly on the site of his house stands the residence now occupied by Mr. O. F. Snapp, and known as the "Tanquary House." Littler's Tavern stood a few hundred yards west, on the Braddock Road, and is now the property of the Timberlake estate.

Morgan ap Morgan, 1000 acres on Mills' Creek, in what is now Berkeley County, W. Va. Born in the Principality of Wales in 1688, Morgan ap Morgan was educated in London, and came to Delaware during the reign of Queen Anne and commenced business as a merchant at Christianna. He was a staunch Church of England man and was a vestryman of New Castle County. He was also coroner of the county for the years 1726, 1727, 1728, and 1729. At Christianna he married Catherine Garretson, a native of the place. The last record to be found of Morgan ap Morgan in Delaware is a deed bearing date November 5, 1730, when Morgan ap Morgan, taylor, of Mill Creek Hundred, New Castle County, sells his acre-lot with dwelling thereon to John Harris.

Upon the organization of Orange County, Va., in 1734, Morgan ap Morgan was named in the first commission of the peace, and was sworn justice February 18, 1734. He took the oath as captain of Orange County militia February 17, 1735, and continued active and prominent in the affairs of the county until the organization of Frederick County in October, 1743. He was appointed senior justice of the new county and colonel of militia. About 1740 a chapel of ease was built on his land for the use of the members of the Established Church, for which he was largely responsible, and which is still called "Morgan's Chapel." He died in 1766 and was buried in the graveyard of this chapel. The state of West Virginia has recently repaired the old tombstone and placed another one with suitable inscription at his grave. That state has also erected a monument to Col. Morgan ap Morgan in the nearby village of Bunker Hill, upon which is an inscription, giving the date of his arrival in Virginia as 1726, which is incorrect.

Col. Morgan ap Morgan left a large family of sons and

daughters, whose descendants may be found in the South and West; and in Berkeley County, W. Va., some still reside; Morgan Morgan VIII, in direct descent, being now a resident of Martinsburg, W. Va.

Hugh Parral, 466 acres joining John Calvert, near Kernstown, Frederick County, Va. Hugh Parral had other tracts in Frederick County by patents from Lord Fairfax, and at the time of his death had surveyed and filed claims for additional lands which had not yet been patented to him. His will, probated October 5, 1748, leaves 200 acres to his son Daniel, adjoining Dr. Daniel Hart and John Millbourne. He makes bequests to his sons Joseph and John; leaves 300 acres on the southwest side of Red Bud Creek "to my loving kinsman, John Bruce"; mentions his son Edward, "my daughter Christian" not yet of age, and "my Cousin Robert Calvert." His wife Ann was to have possession of certain property during her life or widowhood. Witnesses, Thomas Wood, James Bruce, Isaiah Calvert, and Richard Calvert. Robert Calvert qualified as executor, with William McMachen and Richard Calvert as sureties.

James Davis, 1175 acres, on Tullis' Run, in what is now Berkeley County, W. Va. The will of James Davis was probated December 7, 1756, and left his home plantation to his son Jacob. He mentions "my eldest son, James Davis Jr.," and his son John; his son Edward was to have certain land joining Peter Hedges; refers to his brother Robert Davis; and appoints as executors "Mr. James Hedges, Gent.," his son James, and his wife Sarah. Witnesses, Samuel Burrows, Isabel Burrows, and John Parks.

Thomas Babb, 600 acres on Babb's Run, in Frederick County, Va. His will was probated November 4, 1760, and left his home plantation to his son Sampson Babb. He made bequests to his sons Philip, Joseph, and Peter, and to his daughter Elizabeth. Witnesses were James Steward and Janet Steward.

Thomas Babb owned property, and was taxed in Bethel Township, Chester County, Pa., in 1730.

Edward Davis, 875 acres on Tullis' Run, in what is now Berkeley County, W. Va.

On April 10, 1738, as shown in the second deed book of Orange County, Va., Davis disposed of this tract of land in three separate parcels:

(1) To Peter Hedges, for £30 5sh., 300 acres on the west side of Sherrendo River and Opeckon Creek, on a branch of Hungoluta River called Tulise's Branch; adjoining James Davis's land, and part of 875 acres granted to Edward Davis on November 12, 1735; witnesses, Richard Morgan, Solomon Hedges, and Joshua Hedges;

(2) To Richard Morgan, for £30 5sh., 300 acres, described as above, and adjoining Solomon Hedges; witnesses, Joshua Hedges, Solomon Hedges, and Peter Hedges;

(3) To Solomon Hedges, for £18 5sh., 275 acres, described as above, and adjoining Peter Hedges and Solomon Hedges; witnesses, Richard Morgan, Peter Hedges, and Joshua Hedges.

In most instances cited above Edward Davis signs "Edward Devis."

All three tracts in the above conveyances are described as lying "near the mountain."

"Hungoluta" is an attempt at Cohongoluta or Cohongoruton, which were old names of the Potomac from its junction with the Shenandoah at Harper's Ferry to the Alleghany Mountain.

In the above conveyances Edward Davis is described as "late of Orange County."

John Mills, 1315 acres, in what is now Berkeley County, W. Va.; described in the patent as being "On a Branch of Opeckon, near but not adjoining, Lewis DeMoss' land." The records of Frederick County, Va., show that in 1743 John Mills made several deeds conveying portions of this tract to each of his sons, Thomas, Henry, Hurr, and John Jr. In each of these deeds he is described as "John Mills Sr., of Prince George County, Maryland, Farmer." But his sons are all of Frederick County, and John Mills Jr. is referred to as "cordwainer." No wife joins John Mills Sr. in these deeds, she, no doubt, being deceased.

On this tract of land stood the Mills' Creek Baptist Church, the first of that denomination in the Shenandoah Valley, and

Surveyed for Abraham Hollingsworth 582 acres of
Land called Abrahams delight lying within the
limits of an order of counsel granted to ~~Abraham~~
Alexander Ross and others for 10000 acres
beginning at a white oak & hickory & Red Oak
near the head of D Meadow and running thence
N 15 W 149 po to D Red oak & thence N 85 E 850 to a
white oak and hickory by D branch of the Meadow
thence S 19 E 50 pole two Red Oaks thence N 15 E
60 po to two white oaks & a Red Oak by the edge
of the Meadow thence crossing the same N 19 West
25 pole to 2 white oaks thence N 55 E 320 To
2 white oaks and a hickory N 35 west 200 po
to D white oaks thence South 55 W 80 po
to 2 Red oaks thence S 65 W 234 po to the beginning
this 23 day November 1732   R O Brooks

                                      C H M B O Brooks

probably the first in Virginia. It stood in what is now the village of Gerrardstown, and was organized about the year 1743.

John Hood, 1175 acres, at the mouth of Back Creek on Potomac River. On April 11, 1746, "Rachel Hood, widow and relict of John Hood, and Tunis her son" sold 200 acres of this land to Joseph Carrol, and it is stated in the deed that this 200-acre tract is part of 1175 acres granted to John Hood November 1, 1735. The land conveyed is described as lying on the south side of Back Creek at its mouth. Witnesses to this deed were James Porteus, Gabriel Jones, and Lewis Stephens.

That John Hood died prior to June 14, 1744, is shown by a minute of that date granting administration on his estate to Joseph Carroll, with Isaac Parkins and Lewis Stephens as bondsmen; and on September 14, 1744, Rachel Hood, his widow, qualified as administratrix, with James Davis and Jeremiah Jack as bondsmen. The appraisement of this estate was recorded December 6, 1744, and Andrew Campbell, Richard Beason, and Robert Davis were the appraisers.

Among the records of Orange County, Va., may be found a petition presented in 1735/6 signed by John Hood and Tunis Hood his son.

As previously stated, the names of the remainder of the seventy families are unknown. That their patents are not to be found with the foregoing, may possibly be the result of the controversy between the proprietors of the Northern Neck and settlers who relied on Crown patents, which had commenced immediately after Alexander Ross and Morgan Bryan had secured their Order in Council.

That there were others of the Ross and Bryan colony and that at least one of them was seated on his land is proved by survey made for Abraham Hollingsworth on November 23, 1732, by Ro. Brooks, a photostat of which is here presented. This instrument reads as follows:

"Surveyed for Abraham Hollingsworth 582 acres of land called Abrahams Delight lying within the limits of an order of counsel granted to Alexander Ross and others for 100000 acres beginning at a white oak a hickory & Red Oak near the

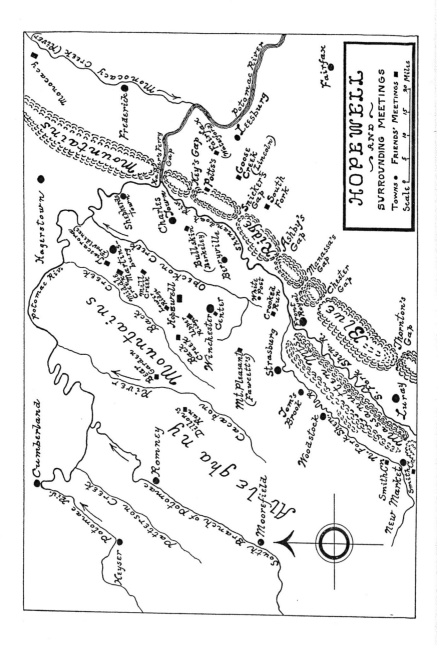

HOPEWELL
~ AND ~
SURROUNDING MEETINGS

Towns ●   Friends' Meetings ■

Scale 0   5   10   15   20 Miles

head of a meadow and Running thence S 15 w 143 p to a Red
oak thence S 36 E 160 to a white oak and hickory by a branch
of the meadow thence S 18 E 60 poles two Red Oaks thence
N 15 E 60 poles to two white oaks & a red Oak by the edge of
the Meadow thence crossing the same N 12 west 25 poles to 2
white oaks thence N 55 E 320 to 2 white oaks and a hickory
N 35 west 200 poles to a white oak thence South 55 w 80 poles
to 2 Read oaks thence S 65 w 234 poles to the beginning this
23 day of November 1732.

R o   Brooks
Ch   br   B O   Brooks"

Most of this land and the foregoing survey are still in the
possession of the Hollingsworth family. The tract is, it will
be noted, within the land granted to Alexander Ross and others.
The tradition in the Hollingsworth family is that Abraham
had been living here for a number of years previous to the
date of this survey. The historian Norris, writing in 1889,
fixes the date of his arrival as 1729, which may be correct,
since the minutes of the Nottingham Monthly Meeting, of
which Abraham was a member, show that about this time he
was under dealings and was absent from his former home.
The family tradition also says that Abraham Hollingsworth
paid three times for this land: "First, a cow, a calf, and a piece
of red cloth to the Shawnee Indians; next a sum of money to
the King's agent; and finally a sum of money to Lord Fairfax."

Perhaps this may be an example of the experience of the
thirty-six families whose patents have not been found, and
who (as the clerk of Hopewell wrote to the Meeting for Sufferings in Philadelphia in 1758, "tho' we have Lawfully purchased the Lands allready of the Several Governments") did
not secure a satisfactory title, recorded many years later, and
in consequence lost their identity, as members of the Ross &
Bryan colony.

CHAPTER III

THE SETTING UP OF HOPEWELL MEETING

Pennsylvania from the beginning was a Quaker colony and was controlled by William Penn and other Friends for two generations, but by the year 1725 or thereabouts the policy of the colony began to change. Slowly but surely control shifted from Friends into other hands on account of the large number of incoming settlers who were not Friends and who did not share their principles and practices in either religion or government. Men who were not Friends and not in sympathy with them were ambitious to get a larger measure of political power, which they gradually succeeded in doing. Accordingly, by the time of which we now speak, after years of quiet and peaceable policy in handling affairs in the Pennsylvania colony, Friends ceased to dominate the government. Moreover, they frequently found themselves in situations not in accord with their political beliefs and religious principles. Under these conditions, when Friends in Pennsylvania learned of the new and unsettled country west of the Blue Ridge in Virginia, many of them decided to seek new homes and establish a community in which they would have more liberty in carrying out Friends' principles. Accordingly, a Friends' colony was established in the lower Shenandoah Valley under the leadership of Alexander Ross and Morgan Bryan. At once, as might be expected, religious services were held and steps were taken to perfect a religious organization under recognized authority and in proper relationship with Friends' organizations already existing in Pennsylvania and Maryland. Our task in this chapter will be to show in detail how this was done—how Hopewell Meeting was established.

Alexander Ross, the pioneer mover in this southern migration, appeared before the governor and council of the colony of Virginia on October 28, 1730, as stated in the preceding chapter, to make provision in a supply of land for the new settlement. In a year or two the colony crossed the Potomac and established their homes on the rich limestone lands of the lower Shenandoah Valley, along the banks of the Opeckon, the Tuscarora, and other streams.

From their first arrival these Friends held religious meetings—out of doors, no doubt, in some cases, under the great trees of the primeval forest. As soon as they finished their log cabins the services were held in front of the cabins and in some of the larger ones. It is well known that some of the dwelling houses were so constructed as to be suitable for the accommodation of meetings. In the early records are numerous items that tell of meetings that were held in the homes of Friends.

The following quotation, from East Nottingham Monthly Meeting Book, now kept in the fireproof vault of the Friends' Historical Society, at Park Avenue and Laurens Street, Baltimore, is proof of the existence and recognition of Friends' religious meetings on Opeckon prior to the official "setting up" of Hopewell Meeting:

Att our Mo/y Meeting of E. Nottingham held the 21st day of the 7th mo. 1734—Elizabeth Hollingsworth married out of meeting—to Samuel Jackson, her statement of same read at E. Nottingham Monthly Meeting— and Alexander Ross is desired to take care that it be read in a First-day Meeting at Opeckon and make report as soon as possible.

In those early days, to marry a person not a member of the Society was sufficient breach of discipline to disown the offending member, as is indicated by the above proceeding. Had there not been a group meeting in the Opeckon country the request that Alexander Ross read the statement in a First-day meeting would not have been made of him.

This colony of Friends came to the Opeckon country not as land speculators, but as bona fide settlers desirous of establishing homes. The governor and council of Virginia were anxious to have such settlers, but at the same time they required each grantee to live on his land two or three years, build a cabin, clear ground, and grow crops before he could take full title, or get a clear deed for his land. Ross and his partners, as shown by the order in council reproduced on the next page, applied for their grants of land in October 1730. They asked for 100,000 acres "lying on the west & North Side of the River Opeckan & extending thence to a Mountain called the North Mountain & along the River Cohongaruton [Po-

At a Council held at the Capitol.
the 28th day of Octr 1730

Present

The Governour

Robt. Carter   John Robinson
James Blair   John Grymes
Wm Byrd   Wm Dandridge
Cole Diggs   Wm Randolph Esqs.

Alexander Ross & Morgan Bryan of the province of
Pensilvania having by their petition to this board set forth
that they & divers other Families of the sd Province amounting to
one hundred are desirous to remove from thence & settle themselves
in the Government & praying that 100000 acres of land
lying on the west & North Side the River Opeckan & extending thence
to a mountain called the North Mountain & along the River
Cohongauton & on any part of the River Therein do not
already granted to any other person may be granted them in
as many Tracts or Dividends as shall be necessary for the
Accommodation of the asd Number of families The Governour
with the advise of the Council is pleased to order as it
is hereby Ordered that the said Alexander Ross & Morgan
Bryan the Petitioners in behalf of themselves and their
partner have liberty to take up the said Quantity of
100000 acres of Land within the Limits above described and
that upon the above Number of families coming to dwell
there within two Years Patents shall be granted them in
Such manner as they shall agree to divide the same and
in the mean time it is Ordered that the said lands be
reserved free from the Entry of any other person ——

tomac] & on any part of the River Sherundo not already granted to any other Person," etc.

Patents were issued to Alexander Ross and his partners in November 1735. This is evidence that they had been living on their lands for several years. No doubt Ross and others had explored these regions in 1730 or earlier. They applied for lands in October of that year. On November 23, 1732, Robert Brook had surveyed "Abraham's Delight" within the limits granted to Ross and others.

On November 4, 1730, the council at Williamsburg ordered that Joseph Smith's petition for 20,000 acres on the north side of the River Opeckan be held in abeyance until the "return of Alexander Ross & Morgan Bryan & their Partners from Pensilvania"; and on October 27, 1732, Alexander Ross and his partners petitioned for an additional large tract, 20,000 acres, which evidently lay on the north side of the Potomac. All this shows that these Friends were in close touch with affairs in Virginia from 1730 on.

*At a Councill held at the Capitol the 4.
day of Nov.r 1730.*

PErsent

The Governour

Robt. Carter   John Robinson
James Blair   John Carter
Wm Byrd   John Grymes
Cole. Diggs   John Custis Esq.r

Joseph Smith Gent haveing petitioned for twenty thousand acres of Land lying on the north side of the River of Opeckan It is Ordered that the s.d Petition be referd untill the return of Alexander Ross & Morgan Bryan & their Partney from Pensilvania in order to discover whether the Lands mentioned in the s.d Petition interfere with the Land granted to them

October the 27: 1732
present
The Governour

Mr. Com.° Blair   John Grymes
Wm Byrd   John Custis
Cole Diggs   Wm Randolph &
John Robinson   John Taylor Esqrs.

On the petition of Abr. Ross & *their associates* ~~n~~ for a Grant of 20,000 acres of Land joining on the S.° Side of the Line of the Province of Pensilvania, on the west side of the Boundary of my Lord Baltimores Grant for the province of Maryland & joining to the Land lately entr'd for by John Robinson Esq.° It is ordered that the Entry of the — petitioners for the S.° Tract be reserved & that if upon settling the Boundaries of Pensilvania & Maryland the said Land shall appear to be within this Government the Pet.rs be prefer'd to a Grant thereof

There were uncertainties as to boundaries and disputes between rival claimants, lords proprietors and others, as shown in the accompanying reproductions of records, but Ross and his associates on the Opeckon were zealous in their religious devotions and earnest in their efforts at regular procedure. The following photo engravings from the East Nottingham Monthly Meeting records make the several steps plain.

Att our mo:ly Meeting of E. Nottingham held ye 18th Day of ye 3d: mo: 1734.

Alexander Ross hath Proposed to this meeting on behalf of ffriends att Opeckon that a Meeting for worship may be Settled among'st them which is Under ye Consideration & Care of this Meeting Untill a Suitable time to Give them a Visit.

Because of the interesting matter contained in these photographic excerpts from the records, they are given (repeated) in type for greater ease in reading.

Att our moly: Meeting of E. Nottingham held ye 18th Day of ye 3d: mo: 1734.

Alexander Ross hath Proposed to this meeting on behalf of ffriends att Opeckon that a Meeting for worship may be Settled among'st them which is under ye Consideration & Care of this Meeting Untill a Suitable time to Give them a Visit.

Att our Mo:ly Meeting of E. Nottingham held ye 17:th Day of ye 6th Month 1734.

Friends being again Mindfull of ye request of friends att Monoquesie & Opeckon, Do in order to Give them a Visit app:t Jeremiah Brown William Kirk Joseph England & John Churchman — Left for additi: on by appointing more att Next meeting . . . .

Att our Moly: Meeting of E. Nottingham
held ye 17th Day of ye 6th Month 1734.

Friends being again Mindfull of ye request of
friends att Monoquesie & Opeckon, Do in order to Give
them a Visit appt: Jeremiah Brown William Kirk
Joseph England & John Churchman—Left for Addition by appointing more att Next meeting. . . . . .

*Att our moly meeting of E Nottingham held
the 21st Day of the 10th mo 1734.*

*The friends appt to visit, frds att Opeckon
Do Report that they have So Done and that they
think it Would be of Service if a meeting were
Settled there, which this Meeting Doth acquiesce
with, and Orders that it be Sent to ye Next
Quarterly meeting.*

At our moly. Meeting of E. Nottingham held
the 21st: Day of the 10th mo 1734.

The ffriends Apptd: to Visit, ffrds: att Opeckon
Do Report that they have So Done and that they
think it Would be of Service if a Meeting were
Settled there, which this Meeting Doth Acquiesce
with, and Orders that it be Sent to ye Next
Quarterly Meeting.

The quarterly meeting was held less than two months
later, and by it favorable action was taken upon the report.

10th of 12th mo. 1734/5.

At our Quarterly Meeting held at Concord for the County of Chester,
etc., the 10th of 12th mo. 1734/5.

Nottingham Monthly Meeting in the behalf of Friends Settled at
Opeckon request that they may have liberty of having a meeting of worship
settled amongst them. After some consideration had thereon Friends at
this meeting do for their encouragement allow them to have and keep a
meeting for worship settled till further order.

The foregoing is from the quarterly meeting minutes, held at Concord, and preserved in the Friends' Historical Library at Swarthmore, Pa. It shows that the request of Alexander Ross and other Friends at Opeckon for liberty to hold a meeting for worship was granted by the end of the year 1734, the request having been submitted to East Nottingham Monthly Meeting nine months before. Considerable time passed between request and the official granting of permission, but in the meantime, no doubt, the Friends on Opeckon were carrying on their meetings for worship, confidently relying upon the expectation that official recognition would be given. The fact that there was a meeting for worship at Opeckon in the summer of 1734 was recognized by the monthly meeting of East Nottingham in requiring Alexander Ross to read before it the statement of Elizabeth Hollingsworth.

Without delay East Nottingham Monthly Meeting acted following the favorable action of the Quarterly meeting:

Att our Moly: Meeting of E. Nottingham held
the 15th Day of ye 12th Month 1734/5.

The Quarterly Meeting having granted ye
Request of Opeckon ffriends, & a meeting allow'd
them   Joseph England · John White   Jeremiah
Brown & Jno Churchman, are apptd, to write to
them to Inform them thereof and to advise
them to be Unanimous in ye place whereon
they Sett or build their Meeting-house

Att our Moly: Meeting of E Nottingham held the 15th Day of the 1st mo 1734/5

The friends appto to write to friends of Opeckon to Inform them of ye Settlemt of ye meeting a-mongst them do Report yt they have So Done.

Att our Moly: Meeting of E. Nottingham
held the 15th Day of the 1st: Mo 1734/5
The friends apptd: to Write to ffriends of Opeckon
to Inform them of ye Settlemt of ye Meeting A-
mong'st them do Report yt [that] they have So Done.

The meeting for worship at Opeckon was established and
soon it was flourishing, for by a minute of the quarterly meeting, held at Concord the following summer, we see that the
Friends at Opeckon were asking for permission and authority
to hold a monthly meeting, that is, a meeting for business and
discipline. We quote the minute in full.

11th of 6th mo. 1735.

Where as divers Friends that are settled at Oppeckon, together with the
Friends settled at Monocquacy, having moved this meeting to grant them
liberty of keeping a Monthly Meeting for Discipline etc., amongst them—
this meeting taking the affair into their Solid consideration, do at this time
request our Friends, Joseph Gilpin, Henry Oburn, Benj. Fredd and John
White to pay the Friends of the above said place a viset in order to inform
themselves how far a meeting of that weight and importance may be kept
and maintained with reputation and make report thereof to our next meeting.

The foregoing is from page 139 of the minute book covering the period 1683-1813 of the quarterly meeting, held at

Concord, Pa., which book is now preserved in the Friends'
Historical Library at Swarthmore, Pa.

Very promptly, considering the difficulties of communication and travel in those times, action was taken regarding the
Friends at Opeckon, and a monthly meeting was granted them.
The following extended quotation from the minute book of
the quarterly meeting referred to above sets the matter clearly
before us.

> At our Quarterly Meeting held at Concord—the 10th. of the 9th Mo.
> 1735.
>
> Pursuant to the directions of the last Meeting the Friends that visited
> those Friends living at Monoquacy and Opeckon report that upon mature con-
> sideration of the affair, judge that it would be well and necessary under
> divers conditions that the Quarterly Meeting would grant them the liberty
> of having a Monthly Meeting set up among them, and they from Oppeckon
> renewing their request who do also signify that upon a friendly conference
> had with those of Monoquacy have unanimously agreed on the time and
> place for the better accommodating the same. This Meeting under a solid
> consideration there of do judge it necessary and convenient for the encourage-
> ment of those Friends and their families who are removed so remote from
> Nottingham Monthly Meeting of which most or all were members, that they
> have the liberty of having a Monthly Meeting for Discipline and Church
> Affairs, in the hopes and with the desire it may be for the prosperity of
> Truth, the good of them and their posterity. Therefore accordingly do
> allow that the Friends now residing at Monoquacy and Oppeckon and there-
> abouts (being members of Nottingham Monthly Meeting) have and keep a
> Monthly Meeting for Discipline amongst them and that it go under the
> name as they themselves call it Hopewell, and be kept on the 1st. second day
> in every Month till further order—Provided never-the-less if there are any
> person or persons under dealing by Nottingham Monthly Meeting such are
> not deemed members of Hopewell Monthly Meeting until they have made
> or given Nottingham Monthly Meeting satisfaction.

Thus it appears that Hopewell Friends' meeting for worship was set up in 1734, and the monthly meeting for business
and discipline in 1735, both under authority of East Nottingham Monthly Meeting, which was in Cecil County, Md.; and
of Chester Quarterly Meeting, held at Concord, Chester
County, Pa. Hopewell thus became a branch of Philadelphia
Yearly Meeting. Because Chester Quarterly Meeting was
held usually if not always at Concord it was in time called
Concord Quarterly Meeting, especially after the establishment
of Western Quarterly Meeting, part of which was in Chester

County. In 1790 Hopewell and other Friends' meetings in Virginia became branches of Baltimore Yearly Meeting.

The name Hopewell was adopted by the Friends on Opeckon, it is most likely, from Hopewell in Lancaster County, Pa., from which place many of the early Friends came to Virginia. See "The Jolliffe Family of Virginia," by William Jolliffe, 1893, page 182. At first this meeting was usually called Opeckon (Opeckan, Opequon, etc.) because of its location, which is about four miles northwest of Opeckon Creek, or River. The majority of Friends' meetings were named for streams or other natural features of the localities in which they were situated.

Following the custom of their home meeting the Hopewell Friends set up the usual books of record, which were faithfully kept from the very beginning. At this time, two hundred years later, we have a continuous record of the meeting's activities, which were considered important enough to record, with the exception of the first twenty-five years. The monthly meeting minute book for the years 1734 to 1759 was lost in the fire which destroyed the home of William Jolliffe in 1759 or thereabouts.

However, the following two pages, of several which have been preserved for us, are reproduced in facsimile to show the care and accuracy with which the records were kept; and so far as known to the committee, these minutes are the earliest existing church records in the lower Shenandoah Valley. A printed reproduction follows:

(1)

At our Monthly Meeting of Hopewell at Opeckan
    the fourth Day of the Second month A. D. 1748.
The Representatives being Call'd they Appeared.
The ffriends appointed to See Cha. Parkins & Patience Milborns Marriage Accomplished report that it was Decently Consumated.
The ffriends appointed to See Wm. Brown & Hannah Moons Marriage Accomplished report that it was decently Consumated—
James Wright & Jos Lupton is appointed by this Meeting to enquire into William Hoge's Junr. Conversation & what else may be necessary, & also concerning his Sons William & Solomon & prepare a Certificate accordingly to Richland Monthly Meeting in Bucks County.
This meeting Appoints the Clerk or Some other ffriend to Read
    the Testimony
against Richard Moon & Susanna Beeson on a first Day after the

At our Monthly Meeting of Hopewell at Opeckan
the fourth Day of the Second month A:D: 1748 —

The Representatives being Call'd they Appear'd.

The friend appointed to See Cha: Parkins & Patience Milborns Marriage
Accomplished report that it was Decently Consumated —

The friends appointed to See Wm: Brown & Hannah Moons —
marriage Accomplished report that it was decently Consumated —

James Wright & Jos: Lupton is appointed by this Meeting to enquire into
William Hoge's Jun:dr Conversation & what else may be necessary, & also
concerning his Sons William & Solomon & prepare a Certificate accordingly
to Richland Monthly Meeting in Bucks County. —

This meeting Appoints the Clerk or Some other friend to Read the Testimony
against Richard Moon & Susanna Brown on a first Day after the
Meeting of Worship at Hopewell meeting House, also Richard Beeson Jun:d to
Read the said Testimony at Providence meeting House on a first Day as afs:d

William Platt & Alice Lowden appeared at this Meeting & Declared their
Intentions of taking each other in Marriage this being the first time, this
Meeting appoints James McGrew & Simeon Taylor to enquire into the said Wm:s
Conversation & clearness in Respect to Marriage & what else may be needful
and make report to the next monthly Meeting Accordingly. —

Ja: McGrew & Jn:l Platt is appointed to enquire into Rich:d Merchants Conversation and
what else may be necessary & prepare a Certificate Accordingly to North Carolina or else
Alex:dr Ross & his Son Geo: are appointed to enquire into Wm: Jolliffs
Conversation & what else may be needful & prepare a Certificate to
Middletown Monthly Meeting in Bucks County. —

This Meeting appoints Tho: Mills & Hur: Mills to Speak to Jn:l Ross &
& acquaint him to come to y:e next Monthly Meeting & make Satisfaction
for his Misbehaviour :: else he may expect to be Testified against. —

This Meeting appoints Rich:d Beeson Jun:r & Morgan offerdwell to enquire into Wm: Gardens
Conversation & what else may be necessary & make report thereof to y:e next monthly Meeting

the 2.3 mo. 1748

At our Monthly Meeting of Hopewell at Opeckan
The Representatives being Call'd they Appeared. _____

William Hiatt & Alice Lowden appeared at this Meeting and
Declared their intentions of taking each other in Marriage this
being the Second time the friends appointed to enquire into
the Said Wm. Conversation & clearness with others in respect to
Marriage report that they find nothing to Obstruct their proceedings
Therefore this Meeting leaves them to their Liberty to consumate
their Said Intentions when they See meet, and this Meeting appoints
James McGrew & Simeon Taylor ___ to See that the marriage be
Decently Accomplished & make report thereof to the next Monthly
Meeting Accordingly. _____

Tho. Mills & Thur Mills acquaints this Meeting that they have not
Spoak with Jno as they was appointed, but they are appointed to Continue
their care to make report to the next monthly meeting.

William Gardener heretofore hath requested to come under the care
of this Meeting, this Meeting after Deliberate consideration thereof
grants his request, and takes him under care _____

The Meeting Concluded

Meeting of Worship at Hopewell meeting House, also Richard Bee-
    son Junr. to
Read the Said Testimony at Providence Meeting House on a first
    Day as affsd.
William Hiatt & Alice Lowden appeared at this Meeting & Declared their
Intentions of taking each other in Marriage this being the first time, this
Meeting appoints James MaGrew & Simeon Taylor to enquire into
    the Said Wms
Conversation & clearness in Respect to Marriage & what else may be needful
and make report to the next monthly Meeting Accordingly.
Ja. MaGrew & Jno. Hiatt is appointed to enquire into Richd. Mer-
    chants Conversation and
what else may be Necessary & prepare a Certificate Accordingly
    to North Carolina or elsewhere
Alexan. Ross & his Son Geor. are appointed to enquire into Wm. Jolliffs
Conversation & what else may be needful & prepare a Certificate to
Middletown Monthly Meeting in Bucks County.
This Meeting appoints Tho. Mills & Hur Mills to Speak wth. Jno. Ross
& acquaint him to come to ye next Monthly Meeting & make Satisfaction
for his Misbehaviour, or else he may expect to be Testified against.
This Meeting appoints Richd. Beeson Junr. & Mordica Mendingall
    to enquire into Wm. Gardeners
Conversation & what else may be necessary & make report to ye
    next Monthly Meeting.
                    The Meeting Concluded
                            (2)
                                    the 2d. 3 mo. 1748
At our Monthly Meeting of Hopewell at Opeckan
The Representatives being Call'd they Appeared.
William Hiatt & Alice Lowden appeared at this Meeting and
Declared their intentions of taking each other in Marriage this
being the Second time the ffriends appointed to enquire into
the Said Wm. Conversation & clearness wth. others in respect to
Marriage, report that they find nothing to Obstruct their proceedings
Therefore this Meeting leaves them to their Liberty to consumate
their Said Intentions when they See meet, and this Meeting appoints
James MaGrew & Simeon Tayler—to See that the marriage be
Decently Accomplished & make report thereof to the next Monthly
Meeting Accordingly.
Tho. Mills & Hur Mills acquaints this Meeting that they have not
Spoak with Jno. Ross as they was appointed, but they are appointed
    to Continue
their care & make report to the next monthly meeting.
William Gardener heretofore hath requested to come under the care
of this Meeting, this Meeting after Deliberate consideration thereof
grants his request, and takes him under care—
                    The Meeting Concluded

And below is given also the wording of the third page of the Hopewell minutes of 1748, preserved from destruction by fire.

(3)

Evan Thomas Junr. & Wm. Jolliff Junr. having transgressed the rules of our Discipline have given in the following paper which this meeting having well Considered of & hoping to be the truth from their hearts have taken as Satisfaction. WE Evan Thomas Junr. & Wm. Jollif Junr. both belonging to the Society of the Christian people Called Quakers, but through carelessness & unwatchfulness have— suffered ourselves to be so far overcome with passion & anger which tended to fighting & quarreling with each other— for which Action we Acknowledge our Selves highly to blame, it being a breach of the known rules of our Discipline & being heartily sorry for it we do hereby— Publickly Condemn the Same, hoping wth. divine assistance to be more careful & circumspect in our lives and— Conversations for the time to come.

Evan Thomas Junr.

&

Wm. Jolliffe Junr.

No small degree of success has been attained in replacing the loss suffered in the destruction of the earliest Hopewell records. A careful search in the records of other meetings— East Nottingham Monthly Meeting, Chester and Concord Quarterly Meeting, and other meetings in Maryland, Pennsylvania, Virginia, North Carolina, and elsewhere—has been rewarded with many facts of our pioneer history. Moreover, the journals of early visiting Friends supply many items of value. John Fothergill, who visited Hopewell in 1736 and wrote of it, was an eminent Friend, and his journal is one of the earliest authentic accounts of travels in this region.

At first, as is obvious from the foregoing records, the Friends of Monocacy, Maryland, were included in Hopewell Meeting; and it seems evident too, from various minutes here and there, that the Friends of Fairfax were also included within the verge of Hopewell for the first nine or ten years.

As time passed, Hopewell Monthly Meeting became the mother church of many other Friends' meetings in Virginia and elsewhere. It is to them, as well as to Hopewell, that this history relates.

CHAPTER IV

THE ROAD TO OPECKON

"Did you know that there was a wagon road to Opequon from Pennsylvania as early as 1734?"

Thomas H. Fawcett of Cheyney, Pa., asked this question in a letter which he wrote February 21, 1935, to Richard E. Griffith, Sr., of Winchester.

Then Mr. Fawcett goes on to cite a survey of a tract called "The Forest," which survey was made for one John Mcgruder April 9, 1734, in the description of which the following lines occur: "beginning at a bounded hickory standing about half a mile above the Wagon Road that goes from Conestoga to Opeckin [where said road] crosses a creek called Ketankin [Catoctin] Creek which falls into Potomack River about six miles above Manocacy."

Mr. Fawcett in his extended correspondence with Mr. Griffith assembles so many items of interest concerning early settlers in the Opeckon region and their relations with Hopewell Meeting that the author of this chapter is indebted mainly to him for both the matter herewith presented and the caption thereof. Inasmuch as Mr. Fawcett collected these items specially for this history of Hopewell, his words are often freely used without quotation marks; but whenever he uses quotation marks they are carefully preserved herein, except in the longer passages, which are set in smaller type without quotation marks.

The *Historical, Genealogical, and Biographical Account of the Jolliffe Family*, by William Jolliffe, Philadelphia, 1893, contains an excellent account of the first settlement of the Quakers in the Valley of Virginia. Another valuable work is Smith's History. About the year 1752, by direction of Philadelphia Yearly Meeting, accounts of the founding of the several constituent meetings were prepared and sent to Samuel Smith of New Jersey, who made use of them in his *History of Pennsylvania*. A part of this work was printed in *The*

Register of Pennsylvania, edited by Samuel Hazard. The following quotation is from Vol. VII, January to July, 1831, page 134.

About the year 1725, Henry Ballinger and Josiah Ballinger, from near Salem, in West Jersey; and soon after them James Wright, William Beals, and others from Nottingham, settled in the upper parts of Prince George's County, Maryland, near a large creek called Monoquesey [Monocacy]. About the year 1726, they applied to New Garden monthly meeting for liberty to hold a meeting for worship on first days, which was granted, and held at the house of Josiah Ballinger and others till the year 1736, when a piece of ground was purchased and a meeting-house built, which is called Cold Spring meeting-house, where meetings are still kept.

About the year 1732, Alexander Ross and Company obtained a grant from the Governor and Council at Williamsburgh in Virginia, for 100,000 acres of land near a large creek called Opeckon in the said colony, which about that time was settled by the said Alexander Ross, Josiah Ballinger, James Wright, Evan Thomas, and divers other Friends from Pennsylvania and Elk River, in Maryland, who soon after obtained leave from the quarterly meeting of Chester, held at Concord, to hold a meeting for worship, soon after which land was purchased and a meeting-house built, called Hopewell, where meetings are still held twice a week.

About the year 1733, Amos Janney from Bucks County, and soon after divers other Friends settled about forty miles lower in Virginia than Opeckon, who obtained leave to hold a meeting for worship on first days, which was held at the said Amos Janney's and other Friends houses till the year 1741, when a piece of land was purchased, and a meeting-house built thereon, called Fairfax, where meetings are since held twice a week.

About the year 1733 or soon after, Richard Beeson and divers others settled near a branch of Opeckon, called Tuscarora, where a meeting was held at said Beeson's house for some time, till the number of Friends being increased, land was purchased and a meeting-house built, called Providence, where meetings are since held twice a week.

About the year 1736, Friends in those back settlements applied to Chester quarterly meeting for liberty to hold a monthly meeting, which was granted, and was held twice at Hopewell and once at Cold Spring, alias Monoquesy, and so continued till the year 1744, when the number of Friends being much increased, they applied to the said quarterly meeting to have the monthly meeting divided, which was granted, so that since the year 1744, Hopewell and Providence make one monthly meeting, which is held by turns at Hopewell and Cold Spring, and the meeting at Fairfax makes another.

The foregoing is valuable, being based on almost contemporary records, but it may contain some errors. Fairfax meeting is located in or near Waterford, Loudoun County, Va. The date 1733 is probably too early for Providence meeting.

After the monthly meeting was divided in 1744, Hopewell monthly meeting would not have ever been held at Cold Spring, or Monoquecy, for Monoquecy was part of Fairfax monthly meeting, which sometimes met there. It is easy enough to learn from the various minutes, quoted above in Chapter III, when Hopewell meeting was officially established; but the problem of the date when Friends first went to the Shenandoah Valley of Virginia can be studied in the life of Alexander Ross, the most prominent Quaker settler there, at first. Many particulars regarding him have been presented in a preceding chapter, but additional items concerning him and others who became more or less familiar at Hopewell may not be amiss.

New Garden monthly meeting, in Chester County, Pa., was divided, and the first monthly meeting was held at Nottingham, in Cecil County, Md., 4 Mo. 20, 1730. There is a photostatic copy of the early minutes, both men's and women's, in the archives of the Pennsylvania Historical Society. The originals are in Baltimore. In the said minutes the following items appear.

6 Mo. 15, 1730: Alexander Ross and others appointed to labor with Samuel White.

8 Mo. 17, 1730: Richard Beeson and Ann Brown declare their intentions of marriage the first time. Miriam Coppock and Kathraine Ross to inquire. Kathrine Ross and Dinah Brown to attend quarterly meeting.

9 Mo. 21, 1730: Richard Beeson and Anne Brown second time. Kathraine Ross and Miriam Coppock to attend the marriage.

11 Mo. 16, 1730/31: Alexander Ross and others to labor with John Gartrill.

1 Mo. 20, 1730/31: John Butterfill and Mary Brown first time. Kathraine Ross and Dinah Brown to inquire.

2 Mo. 17, 1731: Rachell Oldham, Mary Elgar, and Kathraine Ross to attend quarterly meeting.

7 Mo. 18, 1731: Kathraine Ross and Dinah Brown to join with men to draw a testimony again Sarah Morgan.

8 Mo. 17, 1731: Kathraine Ross, Rachell Oldham, Mary Beals, and Dinah Brown to quarterly meeting.

11 Mo. 15, 1731/32: Alexander Ross and others to attend quarterly meeting.

Elisha Gatchell was a prominent Friend of Nottingham, and the Gatchell name still appears upon the records of that meeting. The exact dates at which Alexander Ross and his associates settled in Virginia have not been determined. Their large grant of land was obtained in 1730. In 1732 they applied for 20,000 acres more. "Abraham's Delight" was surveyed in the fall of 1732—evidently it had been named earlier. Tradition places Hollingsworth on his land in 1729.

The first case of discipline from the new settlement in Virginia related to a marriage. 9 Mo. 17, 1733, Katherine Ross and Mary Litler were appointed to labor with Elizabeth Renfro. Later John Littler and Alexander Ross were appointed from the men's meeting. Elizabeth had been the widow of Joseph Hollingsworth, and had been married out of the unity of Friends by a priest. ["Priest" here does not necessarily mean a Catholic priest.]

One of the first marriages of Friends at Opeckon was that of John Ross and Lydia Hollingsworth; but they had to go all the way to Nottingham and back to declare their intentions. John Ross was a son of Alexander, and Lydia Hollingsworth was a daughter of Stephen. At Nottingham under date of 8 month 18, 1735, it was recorded that John and Lydia had appeared and had produced from the "weekly-meeting of Opeckon" what could be desired with respect to their conversation and clearness. On 9 month 15, 1735, they appeared at Nottingham the second time, and were allowed to proceed. Josiah Ballinger and Isaac Parkins were appointed to attend the marriage, "which is to be accomplished at Opeckon," to make report thereof, and to send the marriage certificate as soon as possible. William Jolliffe states that the marriage took place at Hopewell, then in Orange County, Va., on October 11, 1735.

Minutes of Chester Quarterly Meeting under date of 9 month 10, 1735, show that after being visited on request, Friends at Manoquacy and Oppeekon and thereabouts (members of Nottingham) were given permission to have and keep a monthly meeting for discipline amongst them, the said meeting to go under the name "as they themselves call it," Hopewell.

Providence meeting, which seems to have been the same as Tuscarora, near Martinsburg, was officially established in 1738. The minutes of Chester Quarterly Meeting, under date of 9 month 13, 1738, show that Hopewell Monthly Meeting presented the case of Friends "living near or about Richard Beeson's," who requested the liberty of building a meeting-house for worship. Liberty was granted. On 6 month 10, 1741, Hopewell was reported in the same quarterly meeting as saying that the Friends near and about Richard Beeson's had built a meeting-house, met there twice a week, and wished a preparative meeting by themselves, they being a considerable distance from any other meeting. The request was allowed.

In 1758, under stress of the French and Indian War and fear of "an Indian enemy," the attendance at Providence fell so low that the preparative meeting there was discontinued. This discontinuance was apparently first suggested or allowed by Hopewell Monthly Meeting, Providence being a branch of Hopewell, and soon recognized as necessary by Chester Quarterly Meeting. The latter was divided in the 11th month, 1758. In this division Hopewell became a part of Western Quarterly Meeting, whose minutes contain the following entry:

11 Mo. 20, 1758. It having been for weighty reasons recommended by the Quarterly Meeting from which we are divided that Providence Particular Meeting (in Virginia) should be discontinued, by an account now received from Hopewell Monthly Meeting we are informed that advice is complied with.

Providence was also known as Beeson's Meeting. Richard Beeson Sr. requested a certificate from New Garden to Hopewell on the 27th day of 1st month, 1736. Richard Beeson Jr. requested one from Nottingham to Hopewell on the 20th day of 3d month, 1738. There are some indications that Providence meeting-house was used by Tuscarora Meeting between 1760 and 1775, and perhaps later.

John Fothergill visited Hopewell in 1736; John Churchman in 1741 and again in 1760. Edwin Peckover was here in the winter of 1742.   He recorded several interesting items about Hopewell and Providence, quoted by Mr. Fawcett from *The Journal of the Friends' Historical Society*, Vol. I, 1903-4, page 99:

> The Place is called Opecken or Shaunodore River, where many ffamilies have removed from Pennsylvania, and they have two pretty good Meeting Houses. Abundance of people often come in besides ffriends, and it Looks as tho' things went on pretty well amongst them. They have five or six publick ffriends. I think it has not been settled above Ten or Twelve Years at most. I believe they must enlarge their Meeting Houses; they are about Sixteen Miles apart. One is called Hopewell Meeting, the other Providence or Beestons Meeting. We had two meetings out of Doors with them, and had, I hope, good Service. Then set forwards towards Pennsylvania.

Other early visitors were William Reckitt (1757) and Daniel Stanton (1760).

Good evidence of the growth of population and the large number of Friends, as indicated by Edwin Peckover, is to be seen in the fact that Hopewell Monthly Meeting in 1744 was divided, Fairfax and Monocacy being given a monthly meeting of their own. This arrangement was made at the request of Fairfax and Monocacy, with the concurrence of Hopewell.

We have seen, however, how seriously the growth and work of the Valley meetings were interfered with by the French and Indian War. Very few Friends, if any, actually suffered death or violence from the Indians, but many out of fear moved eastward across the Blue Ridge and some took up arms or joined in building military defenses. In 1756 it was recorded by the quarterly meeting in Pennsylvania that Hopewell was in an unsettled condition through fear of the Indians, and in 1758 the willingness to discontinue Providence Meeting was attributed largely to the fact that "all of them have been concerned in building a Fortification and dwelling therein for defence against the Indian Enemy." Under such conditions it was thought they could not reputably keep up a meeting for worship under the Friends' name.

Mr. Griffith is of the opinion that the fortification referred to may have been Neeley's Fort or Fort Evans.

In 1736 certificates were signed on the dates indicated and for the persons named below, most of them to Hopewell:

2 mo. 24, Richard Beeson, wife, and family, at New Garden;

3 mo. 1, Thomas Babb Jr., at Newark or Kennett;

5 mo. 26, Jane, wife of John Smith of Opeckon, "Shee being removed a Considerable time"; at Chester;

5 mo. 31, William Farquer and wife Ann, at New Garden; settled near Monocacy;

9 mo. 27, Mordica Mendenhall and wife, at New Garden.

On 12 month 28, 1737/8, an acknowledgment was received from Opeckon by Chester Monthly Meeting for Samuel Britton, and a certificate was granted him. On 2 month 1, 1738, a certificate to Hopewell was requested at Newark or Kennett for John Harrey; not granted apparently.

Other early certificates to Hopewell granted by different meetings are tabulated below, together with some from Hopewell.

1741

3 mo. 2, Joseph Hollingsworth and wife, certificate signed at Newark or Kennett;

5 mo. 4, George Gregg Jr., certificate requested at Newark or Kennett;

6 mo. 5, John Moon, certificate signed at Falls Monthly Meeting;

6 mo. 17, Mary Taylor, wife of William, certificate requested at Goshen; she and her husband were settled at Hopewell;

7 mo. 14, Henry Taylor, certificate signed at Goshen;

1 mo. 3, 1741/2, Francis Hogue, wife, and children, certificate signed at Falls. They were in Loudoun County, Va., in 1757.

1742

10 mo. 1, Abel Janney reported at Falls to have gone to "Pertomoch"; 7 mo. 1, 1752, certificate signed at Falls for Abel Janney and wife to go to Fairfax; Abel and his wife lived in Loudoun Co., Va.;

11 mo. 17, 1742/3, Charles Davies and wife Hannah, certificate signed at Goshen;

12 mo. 19, 1742/3, John Crompton and wife, certificate granted at Nottingham; 2 mo. 9, 1748, certificate for them

received at Nottingham from Fairfax; they lived in Loudoun Co., which was a part of Fairfax Co. until 1757;

12 mo. 28, 1742/3, Thomas Fawcett, wife Lydia, and son Richard, certificate requested at Chester.

1743

5 mo. 6, Henery Whitesides, certificate signed at Falls; appears by a later minute that he did not go to Hopewell;

7 mo. 3, Jacob Jenney and wife, certificate signed at Newark or Kennett; 6 mo. 6, 1752, certificate received at Newark from Fairfax; they lived in Loudoun;

8 mo. 5, Jacob Janney and wife, certificate signed at Falls;

8 mo. 5, Thomas Clows and wife, certificate signed at Falls;

8 mo. 17, Mary Kinison, widow of Edward, disowned at Goshen; reported to have moved into the Colony of Virginia and joined the Church of England;

9 mo. 5, Isaac Nichols and wife and Hermon Cox, certificate signed at Newark or Kennett.

1744

5 mo. 14, John Hough and wife, certificate signed at Newark or Kennett.

1745

3 mo. 27, John Fawcett and wife Rebeccah, certificate signed at Chester;

12 mo. 24, 1745/6, Rachell Fawcett, wife of Richard, certificate signed at Chester.

1746

4 mo. 4, William Mead, wife, and family, certificate signed at Falls;

5 mo. 26, William Marshal, certificate signed at New Garden; going to Virginia, probably to Fairfax or Hopewell. [They lived in Loudoun.]

1747

1 mo. 27, Richard Ireson and wife Sarah brought into Philadelphia Monthly Meeting a paper signed by them, to obtain a certificate to Friends at Hopewell, Va., where they resided;

4 mo. 29, Richard Ireson and wife Sarah, certificate signed

at Chester; one produced from Philadelphia and one requested to Hopewell.

1748

3 mo. 6, Phillip Babb, certificate signed at Newark or Kennett;

4 mo. 20, Azariah Pugh, certificate signed at Goshen.

1749

7 mo. 4, John Beason, certificate at Hopewell for self, wife, and son; 8 mo. 21, received at Warrington; 6 mo. 17, 1758, certificate signed for John Beeson to New Garden, N. C.

1750

2 mo. 20, James McGrew and wife, certificate signed at Hopewell; 4 mo. 16, received at Warrington;

6 mo. 20, Lydia Malin, certificate signed at Goshen;

12 mo. 16, Morris Rees Jr., certificate requested at Nottingham; delayed because Rees was tardy in paying a subscription of £5 towards the rebuilding of meeting-house; obstruction removed and the certificate was signed 4 mo. 18, 1752.

1752

10 mo. 21, Mary Beeson, certificate signed at Warrington.

1753

1 mo. 15, David Malin, certificate signed at Goshen;

8 mo. 18, Jacob Rees, certificate signed at Nottingham;

8 mo. 18, Morris Rees, wife, and two younger children, Hannah and Thomas, certificate signed at Nottingham;

8 mo. 20, Thomas Pugh, complained of at Goshen for offence committed in Virginia.

1754

4 mo. 15, Parthania Bane, certificate signed at Goshen;

9 mo. 9, Susanna Adams, reported to have gone with her husband (not a Friend) towards Virginia; certificate signed, directed to Hopewell or elsewhere.

1755

3 mo. 1, Robert Read and wife, certificate signed at Newark or Kennett;

12 mo. 1, John Branson, wife Martha, and children,

certificate signed at Hopewell; 1 mo. 17, 1756, received at
Warrington; 7 mo. 17, 1756, certificate signed at Warrington to Burlington.

1756

12 mo. 6, Morris Rees the Elder and wife, certificate
signed at Hopewell; 12 mo. 18, received at Nottingham.

1758

1 mo. 2, Thomas Rees and wife Hannah, certificate signed
at Hopewell; 2 mo. 18, received at Nottingham; 3 mo. 18,
certificate received at Nottingham for Thomas Rees, son of
Morris, from Hopewell, dated 1 mo. 2, 1758; 12 mo. 16,
1758, certificate signed at Nottingham for Thomas Rees and
wife Hannah to Hopewell;

3 mo. 18, Sarah Hawkins, daughter of Joseph Jones, who
had lived within the verge of Hopewell, condemns at Nottingham her outgoing in marriage and shows a testimonial of
her good behavior signed by divers Friends;

5 mo. 20, Stephen Ross, apprentice to John Daye, presented a certificate at Nottingham from Hopewell, signed 4
mo. 3, 1758;

7 mo. 15, Messer Beeson, apprentice to Messer Brown,
disowned at Nottingham; a copy of the testimony delivered
to George Ross of Hopewell, as desired by Hopewell;

10 mo. 4, letter sent to Virginia from Falls, telling of misconduct of Samuel Mead;

12 mo. 6, William Janney reported at Falls to have gone
to Virginia (probably to Fairfax).

1761

John Branson, wife Martha, and children, certificate from
Burlington received at Hopewell.

Some of the foregoing items from Falls Monthly Meeting
have been furnished by Elizabeth Palmer as well as by Thomas
H. Fawcett.

Writing under date of August 19, 1934, Mr. Fawcett says:
"There is very little more than what I sent you in the minutes
of Chester Quarterly Meeting in regard to Hopewell. I will
list the representatives who appeared from that meeting from
time to time. Most of these were from the Fairfax or Mono-

quacy parts of the meeting; and after those were separated
[in 1744] to form Fairfax Monthly Meeting, very few came.
In 1755 the practice of recording the names of representatives
was discontinued."

The list of representatives from Hopewell given by Mr.
Fawcett is as follows:

3 mo.   9, 1737, John Bailes and George Matthew
6 mo.   8, 1737, Amos Jenney and Henry Ballinger
3 mo.   8, 1738, John Smith and William Matthews
9 mo. 13, 1738, Thomas Mills and Williams Forker
6 mo. 13, 1739, James Wright and George Matthew
6 mo. 11, 1740, Amos Jenny and George Matthews
6 mo. 10, 1741, Richard Brown
3 mo. 10, 1742, Henry Ballenger
6 mo.   9, 1742, Amos Jenney and Thomas Mills
6 mo.   8, 1743, Edward Norton
9 mo. 14, 1743, Thomas John
12 mo. 13, 1743, Jacob Jenny
3 mo. 14, 1744, Amos Jenney
6 mo. 13, 1744, Richard Brown
3 mo. 13, 1745, Amos Jenney
3 mo. 14, 1750, John Mendenhall

In 1745 six copies of "The Great Case of Tythes," by
Anthony Pearson, were distributed by Chester Quarterly
Meeting—two to Hopewell, two to Fairfax, one to Deer
Creek, and one to Monoquacy.

In the minutes of the Western Quarterly Meeting are
found some items of interest relating to Hopewell and neighboring meetings in the period from 1758 to 1760. In 11
month, 1758, Benjamin Thornbury attended the quarterly
meeting as representative from Hopewell. It was at this
meeting that the discontinuance of Providence Particular Meeting was recognized. Hopewell Monthly Meeting sent in an
account that "they have lately Performed a Sattisfacory Visit
to the particular Families of Friends belonging thereto"; but
at the same time it was reported that the members of Hopewell were under "considerable Difficulty"; and faithful
Friends were urged to visit Hopewell. Especially was Fairfax Monthly Meeting requested "not to forget them during

the Winter Season." Joshua Brown and Richard Buller were then planning to visit Hopewell.

At Western Quarterly Meeting in 5 month 1759 no account was received from Hopewell, but three months later Hopewell was represented by Jonathan Perkins. In 11th month of the same year Robert Haines, William Neil, and Richard Beeson were representatives of Hopewell, but Neil and Beeson were marked absent. At the quarterly meeting in 2 month 1760 no personal representative was present from Hopewell, though a report in writing was sent in. In the 5th month of that year Hopewell was represented by Robert Haines and Andrew McCoy; and three months later Jesse Pugh and Jonathan Perkins were present from Hopewell. At this time (8 mo. 18, 1760) an interesting minute appears regarding the meeting at Crooked Run:

> Hopewell Monthly Meeting Mentions that the Friends living on Crooked Run, having been for Several Years past indulged with liberty of holding a Meeting for Worship twice a Week, which they say hath been kept up to good Sattisfaction; the friends seeming to Increase in Number & Strength, that Meeting joins them in Application to have a Meeting Settled there twice a Week vizt. on first & fourth Day [an omission] once a Month, living about 20 Miles distant from Hopewell; This Meeting therefore taking the same into Consideration, doth Appoint Joshua Johnson, Thomas Casleton, John Churchman, John Jackson & William Farquer to give them a Visit & endeavour to judge whether the sd. Request may be granted with Reputation to Truth, & make Report in Writing to next Quarterly Meeting.

At the quarterly meeting 11 mo. 17, 1760, George Ross represented Hopewell. Joshua Johnson, Thomas Carleton, and John Churchman, of the committee appointed three months before, reported a visit with the Friends of Crooked Run and recommended action favorable to their wishes; "With which this Meeting Concurs & grants the sd. Request, both with Respect to their Meeting for Worship, & preparative Meeting at ye time proposed."

After 1730, as must be apparent, the "Road to Opeckon" was an important highway. The number of Friends who passed over it, coming into the lower Shenandoah Valley and adjacent regions from Pennsylvania, Maryland, New Jersey, and Delaware, was considerable, though we have no means of estimating the number with any degree of accuracy. At the same time many other pioneers of different religious denominations and various nationalities were also coming in: German Lutherans and Reformed; Mennonites; Scotch-Irish Presbyterians; and English Episcopalians.

The Lutherans, the German Reformed, the Presbyterians, and the Mennonites, like the Friends, came mostly from Pennsylvania; the Anglicans all, or nearly all, came across the Blue Ridge from the older settlements in eastern Virginia. A few Baptists, English and Welsh, also came in, mainly, perhaps, from New Jersey.

The Anglicans located chiefly on the southeastern border of the Valley, along the Shenandoah River and near the Blue Ridge, over which they had come. Most of the Scotch-Irish went far up the Valley and beyond it, into what are now the counties of Augusta and Rockbridge, but some made their homes near the Friends, in and not far from Winchester. The Germans spread over most of the lower Valley, west of the English, and filled it up towards the southwest until they joined the Scotch-Irish and dovetailed with them along the line that now divides the counties of Rockingham and Augusta.

All the land in the lower Shenandoah Valley, together with much east and west of it, lay within the Northern Neck, the princely domain of Thomas Lord Fairfax, who after some years established himself at Greenway Court, 12 miles southeast, almost due south, of Winchester. Among the Germans Jost (Joist) Hite was a leader, corresponding somewhat with Alexander Ross among the Friends. Hite, with his sons, his sons-in-law, and others, came to Opeckon and settled near Ross and his associates, farther southwest. Hite and those who took up land with him and under him had much litigation with Fairfax over titles.

When Hite, Ross, and others came into the Shenandoah Valley, county lines, as well as grant and purchase lines, were not well defined, but the region was theoretically in Spottsylvania County. Beginning in 1734, it was in Orange County. In 1738 an act of the colonial assembly was passed consigning Orange County west of the Blue Ridge to two new counties, to be created, Frederick and Augusta. Frederick was organized in 1743, Augusta in 1745. Frederick County at first,

and until 1753, extended from the Potomac up the Valley to
Toms Brook, now in Shenandoah County. On the east side
of the Massanutten Mountain it came up a mile or two above
the site of Front Royal. In 1753 Frederick County was
extended up to the Fairfax Line, a mile southwest of New
Market; there it remained until 1772, when Shenandoah
County was created.

It will be seen, therefore, that Ross, Hite, and others were
at first in Orange County, Va., but after October 1743 in
Frederick. After that date Hopewell and Providence were
in Frederick County. Crooked Run, The Ridge, Mt. Pleasant, and various other early meetings were in Frederick County
from the first. Smith Creek was at first in Orange, then in
Augusta, and then on the borders between Frederick and
Augusta; and later it was on or near the line between Shenandoah and Augusta. In 1778 Rockingham, formed from
Augusta, took in part of the Smith Creek region.

On April 26, 1737, as the Orange County records show,
Isaac Parkins, with Lewis Neill and Lewis Stephens his
sureties, gave bond to administer on the estate of Joseph Hollingsworth. On August 24 of the next year the Hollingsworth estate was appraised by Joist Hite, Hugh Parrott, and
Peter Holken.

In September, 1741, was recorded the will of Elisha
Perkins, yeoman. By this will the testator's son John was to
have 400 acres "entry land and my land called the Swan
Pond"; also 150 acres bought from George Williams of
Prince George County, Md.; and "my home plantation."
He left a pacing colt to his loving friend Mary Swearingen,
daughter of Van Swearingen. After the payment of debts
the remainder was to be divided between six children, Ute,
John, Elisha, Elizabeth, Phillis, and Margaret. The widow
refused to abide by the will and claimed her dower.

This Elisha Perkins was doubtless the same man who, as
shown in the Orange County records, had various ups and
downs in matrimony. In one record "his wife Margery" is
referred to, but later records make it uncertain whether
Margery really was his wife.

Mr. Richard E. Griffith Sr. of Winchester, Va., and Mr.

Thomas H. Fawcett of Cheyney, Pa., have assembled numerous items of interest concerning various members of the Parkins (Perkins) family, many of whom were prominent residents of Frederick County, Va. In a preceding chapter will be found a sketch of Isaac Parkins, who was one of the original grantees, with Ross, in the Hopewell region.

The road to Opeckon, gathering within itself various trails from the north and northeast, became a great thoroughfare not only into the Shenandoah Valley of Virginia, but also through it into the west, the south, and the southwest. Over it passed toilsomely but hopefully the Friends and many others, into achievement and into history.

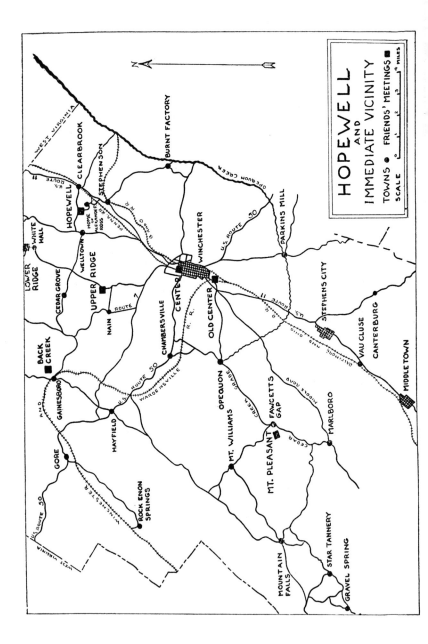

HOPEWELL
AND
IMMEDIATE VICINITY

TOWNS ● FRIENDS' MEETINGS ■

SCALE

0 1 2 3 4 MILES

CHAPTER V

MEETINGS WITHIN THE VERGE OF HOPEWELL

In Chapter III the setting up of Hopewell, first as a meeting for worship in 1734 and then as a monthly meeting for business and discipline in 1735, has been shown in detail. In this chapter we undertake to give the early history of the various meetings that were established at different times within the verge of Hopewell.

The following paragraphs are quoted from Janney's *History of the Religious Society of Friends,* Vol. III, pages 248, 249:

About the year 1732, Alexander Ross and company obtained from the Governor and Council at Williamsburg, in Virginia, a grant for one hundred thousand acres of land in that colony, situated near the Opequan Creek, a tributary of the Potomac. A settlement was soon after begun there by Alexander Ross, Josiah Ballenger, James Wright, Evan Thomas, and other Friends from Pennsylvania and Elk River in Maryland. Under authority of Chester Quarterly Meeting, they established in 1744 [1735] a Monthly Meeting called Hopewell, which thus became a branch of Philadelphia Yearly Meeting.

In the year 1733, Amos Janney from Bucks County, Pennsylvania, removed to Virginia, and settled about ten miles south of the Potomac, near the place where the town of Waterford has since been built. In a Memorial concerning his wife, Mary Janney, he is mentioned as a valuable Friend and true helper Zion-ward; and she is described as a devoted Christian, whose meekness, gentleness, and kindness rendered her company truly agreeable and instructive.

When they came to Virginia, the neighborhood where they settled was almost uninhabited; but other Friends coming soon after, and settling near them, a meeting for worship was held at their house. A meeting-house was built for its accommodation in 1741, and called Fairfax; it being then included in the county of that name, but subsequently the county was divided, and the northern section where Friends were settled was called Loudoun [1757]. Fairfax Monthly Meeting was established in 1744.

Jacob Janney removed from Bucks County, Pennsylvania, about the year 1745, and settled eight miles south of Fairfax Meeting-House. He and his wife, Hannah Janney, were exemplary in their lives, and steadfast in support of their Christian testimonies. A meeting was settled near them called Goose Creek, which at first was subordinate to Fairfax Monthly Meeting, but afterwards becoming very large, it was established as a monthly meeting.

Fairfax meeting was at Waterford, Goose Creek is at

Lincoln, both now in Loudoun County, Va. At this date (1935) Fairfax Meeting, at Waterford, is closed; and the few Friends remaining at Waterford are members of Goose Creek Meeting, at Lincoln.

MONOCACY (MONOQUECY, ETC.)

The Monocacy Valley is in Maryland, almost directly across the Potomac from Waterford (Fairfax Meeting) and Lincoln (Goose Creek). In 1726 a meeting for worship was settled at Monocacy, under the authority of New Garden; and in 1736 a meeting house was built and called Cold Spring. The preceding year, 1735, the Monocacy Friends had been recognized as a part of Hopewell Monthly Meeting. In 1744 when Fairfax Monthly Meeting was set up, Monocacy was put under the authority of Fairfax.

FAIRFAX

In 1734 or soon thereafter Friends in Fairfax, then in Prince William County, Va., set up a meeting for worship. In 1741, as shown by Janney and others, they built a meeting house at Waterford where the Fairfax meeting was held for many years. The name Fairfax no doubt was taken from the name of the new county of Fairfax, which was carved out of Prince William about the time that the meeting house at Waterford was built. From 1735 until 1744 Fairfax was a part of Hopewell Monthly Meeting; then Fairfax was made a monthly meeting, including Monocacy.

PROVIDENCE AND TUSCARORA

As stated in the preceding chapter, Providence Friends' Meeting was established in the year 1738, the request having been presented to Chester Quarterly Meeting by Hopewell Monthly Meeting. It probably was first held at the home of Richard Beeson, and at times was called Beeson's Meeting. By 1741 a meeting house was erected, and in 1748, as shown in the Hopewell minutes of that year, it was called Providence Meeting House. Indeed, this meeting house was perhaps called Providence as soon as it was built, for Edwin Peckover, a Friend who visited the region in 1742, wrote of it as "Providence or Beestons Meeting."

Evidently the French and Indian War interrupted the

Friends' meeting at Providence very seriously, and, as shown in Chapter IV, the preparative meeting there was discontinued in 1758.   After that time the Friends of Tuscarora are frequently mentioned, sometimes in connection with the old meeting house at Providence.   It seems a valid conclusion that Providence meeting house was on or near Tuscarora Creek, and that the Tuscarora meeting of later years was the successor of the earlier Providence meeting.   Various items in point are submitted.

On the 6th of 10th month, 1760, the "scattered Friends" living on Mill Creek, Middle Creek, and Tuscarorah asked Hopewell for a meeting for worship during the winter.   Two months later a committee reported at Hopewell and recommended the "old Meeting house of Providence" as the "properest place to hold a meeting for worship."   This recommendation was approved by the monthly meeting.

On the 3d of 11th month, 1766, Friends living at Tuskarora and Mill Creek were indulged with a meeting, to be held one First Day at Morris Rees Jr. and the next at "Providence old Meeting House," during the winter season. Two years later the Friends of Tuscarora were allowed to hold a meeting for worship "at the Old meeting house at that Place."

In August of 1771 Tuscarorah and Middle Creek were granted liberty for their meeting to circulate—one First Day at one place, the next at the other place.   On the 7th of 6th month, 1773, Friends of Middle Creek and Tuscarorah requested liberty to hold their meeting "Constant at Middel Creek."   The request was granted.

On the 4th day of 4th month, 1796, the meetings of Tuscarora and Middle Creek were united in one meeting to sit with Middle Creek.   On the 2d of 11th month, 1801, permission was given for a meeting at Tuscarora on the 5th day of the week.   In 1822 it was reported at Hopewell that the Tuscarora graveyard was enclosed with a stone wall.   At the same time it was stated that the graveyards at Mt. Pleasant and Crooked Run were also enclosed.

SMITH CREEK

The Friends' meeting at Smith Creek, now in the counties of Shenandoah and Rockingham, Virginia, was never large, but it was in existence at an early date. The burning of the earliest Hopewell records destroyed particular information prior to 1759, but luckily a few items have been preserved in other sources. In 1738, for example, Robert Scarborough wrote a letter in which he stated that he lived within about a mile of a Friends' meeting. His land has been definitely located, and lay on Smith Creek four and a half or five miles southwest of New Market. This town is in Shenandoah County, but the Scarborough land is now in Rockingham County. William Reckitt in 1757 and other Friends at various times visited Friends on Smith Creek and indicate in their journals that there was a meeting in the region. After 1759 occasional references to Smith Creek appear in the Hopewell records.

Under date of the 3d day of 11th month, 1760, Jesse Pugh, Benjamin Thornbrough, and Robert Hains were appointed to pay a visit to the several families of Friends living on Smith Creek who desired to be "joind in membership with us" [Hopewell]. Evidently the Smith Creek meeting was in abeyance at that time. Like various other meetings, it was set up, carried on, neglected, and revived from time to time.

On the 3d day of 6th month, 1771, the following minute was recorded at Hopewell:

Crooked Run preparative Representatives informs this meeting that they have had Several Oppertunityes in seting and Conversing with Smith Creek friends and are of the Judgment With Divers of Smith Creek friends that it might be best to have their meeting some Place more Convenient but they not seeming abel to fix A Spot among themselves Desier the assistance of this monthly meeting. Benjamin Thornbrugh, Jesse Faulkner, Samuel Pickering, and Abel Walker is added to their assistance and report of their service when performed. William Pickering and Robert Hains is added to the above.

Next month the committee reported that they had visited Smith Creek Friends. Evidently, however, they had not been able to reach a satisfactory conclusion, for they recommended the appointment of another committee. Another committee was appointed, and on the 4th day of 5th month, 1772, reported an opinion that it would be best to indulge the

Smith Creek Friends in holding their meeting for worship some time longer, but not at the usual place. "Therefore this [meeting] Appoints that they build A house On or near Jackson Allens Land on the South Side of the North fork of Shannando to meet in."

At the same time the Smith Creek Friends were enjoined to give account to Crooked Run preparative meeting how the Smith Creek meeting was kept up. Robert Hains was appointed to send the Smith Creek Friends a copy of the foregoing minute.

On the 2d of 6th month, 1777, a meeting was established at Smith Creek twice a week for the summer season. Late in 1778 Friends appointed to visit Smith's Creek and Middle Creek meetings reported their purpose that those meetings be established. Hopewell meeting concurred and the clerk was instructed to forward notice of the same to the quarterly meeting.

On the 5th of 6th month, 1817, it was recommended by a committee at Hopewell that Abraham Branson and William Jolliffe be appointed as trustees "to proceed forthwith" to sell the meeting houses at Stafford, Southland, and Smith Creek, with the several lots of land on which they were built, reserving the graveyard at each place. The Smith Creek meeting house, however, was not sold until 1839, and meetings were held in it occasionally, at least, until 1830 or thereabouts.

The Friends' meeting house, Smith Creek, that was sold in 1839 stood about four miles northeast of New Market, near the present village of Quicksburg, where the graveyard may still be found. This location is a short distance northwest of the north fork of the Shenandoah River. If, therefore, a meeting house was built in or about 1772 on or near Jackson Allen's land "on the South Side of the North fork of Shannando," it seems evident that there were from first to last three Smith Creek meeting houses: (1) One somewhere southwest of New Market; (2) another later, on the same (south) side of the river, probably between the river and Smith Creek; (3) and finally a third on the northwest side of the river, in the angle between the river and Holman's Creek, and about a mile northeast of Quicksburg.

In 1822 and thereabouts there was a road just southwest of Mt. Jackson, between Mt. Jackson and Quicksburg, known as the "Quaker Road." This road very probably led to or passed near the Friends' meeting house near Quicksburg.

CROOKED RUN

The Friends' meeting at Crooked Run, a locality now in Warren County, Va., dated from 1758 or earlier. At Hopewell Monthly Meeting on the 4th day of 8th month, 1760, was entered the following minute:

The friends liveing on Crooked Run haveing been for Several years past Indulgd by this monthly Meeting with Liberty of holding a meeting for Worship twice a week which hath been kept up to good Satisfaction and they Lately having built a new Meeting house and Seeming to Increase both in number and Strength they now desire This Meeting to make application to the Quarterly Meeting that their Meeting afforesaid be Established as a meeting for Worship Twice a week viz on first day and fourth day and they likewise request Liberty to hold a preparitive Meeting on the week day afforesaid. They Living about Twenty miels distance from this meeting all which we after deliberate Consideration Submit to the Quarterly Meeting for approbation.

William Reckitt made record of visiting Moses McKoy at or near Crooked Run in 1757, and of holding a meeting there. This might be regarded as an indication that the "Several years past" 1760 reached back to 1757 or earlier. In a report made at Hopewell in 1822 concerning titles to meeting-house properties it was stated that the 99-year lease for the meeting-house lot at Crooked Run was three-fourths gone. This would fix beginnings there in or about 1748. It appears, however, that the calculation of 1822 was not accurately made, since the lease in question has been found on record in Winchester. It was made by Thomas Branson of Orange County, N. C., to John Painter of Frederick County, Va., and dated 6th month 1st, 1758, to run 99 years. It conveyed 4 acres of land on the southeast side of Crooked Run, "for a Friends' Meeting house & burying ground, for that use, and no other."

It is probable that there was an indulged meeting at Crooked Run much earlier than 1758.

Doubtless the request in 1760 for a preparative meeting at Crooked Run was granted. In the Hopewell record of the 3d day of 6th month, 1771, Crooked Run preparative is recognized in connection with a difficulty that Smith Creek Friends were having to agree upon a place for meeting. In 1772 Smith Creek Friends were directed to report to Crooked Run preparative meeting. In the spring of 1776 Hopewell approved a request of Crooked Run to hold their preparative meeting on 7th day constantly, preceding the monthly meeting at Hopewell, and their select meeting on 3d day after the monthly meeting, at the 10th hour of the day.

In 1781 a monthly meeting was established at Crooked Run, as appears from the following minutes at Hopewell:

The subject of a division in the monthly meeting coming under consideration which after a weighty deliberation thereon, Richard Ridgway, Sen., James Steer, William Pickering, Josiah Jackson, Abel Walker, Lewis Walker, James Mendinghall, & Anthony Lee are appointed to unite with Women Friends in a solid conference, with Centre and Mount Pleasant Friends, in order to have them united with Crooked Run friends, in a Division of the Monthly meeting as aforesaid and make report of their service, to next monthly meeting. 5th of 11th mo., 1781.

The Committee appointed to unite with Women Friends, with respect to the Division of the monthly meetings mostly met at Centre, with Centre and Mount Pleasant Friends, which after a solid conference with them on the subject, there appeared to be a pretty general concurrance in sentiment to unite with Crooked Run Friends in a Division of the monthly meeting to be held alternately at Crooked Run & Centre, with which this meeting concurs, and requests the clerk to forward the same to the Quarterly meeting. 29th of 11th mo., 1781.

Crooked Run preparative meeting had requested in the summer of 1780 that a monthly meeting be settled there.

At the time of this division of the meetings it is probable that the number of Friends living in the Shenandoah Valley totaled 1000 or more. Two or three years after the division the members of Hopewell Monthly Meeting appear to have numbered 600. This estimate is made upon the following data: On the 5th of 4th month, 1784, a Hopewell minute shows that "our proportion to the yearly meeting stock" was 6 pounds and 15 shillings, calculated on 22 shillings and 6 pence "to the hundred." Thus it would appear that the Hopewell membership was 600. Just what preparative meetings Hopewell included at that time may be uncertain. The preceding year, 1783, Hopewell raised a quota of £20 to forward to the quarterly meeting, and the committee apportioned the sum as follows: To Hopewell 12 pounds and 10 shillings;

to Middle Creek 5 pounds and no shillings; and to Back Creek 2 pounds and 10 shillings; Virginia currency. If the 600 members of 1784 were all found at Hopewell, Middle Creek, and Back Creek, it is easily conceivable that the membership at Bullskin, Crooked Run, Smith Creek, Mt. Pleasant, Center, and elsewhere raised the total to 1000 or more.

THE RIDGE (UPPER RIDGE)

The "Ridge" is Apple Pie Ridge, which lies two miles or less northwest of Hopewell, parallel in its general course with Little North Mountain and other ranges of the Alleghanies.

It appears that Friends' meetings were in existence prior to 1759 at Crooked Run, Old Providence meeting house, and "Luptons." The last named was probably on the Ridge, the place known as the Upper Ridge in later times.

In 12th month, 1787, as Hopewell records show, a meeting was allowed at William Lupton's for the winter months. During the winter and spring of 1790-91 meetings were held near the house of Mordecai Walker "with a good degree of satisfaction," but in 6th month 1791 it was thought best to discontinue them. A month later Friends about the Ridge near Mordecai Walker's requested liberty of holding a meeting in the afternoon on First Days for the summer season, and James Steer, Abel Walker, Josiah Jackson, and Charles Dingee were appointed to unite with women Friends in a visit to those Friends, sit with them, and judge as to their request.

The next month (8th of 1791) a favorable report was made, a meeting was granted, and Joshua Cope, Isaac Brown, and James Mendenhall were appointed to attend the first meeting.

The third member of this committee was evidently the eminent James Mendenhall (1751-1816), who was a minister for nearly 40 years, a relative, perhaps a son, of Martha Mendenhall (1713-1794), who was a minister about 62 years. Sketches of Martha and James Mendenhall are found in "Memorials Concerning Several Ministers and Others Deceased," a small volume published in 1875 by order of the Baltimore Yearly Meeting.

In 1799 Friends on the Ridge near William Lupton's were granted a meeting. This meeting was established again in

1800.   It was often spoken of as Lupton's Meeting and, after another meeting had been set up lower down on the Ridge near Joseph Hackney's, as the "Upper Ridge." In 1822 a committee on titles to church properties reporting to the monthly meeting at Hopewell said, "At the Upper Ridge the Title is good."

MILL CREEK

During the winter of 1759-60 Friends living on or near Mill Creek (Mills's Creek), in now Berkeley County, W. Va., were given liberty to hold a meeting twice a week during the winter season at the former dwelling house of Hur Mills. The next autumn, on the 6th day of 10th month, 1760, at Hopewell Monthly Meeting Jesse Pugh, Enos Thomas, Jonathan Parkins, William Dillon, Henry Rees, and Joseph Lupton were appointed to visit "a scattered number of friends Liveing on Mill Crick, Middle Crick and Tuscarorah," who by reason of distance could not well attend at Hopewell, and who therefore were desirous of being indulged with liberty to hold a meeting for worship during the winter season.   But they could not agree among themselves upon a meeting-place. The committee of six from Hopewell was to assist them to an agreement.

On the 1st day of 12th month, 1760, the committee reported and expressed the opinion that "the old Meeting house of Providence" was "the properest place" to hold the desired meeting for worship.   Hopewell meeting, after mature consideration, allowed the said Friends to meet at the aforesaid meeting house during the winter season in order to hold a meeting for worship twice a week, namely on First Day and Sixth Day.

Thereafter from time to time during a number of years references appear to the Mill Creek meeting, but it evidently was always a small meeting.   The French and Indian War, which had been in progress since 1755, had no doubt scattered many families, Friends with others.   On the 1st day of 2d month, 1762, it was noted at Hopewell that there were eight families of Friends on or about Mill Creek and Middle Creek who were too far from Hopewell to attend there in the winter season, and they were accordingly allowed to hold a meeting for worship twice a week, as before, "till the first of the 5th month next," but this meeting was to be "at the School house." And the eight families were to be accountable to Hopewell Monthly Meeting how the meeting at the school house was kept up.

In the spring of 1764 Hopewell granted liberty, on request, to the Friends on and around Mill Creek to hold a meeting for worship at the dwelling house of Morris Rees Sr., on each First Day of the week. Two years later (1766), "At the request of friends living at Tuskarora and mill crek," they were indulged to hold a meeting every other First Day, "that is to say one first day at Morris Rees Jr. and the next at old Providence Meeting House during the winter Season."

No evidence has thus far been found of a meeting house for Mill Creek.

BACK CREEK

On the 24th day of 12th month, 1759, Hopewell Monthly Meeting agreed that the Friends living on Back Creek might have liberty to hold a meeting for worship twice a week, on First Day and Fourth Day, at the dwelling house of Thomas Pugh, during the winter season, and that they were to be accountable to Hopewell how the indulged meeting was kept up. It is possible that similar meetings may have been held at Back Creek prior to this date—earlier records were burned. On the 4th day of 8th month, 1760, the following minute was entered at Hopewell:

This Meeting after Deliberate Consideration appoints our friend Sarah Pickering an Elder for Back Creek Till further orders whome we Recommend to the Quarterly Meeting for approbation.

In the late autumn of 1767 Back Creek Friends requested leave of Hopewell to hold their meeting once a month at "Bare Gardin," at Evan Rogers's, "during this winter Season viz the first Day in each month next after our monthly Meeting." The request was granted.

The meeting once a month at Bear Garden was probably for the convenience of Evan Rogers and his neighbors rather than for that of the Friends of Back Creek, inasmuch as Bear Garden was distant nine or ten miles or more from Back Creek, and across a mountain or two.

In 12th month 1777 meetings were established to alternate between Back Creek and Bear Garden, and the establishment of Back Creek meeting was placed before the quarterly meeting. In the spring of 1786 Hopewell decided to settle a preparative meeting at Back Creek, apparently for Back Creek and Bear Garden, and forwarded the proposal to the quarterly meeting. The latter evidently agreed, for early the next year Back Creek preparative was given oversight of the meeting for worship at Bear Garden.

On the 6th day of 5th month, 1793, Back Creek informed Hopewell Monthly Meeting that some Friends near Evan Rogers requested the liberty of holding a meeting there on First Day afternoon, one in two weeks. The request was granted, and Lewis Walker and Richard Ridgway were appointed to attend the indulged meeting and report. This record shows that Back Creek meeting was in operation and good standing in 1793. The meeting at or near Evan Rogers's was evidently another meeting, at another place, in the vicinity of Bear Garden.

Back Creek meeting house was located in Frederick County, about 10 miles northwest of Winchester and about 12 miles due west of Hopewell. The site is fixed by the burial ground which is near the present village of Gainesboro.

MIDDLE CREEK

At Hopewell on the 1st day of 12th month, 1760, a committee that had been appointed to visit Friends on Mill Creek, Middle Creek, and Tuskarorah reported that they had met on that service, and they recommended the "old Meeting house of Providence" as the properest place to hold a meeting for worship. Hopewell Monthly Meeting approved the recommendation and allowed the said Friends to meet at the aforesaid meeting house during the winter season in order to hold a meeting for worship twice a week, namely, on First Day and Sixth Day.

In the 2d month of 1762 the eight families of Friends on or about Mill Creek and Middle Creek were indulged with liberty to hold a meeting for worship twice a week "at the School house till the first of the 5th month next," to be accountable to Hopewell Monthly Meeting how the same was kept up.

On the 5th day of 8th month, 1771, Hopewell Monthly Meeting recorded a request of Tuscarorah and Middle Creek for their meeting to circulate, one First Day at one place and the other at the other. Hopewell after solid consideration granted the request until further order. As usual, an account of how the meeting was kept up was to be rendered, "and that monthly."

Two years later, that is, in the 6th month of 1773, Friends of Middle Creek and Tuscarorah requested liberty to hold their meeting "Constant at Middel Creek Both on first and week Days." The request was granted with the usual requirement of giving account.

Toward the end of 1778 Friends who had been appointed to visit Smith Creek and Middle Creek meetings recommended unanimously that those meetings be established, and the same was forwarded to the quarterly meeting. In 1787 Middle Creek was given oversight of Tuscarora, as appears in the following minute made at Hopewell on the 5th of 2d month, 1787:

The friends appointed to visit Middlecreek meeting, & friends at and near Tuscarora, report, that most of them attended to the service and are free that their request should be granted, with which this meeting concurs, they rendering an account to Middle-creek preparative meeting how the same is kept up, and Mordecai Walker, Richard Ridgway, and Abijah Richard are appointed to sit with them at their first meeting, which is to be next first day & report thereof to next Mo. meeting.

On the 4th day of 4th month, 1796, at Hopewell Monthly Meeting, Friends of Middle Creek proposed that Tuscarora meeting be joined to theirs. Abel Walker, James Steer, John McPherson, Jonathan Wright, and Joseph Steer were appointed to attend the aforesaid meetings and judge of the propriety of the request.

BEAR GARDEN

The first reference in Hopewell records to Bear Garden seems to be under date of 2d day of 11th month, 1767, when Back Creek Friends asked leave to hold their meeting for worship once a month "at Bare Gardin at Evan Rogers' during this winter Season." The request was granted. In 1777 meetings were established to alternate between Back Creek and Bear Garden. In the 9th month, 1780, Bear Garden was "further indulged as heretofore." In 1784 Bear Garden Friends requested liberty to hold a meeting—James Steer, Mordecai Walker, Nathaniel White Jr., Richard Ridgway Sr., James Mendinghall, and Abijah Richards were appointed to unite with women Friends in visiting and sitting with them, judge of their strength and fitness, and report.

Two months later, that is, in the 7th month of 1784, the Bear Garden Friends were indulged with a meeting for worship once a month, and Jonathan Wright and Anthony Lee were sent to attend their first meeting. On the 2d of 12th month, 1784, the committee reported attendance at Bear Garden, also the request of Friends there to be allowed to hold their meeting four times a month, for the winter season. This, after deliberate consideration, was concurred with, and Richard Ridgway Jr. and Jonathan Wright were appointed to attend their first meeting. In 1787 Bear Garden was given liberty to hold meeting twice a week, rendering an account to Back Creek preparative meeting how the same was kept up. On the 4th of 8th month, 1794, Bear Garden meeting was established, according to the record at Hopewell; and on the 3d day of 12th month, 1804, it was reestablished.

STAFFORD

At Hopewell on the 7th day of 8th month, 1769, was considered a request of Friends living near Potomack Run in Stafford County, Va., for liberty to hold a meeting for worship. Certificates were produced and read, one for Joseph Wright and family; one for John Antram and family; and one for Daniel Antram and family. These were lodged until a committee might ascertain whether those persons were settled within the verge of Hopewell, whether they had complied or were likely to comply with their contracts in purchase of the lands they were settled upon, and whether they were capable of holding a meeting. To ascertain these matters of inquiry John Fawcett, Robert Hains, John Lupton, Joseph Lupton, John Branson, and Richard Ridgway Sr. were appointed.

At the next monthly meeting at Hopewell four of the

above committee made report, expressing the opinion that the said Friends in Stafford were not within the verge of Hopewell, being about 20 miles "nigher to fairfax"; but that they seemed in a likely way to comply with their contracts reputably, and were, if they proved careful, a sufficient number and compactly enough settled to hold a meeting for worship reputably. However, the Stafford Friends were willing to join Fairfax Monthly Meeting, if that meeting and Hopewell should think it best. Accordingly, John Lupton and James Steer were appointed to attend the next monthly meeting at Fairfax [Waterford] with a copy of the Hopewell minute, and see if Fairfax Friends were willing to accept the certificates of Stafford Friends.

At Hopewell on the 2d day of 10th month, 1769, Friends Lupton and Steer reported that Fairfax Friends did not seem free to receive the certificates of Stafford Friends, and Hopewell accordingly gave further deliberate consideration to the matter, finding freedom to accept the said certificates and referring the request for a meeting in Stafford to further consideration.

On the 5th day of 11th month, 1770, William Lupton, Richard Ridgway, Jonathan Parkins, and Abel Walker were sent as a committee to Stafford for further investigation.

In the absence of definite records, we may pass over a period of ten years to a minute at Hopewell of 4th day 9th month, 1780, in which we find the decision that Stafford along with Bear Garden, Culpeper, and Mt. Pleasant, "be further indulged as heretofore." This indicates that a meeting for worship had been allowed in Stafford for some time prior to 1780.

A meeting house was built in Stafford, but the date has not been ascertained. The meeting there was laid down in 1807. The meeting house was for sale in 1817, but Friends still held title to the property in 1822.

NEW QUARTERLY MEETING

On the 3d day of 7th month, 1769, a minute was recorded at Hopewell concerning steps that were being taken to set up a new quarterly meeting. A committee that had been appointed for the purpose had attended Warrington Monthly

Meeting and now reported that Warrington agreed to unite with Hopewell and Fairfax in requesting a quarterly meeting to be settled "on this side Susquehannah, to be held twice a year at Warrington and twice a year at Fairfax."

Warrington Monthly Meeting was located in York County, Pa., and Fairfax Monthly Meeting was at Waterford, Loudoun County, Va. They and Hopewell were in neighboring regions, not distantly separated. From Hopewell and Waterford to York the distance is much less than that to Chester. This proposal for a quarterly meeting on the southwest side of the Susquehannah was evidence, too, of growth in numbers and prosperity among the new communities of Friends in Virginia.

John Hough, representing Fairfax Monthly Meeting, informed Hopewell that Fairfax Friends were agreed to join with Hopewell Friends in the move for the new quarterly meeting. Accordingly, Robert Hains, John Rees, John Berry, and W. Jolliffe were appointed to attend the next monthly meeting of Fairfax to forward the request.

The next month (8th of 1769) the committee reported that three of them had attended Fairfax Monthly Meeting and that Fairfax Friends had agreed to present the request for a new quarterly meeting to the next quarterly meeting of Chester. [Western Quarterly Meeting?]

Evidently the request did not meet at once with a favorable answer, for somewhat over two years later, that is, on the 7th day of 10th month, 1771, the following minute was entered at Hopewell:

"This meeting Appoints William Pickering, Enos Ellis, Samuel Pickering, John Lupton, Joseph Lupton, and Benjamin Thornbrugh to meet the Committee from the Quarterly Meeting to meet at pipe Creek in Maryland the 23d of the 10th mo. to Confer With them Conserning Holding of A Quarterly meeting and make Report to the Next monthly meeting."

And on the 4th day of 11th month, 1771, it was recorded that four of the Friends appointed for the service had met the committee from the quarterly meeting at Pipe Creek.

After repeated conferences and long delays, Warrington and Fairfax Quarterly Meeting (including Hopewell) was authorized in 1776; and ten years later, 1786-7, Fairfax Quarterly Meeting (including Hopewell, Crooked Run, Westland, and Goose Creek) was established.

FAWCETT'S (MT. PLEASANT)

On the 1st day of 4th month, 1771, Hopewell representatives reported that there were several families of Friends and some friendly people living near Marlboro Forge, in the southwestern part of Frederick County, who were unable because of distance to attend any particular meeting for worship, with convenience, and who therefore requested the liberty of holding a meeting for worship on each First Day of the week. The request was granted with the proviso that they render an account duly how the meeting was kept up. The meeting was to be held "for the present" at the house of John Fawcett. On the 2d day of 6th month, 1777, the meeting at Fawcett's was established twice a week. At this time it was known as Fawcett's Meeting. In 1785 John Fawcett by will devised two acres of land for this meeting. At various times later it appears as Mt. Pleasant.

The site of Mt. Pleasant (Fawcett's) Meeting can still be determined with certainty by means of the burial ground. Recently Mr. Clark Fawcett of Opequon, Frederick County, Va., has made financial provision for the upkeep of the graveyard of Mt. Pleasant Meeting, which was first held in the house of John Fawcett and attended by many others of the same family name.

CENTER

It appears that Center Meeting, on Abram's Creek, near the Parkinses and Hollingsworths, just southwest of Winchester, was set up prior to the outbreak of the Revolution; was interrupted somewhat by that war; but was carried on, under various difficulties, for a period of 40 years or more at the original location, when it was moved into the town where it still is.

On the 2d day of 9th month, 1776, a request was presented to Hopewell Monthly Meeting "by friends near Isaac Parkins for Liberty of Holding A Meeting for Worship." Jesse Pugh, William Pickering, Robert Hains, Jacob M'Kay, Richard Ridgway, James Steer, Mordecai Ellis, and Lewis

Walker were appointed to meet with Friends near Isaac Parkins and have conference with them. The month following the committee reported and recommended "that it may be best to Grant them the Indulgence for the Winter Season twice A week, their Weekday Meeting to be held on the Sixth day of the week Except that week the Preparative Meeting is held."

On the 2d day of 6th month, 1777, further indulgence was granted to Fawcett's, Smith Creek, and "Senter."

About the time that the Friends near Isaac Parkins were given leave to hold meetings they also began to build a meeting house. This fact is shown in the journal of James Pemberton, one of the exiles from Philadelphia, who were brought to Winchester in the autumn of 1777. Near the end of November Pemberton and John Hunt walked out to "R. Hollingsworth meeting (called the Center)" and conferred with them about a meeting house, which was already partly built. Plans were soon laid, Pemberton states, to complete it.

On the 4th day of 9th month, 1780, at Hopewell, "Friends appointed to visit the several indulged meetings belonging to this Mo. meeting" reported that they had performed the service assigned to them and were of the mind that it might be best to purpose Centre Meeting to the quarterly meeting, in order for its establishment, "with which this meeting concurs"; and that Beargarden, Culpeper, Mt. Pleasant, and Stafford be further indulged, as heretofore. Members were gently admonished to visit the meetings named, for the use and benefit of the said meetings.

Six months later, that is, in the 3d month 1781, at Hopewell, Friends who had been appointed to consider the expediency of constituting one or more preparative meetings stated:

We all met at Centre meeting House, and after a deliberate & weighty consideration, and friends speaking their sentiments thereon, do unanimously agree to give it as our sense and judgment, that Mount Pleasant friends in conjunction with Centre friends unite, there may be a preparative meeting settled at Centre meeting house, as also we are of the mind that the Monthly meeting continue and extend its further necessary care with respect to settling one or more preparative meetings.

The report was signed on behalf of the committee by Rees Cadwallader.

On the 7th of 5th month, 1781, the Friends appointed to attend Centre at their first preparative meeting reported that they "mostly met," and after a solid conference with Centre and Mt. Pleasant Friends agreed to recommend that Centre Preparative Meeting be held at Centre on the 4th day of the week in each month, preceding Hopewell Preparative Meeting. With this Hopewell concurred.

CULPEPER

At Hopewell on the 4th day of 9th month, 1780, a minute was recorded in which occurs the following:

> . . . that Beargarden, Culpeper, Mount Pleasant & Stafford be further indulged as heretofore & that it might be of real use & benefit for this meeting to visit them from time to time.

Very little is known of the Culpeper meeting. The practice of referring familiarly and indiscriminately to both the county and the county-seat as "Culpeper" adds to the difficulty of locating this meeting. The first mention in Hopewell minutes of a meeting in Culpeper appears 8 mo. 3, 1778, when a meeting on First Days was allowed at the home of John Garwood, who lived near the Blue Ridge, on the eastern side, in that part of Culpeper County which in 1833 became Rappahannock. John Garwood had held meetings in his home prior to 1778.

In 1782 Hugh Judge visited John Garwood and wrote: "We were now within the verge of Culpeper meeting, and concluded to have a public meeting at the meeting house at two o'clock in the afternoon."

This shows that Culpeper meeting-house was near John Garwood's. At that time, Judge states, two families kept up the meeting.

In 1784 Culpeper preparative meeting was a member of Crooked Run Monthly Meeting; and in that year its proportion of the annual contribution was set at 9 pence. In 1796 its proportion was 10 pence.

WESTLAND

Westland meeting seems to have had its beginnings in 1782 or earlier. A minute of 4th day 11th month, 1782, at Hopewell states that the quarterly meeting had signified their unity in granting the request of Friends over the Alleghany Mountain as to their meeting for worship on the First Day and the Fifth Day of the week, and their preparative meeting on the 2d Fifth Day in each month, to be called Westland Meeting. Janney (III, 500) says that Westland was the first meeting for worship established west of the Alleghany Mountains.

On the day named above James Steer, Josiah Jackson, Nathaniel White, Jr., and Joseph Hackney were appointed to attend the opening of the preparative meeting at Westland, to assist as occasion might require, and to make report to the next monthly meeting at Hopewell.

In the summer of 1785 the Friends at Westland were asking to have a monthly meeting settled among them. After a delay and deliberation of three months Hopewell Monthly Meeting united with the request and forwarded the same to the quarterly meeting. This monthly meeting of discipline at Westland was to be held circular, alternating on the west side and the east side of the Monongahela River.

Redstone Meeting, on or near Redstone Creek, also was at this time on the eastern side of the Monongahela River.

Inasmuch as there was a continual movement of pioneers into and across the Ohio Valley following the Revolution, Redstone and Westland appear frequently in the Hopewell records of that period. The meeting which was made circular in 1785 with Westland was probably the one known as Monongahela.

REDSTONE

Redstone Friends' meeting was on or near Redstone Creek, in Fayette County, Pa., six or seven miles east of Brownsville. Like Westland and Monongahela it was on the track of the westward migration from Virginia, Maryland, and eastern Pennsylvania. The Friends at Redstone seem to have been allowed a meeting in 1780 or soon thereafter.

On the 3d of 5th month, 1779, at Hopewell, was entered a minute of a committee that had visited Redstone. Another committee, apparently, was appointed at that time to visit Redstone with a committee from quarterly meeting. On the 18th day of 6th month, 1780, the following was entered in the record:

The friends appointed to visit Friends at Redstone made the following report, viz. We of the committee appointed by the Quarterly Meeting to visit the Friends settled westward of the Allegany Mountain, have attended to the service, had several conferences with them, and inspected into their situation, number, and the meetings from whence they came, find that there is seventeen families, members of our society, eight Women and children whose husbands have not a right, one man whose wife and children have not, six young men amounting in the whole to upwards of one hundred fifty persons that have a right of membership amongst us, many of the children grown up, to the state of men and women, and some of them appear hopeful. They are not settled so near and compact together as would have been pleasant to us, yet we have a comfortable hope that divers among them are concerned to seek after an improvement in the Truth. We therefore unanimously agree to report as our sense, that it will be best for Hopewell Monthly Meeting to observe the Direction of the yearly meeting in receiving of Certificates from all such as shall produce them, where upon inspection it don't appear they have misconducted since their removal from the meeting they belonged to, which is nevertheless submitted to the Quarterly Meeting. Signed by John Hough, William Matthews, Joseph Elgar, Joseph Janney.

In view of the fact that Samuel M. Janney (III, page 500) states that Westland was the first meeting for worship established west of the Alleghany Mountains, it is probable that the setting up of a meeting at Redstone was delayed for several years. In 1806 Redstone had a quarterly meeting.

MONONGAHELA

On the 6th of 1st month, 1783, it was reported at Hopewell that Friends on the east side of the Monongahela were desirous of having a meeting, and Isaac Brown, Joseph Hackney, Nathaniel White Jr., and Richard Barrett were appointed to sit with them, judge of their fitness, and make report to the next or a future monthly meeting. During the next year or two other committees were sent to Westland and to the Friends east of the Monongahela. On the 5th of 9th month, 1785, a committee reported to Hopewell in favor of allowing the Friends east of the Monongahela a meeting for worship and also a preparative meeting. On the same date Hopewell Monthly Meeting united with Westland in a request to the quarterly meeting to establish a monthly meeting for Westland and the Friends east of the river, to be held circular, that is, alternately on the west side and the east side of the river.

This meeting on the east side of the Monongahela is believed to have been the one sometimes referred to as Monongahela. It seems to have been unusual in its setting up in that it was established as a meeting for worship, a preparative meeting, and part of a monthly meeting for discipline at the same time, or nearly the same time.

BERKELEY (BULLSKIN)

At Hopewell Monthly Meeting, 1st of 8th month, 1785, the Friends appointed to visit the Friends at Bullskin reported that they had made the visit and were of the mind it would be best to indulge them with holding a meeting on First Day and Fourth Day of the week, which after deliberate consideration was concurred with. The new meeting was to give account monthly how it was kept up. Richard Ridgway Sr., Nathaniel White Jr., Mordecai Walker, and Joseph Hackney were appointed to attend the first meeting at Bullskin and report to the next monthly meeting at Hopewell.

In the 4th month of 1792 a committee was appointed at Hopewell to visit all the indulged meetings within the verge of that monthly meeting. By the following month the committee had visited "Belskin" and Tuscarora. At this monthly meeting the mid-week meeting at Bullskin was discontinued on preparative week.

In the year 1794 the name of this meeting was changed from Bullskin, the name of a near-by small stream, to Berkeley, the name of the county, as it then was, in which the meeting was located.

THE LOWER RIDGE

In 12th month 1796 Friends at Hopewell gave reconsideration to a request of Friends near Joseph Hackney's for liberty to hold a meeting. There is some indication that those Friends had already been allowed to hold meetings for certain periods. At any rate, they asked leave to meet on each First Day and Fourth Day, except the Fourth Day preceding Hopewell preparative meeting, during the winter season of 1796-97, and this request was granted. David Lupton, Mordecai Walker, and Isaac Smith were appointed to attend the opening of the said meeting, and report. They reported the following month.

In the late autumn (1797) Friends "on and near the Ridge near Joseph Hackney's" requested a meeting for the winter season in "their Schoolhouse," and Jonathan Pickering, John McPherson, Jonathan Wright, James Steer, and William

Downing were appointed to sit with them and judge of their request. The committee recommended that the meeting be discontinued "for awhile," but the matter was soon reconsidered and the meeting was authorized.

The next year (1798) Richard Ridgway, William Hitt, Stephen McBride, John McPherson, Nathan Haines, Evan Rogers, Witham Downing, and Jesse Faulkner were appointed to sit with the requesting Friends, and shortly thereafter their meeting was longer indulged.

In 11th month 1813 Friends at "Lower Ridge" requested liberty of holding a meeting for worship at "their School House" on First Day and Fourth Day for the winter season. The request was granted and Jonathan Wright, Isaac Smith, Edward Beeson, and Joshua Lupton were appointed to attend the opening meeting.

By this time (1813), as it appears, the meeting near Joseph Hackney's was designated as the "Lower Ridge," the one near William Lupton's as the "Upper Ridge."

A meeting house must have been erected at Lower Ridge at an early date, for an investigating committee appointed at Hopewell in 1817 reported, "We found the title good for the lot of land on the Ridge near Joseph Hackney's, but the house thereon likely to sustain loss from decay." This house may have been "their Schoolhouse" which was in use in 1797, etc. The committee in 1817 recommended:

> We propose Thomas Barrett and Aaron Hackney as Trustees in the room of Joseph Hackney, decd. and David Faulkner removed to Ohio, with Liberty to rent out the house from time to time and after paying for the useful repairs, pay any surplus of rent to this [Hopewell] meeting.

SOUTHLAND

Southland Friends' meeting was near Mount Poney, 3 miles southeast of the town of Culpeper. In 1782 Hugh Judge found, near Mount Poney, Jonathan Bishop and his family, and had a religious opportunity with them. On 5 mo. 3, 1788, Crooked Run Monthly Meeting granted a First-Day meeting to "Friends near Mount Poney." On 9 mo. 5 of the same year Crooked Run Monthly Meeting allowed "Friends of Southland Meeting near Mount Poney" liberty to hold meetings on the 4th day of each week.

In 1789 Job Scott visited Southland twice, first in 4th month and again in 12th month.

In 5 mo. 1796 Southland's proportion in the annual contribution was 3 shillings and 6 pence. The same year Southland requested the privilege of holding a monthly meeting. The exact date of the granting of this request has not been ascertained because of the loss of the Crooked Run minutes covering the next few years, but it was probably 1797.

In the years 1798, 1799, and 1800 Crooked Run gave certificates of removal to Southland to the following persons: John Woodrow, Peter Cleaver, Alice Clever, Rachel Inskip, Sidney Crumpton, and Rachel Halloway and children.

This shows that Southland was a monthly meeting in 1798, 1799, and 1800. Record that Southland was a monthly meeting in 1799 has been found in the minutes of Fairfax Quarterly Meeting. From the same source it appears that Southland Monthly Meeting was laid down in 6 mo. 1804; the members returning to Crooked Run Monthly Meeting, and that in the 2d month of the next year Southland Preparative Meeting was also laid down.

By the year 1808 the meeting at Southland had evidently been long neglected, for in that year a committee was appointed at Hopewell Monthly Meeting to dispose of the Southland meeting house and other property. At later times steps were taken to sell the house and lot at Southland, excepting the graveyard, but in 1822 Abraham Branson, reporting at Hopewell for a committee, listed Southland as meeting property still held. At that time the graveyard was not enclosed.

DILLON'S RUN

Under date of 7th of 4th month, 1800, a minute was recorded at Hopewell Monthly Meeting to the effect that a meeting was established at Dillon's Run.

In 1822 Abraham Branson, reporting at Hopewell on behalf of a committee that had been appointed to investigate titles to the various meeting houses and meeting house lots, graveyards, etc., held by that monthly meeting, listed "Dillens Run Meeting House" as among the various pieces of real estate held at that time, and also stated, "We believe that the title is good for the Meeting House lot at Dillion Run."

In Hampshire County, now West Virginia, there was a Friends' meeting that was known as Great Cacapon. This is believed by some to have been identical with Dillon's Run.

Several other meetings have been found named that evidently were within the verge of Hopewell, that have not thus far been definitely located either in time or place. Great Cacapon, Little Cacapon, and North Fork were in Hampshire County, now West Virginia. Great Cacapon, it is believed, was identical with Dillon's Run.

A number of years ago, as Friend Arthur Robinson relates, Catherine Fry was a minister at North Fork Meeting in Hampshire County. She occasionally came to Hopewell, and her ministry was favorably received at many Friends' meetings.

On the 7th of 12th month, 1795, request was presented at Hopewell for liberty to hold a meeting "near John Fallis," which was granted, and a committee was appointed to attend the "first setting thereof." John Fallis lived on Little North Mountain, on the line between the counties of Frederick and Berkeley.

In 1822 Abraham Branson, reporting at Hopewell for a committee, listed "School House" as meeting property. This may or may not have been "their Schoolhouse" near Joseph Hackney's in 1797, etc.; for "Lower Ridge" and "School House" are both listed in 1822.

It seems probable that in or about 1830 there was a Friends' meeting near Howard's Lick, in Hardy County, now W. Va.

According to a tradition preserved by the older members of Hopewell, there was a meeting at Gravel Springs, somewhere in the southwestern part of Frederick County, Va.

As is well known, there was a Friends' meeting called South River, near Lynchburg; and there were Friends living on the South River of Shenandoah; but it is not definitely known whether they had a meeting.

At Hopewell on the 6th of 3d month, 1817, a committee who had been appointed on the case of meeting house lots made the following report:

We the Committee appointed to inspect into the situation of the different titles for lots of land belonging to Friends within the compass of this Monthly Meeting, propose what further care may be required on the occasion agree to report as follows: Viz: First—the title for the lot on which Hopewell Meeting House stands, appears to be well secured but Abel Walker, one of the trustees being far advanced in age and Amos Joliffe the other trustee decd. We propose that Isaac Pigeon & Edward Walker be appointed by this meeting to suceed them in Trust—Secondly—we found the title good for the lot of land on the Ridge near Joseph Hackneys, but the house thereon likely to sustain loss from decay. We propose Thomas Barrett and Aaron Hackney as Trustees in the room of Joseph Hackney, decd. and David Faulkner removed to Ohio, with Liberty to rent out the house from time to time and after paying for the useful repairs, pay any surplus of rent to this meeting.

Thirdly—We find a deficiency on the title to the lot of ground near Pughtown on which Back Creek meeting house stands. The Trustees named in the Title Bond being all decd., as also, the grantor, without having made a Deed of Conveyance to Friends for the said lot of ground containing about   acres of land, we therefore propose Thomas Barrett & Jonathan Pickering to be appointed Trustees in that case on behalf of this meeting with full power and authority to use such means as the laws of the land has provided in like cases, for obtaining a title according to the time & intent of the aforesaid Title bond, and the parties thereunto, and call on this meeting for the expenses concerning thereon.

Fourthly—We apprehend the title is good for the lot at Mount Pleasant but the house thereon is in a state of decay, we propose Joshua Lupton and Joseph Fawcett as Trustees for this Meeting, in that case to rent out the property, etc.

Fifthly—Discrepency in Title of the lot of ground on which Middle Creek Meeting House stands. We therefore propose Jacob Rees and John Lee to be appointed Trustees on behalf of this meeting in that case to use such means as is provided by law in such cases for obtaining a legal title to and for the said lot of ground & call on this meeting for the expense thereof.

We further propose that as Friends Title to the land on which Crooked Run Meeting House & School House stands is by a lease for ninety-nine years from its commencement that Samuel Swayne and Amos Lupton be appointed Trustees in behalf of this meeting, in that case with Liberty to rent out the property and after defraying the expense of repairing the graveyard and buildings pay the surplus (if any) to this meeting.

We are of the mind that further attention is necessary to other lands belonging to our Society within the limits of this meeting that we have not as yet been able to fully investigate all of which we submit to the Monthly Meeting signed by the Committee.

Jacob Rees	Joshua Lupton
Thomas Barrett	John Lee
John Wright	Jonathan Pickering

which is concured with and the Friends named as Trustees are appointed to the Service and the Committee continued to what further service may be necessary.

Three months later the committee appointed "to the care of Meeting House lots of land" proposed that Abraham Branson and William Jolliffe be appointed as trustees to proceed forthwith to sell the meeting houses at Stafford, Southland, and Smith Creek, with the several lots of land on which they were built, reserving the burying ground at each place, and to apply money arising from the sales to enclose the graveyards; also to provide a memorial to the Virginia legislature seeking aid in making legal titles for said lots; and have the balance, after defraying all expenses, ready for the disposal of Hopewell Monthly Meeting. The committee who had succeeded to this work were Jacob Rees, William McPherson, John Wright, John Lee, and Thomas Barrett.

Special items relating to Center meeting house at this time (1817) are given in the chapter on "Meeting Houses at Hopewell and Center," and extended particulars about the disposal of the meeting house at Smith Creek at a later period are presented in another chapter under the title "Items and Incidents."

In 5th month 1822 a Hopewell minute listed the meeting properties at that date, as follows: Hopewell, Back Creek, Middle Creek, Berkeley, Center, Crooked Run, Mt. Pleasant, Stafford, Southland, Providence, Upper Ridge, Lower Ridge, School House, and Dillon's Run. [Smith Creek should have been included.]

The same year, three months later, reporting for a committee, Abraham Branson presented the following facts: Robert Painter had given title of land to Friends of Stafford for their meeting house lot, but no deed had been executed. The Crooked Run lot was held by a lease of 99 years, three-fourths of which had expired. Tuscarora graveyard was enclosed with a stone wall. The several meeting places where properties were held at that time (1822) were Hopewell, Middle Creek, Back Creek, Center, Berkeley, Mt. Pleasant, Smith Creek, Southland, and Lower Ridge. [Also Upper Ridge.]

These observations were added by the committee in their report:

At several of the last mentioned places the meetings are laid down and the grave yards with the exception of three, Viz: Mount Pleasant, Crooked Run and Tuscarora, remain unclosed. We believe that the title is good for the Meeting House lot at Dillion Run. At the Upper Ridge the Title is good signed on behalf of the Committee by,   Abraham Branson.

During the next five years over $60.00 was spent in the effort to perfect the title to the lot of ground at Back Creek meeting house, with doubtful success. It was not until 1933 that the old title bond for the lot at Back Creek was found and the title thereby finally perfected.

CHAPTER VI

VISITING FRIENDS
To Hopewell and From Hopewell, 1736-1830

Notwithstanding the fact that the Hopewell records up to 1759 were destroyed by fire, fragmentary information from various sources has been gathered for that early period. From 1759 on the records are complete. Altogether, one is surprised at the large number of visitors, men and women, whose names have been preserved. Many came to Hopewell; many went out from Hopewell. Among them were persons of eminence in Friends' history.

Down to 1830 visiting Friends came to Hopewell and adjacent regions from no less than 68 different meetings in 13 different colonies, states, and foreign countries. Prior to 1776 the political divisions that we now know as states were properly termed colonies or provinces. The several colonies, states, and foreign countries from which visiting Friends came to Hopewell were New York, New Jersey, Pennsylvania, Maryland, Virginia, West Virginia, North Carolina, Tennessee, Ohio, Indiana, Wales, Ireland, and England.

Some of the meetings from which those visiting Friends brought credentials were New Garden, Goshen, Concord, Exeter, York, Chester, Abington, Warrington, and Philadelphia, in Pennsylvania; Deer Creek, Pipe Creek, Fairhaven, and Nottingham, in Maryland; New Garden, Cane Creek, Deep River, Center, and Springfield, in North Carolina; Miami, Short Creek, Concord, Stillwater, and Green Plain, in Ohio; Burlington, Evesham, and Salem, in New Jersey; Marlboro' and Westbury in New York; Liverpool, Nottingham, Tottenham, Sheffield, and London, in England.

As was natural from conditions of settlement, the most numerous and intimate relations of the Hopewell Friends were with the various meetings in Pennsylvania and Maryland, though exchanges of visits between Virginia and New Jersey were also frequent. Fraternal relations were also established at an early date between the Friends of Virginia and various

INTERIOR VIEW OF HOPEWELL MEETING HOUSE

Looking west; showing Gallery, old benches (at the left), original Clerk's table, and above it picture of Elizabeth Fry visiting Newgate Prison

meetings in the Carolinas. In the latter part of the 18th and the early part of the 19th century settlement spread rapidly from Virginia southward and westward. After Ohio became a state in 1803 the movement of Friends to that region was large, and fraternal visits between the Ohio Valley and the Virginia Valley became frequent. By 1830 or earlier a Friends' monthly meeting was in existence on Blue River, in Washington County, Indiana. Among distant Friends' meetings in the South with which Hopewell had occasional exchanges were Lost Creek, in Jefferson County, Tennessee; Wateree, in Kershaw County, and Bush River, in Newberry County, South Carolina; and the more distant one at Wrightsboro' in McDuffie County, Georgia.

One of the earliest Friends who came from a distance to visit Hopewell was the eminent John Fothergill, from England. He came to Hopewell and other meetings in Virginia in 1736. His brief observations here did not give him much encouragement—he wrote his conclusions in a rather doleful strain; but no doubt the contrast which he found here in pioneer life and frontier scarcity, so different from the settled ways and comfortable security of Old England, led him to a more pessimistic view than was really justified. However, this was Fothergill's third visit to America, though his first to the Shenandoah Valley. After his return to Europe he continued actively in missionary work there. In 1742, in Ireland, he attended 60 meetings in a period of about 11 weeks, though his health was noticeably failing. He died in 1744, aged 69.

In 1746 John Woolman, of New Jersey, who became famous as a preacher, writer, and social reformer, came to Hopewell. He visited also Fairfax and other meetings. Woolman in 1746 was only 26 years old, and was just beginning his extended and long-continued journeys of good will and good works. From a statement by Samuel M. Janney, in his History of Friends (Vol. III, page 312), it appears that Woolman on this mission was in the company of Isaac Andrews, a minister of Haddonfield, New Jersey. Some of the meetings, Woolman states, were "comfortable and edifying," but which ones he does not reveal. We trust that the meetings at Hopewell were among those that gave him comfort and uplift.

This tour through Virginia and Maryland deepened Woolman's convictions that he should speak out against slavery and the slave trade. And he did. In 1754 his treatise on slaveholding was printed and widely circulated. (See Janney, III, 312, 313.)

During the early part of the French and Indian War, from the defeat of Braddock near the site of Pittsburgh in 1755 till the capture by the English of Fort Duquesne in 1758 and of Quebec in 1759, inroads of the hostile French and Indians into the Hopewell region were frequent and destructive. Following the defeat of Braddock Colonel George Washington, charged with the defense of the Virginia frontier, built Fort Loudoun at Winchester and other forts at intervals far into the southwest, but the enemy continued to break through; many of the settlers were killed or captured; and many others fled eastward across the Blue Ridge.

We get illuminating glimpses of the conditions here in that distressful period from the autobiography of Friend William Reckitt, a visitor to Hopewell in 1757, and a keen observer. (See Friends' Library, Vol. IX, page 59.) Says Reckitt:

Crossing Potomac we came into Virginia to Fairfax; where we had a meeting on the second day of the week and 12th of the twelfth month. It was a good meeting, truth having the dominion. . . . We lodged at Mary Janney's, a discreet orderly woman, who had several sober, well inclined children. From hence we went to Goose Creek, and had a meeting on third day; it was well. On 4th day we had a meeting at David Pole's, several Friends accompanying us. I had a travail in spirit. . . . We left David Pole's house on 5th day and rode over the Blue Ridge or Blue Mountains, where the Indians had done much mischief, by burning houses, killing, destroying, and carrying many people away captives; but Friends had not hitherto been hurt; yet several had left their plantations and fled back again over the Blue Mountains, where the lands had been rightly purchased of the Indians.

Things seemed dreadful, and several hearts ready to fail. We proceeded on our journey, and came within six miles of Winchester, where the English had a fort. On 6th day we had a meeting at Hopewell, which was an open time. I found my mind much engaged for the poor suffering people, but had to tell them that their greatest enemies were those of their own houses. The meeting ended well. We lodged at Joseph Lupton's, an ancient Friend, who with his wife was very loving to us. The Indians had killed and carried away several within a few miles of their habitation, yet they did not seem much afraid; for they said they did not so much as pull in the sneck-string of their door when they went to bed, and had neither lock nor bar. We had a meeting at Crooked Run [22 miles south of Hopewell] on first day, the 18th of the 12th month. It was a good meeting. On second day we set forward through the woods, and over the hills and rocks, crossing several large creeks. We came in the evening to Moses Mackoy, and had a meeting there next day. They were an unsettled people, yet assented to truth; but were not fully convinced in their minds concerning the sufficiency of it; having an eye to outward shadows. I left them in good will. On 4th day we rode about 30 miles to Smith's Creek, where we had a meeting on 5th day, at the house of William Carroll. It was silent, though they had sent notice several miles, and several came. I told them though I had nothing to communicate by way of preaching or declaration, yet I found freedom to have another opportunity at a proper time and place; which I had next day at the house of John Mills, about ten miles off, somewhat in our way. The meeting was to good satisfaction. The Indians had killed and taken away people within two or three miles of this place not many weeks before; but the Lord preserved us in our journey. Thanksgiving and praise be to him, and that for ever.

Seventh day we set out towards the south parts, . . .

A Joseph Lupton was one of the early treasurers of Hopewell Meeting. He was probably the one who, even in the midst of a bloody war, did not fear the Indians enough to pull in the sneck-string of his door at night. Concerning him Henry W. Scarborough, lawyer and business man of Philadelphia, under date of November 3, 1934, writes:

My ancestor, Joseph Lupton, came from Yorkshire, England, and settled near Newtown, Bucks County, Pa., where he married Mercy Twining, daughter of Stephen Twining. Stephen Twining and his father had emigrated from Eastham, Barnstable County, on Cape Cod, Mass., about 1700 to Bucks County. Subsequently Joseph Lupton removed to Solebury Township, Bucks County, where he married the widow of Samuel Pickering, whose maiden name was Mary Scarborough.

About 1742 Joseph Lupton and his said wife removed to Frederick County, Va., and took along with them some of their own children and some of the children, Pickerings and Luptons, by their first consorts. . . . I think Joseph Lupton was one of the early clerks [he was a treasurer] of the Hopewell Monthly Meeting. I am descended from his eldest daughter, Elizabeth, who married Henry Paxson Jr. Their daughter Sarah Paxson married Joseph Wilkinson of Solebury Township, Bucks County, Pa. Their daughter Elizabeth married Crispin Pearson. Their daughter Mercy married Isaac Scarborough, whose son, Watson Scarborough, was my father.

From the above showing Joseph Lupton in 1757 was evidently an "ancient" Friend.

Just why William Reckitt's meetings on Smith Creek were held in homes instead of in the meeting house is not clear. There was a meeting house on Smith Creek as early as 1737 or 1738. Henry W. Scarborough has a letter written from Smith Creek in 1738 by his ancestor, Robert Scarborough. Therein Robert states that he was settled about a mile from a Friends' meeting.

To be sure, "Smith Creek" is a region of considerable extent. The Smith Creek Valley is well defined from Lacey Spring, 9 miles southwest of New Market, to a point almost at Mt. Jackson, 7 miles northeast of New Market, a total distance of 16 miles. Robert Scarborough's land was near Tenth Legion, five miles southwest of New Market, and the Friends' meeting of 1738 was within a mile of his home. Later, a Friends' meeting house stood near Quicksburg, four miles northeast of New Market, three miles from Mt. Jackson. This one was in use as late as 1830, or thereabouts.

Another Friend of note who visited Hopewell within the period of the French and Indian War was Daniel Stanton. An account of his "Life, Travels, and Gospel" was printed a few years later in Philadelphia. From this we learn of his visit late in December 1760.

We went forward crossing the Patowmac into Virginia; the next meetings were Fairfax, Goose creek, Potts or the Gap, some of which were largely favoured with solid comfort and satisfaction, there appearing many dear Friends with whom I had near unity in spirit; from the last place we travelled till we got over Shanondore river, and lodged at John Vestal's, where we had a solid season in the family; a deep snow falling that night made it the more difficult for us to get forward the next day to William Jolliff's beyond Opeckan, which after a long ride we reached, and were received in love, and the next day were at Hopewell meeting, being the first day of the week, and at their Monthly-Meeting the day following, both which were solid seasons; the next meeting was at Maurice Rees's, in which there appeared to be a necessity for an amendment in the way of truth; from thence we came to Back-creek, and the widow Lupton's had two meetings . . . ; we were also at Winchester, and had a large meeting of Friends and others, in the Court-house, after it was ended, several persons of note not professing with us behaved in a very loving friendly manner; in going from thence I possessed sweet peace in my own mind and went to Robert Hains's where we rested one day, and on first day was at the meeting at Crooked-run.

In the three years that had elapsed since the visit of William Reckitt, who found many of the homes deserted, there had been a turn in the tide. Strongholds of the French at Pittsburgh and Quebec had been taken, inroads of the French and Indians into the English settlements had been arrested, and many of the fugitives had returned. Evidently Stanton came from Goose Creek Meeting, at Lincoln, via Hillsboro and Vestal's (Key's) Gap in the Blue Ridge, over the Shenandoah River, and so on to William Jolliffe's, near Hopewell. Potts's Meeting, or the Gap, was probably at Hillsboro, which is in a gap of a small mountain called Short Hill, or in Vestal's (now Key's) Gap of the Blue Ridge, which is just northwest of Hillsboro. An old trail, now a main highway, passes through Hillsboro and across the Blue Ridge at Vestal's Gap.

In 1765, two years after the close of the French and Indian War, John Griffith, an English Friend with a Welsh name, attended Hopewell Meeting. He wrote: "It was an exceedingly dark, afflicting time." Evidently the people had not yet recovered from the sorrow and destruction of the war. Indeed, occasional massacres by hostile Indians took place in the Shenandoah Valley perhaps as late as 1766. Although the Friends rarely suffered themselves, in their persons or property, they were no doubt distressed by the misfortunes of their neighbors. Besides, as Reckitt implies, some of the Friends in the region of Hopewell had not made satisfactory settlement with the Indians for their lands, and for that reason may have suffered fear of attack, if not actual violence. The Shenandoah Valley lands were more or less in dispute among the Indians themselves, and therefore it was a very difficult matter to quit all claims. The questions of Indian titles dragged on and gave much trouble for many years.

In 1765, moreover, serious disputes were arising between the colonies and the home government in England over taxation and related matters. It was the year of the execrated Stamp Act.

But Griffith perhaps thought more of the spiritual gloom that seemed to deaden religious zeal than he did of the afflicting physical conditions under which the people lived. He declared that great insensibility and lukewarmness appeared almost general. And he spoke plainly to the people. "I was led in as close, plain-dealing, and searching a manner," he asserts, "as ever I remember." Possibly his searching and plain-dealing manner, though really wholesome to those who heard him, was not conducive to their comfort.

But three years later came a comforting visitor; and we may believe that improved conditions warranted more gratifying words. The recorder at Hopewell wrote as follows:

> Our Friend, Rachel Wilson of Old England, being now present on a Religious Visit, produced a Certificate concurring with her Visit; and she having visited most of the Branches that Constitute this Meeting, we can say on our part that her Labor of Love has tended to our Comfort and Satisfaction.

Rachel Wilson was from the monthly meeting of Kendal, and the record of her visit to Hopewell was made on the 5th day of 12th month, 1768.

During the next ten years various Friends came and went —Jacob Janney of Duck Creek; Sarah Janney, Hannah Brook, and Hester Haines of Fairfax; Lacharies Dicks from New Garden, N. C.; and others. In 1778 came Joshua Brown of Little Britain, Pa. A few months later in the same year came Mary Cox from Deer Creek and Ruth Miller from Pipe Creek, both of the state of Maryland.

Joshua Brown's visit to Hopewell was early in 3d month, 1778; and, as Samuel M. Janney informs us (III. 466), he attended at Hopewell the funeral of Thomas Gilpin. The latter was one of 17 Friends who, with three other gentlemen, had been sent by Pennsylvania authorities from Philadelphia to Winchester in September preceding, as prisoners. They were charged with disaffection to the American cause in the Revolution. Isaac Zane, a man of prominence in Frederick County, used his influence in their behalf, else they would have been carried on to Staunton, in Augusta County. John Smith, county lieutenant of Frederick and commandant at Winchester, and later Col. David Kennedy, who had charge in Smith's absence, treated them courteously. In the company were two ministers, John Hunt and John Pemberton. They were permitted to hold meetings, two days each week; and after a while various citizens of Winchester, as well as Friends of the vicinity, attended their meetings. The prisoners were also allowed to attend meetings at Hopewell. There Hunt and Pemberton exercised their gifts in the Gospel. They accordingly should be numbered among the notable visitors to Hopewell, though they left their homes in Philadelphia unwillingly and sojourned in Virginia as exiles.

Among the distinguished men who called on the exiled Friends while they were in Winchester were Col. John A. Washington, brother to Gen. George Washington, and Col. Daniel Morgan, whose home at that time (January, 1778) was a dozen miles east of Winchester.

On March 31, 1778, nearly a month after the death of Thomas Gilpin, John Hunt died. He too was buried at Hopewell and as was the case with most of the early graves— these are not marked.

The next year, 1779, was notable at Hopewell for visitors. Among the Friends who came from a distance were George Dillwyn and Benjamin Reeves from New Jersey, John Simpson from Pennsylvania, Margaret Sidwell from Maryland, and Abel Thomas and Samuel Hughs from Pennsylvania. Within the next year or two came Thomas Thornburgh and William Robertson of North Carolina, Samuel Emlen and Daniel Offley of Philadelphia, and Robert Willis of New Jersey.

In the year 1782 several visitors came to Hopewell from distant quarters. Among them was Hugh Judge, aged 33, miller, minister, traveling missionary, and writer, who through more than half a century of active religious service won a large place in the hearts of Friends. Born in Ireland, a Catholic, he came at an early age with his parents to Philadelphia, where he grew up and joined Friends.

Under approval of Concord Meeting in Chester County, Pa., Hugh Judge in company with Joseph Townsend crossed the Potomac on the 2d day of 2d month, 1782, and lodged at Edward Beeson's, "in the edge of Virginia." The quotation is from Judge's "Memoirs and Journal," a 396-page book published at Philadelphia in 1841. The account of this visit was written by Townsend. He continues:

And on first-day attended the meeting of Friends at Middle Creek; from thence we reached Richard Ridgway's in the evening.

2d mo. 4th. We sat with Friends at their monthly meeting at Hopewell. It was large and measurably owned by the Divine presence; and my companion, Hugh Judge, having laid his minute before the meeting, Friends united with him in his concern, and appointed Richard Ridgway to accompany us in performing the same. There was likewise a woman Friend [Mary Hirst] at this meeting, with a minute from Fairfax monthly meeting, under something of the like concern. The meeting also appointed a number of Friends to engage with her, as way might open.

At the close of the meeting we all conferred together, and two of the women Friends appeared disposed to go with our company to Smith's creek, about fifty-five miles distant from Hopewell. We accordingly set out next morning, and lodged the first night at David Brown's; where we met with several Friends from York county, on a committee of the Quarterly meeting, who were going to the same place, and whose company was truly acceptable.

Next day we came to a place called Stover's-town, or Strasburg, mostly settled by Dutch [Germans] of different denominations; and the minds of some Friends being turned towards the inhabitants of that place, a public meeting among them was proposed to be held that afternoon. This being approved, and notice given, great numbers assembled, and the opportunity was a time of favour, though laborious; I trust, however, that it will not be easily forgotten by a remnant. That evening we arrived at Joseph Allen's within the verge of Smith's creek meeting.

In 12th month, 1784, Hugh Judge was in Virginia again, not at Hopewell, but at Fairfax, Goose Creek, Crooked Run, Smith Creek, and other places. This time his companion was Isaac Jacobs.

In 1790 Hugh Judge entered upon extended and protracted missionary journeys in New York State, New England, and Canada. In 1797 he located his family in New York City, where they resided until 1804, when they removed to a farm which he had purchased at Little Falls, Md. Later they lived a number of years in Baltimore, and finally settled in Belmont County, Ohio. Hugh Judge continued his missionary journeys from time to time, traveling from New York and New England to Indiana, and far south into the Carolinas. It is said that he was at Hopewell again in 1808. He certainly was there in 1814, on his way from Baltimore to Ohio meetings. In his journal he wrote:

11th mo. 24th, 1814, I left home in company with Samuel Hutchinson, and in the evening of the 26th arrived at Abel Walker's. Next day attended Hopewell meeting, and on the day following set out across the mountains for Redstone.

The Abel Walker homestead is two miles northeast of Hopewell, and is now known as the Lupton farm.

Again in the summer of 1821 Hugh Judge may have been at Hopewell, for as he came eastward from Ohio he attended meetings at Dillon's Run, Back Creek, the Ridge, and Winchester. (Journal of Hugh Judge, page 338.) Thirteen years later, late in the summer of 1834, he came east by way of Winchester, and may have visited Hopewell. (See the Journal, pages 366, 367.) But his earthly journeys were near their end. He died at Kennet Square, Pa., on the 21st of 12th month, 1834, in the 85th year of his age, or thereabouts, and having been a minister upwards of 62 years.

Every year visiting Friends, both men and women, came to Hopewell and neighboring churches, some from long distances; and others went out. Especially in the later years of the Revolution and in the decade following that war comings and goings were frequent. In November 1785 John Storer and Thomas Cally of England were in Virginia. The former was from Nottingham, the latter from Sheffield. They produced certificates from their respective monthly and quarterly meetings, also from the yearly meeting of ministers and elders held in London, "setting forth Friends' unity & full approbation with their concern to visit the Churches in America, & they having visited all the Branches of & attended this meeting, whose labour of love amongst us hath been truly acceptable." In the summer of 1787 Richard and Thomas Titus came from Westbury Monthly Meeting on Long Island; and in 1789 Job Scott had several meetings with Hopewell Friends, all "open good meetings and most of them eminently so, even to my own admiration." A meeting in the Presbyterian meeting house at Winchester was a "glorious good meeting."

Job Scott, born in Providence, R. I., in 1751, was a minister of eminence and traveled widely. Hugh Judge in his memoirs mentions him several times. Scott was the author of a journal and also wrote a celebrated essay entitled "Salvation by Christ." Evidently his standards of "good meetings" were high. That those at Hopewell evoked his admiration is significant. The one in Winchester drew forth a strong adjective of approval. Job had skill in apt illustration. He said, for example: "The certainty of Religion, the law, and the light is no more invalidated by the ignorance of man than the truths of astronomy are overthrown by the ignorance of the Indian who maintains that 'if the earth were to turn round, or revolve about the sun, his succotash must certainly fall out of the kettle.' "

When Job crossed the Potomac and entered Maryland he made record that he hoped he was "clear of Virginia." This seems strange. Perhaps Negro slavery in Virginia may have pained him; but slavery was prevalent also in most parts of Maryland. In spite of the mystery we must believe that Friend Scott enjoyed the meetings at Hopewell and Winchester. Friends there abouts at that time were numerous and active. Hopewell stone meeting house, erected in 1759, was enlarged in 1788—doubled in size. Doubtless the meetings that Job Scott attended there were in the enlarged meeting house, even though it was not yet finished; and probably the building was filled with devout worshipers, as it has been many times since then. Hopewell activity in 1789 was at high tide.

Evidence that prosperity continued in northern Virginia is found ten years later in the writings of Henry Hull, who visited the region in 1799. On July 14 of that year he attended a meeting of Friends held in the courthouse of Leesburg, Loudoun County.

We then attended meetings at Goose creek, South Fork, the Gap, Berkeley, Middle creek, Upper and Lower Ridge, Hopewell, Bear Garden, Back creek, and Centre. The following first-day we had a large meeting at Winchester, in the Episcopalian meeting-house, where a great number of the town's people attended, including several preachers, and also the few Friends living there. . . .

After leaving Crooked Run, we rode to Joseph Allen's at Smith's creek, and attended their meeting, where we were comforted together. We were also introduced into near sympathy with our friends Joseph and Eunice Allen, who, a short time previous, had lost two exemplary daughters with the small-pox, and a little while before another was drowned in attempting to ford a creek, on her way to attend the Monthly Meeting. Parting from these dear friends, we went to New Market, where but one Friend's family resides.

The foregoing quotations from Hull's Memoir have been supplied by John A. Kelly of Haverford College, Pa., who says: "Eunice, wife of Moses Walton and later (after 1782) of Joseph Allen, was a daughter of Edward and Hannah (Borden) Rogers and granddaughter of Benjamin Borden, of Frederick County. Henry Hull was probably connected with the Borden family. He was a son of Tiddeman Hull and a grandson of John and Damaris Hull, of Rhode Island.

William Borden, first-cousin of Benjamin Borden, married Alice Hull, daughter of John and Alice (Teddeman) Hull, and removed from Rhode Island to Beaufort, N. C., in 1733."

In 1800 Stephen Grillet, by birth a Frenchman of the nobility and a Catholic, now an American citizen and a Friend, visited quarterly meeting at Hopewell. He says, "My mind had been brought very low, but the Lord was pleased to reveal himself in his ancient power and the meeting was a season of Divine favor." In his sermon he spoke of the "Abominations committed in the dark" and of the "baking cakes to the Queen of Heaven."

Early in the new century came Susanna Horn, "our beloved Friend," from Tottenham, Middlesex County, England; Mary Ellison from Burlington, N. J.; Caleb Shreve from Philadelphia; Evan Thomas from Indian Spring, Md.; Richard Mott from Purchase Monthly Meeting in New York State; John Shoemaker Jr. from Abington, Pa.; Charles Osburn from Lost Creek, Tenn.; Benjamin Beeson from Center Meeting, N. C.; Caleb McCumber from Farmington Monthly Meeting, N. Y.; Mary Naftel from Witham and London; Hannah Lewis from Philadelphia; Tristrum Russel and James Hallock from Marlboro' Monthly Meeting, N. Y.; Patience Sleeper from Green Plain, Ohio; Townsend Hawhurst from Westbury and David Hetchane Jr. from Jericho, Long Island; and many others.

The list of meetings to which Hopewell Friends went out on benevolent and religious missions is less complete, because the regions contemplated in their journeys were often indicated in general or indefinite terms. For example, on 3d day of 10th month, 1768, it was recorded that Esther Haines had returned after having a satisfactory visit to parts of Maryland and Pennsylvania. In 1772 David Fairris and Robert Vollentine went to visit the churches in the Southern Colonies. In the 11th month of 1803 James Steer, an elder, was willing to accompany John Hurst of Goose Creek on a religious visit to Friends "up the Susquehanna River."

But in spite of such general expressions we have found the names of at least 25 different meetings in 10 different colonies and states to which Friends from Hopewell went. The states and colonies were Maryland, Pennsylvania, New Jersey, New

York, Rhode Island, North Carolina, South Carolina, Ohio, Virginia, and West Virginia. A distinction is now made between Virginia and West Virginia, though the actual division did not take place until 1863.

Among the various places (meetings) to which visiting Friends from Hopewell went were New Garden and Deep River, in North Carolina; Bush River in South Carolina; Pipe Creek and Baltimore, in Maryland; Warrington, Westland, London Grove, York, Redstone, and Philadelphia, in Pennsylvania; Miami, Concord, Short Creek, and Cæsar's Creek, in Ohio; Stafford, Fairfax, Crooked Run, Goose Creek, and Smith Creek, in Virginia.

It is recorded that on 6th day of the 9th month, 1762, a certificate was signed for Martha Branson and Esther Wright in order for their visiting some meetings "in the back parts of Virginia and North Carolina"; and the meeting appointed Robert Haines to accompany the said Friends in their visit. Both Martha Branson and Esther Wright appear at later times, Esther and Sidney Wright, for example, going to Maryland in or about 1766; Martha Branson visiting New Jersey in 1766 and Stafford (Va.) in 1774. Within the same period Martha Mendenhall and Esther Haines pay visits to different meetings in Maryland, Pennsylvania, North Carolina, and South Carolina, as well as to several places in Virginia.

In 1781, 1st of 10th month, the following minute was entered at Hopewell: "Our Friend Daniel Brown informs this meeting that he hath had drawings in his mind for some considerable time past to visit some meetings in Maryland, Pennsylvania, & the Jerseys. He being a Minister in esteem with us, with which proposal this meeting concurs, desiring that he may return with the answer of peace in his own bosom, and the Clerk is desired to give him a Copy of this."

In the 8th month, 1785, Ann Pugh and Thomas Pugh informed the meeting that they had a desire to travel in some parts of North and South Carolina in order to see their children, and, if opportunity offered, to attend some meetings "thereaway." Accordingly it was certified that Ann was an esteemed minister, her life and conversation corresponding in good degree with her calling, and that Thomas was also a member in good standing.

Under date of 3d day of 8th month, 1789, was entered the following record:

Jonathan Wright informs this meeting that he hath for some considerable time had drawings in his mind to visit Friends in some parts of the Carolinas, & hath of late had an increasing concern respecting the same, so as to attend the Yearly meeting & as many of the meetings constituting the same as way may open, & some meetings on his way there and returning, which upon deliberate consideration is concurred with, He being a Minister in good esteem amongst us. Also Richard Ridgway informs that he hath drawings on his mind to accompany Jonathan in his intended visit, with which this meeting concurs, he being an Elder in good esteem amongst us.

The same year (1789) James Mendinhall, another minister, was authorized to visit meetings within the verge of Westland Monthly Meeting. Early the next year he was given a minute to attend the quarterly meeting of Warrington, and Abel Walker, an elder in good esteem, offered to accompany James, the meeting approving. Several years later James and Abel went to New Garden, N. C. About 1800 the following record was made:

Our Friend, Joseph Hackney, and wife informs that himself and wife have a prospect of attending the next Yearly Meeting at New Garden in North Carolina, and if way opens to visit some of their relatives in the South, which being considered is concurred with, they being Elders in good esteem amongst us, the clerk is directed to furnish them with a copy of this minute.

In 1804 John McPherson, an elder, was given approval to accompany Jonathan Wright on a visit to New York Yearly Meeting, to Rhode Island, and other places.

As already observed, there was in the early part of the 19th century a movement of population from Virginia and other of the older states to Ohio and other parts of the Northwest Territory, and a consequent increase of communication and travel between the East and the West. Visiting Friends frequently passed back and forth between Virginia and Ohio, as the Hopewell records show. In 1806 David Lupton, a Friend of Hopewell, visiting meetings and families in Ohio, made interesting memoranda, which are given below.

5th Mo., 14th, 1806, I [David Lupton], set out from home in Company with James Mendenhall & Israel Jenny to attend the Mo. Meetings of Short Creek and Concord on their request of haveing a Quarterly Meeting, and rode that Day to Springfield, Next day to Browns, Next Day to Jacob Beesons, Next day to Jonas Cattles, Next day being first day attended Westland Meeting. Rode after Meeting to Workmans about one Mile from

Washington [Pa.], Next day to Wheling where I staid untill fourth Day Morning then went to Concord Meeting after Meeting to Nathan Updegraffs. Next Day attended Short Creek Meeting and after Meeting went to Joseph Steers. Next day visited Uncle Jonathan Lupton whose Wife is very poorly with the apprehensions they will Come to Want, from there to Nathan Luptons. Staid a While and went to Nathan Updegraffs.

Next day being 7th day the 24th of 5 Mo., I attended Short Creek Monthly Meeting after Meeting went to Amos Alipsas to dinner then rode to John Wells and staid that night. Next day attended Flushing Meeting which is on the head Waters of Indian Whiling Creek. Staid that Night at Jacob Pickerings. Next day being second day, went to see Jonathan Parkins and John Marcers Families then to Samuel Pickerings, Staid that Night.

Next day being third day I attended Concord Monthly Meeting held at Planefield, went after Meeting to Samuel Greggs to Dinner from thence home with James Raley. Staid that Night. Next day went to see Robert and Sarah Richie, from thence to Joseph Gills from there to Benjamin Stantons and on to Nathan Updegraffs. Next Morning being 5 day went to see David Evans and James Updegraff but James Wife haveing had a Son that Morning I did not see her then to Short Creek Meeting, after Meeting went home with Nathan Lupton from thence to Asa Cadwalladers. Staid that night.

Next day Rode to Isaac Walkers in Company with Nathan Lupton from thence to Ely Raleys from thence to see John Antram Sr. then to Jonah Cadwalladers. Staid that Night, Next Day being first day was at Redstone Meeting in the fore and after Noon. Next day being Second day the 2nd of the 6th Mo. 1806 attended Redstone Quarterly Meeting. After Meeting a Report was made by the Committee favourable to the Request of Concord and Short Creek Monthly Meetings haveing a Quarter.

Next day set out homeward. Rode to Clements, at Dorothys old place. Next day to Musslemans, Next day to John Adams's at Big Capon. Next Day being Sixth day the 6 of the 6 Mo., 1806. Got Home and found the family all in Tolerable Good Health.

DAVID LUPTON

David Lupton was a grandson of Joseph Lupton, the "ancient Friend" of 1757, and his first wife, Mercy Twining. David's parents were Joseph Lupton Jr. and his wife Rachel Bull. Nathan Lupton of Ohio in 1806 was probably a son of David, the narrator. Nathan Updegraff was a brother-in-law of David Lupton, having married his sister Ann. David married Mary Hollingsworth. Their son, Jonah H. Lupton, 5th son and 7th of 11 children, married Lydia Walker (his 2d wife), and one of their sons was Hugh Sidwell Lupton, who married Mary Roberts Speakman of West Chester, Pa.

The children of Hugh and Mary are named in the Family Records from Hopewell, given in the second part of this book.

In or about 1812 Mary Barker and Lydia Gardner paid a visit to North Carolina. John McPherson was authorized to accompany them. A few years later Nathaniel White went to Cæsar's Creek, Ohio, and shortly thereafter (1817) Abraham Branson and Jonathan Wright were given a minute to visit the Ohio Yearly Meeting. The next year Abraham Branson, a minister, went to Philadelphia, and in 1820 to Red Stone and Short Creek. Within the same period Sarah Brown, a minister, and Sarah Branson, an elder, visited Philadelphia; Margaret Swayne, a daughter of Sarah Brown, also visited Philadelphia. In 7th month, 1820, Sarah Branson went to the Ohio Yearly Meeting; the next year Jacob Branson and Darling Conrow visited New York Yearly Meeting. The following spring (1822) Isaac Lambourn attended New York Yearly Meeting, and in the 3d month of 1823 Cassandra Brown, a minister, was given approval to attend the yearly meeting at Philadelphia.

It would be edifying to speak of later visits from Hopewell and to Hopewell. As in earlier times, Friends of eminence came and went. For example, John Scott was present at Quarterly Meeting in the troubled times of civil war. "While cannon roared and shook the house to its very foundations, he preached with unusual power the Gospel of Peace." Francis T. King, who was there also, said that the meeting was one of the best and most solemn he ever attended. Samuel M. Janney, renowned Quaker historian, educator, and friend of the Indians, also preached at Hopewell in war time, while the soldiers who were quartered there respectfully stood and listened, having stacked their guns outside.

Among other visitors of note who came to Hopewell in more recent times were Miriam Gover, John J. Cornell, Sunderland P. Gardener, Henry W. Wilbur, La Vergne Gardener, O. Edward Janney and his wife, Anna Webb Janney, and Isaac Wilson of Canada and Baltimore.

VISITING MINISTERS

"How beautiful upon the mountains are the feet of him
that bringeth good tidings, that publisheth peace."

I love this ancient house of stone,
　　With all its sacred history;
Its plain, strong walls do well atone
　　For aught they hide of mystery.

To listening faith they have a voice,
　　They breathe to me a message tender;
They witness of the better choice,
　　And service constant souls may render.

They tell of those who bore the stress,
　　Whose faith and works were blended,
Who caused to bloom the wilderness
　　Ere tasks of love were ended.

Here oft upon his distant way
　　The harbinger of peace attends;
With joy he hails th' appointed day
　　To worship with the Hopewell Friends.

Anon perchance some lack of zeal
　　Found here would eager joy abate,
But praying aid our fault to heal,
　　He patiently would work and wait.

How rich their gifts upon the way,
　　Of "whatsoever things" are best;
To us who worship here to-day
　　Their labors have been greatly blessed.

Like them, dear God, may we appear
　　A "cloud of witnesses" for thee;
And may their spirits hovering near
　　A hallowed benediction be.

CHAPTER VII

FRIENDS AND THE INDIANS

The Shenandoah Valley was probably not actually inhabited by the Indians when the Quaker settlers first appeared here, but many evidences of their recent occupancy remained. Kercheval mentions a village at Shawnee Springs near Winchester and various other settlements. A map of western Maryland and the adjoining parts of Virginia made about 1721 (published in the Maryland Historical Magazine, March 1935) shows two Indian towns on the Potomac and an Indian trader's cabin at the mouth of the Monocacy; but on the map of the Northern Neck of Virginia, made from the survey of 1736-1737, these towns are marked "Shawno Indian Fields deserted." Students of the period believe that the Indian towns in this part of the country were founded in historic times as a part of a migration from south to north, and that they were deserted before the coming of white settlers, as the aborigines moved on into Pennsylvania and Ohio. However, the Shenandoah Valley was by no means free from Indian visitors—it served as one of their great highways from north to south along which war parties traveled. The first wagon road from Pennsylvania to Opequon followed in large measure a well marked Indian trail known as the Conestoga Path. The highway up the Shenandoah Valley is thought to have had in part a similar origin.

Friends did not buy their lands from the Indians when they settled at Opequon—a practice that William Penn had been careful to follow in Pennsylvania. This neglect gave great concern to Thomas Chalkley, the well-known Quaker minister of Philadelphia. He felt unable in his old age and poor health to cross the Blue Ridge to Hopewell, but from John Cheagle's (or Cheadle's) in Caroline County, Virginia, he wrote the following letter:

"Virginia, at John Cheagle's, 21st 5th Month, 1738.
"To the friends of the monthly meeting at Opequon:
"Dear friends who inhabit Shenandoah and Opequon:—

Having a concern for your welfare and prosperity, both now and hereafter, and also the prosperity of your children, I had a desire to see you; but being in years, and heavy, and much spent and fatigued with my long journeyings in Virginia and Carolina, makes it seem too hard for me to perform a visit in person to you, wherefore I take this way of writing to discharge my mind of what lies weighty thereon; and

"First. I desire that you be very careful (being far and back inhabitants) to keep a friendly correspondence with the native Indians, giving them no occasion of offense; they being a cruel and merciless enemy, where they think they are wronged or defrauded of their rights; as woful experience hath taught in Carolina, Virginia and Maryland, and especially in New England, &c.; and

"Secondly. As nature hath given them and their forefathers the possession of this continent of America (or this wilderness), they had a natural right thereto in justice and equity; and no people, according to the law of nature and justice and our own principle, which is according to the glorious gospel of our dear and holy Jesus Christ, ought to take away or settle on other men's lands or rights without consent, or purchasing the same by agreement of parties concerned; which I suppose in your case is not yet done.

"Thirdly. Therefore my counsel and christian advice to you is, my dear friends, that the most reputable among you do with speed endeavor to agree with and purchase your lands of the native Indians or inhabitants. Take example of our worthy and honorable late proprietor William Penn; who by the wise and religious care in that relation, hath settled a lasting peace and commerce with the natives, and through his prudent management therein hath been instrumental to plant in peace one of the most flourishing provinces in the world.

"Fourthly. Who would run the risk of the lives of their wives and children for the sparing a little cost and pains? I am concerned to lay these things before you, under an uncommon exercise of mind, that your new and flourishing little settlement may not be laid waste, and (if the providence of the Almighty doth not intervene,) some of the blood of yourselves, wives or children, be shed or spilt on the ground.

"Fifthly. Consider you are in the province of Virginia,

holding what rights you have under that government; and the Virginians have made an agreement with the natives to go as far as the mountains and no farther; and you are over and beyond the mountains, therefore out of that agreement; by which you lie open to the insults and incursions of the Southern Indians, who have destroyed many of the inhabitants of Carolina and Virginia, and even now destroyed more on the like occasion. The English going beyond the bounds of their agreement, eleven of them were killed by the Indians while we were travelling in Virginia.

"Sixthly. If you believe yourselves to be within the bounds of William Penn's patent from King Charles the second, which will be hard for you to prove, you being far southward of his line, yet if done, that will be no consideration with the Indians without a purchase from them, except you will go about to convince them by fire and sword, contrary to our principles; and if that were done, they would ever be implacable enemies, and the land could never be enjoyed in peace.

"Seventhly. Please to note in Pennsylvania no new settlements are made without an agreement with the natives; as witness Lancaster county, lately settled, though that is far within the grant of William Penn's patent from King Charles the second; wherefore you lie open to the insurrections of the Northern as well as Southern Indians; and

"Lastly. Thus having shewn my good will to you and to your new little settlement, that you might sit every one under your own shady tree, where none might make you afraid, and that you might prosper naturally and spiritually, you and your children; and having a little eased my mind of that weight and concern (in some measure) that lay upon me, I at present desist, and subscribe myself, in the love of our holy Lord Jesus Christ, your real friend,   T. C."

As the early minutes of Hopewell Monthly Meeting no longer exist, it is impossible to know what action was taken in regard to Chalkley's letter. In any event it does not appear that his advice was followed. For a score of years the settlements grew, Friends as well as others advanced farther into the wilderness, and there was no trouble with the Indians. But after Braddock's disastrous defeat in 1755 the French encouraged their Indian allies to make incursions into the

Valley; and the inhabitants were terrified and thrown into the greatest confusion by their attacks, as they cut off the outlying settlers, massacred their families, and burned their houses.

Evidence of the state of affairs is found in the Frederick County Court Martial Records.

"At a Council of War held for Regulating the Militia of Frederick County in order to take such steps as Shall be Thought most Expedient on the present Critical Conjuncture the 14th Day of April 1756

Present

The Right Hon^bl The Lord Fairfax County Lieutenant
John Hite Major

Captains
{
John Lindsey
Isaac Parkins
Richard Morgin
Samuel Odell
Edward Rodgers
Jeremiah Smith
Thomas Caton
Paul Long
}

Proposals having been sent the Several Captains of the Melitia Sig^nd by the Commanding Officer of Malitia & Dated the 7th Day of April 1756

"To get what Vollinteers they could Encourage to go in Search of the Indian Enimy who are dayly Ravaging our Frontier & Commiting their accustomed Cruelties on the Inhabitants and the aforesaid Captains being met together & finding the Number of Men insufficient to go out against the Enimy its Considered that the men be Discharged being only Fifteen

Fairfax"

In the court records for May 4, 1757, it is stated that a grand jury was called but did not appear, occasioned by the commotions in the county on account of the Indians. At one time even the town of Winchester was almost abandoned by its panic-stricken citizens. Washington gives a graphic picture of the situation in one of his letters to Governor Dinwiddie:

"Sir,   "Winchester, 22 April, 1756.

"This encloses several letters, and the minutes of a council of war, which was held upon the receipt of them. Your Honor may see to what unhappy straits the distressed inhabitants and myself are reduced. I am too little acquainted, Sir, with pathetic language to attempt a description of the people's distresses, though I have a generous soul, sensible of wrongs, and swelling for redress. But what can I do? I see their situation, know their danger, and participate their sufferings, without having it in my power to give them further relief, than uncertain promises. In short, I see inevitable destruction in so clear a light, that, unless vigorous measures are taken by the Assembly, and speedy assistance sent from below, the poor inhabitants that are now in forts, must unavoidably fall, while the remainder are flying before the barbarous foe. In fine, the melancholy situation of the people, the little prospect of assistance, the gross and scandalous abuses cast upon the officers in general, which is reflecting upon me in particular, for suffering misconduct of such extraordinary kinds, and the distant prospect, if any, of gaining honor and reputation in the service,—cause me to lament the hour, that gave me a commission, and would induce me, at any other time than this of imminent danger, to resign, without one hesitating moment, a command, from which I never expect to reap either honor or benefit; but on the contrary, have almost an absolute certainty of incurring displeasure below, while the murder of helpless families may be laid to my account here!

"The supplicating tears of the women, and moving petitions of the men, melt me into such deadly sorrow, that I solemnly declare, if I know my own mind, I could offer myself a willing sacrifice to the butchering enemy, provided that would contribute to the people's ease."

[Sparks, Vol. II; pp. 143-4; Ed. 1834.]

In the midst of this destruction Friends seem to have been almost miraculously preserved. Some of them were driven from their homes, but none were killed, and only one house was burned. Information to this effect is found in the minutes and papers of the Meeting for Sufferings of Philadelphia Yearly Meetings. This standing committee of influential Friends was organized at about this time to give aid to any members of the Society who might suffer loss on account of the war or their refusal to take part in military operations.

The case of Hopewell Friends was presented to the Meeting for Sufferings in the following letter:

"from Hopewell Monthly Meeting held at opekan ye 5th of ye 9th Month 1757. To friends Members of ye Meeting for Sufferings held at Philadelphia Most Esteemed frds. at our Monthly Meeting of ye 8th mo: *1757* we Sent to ye Quarterly Meeting an acct Of Some famalys of frds that were Likely to Suffer for want of Some Releife & ye Quarterly Meeting Appointed two frds, to write to us to Inform us that the Meeting for Sufferings would Be at a Loss without ye Names and Numbers of Such parsons who are In distress therefore this Meeting appointed Isaac Holingsworth and Jess Pugh to Enquire Into their Circomstance and to See who think themselves in Need on acct. of Being driven from their habitations On acct: of ye Indian Enemy and we find that Some have Been drove from home almost two years and are not likely To Get home again and Some of ym that are Got home Do Stand in need of Some Help So we proceed to Give ye Names And Numbers of them

 Lidya Malin widow and three Children
 Isaac Wright & his wife & 4 Children
 Azariah Pugh his wife and 5 Children
 W:m Pickering his wife and 4 Children
 Sarah Heaworth widdow has 5 Small Children her Husband Being dead Since they Left their habitation
 Thos. Pugh his wife & Seven Children
 Jacob Rees his wife & Seven Children
 James Wright Junr. his wife & five Children
 Thos. Wright his wife & five Children
 Ann Sutherlin widow having one helpless daughter
 Also our Antient friends James Wright and his wife

Are Much Reduced Being driven from their Habitation and are unable to Labour for a Livelyhood And there May Be More for any thing we know at present Having But a few days to Enquire and if there was Some Trustees appointed to distribute ye Money According to the Nesesity of Each particular - - - - - - -

So having no More at present we Conclude And Remain Your Loving friends   Jesse Pugh
           Isaac Hollingsworth"

The Meeting for Sufferings promptly sent fifty pounds by the hand of Joseph Janney, ten pounds of which was for the use of James Wright and his wife, and inquired further details as to the exact nature and amount of losses of each family. They also said that many Friends were concerned because the land at Hopewell had been settled before it was purchased from the Indians and desired to know whether any Indians still had claims to it or whether it was "safe or prudent to remain in the possession of lands not fairly purchased of those that had a native right in it."

Some four months later another letter from Friends at Hopewell was written giving a more complete and particular account of their losses:

"To The Members of the Meeting for Sufferings in Philad$^{a.}$

Dear Friends

"In Love we salute you & hereby inform you, that according to Appointm^t of our Monthly Meeting of Hopewell to inspect into the several Circumstances of some Friends & th$^r.$ Families, wch you have had some short Acco$^t.$ of, which we have perform'd, as far as we could, having gone to their several Places of Abode, except James Wright jun$^r.$, who is remov'd into another County far distant that we cannot at present give so particular Acco$^t.$ of his Stock, but we are sensible it is very small

"You requested to know whether any of them were visited or attackd by the Indians, we answer no, nor any Friends Houses burnt except one. As to putting out their Children we do not find that any of them are willing or requested us to write to you on that Acco$^t.$; the Ages & Sex of their Children what Stock they have & what lost with the Sums recd are as followeth, vizt.

"The Ages & Sex of Wm Pickering's Children, One Daughter 7 Yrs Old, one son five Years old, one Daughter 3 Yrs old, One Son 1 Yr.

"Tho$^s.$ Wright's Children, One Daughter 9 Yrs. old, a Sons 7 Yrs, one Daughter five Yrs, a Daughter 3 Yrs, One Son 1 Yr.

"Isaac Wrights Children, one Son 7 Yrs, another 5 Yrs, a Daughter 3, a Son abo$^t.$ 5 months

"Thomas Pughs Children, One Daughter 13 Yrs old, a Son 11 Yrs, a Son 9 Yrs, a Daughter 7. One Son 6 Yrs a Daughter 3 Yrs another Daughter 2 Yrs old;

"Azariah Pugh's Children, one Daughter aged 10 Yrs, a Son 8 Yrs, another Son 5 yrs, a Daughter 3 Yrs, a Son 3 months

"Sarah Heworth's Children, one Son 12, a Daughter 10, a Son 8, another Son 6, a Daughter 3 Yrs, a Daughter 1½.

"James Wright junr. Children, one Son 12. another Son 10, a Daughter 8 Yrs a Son 3 Yrs,

"Ann Sutherland Widow, had a sickly Daughter helpless.

"William Pickering has 2 Cows & Calves, 2 Young Cattle, 1 Horse & Mare lost, 2 Cows & Calves & 1 Colt, little Household Goods,

"Thomas Wright has 2 Cows, 1 Heifer, lost, 2 Mares & a Horse, 1 Colt, no much Household Goods.

"Isaac Wright one Horse, very little Household Goods.

"Thomas Pugh has one Horse & Mare, 3 Cows, lost, 2 Cows & 2 Mares but little Household Goods.

"Azariah Pugh 3 Cows & Calves, 1 Mare at mal

"Sarah Heaworth, Widow has 3 Cows & 1 Heifer, two Horses & two Mares, Household Goods pretty well, lost 12 Head of Cattle,

"Ann Sutherland Widow, has 2 Cattle, 1 Horse but little Household Goods.

"The Sums recd.

James Wright sen.	£ 10	Azariah Pugh	£ 3
Wm, Pickering	3	Isaac Wright	3
Ann Sutherland	2	Sarah Heaworth	3
Thos. Pugh	4	James Wright jr.	4
Thos. Wright	3		£ 13
			& 22
			is £ 35

Joseph Lupton
Jesse Pugh"

As there was no reply to the part of the letter inquiring about the Indian claim to the land, the Meeting for Sufferings thought it necessary to appoint a committee to pay a visit to Hopewell. The report of this committee contained an extract from the now lost portion of the minutes of Hopewell Monthly Meeting.

"At our monthly Meeting of Hopewell held by Adjournment from the 26th· to the 27th· of ye· 6th· mo· 1758.

"The meeting Proceeded to consider the following matters, That wheras it hath pleased divine providence to Permit for Some time past the Indians or ancient Natives of these Countries to be moved against, and greatly ravage and distress the Frontier Inhabitants of this & the Neighboring Colonys of whom we are part; the same hath deeply and anxiously affected our minds and the minds of our Brethren in general, who by looking at the effect are thence led to Inquire into the cause & in perticular, whether those natives or some of them, have not been unjustly disposes'd of those lands in some measure thro' our means and in particular the meeting for sufferings constituted by our yearly meeting did some time ago write an Epistle to us importing their doubts respecting the justness of our rights to the lands we in these parts are possess'd of and their concern in that respect continuing and also a concern to assist us in the well ordering our Disciplinary affairs they in conjunction with the Committee appointed by the yearly meeting to visit the monthly and Quarterly Meetings have thought it necessary to appoint the following Friends to visit us (in order to administer such advice and Counsel as they in the wisdom of Truth may be enabled) Viz William Brown, Robert Lewis, Joshua Morris, James Moon, Thomas Lightfoot and Sam: Lightfoot jur· who are now present with us and also Isaac Hollingsworth, Francis Hague, Willm· Farquer William Matthew, & John Hough who at the request of the said Committee were appointed by Fairfax Monthly meeting to join them in the Service They having all together attended and assisted us thro' the course of our meeting business after which they took an opportunity of confering together respecting the Tenure of our Lands and do signifie to us that upon looking into former Treaties and collecting the best information they could get it doth not fully appear that the Government hath purchased any other Indian right to those lands than what was conveyed to them by the six united nations which appears to have been acquired by having conquered the former inhabitants in a war and thereby in some measure subjected them and their lands to the pleasure of the conquerors at that time but since that we apprehend they who were so conquered have acquired some Strength and vigour to assert their right to the land and are supposed to be in part the actors of the bloody ravages felt in those countries and in Pennsylvania the people of which Province being doubtfull there had some unfair measures been used to get land from the Indians have procured a Treaty with some of them which appears to have had a good effect so as to procure a peace with a number of the Delaware & Shawanese nations by making them presents and promising to come to a fair & equal adjustment with them respecting Lands And from the salutary effects attending the conduct of the Pennsylvanians the aforesaid Friends do Strongly recomend to us the Necessity of falling into the like measures by sending a message to the Indians who have been treated with by the aforesaid Government informing them that if they or any of them can make appear that they have a natural right of Inheritance in the Lands we hold, that we are willing, to pay them a reasonable Consideration therefor as being in our Estimation justly due to them (tho' we have Lawfully purchased the Lands allready of the Several Governments, to whom the Belong) provided the Said owners will convey to us their Right to the Lands we hold, and Live in Love & peace with their Brethren the English.

"This meeting having solidly considered the matter & conferred thereon, doth conclude that it may be of advantage to comply with the advice of the said friends, and doth desire them to represent our case to the meeting for Sufferings, and that we request the said meeting, if they should Judge it prudent to forward to the said Indians a message of like import with the above, and in General do and consider what may be for our Interest in the case as soon as possable

Signed By order of said
monthly meeting By   Jesse Pugh   Clark
True Coppy Examin'd"

In 1762 there was further correspondence between the Meeting for Sufferings and Hopewell Monthly Meeting in regard to satisfying the Indian claims, but nothing of a practical nature seems to have been done. In 1777 when a number of prominent Philadelphia Friends were exiled to Winchester because of a suspicion that they were in sympathy with the British, they encouraged the revival of this concern. About this time the following subscription was made and bond entered into by members of the monthly meeting:

"We the Subscribers do promise and oblige ourselves, Our Heirs, Executors & Administrators to pay unto Mordecai Ellis, Abel Walker, Edward Beeson, Lewis Neill, Robert Hains, Andrew MKay, or One of them in Pennsylvania Currency the several sums of Money by us respectively Subscribed, to be applied in such manner as the Meeting for Sufferings in Philadelphia with the consent of the said Members of this Meeting, may hereafter direct for the Benefit of the Indians, who were formerly the Native Owners of the Lands, on which we now live, or thire descendants if to be found, and if not for the service, & benifit of Other Indians,—whenever the same may be done in such Manner, as to avoid Giving Occation of Offence to those in Power at the time of such appropriation Agreeable to the Minute of the Conclusion of the Monthly Meeting of Hopewell this sixth day of the first month 1778."

Andrew M Kay	£ 30	Lewis Neill	£ 30
Enos Ellis	15	David Faulkner	4
Jesse Pugh	6	John Tremble	5
Robert Hains	12	Moses Walton	7
Daniel Brown Senr	5	Jonathan Lupton	3
Richard Ridgway	30	Isaac Parkins	25
Abel Walker	15	James Purviance	3
James Gawthrop	8	Joseph Stratton	5
Mordecai Ellis	10	Levi Hains	3
William Pickering	8	John Berry	5
Mordecai Walker	8	Jacob Pickering	2
Anthony Lee	10	George Shinn	2
Rees Cadwallader	6	Meshack Sexton	15
Samuel Pickering	5	Nathaniel White	3
James Steer	5	Daniel M. Pherson	15
Josiah Jackson	10	Isaac Brown	15
Thomas M. Clun	5	Owen Rogers	2
Richard Ridgeway	5	Jonah Hollingsworth	12
John Griffith	5	John Cowgill	10
Robert Rea	3	Jacob M. Kay	15
James Mendenhall	20	Richard Fawcett	2
Joseph Steer Junr.	15	Thomas Fawcett	3
Jonathan Wright	10	Edward Beeson	30
Samuel Lupton	10	Thomas Pugh	3

Joseph Hackney	10	Thomas Ellis	2
Joshua Coope	5	David Ross	5
John Garwood	5	John Lupton	5
John Serjant	3	Isaac Nevitt	2
Jacob Rambo	3	Edward White	3
Daniel Brown	5	Lewis Walker	3
Absalom Hayworth	2	Joseph Adams	1″5
Henry Wiliams	1″5	Richard Fawcett sen^r	3
Evan Rogers	3	Robert Painter	5
Robert Eyre	5	George Fallar	20
Samuel Pleasants	10	John Holloway	2″10
William Smith	3	Daniel Antram	2″—
William Grubb	15	John Brock	1″0
John Pickering	2	Jacob Fallar	—
Barak Fisher	5	John Antram	1″—
John McCoole	5	John Fallar	2
John Rogers	2	Joseph Wright	1
William Adams	4	William Wright	1—

The real difficulty in the way of paying the Indians for their lands seems to have been the lack of information as to just which tribe had inhabited this region. This Friends were unable to discover. Philadelphia Friends, relying on the passage in the bond which said, "for the benefit of the Indians who were formerly the native owners of the lands on which we now live, or their descendants, if to be found, and if not for the service and benefit of other Indians," called for the payment of the subscriptions. Hopewell Friends were dissatisfied with the proposed use of the money, which, according to the terms of the bond, was to be applied as the Meeting for Sufferings should direct *"with the consent of the said members of this meeting."* The controversy dragged on until after Hopewell and Crooked Run Monthly Meetings had been transferred to Baltimore Yearly Meeting. In 1795 it was referred to Fairfax Quarterly Meeting, to which those two monthly meetings then belonged. The following year and on later occasions subscriptions were collected and the money turned over to the Permanent Committee on Indian Affairs appointed by Baltimore Yearly Meeting. Thus money was finally given by Hopewell Friends for the benefit of the Indians, some of whom had once inhabited their lands.

An outstanding instance of the deep and continued interest that Friends felt for the welfare of Indians is to be found in the will of Sarah Zane, sister of Gen. Isaac Zane, proprietor of Marlboro Iron Works. Sarah Zane, whose home was in Philadelphia, had spent several years, at intervals, in Winchester, where she was a member of Center Meeting. Her will was made in 1819 and recorded in Philadelphia in 1821. Among its numerous provisions were two relating to Indians. The 11th item of her will is as follows:

Whereas about 1759 Captain New Castle, an Indian Chief, or messenger, ordered £30 paid to my father for use of two cousins, a boy and a girl, and the boy soon died and the girl named Betty received part of above by Thomas King, an Indian Chief, but no information has been obtained of her for 40 years; therefore £30 with interest from 1759 to be paid to treasurer of Committee of Yearly Meeting of Friends held in Phila. appointed to relieve the Indians, for benefit of said Indians.

The 17th item directs that $1000 be paid to the treasurer of the committee of the Baltimore Yearly Meeting for the relief and benefit of Indians, to be used in the transactions carried on at Mt. Pleasant, Ohio, for the Indians, "having the tribe of Tuscaroroes first in view if to be found within two years."

Sarah Zane had inherited lands of Isaac Zane in the Shenandoah Valley. It seems to be a reasonable inference that she felt that the Indians had not been adequately compensated, and furthermore that the Tuscaroras had the best claim of title to Valley lands.

CHAPTER VIII

HOPEWELL FRIENDS DURING TWO WARS

Our fathers chained in prisons dark
Were still in heart and conscience free.
    * * * *
Faith of our fathers, living still
In spite of dungeon, fire, and sword.
    * * * *

The Religious Society of Friends has always stood for peaceful methods of settling difficulties—between both individuals and nations. In their Book of Discipline, page 60, occurs this passage:

The first allegiance of mankind is to the will of God—It is the duty of every citizen to uphold and obey all legal enactments, unless they directly violate his deep convictions of the dictates of God.

From its earliest days the Society of Friends has held that war is contrary to the spirit, the life, and the teachings of Jesus, who renounced the weapons of worldly passion and used methods of love and self-sacrifice in their place. We restate our conviction that no plea of necessity in policy, however urgent, can release either individuals or nations from their duty to follow the law of love. "To carry out such a profession consistently will, at times, require the highest resolution, perseverance, and courage." (Page 61, Friends' Discipline.)

Holding these views regarding war has made the pathway of Friends very difficult at times, and remarkable instances have occurred wherein individual Friends have borne the most severe persecution rather than go against their convictions of right. Oftentimes the taunts of "slacker" and accusations of a lack of patriotism are harder to bear than facing the enemy would be. "He is a true patriot who exerts himself at all times to make his country a potent factor in the advancement of the world," and war does not conduce to world advancement.

At the time our country was fighting for her independence, Friends, because of their unwillingness to take up arms, were accused of being pro-British, and in Philadelphia, early in September, 1777, a number were arrested. The approach of the British army to the vicinity of that city heightened all defensive activities. Seventeen of those arrested, with three other gentlemen not Friends, were exiled to Virginia.

It was the original order that these men, deported from their homes, be sent to Staunton to prison, but they were never sent any farther than Winchester. Due largely to the intercessions of Isaac Zane, proprietor of Marlboro Iron Works, a man of influence, and in early life a Friend, they were allowed to remain in Winchester. At first under guards, and even threatened by the residents of the town, they later were given more liberty and were lodged in various Friends' homes. They were also permitted to hold religious meetings and to attend meetings at Center and Hopewell. At least two of them, John Pemberton and John Hunt, often preached at Hopewell and elsewhere.

The names of the twenty exiles, Friends and others, were Elijah Brown, Owen Jones Jr., William Smith, Samuel R. Fisher, Miers Fisher, Charles Eddy, Thomas Fisher, Thomas Gilpin, Charles Jervis, Samuel Pleasants, Thomas Afflick, William Drewet Smith, Thomas Wharton, Edward Pennington, Israel Pemberton, John Hunt, James Pemberton, John Pemberton, Henry Drinker, and Thomas Pike.

These men suffered many hardships, and two, Thomas Gilpin and John Hunt, both Friends, died here away from their families and friends, and were laid to rest in the graveyard at Hopewell. The latter was being cared for by Elizabeth (Walker) Jolliffe, the widow of William Jolliffe Jr., at her large and handsome stuccoed house on the west side of the "Great Road" (the Martinsburg Pike), not far from the present station of Clearbrook, on the Cumberland Valley R. R. This fine old residence was wantonly destroyed by fire within the period of the Civil War, 1861-65.

John Hunt in his last illness was a great sufferer, having been obliged, among other things, to undergo the amputation of a limb. William Smith, one of his fellow exiles, rode all night to secure General Adam Stephen, who was a surgeon, to assist Dr. Macky in performing the operation. When one of the surgeons complimented John Hunt by remarking to him,

"Sir, you have behaved like a hero," he mildly replied "I have endeavored to bear it like a Christian."

These exiles during the period of their detention at Winchester, six months or more, made various efforts and pleas for relief. One of these was a letter to the Governor and Council of Virginia, dated 1st day of 10th mo. 1777.

On March 10, 1778, Congress sent out the following letter and order:

A letter of the 7th from the Executive Council of Pennsylvania was read representing that the affairs of the Commonwealth of Pennsylvania are so circumstanced as to admit the return of the prisoners sent from that state into Virginia, without danger to the Commonwealth or to the common cause of America.

That the dangerous example of their longer continuance in banishment may afford on future occasions, has already given uneasiness to some good friends to the independency of these states and requesting, if Congress has no other reasons for continuing them in Virginia, than the Council are acquainted with, that such orders may be given as shall put those people again under the direction and authority of the President and Council of their state.

Monday Mar. 16th, 1778.

Resolved—That the Board of War be directed to deliver to the order of the President and Council of Pennsylvania the prisoners sent from that state to Virginia.

After various delays the prisoners were allowed to leave Winchester for Pennsylvania, most of them going by way of Waterford, in Loudoun County, Va., and thence across the Potomac. They reached Philadelphia on the last day of April, 1778.

Winchester, during the Revolutionary War, derived much importance from the fact that it was a place of detention for large numbers of prisoners captured by the American armies in several notable battles. Three hundred of the Hessian soldiers taken by Washington at Trenton were, after some months, brought to Winchester. They arrived in the autumn of 1777, shortly after the exiled Friends from Philadelphia. In October 1780 a number of men who had been made prisoners when General Burgoyne surrendered to General Gates at Saratoga were conducted to Winchester, after having been detained for varying periods at Charlottesville and other places. And late in the fall of 1781 were brought many of the army that Cornwallis surrendered to Washington at York-town.

In and near Winchester lived a number of the officers who had figured prominently in the Revolution and the colonial wars: James Wood, Angus McDonald, William Darke, Daniel Morgan, Horatio Gates, Charles Lee, Adam Stephen, and others. George Washington was much at home here. In a small stone building still standing he had had his head-quarters in 1756 and thereabouts while building Fort Loudoun and trying to defend the frontier against the Indians and the French. A well which his soldiers dug (blasted) through 103 feet of solid rock still continues to supply excellent water for the thirsty.

It may have been at Winchester that Washington said, in relation to exempting Friends from military service, "Let them alone, for you cannot induce them to fight for or against us. They are harmless, peaceable, and industrious people, who will produce meat and bread, and if they will not sell it to us we can take it, if we need it. We need bread and meat as much as we need Soldiers." (Southern Heroes, page 331.)

In 1777 when war came, the Friends were generally united as to policy. They would assist neither army. They would allow their goods to be taken for forage without resistance and would take no pay for them. Their meet-ing-houses might be used for barracks or hospitals, and they would at the usual time hold their meetings elsewhere. Their pleasant farm-houses and well-filled barns were at the mercy of any needy trooper. Their vacated city homes could be used for the sick and wounded or the winter quarters of soldiery. They would, in the meantime, quietly attend to their busi-ness or religious duties as far as circumstances would permit.

The writer does not know how closely Friends, at that time, were able to follow out this neutral policy, but there is abundant evidence to show how anxious they were to do what they could without compromising their sense of right.

As in the war for independence, so also in the Civil War, Winchester was a center of importance. In the latter struggle it was a strategic point that was contended for in numerous military operations. It changed hands, we are told, from one flag to the other no less than 76 times. No one who did not live here and experience at first-hand the warfare of those trying years can conceive of the unending anxiety, uncertainty, and heart-rending sorrows that fell upon the soldiers of both armies and upon the inhabitants of this part of the Shenandoah Valley. Toward the end of the war every man and boy between the ages of 16 and 60 was liable to be conscripted, and many Friends had to leave their homes and families and seek refuge in other localities to avoid being pressed into the army, contrary to their religious convictions.

From the diary of Mary W. Lupton, whose home was located about five miles from Winchester, we learn that soldiers, sometimes as many as forty in one day, came to demand this or that—sometimes meals, sometimes provisions of one kind or another; now to ask that chickens be cooked for them, or biscuits made; at another time it was hay or grain or horses or cows that they wanted. Occasionally they would pay for something, but more often would demand what they desired, or would steal whatever they saw or wanted. An instance of some soldiers buying a bee-hive for ten dollars is thus described in this diary:

Thirty-two soldiers have been here to-day. Two of them got the bee-hive on the stand and oh dear! what a time they did have to get it. The bees were very cross indeed and would hardly allow the soldiers to come near them. They threw water on the bees, sprinkled it on by dipping a brush in water, which only aggrevated them more. It was worth something to see the men run from them. A bee got into the head of one man and he took off up the lane, beating first with one hand and then the other. One of them was stung on the nose and oh! how he did pull at it, it was really laughable. He said he would rather have been shot, for then he could have had a furlow.

Another item from this diary is dated Mar. 12, 1862, and says:

Winchester was taken to-day without firing a gun. A beautiful morning, calm and pleasant. The Federals took possession about 8 o'clock and the flag of our Union is floating triumphantly there. Jackson retreated to Strasburg and took about twenty Union men off with him.

It is doubtful if at any of the other 75 times that Winchester changed hands in those four years the change was accomplished without firing a single gun.

In an old wallet of Joseph S. Jackson's was found a list of the Union men carried off on that occasion. They were Wm. Riple, G. H. Snap, G. B. Diffendefer, Amos Wright, David Hinkle, C. Snively, L. L. Hodson, George Aulick, L. P. York, V. Lidner, Job Throckmorton, C. W. Gibbons, C. Chase, Joseph

P. Mahany, Joseph S. Jackson, M. L. Real, John Chrismore, Henry Beson, M. Bean, John Clendenner, and J. L. Bowers. "C. Snively" was Charles Snively; "C. Chase" was Charles Chase, a retired sea-captain; and "M. Bean" was Mordecai Bean, one of the family of Beans who had been associated with General Isaac Zane in the iron-making business. The following were Friends: L. L. Hodgson, Job Throckmorton, Joseph P. Mahany, Joseph S. Jackson, Henry Beeson, and Mordecai Bean. The last-named was detained at various places and finally died in a Confederate prison. Another Friend who never reached home alive was Job Throckmorton. He had been arrested on his way to Hopewell to attend meeting. With others he was taken to a prison camp near Staunton, where he contracted typhoid fever and died. A neighbor, hearing of his death, drove to Staunton in a spring wagon, secured his body, and brought it home for burial.

It was during the imprisonment following the arrest and deportation of these men that Joseph S. Jackson was ordered to cut some firewood. He replied, "I do not cut wood when I am at home, and I do not expect to when I am visiting."

At certain periods during those unsettled times the Hopewell meeting house was used as officers' headquarters or soldiers' barracks. At such times Friends continued to hold their meetings at the usual times, either at the house of some member or at the Ridge meeting house, with comparatively few omissions. One Friend, who failed to answer to his name as an appointed representative to a business meeting, gave at the next meeting, as reason for his absence, that he could not get across the pike to the Hopewell road because of the unbroken stream of troops passing up the pike.

The meeting house in Winchester was occupied at first by the Confederates, who left it in fair condition. Later the Federal troops used it and injured it badly. In time they and various persons of the town dismantled and wrecked it to such a degree that it could never be used as a meeting house again.

The quarterly meeting minutes contain occasional records of no reports being received from Hopewell owing to "Military impediments." However, when military operations were active, horses unavailable, and conditions generally unfavor-

able, the unusual difficulties were overcome by extra effort.
For example, we note that on one occasion when no horse could
be secured Joel Lupton walked from his home on Apple Pie
Ridge across the Valley and across the Blue Ridge to Goose
Creek Quarterly Meeting at Lincoln, in Loudoun County, a
distance of over thirty miles.

When we consider the unfavorable conditions that pre-
vailed in those times we can appreciate the zeal and perseverance of Hopewell Friends in facing and surmounting them.
Not knowing what dangers or interferences they might en-
counter they would go five, ten, or twelve miles on horseback
or afoot, sometimes women alone, twice a week, to meet for
religious services. Fellow sufferers in a world of turmoil
and bloodshed, they thus sought strength and guidance from
a Divine Source, and they must have received a constant re-
newal of strength and courage to press forward in their several
pathways, else they could not have been so faithful.

Various incidents of those times have special interest and
significance. For example, there is the story of a flag—the
Union flag that floated for a considerable period over the main
fortification occupied by General Robert H. Milroy and his
forces. This flag, with its 34 stars, was left flying to cover
the retreat of the Federals on June 15, 1863, when Lee's
army, headed for its second invasion of the North, drove them
out. The fort, over which the flag was raised, was on a hill
beside the North Frederick Grade, at the northwest side of
Winchester. When the Confederates next morning stormed
the fort they found the flag waving over an empty camp and
deserted embankments.

As Jefferson Davis was collecting Union flags the boys in
Gray packed Milroy's flag carefully in a box to ship to him in
Richmond. It so happened that Mary Joy, a young girl who
was working in the home of Joseph Jackson, had married a
Union soldier a short time before. He had gone back to his
regiment, and Mary feared that he might be among the
prisoners taken by the Confederates in their capture of Winchester. Some of them had been brought back to Fort Milroy; so she, with a basket of provisions, climbed the hill to the
fort and, sure enough, there among the captured Federals she
found her husband. He, shortly before, while prowling about

the place, had discovered the box containing Milroy's flag. He and another prisoner had quietly removed the flag from the box and when Mary came they bound it around her as a petticoat and told her to take it to Annie Jackson, a daughter of Joseph, whom they knew to be a strong Union girl. When Mary Joy returned to the Jackson home with her flag petticoat Annie Jackson was chatting with some Confederate soldiers, but Mary called her out of the room and soon transferred to her the flag she had brought.

Then began days of rapid movings of the celebrated flag. Both parties wanted it. The Jacksons were suspected by the Confederates, and one searching squad after another came to the house. The flag was taken from one hiding place to another—in ash barrels, under mattresses, in dark corners of the cellar, under the eaves of the roof—and it was not found.

Mary Joy was not the only girl to be married in those days. Cupid managed to keep busy in spite of all besetments and difficulties. Several months after Milroy had been driven out of Winchester and so many of his troops captured, Jonah L. Rees came from Ohio to the Shenandoah Valley, the home of his ancestors, to claim Annie Jackson as his bride. He was stopped at Martinsburg. The Confederates were in control, and they would not honor his pass—which is still preserved by his daughter, Annie J. Rees. We do not know how Jonah Rees at Martinsburg managed to get information of his detention to his lady in Winchester, but he did. Her father, Joseph S. Jackson, then took her, with her sister and two friends, Harriet Griffith (afterwards Mrs. Ellis) and Mary Lupton (afterwards Mrs. Smith), to Martinsburg, in an ambulance. Jonah and Annie were married in that city by an Episcopal minister, for which transgression of the Rules of Discipline they later had to make acknowledgment to the meeting.

The next day after the marriage Winchester again changed hands—this was the middle of February, 1864. Had they known it, the bridal pair might have been escorted to Winchester by a Federal regiment, but they took a train to Philadelphia. Later they went to Canton, Ohio, to live. The war ended, but the years went on. Blue and Gray slept on the grassy hillsides together. And what of Milroy's flag? Annie Jackson Rees had it in Ohio. A few years after the war her mother in Virginia had sent it to her by the hands of Capt. William Starr, a Union veteran of Ohio. After keeping it nearly sixty years she sent it to General Joseph W. Keifer of Springfield, Ohio. She had known him during the war, as well as many other Ohio soldiers. The old flag now rests, after its various wanderings, in Columbus, a colorful memento of the days when Hopewell Friends and others were often disturbed from the even tenor of their ways.

Real heroism was often called for in those perilous times on the part of non-combatants as well as others, as is evidenced by numerous authentic instances. On one occasion the contending armies fought a pitched battle around the house of Joseph N. Jolliffe. For half an hour the strife was acute. The family sought safety upstairs, and afterwards seventeen bullets were found in the rooms below. The chimney was struck by a cannon-ball and came tumbling down upon the roof over their heads, but no member of the family was hurt.

Joseph N. Jolliffe was said to have cast the only vote cast and counted in Frederick County for Abraham Lincoln, when he was candidate for his second term as President. Jolliffe's undaunted and outspoken allegiance to the United States was not calculated to make him popular with his Confederate neighbors. He was complained of on one occasion as a Union man, and General Early sent officers to arrest him. Jolliffe asked the general what he required of him. General Early replied that he wished him to show him the roads in the different parts of that region. "Now, Friend Early, you know the roads around this part of the country as well as I do," was the prompt reply; "and you know I would not show them to you anyway."

He was then asked to take the oath of allegiance to the Confederacy, and on his declining to do this the general asked if he had taken the oath to the United States. He replied that he had promised allegiance, and the general told him to take now the oath of allegiance to the Confederate government. Jolliffe answered, "When you get it established I will, and not before." An officer who was standing by said, "Mr. Jolliffe, you are the first Quaker I ever saw who says *You* instead of *Thee*." General Early responded, "That makes no difference. He has the principles." The general then sent him home with an admonition to pray for the Confederacy.

At one time General Breckenridge made his headquarters at the house of Joseph Jolliffe for some weeks and his staff camped upon the beautiful lawn in front, but when Sheridan got the better of his forces Breckenridge took sudden leave, not even stopping to thank the members of the household for their courtesy and care of him during his unwelcome stay. See "Southern Heroes," page 343.

Breckenridge's sudden departure may have been the result of information which Sheridan received in 1864 by means of an unusual stratagem. The story as handed down concerns a member of the family of Amos and Rachel Wright. The father, opposed to taking up arms, leaving his wife and two daughters, Rebecca and Hannah, went west. This, of course, was after his arrest by General Jackson in 1862 and his subsequent release. Hannah Wright was an ardent upholder of the Confederacy; Rebecca was equally earnest in her support of the Union. On the 14th of September, 1864, a convalescent Confederate soldier called at the home of these young ladies, and naturally they talked of the war; and he told what he knew of the strength of the Confederate forces, which were then much weakened; that the artillery division had been withdrawn from Early's command, etc.

Two days later, as Rebecca Wright was sitting in her schoolroom at the noon recess, an intelligent-looking Negro came to the door, entered the room, and closed the door behind him. He then asked for Miss Wright, the Unionist. She told him that she was the one he was looking for. He told her that he had a letter for her from General Sheridan. She was excited and troubled, but took the little ball of tin foil which the man removed from his mouth. She began to tear off the tin foil with her fingers, when he said, "Don't do that—you will need it to wrap your reply in. I carried this letter to you from General Sheridan in this tin foil, holding it under my tongue. I have a permit to go through the Confederate lines three times a week, and I was instructed to swallow the letter if I was arrested or searched."

The contents of the letter which Rebecca Wright received were as follows:

Sept. 15th, 1864.

I learn from Major General Crook that you are a loyal lady and still love the old Flag. Can you inform me of General Early and his forces, the number of his divisions, or expected intentions? Have any more troops arrived from Richmond, or are any more coming, or reported to be coming? I am very Respectfully your most obedient servant, P. H. Sheridan, Major General Commanding.

You can trust the bearer.

Rebecca wrote what information the convalescent Confederate soldier had all unwittingly given her, wrapped it in the tin foil and gave it to the Negro, who put it under his tongue and departed. He delivered the note to Sheridan near Millwood.

For the next two days Rebecca Wright kept wondering what had become of the Negro; but on the 19th before daybreak the roar of cannon was heard, and the following day was one of suspense and anxiety, but finally looking out from the garret window she spied the Union flag flying and coming into Winchester.

In January 1867, three years after this event, she received from General Sheridan a letter and a beautiful gold watch, chain, and a breast-pin, with an inscription in the case of the watch in commemoration of her services in September 1864. As she wore the watch constantly it attracted some attention and the story leaked out to a reporter, who published it in a Baltimore paper. Winchester, of course, with its southern sympathies, looked upon her as a traitor to the South, and the bitter feeling engendered caused the family to move to Philadelphia.

Later Rebecca wrote to General Sheridan of her troubles and he immediately answered, with a letter which when presented to President Grant, during his first term of office, brought her an appointment to a position in the Treasury Department in Washington. In 1871 she married William Bonsal, but she held her appointment in the public service until her death in 1914.

Aaron H. Griffith, a Friend, greatly respected in the neighborhood, was frequently imprisoned, and during the several periods of his confinement he had much property taken—

horses, harness, and cloth, as well as the machinery from his mills, several of which were located at short distances east and southeast of Winchester.

From these incidents it will be seen that the devastation in Winchester and around that city and Hopewell was greater than the present generation can picture, for armies have little consideration for property rights—they use anything and everything in their range of vision that they care to use, and often wantonly destroy much that they cannot use and need not disturb.

Of course the keen demand for all food supplies made the price of everything very high. Illustrations from Mary W. Lupton's diary are eloquent and convincing—here are a few:

Flour is $16.00 per barrel and produce of every kind very high. Bacon was sold as high as $1.00 per lb., butter $1.00 per lb., apples from $10.00 to $15.00 per bushel, chickens $1.00, honey $1.00 per lb., sugar $2.00 per lb., brass buttons $3.00 per dozen. Ogdon only asks $7.00 for soling a pair of gaiters. A good deal of tobacco has been hauled out of Winchester and burned.

Most of the foregoing high prices, no doubt, were quoted in paper currency, but at one time salt was as high as $1.00 a pint in gold. Indeed, at many times it was almost impossible to get salt at all. One member of Hopewell meeting on a certain occasion purchased a number of milk crocks—he admitted afterwards that he did not need the crocks; but they had been glazed with salt, and he had noticed that they contained small deposits of salt!

Organized charitable institutions did not exist at that time outside of large cities to come to the rescue of communities such as this, whose citizens were stripped of their possessions with little left to live on, but there are always hearts that are softened by the sufferings of others, and so we find record in our minutes of a small meeting in Maryland (among whose members some of our men had sought refuge from Confederate conscription) donating a sum of money to Hopewell Monthly Meeting for relief service. The following entries in our record are in point.

7th day of 9th month, 1865.

The Meeting was informed that a contribution of $460. had been made by Little Falls Preparative Meeting, Harford County, Md., to this Monthly Meeting to be distributed among the loyal Friends of this Monthly Meeting

There was a great increase in the wealth and culture of the Friends in the large cities—they had opportunities that were not available for country Friends; and they seemed to the country Friends to be growing away from our testimony in favor of simplicity. Their homes became more luxurious, their dress, though plain, was of more expensive material, and their ideas were more or less molded by the new literature which came their way.

Country Friends were seldom in the cities—they produced most of their supplies—had no daily papers to keep them in touch with the outside world; and so did not keep pace with the urban Friends. Thus, when in attendance at their yearly meetings, they often found matters coming up in the business sessions which were new to them, but which their city friends seemed to understand and be ready to act upon—hence it is easy to see how the city and country Friends grew apart.

Perhaps the greatest factor in causing the separation came from the wave of Evangelicalism that had recently spread over England, and which brought about a revival of religious life and activity both in England and America. "Evangelicalism had certain important points of contact with Quakerism; its insistence on religion as a vital personal experience; its gospel of salvation for all men, even of the neglected classes and the heathen nations; its passion for morality and social reforms. But its doctrine of the final outward authority of the Scriptures, and the total depravity of human nature, were radically opposed to the early Quaker doctrine of the Inner Light; and the program and methods of this new movement were not in line with the spirit of Quakerism." English Friends came in close touch at many angles with this movement and it exerted a great influence on their views and ideals. American Quakerism did not have so many contacts as the English Friends had with the Evangelical movement, but it did have some very able ministers, who had come into the Society from other denominations and had brought with them doctrinal ideas quite new to Quakerism, and so, when English Friends came to America with their newly absorbed Evangelicalism they found a group in the city centers quite prepared to listen to them, and thus these new ideas got a foot-hold in the Meeting for Sufferings.

These various conditions were calculated to bring friction into the Society. One faction, consisting largely of country Friends, still imbued with the views of 18th-century Quietism, not in sympathy with "the new doctrines and growing worldliness of city Friends, but having themselves imbibed a new revolutionary spirit of democracy and liberty, and chafing under the autocratic authority of the Elders"; and the other faction, "composed chiefly of the Elders and their sympathizers in the cities who were alarmed at the growing disregard of the Discipline and opposition to it, who grew determined to suppress the new tendencies by more rigorous disciplinary measures, and who were especially fearful of any modes of doctrinal expression which seemed unsound by Evangelical tests"; and thus the stage was set for the struggle that culminated in the Separation.

The preaching of Elias Hicks was the spark that started the fire. Elbert Russell says, "the Separation was the joint achievement of four out-standing Quaker saints: Elias Hicks, Samuel Bettle, John Comly, and Thomas Shillitoc." They were all conscientious men, sincerely devoted to the Christian ideal as held by Friends, and devout students of the Scriptures. "They were all quietist mystics, seeking God in the silence of the creature, looking within for the divine leading, following Truth, and doing God's will as Light and Strength were given them. Each deemed himself a special guardian of a particular treasure in the Quaker patrimony:—Bettle, of Authority;—Hicks, of Truth;—Comly, of Peace; and Shillitoc, of Duty. Unfortunately, there was none to maintain patience and love as supreme Christian virtues." . . . "They lost sight of the fact that love is the essence of Christianity, that the fruit of the Spirit of God in the soul is first of all, love."

It was hoped for some time that the schism would be confined to Philadelphia Yearly Meeting, where it began, but it extended to New York, Baltimore, Indiana, and Ohio Yearly Meetings.

Elias Hicks was a Long Island farmer—he had a strong mind and commanding personality, and "felt the breath of a new age when Rationalism and Evangelicalism penetrated into Quaker circles." . . . "He was a powerful minister" and "thus

CHAPTER X

THE MEETING HOUSES AT HOPEWELL
AND CENTER

By the very nature of things much interesting history clusters about the old meeting houses. What a story it would make if we had the complete chronicle of all the sacred structures that have stood and served their day at Hopewell, Providence, Crooked Run, Smith Creek, Mt. Pleasant, the Ridge, Middle Creek, Berkeley, and the various other meeting places that our fathers and mothers knew! In this chapter we can attempt only a few brief sketches of the buildings at Hopewell and Center.

Hopewell meeting house, much as it is now, has been a familiar landmark of the lower Shenandoah Valley for five or six generations. Its staunch walls in colonial days often cast back the echoes of howling wolves and more than once reflected the shadows of painted Indians. When those walls were first erected, those that compose the east end of the structure, George Washington was a young man of 27, and he was the first President of the new United States when they were extended to their present dimensions. In 1833, when the stars fell in a brilliant and protracted shower, Hopewell meeting house in its full size was already a rather old building.

Of course, we are speaking of the present building of native limestone, which was first built in part in 1759 and enlarged by an addition to the western side in 1788-89. The first meeting house on the site was doubtless constructed of logs, and may have been erected as early as 1734 or 1735.

A more fitting name for the structure and the location could hardly have been selected. Hopewell meeting house stands squarely on the cardinal points of the compass and crowns a gently-sloping hill that faces the sunrise. From the summit of this hill one looks out over a wide fertile valley to blue mountains, the long undulating line of the Blue Ridge twenty miles away, edging up to the eastern horizon. It is a rural scene of plenty and, through most of the long years, also

CENTER MEETING HOUSE, IN WINCHESTER
Northwest Corner of Washington and Piccadilly Streets

of peace, though Braddock's ill-fated army passed near, moving westward, in 1755; Daniel Morgan's riflemen mustered not far away in 1775; and soldiers of both armies, Blue and Gray, passed and repassed nearly every day from 1861 to 1865. But the scene presented is usually quiet and undisturbed, one to invite to steady industry and to inspire the worker with hope and courage. Moreover, the outlook from Hopewell is one to quicken a love of nature and an appreciation of the beautiful.

As already suggested, the Hopewell region is rich in history—geography and men have made it so. From times immemorial the Shenandoah Valley has been a highway as well as a hunting ground, and into it, across the mountains and the rivers, come nature's gateways. In the Blue Ridge, in plain sight from Hopewell on a clear day, are six well-known passes —gaps we call them in Virginia: Chester Gap and Manassa's Gap just east of Front Royal; Ashby's Gap back of Millwood and Berry's Ferry; Snicker's Gap, often used by Washington, on a direct course from Winchester, via Berryville and Castleman's Ferry, to Dumfries and Alexandria; Key's Gap, or Vestal's Gap, just east of Charles Town and on the main road towards Hillsboro, Leesburg, and Washington; and Harper's Ferry Gap, where the Shenandoah and the Potomac unite and burst through the rocky mountain barrier.

Up the Potomac a few miles above Harper's Ferry are the shallow Packhorse Ford and other well-known crossings, giving access into the Shenandoah Valley from the northeast.

The view westward from Hopewell is a good deal obstructed. Half a mile away is Pumpkin Ridge. A mile and a half farther westward, and parallel with Pumpkin Ridge, is Apple Pie Ridge, famous for its orchards and historic associations. When the trees on these ridges are dense with foliage they hide the Alleghanies from an observer at Hopewell, though by looking around towards the southwest one may catch glimpses of a few mountain crests. Towards the north and northeast a considerable stretch of Little North Mountain may be seen, as it leads the eye down to the regions of the Potomac, hiding the greater ranges of the Alleghanies behind it.

At the foot of the Hopewell hill, two or three hundred yards southeast of the meeting house, is a copious spring, gushing up through massive and projecting limestone ledges, near the homestead of Alexander Ross. Ross, a leader among the first Friends to settle here, conveyed the tract of land on which Hopewell meeting house stands—ten acres; an oblong rectangle extending from east to west, with a stone firmly planted at each corner.

Two easy driveways lead in to Hopewell from the main highway, the historic Valley Pike between Winchester and Martinsburg. One starts in near Stephenson's Depot and crossing the railroad continues northward to the meeting house, just a mile from the entrance at the highway; the other one starts in at Clear Brook, also crosses the railroad, and continues westward to the meeting house, a mile and one tenth from the entrance at the highway. At Clear Brook, in the angle of the highway and the entrance road, is the stone monument bearing the bronze tablet commemorating Hopewell.

The older part of the stone meeting house at Hopewell, erected in 1759, measures 44 feet from south to north and 33 feet from east to west. The part that was added in 1788 measures 30 feet from east to west and 44 feet from south to north. Thus it is easy to see that the building was practically doubled in size in 1788-1789. In 1910 the whole building was repaired and most of the older wall was rebuilt; but a considerable section of it on the south side is pointed out as being a part of the original wall of 1759. The whole is an excellent example of rubble masonry.

In the earlier years the house was roofed with the almost everlasting shingles of white pine or yellow pine, but the present roof, dating from 1910, is composed of uniform leaves of dark-colored slate. Several massive stone chimneys stand erect and high above the roof. Many of the window sills and several of the door frames show evidence of great age, and within the building are a number of old benches and perhaps a long, narrow table or two that may have been in the meeting house from 1759 or earlier. A gallery and other interior features of olden days have been preserved.

On the Hopewell grounds, a hundred yards west of the meeting house, is a dwelling house, in which the caretaker and his family live. Just east of the meeting house is the burial ground, an acre nearly square in shape, enclosed with a wall of limestone well laid up without mortar. In the edge of the enclosure, next to the church, are several ancient trees. Other trees of larger or smaller size are to be found at different places on the grounds. John Griffith 3rd, who died in 1870, left a bequest of $30 for the care of Hopewell graveyard. His son, Aaron H. Griffith, added sufficient monies to his father's bequest to build the wall around the cemetery. The work was done the same year, 1870, as shown by figures on one of the stones; and the initials "W. D. L." indicate that the artisan who constructed the wall was W. D. Lee.

If we had the earliest minute books of Hopewell meeting we could no doubt ascertain just when the first meeting house was erected, the cost thereof, the name of the master-builder, and other particulars that we should like to know. We do have the books from 1759 down to the present. From them we select a few items. The builder of the stone meeting house, 33 by 44 feet, in 1759 was Thomas McClun. On the 5th day of 10th month, 1761, it was "unanimously agreed to allow Thomas McClun according to his request 12£: 10s: 0d more than his former bargain for Building the Meeting house which augments the sum to 55£: 10s: 0d."

The extra allowance was probably due to a change in plan by which the building was made somewhat larger than at first contemplated.

Soon after the house of 1759 was finished Mordecai Walker undertook to make the fires that were necessary for heating it. For nearly thirty years this building seems to have been adequate. It was in this building that the Pembertons, John Hunt, Thomas Gilpin, the Fishers, and other Friends exiled from Philadelphia during the winter of 1777-78 attended meetings. John Pemberton and John Hunt were ministers, and at Hopewell on the 2d day of 2d month, 1778, John Hunt, in the words of James Pemberton, "spoke largely and prophetically." Shortly afterwards Thomas Gilpin and John Hunt were given places in the burial ground. If their graves were marked at the time, their identity has long since been lost.

Probably during the troubled times of the Revolution the size of Hopewell meeting house was sufficient, but with the return of peace and the revival of prosperity after the war larger quarters were needed. On the 3d day of 3d month, 1788, was entered this minute:

> This meeting agrees to ask the advice of the Quarterly meeting, with respect to enlarging our meeting House, to accommodate the same.

Four months later it was noted that the Quarterly Meeting had agreed, and that the house would be enlarged by advancing the west side 30 feet farther out. Abel Walker, Nathan Littler, Lewis Neill, Amos Jolliffe, Isaac Brown, William Pickering, Anthony Lee, William McPherson, and Josiah Jackson were appointed to take charge of the work and to raise the necessary money by taking subscriptions in each meeting. The task of enlarging, finishing, and equipping with additional furniture, etc., and completing payments occupied several years. In 1793 a committee of eight was appointed to take in subscriptions for finishing the meeting house, and early the next year the work was "nearly done." Edward Beeson, Nathan Updegraff, Aquilla Janney, James Steer, and Walter Denny were appointed to settle with those who had charge of the work. On the 7th day of 4th month, 1794, the committee reported that the amount of the expense was 139 pounds 0 shillings 6 pence, of which sum 34 pounds 7 shillings 5 pence remained unpaid. Direction was given to raise the balance as soon as possible.

In 1796 a considerable amount of money belonging to the meeting was stolen, but additional repairs were undertaken. In 1812 the north side of the meeting house needed a new roof, the cost of which was estimated at about $65.00. In 1819 Jacob Rees reported that all costs for the meeting house roof had been settled.

"A righteous man regardeth the life of his beast." The Friends were always considerate of the welfare and comfort of the horses that they rode or drove to meeting. Shelter was provided for them. On the 4th day of 11th month, 1771, for example, Abel Walker, Richard Ridgway, and John Berry were appointed to employ workmen to build a stable and repair the graveyard. Even to-day, when automobiles are used almost exclusively, a commodious hitching shed for horses still remains on the Hopewell grounds, near the meeting house. This shed may also be serviceable for sheltering cars. Many attendants at Hopewell remember another large structure, shed and stable, that used to stand near the southeastern entrance to the grounds. That one and the one still remaining were both in use for many years.

In 1772 Jonathan Parkins, Richard Ridgway, Abel Walker and Thomas McClun were appointed to look into the title to the meeting house lot. In 1796 and again in 1817, perhaps at others times also, attention was given to titles. Friends as a rule have been properly careful of such matters.

Soon after the setting up of Hopewell a small group of log cabins began to rise at Shawnee Spring, 7 miles southwest of Hopewell. They were the beginning of the town of Winchester, which occupies the site of a village or at least a camping-ground of the Indians. After Winchester had grown to be a good-sized town and had assumed a place of much importance in colonial history, Center Friends' Meeting was established, first just southwest of the town, adjoining the Parkins and Hollingsworth homes, and later in the town itself, where it is still carried on. Inasmuch as Center from its beginning and Hopewell have been so closely linked in nearness of place and active coöperation, a number of particulars concerning the Center meeting houses are herewith presented.

In 1776, as Hopewell records show, leave was given the Friends "near and at Isaac Parkins" [Isaac Parkins Jr.] to hold a meeting for worship. About that time they began to erect a meeting house, but the Revolution doubtless interrupted the work. The name Center was soon adopted. The Hollingsworths lived near. On the 21st of 11th month, 1777, James Pemberton, one of the exiles from Philadelphia, wrote in his journal: "Walked to R. Hollingsworth meeting (called the Center) dined at Josiah Jacksons." The next day he wrote:

A fine clear morning & moderate—walk'd in comp—with I. Hunt etc. to R. H.'s in order to have a conference with ye ffrds who constitute the Center Meeting respecting the building a Meeting house which some of our ffrds thought would tend to promote the cause of Truth if erected in the town of Winchester, which was proposed to their consideration & left with them: they had sometime before concluded to build a house abt a mile distant, and after conferring together this time they agreed to proceed in compleating that wch was before partly built, & they united in opinion the place was more convenient for them than to alter it. & some ffrds called to inform us that they had entered into a subscription in order to finish it as speedily as they could—

On the 19th of 4th month, 1778, first day of the week, Israel Pemberton, John Pemberton, James Pemberton, Henry Drinker, and Samuel Pleasants, who had been lodging in the house of David Brown and wife Sarah at or near Springdale, left Brown's for Pennsylvania, going by way of Winchester. "We went to Centre Meeting in the morning." See "Exiles from Pennsylvania," page 226. This may mean that Center meeting house was completed and in use at that time.

The original site of Center meeting house, as James Pemberton indicates, was about a mile southwest of Winchester. That was in 1777. Now the city has grown out to and even beyond that locality, but the spot may still be identified by means of the graveyard.

In 1781 a preparative meeting was settled at Center, including the Friends of Mt. Pleasant (Fawcett's Meeting), near Marlboro Iron Works. In 1817 Sarah Zane, a sister of General Isaac Zane of Marlboro, conveyed a lot of ground in Winchester, the whole square of the 600 block, on the west side of South Washington Street, to the Friends of Center, and in the 5th month of 1817 steps were taken towards erecting a meeting house thereon. Within the next two or three years the new building was finished and in use, but the property at the old site was carefully secured. In the 2d month of 1820 Samuel Brown and Amos Lupton were appointed trustees to receive title to the graveyard "at the old Meeting House lot."

The new meeting house in Winchester was used until the Civil War, when it was destroyed. The following report, prepared in 9th month 1865 and presented to the meeting, is apropos.

To Centre Preparative Meeting

Dear friends,

Your committee appointed at the last preparative Meeting to investigate the causes of the destruction of the said Meeting House, we find that it was first occupied as a Hospital by the Southern Army in the summer of 1861 for a few weeks, but it was left by them in a pretty good condition. Meetings were held there afterwards, until about the 12th of 3rd Mo. 1862, on which day Banks Army arrived in Winchester.

As near as we can ascertain on the next day (the 13th) the Military authorities demanded the Key and took possession of the Meeting House. Friends never used it afterwards.

The entire fencing around the lot and a portion of the inside work of the Building were destroyed by Banks Army during the time that he occupied Winchester.

We next find that in the winter of 1862-1863 while Gen. Melroy occupied the town the balance of the inside wood work including window frames and door frames was destroyed by the troops under his (Melroy's) command. The walls remained standing until about the 9th month 1863 then they fell down. After the fall of the building the remaining materials were used or destroyed by a portion of the Citizens of the Town. There was no army here at that time.

Your committee upon examining the premises find no part of the Building left, except a small part of the foundation wall.

In concluding this brief, but we hope satisfactory account of the destruction of our Meeting House we gratefully acknowledge the kind assistance of the Women Friends in furnishing dates and other important information contained in the report.

With regard to the cost of the Building your committee would express the opinion that considering the present high price of materials and labour it will requre $2500 or $3000 to replace it.

We would also express the opinion in which we believe the entire Meeting will unite, that the new Meetng House should be located in a more convenient and central part of the Town.

Winchester 8th Mo. 9th 1865

CHARLES L. WOOD
JOHN W. MARVIN

Fairfax Quarterly Meeting held at Goose Creek, Loudoun County, Va., on the 20th of 11th month, 1865, communicated to Hopewell Monthly Meeting that the monthly meetings were directed, in accordance with the recommendation of the Yearly Meeting, to open books for subscriptions to the fund to rebuild Centre Meeting House in the town of Winchester. Elkanah Fawcett, Joel Lupton, Daniel Walker, and Hugh Sidwell were appointed as a local committee to take subscriptions. Some time later Joseph S. Hackney, Hugh Sidwell, and Daniel Walker were named for the same purpose.

The work evidently did not go forward rapidly. On the 4th of 11th month, 1869, a committee from Center conferred with Friends at Hopewell and agreed that such a building as would be needed in Winchester would cost about $3000. The committee was continued and authorized to make sale of the lot belonging to Friends in Winchester and purchase other property on which to build a meeting house if they found it most expedient to do so.

Later the committee reported that they had purchased a lot on which to build. Elkanah Fawcett, Charles L. Wood, Daniel T. Wood, and Joseph S. Jackson were appointed trustees for the said lot, and a deed was to be made to them.

At Hopewell Monthly Meeting on the 7th day of 12th month, 1871, representatives were present except Hugh S. Lupton, for whose absence a reason was given. The committee appointed at a former meeting to purchase a lot and build a meeting house at Center in Winchester reported the house to be in readiness to hold meetings. Dr. Richard Sidwell, treasurer, in account with Hopewell Monthly Meeting, reported that he had received cash and donations to the amount of $5349.75. He had paid bills to the amount of $5206.58, leaving in his hands a balance of $143.17. Subscriptions still uncollected amounted to $354.00.

But there were still several bills for materials and work on the meeting house unpaid:

John Diffendaffer and Son,	$850.82
Baker and Bros.,	65.07
Alfred Seals,	19.00

Deducting the amount of cash in the hands of the treasurer, $143.17, left a balance of $791.72 to be provided for.

On the 8th of 2d month, 1872, the first monthly meeting was held at the new Center meeting house, in Winchester, the present building, located on the corner of North Washington Street and West Piccadilly. A month or two later other bills were paid, among them a balance of $18.00 to John W. Marvin as rent, for the use of his room in which Center Meeting was held in 1871.

John W. Marvin, known as Dr. Marvin, was a well-to-do and scholarly Friend who had opened a boarding school in Winchester in 1838 on Sharpe Street. Center Meeting in 1871 was held in one of the buildings of this school.

The burial ground at Old Center, southwest of town, now on the edge of the city, was used for years after the meetings were held in town. A few tombstones and a deep furrow around them, the foundation of the wall now removed, hard by the northwest side of the Valley Pike, still show clearly the location of the cemetery at Old Center. Four tombstones

bear legible inscriptions: (1) "Samuel Brown," who died 8th
month 10th 1852, aged 69; (2) "Hannah M. Brown," who
died 8th month 15th 1849; age not stated; (3) "Mary M.
Brown," 1832; (4) "S. A. F. B."

This graveyard was deeded as a gift to Hopewell Monthly
Meeting by Isaac Parkins Jr. in 1820, but all record of the
deed was lost for many years. It was found only in the spring
of this year (1935). It shows that Friends have a clear title
to the ground.

CHAPTER XI

SCHOOLS AND CULTURAL ACTIVITIES

It is a well known fact that Friends were interested in giving their children educational advantages, as far as environment and circumstances permitted, and that the establishment of a school was one of their first thoughts when settling a community; consequently, we feel sure that Hopewell Friends, when settling here, must have given attention to this important matter. Data of this early period would be more full if the first records of the Monthly Meeting had not perished in a fire in 1759.

As early as 1st of 2nd Month, 1779, we find the following minute:

"Friends of Hopewell particular meeting request the Liberty of Building a Schoolhouse on the Meeting House lot for the use of the Society. With which the Monthly Meeting concurs and grants." The same year, we find a committee appointed, "to take the necessary care of inspecting into schools according to the direction of the Yearly Meeting, and render an account when called upon."

In Record Book 2, page 296, we find this minute:

The Committee to take into consideration, and to visit schools, made the following report in writing. We, the committee appointed in the case of schools and the education of children under pious Tutorers agree to report that we have several times met and visited most of the schools among Friends belonging to this Monthly Meeting and find a disposition prevailing among Friends to endeavor to come up to advice of the Yearly Meeting in 1778, as near as their circumstances will admit of, so that there is one school within the verge of Hopewell Particular meeting under the direction of a committee. One school-house built and a dwelling house for a school master on the way, on a lot of ground containing four acres for that purpose, and some more under consideration, though a remisness in some others is too prevalent. Signed on behalf of the Committee by Anthony Lee. Which after deliberate consideration is concurred with, and the clerk is directed to forward this same to the Quarterly Meeting.

At Hopewell meeting on the 5th day of 4th month, 1784, were received for distribution a number of books: 7 dozen of William Penn's "Tender Counsel," 6 dozen and 3 German

books, 5 of Phipps, 5 of Penn's Epistles. These were divided
among the different meetings. These books, of course, had
a positive educational value. The German books, no doubt,
were procured in consideration of the large number of German
people in the neighborhood of Winchester and other parts of
Frederick County. From time to time occasional German
names appear among the lists of Friends thereabout.

A record of 1st of 1st month, 1787, says, "At this meeting
the Extracts (of the Yearly Meeting) were produced and
read, and the many seasonable advices and directions therein
contained, claiming the future attention of this meeting, par-
ticularly that of schools, and it is desired that the Committee
appointed for that service may be animated to proceed therein,
so as to be prepared to send up a satisfactory report to the
meeting next year, and that Friends may individually labour
to guard against those things, which so much are the cause of
the body being exercised on Our account, ———."

References occur in 1787, 1788, and 1789 to requests
being made by Friends living near the school house close to
William Lupton's, to hold a meeting for worship in the winter
season at this school house, which was evidently under the
care of Hopewell Monthly Meeting.

On 6th of 3rd month, 1797, "Friends on and near the
Ridge near Joseph Hackney's request to have the liberty to
hold a meeting in their school-house." This shows that
Friends had a school house at the place indicated, which we
think was one of the first schools in Frederick County. It was
near the site of the brick school house south of White Hall,
still standing. Here many of the early Quaker settlers received their education. The teachers of this school were
Friends, but the school was open to children of non-members,
as well as to those who were members. John Griffith, a
Friend, born 1777, died 1870, acquired his entire education
at this school, and his seven sons and three daughters received
most of their training there also; and they were considered
well educated according to the standard of the times. William Thornburg was a teacher in this school some time between
1815 and 1835. In the minutes of the Orthodox branch of
Friends, two schools at Hopewell are mentioned in 1834 and
also in 1835. One of these was doubtless the school already

referred to. Samuel F. Balderson, Mahlon Schofield, and
Robert Bond are spoken of as teachers here at different times;
the last-named being clerk of the Orthodox Meeting.

Under date of 4th of 7th month, 1800, we have record of
an "Indulged" meeting at Dillon's Run being held in the
school house near Asa Lupton's; and in 1801 a committee was
appointed to consider, "as handed down in the Extracts," the
"pious guarded Education of our Youth and state of schools
amongst us, and report to next meeting." Some months later,
in 1802, the committee reported it had paid some attention
thereto, but was continued. It is a well established fact that
a school house stood on the Friends' meeting house lot at
Crooked Run at an early date; and there was also a school in
connection with the Mt. Pleasant Meeting.

On 10th of 8th month, 1815, the meeting seemed to
have a deep concern that greater attention be paid to education,
as shown in the following minute: "The committee on the
subject of schools as recommended in the Extracts reported as
follows, 'We, the committee appointed on the subject of
schools, agreed to report that attention has been paid thereto,
and find there has been three schools taught by members of
our Society within the limits of our meeting; but with respect
to friends generally attending to the education of their children, a renewed attention seems necessary, it being obvious
that great uneasiness prevails on that account.' "

The importance of better educational advantages probably
led Baltimore Yearly Meeting in 1815 to buy property in
Montgomery County, Maryland, for a school, which was later
established under the name of "Fair Hill Boarding School."
Hopewell Monthly Meeting contributed financially toward
starting this school, and also aided from time to time in its
support, as shown by record of committees to collect funds for
it. Pupils from this monthly meeting also attended the
school. Some years later, probably about 1850, this school
was given up; and when Baltimore Yearly Meeting sold the
property the proceeds were divided, and part of them used to
help finance the Baltimore Friends school; and part was invested for the use of children of the country meetings. This
fund has proven and is still proving valuable, as many children
from the country meetings belonging to Baltimore Yearly

Meeting borrow from it, without interest, to help them get more advanced education, being expected if possible to pay back the borrowed sums when they get to earning for themselves. In 1882 the following minute occurs in the records of Hopewell, which doubtless refers to this fund: "A communication was read from Baltimore Yearly Meeting on the subject of Education, advising Friends to use to advantage the fund appropriated for distribution throughout the different Monthly Meetings."

There was also a "Ridge school" some miles south of the one already mentioned, where many of past generations received instruction. This was held in one end of the Ridge Meeting House, a picture of which is given showing the old stone horse-block, where, no doubt, many of our ancestors mounted and dismounted from their horses in school days and on meeting days.

At a monthly meeting held the 10th of 8th month, 1848, this minute appears: "Women's Meeting having laid before us an exercise amongst them of promoting the Education of our Youth by the establishment of a school amongst us for that purpose, the following committee was appointed to unite with women friends on consideration of the subject and report their view of the case to next or a future meeting." At the next monthly meeting the committee reported, but the substance of the report is not recorded. "After claiming the attention of the meeting it was thought best to be left under consideration of the members individually until a future meeting."

This was continued from month to month until 7th of 12th month, 1848, when we find this minute: "The subject of the school as proposed by Women Friends being under consideration it was proposed that a committee be appointed to unite with a like committee of women friends (if they think proper to appoint one) and take the subject under their care, and try what funds can be raised according to the report of the committee in the 9th month." This committee was continued as shown on the record book, for four months, and then the subject continued under the committee to report when ready. From tradition we are sure this school was established, although we find no further report in the records; but the parents of some of us have told of their school days at that place, parents who would have been too old to have gone to a later school there, which is spoken of subsequently in our annals.

This later effort was made in 1883, thirty-five years after the other, at which time a committee was appointed "to unite with the Yearly Meeting Committee on Education to consider the establishment of a Friends school under care of the Monthly Meeting to be held at the Ridge, with which the women unite." Two months later, "The committee appointed at a previous meeting on Education are requested to consult with the Public school authorities in regard to a school at the Ridge and report at next meeting." No further report of this attempt appears, but a school, with a Friend as teacher, was conducted for a time either at the Ridge meeting house or at the public school house near by.

David W. Branson conducted a school in a room fitted up over his carriage house, which his children, those of his two brothers, and of some of the neighbors attended, there receiving their start in the field of learning.

There were also a number of small schools taught in Friends' families, in different parts of the community. Transportation then, as in pioneer days and later also, was a serious consideration; accordingly, schools near at hand were desired.

A few copies of the Epistles sent each year from London Yearly Meeting and copies of other books occasionally sent to Hopewell Meeting by London, Ireland, and by the "Meeting for Sufferings" in Philadelphia were apparently treasured and carefully handed around to Friends and others for perusal. Some of those books were for the school—but with a list such as the following, one wonders which were deemed suitable for children! And how many may still lie hidden away in some of the neighborhood attics?

"Primitive Christianity," revised by Wm. Penn;

"The Anarchy of the Ranters";

"Principles and Practices of the Christian Religion," by Sam'l Fuller;

"Baptism"—printed in the Dutch language;

"Essay upon Silent Worship," by Mary Brook;

"Catechisms";

"Spirit of Prayer";
"Berkeley's Apology" (Barclay).

It would be interesting to know more about how those early schools were conducted; but whatever their methods and their equipment, the results attained were remarkable, considering the contrast between the wide opportunities of to-day and the restricted conditions that surrounded our ancestors. Sterling worth, high standards of conduct, and a broad diversified knowledge were outstanding characteristics of the better educated men of those days.

The obituary of one of the early teachers named above is reproduced below. It is not only a fitting tribute to a worthy man, it also is a contribution to our educational history.

ROBERT BOND

Robert Bond, aged about 66 years; an esteemed member and overseer of Hopewell Monthly Meeting in Frederick County, Virginia, died on Fifth-day evening, the 5th of 12th mo. 1850.

This dear Friend died in the faith and hope of the Gospel, which he honoured by an exemplary and dedicated life. His many friends have the consoling belief that he has joined the cloud of witnesses, who surround the Throne of infinite purity. His memory is precious to a large number of scholars who were benefited by his teaching during a period of more than 20 years in the same school-room; very many of whom had no other teacher.

His counsel and his influence were always given with an earnest zeal to promote the lasting welfare of his pupils. Many worthy men and women, who, in after years, filled honourable positions of trust attributed much of their success to his wise counsel and influence.

HOPEWELL LIBRARY

Many years ago a carefully selected library was maintained in the meeting-house at Hopewell. The number of volumes was small, but the books embraced in the collection were well suited to religious and educational purposes. On the 6th day of 4th month, 1868, a report on the library was made to the meeting. This report was signed by Charles L. Wood and Lydia Lupton on behalf of a committee that had been appointed some time before. So much interesting information is contained in this report that it is given below in full.

To Hopewell Monthly Meeting

The committee appointed at last monthly meeting for the purpose of examining the condition of Hopewell Library, are prepared to make the following report. First, we find upon examination of the bookcase heretofore used, that it will be too small to contain the books; as the numbers will be considerably increased. We, therefore, recommend that the meeting make an appropriation sufficiently large to have a more commodious case made.

Second, a part of the committee met at the house of Joseph Branson (where the books have been kept since their removal from Hopewell during the rebellion) and found a list of names and numbers calling for forty four volumes, names and numbers in them. There were therefore ten books called for in the list which were not to be found neither could any record of the names of the persons who may have them be found. The committee would recommend that the members of the Monthly Meeting look through their private libraries, and see if some of the missing volumes can be found.

3rd, We found nine volumes belonging to private parties, which have been loaned to the Library for a season and are still in it. They are not named or numbered in the list, and the committee are of the opinion there are more of the same kind, as we found but five of the volumes belonging to the set of eight of George Fox's works.

4th, We found two volumes of B Turks works which appear to have been given to Hopewell Preparative which are not mentioned in the list.

5th, We found the second volume of Janney's History of Friends with the Library books, but found no number or name in the book, or the list to indicate where it belongs, but we are of the opinion it belongs with them and that the first volume should be there also, but it was not among them.

6th, We found six little pamphlets called Treasury of Facts which have not been properly numbered.

Lastly, we would recommend that a standing committee of two, one man and one woman friend from each particular meeting be appointed to examine all books that may be donated to the Library and to make such purchases of books, from time to time, as donations of funds may be placed in their hands for that purpose. Also that an efficient Librarian be appointed whose duty it shall be to keep a record of all books received and also all loaned out and to whom they have been loaned, and to see that but one book is taken out by the same person at the same time, and that no book is kept out more than one month at a time, but that they may be permitted to renew the loan for one month longer. It was also suggested that if any friends have books in their private libraries, they wish to have more extensively read are left at liberty to contribute such books as will be acceptable to the committee as proper to be in a Friend's library, and when so contributed shall be considered as the property of the Monthly Meeting.

Four months later, to wit, on the 10th day of 8th month, 1868, Jonah H. Lupton and Archibald Robinson on behalf of a committee submitted the following report:

To Hopewell Monthly Meeting

The committee appointed at a former Meeting to procure a bookcase for the purpose of holding the books of Hopewell Library are now prepared to report that they have had one made which they think suitable for the purpose at a cost of ten dollars. A book was procured for the purpose of keeping the records at a cost of one dollar.

FIRST-DAY SCHOOLS

In pioneer days, Sunday Schools were not in existence, so of course it was many years before this method of giving religious instruction became general among Friends.

Friends' first effort in this direction here was made by David Branson, a member and minister at Hopewell, who had a small school at his own house, probably some time in the 1870's, on First-Day afternoons.

One who attended this school says, "It did not make much of a hit with us children because we were called in from our play to attend it."

The first record we have of an organized Sunday School at Hopewell was in 1886, when one was established to meet through the summer months, after the religious meeting on First Day. Whether the other branch of Friends held a Bible School at Hopewell earlier than that, has not been ascertained. However, at the present time, the two branches hold their schools jointly each Sunday; and the combined school has about 65 on its roll now, with a fine group of young people.

A First-Day School was also started at the Ridge Meeting House about the same time the one at Hopewell began, but it has long since passed, as no meeting has been held there for years, the meeting house having been destroyed by fire.

Winchester, which is a part of Hopewell Monthly Meeting, also maintains a First-Day School, but we are unable to say when it was first started. It meets regularly each Sunday after the religious meeting.

HOPEWELL YOUNG FRIENDS ASSOCIATION

In 1898 through the instrumentality of a young Friend, Tacy Branson Doing, the subject of starting a Young Friends Association at Hopewell was brought up, resulting in an organization which lasted over a period of nearly twenty-eight years.

This work, however, was not confined to young Friends only, as persons of all ages took part, but the officers who conducted the exercises were chosen mostly from the younger part of the membership. The regular meetings were held at Hopewell most of the time, but were interspersed with parlor meetings.

The exercises of the organization were varied, including subjects of historical nature, denominational interest, current events, and original papers, many of which were of decided value and called forth very helpful discussion. At first, music formed no part of the programs, but later hymns became a regular feature of the meetings.

From this organization many recommendations went to the monthly meeting from time to time, suggesting changes and improvements which, in the retrospect, have proven worth while. Some of these will be mentioned further on.

In 1903 a small meeting was held once a month at the Ridge Meeting House (later destroyed by fire), and the Young Friends Association divided itself into committees of six or more to aid this struggling meeting by one of these committees attending each month and contributing something to the religious life of the meeting.

That same year, through this organization, the Quarterly Meeting was held, as it was for several years following, on First Day in Winchester instead of at Hopewell, in the effort of thus making it a more orderly occasion, since it had become rather a picnic for many who were neither members nor interested in the religious values of the meeting. This change had the desired effect, and now the Quarterly Meeting, held again regularly at Hopewell, is more in keeping with the wishes of Friends, who are glad to welcome any who come to worship with them in their simple method of service.

The Young Friends Association interested itself in trying to add to the value of the regular religious meetings by arranging for the presentation of some definite topic in the early part of the meetings for worship, which might form a basis for thought and expression. Also "A Study of Doctrine and Discipline," by Henry W. Wilbur, was used to widen the knowledge of young Friends concerning the methods of conducting our business meetings.

Since the separation of Friends into two branches in 1827 the meeting house at Hopewell had been used by the two, one branch using one end and the other the other end. The older half of the building gradually fell into bad condition, so in 1908 the Y. F. A. expressed a great desire that some action be taken to repair the building; and finally after the matter was under consideration for some time the wall of the east end was torn down and rebuilt. During the time of the rebuilding the two meetings met together, and have continued to do so ever since.

Another improvement this organization introduced was the putting in of a cistern, thus providing good drinking water, which has proven a great boon. Not infrequently two meetings are held at Hopewell on the same day, morning and afternoon, and a lunch served, when good water is a necessity.

Various kinds of philanthropic work claimed the attention of the Association, such as contributing to the hospital in Winchester, doing sewing, knitting, and other work for sufferers in the World War, and contributing financially to denominational interests.

The Swarthmore Chautauqua was introduced into this community through this Association, and came to Winchester successfully for several years. Articles on peace were written, and a number published in the two local papers which were operating here at that time.

Suggestions for the better heating of the meeting house were first introduced by this body, as was also the erecting of a sign on the Martinsburg Pike showing the location of the meeting house. This was the initial step toward the placing beside the highway of a permanent monument—the one which has been erected as a part of our 200th anniversary exercises.

Improvement of the near-by graveyard at Hopewell has been more than once under consideration, and we hope that later on this concern will be carried into effect.

In 1912 or 1913 the Hopewell organization joined the general conference of Young Friends Associations, with which it kept in touch through delegates sent to the annual meetings. These delegates reported upon the activities of other associations. This procedure was kept up for a number of years, but in time, as has been the case in many other organizations, the interest waned until in 1928 this previously useful and active body held a meeting which proved to be its last one, although it was never decided that the work be dropped permanently.

THE YOUNG FRIENDS MOVEMENT

Although since the founding of the Society of Friends there has been an interested and active group of younger Friends who cared enough to carry on the principles and ideals of the Society as they grew older, there never was a definite organization of Young Friends formed in the Baltimore Yearly Meeting until the year 1919. It was then that the purposes of this movement, to stimulate a study of Christianity as Friends see it, and its application to the life of to-day, to increase the usefulness of the Young Friends to the Society in general through promotion of friendly relations between all its branches, and by greater participation in the religious and business conduct of the home meetings, were definitely outlined; and the Yearly Meeting recognized this movement as a real and important part of its activities in 1920. Since that time the organization has continued to be a very active part of the program of the Society of Friends and from it have come many worth-while ideas and accomplishments.

The Young Friends Movement is composed of groups of young Friends from all the meetings included in Baltimore Yearly Meeting, and each group is represented on an executive committee which plans the activities of the year, which include chiefly worth-while conferences at various times during the year, and frequent pilgrimages of the different groups to visit other Young Friends' organizations in the Yearly Meeting.

The younger members of the meeting at Hopewell have never been definitely organized as a Young Friends' group, although they have been members and have taken active part in such organizations as the Young Friends Association, which included older Friends as well. As may well be imagined, this local group has greatly benefited by the opportunities it has had in its meetings and in its association with the other members of the whole Yearly Meeting Movement. Such opportunities have been afforded many members of the Hopewell group, and it has been represented by one, two, and often many more members at practically all of the Young Friends' mid-winter conferences, usually held in Baltimore; at the summer conferences at Camp Keewadin, near Annapolis; at the Young Friends' meetings held in conjunction with the Friends' General Conferences at Cape May, New Jersey; and even at the Leadership Training Institutes for First-Day School teachers; also at Camp Keewadin. A young Friend and member of the Hopewell Meeting had the privilege to study, during the winter and spring of 1935, at the Woodbrooke School in England, where one has the opportunity of meeting Friends and Friendly people from all the countries of the world.

Through the broadening horizon of friendships and the earnest study and application of the principles for which the Society of Friends stands, the Young Friends Movement is working toward the real ideal of the organization—to make religion, as the Friends see it, an active and vital part of every day of our lives.

CHAPTER XII

INDUSTRIAL OPERATIONS

At the period when Friends first settled in the Shenandoah Valley, manufacturing as a business, as it is known to-day, was an undreamed-of occupation. The only motive power then known originated in men, beasts, and water; and as yet the use of water power was in a primitive stage. The small mills, serving their respective neighborhoods, and the furnaces and forges of iron works were, perhaps, the nearest approaches to modern industrial operations then known.

For some reason, as the mechanical arts developed, Friends evidenced a decided aptitude for these vocations, and until the Civil War period, and indeed for some years afterward, a large percentage of them were so employed, though a majority of those in Virginia were agricultural.

Iron-making seems to have been an important industry in which certain Friends were engaged at an early date. In 1734 a Friend named Israel Friend settled on a large tract of land on the Potomac River about two miles west of Harper's Ferry and shortly thereafter commenced mining iron ore. It is not known whether he had a furnace, and it may be that he hauled his ore across the river to his Antietam furnaces in Maryland. He died in 1753 and the property passed into other hands, by whom the operations were enlarged and a furnace called "Keeptryst" erected.

Among the early Friends who settled in what is now Jefferson County, W. Va., were the Vestals. Their land lay upon the west bank of the Shenandoah, about seven miles south of Harper's Ferry. The records of Frederick County show that William Vestal, in partnership with John Tradan, Richard Stevenson, and Daniel Burnet, on May 10, 1742, entered into an agreement with Thomas Mayberry to build for them a "Bloomery for making Barr iron, upon the present Plantation of William Vestal lying upon Shunandore." Mayberry agreed to build the bloomery and complete "not only the Wooden Works, but all & Sundry the Iron Works thereunto

Appertaining, and all and Sundry Dam & Dams, Water & Water Courses, in as Ample & full manner as may be Required." Mayberry was to be paid £400 "Curr. Money of Pennsylvania" and to have a one and one-half share in the enterprise. Shortly after the French and Indian War the Vestals removed to North Carolina, and the bloomery property passed to other hands, but continued in operation until the Civil War.

The largest iron works with which Friends seem to have been concerned were those in southwestern Frederick County, on Cedar Creek. This operation was started by Lewis Stephens, not a Friend, who in 1763 sold an interest to John Hughes and John Potts Jr. of Philadelphia and John Potts Sr. of Potts Grove, Pa. In 1767 Isaac Zane Jr. of Philadelphia acquired an interest, and in the course of a few years purchased all the shares of the other owners. He named it "The Marlboro Iron Works" and carried on very extensive operations. Other Friends associated with him in the business were the Taylors, Bonds, Beans, and Fawcetts. This association probably ceased during the Revolution when Isaac Zane accepted the commission of a colonel in the Virginia militia, and the Marlboro Iron Works cast cannon, cannon balls, and other munitions of war for the use of the American army. A Presbyterian preacher, named Philip Vickers Fithian, who talked with him in 1776 states in his diary that Isaac Zane called himself "a Quaker for the times." The output of the Marlboro Iron Works was 4 tons of bar iron per week, and 2 tons of castings. About 150 persons were employed, and 25,000 acres of land belonged to the project. The largest furnace, together with a forge and foundry, was located at the present village of Marlboro, and a smaller furnace, that came to be known in later years as Taylor's Furnace, was located a few miles southwest, and was sometimes called "Bean's Smelter." After the death of Isaac Zane Jr. in 1795 the property was sold, and the manufacture of iron was not resumed by the purchasers.

In 1793 Benjamin Fawcett operated an iron furnace in Rockingham County, known as Mt. Ery, and at a later period had in the same county an establishment named Haho Furnace, in partnership with Benjamin Savage. A Friend named

Solomon Matthews, very prominent in business affairs, appears to have been the founder of Mt. Ery Furnace, which was located on Linville Creek.

Friends early established grist mills on streams running through their plantations, for their individual use, and only a few years after their arrival were operating commercial flour mills. It is known that Isaac Parkins had a flour mill on his property as early as 1736—probably in connection with a sawmill—as an order is entered in the minutes of the Frederick County Court, December term 1743, being the second meeting of this court, directing that he be paid tobacco to the value of $62.00 for "1000 feet of sawn plank" furnished by him and used in the erection of the first court house and county jail. The Parkins family owned and operated one or more flour mills on Abram's Creek from 1736 to 1874. In 1812 they were operating three mills one mile south of Winchester on Abram's Creek under the name of "The Union Mills, Nathan Parkins & Co. Owners." The shipping book of this firm for the period August 1812 to January 1819 is preserved. The receipts given by the wagoners during 1812 show that they hauled for the firm 169 barrels of flour to Ambrose Vass, merchant at Alexandria; 318 barrels to Hollingsworth & Sullivan, merchants at Baltimore; and 184 barrels to J. & H. Strider at Keeptyrst Furnace near Harper's Ferry. The average price in 1812 was $9.50 a barrel, delivered at the port. During 1815 the shipping book shows that 232 barrels of flour were hauled to Ambrose Vass and John Swayne, merchants at Alexandria; 445 barrels to Adams & Jonas and N. Parkins, merchants of Baltimore; 83 barrels to J. & H. Strider at the Keeptyrst Furnace; and 1412 barrels were sold to wagoners at the mill. In 1815 the average price was $5.00 delivered at the port. Just prior to the Civil War, Alfred Parkins, great-grandson of Isaac Parkins Sr., operated eight flour mills in the counties of Frederick and Clarke.

John Litler owned and operated two grist mills, a fulling mill, and a sawmill before 1745, and was a founder of the tavern located at Brucetown, on the Braddock Road, which later became so widely known as "The Blue Ball."

Of all the early Friends, perhaps the family most engaged in manufacturing was the Carter family, who removed from

Bucks County, Pa., to Frederick County, Va., before 1736 and settled on the Opequon at the point where it is now crossed by the Berryville-Winchester highway. They established their home on the east bank of the Opequon, and on the west side they erected a large "ordinary" or tavern. Nearby on Abram's Creek, near its mouth, they built a flour mill and distillery. This mill site is one of the oldest in the lower Valley, that has been in continuous operation. The present mill erected on the old foundation, and called the "Spout Spring Mill," was built in 1866 by the late Daniel T. Wood, a much esteemed elder of Center Meeting, Winchester. John, James, Joseph, Arthur W., and Watson Carter acquired other lands a few miles down the Opequon and on Red Bud Creek, and utilizing the remarkable fall of these streams, in the ensuing years, they built five mills within a distance of two miles. These consisted of a paper mill, perhaps the first enterprise of its kind in the Valley; a "Flax Oyle mill," a sawmill, a flour mill, and a flax-breaking mill. Another Friend, Lewis Neill, also had a mill on the Opequon near the same place. With him the Carters had a difference about the riparian rights. The following letter from Lord Fairfax to his nephew, Col. George William Fairfax, deals with this discussion:

"July 5, 1758."

"Dear George:

Mr. Neill has been with me and complains that Joseph Carter takes in all the water, which very much hurts his plantation. He desires if he [may] have thirty or forty acres which I really think is very reasonable. He likewise desires his brother's and his deed may be made separate.

"I should be likewise glad if some Golden Pipen, Nonparel, Aromatick and Medlar Apple grafts by him, which he will take care to convey to me. My service attends Mrs. Fairfax and all friends. I remain

Yours,
Fairfax."

("Fairfax Letters," Pub. by Munsell, Albany, 1868.)

Joseph Wood, a native of Chester County, Pa., settled in early life in Berkeley County, Va. In 1783 he purchased land on Hogue Creek in Frederick County and there erected a flour mill. In 1787 he removed to one of the Parkins mills which he operated for some years. In 1804 he purchased land on Red Bud Creek, about four miles northeast of Winchester, where he erected a large mill and lived until his death in 1815. Joseph Wood was much esteemed among Friends and was active in the development of the milling industry in early days. His mill property descended to his son Isaac Wood, who became very successful in business, adding the "Spout Spring Mill" to his holdings, as well as a mill in Loudoun County. In early life Isaac Wood was in unity with Friends, but marrying out of meeting, he became associated with another church. His mill on Red Bud descended in 1855 to his son Charles Littler Wood, who erected on the original site, shortly after the Civil War, a large mill with the newest machinery, and with what was said to have been the largest water wheel in Virginia. Charles L. Wood was for many years an elder and trustee of Center Meeting. As before stated, his brother Daniel T. Wood inherited the "Spout Spring" property. Through industry and care he was able to add greatly to his inheritance, and because of his integrity of character was highly regarded throughout his long life.

In 1799 David Lupton erected on Babb's Run, about seven miles northwest of Winchester, the Cedar Grove Mill, John Chenowith being the designer and millwright. David Lupton's son Nathan was associated with him in the operation of this mill, together with a mill David Lupton owned on Great Cacapon River, in Hampshire. They were largely engaged in exporting flour, and in 1814 and 1815 Nathan Lupton sailed from Alexandria with cargoes of their flour which he sold in European ports. Letters from him at Lisbon, Portugal, in 1815 show that he sold his flour there at $8.33, when Parkins & Co. could command a price of only $5.50 in Alexandria.

The date of the erection of the mill by Abraham Hollingsworth at "Abraham's Delight" is lost in antiquity. But that he had a mill there at an early date is shown by the diaries of the Moravian Single Brethren, who, at the noonday stop on October 18, 1753, purchased there feed for their horses. This homestead, settled prior to 1733, is still in possession of the Hollingsworth family, and the great Hollingsworth spring near by the mansion turned the wheels of the mill together with a fulling mill erected by the family shortly after the

Revolution, until it was purchased by the city of Winchester in 1890, since which time it has supplied the city with water. Another member of this family, Solomon Hollingsworth, became widely known as a manufacturer of wool-carding machines, which he constructed at his factory in Winchester, until his removal to Ohio about 1815.

Perhaps the best known of the Hollingsworth mills in Virginia was the one erected by Isaac Hollingsworth in 1827 near the site of the first Parkins mill, on land he purchased from his father-in-law, Isaac Parkins Jr. This mill had a capacity of 25 barrels of flour per day, and was considered the finest in the lower Valley. Isaac Hollingsworth in early life had been a stone mason, and this mill, constructed of stones which he himself dressed, with its three storied galleries or porches, was, of itself, a beautiful building. Unfortunately, the building was burned in 1911, but the mill had been in almost continuous operation until that time.

Other Hopewell families owning flour and grist mills in the early days were the Luptons, Jolliffes, Chenowiths, Neills, Wrights, Bruces, Fromans, Bordens, Berrys, Woods, Browns, Bransons, Hackneys, Hoges, Haineses, Morgans, Worthingtons, Beesons, Holmeses, and other large landowners. These mills, however, were generally confined to grinding the products of the owners' plantations, and perhaps for the accommodation of near neighbors.

It was not until about 1820 that the inventions of Arkwright and Hargreaves in textile machinery came into use in the Shenandoah Valley. Before that time the manufacture of woolen, cotton, and linen fabrics was generally under the care of the women and servants of each individual family. The raw materials were grown, carded, spun, and woven mainly on the plantation, and only in the case of woolens was it necessary to employ outside aid; the raw wool sometimes being taken to a community carding machine and the woven fabrics to some near-by fulling mill to be fulled and shrunk.

Perhaps the first of Hopewell Friends to engage in the textile industry on a commercial scale was John Griffith 3rd of Apple Pie Ridge, in Frederick County. In 1828, with his sons Aaron H. and Joseph Griffith and his nephews, Asa and Israel Hoge, he formed the firm of Griffith, Hoge & Co. and established the Friendly Grove Factory one mile south of Winchester on Abram's Creek where they manufactured flannels, worsteds, blankets, and linseys.   In 1835 Aaron H. and Joseph Griffith bought all of the interests and established an additional and larger woolen mill three miles east on the same stream, which they called the Brookland Woolen Mills.   In 1850 Aaron H. Griffith acquired his brother's interest, and disposed of the Friendly Grove mill.   He enjoyed remarkable success and received a number of medals and awards at different expositions for the excellence of his cloth.

About this time Aaron H. Griffith established his brother Richard S. Griffith in a woolen mill at Wetheredville, Md., near Baltimore, under the firm name of R. S. Griffith & Bro., and with his son Isaac H. Griffith and other partners operated until the close of the Civil War the "Henry Clay Mills" at Wilmington, Del., under the firm name of Griffith, Du Pont & Co.   With his son J. Clarkson Griffith and others he established in Philadelphia the firm of Griffith, Hance & Co., manufacturing chemists.

Losses caused by the Civil War closed all of these enterprises except the Brookland Woolen Mills.   These were continued in operation by Aaron H. Griffith until his death in 1877, and after that date were operated by his sons, Isaac H. and John Griffith until 1904.

John Griffith 3rd and Aaron H. Griffith were elders of the Orthodox Hopewell Meeting, and Aaron H. Griffith and his son John Griffith both served many years as clerks of the same meeting.

Charles L. Wood was a member of the partnership of Thomas B. Wood & Bro., a firm that erected a textile factory known as the "Morgan Mills" about four miles northeast of Winchester on Red Bud Creek.

The Funston and Ridgeway families, members of Crooked Run Meeting, had a carpet factory operated by horsepower at White Post, Va., and the Job family owned and operated a textile factory for several generations at Brucetown, Va.

As previously stated, sawmilling was one of the industries in which Friends were engaged almost immediately after their arrival in the Shenandoah Valley.   These mills were primitive affairs of the old "up and down" type, and, of course, driven by water power. Their capacity was very limited, and nearly all lumber was hand hewn. The introduction of the circular saw greatly stimulated lumbering in the Valley, portions of which were heavily timbered with valuable hardwoods. Probably the first Friends to engage in lumbering on a commercial scale were the brothers Lewis and Joel Lupton. In 1835 they secured the contract to furnish all of the ties and trestles for the railroad then being built from Harpers Ferry to Winchester, as well as the lumber for the wooden rails then used. They successfully completed this contract, and used probably for the first time methods employed ever since in construction practice. In 1848 the legislature of Virginia chartered the Winchester & Front Royal Turnpike Co., four miles of which were to be a plank road, and in 1851 a charter was granted to the North Frederick Turnpike Co., four miles of which were to be plank. Lewis and Joel Lupton secured the contract to furnish the lumber and build the plank sections of each of these roads, and likewise successfully completed these projects.

It was during this period that the remarkable talent for mechanical invention possessed by Joel Lupton and to a lesser extent by his brother Lewis, became apparent. Lewis Lupton suspended a heavy blade of iron in a diagonal direction beneath a wagon, and used the device to scrape aside loose earth from the right of way. Cartmell's History states (p. 453) "Some enterprising machinists of Kennet Square, Pa., seeing it in use, took advantage of their opportunity, and soon had this useful piece of road machinery in general use, claiming exclusive rights." The Lupton brothers also invented improvements to the old "Scotch drum" cylinder threshing machine, which they manufactured. Joel Lupton conceived the idea that to mow grass successfully, the motion of shears must be used, and built a mowing machine with this idea incorporated, which he sold to a man named Hubbard of New Jersey. In the famous law suits between Hubbard and Cyrus McCormick over the reaper patents, Joel Lupton was an important witness and identified his machine. He also invented and built an adding machine, improvements for the cotton gin, a bee hive, an automatic die and stamping machine for rapidly and cheaply making the metal clamps used in holding the teeth of peg-tooth harrows. His home became locally famous after he

equipped the window sash with cords and weights, undoubted-
ly the first used in the Shenandoah Valley.   In 1856 he was a
partner in the firm of Lavender, Lowe & Lupton engaged in
the manufacture of paper from rattan, with factories in New
York, Baltimore, and Winchester.   He died in 1883 in his
79th year and was buried at Upper Ridge Meeting, of which
he was a member.   He was a sincere Friend his entire life.

Among the members of Hopewell Monthly Meeting in
early times there seem to have been at least two watch and
clock-makers and gold and silversmiths.   The first of whom
there is record was William Richardson, silversmith and watchmaker.   Just when his business was begun has not been ascertained, but the records of Frederick County show that the
executors of Lord Fairfax, March 7, 1782, paid him "for
silver   mountings   &   trimmings   on   his   lordships   coffin,
£11-16-0."   Perhaps the silver plate engraved with the Fairfax arms, said to have been on the coffin of Lord Fairfax and
now exhibited at the Handley Library, in Winchester, was
executed by William Richardson.   He evidently was in business in 1781 when Lord Fairfax died.   The Winchester
Centinel of 1787 states that the watchmaker shop of William
Richardson had been broken into, but that fortunately two of
the villains had been caught.   In November 1789 the same
paper carries his advertisement as "watchsmith" and states that
his shop is two miles south of town.   His name appears in the
records of Hopewell Monthly Meeting; but from the location of his home it is probable that he attended Center Meeting.

Goldsmith Chandlee, who appeared in Winchester before
1784, was another Friend who engaged in the manufacture of
clocks and watches; he was also a brass founder and silversmith.   In addition he manufactured mathematical and sur-
veyors' instruments.   His business was located on the northwest corner of Cameron and Piccadilly streets in Winchester,
where he owned several buildings and also resided.   A number of his "grandfather" clocks are to be seen in the Valley,
still running.   One inherited by Howell M. Bond of Apple
Pie Ridge and one in the possession of the heirs of Samuel
Pidgeon of Clarke County are remarkable for their accuracy.
Another, which he made for Col. Thomas Bryan Martin,
nephew of Lord Fairfax, still remains in the land office of the

Proprietary at Greenway Court. Goldsmith Chandlee enjoyed the highest reputation for integrity, and was frequently chosen as an arbiter to settle differences, often appointed by the courts to administer estates, and named executor in many wills. As executor of the estate of Dr. Robert Dunbar, he was concerned in the final settlement of the Fairfax estate. The articles he manufactured were of high quality, and after his death his administrator's account shows sales of his clocks in 1823 at prices ranging from $87.50 downwards. At this sale his surveyors' compasses sold for $65.00; protractors $9.00; dividers $2.50; quadrants $5.75; squares $2.50; and graduated rules $1.50.

Chandlee also made money scales and apothecary scales and weights, for which at that time there was a large demand. He sometimes acted as a banker and was regarded as one of the foremost citizens of Winchester. All his life he was earnestly devoted to the principles of Friends. He attended Center Meeting, and served many years as clerk of Crooked Run Monthly Meeting and Fairfax Quarterly Meeting. He died in 1822 and was buried in Center Meeting graveyard on the Valley Pike.

The unusual number of pack-horse trails converging on Winchester in the early frontier days, and the construction of the military roads from Winchester to the west and northwest at the time of and after the ill-fated Braddock expedition in 1755, made the town an important center in the fur trade of the Middle Atlantic States in the latter part of the 18th and early 19th century. There naturally sprang up a considerable business in the manufacture of hats and gloves. Among Friends engaged in this business was Nathan Updegraff, who established in 1780 a factory for the making of beaver hats and fur and cloth caps. His efforts met with marked success, and about 1790 he expanded his plant and erected larger buildings on the lots now designated Nos. 43-5-7, on South Loudoun Street in Winchester. He was an earnest Friend, much devoted to the advancement of the Society, attending Center Meeting and Crooked Run Monthly Meeting until his removal in 1801 to Ohio. There he was concerned with various industrial activities.

Another Friend who was engaged in the manufacture of

hats was Joseph Steere Jackson. His establishment at No.
135 North Loudoun Street in Winchester made beaver, felt,
straw, and silk hats, as well as fur and cloth caps. He manufactured hats for the wholesale trade and also conducted a
retail business for custom-made hats, employing journeymen
and apprentices. His account book now in the possession of
his grand-daughter, Miss Annie J. Rees, commencing May
4, 1840, and ending March 10, 1855, shows that in 1842 he
made for the retail trade 364 hats and caps; and that in 1854
the business had increased to 1886 hats and caps per year.

The type and style of hat used by men Friends cost $6.00;
for others the prices ranged from $12.00 for a "shappo" down
to $2.50 for a "slouch hat." Caps made from otter fur sold
for $10.00 and $12.00 each. His book shows that he paid
$2.50 per barrel for muskrat skins in 1847, and the same year
12½ cents each for rabbit skins. In 1841 he purchased seal
skins at $8.12 each, sheep skins at 62 cents each, otter skins at
$4.00 each, and beaver skins at $3.75 each. The Civil War
closed his business, and he himself was carried away and imprisoned for a considerable period. These losses and sufferings were met with the calmness of a consistent Friend, which
was typical of his character. After the Civil War he removed
to his farm four miles north of Winchester, where he lived
until his death in 1896. He was a regular attendant of Center
Meeting as long as his health permitted.

Another of the industries arising from the fur trade that
flowed to Winchester in the early days was that of tanning.
When the Shenandoah Valley was still the frontier, it was the
practice for the pioneer to tan his hides in a measure at home.
If the skins were to be used in his family, or sold locally, they
were taken to some near-by tanyard to have the process completed. These tanyards were at first operated for the accommodation of individual plantations, and, perhaps, near-by
neighbors, but in later years were developed into industries of
considerable proportions. Among Friends, Meredith Darlington had a tanyard in operation a number of years before
the Revolution, at a point on the old South Branch road about
three miles west of Winchester, now the property of the estate
of the late Julian W. Baker Sr. About the same time, or
perhaps earlier, another tannery was located north of Clear-

The Upper Ridge

Meeting-house End   Schoolroom

The two parts of the house were separated by a partition

Stone Horse-block

brook, conducted by the Ridgeway family. In 1816 Isaac Pidgeon had a similar tanyard on his plantation in Clarke County. In 1808 John Brown purchased from the Conrad heirs the large tanyard on the east side of Kent Street, Winchester, comprising the entire square between Sharpe Street, Cork Street, Kent Street, and East Lane. A portion of this property, 127 years later, is still owned by John Brown's descendants. At this stand Brown operated a large tanyard and in connection with it a soap factory until his death in 1837.

After John Brown's death his son Richard continued the operation of the tannery until his death in 1884. After his death his sons Richard Richardson, John Isaac, and Charles Murphy Brown closed the old tanyard, the bark mill of which had been run by horse power, and purchased in 1885 of J. C. Maxwell the steam tannery on the west side of Kent Street, which they operated until about 1890. All these members of the Brown family were consistent Friends and regular attendants of Center Meeting, one generation or another attending in their day at one or more of the sites occupied by Center in its long history.

In 1847 Hugh Sidwell purchased the property that is now designated as Nos. 28-30-32 North Cameron Street in Winchester, and established thereon a tanning business of considerable proportions called "Cecil Tannery." Sidwell's son Richard, after the death of his father, continued the business until 1879 when the property was sold to J. C. Maxwell. Hugh Sidwell and his son Richard were highly esteemed citizens of Winchester. They were active in the affairs of Friends, and their names frequently appear in the minutes of Hopewell Monthly Meeting.

CHAPTER XIII

FRIENDS OF EMINENCE

It would be difficult, perhaps impossible, to estimate correctly the value of the 200 years of service that Hopewell Monthly Meeting has rendered to those residing within its verge, whether members of our Society, of other denominations, or of no denomination. However, the fact that a Christian organization has a great value in any new country is easily recognizable. For nearly a quarter of a century, on the frontier west of the Blue Ridge and south of the Potomac, the members of Hopewell maintained as best they could the principles of the Religious Society of Friends in the face of savages engaged nearly continuously in warfare with all men, save themselves, on the one hand, and on the other as subjects of a government whose laws forbade the very existence of their religion.

When Alexander Ross and other Friends arrived in the Shenandoah Valley that section of the country had not been even nominally organized into a parish by the colonial government, and no effort was made to do so until 1734 when Orange County was established. At that date the Valley was included in the parish of St. Mark's and so remained until the county and parish of Frederick were set up in 1743. During those nine years, therefore, Friends of Hopewell resided within the bounds of St. Mark's Parish. The early records of this parish having been lost or destroyed, it is not definitely known what, if any, efforts were made by the Established Church to hold religious services in the vast region lying west of the Blue Ridge prior to 1743.

In 1744 a vestry was elected for Frederick County and Parish, but seems to have been an unfortunate choice since it was dissolved in 1752 by act of the Assembly, after being charged with wasting the public monies. Bishop Meade states ("Old Churches, Ministers, and Families of Virginia," Vol. II, page 285) that the first minister stationed in the Valley was the Rev. Mr. Gordon. "When his ministry commenced and ended, not known. The Rev. Mr. Meldrum comes next, and continues until 1765." The records of Frederick County, however, show that the Rev. John Gordon caused the arrest and prosecution of a man on November 20, 1746, in connection with the theft of the reverend gentleman's silver watch, and we therefore conclude that he was settled in the parish at that time.

Of the dissenting sects, the Presbyterians were probably the first to effect a church organization after the setting up of Hopewell; and, although they enjoyed the services of visiting ministers at considerable intervals, Dr. Graham says ("Planting of Presbyterianism in the Northern Neck of Virginia," page 26) that no pastor was regularly settled among them until 1754, when the Rev. John Hoge became the pastor of the Opequon Church at Kernstown, and supplied them at intervals until 1772. No other Presbyterian pastor came to be settled in the lower Valley until the Rev. Hugh Vance was installed at Tuscarora in 1772.

In 1743 a Baptist church was constituted on Mills's Creek, in now Berkeley County, W. Va. Soon thereafter the Rev. Henry Loveall became its pastor. Other leaders soon succeeded him, notably Elder John Gerrard in or about 1755. (Semple's History of Virginia Baptists, pages 375, 376.) Disturbed by the inroads of the French and Indian War, Mr. Gerrard and many of his flock moved east of the Blue Ridge where in 1756 they assisted in organizing Catoctin Baptist Church, in what became Loudoun County the next year. At a later date unknown Mr. Gerrard and probably others returned to Mills's Creek. The site of the church there is preserved in Gerrardstown.

Of the other dissenting denominations who were present in the Valley from an early date, the Lutherans do not appear to have had a regular pastor until after the Revolution, and the German Reformed some years later. There were doubtless ministers among the early Mennonites, but they were located mainly in what is now Page County, Virginia, and thus at a considerable distance from Hopewell.

Through the trying pioneer period, with all its commotions and hardships, meetings for worship were continuously held at Hopewell, and notwithstanding the horrors of Indian

warfare and the sufferings imposed on Friends by their refusal
to bear arms, the surviving records show that the organization
of the meeting was preserved, the principles of the Society
maintained, and Christianity preached to all who would listen.

We believe, therefore, that it will be of interest to mention
briefly some who were ministers among us at that time; also
others not ministers and not previously mentioned who, by
their services to Hopewell Meeting and the community in
general, appear to have been of eminent ability and usefulness.

Evan Thomas came to the Shenandoah Valley in the colony
led by Alexander Ross, and was perhaps the first minister to
live within the verge of Hopewell Monthly Meeting, where
he resided until his death in 1753.   It was said of him that
"he came to be early engaged in the work of the ministry,
and was a serviceable instrument . . . He was zealous of the
honor of God and the promotion of his blessed truth."

James Wright and Mary Wright his wife both appeared
in the ministry at Hopewell soon after its setting up, and by
their lives and characters gained a reputation for steadfastly
upholding the truth that has survived to this day.   James
Wright traveled extensively in the ministry and was highly
regarded among Friends.   During the Indian massacres he
was the object of affectionate regard by the Meeting for Sufferings in Philadelphia, who referred to him as "our Antient
Friend."

Isaac Hollingsworth, son of Abraham, was also prominent
among early Friends of Hopewell because of his great efforts
for the promotion of the interests of our Society.   Meetings
were held in his house, built in 1754 and still standing, and
which he constructed with moveable partitions so that large
numbers might be conveniently seated in one room.   He was
active in inducing Friends to remove to the Hopewell settlement, and laid out an addition to the town of Winchester.
His activities in this connection were contemporaneous with
those of Lord Fairfax, who at the same time made an addition
to Winchester.   The following letter written by Lord Fairfax
to his cousin, George Fairfax, is of interest:

Sept'r 10th 1758.
Dear George:

    Mr. Stephens in his way to the office called here and I take the oppor-
tunity of sending by him a letter left here for you, as also Mr. Lemon's plot.

When you see Mr. Carlyle pray desire him to set aside a hogshead of rum and barrel of sugar which I shall soon send my wagon for. I believe I shall be down in your parts before you set out for Williamsburgh. Mr. Bayliss has very much disappointed us, in not sending down a petition for the addition to Winchester, which as Mr. Wood is doing may occasion some confusion. Hollingsworth is likewise desirous of doing the same thing, as also Mr. Cochrane. My service attends the families at Belvoir and Alexandria. I remain

Your humble servant and kinsman,

FAIRFAX.

("Fairfax Letters," pub. by Munsell, Albany, 1868.)

After the death of Isaac Hollingsworth Hopewell Friends, in the course of a memorial, gave the following estimate of his character:

He received a gift in the ministry when about twenty-one years of age, and was, we believe, a faithful labourer in his master's work; being much concern'd for the promotion of truth and the eternal well-being of mankind: Of a sober and grave deportment, diligent in attending religious meetings, ... He visited the churches in divers parts of the neighboring colonies; and we find by accounts from thence his services and labours of love were well accepted among them.

Isaac Hollingsworth died in Loudoun County, where he had located in 1757, on the 10th of the 9th month, 1759, aged about thirty-seven years, and was interred in the Friends' burying ground at Waterford on the 12th of the same month.

Martha Mendenhall, who lived in what is now Berkeley County, W. Va., was another minister of the early period. She traveled extensively in America on religious visits and met with much success. The Hopewell records state "she became an able minister of the Gospel, and visited the meetings of Friends in other parts of this continent ... being humble and meek in deportment, she was beloved by most who knew her." She died on the 28th of the 10th month, 1794, in the 82d year of her age, and the 62d year of her ministry, and was the next day interred in the Friends' burying ground at Tuscarora, about two miles west of Martinsburg.

It is much regretted that little is known of Simeon Taylor, the first clerk of Hopewell Monthly Meeting. On the 28th of the 4th month, 1738, a certificate issued by East Nottingham Monthly Meeting was received for Simeon Taylor and wife. He resided on a plantation in what is now Clarke

County, on the east side of Opequon Creek at the mouth of Yorkshireman's Branch, now called Litler's Run, and in his day and generation, doubtless, faithfully served our Society. Hopewell records show that on the 2d of the 4th month, 1764, a Simeon Taylor, with his wife and children John and Ann, obtained a certificate to New Garden Monthly Meeting in North Carolina, and it is likely this was our first clerk.

The second Friend to perform the service of clerk for our meeting was Jesse Pugh. Nothing is known of him except that he lived in the western part of present Frederick County on Back Creek. The correspondence between the Meeting for Sufferings at Philadelphia and Jesse Pugh indicates that he was watchful of the interests of Friends and zealous in their service.

The next and third clerk of Hopewell Monthly Meeting was William Jolliffe Jr., son of William Jolliffe, barrister. The latter removed from Nansemond County, Virginia, about the time Frederick County was erected and was admitted to practice at the bar of the Frederick County Court January 13, 1743. It is uncertain whether William Jolliffe Sr. was a Friend, although he was buried at Hopewell Meeting. A member of a family belonging to the gentry of old England, he was known as the "Quakers' lawyer" and attended to practically all of the law business of Hopewell Friends. In this he was succeeded by the attorney Alexander White, and he in turn by Cuthbert Hayhurst, and Hayhurst by Joseph Sexton, these last two being Friends.

William Jolliffe Jr. was born in eastern Virginia about the year 1721 and came with his father to the Shenandoah Valley. He married Lydia, daughter of Stephen Hollingsworth and widow of John Ross; for his second wife he married Elizabeth, daughter of Abel and Sinah Walker. William Jolliffe Jr. was appointed clerk the 26th of the 3d month, 1759, and served until his death in 1770. He was much engaged in business, and in addition to the lands he inherited and acquired by marriage he secured patents for other large tracts from Lord Fairfax. He purchased the estate of Colonel John Neville, about one-half mile south of his father's plantation, "The Red House," and lived on the Neville place until his death.

In the settlement of Friends in the section that is now Jefferson County, W. Va., and near to the county-seat, Charles Town, perhaps the first Friend to arrive was Robert Worthington, who settled on Evitt's Marsh on a tract of 3000 acres granted him from the Crown, and which he named "Quarry Banks New Stile" for his old home in Cheshire, England, which was named "Quarry Banks." The date of his arrival in the Shenandoah Valley is not definitely known, but among the papers relative to the settlement of his estate on record in Orange County is a deposition made by his widow, which states that she and her husband were married in Friends' Meeting at Burlington, New Jersey, 13th of 6th month, 1729, "and quickly after the said marriage . . . removed to this Country."

Robert Worthington was a consistent Friend and devoted to the interests of our Society. This is shown by the records of Moate Monthly Meeting and Dublin Monthly Meeting in Ireland, which he attended during his residence in that country, and of the Monthly Meetings of Salem, N. J., and Philadelphia, Pa., in America. After his settlement in Virginia he was largely engaged in business as a merchant and exporter as well as a farmer, and was instrumental in promoting the settlement of the lower Valley. After his death "Quarry Banks" and a portion of his land came into the possession of his youngest son Robert. The latter by marriage out of meeting withdrew from our Society in 1760, and shortly thereafter he with others erected near his mansion house St. George's Chapel, said to have been the most costly chapel in Virginia at that time. The ruins of this chapel are a well known landmark two and a half miles northwest of Charles Town. His son Thomas, born and reared at "Quarry Banks," removed to Ross County, Ohio, and became the sixth governor of that state.

The remainder of the "Quarry Banks" estate was divided among the older children of Robert Worthington Sr. and was purchased from them at various times by Lawrence and Samuel Washington, the latter of whom built, on a part of this land, his mansion "Harewood" where he resided at the time of his death in 1781. It is of interest to note that Samuel Washington's son, George Steptoe Washington, married Lucy Payne, whose parents, John and Mary Payne, served for many years as the clerks of Cedar Creek Meeting in Hanover County, Va. At "Harewood" Dorothy Payne Todd, sister to Lucy (Payne) Washington and widow of John Todd of Pine Street Meeting, Philadelphia, was married to James Madison, later fourth President of the United States.

In this same section of the Valley (Jefferson County) lived Edward Lucas, who removed from Bucks County, Pa., and settled some time prior to 1740 on a plantation which he named "Cold Spring." Robert Lucas, father of Edward, came from Deverall, Lingbridge, Wilts, England, in 1679 and was a member of the Pennsylvania Assembly in the early days of the "Holy Experiment." After Edward Lucas removed to Virginia he attended Tuscarora Meeting and took an active part in the Friends' settlement in that part of the Valley. He was the grandfather of Robert Lucas, eleventh governor of Ohio; the great-grandfather of Edward and William Lucas, both of whom were elected to Congress from the Valley district; and the great-great-grandfather of Daniel Bedinger Lucas, United States Senator from West Virginia.

About the same time, and also from Bucks County, Pa., Joseph Darke came to the Valley and settled near the Opequon Creek. He attended Middle Creek Meeting and was prominent among Friends and in the affairs of his community, as were his children, except William, who embraced a military career, reaching the rank of brigadier-general and achieving renown as "the hero of St. Clair's defeat."

In 1744 James Harlan came with his family from Kennet Monthly Meeting, Pa., and settled on the east side of Back Creek Mountain in (now) Berkeley County, W. Va. With his son George he suffered much during the French and Indian War for their peace principles. They were subjected to fines and imprisonment, but steadfastly maintained the Friends' unwavering stand for peace, and were much respected among Friends. In them was found true the declaration, revealed in court records, of a certain Quaker of Nantucket. To him a magistrate said, "Your principle is passive obedience and nonresistance." "On the contrary," was the reply, "our principle is active obedience (to God) and passive suffering." They were members of Tuscarora Meeting and are buried in the graveyard that adjoined the old meeting house. George

Harlan's son James married Sarah Caldwell and removed to Kentucky. They were the grand-parents of John Marshall Harlan, associate justice of the United States Supreme Court. On the Supreme Court Bench with Justice Harlan sat Associate Justice Noah Haines Swayne, son of Joshua Swayne, who removed from Philadelphia to Frederick County, Va., about 1784, where he attended Crooked Run Meeting for some years, removing from thence to Culpeper County where his son Noah was born the 7th of 12th month, 1804. Joshua Swayne and his family attended Mt. Pony Meeting in Culpeper County and were consistent Friends. Justice Swayne was educated at Friends' School, Waterford, Va., and read law in Warrenton, Va. He was appointed to the Supreme Court by President Lincoln in 1862, where he continued to serve until his resignation in 1881.

A Friend who does not appear to have been associated in business with Alexander Ross and his company, yet was largely concerned in the settlement of the Shenandoah Valley, was Robert McKay Sr., who came to Virginia from Cecil County, Maryland, to which place he had come some years before from near Freehold, Monmouth County, New Jersey. While residing in Cecil County he was a member of Nottingham Monthly Meeting, the minutes of which record the marriage intentions of three of his children, viz.: Margaret, who married Joshua Job; Hannah, who married George Hollingsworth; and Robert Jr., who married Patience, daughter of Andrew Job. In the New Garden records may be found the marriage of his daughter Mary and George Robinson of Brandywine Hundred, New Castle County, Delaware.

Robert McKay Sr. carried on very extensive transactions in land. For example, on the 21st of 10th month, 1731, he secured from the Governor and Council an order for 100,000 acres. In this grant he had as a partner Joist Hite, leader of the German settlers in the lower Shenandoah Valley. In the bill of complaint filed by Hite in 1749 in his suit against Lord Fairfax relative to the titles for this land, it is stated that both Hite and McKay were residents of Pennsylvania when the Council made this order, but no doubt they arrived in the Valley shortly thereafter. The terms of this order required McKay and Hite to settle 100 families on their land in two years, which it appears they were unable to do, as the Governor and Council in a subsequent order extended the period; but in 1737 when their settlers were enumerated by Col. Morgan ap Morgan, representing the Governor, and Peter Wolfe, representing McKay and Hite, it was found that sufficient settlers were actually in residence to comply with the terms of the original order.

The business of McKay and Hite developed very largely, and feeling the need of aid they took into partnership William Duff, a Friend residing in King George County, Va., and a certain Robert Green of Orange County. Some time before his death in 1752 Robert McKay Sr. withdrew from the firm, which soon became involved with Lord Fairfax in lawsuits which were not settled until after the Revolutionary War, when all the original litigants had long been dead. Among the various tracts of land held by Robert McKay Sr. and his partners was one of 7009 acres on Linville Creek, in what is now Rockingham County, which they secured in 1739. In June, 1746, 1200 acres of this land was transferred to Robert McKay Sr. This valuable tract after his death descended to his sons, Robert Jr., Zachariah, Moses, and James, who possessed the greater part of it until 1768, when they sold 300 acres of it to Tunis Vanpelt and 600 acres to John Lincoln. Portions of both these tracts were acquired by Captain Abraham Lincoln, grandfather of President Lincoln, and were sold by him in 1780 when he was preparing to move to Kentucky. On Captain Lincoln's land was a meeting house which was built in or before 1756, while the land was still owned by the McKays. They doubtless built the house, or aided in building it. The Baptists of the neighborhood, organized in August 1756, with Rev. John Alderson as pastor, acquired it and used it thereafter.

Robert McKay Sr. lived on or near the South (main) Fork of the Shenandoah River several miles above Riverton. This placed him in Augusta County after 1744, when the line between Frederick and Augusta was surveyed, and in Augusta County his will is on record. The place of his residence is indicated by an order of Council of June 12, 1734, when Robert Brooke was directed to survey land claimed by William

Russell within the grant of 100,000 acres made to McKay and Hite:

It is ordered that Mr. Robert Brooke do survey the ten thousand acres of land granted the said Russell, in the fork of Shenando so as the said survey do not extend near to the said Robert McKay's present settlement than one mile, nor above ten miles along the river from his beginning place at the mouth of the said fork, and if within these bounds he cannot have the aforesaid quantity of 10,000 acres, that then the survey be extended back in a straight course from the river towards the north branch to complete the same.

The will of Robert McKay Sr. was dated the 7th of the 10th month, 1746, and probated the 19th of the 8th month, 1752. His sons were appointed executors. James qualified by making oath; Zachariah declined to serve; Moses and Robert Jr., who were Friends, as the record shows, qualified by affirmation.

James McKay married Mary, daughter of Captain Thomas Chester, who lived in the gap of the Blue Ridge that now bears his name; Moses McKay married Mary Job; Leah McKay married first William Taylor, and second —— Leith. The marriages of the other children of Robert McKay Sr. appear in the Nottingham and New Garden Meetings records as before mentioned.

Robert McKay Jr. lived on a tract of 828 acres of land on both sides of Crooked Run in what is now Frederick and Warren Counties, which he held by a Crown patent bearing date October 3, 1734. He was closely associated with Friends of Hopewell and Crooked Run meetings all his life and devoted to the interests of our Society. Meetings were held at his house, and the Journal of John Fothergill records that on the 15th of 9th month, 1736, John Fothergill went "from Alexander Rosse's to a meeting the following day near Shenando River held at Robert McKay's the Younger—pretty open and comfortable."

In the years 1754-55 a determined effort was made by the colonial government to force Friends to bear arms against the French and Indians, and upon their steady refusal some of them were beaten and imprisoned. The records of Frederick County show that in September, 1754, the following Friends, Joseph Roberts, Edward Tyler, Dennis Bond, James Henry, Thomas Howell, Benjamin Kelley, Henry Hampton, and

James Welch, were imprisoned in the county jail at Winchester, where they were kept for over a year. On one occasion, Hopewell Friends held a meeting beneath the jail windows until dispersed by soldiers who seized one of them, George Hollingsworth, and threw him into prison. Upon his being brought to trial he was fined £5 Sterling for "disorderly meeting & assembling." Friends in eastern Virginia waited upon Governor Dinwiddie at Williamsburg and finally secured the release of their brethren in Winchester.

The Friends of Hopewell Monthly Meeting and the people of Winchester have reason to remember with gratitude Sarah Zane of Philadelphia, a frequent visitor to Winchester before the death of her brother, General Isaac Zane Jr. After his decease in 1795 she for a time resided in Winchester, engaged in settling his estate. Before his death General Zane had given to the Winchester Academy five acres of ground west of Stewart Street and north of Clifford Street in Winchester, but died before he could execute a deed for the property. Sarah Zane with her sister and brother, Hannah Pemberton and John Zane, confirmed this gift in 1798 by deed to "John Smith, Robert Macky, Alexander Balmain, Edward Smith, Raleigh Colston, Robert White Junr., John Peyton, Cornelius Baldwin, John Kean, Nathaniel Burwell and Daniel Conrad, surviving Trustees of the Winchester Academy, for the purpose of erecting an Academy House thereon." This was the first of many gifts for which this generous Friend became so well known. As previously mentioned she in 1817 presented an entire block in Winchester to Friends for the use of Center Meeting. She died in Philadelphia in the spring of 1821. By her will, after making bequests to her family, to meetings in Philadelphia, and provisions already shown in Chapter VII for the care of Indians, she directs that her executors pay $500.00 to each of the yearly meetings of Ohio and Baltimore; and

Twentieth—I give to the select members belonging to the Monthly Meeting of women Friends held at Hopewell Frederick County Virginia Five hundred Dollars to be realized in the Town of Winchester in the same County the interest or income issuing therefrom to be annually paid into the Treasury of the abovesaid Monthly Meeting stock toward the relief of the Poor belonging thereto.

Twenty-first—I give to my dear Friends Composing Center Preparative

Meeting belonging to Hopewell Monthly Meeting the sum of Five hundred Dollars toward enlarging Friends Meeting House in Winchester if that Meeting think it expedient and to assist in building a Stone wall so as to enclose the whole lot whereon the said Meeting House is erected.

Twenty-second—I give to the citizens of Winchester abovesaid one thousand dollars to purchase a Fire Engine and Hose to be Kept in best repair with my affection and gratitude.

Twenty-third—I give to my much respected friend Charles Magill of Winchester Virginia my large silver Tankard in remembrance of his friendship with one thousand dollars in specie under grateful sense of the Kind accomodations in his office for Books.

Twenty-fourth—I give to my very dear friend Mary Buckner Magill wife of Charles Magill one hundred Eagles in Gold Coin Currency of the United States equal to one thousand Dollars in most grateful affectionate remembrance of the sincere and firm friendship that hath subsisted between us for a number of years. . . .

Twenty-ninth—I give to my friends Goldsmith Chandlee, Samuel Swayne, and Samuel Brown five hundred Dollars to be realized in Such Manner as their Judgment may dictate so that an interest may be obtained toward the support should it be necessary of Venus and Daniel two people of colour emancipated by me from the Marlboro Estate in the year 1796 Frederick County Virginia.

Following Sarah Zane's bequest to the citizens of Winchester, a volunteer fire company was formed there and called by her name, and a hand engine built by Joseph Share & Sons of Baltimore, Md., was purchased which did good service for over thirty years, and is still carefully preserved in the engine house of the Sarah Zane Fire Company, on North Loudoun Street.

The Shenandoah Valley Historian Norris in writing of Sarah Zane states: " . . . she spent much of her time in Winchester. She boarded with Mrs. Christian Streit; she also stayed with the Baldwin and Macky families. She was a woman of fair size, compactly built, and rather good looking, with an extremely benevolent, pleasant and kindly face. She will always have a warm place in the hearts of Winchester people."

Her private benefactions, of which there is no record, extensive and generous, made her much beloved, and the arrival of her coach in Winchester always caused much rejoicing among the poor and afflicted.

CHAPTER XIV

ITEMS AND INCIDENTS

A LETTER OF 1738

About 1737, two years after Hopewell Monthly Meeting was established, Robert Scarborough left Bucks County, Pa., and settled on Smith Creek, Va., some five miles southwest of the cross-roads where the town of New Market later grew up. In 1738 Robert Scarborough wrote a letter to his brother, a Friends' minister of Solebury Township, Bucks County, Pa., that has proved of decided historical value, for therein Robert Scarborough states that he lived about a mile from a Friends' meeting. This indicates that a number of Friends were living on Smith Creek at that time and that they were holding a meeting for worship, doubtless under the authority of Hopewell Monthly Meeting. Thus the Scarborough letter takes the place of some of the early Hopewell records that were burned in 1759 or thereabouts.

The Augusta County order book of 1762 names Thomas Moore, Quaker. Rockingham County records list John Quaker Moore as a large landowner on Smith Creek or in that vicinity in 1789. There is abundant evidence to show that a number of the Moores as well as several of the Allens of the Smith Creek country were Friends.

At the close of the French and Indian War, about 1763, Robert Scarborough moved westward and located in the limestone sinks near Union, now Monroe County, W. Va. Some of his descendants still live in West Virginia. His eldest son John, who as a child accompanied him from Bucks County, Pa., to Smith Creek, returned to Solebury about 1757, as is shown by his certificate from Hopewell meeting. John deposited his certificate with the Buckingham meeting.

HAWORTH NEIGHBORS

Neighbors of Robert Scarborough on Smith Creek were the Haworth brothers, Absalom, Stephanus, and James. Their mother was Sarah Scarborough, sister to Robert. The survey book of John Bayless gives the location of the lands of

Scarborough and the Haworths on Smith Creek and the Daniel James branch of Smith Creek.

With the Haworths to Smith Creek came their brother John Haworth, though he did not remain there permanently. This John Haworth was an ancestor of Herbert Clark Hoover, 31st President of the United States, as shown by the outline below.

1. Herbert Clark Hoover, born at West Branch, Iowa, August 10, 1874.   He was a son of

2. Jesse Clark Hoover and his wife Huldah Minthorn. Huldah was a daughter of

3. Theodore Minthorn and his wife Mary Wasley. Mary was a daughter of

4. Henry Wasley and his wife Ann Toole.   Ann was a daughter of

5. Aaron Toole and his wife Rachel Haworth.   Rachel was a daughter of

6. John Haworth and his wife Mary Garner, who were members of Buckingham, Hopewell, Haverford, and Goshen meetings.   John Haworth was a son of

7. George Haworth and his wife Sarah Scarborough, members of Buckingham Monthly Meeting.   Sarah was a daughter of

8. John Scarborough and his wife Mary.   John settled in Langhorne, Bucks County, Pa., in 1682; was a member of Middletown and Falls meetings; was founder of Buckingham Monthly Meeting; moved to Solebury Township in 1700. He was a son of

9. John Scarborough of London, a member of Peel Monthly Meeting.   In 1682 he came to Bucks County, Pa., but in 1684 he returned to London, where he is buried.

AFTER THE FIRE

At a meeting held at Hopewell on the 2d day of 6th month, 1760, the committee that had been appointed to set the minutes in order for recording reported that they had met, but one of the minute books having been lost by an accidental fire they could not go back any further than to the point where William Jolliffe had been appointed clerk. Accordingly, the work was continued under their care, to be done any time within a year; and they were to begin as far back in re-producing the records as they could make them correct—that is, as far as they had notes and reliable testimony. It does not appear, however, that anything in the way of definite re-production of the burned minutes was accomplished. Jonathan Parkins was appointed to record all meeting testimonies and papers, for which he was to be paid by the meeting a reasonable sum. On the 1st day of 7th month, 1765, he brought in his account, amounting to 1 pound and 12 shillings for recording 64 pages in the meeting book. The charge was allowed and John Rees and Joseph Lupton were ordered to pay him.

It seems reasonable to conclude that Jonathan Parkins was employed because he was a good scribe, William Jolliffe con-tinuing as clerk. On the 6th day of 8th month, 1770, Robert Hains was appointed clerk "for this year in the Room of William Jolliffe Deceased."

TO ADAM STEVENS

The attitude of Friends towards military service was often misunderstood and they frequently were subjected to harsh treatment and extra financial burdens because of their unwill-ingness to bear arms or train in the militia companies. On the other hand, other persons not Friends occasionally at-tempted to escape military service by pretending to be mem-bers of this or that Friends' meeting. To prevent such evasions the several meetings were required to make out lists of their members and certify them to the proper county of-ficers. An instance of this is found in the Hopewell records under date of the 4th day of 1st month, 1768: "This Meet-ing orders the Clerk to return to Adam Stevens a list of Friends names belonging to Hopewell monthly Meeting agreeable to an act of assembly directing the same."

Adam Stevens (Stephen) was no doubt the same man who later was a major-general in the Revolution. Following the battle of Germantown, in October 1777, he was dismissed from the army on a charge of intoxication and other conduct unbecoming to an officer. This explains why he was within reach of Hopewell in the spring of 1778, when his services were secured as an assistant in amputating John Hunt's leg. Shortly after this General Stephen secured approval by the

General Assembly of Virginia for laying out the town of Martinsburg on 130 acres of his land, in the county of Berkeley. In 1768 and until 1772 the area which went into the counties of Berkeley and Jefferson was in Frederick County, the county in which Hopewell Meeting is located.

SLAVERY

We find that it was not unusual in the early days for Friends to hold slaves, but little by little the conviction that the practice was not in accordance with Christian ideals led to a growing sentiment against it.

John Woolman, a Friend living in New Jersey, was so impressed with the wrongfulness of slavery that he brought the matter before the Philadelphia Yearly Meeting in 1758 and the meeting sent out a committee of four, of whom John Woolman was one, to visit slaveholders in the meetings comprising that yearly meeting, urging Friends to "set them [the slaves] free making a Christian provision for them." John Woolman also visited meetings in Maryland, Virginia, and North Carolina on this mission. Gradually Friends were convinced that slavery was wrong, and Baltimore Yearly Meeting, of which the Valley of Virginia later constituted a part, in 1772 made it a disownable offense for its members to hold slaves.

The meetings spent some years reasoning and treating with their slaveholding members before bondage was entirely eliminated, as we find record of committees appointed from time to time to visit and advise with such members.

On 5th day of 4th mo. 1773 we have record: "William Jolliffe, by his Last Will left his negro woman to be free and desired that a couple of friends might be appointed to take care of her. Accordingly the meeting appoints Rees Cadwallader and David Ross to take necessary care of her and make report of their service when called upon."

On 5th day of 2nd mo. 1776 was made this entry: "The friends appointed to assist Jackson Allen in setting his slaves free report they have had an opportunity with him and have advised him to let the aged ones have their freedom if they choose it and for him to administer to their necessities, if their circumstances should require it, and for the younger ones to give them learning, as other orphan children and to be set free, the boys at the age of 21 years and the girls at 18, with which this meeting concurs and leaves it some longer under Jackson's Consideration."

Setting slaves free in 1776 was a matter of considerable difficulty, but evidently Jackson Allen was minded to a purpose. In the court order book of Shenandoah County, under date of May 28, 1776, appears this record: "The Court being informed that Jackson Allen of this County have set three of his Negroes free, Ord that he be sum'd to apr. at the next Court to shew Cause why they should not be sold according to an act of Assembly in that case made and provided."

In 1777 at Hopewell the following entry appears: "This meeting appoints Abel Walker, Richard Ridgeway, Rees Cadwaledar and Jacob M'Kay to provide a book and record such manumitions of negroes as shall and hath been produced to this meeting and also to inspect into and take the necessary care in regard to those that are set free where ever they think it necessary."

As late as 1782 we find that William Askew was disowned from membership for neglect in attending meetings, for using corrupt language, and for purchasing two Negroes. Thus it becomes evident that the testimony against slavery, like most reforms, took time to become established. Slavery was not entirely abolished among Virginia Friends in 1817, ten years after the act of Congress against the foreign slave trade and only 46 years before the proclamation of emancipation.

AT WAYNEOAK

One of the results of the American Revolution, 1775-1783, was the disestablishment of religion, that is, the withdrawal of state support from ecclesiastical bodies. In Virginia it was the end of support given by the government, through taxation and otherwise, to the Anglican Church. This of course was a serious blow to the clergy and to the financial resources of the Episcopalians. In 1784 and 1785 several bills were presented to the General Assembly of Virginia to establish by a small rate of tax a provision for the teachers of religion. The benefits of this plan would not have been limited to any one religious denomination, but the principle involved, that of giving the state control over religion, even in a small measure, alarmed many persons, especially Baptists, Presbyterians, Methodists, Friends, and others. James Madison, among others, drew up a memorial and a remonstrance against the proposals. Although the Friends and the Mennonites would likely have been exempted in the application, if the bill of 1784-85 had become law, they, the former especially, joined in opposition to it. In the minutes of Hopewell Monthly Meeting under date of the 2d of 5th month, 1785, we find the following:

This meeting is informed that there is in agitation a Law termed a Support for Religion, which we are apprehensive if confirmed will be a considerable burden to us as a Society. Richard Ridgway Sen. & James Mendinghall are appointed to attend the Yearly Meeting to be held at Wayneoak in Virginia this month in order to take into consideration, & unite with Friends of that meeting in remonstrating against it or what may be most suitable to lay before the Assembly, in order to show our dislike to such a Law, & be most to the support of our Christian Testimony against an Hireling Ministry, and the Clerk is directed to furnish a Copy of this Minute.

On the 2d of 6th month of the same year the following record was made at Hopewell:

Richard Ridgway Sen. reports that he attended the Yearly Meeting at Waynoak in Virginia, & friends of that meeting have provided a Memorial in order to lay before the next meeting of the Assembly. A copy of which was produced to this meeting, & read to satisfaction, & is expected to be signed by Friends in General.

As is well known, the bill failed to become a law.

FUND FOR THE POOR

Thrift and economy are cardinal business principles with the Friends, but they of course, like other religious bodies, have always had some members of their society who have needed material assistance. In 9th month 1792, at Hopewell, Edward Beeson, Abraham Branson, and Stephen McBride were appointed to settle with Anthony Lee and Eleanor Barrett and see for what amount each preparative meeting within the verge of Hopewell was indebted for keeping the poor, and endeavor to have the money forwarded to discharge the indebtedness; and report to next monthly meeting.

A PASTURE LOT

On the 3d day of the 9th month, 1792, at Hopewell Monthly Meeting it was reported: "There appears to be the sum of 53 Lbs. 7 shillings and 6 pence subscribed by the members of our Monthly Meeting for the purpose of purchasing a piece of ground for a pasture, for the use of the Yearly Meeting (including them that subscribed at the Yearly Meeting)."

The pasture ground purchased, or proposed for purchase, was no doubt located somewhere in or near the city of Baltimore, situated conveniently for the use of those Friends who rode or drove horses to the Yearly Meeting. A pasture lot in Baltimore seems to us incongruous, but it was less so a century and a half ago. The census of 1790 gave Baltimore a population of a little more than 13,000, so we may guess that it was not over 15,000 in 1792.

In the first month of 1793 it was announced at Hopewell that the sum apportioned for that monthly meeting to raise for the purpose of making room to accommodate the Yearly Meeting was 23 pounds and 15 shillings, Pennsylvania currency. Two months later John Griffith was appointed "to receive our proportion towards the enlargement of the Yearly Meeting House at Baltimore, and pay it in the Quarterly Meeting."

OHIO PIONEERS

Martha M. (Mrs. George S.) Pilcher, writing from Athens, Ohio, January 27, 1927, in answer to inquiries about Hopewell Friends, said:

"I have traced my mother's family, the Pickerings, who once belonged to Hopewell Meeting, then came to Concord, Ohio, lived in Belmont County. . . . My great-grandfather Levi Pickering belonged to the Quaker Church in Barnesville, Belmont County, and is buried there. My grandfather brought his family down to Athens County."

In the same letter Mrs. Pilcher states further:

"In the years 1803-1805 the Hopewell Monthly Meeting sent to Concord in Ohio members of the families of Lupton, Piggot, Jenkins, Pickering, Miller, Ellis, Steer, Bevin, and to various other meetings in Ohio in 1804 McPherson, George, Walton, Walter, Wickersham, White, Wilson, Allen, Adams, Branson, Cope, Crampton, Fawcett, Hackney, Janney, Lloyd, Little, Lupton, Pickering, Steer, Smith, Swayne, Tounsend, and Taylor.

"Crooked Run Monthly Meeting, Va., sent to Concord 1803-06 a great number of families. Thomas Fawcett was first to be buried in the Mt. Pleasant Cemetery, Frederick Co., Va. . . . . .

"Religious freedom—our forefathers paid heavily for their freedom. We have also received from our forefathers an inheritance of a sense of humor, an inheritance that should be cherished today. Steadfastness is another one of the things we have inherited from past generations. The early Quakers were interested not only in politics but also in human brotherhood."

Mrs. Pilcher's grandparents joined the Methodists—none of the family have been members of the Society of Friends since then.

FRIENDS IN OHIO

On the 29th of 4th month, 1804, Nathan Updegraff wrote to his brother-in-law, David Lupton, of Frederick County, Va.: "Joseph Steer & Wife and Grace Parkins were at our meeting at Short creek to day and came home with us from Meeting. they Appear quite as well reconciled with their new place of residence as could be expected. . . . The population of this Country Still increases. people have been moving almost daily the course of this Spring our Settlement will I believe Shortly be filled up and that pretty much with friends. its likely we will have a Quarterly Meeting Shortly Over the Ohio, as I expect a request of that kind will go forward to our next Quarter."

On the 2d day of 6th month, 1806, Short Creek and Concord monthly meetings were granted a quarter by Redstone Quarterly Meeting. See diary of David Lupton in Chapter VI.

NEW YEARLY MEETING

Writing from Short Creek, Ohio, the 29th of 8th month, 1813, Nathan Updegraff said: "we were in hopes you [David and Mary Lupton] would have come to Sit with us at the opening of our New Yearly Meeting, the attendance of which I think you would have not regretted. I think it was a good Meeting. the Business was transacted much in the harmony & brotherly condesention, as much so as could be expected from a collection of friends from so many different parts &

used to so many different manners & customs. We were also favoured with the company of a Number of friends from different parts & from different Yearly Meetings Viz Jessee Kersey, Daniel Quinby, Daniel Haverling, John Letchworth, Abraham Branson, Nathan Sharpless, Philip Price, Caleb Bently, Deborah Stabler, Sarah Proctor, & Edith Schoolfield & a Number of others Whose Company & Services & gospel labours amongst us I may say was Satisfactory."

MARRIED AT HOPEWELL

Many persons hearing of the plan to publish this book have written to the committee expressing interest, and in some instances sending in items of information. One who did this is Mary Yager (Mrs. Henry R.) McKay, of Luray, Va. She says:

"My husband and I are direct descendants from the first pioneers who settled the west side of the Blue Ridge—Jost Hite, Robert McKay, William Duff, and Robert Green. My husband, Henry Relfe McKay, came down from Robert McKay. Great-great-grandfather Andrew McKay married Jane Ridgeway, a Quakeress. We have a copy of their troth, pledged in old Hopewell Meeting House. Several other McKays married Quakers. . . . Jost Hite's eldest daughter Elizabeth married Paul Froman, a Quaker from New Jersey. Their daughter Christina was my great-great-grandmother. She married John Overall. My own grandmother was Christina Overall Yager."

SMITH CREEK MEETING HOUSE

On the 6th of 8th month, 1829, Hopewell Monthly Meeting recorded a communication from Benjamin Allen respecting Smith Creek meeting house and lot. Joseph Hackney, Thomas Wright, Josiah Fawcett, and John Bond were appointed to take the subject into consideration and report when ready.

Nearly four years later, to wit, on the 9th of 5th month, 1833, the committee reported that they had investigated the subject. They had found that Benjamin Allen, a Friend in Ohio, who formerly resided near the Smith Creek meeting house, had lately written to John Bond, informing him that many years past he (Allen) had expended money in acquiring a title to the said property, and that he wished him (Bond) to inform the monthly meeting of it. He requested Friends to refund to him his money.

The committee had requested Allen to send the deed or state where it might be obtained; also to send an itemized account of his expenditures in the case. John Bond, Thomas Wright, and Isaac Smith reported as the committee.

On the 6th of 3d month, 1834, John Bond on behalf of the committee reported that they were willing to allow the said Allen the sum of $8.25 for the monies expended and for his trouble. The committee also proposed that some Friend or Friends be appointed to take charge of the property and make sale of it as soon as convenient. Four months later John Bond and Thomas Wright were appointed to take charge and make sale.

On the 7th of 3d month, 1839, the said appointed trustees reported to Hopewell Monthly Meeting as follows:
Dear Friends:

We the subscribers having been appointed by the meeting to make sale of the meeting house and lot at Smith Creek belonging to Friends report, that through the intervention of Moses Walton, who resided in the vicinity of the property, we have contracted with and sold it to John Neff whose land joins it for the sum of Sixty Dollars, one half of which sum he has paid and the other half is to be paid on the 1st. of the 5th Month next and we hold his note to that effect. In consequences of the service of Moses Walton we have agreed and paid him $4.00 out of the sum which we have received and John Bond $2.75 on account of money sent by him to Benjamin Allen, who had a claim on the property which the meeting directed be liquidated and also, one dollar expended in correspondence with Benjamin Allen, and in obtaining the original deed for the property.

JOHN BOND
THOMAS WRIGHT

The site of the building, which was perhaps the third meeting house of Friends in the Smith Creek region, can be fixed by means of the graveyard. The lot of land was until recent years part of the farm of Jacob G. Neff, a grandson of John Neff, to whom the land was sold in 1839. John Neff and both his wives have tombstones in the graveyard, with legible inscriptions. About 1840 the meeting house was torn down and some of the logs therein were used in the construction of "Liberty," a building on Holman's Creek which was used for school and church purposes for many years, then was remodeled, since when it has been used mainly as a church. See Wayland's History of Shenandoah County, Va., page 171.

BAD ROADS

In or about the year 1869 Charles L. Wood, Daniel Walker, and Richard Sidwell were appointed by the Hopewell Meeting to state to the court of Frederick County the "bad condition of the road leading from the Martinsburg Turnpike through the Washington Farm to Hopewell Meeting House," and ask the court to take some action to have the said road put in a better condition.

The road referred to in this appeal to the county court was evidently the one leading in to the meeting house from the south, which leaves the main highway (Martinsburg Turnpike) a short distance northeast of Stephenson's Depot, and approaches the meeting-house hill alongside the Washington homestead and the great spring near by. The Washington farm was originally the home place of Alexander Ross, who conveyed the land for the meeting house, burial ground, etc., at Hopewell.

A LITTLE LOG BUILDING

In 1927 Friend Lewis Pidgeon, writing from Wadesville, Va., recalled a number of interesting facts concerning Friends in Frederick County, Va. Some are herewith presented.

"The last one [Friends' meeting] laid down was the Ridge meeting, held in a little log building on Apple ridge, about five miles northwest of Winchester. Here a meeting was held twice a week, and then once a week, until a few years ago when it was discontinued, except once a year, until the summer of 1925, shortly after which the building was destroyed by fire." . . . . .

A TRAVELING CLOCK

"The monthly meeting [at Hopewell] was at one time so large and important that we are told Friends have journeyed on horseback from places as far away as Ohio to attend the meeting. ... I remember an old gentleman, Elkana Fawcett, who lived nine miles or more from Winchester and who came there to meeting twice a week, usually traveling on horseback and seldom missing a meeting, and almost never five minutes late. My father [Samuel Pidgeon] went to Hopewell, about five miles away, twice a week, always allowing an hour and a half to travel the five miles, and mostly it took that long to get through (not over) the roads of that day. He started so regularly that we heard people along the road say that they set their clocks by him."

AT WINCHESTER AND HOPEWELL

"We have at Winchester a First-Day school (Sunday-school) of four interesting classes, and at Hopewell one of eight classes. The latter, though called a Friends' school, has a good many pupils who are members of other churches. . . . We have a Young Peoples Association and a 'Class Social' —both of a literary and social nature. . . . As I said before, we have no pastor. Friends have generally believed in a free Gospel ministry, and anyone seeming to have a gift in that line is encouraged to exercise the same. While we have never had a theological seminary, there have been in recent years chairs for Biblical teaching established in several schools and colleges. . . . . .

"Weekly meetings are held for worship at both Winchester and Hopewell. Once a month, alternating between the two places, there is a business session called the monthly meeting. Delegates are appointed to attend Quarterly Meetings, in May at Hopewell, in August at Lincoln, Loudoun County, Va., and in November in Washington, D. C. There was a fourth one which met in February, but it has been discontinued." . . . . .

[The Quarterly Meeting that was held in Washington in November is now held in the same city in February.]

GUNS OUTSIDE

"During the Civil War our meeting house at Hopewell was used a while as a hospital, and meetings were held at a residence. When time came for the Quarterly Meeting [in May] the officers were asked to have the building put in proper shape for the occasion, which they willingly did. The soldiers were invited to attend, and requested to leave their arms outside. They came, stacking their guns outside the door. Samuel M. Janney, a well-known minister in the Society, and author of Janney's history of Friends, was present and preached a powerful sermon on peace." . . .

GUNS INSIDE

Friend Lewis Pidgeon omits to relate that a generation or two before the Civil War the Friends themselves carried their rifles to Hopewell Meeting and stacked them in a corner of the room during worship—or business meetings. This fact was recalled at the Quarterly Meeting in May, 1935, in a reminiscent conversation by a Friend of the community who had gotten the information from his father or his grandfather. But the rifles were carried not with any reference to Indians or other human beings, but for defense against the wolves which still infested the country, and which could often be heard howling and yelping on the ridges west of Hopewell while meetings there were in progress.

The same gentleman related that on one occasion a woman who came to meeting at Hopewell, on horseback, and carrying a baby in her arms, was chased by a pack of wolves as she was returning home; but she outran them and reached home in safety.

FREDERICK FAMILIES

Henry T. Louthan writing from Duane, King William County, Va., April 30, 1935, gives many facts of interest. He says: "My grandfather, John Louthan, who was born in Frederick County, Va., but lived the greater part of his life at Millwood and later at 'Milton Valley' in Clarke County, married Lydia Carter, a daughter of James Carter and wife Rachel Neill. I have my grandfather Louthan's family Bible. Rachel Neill, born May 8, 1772, was a Friend and a member at Hopewell."

Mr. Louthan gives several family lines, as follows:

THE CARTER-LOUTHAN LINE

I. Joseph Carter, from England, landed on the bank of the Delaware River in 1687; was a Friend, and a member of Penn's colony. His wife was Catherine ——. He removed from Bucks County, Pa., to what is now Frederick County, Va., either in or prior to 1739, for his name appears in 1739 with 54 other signers in a petition for a court house to be established in Frederick County, as Orange County C. H. was too far away.

In 1743 Lord Fairfax granted to Joseph Carter 600 acres

on Opequon Creek, six miles from Winchester, on the road to Berryville.

Joseph Carter and his wife Catherine had the following children. 1. Catherine, 2. Sarah, 3. Joseph, 4. Mary, 5. Rachel, 6. James, born August 19, 1732 (evidently in Pennsylvania).

II. James Carter (born 1732; died October 27, 1798) married Ann ——, who was born August 5, 1734. He owned large tracts of land in Frederick County, two large flour mills, a flax oyle mill, and a sawmill. There is a record of his helping the American Revolutionary cause by giving one horse and by selling or giving 495 pounds of beef. See Frederick County Order Book 18, pages 14, 17, 35. These first two generations of our Carters all seem to have been Friends.

The children of James Carter and his wife Ann were: 1. Catherine, 2. Mary, 3. Sarah, 4. Rachel, 5. Joseph, 6. James (born February 9, 1768; died October 10, 1831), 7. Arthur W. (born May 14, 1772; died January 12, 1846).

I have a portrait of Ann, wife of James Carter (1732-1798). It is painted in the costume of the Friends. On the back of the portrait are these inscriptions:

"Ann Carter Aged 86
August 5th, 1820."
"Ann Carter died on Jany 1824
aged 88 years 5 mos & days."

III. James Carter (1768-1831) married, Sept. 17, 1790, Rachel Neill (born May 8, 1772), daughter of John Neill and wife Ann Hollingsworth. Their children were: 1. John, born Sept. 19, 1791; 2. Ann, born July 19, 1793; 3. Thomas, born March 15, 1795; 4. Maria, born Nov. 10, 1797; 5. Jabez, born June 15, 1799; 6. Ruth, born Aug. 15, 1804; 7. Lydia, born Sept. 30, 1805; married John Louthan; 8. Phoebe, born Nov. 23, 1808; married George Louthan; 9. Rachel, born Dec. 27, 1810; married William Anderson; 10. James, born Sept. 10, 1813; married Lucinda Dunn of Indiana and lived at Bloomington, Indiana.

III. Arthur W. Carter (1772-1846) was the father of William Arthur Carter (Feb. 18, 1799—Sept. 29, 1857), who built the brick residence, now called Carter Hall, about two miles west of Stephens City, in 1832. Carter Hall was bought by Berryhill McLean Carter, a son of William Arthur Carter, and he lived there until his death, August 28, 1932. Arthur W. Carter joined the Baptists and is said to have been the first of this family of Carters who was not a Friend.

IV. Lydia Carter (born 1805) married John Louthan of Millwood and "Milton Valley," Clarke County, Va., August 3, 1824. Their son

V. Carter McKim Louthan (born May 11, 1838) married Mary Ella Brown, Feb. 1, 1866, a daughter of Capt. Charles Brown and wife Ann Maria Kelly, of "Melrose," Rappahannock County, Va. Their son

VI. Henry Thompson Louthan (born Nov. 5, 1866) married Elizabeth Rowland Hurt, a daughter of James Thomas Hurt and wife Ann Eliza Ewing Thomas, of "Thornhill," Caroline County, Va., March 25, 1903. They have two children: 1. Mary Tyler Louthan, born May 9, 1904; 2. Carter Thomas Louthan, born July 23, 1906.

THE NEILL-LOUTHAN LINE

1. Lewis Neill, of Lurgan, Ireland, and Frederick County, Va., married Lydia Hollingsworth about 1737. See Jolliffe's book on the Jolliffe, Neill, and Janney Families of Virginia, pages 175-191, for a history of the Neills.

2. John Neill married Anne Hollingsworth, June 15, 1771.

3. Rachel Neill married James Carter, Sept. 17, 1790. They lived at Red Bud Mills, on the west side of Opequon Creek, in Frederick County, but not far from Spout Spring, now in Clarke County.

4. Lydia Carter married John Louthan (born January 10, 1804), a native of Frederick County, Va., who after his marriage lived at Millwood, and from 1849 on at "Milton Valley," Clarke County.

5. Carter McKim Louthan (born 1838) married Mary Ella Brown, February 1, 1866.

6. Henry Thompson Louthan (born 1866) married Elizabeth Rowland Hurt, March 25, 1903. They have two children, Mary Tyler and Carter Thomas, and are now living (since June 1, 1932) at "Retreat," near Duane, King William County, Va.

Lewis Neill and his two brothers John and William took

passage from Lurgan, Ireland, in 1730, and landed in Pennsylvania; and family tradition says that they settled near Lancaster. But John and Lewis were soon attracted to the Shenandoah Valley. They left Pennsylvania about the year 1733 in company with a number of Friends and took up their residence in Virginia, now Frederick County. There is no record known that William Neill ever left Pennsylvania.

Lewis Neill and his brother John, though members of the Society of Friends in Ireland, did not bring their certificates with them, and were not actually members of the society afterwards, though they always leaned towards that body in their religious beliefs. See Jolliffe, page 178.

Lewis Neill in later life must have attended Friends' meetings quite regularly, but William Jolliffe says he can find no record of his ever having joined them in Virginia. But he worked with his own hands as a mason upon the walls of Hopewell, as did also some Hollingsworths, and contributed to the erection of the stone meeting house [in 1759].

Lewis Neill fixed his home on the banks of the Opequon at a point now known as Burnt Factory. He built a grist mill and opened his residence as an ordinary. He acquired much land and was wealthy.

THE HOLLINGSWORTH-LOUTHAN LINE

Sections I, II, and III below are made up from "Descendants of Valentine Hollingsworth Sr.," by J. Adger Stewart (Louisville, 1925) and "Immigration of Irish Quakers to Pennsylvania," by Albert Cook Myers (Swarthmore, 1902).

I. Valentine Hollingsworth Sr., first of this family in America, was born in Parish Sego, County Armagh, Ireland, about 1632, son of Henry and Catherine Hollingsworth. He married, Apr. 7, 1655, Ann, daughter of Nicholas Ree, of the same county. She died Feb. 1, 1671, and he then married Ann, daughter of Thomas and Jane Calvert, of Parish Sego, County Armagh, Apr. 12, 1672. In 1682 he and his family, including his son-in-law Thomas Connaway and indented servant John Musgrave, sailed from Belfast to the Delaware River, arriving a few months after William Penn's ship, the *Welcome*. He settled on a plantation of nearly 1000 acres in Brandy Wine Hundred, Del. Shortly after his arrival a meeting was established at his house, and in 1687 he granted "unto ffriends for a burying place half an acre of land for ye purpose, there being already ffriends buried in the spot." He was a member of the first Pennsylvania Assembly 1682-83, and of the Assemblies of 1687, 1688, 1695, and 1700. He was a signer of Penn's Great Charter and a justice for New Kent County. He was an overseer of Friends' meeting many years. His second wife died Aug. 17, 1697, and his death occurred about 1711. Both Valentine Hollingsworth Sr. and his second wife are buried in the Friends' graveyard at Newark, Del., which he had given them in 1687. By his first marriage he had 11 children.

II. Thomas, the third child and second son, was born in County Armagh, Ireland, in March 1661 and accompanied his father to America. He was killed by a buffalo near Winchester, Va., in 1733, while on a visit to his son Abraham. His home, however, after his arrival in America, was always Rockland Manor, New Castle County, Del. He married (1), about 1684, Margaret ———, who died Aug. 1, 1687. He married (2) Grace Cook of Concord, Pa., Jan. 31, 1692.

III. Thomas's son Abraham by his first marriage, born Jan. 18, 1686, married Ann, daughter of George Robinson, March 13, 1710. The same year he moved to Cecil County, Md.; and in 1732 (tradition says 1729) was living at "Abraham's Delight," soon Orange (now Frederick) County, Va., as shown in Chapter II.

IV. Lydia Hollingsworth (born about 1718) married Lewis Neill of Frederick County about 1737.

V. John Neill married his first-cousin, Ann Hollingsworth, and left nine children.

VI. Rachel Neill married James Carter, Sept. 17, 1790.

VII. Lydia Carter, Aug. 3, 1824, married John Louthan of Millwood and later of "Milton Valley," near Berryville. John Louthan for a number of years owned flour mills at Millwood. In 1849 he bought "Milton Valley" and located there. He had 12 children and was very prosperous.

VIII. Carter McKim Louthan (born 1838) married Mary Ella Brown, Feb. 1, 1866. He was a Confederate soldier and after the war studied law privately. He received his academic education at the University of Virginia. He was commonwealth's attorney for Clarke County about eight years, and later was her superintendent of schools. When he resigned the latter position about 1885 he was succeeded by Lewis N. Hoge, a Friend, and a member at Hopewell. William Page Louthan, a brother of Carter M., was an M. A. of the University of Virginia and in 1860-61 was professor of Greek in Richmond College. He died in 1861 at the age of 25.

IX. Henry Thompson Louthan (born 1866) married Elizabeth Rowland Hurt of Caroline County, Va., March 25, 1903. Their children: 1. Mary Tyler, born May 9, 1904; A. B. 1926 of the University of Michigan; 2. Carter Thomas, born July 23, 1906; B. S. 1926 and LL. B. 1928 of the University of Virginia; now practicing law in New York City.

Henry T. Louthan is an A. B and A. M. of the University of Chicago, and has held professorships in the College of William and Mary, Mercer University, and Staunton Military Academy. The Louthans, beginning with John and Lydia Carter Louthan, have been mostly Baptists.

AS WHEELS GO ROUND

In the Pidgeon family of Hopewell is preserved an interesting relic in the form of a tax certificate of 1814, which illustrates how moneys that are paid on harmless equipment by friends of peace may sometimes, by a roundabout process, be used in war, or to pay war debts. The relic before us shows how Isaac Pidgeon, grandfather of Lewis, was required to pay $4.00 a year on his chaise, or "chair," a carriage with springs, and no doubt a protective top, much as his descendants to-day pay a license to operate an automobile. Isaac Pidgeon, however, paid his tax to the Federal instead of the state government. The wording of the "license tag" of 1814 follows:

No. 187   ----

This is to certify that *Isaac Pidgeon*   in the County of *Frederick* in the ninth Collection District of Virginia has paid the duty of *Four* _____ dollars *for the year ending the 31. March 1814*

for and upon a *Two* wheel Carriage for the conveyance of persons *said Carriage having Steel Springs*

called a *Chair*   owned by *him*

This certificate to be of no avail any longer than the aforesaid Carriage shall be owned by the said *Isaac Pidgeon* unless said certificate shall be produced to the Collector by whom it was granted, and an entry made thereon specifying the name of the owner of said Carriage, and the time when *they* became possessed thereof.

GIVEN in conformity to an act of Congress of the United States pas-:d the 24th July 1813.

                         (Signed) *W. Davison*
                              Collector of the Revenue
                    For the Ninth Collection District, Virginia.

Winchester
May. 5. 1814

Italics are used to indicate the words and letters written into the printed form.

As early as 1790 the Secretary of the Treasury proposed that excise taxes be laid upon snuff, tobacco, carriages, etc. In June, 1794, carriages among other "luxuries" were taxed. The measures, especially the law to tax carriages, were resisted on constitutional grounds, but the Supreme Court, in Hylton *vs.* the United States, upheld the act. In 1801, when the party of Jefferson came into control of the Federal government, all forms of internal taxation at Washington were abandoned. In the War of 1812, however, it became necessary to supplement the national income, and on July 24 and August 2, 1813, Congress passed acts reimposing taxes on carriages, sugar refined in the United States, distillers of spirituous liquors, retailers of wine and other drinks, legal instruments, sales at auction, etc. It was under the act of July 24, 1813, as shown in the certificate, that Friend Isaac Pidgeon paid tax on his "chair."

The moneys raised from the acts of 1813 did not come in soon enough to be of much service in the War of 1812, but they were available in settling up the claims following the end of the war. New measures of taxation were passed in January, 1815; but in December, 1817, all such acts were set aside and were not again resorted to until the Civil War.

CHAPTER XV

PLACES OF MEETINGS

A GEOGRAPHICAL AND HISTORICAL DIRECTORY

In the following pages are located the several Friends' meetings with which the Friends of Hopewell had relations or communications.

ABINGTON MEETING was (and is) in Montgomery Co., Pa.

ALEXANDRIA MEETING was first near Woodlawn, in what is now Fairfax Co., Va.; later in the city of Alexandria. Alexandria Monthly Meeting was opened in 9th month, 1802. (See Janney, IV, 113.) Subsequently it was moved to 1811 I Street, N. W., Washington, D. C., where it is still known as Alexandria Monthly Meeting.

ALUM CREEK MEETING was held at Owl Creek, Knox Co., Ohio. It was in existence as a monthly meeting in 1834.

BACK CREEK meeting house, built in 1777, was located near the present village of Gainesboro, Frederick Co., Va. The Friends' burial ground there has in late years been enlarged into a community cemetery, surrounded with a fine stone wall, and incorporated. Back Creek Meeting was laid down in 1829.

There was also a Back Creek meeting in Randolph Co., N. C.

BALTIMORE MEETING was first known as Patapsco. It was removed to Asquith & Fayette streets, "Baltimore Town," on the 22d day of 2d month, 1781. Later it was located on Lombard Street; and now it is on Park Avenue & Laurens Street. There is a Friends' school adjoining this meeting house, but the school has grown too large for the quarters and a new building outside the city now accommodates some of the grades.

BEAR GARDEN meeting house was in Hampshire County, now West Virginia, at the eastern foot of Bear Garden Mountain, and about 2 miles north of Highway No. 50. The site can still be located by means of the burial ground. There was a meeting for worship at Bear Garden as early as 1767. It was indulged in 1780 and earlier, and established in 1794. It evidently was not well kept up, for it was reëstablished in 1804.

BENJAMINVILLE. This meeting was somewhere in the state of Illinois. It was in existence in 1875.

BERKELEY MEETING. This meeting was at first known as Bullskin, and was located about three and a half miles southwest of Charles Town, now Jefferson Co., W. Va. In 1794, when the name was changed, it was in Berkeley Co., Va. See Bullskin.

BLACKWATER. Probably in the southeast part of Virginia, near the line of North Carolina. In or about 1775 Esther Hains of Hopewell was approved "to visit in lower parts of Virginia and had a satisfactory visit. Attending Blackwater Yearly Meeting."

The Blackwater River rises near Petersburg, Va., flows southeast through the counties of Prince George, Surry, Sussex, Isle of Wight, Southampton, and Nansemond, into North Carolina, near to the counties of Perquimans and Pasquotank. About 1793 Jonathan Wright, a minister, went from Hopewell to Black Water Yearly Meeting in Virginia.

There is a Blackwater (village, etc.) in southwest Virginia, in Lee County.

BLUE RIVER. This meeting was on or near Blue River, Washington Co., Indiana. Under date of 7th day 10th month, 1830, it was recorded at Hopewell that Joseph Cadwallader came from Blue River Monthly Meeting.

BRADFORD MEETING was in Pennsylvania, and with Sadsbury, Uwchland, and Robeson Monthly Meeting formed East Caln Quarterly Meeting.

BROADWAY. About 1795 Jesse Kersey came to Hopewell from "Broadway Monthly Meeting." It was probably at Broadway on the Appomattox River, below Petersburg, in Prince George Co., Va. See "Virginia Magazine of History and Biography," July 1935, page 264; Jefferson's "Notes on Virginia," edition of 1853, page 3; and John Reid's map of 1796. Broadway in 1796 was at or near the site of the present city of Hopewell.

BUCKINGHAM Monthly Meeting, founded 1720, was lo-

cated at Lahaska, Buckingham Township, Bucks Co., Pa. It
at one time belonged to Falls Monthly Meeting and Bucks
Quarterly Meeting.

BULLSKIN meeting house was on or near Bullskin Creek, a
few miles southwest of Charles Town, in (now) Jefferson
County, W. Va. The site was in Frederick County, Va., until
1772; after that in Berkeley County until 1801; since then in
Jefferson County. The location of the meeting house is indicated by the grave yard, which is surrounded by a stone wall,
but overgrown by trees and vines. It is about half a mile
northwest of the main highway between Charles Town and
Rippon, between the forks of the Bullskin, somewhat nearer
to the south fork. The name was changed from Bullskin to
Berkeley in 1794. See Berkeley.

BURLEIGH. On the 4th day of 3d month, 1782, at Hopewell, it was recorded: "Our Friend Edward Stabler produced
a Copy of a minute to this meeting from Burleigh Monthly
Meeting."

In 1785 Edward Stabler lived in Petersburg, Va. (See
Hugh Judge's Journal, page 47.) This was probably Edward Stabler Sr. Edward Stabler, the celebrated minister,
was born in Petersburg in 1769; located in Alexandria in 1792;
and made his first appearance in the ministry in 1806. (See
Janney, IV, 112, 113.)

Burleigh, Binford, Leacock, and Stanton's composed a part
of Gravelly Run Monthly Meeting. Gravelly Run was in
Dinwiddie Co., Va., about 12 miles south of Petersburg.

BURLINGTON MEETING was in Burlington Co., N. J. With
Mt. Holly, Rancocas, Bordentown, and Trenton it formed a
part of Burlington Quarterly Meeting, which was established
in 1682.

BUSH RIVER was in Newberry Co., S. C. Another meeting of the same name was in Harford Co., Md. Nottingham
Monthly Meeting, first held on 12th of 4th month, 1730,
was composed of three preparative meetings, E. Nottingham,
W. Nottingham, and Bush River, the last being on the west
side of the Susquehanna River.

BYBERRY was in Pennsylvania, in the county of Philadelphia or Montgomery. In 1683 a meeting of worship was

settled among the Friends at Poetquesink and held at John Hart's house. It afterwards became Byberry Meeting. It was a monthly meeting in or about 1805.

CAESAR'S CREEK was in the southwestern part of Ohio, near Waynesville and Wilmington. It was a monthly meeting in 1813 or thereabouts.

CALN was in Chester County, Pa. On the 12th day of 11th month, 1784, Bradford Monthly Meeting was held at Caln.

CANE CREEK, established in 1751, was in Alamance Co., N. C. There was also a Cane Creek meeting in Union Co., S. C., which was extinct in 1896.

CARVER'S CREEK Monthly Meeting, established in 1746, was in North Carolina.

CEACIL (CECIL) Monthly Meeting was in Cecil County, Md. In "A Retrospect of Early Quakerism" is this statement: "At our Monthly Meeting held at our Meeting House in Cecil County the 9th of Ninth Month 1698, it being our first Monthly Meeting," etc.

CEDAR CREEK MEETING was in the region of Richmond, Va. In or about the year 1800 Catlett Jones came to Hopewell from "Cedar Creek Monthly Meeting in Hanover Co." Mt. Pleasant Meeting, in Frederick County, Va., was probably referred to sometimes as Cedar Creek.

CENTER was the name of several Friends' meetings, in different states: (1) Center Quarterly Meeting, comprising Center, West Branch, Dunning's Creek, and Bald Eagle; post office Half Moon, Center Co., Pa.; (2) in Pennsylvania or Delaware, about 8 miles southeast of Kennett Square, Chester Co., Pa.; (3) in New Jersey; (4) in Guilford Co., N. C.; (5) in Ohio, perhaps in Clinton Co., in 1812 and thereabouts; (6) in Frederick Co., Va., first just southwest of Winchester; about 1819 moved into the town, where it is still. See Winchester.

CHESTER MEETING was in Delaware Co., Pa. Earlier it was known as Chichester and Upland. It was established in 1675 by Friends of Chichester and Upland, Robert Wade being one. Moorestown Meeting, N. J., was first known as Chester.

CHESTERFIELD was in Burlington Co., N. J., which was spoken of in 1783 and thereabouts as in "West New Jersey."

CHICHESTER. See Chester.

CINCINNATI, Ohio. References have been found to a Friends' meeting in Cincinnati in 1828 and 1829.

CLEAR CREEK Monthly Meeting was in Putnam County, Illinois.

CONCORD. A Concord Friends' meeting was (and is) in Chester Co., Pa.; another was in Franklin Co., Pa.; and a third was in Ohio. Concord Monthly Meeting, Ohio, was first held the 19th of 12th month, 1801. See letter of Nathan Updegraff of 26th of 12th month, 1801, from Short Creek, Ohio. In 1806 it was held at Plainfield, Coshocton Co., O.; also near Wheeling and Short Creek. On the 2d day of 6th month, 1806, Redstone Quarterly Meeting granted the request of Concord and Short Creek monthly meetings to have a quarter. See the memoranda of David Lupton in the chapter on Visiting Friends.

CROOKED RUN Monthly Meeting was located near the village of Nineveh, now in Warren Co., Va., on the main road between Winchester and Front Royal; about 13 miles from the former and 7 from the latter place. A meeting house was built at Crooked Run prior to 1759. A monthly meeting was settled there in 1781-82. The Crooked Run Meeting was laid down in 1810—so few Friends attending. In 1812 selling the house was considered, but it was still held in 1828, though in bad condition. The site is now occupied by the Nineveh Presbyterian Church.

CULPEPER MEETING was located south of Chester Gap, in what is now Rappahannock Co., Va., near the home of John Garwood. John Garwood lived on the north fork of Rush River, near the site of the present town of Washington, county-seat of Rappahannock Co., where he purchased five tracts of land, the first two in 1768, the last in 1794, as revealed by Culpeper Co. records. Culpeper Meeting had a meeting-house in 1782, as shown by Hugh Judge. Meetings had been held in the home of John Garwood in 1778 and earlier.

CURLS. This meeting was probably at or near Curles

Neck, in Henrico Co., Va. On the 4th day of 1st month, 1773, "Sidney Wright returned [to Hopewell] from Yearly Meeting at Curls." In 1785 Hugh Judge was at Curles, just a day or two after he was at or near Petersburg, Va. See his Journal, page 47.

DARBY CREEK, still Darby Meeting, is in Pennsylvania, near Philadelphia, between Philadelphia and Chester. It was settled in 1682.

DEEP CREEK was in Yadkin Co., N. C.; still active in 1896.

DEEP RIVER MEETING was in Guilford Co., N. C.

DEER CREEK was in Harford Co., Md., 5 miles northwest of Port Deposit, 5 miles southeast of Broad Creek, and 4 miles southwest of Conowingo Bridge.

DILLON'S RUN MEETING, established in 1800 or earlier, was in Hampshire County, now West Virginia, near Lupton's Mill, about a mile northwest from the present postoffice of Dillon's Run. The burial ground is still known as the Quaker Graveyard. It is now a community burying ground —in Park's Hollow.

DUCK CREEK was near Smyrna, in Lancaster Co., Pa. Little Creek was near Duck Creek. In 1781 the monthly meeting for Duck Creek was held at Little Creek. There was a Duck Creek Friends' meeting also in Henry Co., Ind.

DUNNING'S CREEK was in Bedford Co., Pa., 11 miles northwest of the town of Bedford.

EAST NOTTINGHAM was in Cecil County, Md. This was the mother church of Hopewell, in Virginia.

ELK MEETING was in Carroll (?) Co., Ohio. There is a reference to Elk Meeting in the Hopewell records, date of 4th day 10th month, 1827.

EVESHAM MEETING, in New Jersey, established 1760; was spoken of in 1779 as in the "West Jerseys." It was located about 3 miles southeast of Moorestown.

EXETER MEETING was in Berks Co., Pa. On the 29th day of 11th month, 1781, Exeter Monthly Meeting was held at Maiden Creek.

FAIRFAX MEETING was in Waterford, in what is now (since 1757) Loudoun Co., Va. The first meeting house was built in 1741. Fairfax Monthly Meeting was established in 1744. See Janney's History of the Friends, Vol. III, page 249. It would seem that the Friends held meetings in Fairfax as early as 1735 or 1736. The region was then in Prince William County.

FAIRFIELD Friends' meeting was in Highland Co., Ohio, one mile south of Leesburg.

FAIRHAVEN was in Talbot County, Md.

FALL CREEK, or FALLS CREEK, was in Highland Co., Ohio. There was also a meeting of the same name in Indiana in 1848, 1856, etc.

FALLS MEETING was in Bucks Co., Pa. A meeting was there as early as 1683. (See Janney, II, 382.) In or about 1805 John Stabler of Falls Mo. Mtg. came to Hopewell with Hannah Yarnall of Byberry and Catharine Leeds of Horsham.

FARMINGTON Monthly Meeting was in Ontario Co., N. Y. Settlement there was begun by Friends from Berkshire, Mass., among whom were Nathan Comstock, his sons Otis and Darius, and Robert Hathaway. The first house of worship there was erected by Friends in 1804.

FAWSETT (Fawcett). See Mt. Pleasant.

FLUSHING MEETING was on the head waters of Indian Whiling Creek, in Belmont Co., Ohio. There was also a Friends' meeting at Flushing, N. Y. David Lupton of Hopewell visited Flushing (Ohio) meeting in 1806.

GAP MEETING. See Potts's Meeting.

GENITO was in Fluvanna Co., Va.; extinct in 1896.

GENOA MEETING was in Nebraska; in existence in 1877.

GOOSE CREEK Monthly Meeting is held at Lincoln, Loudoun Co., Va. This meeting was visited by William Reckitt in 1757. At Lincoln are now several Friends' meeting houses: one of stone, built 1765, now used as a dwelling; one of brick, erected in 1817; and another dating from 1880, or later. Lincoln was the home in his later years of Samuel M. Janney, the poet and historian.

Friends were also located at an early date on Goose Creek south of the James River. About 1800 Christopher Anthony came to Hopewell from Goose Creek "Bedford's," Stephen

Morland his companion. The Goose Creek Monthly Meeting in Bedford County, Va., was set up in 1794; laid down in 1814.

GOSHAM. See Goshen.

GOSHEN Monthly Meeting, sometimes written Gosham and Goshan, was in Chester Co., Pa., 4 miles northeast of West Chester. There was also a Goshen Friends' meeting in Tuscarawas Co., Ohio; another in Logan Co., Ohio; and a fourth in Indiana, in 1832. See Hugh Judge's Journal, page 361.

GRAVELLY RUN was in Dinwiddie Co., Va., about 12 miles south of Petersburg. See Burleigh.

GRAVEL SPRINGS, according to tradition, was in the southwestern part of Frederick Co., Va.

GREAT CACAPON was in Hampshire Co., Va., now W. Va.; perhaps to be identified with Dillon's Run.

GREEN PLAIN MEETING, often written Green Plane, was in Clark Co., Ohio, southeast of Springfield and near Selma. References to it have been found in the Hopewell records of 1823, 1828, etc.

GUINEDD. See Gwynedd.

GUNPOWDER is in Baltimore Co., Md., 16 miles north of Baltimore City, 18 miles west of Little Falls Meeting. The nearest railway station is Sparks.

GWYNEDD MEETING, formerly North Wales, was in Montgomery Co., Pa. The name was also written Gwynard, Guinedd, Gwinidd, etc.

HADDONFIELD is in Camden Co., N. J.; sometimes written Hatenfield.

HARDSHAW-WEST Monthly Meeting was held at Liverpool, England, on the 4th day of 3d month, 1825. Elizabeth Robson on that date received a certificate which was later presented at Hopewell.

HARRISON PURCHASE. Under date of 2d day 11th month, 1801, it was recorded: "Richard Mott from Harrison Purchase in the State of New York and Daniel Titus from Westbury on Long Island" came to Hopewell. See Purchase.

HATENFIELD. See Haddonfield.

HAVERFORD. See Radnor.

HERFORD has not been definitely located. Was perhaps Harford County, Md.

HONEY CREEK Friends' meeting was in Vigo Co., Ind.; in existence in 1835.

HOPEWELL; 7 miles northeast of Winchester, in Frederick Co., Va.; named, it is said, for Hopewell in Lancaster Co., Pa. Prior to 1744, says Thomas H. Fawcett, Hopewell included Monoquacy and Fairfax.

HORSHAM is in Montgomery County, Pa.

INDIAN SPRING Monthly Meeting was held at Sandy Spring, Md., Montgomery Co. Later Indian Spring was laid down and the work carried on at Sandy Spring.

JERICHO was on Long Island, N. Y., near the border between the counties of Queens and Nassau.

KENDAL, England. In 1768, 12th month, Rachel Wilson from the monthly meeting of Kendal, in "Old England," was present at Hopewell.

KENNET is in the town of Kennet Square, Chester Co., Pa. Prior to 1754 Kennet was known as Newark, and originally as New Castle. See Michener, pages 92-95.

KINGWOOD MEETING was located in Hunterdon Co., N. J.

LEE'S CREEK was in Clinton Co., Ohio, about 9 miles east of Wilmington.

LITTLE BRITAIN MEETING was in Lancaster Co., Pa.

LITTLE CACAPON was in Hampshire Co., Va., now W. Va.

LITTLE CREEK was near Smyrna, in Lancaster Co., Pa. Little Creek and Duck Creek were near each other.

LITTLE FALLS Friends' meeting was in Maryland.

LIVERPOOL, England. In 1827 Elizabeth Robson, "from Liverpool, Great Britain, attended this meeting [Hopewell] and most of its branches." It is stated in another place: "Our friend, Elizabeth Robson, a minister from Great Britain, attended this meeting and most of its branches, and produced a certificate from Hardshaw-west Monthly Meeting held at Liverpool the 4th of the 3rd mo. 1825; endorsed by Lancashire."

LONDON, England. In 1785 John Storer from Nottingham and Thomas Cally from Sheffield produced at Hopewell certificates from their respective monthly and quarterly meetings, also from the yearly meeting of ministers and elders held in London.

London Grove was in Chester Co., Pa., in the township joining to Marlboro.

Lost Creek Monthly Meeting was in Jefferson Co., Tenn.

Lower Ridge. See under Ridge Meeting.

Lupton's Meeting was the name often applied to the Ridge Meeting. See the Ridge.

Maiden Creek, a meeting within the verge of Exeter Monthly Meeting, which was in Berks Co., Pa.

Marlbrough (Marlboro) Monthly Meeting was in Marlboro Township, Ulster Co., N. Y. Under date of 10th day 2d month, 1819, was recorded at Hopewell the visit of James Hallock from Marlbrough; and on the 4th day of 11th month, the same year, a minute was made of the visit of Tristrum Russel from Marlbrough Monthly Meeting, New York State.

There was also a Marlborough in South Carolina, which was visited by Hugh Judge in 1785; and another in Randolph Co., N. C.

A meeting first held at the house of John Fawcett, in the southwestern part of Frederick Co., Va., and later known as Mt. Pleasant, may sometimes have been spoken of as Marlboro, because it was near Marlboro (Zane's) Iron Works, on Cedar Creek. Possibly it was also referred to occasionally as Cedar Creek, though Cedar Creek meeting, properly so called, was in Hanover Co., Va.

Medford. See Upper Evesham.

Miami Monthly Meeting, located on the Little Miami River in Warren County, "was the first to be established in southwestern Ohio."

It was the center from which Quakerism spread over western Ohio and throughout Indiana,—the territory now embraced in Wilmington, Indiana, and Western Yearly Meeting. The settlement of Friends in the section about the present site of Waynesville began in the closing years of the eighteenth century. A meeting for worship was established about 1801. Miami Monthly Meeting was opened 10 Mo. 13, 1803, by permission of Redstone Quarterly Meeting, held at Westland, Pa., 9 Mo. 5, 1803.

Prior to the establishment of Miami Monthly Meeting, the Friends moving into this section left their certificates of membership at Westland Monthly Meeting, Washington County, Pa., or at Concord Monthly Meeting, Belmont County, Ohio. The former meeting had been in existence since 1785; the latter was not set up until about the end of 1801. Usually the records of certificates received do not mention the place of settlement of the new members, but one exception to this rule has been noted. Under date of 12 Mo. 25, 1802, Westland minutes record the receipt of nine certificates from Bush River Monthly Meeting, S. C., with the statement that the persons named were settled at Little Miami. These certificates were dated 9 Mo. 25, 1802, and were for the following named persons, Samuel Kelly, wife Hannah, and six children; Abijah O'Neal, wife Anna, and seven children; James Mills, wife Lydia, and nine children; Robert Kelly, wife Sarah, and two children; Alexander Mills, wife Eunice, and four children; Layton Jay, wife Elizabeth, and six children; Ellis Pugh and wife, Rachel; Mary Paty, wife of Charles; Ann Horner, wife of Thomas. There are indications that some of the men mentioned above, including Abijah O'Neal, Samuel Kelly, and James Mills, had been settled on the Little Miami for two or three years previous to the date of their certificates.

MIDDLE CREEK meeting was in the village of Arden, in Berkeley Co., now West Virginia, southwest of Martinsburg. It is said that Arden was founded in 1775 by Jacob Moon, a Friend, who named it for his former home village in England. In 1778 the establishing of a meeting at Middle Creek was under consideration at Hopewell. In 1791 a preparative meeting was held at Middle Creek; and in 1796 Tuscarora and Middle Creek united in one meeting, to sit with Middle Creek. The meeting house was a stone building and remained in the hands of the Friends until just before the Civil War, when the lot and burying ground passed to the Southern Methodists.

MIDDLETOWN. (1) A Friends' meeting in Bucks Co., Pa. (2) A Friends' meeting in Ohio, on the Great Miami River, between Cincinnati and Hamilton. In 2d month 1748 William Jolliffe was given a certificate to Middletown (1) from Hopewell.

MILL (MILLS') CREEK. In Berkeley Co., Va., now W. Va. Mill Creek and Middle Creek Friends, 8 families, were granted a meeting for worship on the 1st day of 2d month, 1761, at the home of Morris Rees Sr.

There was a Mill Creek Friends' meeting in Ohio, perhaps in Hamilton County. It was referred to at Hopewell in 1819.

MILFORD Friends' meeting was in Wayne Co., Ohio. In

1832 there was a Milford preparative meeting on the Eastern Shore of Maryland.

MONALLEN, also written Menallen, is in Adams County, Pa., 9 miles north of Gettysburg.

MONONGAHELA. Friends on the east side of the Monongahela River and Friends at Westland on the 5th day of 9th month, 1785, requested a monthly meeting. About that time or shortly thereafter a circular monthly meeting was etsablished, to alternate between the west side and the east side of the river. The meeting on the east side, apparently, was known as Monongahela. Possibly it was the same as Redstone.

MONOQUACY, also written Monocacy, was on or near the Monocacy River, in Maryland. It was included in Hopewell Monthly Meeting until 1744. This meeting, for worship, was laid down in 1762.

MOORESTOWN Friends' meeting, N. J., was first known as Chester. See Chester.

MOUNT HOLLY was described at Hopewell in 1791 as "in the Jerseys." It was in Burlington Co., N. J.

MOUNT PLEASANT Meeting was located 8 miles southwest of Winchester, in Frederick Co., Va., on the northwest side of the Cedar Creek Grade. In 1771 it was held in the house of John Fawcett. In 1777 it was spoken of as "Fawsett." Sometimes, perhaps, it was referred to as Cedar Creek, but Cedar Creek, more properly, was in Hanover Co., Va. Mt. Pleasant meeting was apparently discontinued in 1809.

There was also a Mt. Pleasant Friends' meeting in Berkeley Co., S. C., and a third one in Jefferson Co., Ohio.

MUNSY MONTHLY MEETING was in Pennsylvania; changed later to Fishing Creek Monthly Meeting, held at Millville, Columbia County. In the 1st month 1801 Jesse Hains came to Hopewell from Munsy Monthly Meeting, with William Ellis of the same meeting as his companion.

NEW GARDEN. There were at least five Friends' meetings by this name: (1) in Chester Co., Pa.; (2) in Guilford Co., N. C., set up in 1754; (3) in Rowan Co., N. C.; (4) in Columbiana Co., Ohio; (5) in Wayne Co., Ind.

NEW HOPE was in Greene Co., Tenn.; still active in 1896, according to Stephen B. Weeks's map of that year.

NORTHAMPTON was described in 1780 as in West New Jersey.

NORTHERN DISTRICT of Philadelphia, Pa. The meetings of this district were held most frequently at the Bank Meeting House on Front Street, but the meetings were transferred in 1789 to a new structure in Key's Alley. The original Bank Meeting House was erected in 1685. See "A Retrospect of Early Quakerism," by Ezra Michener, 1860, pages 52, 54.

NORTH FORK was in Hampshire Co., Va. (now W. Va.), on a branch of Capon River.

NOTTINGHAM MEETING is in Cecil County, Md. The Nottingham Monthly Meeting was settled in the summer of 1730. See Janney's History of the Friends, Vol. III, page 258. Nottingham, England, is also referred to in Hopewell records.

OBLONG. A village in Northeast Township, Dutchess Co., N. Y. On the 5th day of 1st month, 1784, at Hopewell, it was recorded: "Our esteemed Friend Aaron Lancaster produced a certificate from the Mo. Meeting at Oblong in the province of New York." In or about 1800 Daniel Haviland came to Hopewell from Oblong Monthly Meeting. From the journal of Hugh Judge it appears that Oblong was in the southeastern part of New York State.

OLDHAM was in Guernsey Co., Ohio.

PASQUOTANK County is in the northeastern part of North Carolina, just east of Perquimans County. Weeks says, "In 1800 there were three strong meetings in Pasquotank, with one monthly meeting."

PERGUIMONTO was a quarterly meeting in North Carolina in 1772. The name as here written is probably a variation of Perquimons or Perquimans.

PETERSBURG Friends' meeting was in South Carolina. There were also Friends living in Petersburg, Va.; at least in 1785 Hugh Judge lodged several days in Petersburg with Edward Stabler, who evidently was a Friend. No evidence has been found of a Friends' meeting in Petersburg, Va.

PHILADELPHIA, a Friends' center. On 10th day 7th month, 1828, and at other times, the Philadelphia Monthly Meeting was at Cherry Street. The meeting of the above date is mentioned in old records at Hopewell.

PIPE CREEK MEETING was in Carroll Co., Md., 40 miles west of Baltimore, and half a mile from Union Bridge Station.

PLAINFIELD MEETING was in Coshocton Co., Ohio. Probably there was one also at Plainfield, N. J., and perhaps one in Maryland.

POTTS'S Friends' meeting was visited by Daniel Stanton in 1760. Other later references to it have been found. It was also known as the Gap Meeting, and was at or near Hillsboro, Loudoun Co., Va.

PRAIRIE GROVE Friends' meeting was in Iowa, and was in existence in 1877.

PROVIDENCE MEETING was in Montgomery Co., Pa. Another was near the Potomac River, in Virginia, in what is now Berkeley Co., W. Va. The latter was organized at an early date and a meeting house was built on the land of Richard Beeson. This Providence and Fairfax were nearly as old as Hopewell. See Tuscarora.

There was also a Providence meeting in South Carolina, which was visited by Hugh Judge in 1785. See his Journal, page 44.

PURCHASE, in New York State. Under date of 18th day of 11th month, 1805, Fairfax Quarterly Meeting, held at Hopewell, recorded: "Richard Mott attended this Meeting from Purchase Monthly Meeting, New York. Also John Shoemaker Jr. from Abington Monthly Meeting in Pennsylvania." See Harrison Purchase.

RADFORD is in Pulaski County, Va.

RADNOR MEETING is near Haverford, Pa.—it formerly was Haverford. It is named in Hopewell records in 1802, and thereabouts.

RAHWAY, New Jersey. Under date of 3d day 9th month, 1781, it was recorded at Hopewell: "Our Esteemed Friend Robert Willis produced a certificate to this meeting from Rahway Mo. Meeting in East New Jersey, held the 15th day of the 3d month, 1781."

REDSTONE MEETING was in Fayette Co., Pa., 6 or 7 miles east of Brownsville, near a place called Quaker Rock, now on Route 40; also, in early times, near Jonah Cadwallader's. See David Lupton's memoranda of 1806; also T. Chalkley Matlack, Moorestown, N. J. In 1780 there were 17 families in this locality; 150 persons with right of membership; and other friendly people.

RICHLAND MEETING was in Bucks Co., Pa.

RICHSQUARE was in Northampton Co., N. C.

RIDGE MEETING was located on Apple Pie Ridge, 2 miles west of the Valley Pike (highway from Winchester to Martinsburg). The Ridge meeting house was erected in 1791; and in 1800 the meeting was spoken of as being near William Lupton's. The site was about 4 miles southwest of Hopewell. It was called the Upper Ridge after a second meeting, the Lower Ridge, was established about 2 miles northwest of Hopewell. Lower Ridge Meeting was in the village of White Hall, near Joseph Hackney's. See Lupton's.

RIGHTSBOROUGH. See Wrightsborough.

ROBINSON Monthly Meeting, in existence in 1794, but has not been definitely located.

SADSBURY QUARTERLY MEETING is held in Christiana, Lancaster Co., Pa.

SALEM MEETING was in Salem Co., N. J. There was also a Salem Friends' meeting in Columbiana Co., Ohio, and another in Union Co., Indiana. The last was known also as Silver Creek.

SANDY SPRING was in Montgomery Co., Md. See Indian Spring.

SHEFFIELD, England. On the 19th day of 11th month, 1785, John Storer from Nottingham and Thomas Cally (Colley) from Sheffield presented certificates at Hopewell, from their respective monthly and quarterly meetings "where they belong in England, also from the Yearly Meeting of Ministers & Elders held in London."

SHORT CREEK MEETING was in Harrison Co., Ohio. It and Concord were granted a quarter in 1806.

SILVER CREEK. See Salem, Ind.

SINKING CREEK was an indulged meeting of Westland Monthly Meeting, about 1791.

SMITH CREEK Friends' meeting was held at several places near New Market and Mt. Jackson, Shenandoah Co., Va., over a period from 1738 to 1838, or thereabouts. In 1738 Robert Scarborough, who lived four or five miles southwest of the site of New Market, on Smith Creek, wrote that he was near a Friends' meeting. In 1771, as Hopewell records show, a more convenient place for Smith Creek Meeting was being sought. In the 5th month 1772 it was proposed to build a meeting house on or near Jackson Allen's land, on the south side of the north fork of Shannando River, to give account to Crooked Run. For many years after 1800 a Friends' meeting house stood 3 or 4 miles northeast of New Market and about the same distance southwest of Mt. Jackson, on the north side of the north fork of Shenandoah River. This meeting house and the lot whereon it stood were sold to John Neff in 1839. The burial ground marks the site.

SOLESBURY Meeting was in Bucks Co., Pa.

SOUTH FORK Meeting was in Loudoun Co., Va., 6 or 7 miles southwest of Lincoln (Goose Creek Meeting). In 1784 Hugh Judge was at South Fork. It was on or near the south fork of Beaverdam Creek. Yardley Taylor's map of Loudoun County, made in 1853, shows South Fork Friends' Meeting still active. The old burial ground, near the village of Unison, marks the site of the meeting house.

SOUTHLAND Meeting was located near Mount Pony, which is in Culpeper Co., Va., three miles southeast of the town of Culpeper. It dated from 1788 or thereabouts. Jonathan Bishop and perhaps other Friends lived near Mount Pony as early as 1782. Southland was made a monthly meeting about 1797.

Mrs. C. H. Wine of Culpeper has been of much assistance in gathering information about Southland Friends' Meeting, which was located between Mt. Pony and Stevensburg. She has transmitted a letter written at Raccoon Ford, Culpeper Co., Va., Sept. 18, 1935, by Philip Pendleton Nalle, A. M., a gentleman who has spent his long life in the vicinity. Following are parts of his letter:

About 1783 the state laid off several towns in Culpeper County (then in-

A Quarterly Meeting at Hopewell

Back Creek Meeting House

cluding Madison and Rappahannock). One of them was Stevensburg, about seven miles from Culpeper [town], on the Fredericksburg road. After a while a Quaker settlement was formed there and grew rapidly. It soon became larger than the Court House, for the Quakers were thrifty. But slavery distressed them, and they began to shift off to Ohio.

By 1820 or before there were few of them left. They had a cemetery of several acres; and the church near by, used by the Baptists in the 1850's, may have been the Quaker church. It was plain and rough. Both church and tombstones disappeared during the War of the States, and the cemetery has been in cultivation for many years.

A Methodist church stands about where the Baptist structure stood. Going east along the "straty boulevard" the road joins the right-hand [road] going to Raccoon Ford. Right here at the corner the cemetery began, an acre or more perhaps, and running along the left, going to Raccoon Ford, reached maybe 150 or 200 yards. I remember the tombstones and heard sermons in the church.

I was occupied with genealogy for a short while. My life has been spent mainly in the effort to get rid of the fog and denseness that cover the Christian faith. I am in my 87th year now, and am still learning. Wishing you good standing in His family, I am,

Yours very truly,

P. P. Nalle, Jr.

SOUTH RIVER Monthly Meeting was in Campbell Co. (Bedford prior to 1782), Va. The monthly meeting there was set up in 1757. It survived until 1858.

SPRINGBOROUGH Monthly Meeting was in Warren Co., Ohio, in 1825 and later—possibly earlier.

SPRINGFIELD Friends' meeting was in Guilford Co., N. C., near the line of Randolph Co. There was also a meeting of the same name in Delaware Co., Pa., and perhaps another in Ohio.

STAFFORD Friends' meeting was probably in the southeastern part of Stafford Co., Va., on or near Potomac Run (Creek). It was indulged in 1780, "as heretofore." In 1817 steps were taken to sell the meeting house "at Stafford"; the burying ground to be reserved. This was done at a number of places.

STILLWATER was in Tuscarawas Co., Ohio. It is found in Hopewell records in 1816, etc.

TOTTENHAM, England. About 1805 came to Hopewell Susanna Horn, "our beloved Friend, from Tottenham, Middlesex Co., England."

TUSCARORA meeting house was located 2½ miles northwest of Martinsburg, now in West Virginia, on the Tuscarora Pike. The meeting at this place seems to have been called Providence, as well as Tuscarora. On 1st of 12th month, 1760, the Friends of Tuscarora, Mill Creek, and Middle Creek were given leave to hold their meetings during the winter season in the "Old Meeting House of Providence." In 1768 the Friends of Tuscarora were granted liberty to hold a meeting for worship on each 1st day during the winter season in the "Old meeting house at that Place." Tuscarora was still holding in 1792.

UPLAND. See Chester.

UPPER EVESHAM, later Medford, was near Haddonfield, New Jersey.

UPPER RIDGE. See under Ridge Meeting.

UWCHLAN (UWCHLAND) was in the Welsh Tract, near Chester, Pa. The meeting there was established in 1720.

WAN OAK. In the 11th month 1792 Jonathan Wright went from Hopewell to "Wan Oak." In 1785 Hugh Judge (Journal, page 47) had been at "Wainoke," not far from Curles and Richmond. In Hopewell records the name has been found also as "Waynoak" and "Wayneoak." This meeting was doubtless Weyanoke, in Charles City Co., Va.

WARRINGTON Monthly Meeting, established in 1747, was held in York Co., Pa., 14 miles northwest of the city of York. The present Warrington Quarterly Meeting is held at Menallen, Adams Co., Pa.

WATEREE was in Kershaw Co., S. C.

WATERFORD, now Loudoun Co., Va., the place where Fairfax Friends' Meeting was held.

WESTBURY is in Nassau Co., N. Y., on Long Island. A monthly meeting was there in 1786.

WESTFIELD was in Surry Co., N. C. There was also a Westfield Friends' meeting in Ohio in 1857, etc.

WEST GROVE was in Chester Co., Pa. There was also a West Grove in Wayne Co., Ind.

WESTLAND meeting house was in Washington Co., Pa., a few miles west of Brownsville. Here was established a meeting for worship and also a preparative meeting in 1782, the first meeting for worship, says Janney, west of the Alleghanies. A meeting house was built in 1785, in place of the former which was burned. Possibly there was also a Westland Friends' meeting in North Carolina.

WEST RIVER, Maryland. The following is from "An Account of the Meetings for Worship and Discipline of the Society of Friends, Composing Baltimore Yearly Meeting," by Levi K. Brown.

"From ancient records it appears that the first Yearly Meeting in Maryland was held on West River, in the year 1672. For many years thereafter it was held, alternately, at West River, on the Western Shore, and at Tredhaven, on the Eastern Shore of Maryland. In 1790, the Yearly Meeting was removed to be held in Baltimore, at which time the meetings composing Fairfax and Hopewell Monthly Meetings in Virginia, and Warrington Monthly Meeting in Pennsylvania, which had previously belonged to Concord Quarter, Philadelphia Yearly Meeting, were attached to Baltimore, and those meetings on the Eastern Shore of Maryland now comprising 'Southern Quarterly Meeting,' were united to Philadelphia Yearly Meeting."

WHITE OAK SWAMP was in Henrico Co., Va. In or about 1800 James Ladd came from White Oak Swamp Mo. Mtg. to Hopewell.

WHITE WATER was in Wayne County, Ind. The name is found in Hopewell records in 1826, 1842, etc.

WILMINGTON Friends' meeting was in Newcastle Co., Del. There was (perhaps still is) also a Friends' meeting at Wilmington, Clinton Co., Ohio.

WINCHESTER, Virginia. In or about 1819 Center Meeting, located near the homes of Parkins and Hollingsworth just southwest of Winchester, was moved into town, but still called Center. In town the meeting house was first in the 600 block (had the whole square), on the west side of S. Washington Street. This building was destroyed during the war, 1861-65. In 1870 or 1871 another house of worship was erected on another lot, corner of N. Washington & W. Piccadilly. In this building, the one still in use, the first monthly meeting was held on the 8th of 2d month, 1872. The burial ground at Old Center, near the homes of Parkins and Hollingsworth, was used for many years after 1819, and may still be located.

WITHAM, England. Under date of the 6th day of 10th month, 1817, it was recorded at Hopewell that Mary Naftel from Witham Monthly Meeting, also the Yearly Meeting at London, was present. With Mary had come Hannah Lewis of (or from) Philadelphia.

WRIGHTSBOROUGH was on Town Creek, 16 miles from Appling, in McDuffie Co., Ga. On July 3, 1770, the general assembly of Georgia granted to Joseph Maddock (or Mattock) and Jonathan Still a tract of 40,000 acres of land in St. Paul's Parish, to be held in trust for the Quakers. Here they began their town, which they named for Sir James Wright, governor of the colony.

YORK MEETING was in the town of York, county of York, Penna.

CHAPTER XVI

CONCLUSION

THE QUAKER'S FAITH

By RUFUS M. JONES

The Friends, or Quakers as they are popularly called, had their rise in the turbulent and chaotic years of the English Commonwealth period (1642-1660). The originator of this movement and the founder of the religious Society of Friends was George Fox (1624-1691), who was untrained in school learning, but a man of unusual native capacity, of extraordinary depth of life, swift of insight, a born leader, a spiritual genius, a fine union of mystic, prophet, and practical reformer, a rugged, fearless champion of a fresh and novel type of Christianity. He drew about him from the groups of sectaries who were eager for a more complete reformation of the Church a large and impressive following, among whom the most notable figures were William Penn, the founder of Pennsylvania; Robert Barclay, scholar and theologian; and Isaac Penington, mystic and saint. The movement spread in England in the face of a fierce and brutal persecution, and from 1657 onward the Quakers invaded America and soon became an important factor both in the religious and political life of the colonies.

George Fox and his companions were primarily concerned to get free from the forms and systems which had accumulated through the centuries and to revive as far as possible the simplicity and power of the primitive, apostolic Church. They put the main emphasis on life and experience. Quakerism is thus an attempt to express a religion of life. The Society of Friends was designed to be a living, growing fellowship or brotherhood rather than a sacred and authoritative institution. It was not meant to be a new sect or denomination, but the germ and seed of a world-wide spiritual Christianity. In fact, one of George Fox's favorite names for his movement was "the Seed"; that is, the spiritual nucleus.

The reality of God as a living Presence in the world and

in men lies at the very centre of the Quaker faith. Friends are not much interested in formulating abstract theories and statements about God. They prefer to begin with personal experience of Him. They are convinced by their experience that He is not remote or far away. Every day is a day of creation. All history is sacred history. All places are holy places for the true worshipper. They find Him walking with them in the cool of the day and also in the stress and strain of business and duty. They think of man's soul as a revealing place for God. Man is made in the divine image. He is a spiritual being. He is more nearly like God than is any other being in the universe. He has within himself an inner sanctuary where the human and the divine can meet and commune. He feels the august call of duty. Something in his deeps tells him that right is eternally right and wrong is forever wrong. He judges and condemns himself when he takes the wrong course. He has spiritual hungers and thirsts. He all the time seeks for something beyond himself. He is *made* for the divine life and he is restless until he finds God. The real drama of human life is here within. The place to look for God is not above the sky, but in the inner life and spirit of man. The heart of religion, for Friends, is experience of God and joyous worship of Him.

Through His presence felt within, Friends find their peace and power and fortification, not only in green pastures and by quiet waters, but also in the valley of shadows and in the press of storm and danger. They live and think and act in the quiet faith that God is Spirit, close as breathing, and near as one's own limbs. This is of course not a new idea, but it is a strangely neglected one and one that needs constant reemphasis and personal witness.

Friends gather in hush and silence in order to feel and hear before they speak. They try to leave behind the problems of house and office, of business and duty, of worry and perplexity, to settle into deep calm with an intensity beyond speech and to feel the currents of the divine life circulate through them and refresh and revitalize them. The rush and turmoil of this busy and material life tend to make men forget their spiritual heritage and divine destiny. They live in the outward and temporal and lose their contacts with the inner world of health and healing. Worship, which is as necessary for full and complete life as breathing, wanes away and becomes a lost art. Friends have aimed to restore its vital power and to put it at the centre of life. This is not something that one man can do for the rest. It cannot be delegated. It is both individual and corporate. Each person seeks and finds for himself, but he does more than that; he helps to produce an atmosphere and spirit in which all the others who compose the waiting group are strengthened and assisted in their aspirations and in their correspondence with the Eternal Spirit. These occasions of worship are often times of intense listening, of convincing experience, of quiet peace and deep joy.

The underlying faith that God is Spirit comes to light again in the Quaker's natural and simple way of thinking of Christ as a revelation of God in life and history. There are not two worlds, a divine one far away, off in another realm, and an undivine one down here where we live, so that He who comes to reveal God must come mysteriously out of a distant heaven to dwell as an alien and foreigner here among men. Not that. God is spirit and dwells in His world. He has always in some measure been here. He has in all ages stirred men's hearts with love and desire. He has quickened aspiration and awakened ideals. He has stage by stage prepared the way for higher and holier living. He has been working in and through the unfolding events of history, and at length in Christ, who is both human and divine, He has found a perfect organ for revealing His life and character and will. Christ is the new Adam, the head of a new humanity, the spiritual guide and saviour for whom the race was waiting. When Friends think of God then, they think of Him as like Christ. They start with those traits of heart and character which have been made known to us in the Life we know and love, and they feel and believe that that Life of tenderness and grace and truth is a perfect unveiling of the Nature of God. God is like *that*.

Religion for Friends is not something apart from life and business, not something for special days or sacred places. It is the whole of life. It is a way of life. It is something that one does and is. Like breathing or digestion, it carries vital energy and power into every pulse of thought and stroke of work. It does not have to do primarily with another world, or with a state after death; it has to do essentially with now and here.

The Quaker sees his world and he sees human life in the light of Christ's love and sacrifice. He sees how precious man must be if Christ loved him that way. He sees what immensely important spiritual tasks there are for us to do, if Christ was ready to go the way of the cross to show how the new spiritual order which he called the kingdom of God is to be built. The Quakers, then, awakened and kindled by that divine example, have always had a warm and glowing passion for human service. They have uncommon faith in the transforming power of love. They make it an inherent part of their religion to practice the spirit and method of love in the various walks of life. They feel to a high degree the preciousness, the absolute worth, of the human life, made in God's image and big with divine possibilities, and they count nothing too hard or too difficult or too costly if they can save or elevate or liberate any life, even that of a little child. They have been the champions of less favored races. They have been friends and helpers of friendless people, of those who were neglected or exploited. They have opposed war on Christian principle and on the grounds of love and humanity. It seems to them unthinkable as a method of solving international issues. They have insisted that Christians should exhibit a way of life that would eliminate the causes of war. In any case they themselves stand unalterably for the application of Christ's way of life not only to relations between nations, but to relations between races and to all social and economic problems as well.

Friends as a religious people are concerned to live in simplicity and sincerity, to speak and to practice truth, to maintain a clean and quiet type of life and to proclaim their faith by deed and action rather than by words and phrases. Their ministers are unordained and unclerical, speaking as they feel themselves to be moved and led by the Spirit. They bear testimony to what they have seen and heard and felt.

The Society of Friends numerically is a small body. It is composed in America of only about one hundred thousand persons. Its work is quiet, unostentatious and humble, but it is a spiritual *seed*, still living and growing, and bearing within itself the hope and promise of larger possibilities of life and service.

QUAKER WORSHIP

As Set Forth in a Publication of the Friends' General Conference

The Society of Friends extends an invitation to all who will to join us in the worship of our Heavenly Father after a manner which we have found helpful. We are glad to welcome you to our meetings, and to wish for you, and for ourselves, that by right use of this opportunity we shall all draw from it the guidance and strength needed to meet the problems of these days in a truly Christian spirit.

For those of our visitors who are not familiar with our method of worship we venture the following brief explanation of the ideal meeting toward which we strive.

We aim to have all our external arrangements conform to our ideas of reverence, of simplicity, of democracy. The seats are all free. Those facing the body of the meeting are usually occupied by members of a committee of oversight. No collection is ever taken in these religious gatherings.

God, according to our conception, is not some far-off Being, unknown and unknowable, but our loving, ever-present Father. Every human soul is closely akin to the Divine, and may receive directly and respond to revelations of His will, as Jesus did, and as have the prophets and holy men of all ages. Therefore for us, worship cannot consist of ritual or form, but is rather the conscious effort of man to put himself into such a condition of mind and soul that he can, to a degree at least, know the will of God.

We meet at the appointed time and sit in reverent silence. This silence must not be regarded as an end in itself, but must be filled with a passionate desire to know God, to know His will and to surrender our wills to His. Silent prayer, thanksgiving and meditation are powerful aids in attaining to this state. Often in such a meeting, comes to one, or more, of those present the conviction that he has a thought that should be shared with the others. If he believes that he is acting under a Divine impulse, he rises and delivers his message. We have usually found that a few words fitly spoken are of far more value than the long sermon. If any one feels the impulse to vocal prayer, the rest will sit with bowed heads.

In such a meeting as this there is a responsibility resting on every one present. Each should try to raise the spiritual temperature by the fervor of his own spirit. By sympathetic attention we should try to help any one who may speak. By his own individual faithfulness he should be ready to speak or to remain silent according to which seems the more consonant with God's will.

In this bustling world of ours, too few are such chances for calm meditation, for sane thinking, for attaining to that detachment of spirit where we can see life in a truer perspective.

May we all in joint communion find the strength and peace which Whittier voices in the following words:

"And so I find it well to come
For deeper rest to this still room,
For here the habit of the soul
Feels less the outer world's control;
The strength of mutual purpose pleads
More earnestly our common needs,
And in the silence multiplied
By these still forms on either side,
The world that time and sense have known
Falls off and leaves us God alone."

PART TWO

DOCUMENTARY

MARRIAGE CERTIFICATES FROM HOPEWELL
1748-1830

To illustrate the form of certificate and for other reasons, a few certificates are given in full, but most have been abridged. Names of the man and woman married have in each case been printed in *italics*. In later years printed and engraved forms were used, blank spaces being filled in with the usual information regarding the contracting parties.

As a rule, the grouping of signatures on the certificate had significance, and has been preserved. The groom's family signed in the right-hand column; the bride's family in the next column to the left; other relatives in the third column; and other persons, relatives, neighbors, and guests, frequently some not Friends, in the fourth column at the left. In copying the names into the record books the original order and arrangement of the signatures was not always observed.

Consent of parents, as well as of other members of the meeting, was regularly sought; hence the statement that consent of parents was given is no indication that the contracting parties were under 21 years of age.

AN EARLY MARRIAGE AT HOPEWELL

Record copied from a loose sheet in the minute book from Baltimore

At our Monthly Meeting of Hopewell at Opeckon the fourth Day of the Second Month A. D. 1748:

William Hiett and Alice Lowden appeared at this Meeting and declared their intention of taking each other in marriage, this being the first time, this Meeting appoints James McGrew and Simeon Taylor to inquire into the said William Hiett's conversation and clearness in respect to marriage and what else may be needful to make report to the next Monthly Meeting accordingly.

At Our Monthly Meeting of Hopewell at Opeckon 2nd day of 3rd month 1748:

William Hiett and Alice Lowden appeared at this Meeting and declared their intention of taking each other in marriage, this being the second time, the friends appointed to inquire into the said William Hiett's conversation and clearness with others in respect to marriage, report that they find nothing to obstruct their proceedings.

Therefore, this Meeting leaves them to their Liberty to consumate their said intentions when they see meet, and this Meeting appoints James McGrew and Simeon Taylor—to see that the marriage be decently accomplished and make report thereof to the next Monthly Meeting accordingly.

A TYPICAL MARRIAGE CERTIFICATE

WHEREAS *Asa Lupton*, Son of William Lupton Deceased & Grace Lupton, in the County of Frederick in Virginia, and *Hannah Hank* of the same place, Daughter of John Hank Deceased & Margaret Hank of Rockingham County, having Declared their Intentions of Marriage with each Other before several Monthly Meetings of the People Called Quakers at Hopewell in the County of Frederick aforesaid, According to the good Order used amongst them and having Consent of Parents, their said proposals of Marriage was allowed of by the Said Meeting.

NOW these are to Certify whom it may Concern That for the full Accomplishing their said Intentions this 17th Day of the Fifth Month in the Year of Our Lord One Thousand Seven Hundred & Eighty Seven, they the Said Asa Lupton & Hannah Hank, Appeared in a Publick Meeting of the Said people at Hopewell in the County of Frederick Aforesaid, and the said Asa Lupton taking the said Hannah Hank by the Hand, did in a Solemn Manner Openly declare that he took her to be his Wife promesing to be unto her through Divine assistance a Loving and faithfull husband untill Death should Separate them, or words to the Same Effect, and then and there in the Said Assembly she the Said Hannah Hank did in Like manner Openly Declare, That She took him the Said Asa Lupton to be her Husband, Promising with Divine Assistance to be unto him a Loving and faithful wife untill Death Should Separate them, or words to the same Effect.

MOREOVER they the said Asa Lupton and Hannah Hank, she According to the Custom of Marriage Assuming the name of her Husband, did as a further Confirmation thereof then & there to these Presents Set their Hands.

Asa Lupton
Hannah Lupton

AND we being Present at the Solemnization of the said Marriage and Subscription in Manner Aforesaid do as Witnesses hereunto also Subscribe our Names the Day and Year above Written.

Martha Mendenhall	Richard Ridgway	Jonathan Pickering	Grace Lupton
Hannah Pickering	Lewis Walker	Joseph Steer Junr.	Samuel Lupton
Martha Walker	Nathaniel White Jun.	James Steere	Jesse Lupton
Marget Ridgway	Chas. Dingee	Isaac Steer	David Lupton
Hannah Wright	Richard Barrett	Phebe Steer	John Lupton
Catherin Lewis	Joseph Hackney	Elizabeth Woodrow	Ann Lupton
Mary Walker	Abraham Branson	Abigail Steere	William Lupton
Rebekah Roberts	John Cougill	Samuel Jackson	Bathsheba Lupton
Rachel Walker	Jacob Smith	Hannah Steere	Mary Lupton
	David Ross	Grace Steere Jun.	Rebekah Lupton
	Nathan Littler	Rachel Steer	Joshua Lupton
	Abel Walker	Lydia Rees	Nathan Lupton
		Isaac Steer Jun.	Mary Lupton Jun.
		Grace Jackson	Betty Lupton
		Joseph Steer 3ed.	Rachel Lupton
			Ruth Lupton
			Joseph Lupton
			Lydia Woodrow
			John Woodrow

ROGERS—BALLINGER

Evan Rogers, Son of John Rogers of or near Back Creek in the County of Frederick and Colony of Virginia, and *Sarah Ballinger,* Daughter of Josiah Ballinger, deceased, of Opeckan in the Colony afforesaid; the 15th day of 4th Mo., 1749; at Hopewell.

Evan Rogers
Sarah Rogers

Witnesses who signed this Marriage Certificate:

Martha Beeson	Evan Thomas	John Roger
Ann M'Cooll	William Dillon	Ellinor Roger
Lydia Wright	James M'Cooll	Mary Ballinger
Sarah Wright	Daniel Dillon	James Wright
Lucy Wright	James McGrew	Josiah Ballinger
Esther Wright	Henry Lewis	Owen Roger
Sarah Mills	Jacob Jenkins	Mary Lewis
Hannah Pugh	Lucy Pugh	Elizabeth Jenkins
Lydia Dillon	Isaac Wright	Sidney Rogers
Mary McGrew	James Wright	James Ballinger
Lydia Barret	Thomas Wright	
Mary Ridgway	Thomas Mills	
	Joseph Lupton	
	Thomas Pugh	
	Jesse Pugh	

LUPTON—BULL

Joseph Lupton, son of Joseph Lupton of Opeckan in ye County of Frederick and Colony of Virginia, and *Rachel Bull,* daughter of Richard Bull of ye County of Chester of province of Pensilvania; 17th day of 8th month, 1750; at Isaac Hollingsworth's home, Opeckan.

Joseph Lupton Junr.
Rachel Lupton

Witnesses who signed this Marriage Certificate:

John Thomas	Mary Wood	Mary Barret	Mary Lupton
Evan Thomas	John Barrett	Phebe Barret	William Lupton
Thomas Wright	William Barrett	Paisence Perkins	John Lupton
John Williams	Jesse Pugh	Margret Carter	William Pickering
Jonathan Parkins	Enos Thomas	Rachel Hollingsworth	Ann Lupton
Abner Clarke	Evan Thomas	Elizabeth Southerland	Marcy Lupton
	Charles Parkins	Albenah Thomas	James Haworth
	George Ross	Lydia Ross	Sarah Haworth
	Thomas Barrett	Martha Thomas	Sarah Pickering
	Messer Brown	Rachel Thomas	Enos Pearson
	William Pugh	Tabitha Jacocks	Jonathan Lupton
	John Pugh Jr.	James Wright Sr.	
	James Barrett	Evan Rogers	
	Wm. Jolliffe	James Wood	

LUPTON—FROST

John Lupton, son of Joseph Lupton of Opeckon in the County of Frederick and Colony of Virginia, and *Sarah Frost*, daughter of John Frost of the County afforesaid; 26th day of 6th month, 1755; at Opeckan.

John Lupton
Sarah Lupton

Witnesses who signed this Marriage Certificate:

James Wright Sen.	Martha Thomas	Joseph Lupton
Jesse Pugh	Albenah Thomas	William Lupton
Thomas Wright	Lydia Jolieffe	Joseph Lupton Jr.
John Thomas	Esther Wright	Jonathan Lupton
Enos Thomas	Amey Higins	Mary Frost
James Barrett	Rebeckah Handshaw	Mercy Haines
Jacob Chandler	Mary Wright	William Pickering
John Scarborough	Phebe Barrett	James Hayworth
	Rachel Hollingsworth	Sarah Hayworth
	Elisabeth Parkins	

REES—THOMAS

Henry Rees of Frederick County in ye Colony of Virginia, Son of Thomas Rees and Margaret his wife, and *Martha Thomas*, Daughter of Evan Thomas and Catherine his wife, deceased; 6th day of 4th month, 1758; at Opeckan.

Henry Rees
Martha Rees

Witnesses who signed this Marriage Certificate:

Eliz. Chandler	Sidney Wright	Jacob Moon	Margret Rees
Mary Brooks	Cathrine Ross	David Rees	Henry Bowen
Margret Richeson	Mary Litler	Geo. Ross	Evan Thomas
Zilpha More	Evan Rogers	Jesse Pugh	Albena Thomas
Jane Ridgway	Benj. Thornbugh	James Jolife	
Mary Wright	Wm. Pickering	Tho. Wright	
Mary Balenger	Jno. Ridgway	Wm. Barret	
Esther Wright	Wm. Gadis		
Sarah Pickring	Geo. Ruble		
	Jno. Gadis		

MOOR—HAINES

Joseph Moor, of Crooked Run, Frederick County, in the Colony of Virginia, and *Mary Haines*; 15th day of 10th month, 1760; at Crooked Run.

Joseph Moor
Mary Moor

Witnesses who signed this Marriage Certificate:

Elizabeth Berrey	Benjamin Moor	Mary Haines
Elizabeth Branson	George Jammison	Anthony Moor
Margaret Mackay	Richard Ridgeway	Robert Haines
Rebekah Branson	John Painter	Zilphay Moor
Susannah Painter	A. Mackay	Rebekah Haines
Phebe Jobe	Jacob Mackay	

M'COY—RIDGEWAY

Andrew M'Coy, son of Robert M'Coy in the County of Frederick and Colony of Virginia, and *Jane Ridgeway*, Daughter of John Ridgeway of the County and Colony aforesaid; 27th day of 11th month, 1760; at Hopewell.

Andrew Mackay
Jane Mackay

Witnesses who signed this Marriage Certificate:

Margaret Mackay	Jacob Mackay	John Ridgeway
Mary Fallis	Richard Ridgeway	Robert Mackay
Mary Moor	Henry Rees	Richard Ridgeway
Sidney Wright	Jesse Pugh	Joseph Moor
Albenah Thomas	John Lupton	Benjamin Moor
Rebeckah Hancher	Wm. Pickering	Robert Haines
Elizabeth Ballinger	Isaac Fallis	
Phebe Jobe	Robert Painter	
Rebeckah Haines	Jacob Fallis	
Martha Rees		

JOLLIFFE—WALKER

William Jolliffe Jr., of Opeckon in the County of Frederick and Colony of Virginia, and *Elizabeth Walker* of the same place, Daughter of Abel Walker and Sinah Walker, dec'd; 9th day of 4th month, 1761; at Opeckon.

William Jolliffe Jr.
Elizabeth Jolliffe

Witnesses who signed this Marriage Certificate:

Esther Wright	William Dillon	Wm. Jolliffe Sr.
Lydia Cunningham	Henry Rees	James Jolliffe
Albenah Thomas	Jonathan Perkins	Edmund Jolliffe
Sarah Milburn	George Ross	Abel Walker
Martha Melson	Edward Beeson	Lewis Walker
Sarah Haworth	John Ridgeway	Mordecai Walker
	George Cunningham	Mary Campbell
	James Steward	Sinah Walker
	Alexander Ross	Margaret Dorster
	Robert Bull	Hannah Jolliffe
	Thomas Butterfield	
	Evan Thomas	
	Edward Dodd	

BULL—MILBURN

Robert Bull, of Frederick County and Colony of Virginia, and *Sarah Milburn*, Widow of Robert Milburn of the same place; 7th day of 5th month, 1761; at their publick Meeting House.

Robert Bull
Sarah Bull

Witnesses who signed this Marriage Certificate:

Wm. Jolliffe jun.	Patience Perkins	Edward Dodd	Mary Littler
Eliz. Conyers	Hannah Perkins	Joseph Lupton	Samuel Littler
Morgan Morgan jur.	Sarah Bruce	Rachel Lupton	Nathan Littler
Geo. Cunningham	Rebekah Beaumont	Morris Rees	John Littler
Wm. Hobson	Hannah Rees	Morris Rees Jur.	Rachel Bruce
Tho. McClunn	Bethlehem Moseley	David Ross	Catharine Littler
Abel Walker	Elizabeth Jolliffe	Jonathan Ross	Elisabeth Littler
Thomas Jones	Mary Taylor	Mary Milburn	George Ross
Hannah Rees	Lydia Cunningham	John Milburn Jur.	Alexander Ross
Rachel Medcalf	Mary Frost	Thomas Rees	
Eliz. Chinaweth	Ann Taylor	Tho. Butterfield	
Mary Bowen	Mary Burney	Albenah Thomas	
Eliz. Cunningham			

McCLUN—PARKINS

Thomas McClun, of Frederick County and Colony of Virginia, and *Hannah Parkins*, Daughter of Isaac and Mary Parkins of the same place; 12th day of 11th month, 1761; at their Publick Meeting House.

Thomas McClun
Hannah McClun

Witnesses who signed this Marriage Certificate:

Albenah Thomas	Isaac Parkins
Esther Wright	Thomas Berry
Margaret Buntin	Charles Parkins
Elizabeth Rees	Isaac Malin
Sarah Lupton	Jonathan Parkins
Ann Lupton	David Parkins
Henry Rees	Isaac Parkins Jun.
Joseph Lupton	Patience Parkins
Samuel Ruble	Rachel Parkins
Jonathan Lupton	Ruth Parkins
Richard Beaumont	
David Rees	

WALKER—BEESON

Abel Walker, son of Abel Walker and Sinia Walker, Deceased, of Frederick County in the Colony of Virginia, and *Mary Beeson*, Daughter of Edw. Beeson, Deceased, and Martha his wife of the same place; 12th day of 11th month, 1761; at their Publick Meeting House.

Abel Walker
Mary Walker

Witnesses who signed this Marriage Certificate:

Benj. Thornburgh	Sarah Rees	Josiah Ballinger	Lewis Walker
John Williams	Ann Herlen	James Mendenhall	Mordecai Walker
Richard Ridgeway	Rachel Morgan	James Wright	Edward Beeson
George Ross	Mary Thornburgh	Lucy Wright	William Jolliffe
Joseph Morgan	Rebeccah Vanmature	Ralph Wright	Elisabeth Jolliffe
Edw. Morgan	Ann Goier	Elis'h Ballinger	Sinia Walker
Mordecai Morgan	Eliz'h Patterson	Jane Pugh	Ann Pugh
Wm. Patterson	Elizabeth Fenecan		Ebenezor Walker
Abraham Vanmature	Catherine Harlin		Micajah Beeson
Owen Williams			William Cambell
			James Ballinger

PAINTER—OSMOND

Robert Painter, Son of John and Hannah Painter, and *Eunice Osmond*, Daughter of John and Martha Osmond; 16th day of 12th month, 1761; at Crooked Run.

Robert Painter
Eunice Painter

Witnesses who signed this Marriage Certificate:

Alexander Oglebey	Samuel Humber	John Painter
Zilpah Moor	Hannah Branson	Hannah Painter
Rebekah Hains	Susannah Painter	John Branson
Margaret Mackay	Thomas Branson	John Painter Junior
Mary Haines	Reuben Braddock	Sarah Humber
	Anthony Moor	Jane Branson
	Robert Haines	Elizabeth Branson
	John Dodd	Armelia Osmond
	Samuel Shinn	
	Andrew Mackay	
	Lionel Branson	

REES—NEILL

Henry Rees, son of Thomas and Margaret Rees of Frederick County in the Colony of Virginia, and *Ann Neill*, Daughter of Lewis Neill of the same place; 26th day of 8th month, 1762; at their publick Meeting House.

Henry Rees
Ann Rees

Witnesses who signed this Marriage Certificate:

Jno. Rees	Charity Dillon	Lewis Neill Jr.	Lewis Neill
Jesse Pugh	Mary Tompson	Abraham Neill	Margaret Rees
George Ross	Esther Wright	Jno. Lupton	Thomas Rees
Wm. Harriss	Albenah Thomas	Thomas Tompson	Enos Thomas
Wm. Boyd	Eliza Ballinger	Evan Thomas	John Neall
Wm. Dillon	Lyda Ballinger	Cuthbert Hayhurst	
Jonathan Perkins			

RIDGWAY—McCOY

Richard Ridgway, Son of John Ridgway and Hannah, Dec'd, in the County of Frederick and Colony of Virginia, and *Margaret McCoy*, Daughter of Robert McCoy and Patience McKay, Deceased, of the County and Colony aforesaid; 22d day of 12th month, 1762; at Crooked Run.

Richard Ridgway
Margaret Ridgway

Witnesses who signed this Marriage Certificate:

Jno. Painter	Robt. Painter	Jacob McKay	John Ridgway
Robert Hanes	Martha Branson	Jane McKay	Robt. McKay
Anthony Moore	Mony Hanes	Rachel Ridgway	Andrew McKay
George Ross	Hannah Painter	Robt. McKay	
John Branson	Elizabeth Berry	Zilphia More	
John Painter Jr.	Susana Painter		

REES—REES

Thomas Rees, Son of Morris Rees and Sarah his wife, and *Margaret Rees*, Daughter of Thomas Rees and Margaret his wife, in the County of Frederick and Colony of Virginia; 14th day of 7th month, 1763; at their "publick meeting"

Thomas Rees
Margaret Rees

Witnesses who signed this Marriage Certificate:

Cuthbert Hayhurst	Wm. Boyd	Morris Rees Sr.
Thomas McClunn	Mary Handsher	Margaret Rees
Wm. Barrett	Jno. Perkins	Henry Rees
Jno. Neill	Esther Wright	John Rees
Aron Hackney	Albenah Thomas	Thomas Rees
	Katherine Littler	Ann Rees
	Abigal Southerland	Ann Dillon

LUPTON—FAWCETT

Jonathan Lupton, of Opeckon in the county of Frederick and Colony of Virginia, and *Sarah Fawcett*, daughter of John Fawcett of the county aforsaid; 23d day of 5th month, 1764; in a meeting at the house of John Fawcett.

Jonathan Lupton
Sarah Lupton

Witnesses who signed this Marriage Certificate:

Hannah Pickering	Ann Lupton	John Fawcett
Jane McCormack	Grace Pickering	Rebecah Fawcett
Mary Fawcett	Hannah Longacre	Jno. Fawcett
Mary Neall	Rachel Fawcett	Richard Fawcett
Joseph Longacre	Esther Wright	William Lupton
John Thomas Jr.	Albenah Thomas	John Lupton
Richard Fawcett	Jonathan Parkins	Wm. Pickering
Richard Iveson	William Neall	Joseph Lupton
Andrew Longacre	Robert Hodgson	Sam'l Pickering
Richard Longacre	James Iveson	Mercy McCormack
John Fawcett Jr.	Elizabeth Iveson	Grace Lupton
Rachel Fawcett	Mary Pickering	
Thomas Fawcett		
Christopher Acklon		

CHANDLER—TAYLOR

Jacob Chandler, of Frederick County in the Colony of Virginia, and *Ann Taylor*, daughter of Jonathan Taylor of the County and Colony aforesaid; 27th day of 9th month, 1764; at Hopewell.

Jacob Chandler
Ann Chandler

Witnesses who signed this Marriage Certificate:

Rich. Ridgway	Evan Rogers	Jesse Pugh	Jonathan Taylor
William Martham	George Ross	John Lupton	Prissilla Marchant
Thomas McClun	Aaron Hackney	Jona. Perkins	
Nathaniel Large	Sarah Pickering	Wm. Lupton	
Elisabeth Jolliffe	Esther Wright	Sam'l Pickering	
Sarah Rogers	Grace Pickering	John Rees	
Margaret Rees	Mary Ballenger	Morris Rees	
Charity Rees	Albenah Thomas	Morris Rees Jr.	
Hannah McClun	Sudney Wright	Lydia Rees	
	Rachel Bruce		

McCAY—RIDGEAWAY

Jacob McCay, of Crooked Run in Frederick County in the Colony of Virginia, and *Rachel Ridgeaway*, of Opecon and County aforesaid; 15th day of 8th month, 1765; at Hopewell.

Jacob McCay
Rachel McCay

Witnesses who signed this Marriage Certificate:

Esther Wright	William Jolliffe	Richard Ridgaway	Robt. McKay
Elisabeth Branson	Eliz. Jolliffe	George Follis	Jno. Ridgeway
Hannah McClun		Isaack McCay	Andrew McKay
Martha Wright		Tho. McClun	Robert McKay
		Robert Hains	

REES—KIRK

Jacob Rees, son of Morris Rees and Sarah his Wife, Deceased, and *Hannah Kirk*, Daughter of Roger Kirk and _____ his wife, Deceased, in the County of Frederick and Colony of Virginia; 11th day of 12th month, 1766; at their meeting place.

Jacob Rees
Hannah Rees

Witnesses who signed this Marriage Certificate:

Thomas Ellis	Henry Bowen	Job Hastings
Martha Mendinghall	John Gaddis	Mary Hastings
Albenah Thomas	Aron Hackney	Sarah Rees
Thos. Butterfield	Jacob Moon	Hannah Rees
Enos Ellis	Jean Moon	Thomas Rees
Eliz. Ellis	Absalom Chinoaworth	Margaret Rees
Joseph Hackney	Ruth Chinoaworth	
Jacob Beeson	Rees Hastings	
Hannah Huton	Jean Bowen	
John Brabson	Margaret Bowen	
Sina Walker	James Mendinghall	
Hannah Hastings		

HAINS—WRIGHT

Robert Hains, of Frederick County in the Colony of Virginia, and *Esther Wright*, of the Said County, Widow; 12th day of 2d month, 1767; at Opecon.

Robert Hains
Esther Hains

Witnesses who signed this Marriage Certificate:

Samuel M'Cray	William Pickering	Anthony Moor
Lydia Ballinger	Evan Rogers	Zilpha Moor
Samuel & Grace	Abraham Taylor	Joseph Moor
Pickering	Anne Chandler	Mary Moor
John Lupton	Mary Barrett	Robert Rea
Thomas M'Clun	Rachel Barrett	Rebekah Rea
Mary Babb	Lydia Barrett	Jonathan Wright
David Ross	Ann Rees	Edward Beeson
Mordecai Walker	Ann Taylor	James Ballinger
Mesheck Sexton	Abigail Steer	Mary Steer
Richard Ridgeaway	Elizabeth Jolliffe	Hannah Steer
Jonathan Perkins	Sarah Lupton	
Josiah Ballinger	Philip Babb	
Elizabeth Ballinger	Hannah Pickering	
	Hannah M'Clun	
	Mary Wright	

CADWALADER—PARKINS

Rees Cadwalader, of Loudoun county of Virginia, and *Ruth Parkins*, daughter of Isaac Parkins of the county of Frederick and Colony aforsaid; 10th day of 9th month, 1767; at Hopewell.

Rees Cadwalader
Ruth Cadwalader

Witnesses who signed this Marriage Certificate:

William Jolliffe	Mary Ballinger	Joseph Cadwallader
Ben. Thornbrugh	Elizabeth Jolliffe	Hannah McClun
George Ross	Elizabeth Ballinger	Isaac Parkins
Henry Rees	Ann Rees	Ebenezer Parkins
William Lupton	Sarah Lupton	John Cadwallader
James Steere	Rebecca Beaumont	Affinity Cadwallader
Cuthbert Hayhurst	Grace Pickering	Thomas McClun
David Ross	Sarah Bruce	Elizabeth Parkins
Simion Hains	Sarah Walker	
Joseph Steer	Ann Hollingsworth	
	Elizabeth Barrett	

BEESON—PUGH

Edward Beeson, son of Edward Beeson and Martha his Wife, and *Jane Pugh*, Daughter of Jesse Pugh and Alice his Wife, Both of the County and Colony of Virginia; 21st day of ye 9th month, 1767; at Back Creek.

Edward Beeson
Jane Beeson

Witnesses who signed this Marriage Certificate:

John Rogers	Henry Lewis	Mordecai Walker	Jesse Pugh
John Wright	Eliza Jinkins	Eliza Pugh	Alice Pugh
James M'Gill	Sudney Lewis	Sidny Wright	Martha Mendinghall
Richard Hayworth	Martha M'Coole	John M'Coole	Thomas Pugh
George Hoge	Owen Rogers	Jacob Beeson	Ann Pugh
Sam'l Pickering	Sarah Jankins	John Gaddis	Charity Ridgway
Isaac Mahlon	Ruth Pugh	Messer Beeson	Mary Walker
Wm. Hoge	Elines Lewis	Edward Beeson	Alice Pugh Jr.
Grace Steer	Gemimah Haworth	Peter Ruble	Abel Walker
Hannah Steer	Ann Haworth	Barak Fisher	Richard Ridgway
Job Pugh	Sarah Rogers	Ebenezer Walker	Lewis Walker
Joseph Steer	Ann Rogers	John Jolliffe	Jas. Mendinghall
Sinia Walker	Sam'l Lewis	Ellis Pugh	Evan Rogers
Mashac Saxton	Rees Gaddis	Joseph Hackney	Richard Beeson
Mary Barrett	John Pickering	Henry Lewis	
Eliz'h Joliffe	Jacob Jinkins	Mary Lewis	
Katherine Day	Jonathan Jinkins	Joseph Day	
Sarah Lupton	Susannah Mahlon	Joseph Lupton	
Esther Hoge	Lydia Mahlon	Samuel Ruble	
Mary Pickering	Ellin Rogers		
Sarah Walker	John Lupton		

WALKER—BRUCE

Lewis Walker, of the County of Frederick and Colony of Virginia, and *Sarah Bruce*, Daughter of George Bruce of the said County and Colony; 17th day of 3d month, 1768.

Lewis Walker
Sarah Walker

Witnesses who signed this Marriage Certificate:

Cuthbert Hayhurst	Katherine Thomas	George Bruce
John Jolliffe	Hannah Rees Jr.	Rachel Bruce
John Wilson	Rachel Barrett	Wm. Jolliffe
Gidion Rickey	Mary Bruce	Abel Walker
Jacob Rees	Lydia Rees	Mordica Walker
Robert Blackburn	James Steer	Ebenezer Walker
Margaret Blackburn	Richard Ridgway	Samuel Littler
Mary Johnston	Charity Ridgway	John Littler
Thomas Muir	Rebekah Littler	Wm. Cambell
Benjamin Johnston	Sarah Littler	Nathan Littler
John Rees	Sarah Ragan	Eliza Jolliffe
William Hudnal	Morris Rees	Joseph Day
Henry Rees	William Sayers	Katherine Day
Evan Thomas		Sinia Walker
Rebeckah Beaumont		Sarah Walker
Ann Rees		David Ross
Abraham Taylor		

SAXTON—STEER

Mashac Saxton, son of George Saxton of the County of Frederick and Colony of Virginia, and *Hannah Steer*, daughter of Joseph Steer of the County and Colony aforesaid; 7th day of 4th month, 1768; at Hopewell.

Mashac Saxton
Hannah Saxton

Witnesses who signed this Marriage Certificate:

Wm. Jolliffe	Job Pugh	Joseph Steer Jr.	George Saxton
Henry Rees	John Barrett	Wm. Pickering	Joseph Steer
Thomas McClunn	Mary Pickering	Sam'l Pickering	Grace Steer
John Rees	Ruth Fawcett	Grace Pickering	John Saxton
	Alice Pugh	Joseph Steer	Margaret Cromwell
		Sarah Lupton	Josiah Jackson
		Thos. Fawcett	Ruth Jackson
		Eliza. Ballenger	James Steer
		Lydia Ballenger	Mary Steer
		Hannah Pickering	
		Samuel Lupton	

FAWCETT—PICKERING

Richard Fawcett, son of Richard Fawcett of Frederick County in the colony of Virginia, and *Mary Pickering*, Daughter of Samuel Pickering of the County and Colony aforesaid; 21st day of 4th month, 1768; at Hopewell.

Richard Fawcett
Mary Fawcett

Witnesses who signed this Marriage Certificate:

Eliza Jolliffe	David Ross	Richard Fawcett
Hanah Pickering	Abel Walker	Samuel Pickering
Jane Kelsoe	Sarah Walker	Joseph Fawcett
Wm. Jollffe	Grace Haines	John Fawcett
Henry Rees	Jacob Pickering	Rachel Fawcett
James Steer	John Lupton	Mary Fawcett
John MaCoole	Sarah Lupton	John Fawcett Jr.
Ann Pugh	Sam'l Coopstitck	Thomas Fawcett
Joseph Hackney	Samuel Lupton	John Longacre
William Barrett	Isaac Lupton	Joseph Longacre
Hannah M'Clunn	Rachel Lupton	Richard Longacre
	Joseph Lupton	Benjamin Fawcett
	Evan Rogers	Lydia Yong
		Thomas M'Clunn

WALKER—BARRETT

Mordecai Walker, of Frederick County in the Colony of Virginia, and *Rachel Barrett*, daughter of Wm. Barrett of the County and Colony aforesaid; 21st day of the 4th month, 1768; at Hopewell.

Mordecai Walker
Rachel Walker

Witnesses who signed this Marriage Certificate:

Joseph Lupton	Lydia Ballinger	Mary Case	Wm. Barrett
James Mendinghall	Sarah Case	Isaac Perkins Jr.	Abel Walker
Thomas Ferrell	Thos. McClunn	Sarah Walker	Lewis Walker
Joseph Hackney	John Barrett	Mary Bruce	Wm. Jolliffe
Josiah Ballinger	Henry Rees	Ruben Case	Eliza. Jolliffe
Joseph Steer	John M'Coole	Edw. Beeson	Ann Pugh
Isaac Sunderlin	Thomas Pugh	Jane Beeson	Mary Walker
Luke Dillon	John Lupton	Alace Pugh Jr.	Sinia Walker
	Evan Roger	Sarah Lupton	Sarah Walker
	James Steer	Hannah M'Clun	Mary Barrett
	Sam'l Pickering	Robt. Beaumont	
		Eliz'h Ballinger	

HACKNEY—M'COOLE

Joseph Hackney, of Frederick County in ye Colony of Virginia, son of Joseph Hackney and Charity his wife, late Deceased, and *Martha M'Coole*, Daughter of Jame M'Coole, late Deceased, and Ann his Wife; 20th day of 7th month, 1768; at Back Creek.

Joseph Hackney
Martha Hackney

Witnesses who signed this Marriage Certificate:

Thomas Nowland	Eliz. Pugh	Lydia Rogers	Thomas Pugh
Josiah Jackson	Esther Hoge	Hannah Hackney	Ann Pugh
George Noble	Lydia Pickering	Mary Gregg	Aaron Hackney
Eliz. Ruble	Hannah Pickering	Margret Rees	John McCoole
Cath. Bramfield	Samuel Ruble	Sidney Wright	James M'Coole
	Samuel Smith	Lydia Barrett	Jesse Pugh
	Job Pugh	Elizabeth Ballenger	Wm. Pickering
	Mordecai Walker	Lydia Mallin	Sarah Pickering
	Rachel Walker	Messer Beeson	
	Philip Nowland	Josiah Ballenger	
		Josiah Rogers	

FAWCETT—BRANSON

Thomas Fawcett, son of Richard and Rachel Fawcett of Frederick County in the Colony of Virginia, and *Martha Branson*, daughter of John and Martha Branson of the County aforesaid; 11th day of the 1st month, 1769; at Crooked Run.

Thomas Fawcett
Martha Fawcett

Witnesses who signed this Marriage Certificate:

Thomas Fearnley	Andrew M'Kay	John Painter	Richard Fawcett
Alexander Obbey	Benj. Fawcett	John Painter Jr.	John Branson
	Richard Longacre	Susannah Painter	Martha Branson
	John Fawcett	William Branson	Rachel Fawcett
	Richard Boyce	Mary Fawcett	Joseph Fawcett
	James Byrn	Lionel Branson	Robert Painter
	Amelia Larrick	Rebecca Branson	Anthony Moore
	Martha Wright	Hannah Painter	John Longacre
	Hannah Wright	Abraham Branson	Isaac Painter
	Eliz. Branson	Will Cryer	Thomas Painter
		Robert Hains	Andrew Longacre
		Joseph Longacre	Joseph Fawcett
		Eliz. Longacre	Lydia Yonag
		John Kemp	
		Esther Haines	
		Mary Haines	

PERKINS—STEER

Isaas Perkins Jr., of Frederick County in the Colony of Virginia, and
Mary Steer, of the said County; 9th day of ye 3d month, 1769; at Hopewell.

Isaac Perkins
Mary Perkins

Witnesses who signed this Marriage Certificate:

Sarah Lupton	Thomas M'Clunn	Mashack Saxton
Samuel Lupton	Hannah M'Clunn	Isaac Steere
Isaac Lupton	James Steere	Joseph Steere Jr.
Samuel Pickering	Abigail Steere	Joseph Steere
Grace Pickering	John Steere	Isaac Perkins
Joseph Lupton	Mary Steere	Joseph Steere
Rachel Lupton	Abel Walker	Grace Steere
John Willson	Mary Walker	Jonathan Perkins
Margaret Crumwell	Ruth Nevit	Ebenezer Perkins
Josiah Ballinger	Mary Ballenger	Josiah Jackson
Eliz. Ballenger	John Lupton	
Ann Lupton	Richard Ridgway	

FERNLY—MELLSON

Thomas Fernly, of Frederick County in the Colony of Virginia, and
Martha Mellson, of the same County; 12th day of 12th month, 1770; at
Crooked Run.

Thomas Fernly
Martha Fernly

Witnesses who signed this Marriage Certificate:

Sarah Walker	John Painter Jr.	Mercy Mackay
Hannah Painter Jr.	Andrew M'Kay	Deborah Hendry
Abigail Elles	Anthony Moore	George Hendry
Mary Wright	Robert M'Kay	Edward Rogers Jr.
Mary Haines	Thomas Fawcett	Robert M'Kay Sr.
Esther Haines	John Kemp	
Martha Fawcett	Jacob M'Kay	
Martha Branson	Caleb Remy	
Mary Elles	his	
	Wm. W. E. Ellis	
	mark	

ROSS—THOMAS

David Ross, of Hopewell in the County of Frederick and Colony of Virginia, and son of John Ross deceased of the County and Colony aforesaid, and *Catherine Thomas*, daughter of Enos Thomas deceased of the County and Colony aforesaid; 20th day of 12th month, 1770; at Hopewell.

David Ross
Catherine Ross

Witnesses who signed this Marriage Certificate:

Jonathan Perkins	John Berry	Evan Thomas
Abel Walker	Richard Ridgway	Albenah Thomas
Mordecai Walker	Patience Berry	George Ross
Jacob Rogers	Margret Ridgway	Alexander Ross
James Lupton	Henry Rees	Stephen Ross
Samuel Lupton	John Handley	John Jolliffe
Gidion Rickey	John Rees	Magnus Tate
Enoch Parson	Phebe Thomas	John Thomas
Mary Walker	Phebe Jolliffe	Alice Thomas
Rachel Walker	Joseph Day	Catherine Steward
Thomas Baldwin	Catherine Day	Eliz. Jolliffe
Eliz. Baldwin	Edmund Jolliffe	Margret Handley
Hannah Rees	Lidia Barrett	——— Gibbins
Eliz. Bayles	Evan Hiett	
John Smith	John Smith Jr.	
Andrew Beard		

M'COOLE—LEWIS

John M'Coole, of Frederick County and Colony of Virginia, and *Eleanor Lewis*, Daughter of Henry and Mary Lewis; 14th day of 3d month, 1771; at the Dwelling House of Owen Rogers in Hampshire.

John M'Coole
Eleanor M'Coole

Witnesses who signed this Marriage Certificate:

John Gaddis	Ruth Jackson	Henry Lewis Sr.
Ann Rogers	Jesse Pugh	Mary Lewis
Mary Jinkins	Wm. Pickering	James McCool
Saray Rogers	Owen Rogers	Henry Lewis Jr.
	Evan Rogers	Martha Hackney
	Barak Fisher	Joseph Hackney
	John Rogers	Sarah Pickering
	Lydia Pickering	John Rogers
	Jasper Cather	Jonathan Jinkins
	John Pickering	Robert Rogers
	Samuel Lewis	Wm. Gaddis
	John Millikin	Sarah Gaddis
	Rees Gaddis	Josiah Jackson
	Jacob Jenkins	

LEWIS—BARRETT

Henry Lewis, son of Henry and Mary Lewis of Hampshire County and Colony of Virginia, and *Lydia Barrett,* Daughter of William and Lydia Barret of Frederick County aforesaid; 21st day of 3d month, 1771; at Hopewell.

Henry Lewis
Lydia Lewis

Witnesses who signed this Marriage Certificate:

Eleanor Barrett	Sarah Babb	R. Rutherford	Henry Lewis
Mary Barrett	Patience Berry	Samuel Berry	Wm. Barrett
Eleanor M'Cool	Margaret Berry	Mary Jinkins	Benj. Barrett
Rachel Walker	Sarah Lupton	Jonathan Jinkins	Samuel Lewis
Sydney Wright	Eliz. Ballenger	John Handcher	John M'Cool
Sidney Rees	Hannah Pickering	Rich. Ridgway	Mordecai Walker
Martha Mendingall	Alice Pugh	John Berry	Robert Rees
Katherine Ross	Abram Taylor	John Adams	David Ross
Mary Jenkins	Ann Taylor	Enoch Fenton	Abel Walker
	Peter Babb	David Berry	Margaret Ross
	Josiah Ballenger	John Lupton	Hannah Fenton

ADAMS—MALIN

William Adams, son of John Adams of Frederick County in the Colony of Virginia, and *Lydia Malin,* Daughter of Isaac Malin deceased of the County Aforesaid; 18th day of 7th month, 1771; at Hopewell.

William Adams
Lydia Adams

Witnesses who signed this Marriage Certificate:

Sarah Babb	George Ruble	John Adams
Rachel Walker	Mordecai Walker	Hannah Adams
Lydia Lewis	William Barrett	Sarah Ruble
Eliz. Ballenger	David Ruble	Isaac Malin
Susanna Baily	James Carter	Henry Adams
Jane Baily	Josiah Ballenger	Henry Lewis
Alice Pugh	Isaac Ruble	Jonathan Perkins
Sarah Walker		Abel Walker

LUPTON—SMITH

Samuel Lupton, of Frederick County and Colony of Virginia, and *Sarah Smith*, Daughter of James Smith of Hampshire County and Colony aforesaid; 18th day of 6th month, 1772; at Hopewell.

Samuel Lupton
Sarah Lupton

Witnesses who signed this Marriage Certificate:

Abigail Steer	Rachel Walker	William Lupton
Mary Ballinger	Rachel Lupton	Grace Lupton
Eliz. Kirk	Eliz. Smith	Samuel Pickering
Margret Bery	Mary Fawcett	Joseph Lupton
Lydia Rees	Jacob Pickering	John Lupton
Joseph Steere	John Pickering	Sarah Lupton
Grace Steere	Mary Hanes	Wm. Pickering
Ruth Wright	Lydia Pickering	Jonathan Lupton
Mordecai Walker	Isaac Lupton	Mercy M'Cormack
Wm. Lupton	Grace Lupton	
Isaac Brown	David Lupton	
Isaac Steere	Jonathan Perkins	
Hannah M'Clun	Abel Walker	

ELLIS—REES

Thomas Ellis, of Barkley County and Coloney of Virginia, and *Margaret Rees*, Daughter of Morris Rees of the County and Coloney aforesaid; 21st day of 10th month, 1772; in a Publick Meeting appointed for that purpose.

Thomas Ellis
Margaret Ellis

Witnesses who signed this Marriage Certificate:

Jonas Likings	Samuel Dutton	Enos Ellis
Rebekah Likings	Joshua Woodrow	Elizabeth Ellis
Hannah Hackney	William Highat	Morris Rees
Martha Hackney	Richard Ridgway	Sarah Rees
Hannah Rees	Elizabeth John	John Rees
Rees Hastings		Aaron Hackney
Hannah Hastings		Joseph Hackney
Margrett Rees		Hannah Ellis
Jone Ellis		Rebekah Ellis
Benjamin Thornbrugh		Jone Ellis
Martha Mendenhall		Mary Butterfield
Ellizabeth Ballinger		
Judith Thornbrugh		
Simeon Woodrow		
Josiah Ballinger		

WRIGHT—BARRETT

John Wright, of Frederick County and Colony of Virginia, and *Phebe Barrett*, daughter of James Barrett of the County and Colony aforesaid; 11th day of 2d month, 1773; at Hopewell.

John Wright
Phebe Wright

Witnesses who signed this Marriage Certificate:

Sarah Lupton	Patience Ballenger	Rachel Walker	Sidney Wright
Rachel Lupton	Jane Taylor	Isaac Perkins	Rachel Hollingsworth
Patience Berry	Phebe Barrett	Lydia Lewis	Ruth Wright
David Lupton	Abel Walker	Mary Walker	Sarah Pickering
John Purkins	Mary Walker	Jonah Hollingsworth	Jonathan Perkins
Jonathan Pirkins	David Berry	Nathan Wright	Hannah Pickering
Thomas Shepherd	Abigail Steere	Mary Perkins	Rees Cadwallader
Nathan Pusey	William Neall	Henry Lewis	Benj. Barrett
	Nathan Wright	Jonathan Wright	Thomas M'Clun
	Wm. Handshaw	Sam'l Pickering	William Pickering
	John Lupton	Mordecai Walker	
	John Berry	James Steere	
	Joseph Lupton	Eliz. Ballenger	

THOMPSON—LUPTON

Joseph Thompson, of Barkley County in the Colony of Virginia, and *Ann Lupton*, Daughter of Joseph and Mary Lupton, Deceased; 15th day of 7th month, 1773; at Hopewell.

Joseph Thompson
Ann Thompson

Witnesses who signed this Marriage Certificate:

Jesse Pugh	Grace Lupton	William Lupton
Jonathan Parkins	Rachel Lupton	William Pickering
William Neall	Sarah Pickering	Joseph Lupton
James Steer	Grace Pickering	Samuel Pickering
David Lupton	Lydia Pickering	John Lupton
Jacob Pickering	Elisabeth Jolliffe	Rees Cadwaleder
Samuel Lupton	Mary Hains	James Maccormick
Isaac Lupton	Grace Lupton	Abigail Steer
Joshua Haines	R——	Rachel Walker
Jacob Rogers Jr.	Lydia Rees	Sam'l Pickering Jr.
John Dillon		
Abel Walker		

THATCHER—WRIGHT

Samuel Thatcher, of Barkly County in the Coloney of Virginia, and *Mary Wright*, of Frederick County and Coloney aforesaid; 8th day of 9th month, 1773; at Crooked Run.

Samuel Thatcher
Mary Thatcher

Witnesses who signed this Marriage Certificate:

Andrew McKay	Robert Haines
Jacob McKay	Esther Haines
Elizabeth Jolliffe	Stephen Thatcher
Sarah Brown	Ann Canby
Jane McKay	James Mendenhall
Joshua Thorp	Abel Walker
Enos Ellis	Martha Mendenhall
Anthony Moon	Ruth Wright
Zilpha Moor	Mary Ellis
Mary Haines	Thomas Fearnby
Rebekah Rea	Martha Farnby
	Martha Fawcet
	Robert Rea

LUPTON—KIRK

Isaac Lupton, of Opeckan in the County of Frederick and Colony of Virginia, and *Elizabeth Kirk*, of the County aforesaid; 17th day of 3d month, 1774; at their Publick Meeting House.

Isaac Lupton
Elizabeth Lupton

Witnesses who signed this Marriage Certificate:

Joseph Steer	William Lupton
John Rees	Grace Lupton
Grace Steer	Sarah Lupton
Joseph Steer Junr.	Joseph Lupton
William Wickersham	Rees Cadwallader
Jonathan Parkins	John Berry
Daniel Brown	Jesse Faulkner
Isaac Brown	David Lupton
Thomas Brown	Sarah Pickering
Sarah Keeran	Ruth Wright
Isaac Steer	Martha Bivan

ELLIS—THORNBROUGH

Nehemiah Ellis, Son of Mordecai Ellis of Berclay County in the Colony of Virginia, and *Sarah Thornbrough*, Daughter of Benjamin Thornbrough of the same place; 10th day of 8th month, 1774; at Middle Creek.

Nehemiah Ellis
Sarah Ellis

Witnesses who signed this Marriage Certificate:

Hannah Ellis	Martha Mendinghall	Mordecai Ellis
Rebekah Ellis	Elisabeth Ellis	Sarah Ellis
Abigail Lee	Esther Haines	Benj. Thornbrugh
Sarah Hutton	Anthony Lee	Susanna Ellis
Samuel Ellis	Judith Thornbrugh	Jane Ellis
Mordecai Ellis Jun.	Thomas Ellis	Elenor Ellis
Jas Mendinghall	Margaret Ellis	Amos Ellis
Jacob Moon	Jane Ellis	Carety Thornbrugh
Lewis Walker	William Ellis	
Edward Beeson	Anne Ellis	
Edward Beeson Jun.		
Ruth Wright		
Elis'h Thornbrugh		
Sarah Walker		
Benj. Thornbrugh		
John Forguson		
Thomas Bright		

THORNBRUGH—HUTTON

Benjamin Thornbrugh, of Berkley County and Colony of Virginia, and *Sarah Hutton*, of the same place; 5th day of 10th month, 1774; at Middle Creek.

Benjamin Thornbrugh
Sarah Thornbrugh

Witnesses who signed this Marriage Certificate:

Mordecai Ellis	Eleanor Ellis
Mary Ellis	Thomas Wright
Anthony Lee	John Finley
Abigail Lee	John Farguson
Enos Ellis	Esther McDonald
Elizabeth Ellis	Agness Mendenhall
Lewis Walker	Margaret Moon
Nehemiah Ellis	Nancy Bright
Sarah Ellis	Ann Ellis
Charity Thornbrugh	
Judith Thornbrugh	
William Ellis	
Rebekah Ellis	
Sarah Walker	

BROWN—WHITE

Thomas Brown, Son of Daniel and Susannah Brown, and *Mary White*, Daughter of Nathaniel and Mary White in the County of Frederick and Colony of Virginia; 17th day of 11th month, 1774; at Hopewell.

Thomas Brown
Mary Brown

Witnesses who signed this Marriage Certificate:

Thomas McClunn	Margaret Brown	Daniel Brown
Ruth Cadwallader	Jesse Falkner	Nathaniel White
Hannah M'Clun	Meshack Sexton	Mary White
Grace Steer	John Berry	Susannah Brown
Ruth Jackson	Samuel Pickering	David Brown
David Berry	John Lupton	Isaac Brown
Patience Ballinger	James Steere	Thomas White
Eliz'h Peterson Smith	Rees Cadwalader	Ann White
Elizabeth Jolliffe	John Rees	Sarah White
Mary Walker	Lydia Rees	Lydia White
Fillis Kerlin	Owen Long	Daniel Brown
Peter Kerlin	Lydia Long	Mary Brown
Susannah Grubb	Sam'l Berry	
	Margaret Berry	

PICKERING—ELLIS

Jacob Pickering, son of Samuel and Grace Pickering in the county of Frederick and Colony of Virginia, and *Hannah Ellis*, daughter of Enos and Elizabeth Ellis in Berkly county and Colony aforsaid; 21st day of 12th month, 1774; at Middle Creek in Berkly county.

Jacob Pickering
Hannah Pickering

Witnesses who signed this Marriage Certificate:

William Ellis	Nehemiah Ellis	Samuel Pickering
Enos Ellis	Sarah Ellis	Grace Pickering
Jonathan Ellis	Dinah Ellis	Enos Ellis
Samuel Ellis	John Pickering	Elisabeth Ellis
Abigail Lee	Lydia Pickering	Mordecai Ellis
Sarah Thournbrough	Samuel Lupton	Thomas Ellis
Sarah Lupton	Benjamin Thornbrugh	Wm. Ellis
Sussanah Ellis	Anthony Lee	Benjamin Pickering
Grace Lupton	John Lupton	Rebecah Ellis
Charity Thournbrough	Richard Ridgway	Samuel Pickering
Judith Thournbrough	Joseph Hackney	Sarah Pickering
	Jacob Moon	
	Samuel Berry	
	Joshua Lupton	
	Ellis Ellis	

PUSY—BROWN

Nathan Pusy, of the County of Frederick and Colony of Virginia, and *Mary Brown*, of the same place, Daughter of Daniel Brown and Susanah his wife; 15th day of 6th month, 1775; at Hopewell.

Nathan Pusy
Mary Pusy

Witnesses who signed this Marriage Certificate:

John Berry	Elisabeth Pervience	Daniel Brown
William Lupton	Patience Berry	Susanah Brown
John Lupton	Mary Walker	Daniel Brown
Abel Walker	Lydia Rees	David Brown
Elisabeth Jolliffe	Marriam Brown	Sarah Brown
Grace Steer	John Fawcet Jun.	Isaac Brown
Ann Rees	Richard Ridgway	Rees Cadwaleder
Samuel Berry	David Ross	Thomas Brown
Margaret Berry	Vance Bush	James Pervience
Mary Jolliffe	Elisabeth Bush	Thomas Wright
Isaac Steer	Robert Haines	Mary Wright
Ruth Jackson	Jonathan Wright	Sarah Wright
Patience Ballinger	Solomon Shepherd	Ann Wright
Rachel Rees	Margaret Brown	Ruth Cadwaleder

PICKERING—ELLIS

Benjamin Pickering, Son of Samuel and Grace Pickering in the County of Frederick, in the Colony of Virginia, and *Rebekah Ellis*, Daughter of Enos and Elizabeth Ellis in Berkley County and Colony Afforesaid; 18th day of 10th month, 1775; at Middle Creek.

Benjamin Pickering
Rebekah Pickering

Witnesses who signed this Marriage Certificate:

Margaret Moon	Mary Walker	Samuel Pickering
Judith Thornbrugh	Mary Rees	Enos Ellis
Benjamin Thornbrugh	Susannah Ellis	Elizabeth Ellis
William Ellis	Lydia Pickering	Jacob Pickering
Abel Walker	Jonathan Wright	Sarah Pickering
John Pickering	Jonas Likens	William Pickering
Jane Pickering	Jonah Hollingsworth	Sarah Pickering
Mordecai Ellis	David Lupton	Martha Mendenhall
Abraham Thornbrugh	Samuel Lupton	Thomas Ellis
Benjamin Thornbrugh	Solomon Shepherd	Samuel Pickering
William Ellis	Jane Rees	Jacob Pickering
Thomas Moon	Zadoc Ong	Anthony Lee
Anne Ellis		Abigail Lee
		Deborah Lee
		John Berry
		Jonas Lakins

PICKERING—ELLIS

John Pickering, Son of William and Sarah Pickering of Frederick County in the Colony of Virginia, and *Jane Ellis*, Daughter of Enos and Elizabeth Ellis of the County of Berkley and Colony afforesaid; 18th day of 10th month, 1775; at Middle Creek.

John Pickering
Jane Pickering

Witnesses who signed this Marriage Certificate:

Jonathan Wright	Enos Ellis	William Pickering
Janas Likens	Elizabeth Ellis	Sarah Pickering
Jonah Hollingsworth	Samuel Lupton	Mordecai Ellis
Solomon Shepherd	David Lupton	Anthony Lee
Benjamin Pickering	Hannah Pickering	Abigail Lee
John Berry	Hannah Pickering	Deborah Lee
Rebekah Pickering	Lydia Pickering	Thomas Ellis
Abraham Thornbrugh	Mary Fawcett	Nehemiah Ellis
Samuel Pickering	Ruth Wright	Sarah Ellis
Benjamin Thornbrugh	Judith Thornbrugh	Samuel Pickering
William Ellis	Margaret Moon	Ellis Ellis
Thomas Moon	Lydia Rogers	William Ellis
Zadoc Ong	Mary Walker	James Wright
Benjamin Thornbrugh	Jane Rees	
	Mary Rees	
	Susannah Ellis	
	Ann Ellis	
	Sarah Thornbrugh	

THORNBRUGH—DOD

Abraham Thornbrugh, Son of Benjamin Thornbrugh of the County of Berkeley and Coloney of Virginia, and *Albanah Dod*, Daughter of Edward Dod of the County of Frederick and Coloney aforesaid; 10th day of 1st month, 1776; at Middle Creek.

Abraham Thornbrugh
her
Albanah A Thornbrugh
mark

Witnesses who signed this Marriage Certificate:

Stephen Thatcher	Judith Thornbrugh
Benjamin Pickering	Charity Thornbrugh
John Wason	Mary Dod
Richard Ross	Nehemiah Ellis
Absolom Miller	Benjamin Thornbrugh
John McDonald	Jun.
Samuel Mendenhall	Joel Thornbrugh
Rebekah Pickering	Margaret Moon
William Ellis	Lewis Walker
Jacob Rogers Jun.	Enos Ellis
Mordecai Ellis	Jacob Moon
Mary Ellis	
Martha Mendenhall	
Dinah Ellis	
Thomas Moon	

CHANDLEE—WHITE

Goldsmith Chandlee, of the County of Frederick and Colony of Virginia, son of Benjamin and Mary Chandlee, and *Ann White*, daughter of Nathaniel and Mary White of the said County and Colony; 15th day of 2nd month, 1776; at Hopewell.

Goldsmith Chandlee
Ann Chandlee

Witnesses who signed this Marriage Certificate:

Grace Steer	Mordecai Walker	Nathaniel White
Lydia Rees	John Berry	Mary White
Sina Walker	John Lupton	Elizabeth Perviance
Lydia Jolliffe	Owan Long	Sarah White
Ann Rees	John Cowgill	James Perviance
Grace Lupton	Joseph Steer Jr.	Thos. Brown
Rachel Lupton	Jonah Hollingsworth	Isaac Brown
Hannah Pickering	David Lupton	John Jolliffe
Phebe Yarnold,	Samuel Lupton	Thodee Ellis
per order	Simeon Woodrow	Henry Smith
Mary Jolliffe	Mary White	Edward Wright
Elizabeth Jolliffe	Thomas McClun	Abel Walker
Mary Walker	Mordecai Yarnall	
Mary Jolliffe	Edmond Jolliffe	
Richard Ridgway	Amos Jolliffe	
Hanna McClun		

FALLIS—ANTRAM

John Fallis, of the County of Stafford and Coloney of Virginia, and *Mary Antram*, of the County and Coloney afforesaid; 10th day of 4th month, 1776; at Stafford.

John Fallis
Mary Fallis

Witnesses who signed this Marriage Certificate:

Alice Green	Rachel Fallis	John Antram
Elizabeth Shinn	Eunice Branson	Elizabeth Antram
Joseph Wright	Rebekah Wright	Daniel Antram
George Shinn	Elizabeth Branson	Caleb Antram
John Brock	Robert Painter	Thomas Fallis
Mary Brock	Eunice Painter	Jane Fallis
Abas. Holloway	Ann Smith	Jacob Fallis
Daniel Brock	Rachel Shinn	Esther Antram
Scholey Wright	William Branson	Rachel Antram
	Mary Wright	
	Abigail Green	
	Sarah Wright	

STEER—LUPTON

Joseph Steer, Son of Joseph and Grace Steer of Frederick County in the Colony of Virginia, and *Grace Lupton*, Daughter of John Lupton in the County and Colony afforesaid; 11th day of 4th month, 1776; at Hopewell.

Joseph Steer
Grace Steer

Witnesses who signed this Marriage Certificate:

Rees Cadwallader	Isaac Lupton	Joseph Steer Sen.
Nathan Lupton	Richard Ridgway	Grace Steer
Joshua Lupton	Abel Walker	John Lupton
Sarah Pickering	Jonathan Parkins	William Lupton
John Hodgson	Samuel Pickering	Joseph Lupton
Deborah Hodgson	Samuel Pickering	James Steer
Josiah Jackson	Asa Lupton	Edmond Jolliff
Ruth Jackson	Mary Parkins	Isaac Nevitt
Mary Lupton	Hannah Saxton	Elisabeth Nevitt
Isaac Parkins	Lydia Pickering	Aaron Grigg
Isaac Brown	Ruth Wright	Elisabeth Grigg
Samuel Jackson	Sary Lupton	Jonathan Lupton
Jesse Lupton	Jacob Pickering	Meshach Saxton
Sarah Lupton	David Lupton	Samuel Lupton
Sarah Pickering	Rachel Lupton	
Mary Walker	Isaac Steer	
	Jane Pickering	
	Massy Lupton	
	Ruth Cadwaleder	

LUPTON—REES

John Lupton, in the County of Frederick in the Colony of Virginia, and *Ann Rees*, Widow of Henry Rees in the County and Colony affsd; 13th day of 6th month, 1776; at Hopewell.

John Lupton
Ann Lupton

Witnesses who signed this Marriage Certificate:

Margaret Rees	Richard Ridgway	Thomas McClun	William Lupton
Samuel Pickering	Abel Walker	Hannah McClun	Joseph Lupton
Samuel Pickering Jun.	Jacob Smith	Joseph Neill	Jonathan Lupton
Grace Pickering	Mordecai Walker	Sarah Lupton	William Neill
William Pickering	Jacob Pickering	Joseph Steer Jun.	Thomas Neill
Joseph Steer	Hannah Pickering	Lewis Neill	Rachel Lupton
Grace Steer	Jonah Hollingsworth	John Neill	Abraham Neill
Sarah Pickering	David Lupton	Sarah Pickering	Grace Steer Jun.
Elisabeth Grigg	Isaac Steer	Hannah Pickering	Rachel Lupton Jun.
Ruth Jackson	Isaac Brown	Mercy Lupton	Elisabeth Neill
Elisabeth Jolliffe	Thomas Gawthrop	Samuel Lupton	
Mary Jolliffe		Joshua Lupton	
		Nathan Lupton	
		Catherine Rees	
		Gideon Rees	
		Lydia Rees	
		Isaac Lupton	
		Grace Lupton	

SMITH—BALLINGER

Jacob Smith, Son of Joseph and Rachel Smith of the County of Frederick and Colony of Virginia, and *Patience Ballinger,* Daughter of Josiah and Elizabeth Ballinger of the County and Colony afforesaid; 15th day of 8th month, 1776; at their Meeting House.

Jacob Smith
Patience Smith

Witnesses who signed this Marriage Certificate:

Joseph Steer Jun.	Isaac Smith	Joseph Smith
Grace Steer Sen.	John Pickering	Josiah Ballinger
Isaac Brown	Ann Horner	Elizabeth Ballinger
Jonathan Wright	Jane Pickering	Rachel Smith
Absalom Haworth	Rachel Hollingsworth	Martha Mendinghall
Henry Lewis	John McCoole	Charity Ridgway
Abel Walker	Elenor McCoole	William Pickering
Jesse Faulkner	Evan Jinkins	Evan Rogers
Joseph Hackney	Ruth Wright	Evan Rogers Jun.
James Wright	Mary Jinkins	Josiah Rogers
Aaron Hackney	Mary Rogers	Sarah Pickering
James Steer	Lydia Pickering	Hannah Pickering
Jacob Pickering	Sarah Babb	
Thomas Barrett	John Rogers	
	Grace Steer Jun.	
	Hannah Hackney	

WRIGHT—PARKINS

James Wright, of Frederick County of Virginia, Son of Isaac and Sidney Wright, and *Phebe Parkins,* Daughter of Jonathan and Elisabeth Parkins of the County Afforesaid; 5th day of 9th month, 1776; at Hopewell.

James Wright
Phebe Wright

Witnesses who signed this Marriage Certificate:

Rachel Walker	Rachel Lupton	Jonathan Parkins
Cuthbert Hayhurst	Evan Rogers	Sidney Wright
Mordica Walker	Ruth Jacson	John Wright
Edward Wright	Grace Pickering	Ruth Wright
John Lupton	Ann Lupton	Elisabeth Milburn
David Lupton	Lidia Pickering	Josiah Rogers
Joseph Lupton	Phebe Barrett	Mary Hollingsworth

LUPTON—HOLLINGSWORTH

David Lupton, Son of Joseph and Rachel Lupton in the County of Frederic and Colony of Virginia, and *Mary Hollingsworth*, Daughter of Rachel Hollingsworth of the County afforesaid; 12th day of 6th month, 1777; at Hopewell.

David Lupton
Mary Lupton

Witnesses who signed this Marriage Certificate:

Susanna Ellis	Narhaniel White	Martha Mendinhall	Joseph Lupton
Sarah Pickering	Daniel Brown	Elizabeth Jolliffe	Rachel Lupton
Abel Walker	Susanna Brown	Mary Walker	Rachel Hollingsworth
Mordecai Walker	Martha Glover	Martha Walker	Ann Neill
Samuel Berry	Josiah Jackson	Lewis Neile	Phebe Hollingsworth
James Parviance	Solomon Shepherd	Isaac Steer	Rachel Lupton Junr.
Cuthbert Hayhurst	Jacob Rogers Junr.	Sam'l Pickering	Jonah Hollingsworth
Isaac Smith	Sam'l Pickering Jr.	Jos. Steer Junr.	William Lupton
James Gawthorp		Abraham Neill	Jonathan Lupton
		Rebekah Janney	Marcy M'Carmick
		Grace Pickering	Grace Lupton
		John Russell	Joshua Lupton
		Henry Smith	Nathan Lupton
			Samuel Lupton
			William Lupton Junr.

SMITH—ALLIN

Isaac Smith, son of Joseph and Rachel Smith of the county of Frederick in the Colony of Virginia, and *Mary Allin*, daughter of Jackson and Betty Allin of the county of Dunmore in the Colony afforesaid; 8th day of 1st month, 1778; at Smiths Creek.

Isaac Smith
Mary Smith

Witnesses who signed this Marriage Certificate:

Abraham Smith	Robert Haines	Jackson Allin
Joseph Moore	Ruth Holland	her
John Moore	Ruth Miller	Betty B Allin
Benjamin Allin	John Hirst	mark
Mercy Lupton	Henry Smith	Joseph Smith
Thomas Wright	Wm. Lupton Jr.	Jacob Smith
Samuel Berry	Hanna Moore	his
Elizabeth Moore	Lydia Woodrow	Joseph O Allen
Abraham Byrd	Patience Osburn	mark
Sam'l Pickering Jr.	Mary Moore	his
Ruben Moore	Sarah Moore	Jacob O Rambo
Samuel Mills	her	mark
Jonathan Wright	Lydia X Moore	her
Sarah Byrd	mark	Lydia X Allen
Sarah Moore		mark
Isaac Woodrow		John Bond
		Barsheba Allen
		her
		Rebekah A Bon.l
		mark
		her
		Ruth X Allen
		mark
		Ruben Allen

[Dunmore was the old name of Shenandoah County.]

FAULKNER—THORNBRUTH

David Faulkner, of Frederick County and Colony of Virginia, and *Judith Thornbruth*, of Berkly County and Colony aforesaid; 4th day of 3d month, 1778; at Middle Creek.

David Faulkner
Judith Faulkner

Witnesses who signed this Marriage Certificate:

Margaret Moon	Jean Faulkner	Benjamin Thornbrugh
Margaret Boyd	Charity Thornbrugh	Sarah Thornbrugh
John McDonald	Albenah Thornbrugh	Thomas Faulkner
Dinah Ellis	Ruth Faulkner	Jesse Faulkner
Elenor Ellis	Thomas Moon	Robert Faulkner
Hannah Daniel	Ellis Ellis	Abraham Thornbrugh
Mordecai Ellis	Enos Ellis	Sarah Ellis
Mary Ellis	James Hodgson	Charity Thornbrough
Anthony Lee	Thomas Ellis	Martha Faulkner
Abot. Lee	Susanna Ellis	

HOGE—JENKINS

John Hoge, of Frederick County in the Coloney of Virginia, Son of William Hoge and his Wife, and *Mary Jenkins*, Daughter of Jacob Jenkins and Elizabeth his Wife of the County of Hamshire and Coloney afforesaid; 14th day of 5th month, 1778; at the Dwelling house of Owen Rogers in Hampshire County.

John Hoge
Mary Hoge

Witnesses who signed this Marriage Certificate:

Josiah Rogers	William Pickering	William Hoge
Mary Rogers	Barak Fisher	Esther Hoge
Sarah Roger	Sarah Pickering	Jacob Jenkins
John Wright	Jesse Pugh	Elizabeth Jenkins
Robert Rogers	Martha Ewin	Owen Rogers
John Lewis	Susanna Ewin	Evan Rogers
John Rogers	Ezekiel Lyon	Henry Lewis
Jobe Pugh	Hannah Lyon	Evan Lewis
Eliz. Lewis	Sebler Ewin	Thomas Barret
Phebe Barret		Israel Hoge
Samuel Lewis		Evan Jenkins
Sarah Rogers		Anne Jenkins
Eli Pugh		Jonathan Jenkins
Catharine Riser		

BERRY—PICKERING

David Berry, Son of John and Patience Berry of the County of Frederick in the Colony of Virginia, and *Hannah Pickering*, Daughter of William and Sarah Pickering of the County afforesaid; 13th day of 1st month, 1779; at Back Creek.

David Berry
Hannah Berry

Witnesses who signed this Marriage Certificate:

Jesse Pugh	Abel Walker	John Berry
John Lupton	Mordecai Walker	William Pickering
Daniel Brown	John Wright	Sarah Pickering
Miriam Brown	Ruth Fenton	Patience Berry
Joel Brown	John Adams	Enos Ellis
Josiah Rogers	John Fenton	John Pickering
William Lupton Jr.	Mary Wright	Samuel Berry
Thomas Pugh	Mary Pickering	John Berry Junr.
Ann Pugh	Elizabeth Rogers	Martha Mendinghall
Sidney Wright	Aaron Grigg	Samuel Pickering
Owen Rogers	Elizabeth Grigg	Grace Pickering
Esther Hoge	Sarah Fisher	Barak Fisher
Phebe Wright	Sarah Powel	Mary Fisher
Even Rogers	Jane Pugh	Margaret Berry
Alice Pugh		Lydia Berry
John M'Coole		Jacob Pickering
		Jonathan Pickering
		Jane Pickering
		Lydia Adams

JENKINS—CUNROD

Evan Jenkins, of Hampshire County and Colony of Virginia, and *Elizabeth Cunrod*, daughter of James and Jane Cunrod of the same place; 14th day of 1st month, 1779; at the dwelling house of Jacob Jenkins in Hampshire County.

his
Evan X Jenkins
mark
her
Elizabeth X Jenkins
mark

Witnesses who signed this Marriage Certificate:

John Lewis	Jesse Pugh	Jacob Jenkins
Henry Lewis	Anne Rees	Elizabeth Jenkins
Misheal Jenkins	Anne Jenkins Senior	James Cunrod
Robert Gaddis	Ann Jenkins Junr.	Owen Rogers
John Butcher	Phebe Barrett	Enos Ellis
	Elizabeth Lewis	Samuel Lewis
	John M'Coole	Jonathan Jenkins
	Elenor M'Coole	John Wright
	Thomas Barrett	Mary Lewis
	Alice Pugh	Jobe Pugh
	Barak Fisher	Israel Hoge
	Solomon Rees	Josiah Rogers
	J..ne Pugh	Robert Rogers

STEER—HOLLINGSWORTH

Isaac Steer, Son of Joseph and Grace Steer in the County of Frederick in the Colony of Virginia, and *Phebe Hollingsworth,* Daughter of Rachel Hollingsworth, Widow, in the County aforesaid; 21st day of 4th month, 1779; at Center.

Isaac Steer
Phebe Steer

Witnesses who signed this Marriage Certificate:

Samuel Pickering	Henry Smith	Rachel Hollingsworth
Grace Pickering	William Wickersham	Joseph Steer Junior
John Lupton	Mary Wickersham	Grace Steer Junior
Ann Lupton	Grace Jackson	James Steer
Joseph Lupton	Catharine Sexton	Jonah Hollingsworth
Samuel Lupton	Phebe Ball	Josiah Jackson
Isaac Lupton	Rachel Parkins	Ruth Jackson
Asa Lupton	John Parkins	Lydia Hough
Nathan Lupton	Mary Parkins Junr.	Hannah Sexton
Joshua Lupton	Hannah Parkins	Isaac Parkins
Elizabeth Lupton	Ann Parkins	Mary Parkins
Rachel Lupton	Ann Jackson	Ann Neill
Mercy Lupton	Susannah Ellis	David Lupton
Ann Lupton		Mary Lupton
Hannah Lupton		Leah Ball
Joseph Wood		Hannah Steer
		Grace Steer
		Rachel Steer
		Abigail Steer

BRANSON—REESE

Abraham Branson, Son of William Branson and Elizabeth Branson his wife of Stafford County in the Colony of Virginia, and *Cathrine Reese,* Daughter of Henry and Martha Reese of the County of Frederick and Colony aforesaid. Deceased; 22d day of 10th month, 1779; at Center.

Abraham Branson
Catherine Branson

Witnesses who signed this Marriage Certificate:

Meshack Sexton	Sidney Wright	Margaret Rees
Daniel Brown	Rachel Hollingsworth	Ann Lupton
James Wright	Martha Rees	Thomas Moon
Mordecai Walker	Jonathan Parkins	Sarah Branson
Anthony Lee	Abigail Steer	Mary McGrew
Richard Ridgway	Rachel Lupton	Gideon Rees
Jacob Pickering	Richard Ridgway	John Lupton
Grace Steer	Abel Walker	Lydia Rees
Grace Pickering	Samuel Pickering	Jesse Holloway
Isaac Steer	William Pickering	John McGrew
Phebe Steer	Caleb Antram	
Margaret Brown	Sam'l Pickering Jr.	
Joshua Lupton	Sarah Pickering	
Nathan Lupton	Susannah Brown	

LUPTON—ALLEN

William Lupton, Son of William and Grace Lupton of the County of Frederick and Colony of Virginia, and *Bathsheba Allen*, Daughter of Jackson and Betty Allen of Smiths Creek of the County of Shannandore and Colony afforesaid; 4th day of 11th month, 1779; at Smith's Creek.

William Lupton
Bathsheba Lupton

Witnesses who signed this Marriage Certificate:

Edward Bond	Mercy Lupton	Jackson Allen
Joseph Moore	Samuel Pickering	Betty Allen
Joseph Rambo	Sarah Pickering	Joseph Allen
Sarah Rambo	Mary White	Mary Moore
Benjamin Allen	Jacob Rambo	Reuben Allen
Nathan Lupton	Martha Branson	Davis Allen
Elizabeth Moore	Ann Smith	Mary Lupton
Ann Pennyworth	Martha Fernley	Mary Smith
Hannah Moore	Grifith Dobyns	Lydia Allen
Rebekah Bond	John Moor	Joshua Lupton
Hannah Bond	John Bond	Samuel Lupton
Susannah Bond	Anderson Moffett	Asa Lupton
	Reuben Moore	
	Jacob Holeman	
	Margaret Holeman	
	Betty Beale	
	Sarah Hawkins	

WRIGHT—BRANSON

William Wright, of the County of Stafford in the Colony of Virginia, and *Eunice Branson*, of the County and Colony afforesaid; 17th day of 11th month, 1779; at Stafford.

William Wright
Eunice Wright

Witnesses who signed this Marriage Certificate:

Joseph Steer Junr.	Elizabeth Antram	Joseph Wright
Robert Painter	Mary Wright	Rebekah Wright
George Shinn	Esther Antram	William Branson
Elizabeth Carter	Levi Antram	Abigail Holloway
John Saxton	Rachel Antram	Abraham Branson
Joseph Antram	John Grigg	Daniel Antram
Mary Saxton	Isaac James	Sarah Wright
John Antram	James Primm	Sarah Branson
John Holloway	Rachel Shinn	William Branson
John Fallis	Mary Fallis	Catharine Branson
Caleb Antrim	Jacob Allentharp	Eunice Painter
Thomas Fallis	Isaac Holloway	Ruth Holoway
Asa Holloway	Jane Fallis	Elizabeth Wright
Susannah Antram	Abigail Green	Anne Grigg
		Elizabeth Shinn
		Mary Green

HOLLOWAY—PAINTER

Jesse Holloway, son of John and Margaret Holloway of Stafford County in the Colony of Virginia, and *Sarah Painter*, daughter of John and Susannah Painter of the County of Frederick and Colony afforesaid; 12th day of 1st month, 1780; at Crooked Run.

Jesse Holloway
Sarah Holloway

Witnesses who signed this Marriage Certificate:

Finly M'Grew	Catherine Branson	John Painter
Robert Rea	Sarah Moor	Susannah Painter
Benjamin Moor	Mary M'Grew	Hannah Painter
Moses Sharp	Mary Ellis	Conrod Devo
Joseph Haines	Margaret Smith	Sarah Devo
Caleb Antram	Sarah Cranson	Isaac Painter
John M'Grew	Mary Fawcett	Sarah Painter
Joshua Swayne	John Humber	David Painter
John Green	Patience M'Kay	Elizabeth Painter
Robert Haines	John Smith	Jacob Painter
John Haines	Robert Hannah	Elizabeth Haines
	Thomas Fawcett	Mary Haines
	Jacob M'Kay	Ann Smith
	Levi Haines	Hannah Smith
	Anthony Moor	Martha Branson
		Martha Fernley
		Abraham Branson

PICKERING—WRIGHT

Isaac Pickering, of Solesbury Township in the County of Bucks and Province of Pennsylvania, and *Sidney Wright*, of the County of Frederick and Coloney of Virginia; 8th day of 3d month, 1780; at Back Creek.

Isaac Pickering
Sidney Pickering

Witnesses who signed this Marriage Certificate:

John Berry	Jesse Pugh	Samuel Pickering
Patience Berry	Lydia Adams	William Pickering
Aron Gregg	Solomon Wright	Grace Pickering
Elizabeth Gregg	John Fenton	Jonathan Lupton
Thomas Pugh	Jacob Pickering	Evan Rogers
Mordecai Walker	Hannah Pickering	Elizabeth Jenkins
Rachel Walker	Samuel Pickering	Eloner Barret
Barak Fisher	Mary Wright	Ann Pugh
Mary Fisher	David Berry	Jacob Jenkins
Alice Pugh	Hannah Berry	Sarah Pickering
Jonathan Pickering	Phebe Wright Senior	Ruth Fenton
Mary Pickering	John Wright	Joseph Lupton
Ruth Jackson	Josiah Jacson	

WOOD—LUPTON

Joseph Wood, of the County of Barkly, Colony of Virginia, Son of William Wood Deceased of the County of Chester and Province of Pennsylvania, And *Rachel Lupton,* Daughter of Joseph Lupton of the County of Frederick and Colony afforesaid; 17th day of 3d month, 1780; at Center.

Joseph Wood
Rachel Wood

Witnesses who signed this Marriage Certificate:

Rees Cadwallader	Rachel Hollingsworth	Joseph Lupton
Walter Denny	Daniel Brown	Rachel Lupton
John Tremble	Susannah Brown	John Lupton
Josiah Jackson	Samuel Pickering	Ann Lupton
Isaac Steer	Jonah Hollingsworth	Jonathan Lupton
Phebe Steer	Hannah Hollingsworth	Grace Lupton
Amos Jolliffe	Mary Parkins	Hannah Lupton
Daniel Brown	Bathsheba Lupton	Samuel Lupton
Thomas Babb	Mercy Lupton	William Lupton
Meshack Sexton	John Parkins	Joshua Lupton
	Mary Parkins	David Lupton
	Margaret Brown	Mary Lupton
	Ruth Jackson	Nathan Lupton
	Hannah Sexton	Jos. Steer Junior
	Sarah Pickering	Grace Steer Junr.
	Mary Jolliffe	Morris Rees
	Rebekah Miller	Isaac Parkins
	David Parkins	

THATCHER—FORKNERE

Stephen Thatcher, of the County of Berkeley in Virginia, and *Ruth Forknere,* daughter of Jesse Forkner of the same place; 5th day of 4th month, "called April," 1780; at Middle Creek.

Stephan Thatcher
Ruth Thatcher

Witnesses who signed this Marriage Certificate:

Enos Ellis	Margaret Ellis	Jesse Faulkner
Mordecai Ellis	Rebekah Pickering	Martha Faulkner
Anthony Lee	Lydia Richard	Thomas Faulkner
Rowland Richard	Elizabeth Ellis	John Griffith
Lewis Walker	James Mendenhall	Jesse Faulkner Junior
Joseph Hackney	Alexander Campbell	Robert Faulkner
Sarah Thornbrugh	Benjamin Thornbrugh	Jean Faulkner
Jacob Moon	John Parks	Mary Thatcher Junior
Edward Beeson	Samuel Parks	Judith Faulkner
Henry Cowgill	William Hancher	Martha Faulkner
Mary Ellis		

HAINES—SMITH

Robert Haines, Widower, of Frederic County in Virginia, and *Margaret Smith,* of the County afforesaid; 12th day of 4th month, 1780; at Crooked Run.

Robert Haines
Margaret Haines

Witnesses who signed this Marriage Certificate:

Anthony Moor	Sarah Holloway	John Smith
Job M'Cay	Mary Ellis	Ann Smith
Joseph Haines	Sarah Branson	Hannah Smith
James Moor	Sarah Painter	Mary Cleavinger
Thomas Cooper	Mary M'Grew	Elisabeth Haines
William Collins	Sarah Devo	Bulah Haines
Robert Hannah	Martha Fawcett	Benjamin Elkins
Moses Waltin	Elizabeth Painter	Asa Cleavinger
Thomas Smith	Martha Branson	Thomas Fawcett
John Haines	Elizabeth Byrn	Abraham Branson
Hannah Hains	Eunice Walton	Isaac Painter
Catharine Branson	Mary Byrn	David Painter
Martha Farnly	Hannah Oglesbey	Lionel Branson
Mary White	Benjamin Moor	Jesse Holloway
Robert Rea	John Mead	Mary Smith
Joshua Swayne	Alexander Oglesbey	Asa Oglesbey
Andrew M'Kay	Rebekah Smith	
Joseph Cleavinger	John Byrn	
Finley M'Grew	Mary Postgate	
Jacob M'Kay	Ann Moor	
Sarah Moor	Rebekah Moor	
Hannah M'Kay	Zilpha Moor	
Patience M'Kay	Rebekah Rea	
	Jane M'Kay	
	Meriam Moor	
	Phebe Moor	

SMITH—WHITE

Mahlon Smith, Son of William and Ann Smith in the County of Lowden, and *Mary White* (formerly Woodrow), Daughter of Simeon Woodrow in Frederic County in Virginia; 16th day of 11th month, 1780; at Hopewell.

Mahlon Smith
Mary Smith

Witnesses who signed this Marriage Certificate:

Abel Walker	Rachel Hollingsworth	William Smith
Jonathan Wright	Mary Walker	Simeon Woodrow
Sinah Walker	Rachel Neill	Lydia Woodrow
Hannah Pickering	Martha Mendinghall	Nathaniel White
Samuel Pickering	Abigail Steer	Nathaniel White Jr.
Cuthbert Hayhurst	Lydia Woodrow	Ezekiel Smith
Joseph Hackney	Elizabeth Woodrow	Mary Smith
James Perviance	Lydia Jolliffe	William Lupton
Elizabeth Perviance	Jane Rees	William Smith
Sarah White	Joseph Smith	Rachel Piggot
Rachel Walker	William Kinsey	Edith Smith
Jonathan Pickering	Mercy Lupton	Hannah Piggot
Ruth Wright	Elizabeth Moore	Henry Piggot
Phebe Barrett	John Berry	Moses Piggot
David Griffith	George Redd	Owen Long
James Reley	David Ross	Joseph Smith
Sarah Pickering	John Tremble	
Elizabeth Wickersham	James Moore	
Mary Smith		

SHIHON—PARKINS

Michael Shihon, of Center of the County of Frederick and Colony of Virginia, and *Mary Parkins,* Daughter of Jonathan and Elizabeth Parkins of Center, in the County and Colony aforesaid; 15th day of 12th month, 1780; at Center.

Michael Shihon
Mary Shihon

Witnesses who signed this Marriage Certificate:

Jonah Hollingsworth	Jonathan Parkins
James Lownes	Rachel Hollingsworth
Joseph Steer Junior	Isaac Parkins
Rees Cadwallader	James Wright
Nathaniel White	Phebe Wright
Samuel Pickering Junior	Ann Parkins
Isaac Steer	Hannah Parkins
Joshua Lupton	
Leah Parkins	
Sarah Brown	
Isaac Brown	
Amy Long	
Samuel Pickering	
Meshack Sexton	
Hannah Sexton	
Ruth Jackson	

HORSMAN—LUPTON

William Horsman, of the County of Frederick and Colony of Virginia, Son of Charles and Elizabeth Horsman of the County of York and Province of Pennsylvania, and *Marcy Lupton*, Daughter of William and Grace Lupton of the County and Colony aforesaid; 5th day of 4th month, 1781; at Hopewell.

William Horsman
Marcy Horsman

Witnesses who signed this Marriage Certificate:

Richard Ridgway	Joseph Steer Junr.	William Lupton
James Steer	Grace Steer Junr.	Grace Lupton
Abel Walker	Martha Mendenhall	Samuel Lupton
Jonathan Wright	David Lupton	David Horsman
David Griffith	Mary Lupton	Jesse Lupton
Isaac Brown	Charity Ridgway	Asa Lupton
	Lydia Woodrow	William Lupton Jr.
	Sarah Brown	
	Isaac Woodrow	

ANTRAM—FAWCETT

Caleb Antram, son of John and Elizabeth Antram, and *Hannah Fawcett*, Daughter of Richard and Rachel Fawcett, both of the County of Frederick in the Colony of Virginia; 5th day of 4th month, 1781; at Mount Pleasant.

Caleb Antram
her
Hannah X Antram
mark

Witnesses who signed this Marriage Certificate:

Nathan Pusey	Hannah Longacre	John Antram
Rees Cadwallader	Rebeckah Fawcett	Richard Fawcett
Ruth Cadwallader	Rachel Fawcett	Elizabeth Antram
Sarah Pancoast	Joseph Longacre	Joshua Antram
John Brock	Elizabeth Longacre	Richard Fawcett Jr.
Jane Brock	Jonathan Lupton	Martha Fawcett
Mary Pusey	Sarah Lupton	John Fawcett Sen.
Mary Pancoast	Samuel Pickering	William Branson Jr.
Elizabeth Pancoast	Mary Fawcett	
	Lydia Fawcett	
	Esther Antram	
	Thomas Fawcett	
	John Longacre	

GREEN—HOLLOWAY

John Green, of the County of Stafford in Virginia, and *Ruth Holloway,* of the same place; 25th day of 4th month, 1781; in Stafford.

John Green
Ruth Green

Witnesses who signed this Marriage Certificate:

George Shinn	John Paxson	Isaac Green
Robert Painter	Mary Paxson	John Holloway Sen.
Eunice Painter	Achsah Paxson	Mary Green Sen.
Elizabeth Shinn	Asa Holloway	Amos Holloway
Mary Shinn	Mary Fallis	John Holloway Jun.
Daniel Antram	Mary Fallis	James Holloway
Rachel Branson	Jane Fallis	Abigail Green
Mary Ficklen	Rachel Antram	Mary Green
Mary Gray	Eunice Wright	Robert Green
Edith Antram	Rachel Fallis	Reubin Green
Elizabeth Samuel	Frances Wright	Thomas Holloway
Daniel Antram Junr.	John Fallis	Lydia Green
Shadey Skidmore	William Branson	Susanna Green
Isaac Branson	William Wright	Isaac Holloway
	Isaac James	Mary Holloway
	Levi Antram	Garrat Gray Senr.
		Lydia Gray

REDD—FAWCETT

George Redd, of the County of Barkly and Colony of Virginia, Son of Adam Redd (and Meriam his wife deceas'd) of Christiana Hundred, New Castle County, Pennsylvania [Del.?], and *Rachel Fawcett,* Daughter of John and Rebeckah Fawcett of the County of Frederick and Colony aforesaid; 15th day of the 11th month, 1781; at Mount Pleasant.

George Redd
Rachel Redd

Witnesses who signed this Marriage Certificate:

Samuel Pickering	John Antram	John Fawcett
Jane Brock	Robert M'Kay	Rebekah Fawcett
Elizabeth Antram	Joseph Longacre	Richard Fawcett Sr.
Mary Jolliffe	Andrew Longacre	Jonathan Lupton
Ezekiel Cleaver Jr.	John Longacre	Sarah Lupton
John Brock	Nathan Pusey	Jno. Fawcett Junr.
Mary Fawcett	Richard Longacre	Hannah Antram
Rachel Fawcett	Morris Rees	Thomas Fawcett
	Jacob Rees	Caleb Antram
	Mary Pusey	Margaret Brown
	Mary Fawcett Junr.	
	Elizabeth Longacre	
	Richard Fawcett	

FAWCETT—BROWN

John Fawcett, Son of John and Rebekah Fawcett, and *Margaret Brown,* Daughter of Daniel and Susannah Brown, Both of the County of Frederick in the Colony of Virginia; 13th day of 12th month, 1781; at Mount Pleasant.

John Fawcett
Margaret Fawcett

Witnesses who signed this Marriage Certificate:

Joseph Steer Jun.	Elizabeth Antram	John Fawcett
Grace Steer Jun.	Mary Wood	Rebekah Fawcett
Mary Brock	Jane Brock	Daniel Brown
Joshua Antram	Richard Fawcett	Susannah Brown
Martha Fearnly	Joseph Lupton	Thomas Fawcett
Mary Pusey	Mary Pancoast	David Brown
	Elizabeth Pancoast	Sarah Brown
	Ezekiel Cleaver Jun.	Daniel Brown Junr.
	Joshua Swayne	Jonathan Lupton
		Richard Fawcett Sr.
		George Redd
		Rachel Redd
		Nathan Pusey
		Mary Fawcett
		Mary Fawcett
		Mary Lupton
		Hannah Longacre

EMBREE—COULSON

Thomas Embree, of Shannandoah County in the Colony of Virginia, and *Esther Coulson,* of Frederick County in the Colony aforesaid, Daughter of Samuel Coulson, Deceased, and Tamer Coulson, near the Monongalia River; 20th day of 12th month, 1781; at Hopewell.

Thomas Embree
Esther Embree

Witnesses who signed this Marriage Certificate:

Abigail Steer	Abel Walker	Tamar Coulson
Elizabeth Woodrow	John Berry	Mordecai Walker
Elizabeth Jolliffe	Lewis Walker	James Parviance
Hannah Sidwell	Jonathan Wright	
Rachel Walker	Nathaniel White	
Hannah Pickering	Jacob Smith	
Jacob Pickering	Benjamin Allen	
Phebe Barrett	Richard Ridgway	
Richard Barrett	William Lupton	
	Abraham Smith	
	David Ross	
	Aaron Berry	
	Henry Lewis	
	Thomas Babb	
	Martha Hackney	
	Joseph Hackney	
	James Steer	
	Samuel Berry	
	Lydia Berry	
	Margaret Berry	

PARKINS—BROCK

Jonathan Parkins Jun., of Frederick County in Virginia, Son of Jonathan and Elizabeth Parkins, and *Jane Brock*, Daughter of John and Jane Brock, of the County afforesaid; 9th day of 5th month, 1782; at Hopewell.

Jonathan Parkins Jun.
Jane Parkins

Witnesses who signed this Marriage Certificate:

James Steer	Abigail Steer	Jonathan Parkins Sr.
Nathaniel White	Hannah Picket	John Brock
Abel Walker	Joseph Smith	Jane Brock
Jonathan Wright	Jacob Pickering	Daniel Brock
Joseph Hacknev	Martha Smith	Alice Brock
John Cowgill	Mary Jolliffe	Stephen Brock
Richard Barrett	Jane Rees	James Gawthrop
David Ross	Martha Hackney	Elizabeth Jolliffe
James Parviance	Hannah Pickering	Martha Mendinghall
Mordeca Walker	Patience Gawthrop	
Joseph Lupton	John Berry	
Samuel Pickering		

COOK—COUZENS

Thomas Cook, from west side of Alligany, Son of John Cook, Deceased, and Rebekah his Wife, of the County of Chester and Province of Pensylvania, and *Susannah Couzens*, Daughter of John and Sarah Couzens from west Side Alligany; 13th day of 5th month, 1782; at Hopewell.

Thomas Cook
Susannah Cook

Witnesses who signed this Marriage Certificate:

Marget Berry	Hannah Berry	Richard Ridgway	Rebekah Cook
Patience Berry	Ruth Cowgill	Culburt Hayhurst	Stephen Cook
Isaac Everitt	Martha Smith	Henry Cowgill	Margret Cook
Hannah Sidwell	Bathsheba Lupton	Thomas Smith	Sarah Cowzens
Elizabeth Woodrow	Henry Smith	Sarah Smith	Isaac Brown
Rachel Walker	Joseph Smith	John Brown	Jonathan Wright
Ezekiel Cleaver	Thomas Smith	James Cowgill	John Berry
	Ann Stroud	Mary Rees	John Tremble
	Sinah Walker	Jane Denny	David Berry
	Ann Pugh	Rachel Picket	
		Hannah Picket	

SMITH—SMITH

Henry Smith, from West Side of Allegania Mountain, Son of Samuel Smith and Mary his Wife (Deceased), and *Martha Smith*, of the same place, Daughter of Samuel Smith of Kent County in Delaware and Tamzon his Wife, Deceased, 30th day of 5th month, 1782; at Hopewell.

Henry Smith
Martha Smith

Witnesses who signed this Marriage Certificate:

Ezekiel Cleaver	Elizabeth Jolliffe	Thomas Smith Jr.
Richard Ridgway	Hannah Sidwell	Joseph Smith
John Berry	Margaret Cook	Thomas Smith Sr.
Lewis Walker	Ruth Jonson	William Lupton
Isaac Everitt	John Brown	Dannel Ballinger
Mordecai Ellis	Mary Lupton	Mary Jolliffe
Nathaniel White	Elizabeth Woodroe	Sarah Brown
Robert Eyre	Martha Mendinghall	Eliz'h Jolliffe
David Berry	James Steer	Ann Pugh
David Lupton	Cuthbert Hayhurst	Patience Berry
Isaac Brown	Sarah Smith	Margaret Berry
Jacob Pickering	Thomas Cook	Hannah Berry
Mordecai Walker	Bethsheba Lupton	Sarah Pickering
Sinah Walker	John Trimble	Jane Brock
Sephen Cook	John Pickering	Rachel Walker
James Parvianch	Rebeckah Cook	
James Cougill	Lidia Woodrough	
Jonathan Wright	Elizabeth Woodrough	
Joseph Hackney	Susanah Cook	
Joseph Steer Jun.	Hannah Piggot	
	Sarah Perkins	

PICKERING—BARRETT

Jonathan Pickering, Son of William Pickering and Sarah his wife of Back Creek in Frederick County and Colony of Virginia, and *Phebe Barrett*, Daughter of Benjamin Barrett, Deceased, and Ellinor his wife of County and Colony afforesaid; 17th day of 10th month, 1782; at Hopewell.

Jonathan Pickering
Phebe Pickering

Witnesses who signed this Marriage Certificate:

Bathsheba Lupton	Evan Rogers	William Pickering
Richard Ridgway	Jacob Pickering	Sarah Pickering
Jacob Pickering	Josiah Rogers	Elenor Barrett
Hannah Pickering	Mary Rogers	Thomas Barrett
Phebe Likins	John Fenton	John Pickering
Abel Walker	Ruth Fenton	Jane Pickering
Sinah Walker	Martha Hackney	Richard Barrett
William Barrett	Henry Lewis	Mary Pickering
Rachel Barrett	William Lupton Sr.	Martha Mendinghall
James Parviance	Mordecai Walker	Rachel Walker
Patience Gawthrop	Jane Parkins	Jonathan Wright
Josiah Jackson	James Steer	Nathan Wright
David Faulkner	Samuel Berry	

NEVITT—BARRETT

Isaac Nevitt, son of Thomas Nevitt, Deceased, and Katherine his Wife, and *Rachel Barrett*, Daughter of James and Sarah Barrett in Frederick County, Virginia; 7th day of 11th month, 1782; at Hopewell.

Isaac Nevitt
Rachel Nevitt

Witnesses who signed this Marriage Certificate:

Aaron Grigg	Josiah Ridgway	James Barrett
Elizabeth Jolliffe	Charety Ridgway	Sarah Barrett
Martha Hackney	Grace Steer	David Barrett
David Lupton	Richard Ridgway	William Barrett
John Brown	Abel Walker	James Barrett
Rachel Ridgway	Mordica Walker	James Barrett Junr.
Rachel Bruce	Jonathan Wright	Thomas Barrett
Henry Williams	Lewis Walker	Rachel Walker
Isaac Brown	Sarah Brown	William Wickersham
Cuthbirt Hayhurst	Mary Brown	Lydia Wickersham
David Ross	Elizabeth Wickersham	Elizabeth Nevitt
	Hannah Piggot	James Steer
	Mary White	Abigail Steer
	Richard Barrett	Isaac Steer
	Lydia Berry	Phebe Steer
	Nathan Wright	Patience Gawthrop
	Martha Rees	Hannah Pickering
		Jonas Likins

PICKERING—LIKINS

Samuel Pickering, Junior, of the County of Frederick and Colony of Virginia, and *Phebe Likins*, of the County and Colony Afforesaid; 14th day of 11th month, 1782; at Hopewell.

Samuel Pickering, Junr.
Phebe Pickering

Witnesses who signed this Marriage Certificate:

Miriam Brown	Isaac Pickering	Samuel Pickering
Sinah Walker	Sarah Pickering	Grace Pickering
Martha Walker	John Rees	Jonas Likins
Mary Rees	Nathaniel White	Rebekah Likins
Mary Jolliffe	Richard Ridgway	Thomas Ellis
Elizabeth Jolliffe	David Lupton	Margret Ellis
Jane Rees	Mary Lupton	Jacob Pickering
Hannah Sidwel	James Parviance	Hannah Pickering
Morris Rees	Isaac Steer	Jonas Likins Junr.
William Wickersham	Joshua Lupton	Ann Strode
Josiah Ridgway	Mary Lupton	Grace Pickering
Jacob Graps	Nathan Lupton	Henry Likins
Hannah Rogers	Casper Seeber	John Pickering
Henry Graps	Richard Ridgway	Benjamin Pickering
Lydia Wickersham	Carity Ridgway	Rebekah Pickering
	Joshua Cope	
	Henry Williams	
	Jonathan Pickering	

ELLIS—PICKERING

Ellis Ellis, Son of Enos Ellis and Elizabeth his wife of Berkley County and Colony of Virginia, and *Mary Pickering*, Daughter of William and Sarah Pickering of Frederick County and Colony Afforesaid; 18th day of 12th month, 1782; at Back Creek.

Ellis Ellis
Mary Ellis

Witnesses who signed this Marriage Certificate:

Mary Wright	Jonathan Pickering	Enos Ellis
Phebe Rees	Enos Ellis	William Picking
Deborah Lee	Michael Shihon	Sarah Pickering
Ealeanor Ellis	Esther Hogue	David Berry
Thomas Ellis	Israel Hogue	Ann Pugh
Samuel Ellis	Walter Denny	Hannah Berry
Rowland Ellis	Jesse Ruble	Jacob Pickering
John Rogers	Jesse Hogue	Hannah Pickering
John Wright	Susannah Hogue	Thomas Ellis
William Humber	Daniel Dillon	Margaret Ellis
Evan Rogers	Deborah McCool	Rebekkah Pickering
Josiah Jackson	Anthony Lee	John Pickering
Ruth Jackson	Arther Howel	Benjamin Pickering
Jeane Denny	Lewis Walker	Jane Pickering
Jacob Rogers Jun.	Josiah Rogers	
	Thomas Pugh	

WRIGHT—RIDGWEY

Jonathan Wright, Son of Thomas and Esther Wright, Deceased, of the County of Frederick in Virginia, and *Hannah Ridgwey*, Daughter of Richard and Margaret Ridgwey of the County of Berkley in Virginia as aforesaid; 16th day of ye 1st month, 1783; at their usual Meeting house.

Jonathan Wright
Hannah Wright

Witnesses who signed this Marriage Certificate:

James Parviance	John Adams	Richard Ridgwey
Mordica Walker	Patience Berry	Margret Ridgwey
Rachel Walker	Lydia Rees	Patience McKay
Josiah Jackson	Abigail Steer	Lydia Woodrow Jun.
Daniel Brown	Catharine Ross	Miriam Brown
Abel Walker	David Lupton	Martha Ridgwey
Isaac Brown	Mary Lupton	Josiah Ridgwey
John Rees	Martha Rees	William Pickering
Mary Hirst	James Raley	Sarah Pickering
Lewis Walker	Martha Walker	Martha Mendinghall
John Cowgill	Sinah Walker	Mary Thatcher
John Berry	Margret Berry	James Steer
John Trimble	Henry Piggott	Aaron Grigg
Jacob Pickering	Sarah Brown	Cuth Hayhurst
Hannah Pickering	Isaac Steer	
Richard Barrett	Elizabeth Jolliffe	
Samuel Berry		
John Brown		

RELEY—HUTTON

John Reley, of the West side of Allegany Mountain, Son of Robert Raley and Ann his Wife, and *Mary Hutton*, of the same place, Daughter of Thomas Hutton and Mary his Wife; 20th day of 2d month, 1783; at Westland.

John Reley
her
Mary M Raley
mark

Witnesses who signed this Marriage Certificate:

Israel Wilson	James Crawford	Asa Lupton	Robert Reley
William Heald	Amos Hough	John Hutton	Thomas Hutton
Clement Rigg	John Jenkinson	John Allmon	Mary Hutton
Thomas Cook	Abraham Smith	Hannah Hutton	John Couzens
Susannah Cook	Isaac Jemkenson	Jane Hutton	Sarah Couzens
Sarah Thomas	Thomas Bishop Jun.	Phebe Hutton	William Wilson
Elizabeth Wilson	George Smith	Jane Reley	Barnabas McNamee
Sarah Bishop	John Heald	Ann Reley	Mary Mcc namee
Ann Jenkinson	James Powell	Thomas Allmon	Isaac Mcc namee
Mary Couzens	Samuel James	Ely Reley	Gideon Mcc namee
Sarah Wilson	Hannah James	Henry Smith	John Mcc Call
Mary Jenkinson	Sarah Smith	John Hirst	Sarah McCall
Ann Brown	Cassandra Hawkins	Mary Hirst	Michael Reley
Elizabeth England	Chas. Wheeler	Abigail Steer	Robert Reley
Joseph Brown	Henry Dixon	William Grubb	
Sarah Mcc namee	Amos Ailes		
	Martha Smith		
	Naomi Smith		

GEORGE—COWGILL

Richard George, Son of Ellis George of Frederick County in Virginia, and *Mary Cowgill*, Daughter of Henry Cowgill of the same place; 12th day of 6th month, 1783; at Hopewell.

Richard George
Mary George

Witnesses who signed this Marriage Certificate:

James Steer	Jonathan Wright	Henry Cowgill
Aaron Grigg	Lewis Walker	Ruth Cowgill
James Raley	Joseph Hackney	Lydia George
John Griffith	James Parviance	Ellis George
Thomas Butterfield	Richard Barrett	William Lupton Jr.
Amy Long	Elizabeth Jolliffe	John Cowgill
Martha Payne	Martha Mendenhall	James Cowgill
	Abigail Steer	Joseph Haire
	Charety Ridgwey	Isaac Haire
	Henry Haire	James Butterfield
	Katharine Cowgill	Jacob Haire
	Rachel Payne	John Thompson
	Sarah Payne	Richard Ridgwey
		Abel Walker

WILSON—REES

Thomas Wilson, Son of Samuel and Catharine Wilson in East Nottingham of the County of Chester in Pensylvania, And *Jane Rees*, Daughter of David and Martha Rees of the County of Berkley in Virginia; 4th day of 9th month, 1783; at Hopewell.

Thomas Wilson
Jane Wilson

Witnesses who signed this Marriage Certificate:

Abel Walker	Lewis Walker	Enoch Rees	Jno. Wilson
Robert Eyre	Mordica Walker	Martha Mendinghall	Thos. Job
Mary Eyre	James Parviance	Sarah Brown	David Rees
Lydia Jolliffe	Nath'l White Sen.	Morris Rees	Martha Rees
Ann Eyre	Jonathan Wright	Mary Jolliffe	John Tremble
Margaret Ridgwey	Michael Shihon	Miriam Brown	Deborah Wilson
Richard Ridgwey	Nath'l White Jur.	Elizabeth Woodrow	Nathan Littler
	Joseph Hackney	Martha Walker	Rebeckah Littler
	Cuthbert Hayhirst	Sinah Walker	Mary Rees
	Timothy Brown	Mary Bennett	Phebe Rees
	David Ross	Hannah Wright	Mary Hastings
		Katharine Ross	Charity Rees
			Jacob Rees Jur.
			Margaret Rees Jun.
			Rachel Littler

SMITH—PAYNE

Abraham Smith, Son of Joseph Smith, Deceased, of Frederick County in Virginia, and *Martha Payne*, Daughter of George Payne of Berkley County in Virginia; 16th day of 10th month, 1783; at Hopewell.

Abraham Smith
Martha Smith

Witnesses who signed this Marriage Certificate:

David Ross	Isaac Brown	Ruth Cowgill	George Payne
John Griffith	James Parviance	Martha Griffith	Rachel Payne
Abraham Tucker	Nathaniel White	Bathsheba Lupton	Rachel Smith
Joseph Smith	Joseph Hackney	Martha Mendenhall	Jacob Smith
John Scoggin	Lewis Walker	Eliz'h Balenger	Seth Smith
Jesse Lupton	Jonathan Wright	Rachel Walker	Levi Smith
Isaac Woodrow	Nath'l White Sr.	Elizabeth Woodrow	Mary Smith
	James Raley	Ann Tucker	Henry Payne
	Jacob Pickering	Rachel Thomas	Hannah Haslet
	Richard Barrett	Katharine Ross	Sarah Payne
	William Horsman	James Steer	Alice Payne
	William Lupton	Abel Walker	John Cowgill
	Henry Cowgill	Mordecai Ellis	Katharine Cowgill
		Mordicai Walker	James Cowgill
		William Grubb	Isaac Haire
			Richard George
			Mary George

BARRETT—THORNBROUGH

Thomas Barrett, Son of Benjamin Barrett, Deceased, and Eloner his Wife of Frederick County in Virginia, and *Elizabeth Thornbrough*, Daughter of Benjamin Thornbrough and Mary his Wife, Deceas'd, of Berkley County in Virginia; 4th day of 12th month, 1783; at Hopewell.

Thomas Barrett
Elizabeth Barrett

Witnesses who signed this Marriage Certificate:

Abel Walker	Martha Griffith	Elenor Barrett
Mordicai Walker	Mary Griffith	Richard Barrett
Michael Shihon	Isaac Brown	Jonathan Barrett
Joseph Hackney	Jesse Faulkner	David Faulkner
Lewis Walker	James Steer	Jonathan Pickering
Jonathan Wright	Lidia Rees	Phebe Thornbrough
Nathaniel White Sr.	Hannah Pickering	Phebe Pickering
Nathan Littler	Rebekah Beaumont	Rachel Walker
James Raley	Katharine Ross	Robert Faulkner
Jacob Pickering	David Ross	John Griffith
Hannah Pickering	Cuth. Hayhirst	Martha Faulkner
	Martha Hackney	

JANNEY—McPHERSON

Aquila Janney, son of Jacob Janney of the County of Louden, and *Ruth McPherson*, Daughter of Daniel McPherson of the County of Berkeley; 12th day of 5th month, 1785; at Hopewell.

Aquila Janney
Ruth Janney

Witnesses who signed this Marriage Certificate:

William Grubb	Amy Long	James Steer	John McPherson
James Parviance	Mary Walker	Charity Ridgwey	Dan'l McPherson
Abel Walker	Eliz'h Parviance	Josiah Ridgwey	Thomas Gregg
Isaac Brown	Jonathan Barrett	Isaac Woodrow	Jonas Janney
David Lupton	Abraham Branson	Goldsmith Chandlee	James Bruce
Isaac Steer	John Rees	Priscila Lyles	Richard Ridgwey
William Barrett	John Tremble	Betsey Gibs	Elisha Janney
	Joseph Hackney	Phebe Steer	Nathan Haines
	Nathan Litler	Martha Walker	Daniel Hitt
	Mordecai Walker	Martha Mendenhall	Wm. McPherson
	Anthony Lee	Rachel Neill	Blackston Janney
	Lewis Walker	Mary Janney	Jane McPherson
		Sarah Brown	John Berry
		Phebe Yarnall	Susannah Grubb
		Elenor Barrett	Sarah Walker
		Sinah Walker	

BARRETT—GEORGE

Richard Barrett, Son of Benjamin Barrett, Decea'd, and Elenor his Wife of Frederick County in Virginia, and *Sarah George*, Daughter of Ellis and Lydia George of the same place; 12th day of 5th month, 1785; at Hopewell.

Richard Barrett
Sarah Barrett

Witnesses who signed this Marriage Certificate:

Sarah Brown	Nath'l White Jr.	Ann Hackney	Ellis George
Phebe White	James Steer	Jas. Butterfield	Lydia George
Anne Eyre	Isaac Brown	Jas Cowgill	Elenor Barrett
Sarah Walker	Daniel McPherson	Nathan Littler	Richard George
Elizabeth Woodrow	Abraham Branson	Martha Hackney	Mary George
Eliz'h Parviance	Mordicai Walker	Joseph Hackney	Rebekkah George
Lydia Bruce	William Barrett	Henry Cowgill	Thomas Barrett
Pricilla Lyles	John Tremble	Henry Williams	Eliz'h Barrett
Margaret Berry	Goldsmith Chandlee	Jacob Haire	Jonathan Barrett
Rebekkah Pickering	Lewis Walker	Joseph Haire	David Barrett
Hannah Pickering	Rich. Ridgway	Elizabeth Jankins	Mishael Jenkins
Martha Walker	Anthony Lee	Henry Cowgill Jr.	Rachel George
Martha Mendenhall	James Parviance	James George	John Barrett
Samuel Littler	Wm. McPherson	Amy Griffith	Lydia Barrett
Isaac Woodrow	John McPherson	Jesse George	Amy Long
Rebekkah Long	William Grubb	Lydia George Jr.	Mary Long
Ruth Cowgill	Abel Walker	Mary Griffith Sr.	
		Mary Griffith Jr.	

GREGG—COULSON

Thomas Gregg, Son of Thomas Gregg and Martha Gregg, and *Sarah Coulson*, Daughter of Samuel Coulson, Deceas'd, and Tamer his wife, Both of Fiat County on the West Side of Allegany Mountain; 10th day of 11th month, 1785; at Hopewell.

Thomas Gregg
Sarah Gregg

Witnesses who signed this Marriage Certificate:

James Steer	John Tremble	Tamer Coulson
Lewis Walker	Abigail Steer	Joseph Gregg
Nathaniel White	Martha Mendenhall	Isaac Gregg
Richard Barrett	Patience Berry	John Griffith
David Ross	Rebekkah Pickering	Martha Gregg
Henry Cowgill	Judith Faulkner	Phebe White
David Lupton	Catharine Ross	Nathan Littler
	Richard Ridgway	Ann Eyre
	Jonathan Wright	Margret Ridgwey
		Cuth. Hayhirst
		John Cowgill

["Fiat County" must have been Fayette County, Pa.]

BRANSON—WHITE

Abraham Branson, of Frederick County in the State of Virginia, Son of William Branson and Elizabeth his wife, Deceased, of Stafford County, and *Sarah White*, Daughter of Nathaniel and Mary White of the County and State aforesaid; 12th day of 1st month, 1786; At their Publick Meeting house.

Abraham Branson
Sarah Branson

Witnesses who signed this Marriage Certificate:

Joseph Hackney	Abigail Steer	Nathaniel White
Charles Dingee	Judith Falkner	Mary White
Lewis Walker	Martha Dingee	Elizabeth Parviance
Nathan Littler	Anna Williams	Thomas Brown
Isaac Steer	Catharin Ross	Goldsmith Chandlee
John Berry	Rachel Thomas	Hannah Chandlee
Richard Barrett	Mary Ballinger	Mahlon Smith
James Steer	Elizabeth Woodrow	Mary Smith
Scholey Wright	Rachel Walker	David Ross
Abse. Fleming	Abel Walker	John Parviance
Ann Cannon	Daniel Brown	
Rachel Woodrow	Mordicai Walker	
	Richard Ridgway	
	Jonathan Wright	

PAINTER—FAULKNER

David Painter, Son of John and Susannah Painter in the County of Frederick and State of Virginia, and *Martha Faulkner*, Daughter of Jesse and Martha Faulkner of Berkley County and State Afores'd; 8th day of 2nd month, 1786; at Middle Creek.

David Painter
Martha Painter

Witnesses who signed this Marriage Certificate:

Andrew Daniel	Mary Hastings	Jesse Faulkner
Hannah Daniel	Judith Faulkner	Isaac Painter
Sarah Hoseir	Phebe Oglesbey	Thomas Painter
Martha Griffith	Ann Eyre	Jacob Painter
Hugh Sidwell	Mary Painter	Thomas Faulkner
Robert Branson	Elizabeth Mills	David Faulkner
Ruth Faulkner	Ruth Thatcher	Henry Mills
Simon Moon	Phebe Reese	Martha Griffeth
Jacob Moon	Hannah Faulkner	Anthony Lee
Rachel Moon		James Mendinghall

LUPTON—GEORGE

Jesse. Lupton, Son of William Lupton, Deceas'd, and Grace his wife in the County of Frederick in Virginia, and *Rebecca George*, Daughter of Ellis George and Lydia his Wife of the Same County; 13th day of 4th month, 1786: at Hopewell.

Jesse Lupton
Rebecca Lupton

Witnesses who signed this Marriage Certificate:

Richard Barrett	Rachel Butterfield	Rich'd Griffith	Ellis George
Henry Cowgill	Richard Ridgway	Mary Long	Lydia George
Richard George	Abel Walker	Jas. Butterfield	Grace Lupton
Mary George	Jonathan Wright	Henry Cowgill	Samuel Lupton
William Lupton	James Steer	Charity Hackney	Bathsheba Lupton
John Griffith	John Tremble	Rachel Cowgill	Sarah Barrett
Mary Griffith	David Ross	Rachel Walker	Rachel George
Martha Griffith	David Lupton	Rachel Neill	Jesse George
Ruth Cowgill	James Parviance	Mary Walker	James George
	Lewis Walker	Hannah Piggott	Amy Long
	Elizabeth Greg	John Griffith	Mary Rees
	Thos. Butterfield	Theder Ellis	Amy Griffith
	Joseph Hackney	Mary Griffith	James Cowgill
	John Barrett Jr.	Ann Hackney	Sam'l Griffith
		Lydia Barrett	

SIDWELL—LONG

James Sidwell, of Berkley County, Virginia, son of Richard Sidwell Deceased and Margaret his Wife, and *Amy Long*, of Frederick County, Virginia, Daughter of Owen Long and Lydia his Wife Deceased; 11th day of 5th month, 1786; at Hopewell.

James Sidwell
Amy Sidwell

Witnesses who signed this Marriage Certificate:

Joseph Hackney	Martha Dingee	Enoch Rees	John Rees
Charles Dingee	Ann Eyre	Rebekah Long	David Rees
Richard Barrett	Hannah Eyre	David Rees	Jacob Rees
Abraham Branson	Katharine Ross	Martha Mendenhall	Rebekkah Lupton
Richard Ridgway	Abel Walker	Sarah Brown	Mary Long
David Ross	Mordicai Walker	Abigail Steer	Rachel George
	Nathan Littler	Martha Hackney	Mary Rees
	James Steer	Rachel Neill	Hugh Sidwell
		Miriam Brown	Richard Sidwell

SIDWELL—HASTINGS

Hugh Sidwell, son of Abraham Sidwell Deceased and Charity his Wife, and *Mary Hastings*, Daughter of Job Hastings Deceas'd and Mary his Wife, Both of Berkley County in the State of Virginia; 7th day of 6th month, 1786; at Middle Creek.

Hugh Sidwell
Mary Sidwell

Witnesses who signed this Marriage Certificate:

Mary Bennett	Henry Beason	James Miller	Mary Hastings
Edward Baldwin	Mary Rees	Jacob Moon	Rees Hastings
Joseph Hackney	Phebe Rees	John Eyre	James Sidwell
Jesse Faulkner	Rebekkah Rees	Hannah Eyere	Mordecai Ellis
John Griffith	Anna Beason	Amy Sidwell	Richard Sidwell
Jonathan Ellis	Mary Eyre	Martha Hackney	Charles McGill
Robert Miller	David Griffith	Abigail Lee	Hannah McGill
	Jacob Beason	William Balden Jr.	

SMITH—RIDGWAY

Thomas Smith, Son of Henry and Alice Smith of the County of Louden in the State of Virginia, and *Martha Ridgway*, Daughter of Richard and Charity Ridgway of the County of Frederick and State Afforesaid; 7th day of 9th month, 1786; at Hopewell.

Thomas Smith
Martha Smith

Witnesses who signed this Marriage Certificate:

James Steer	Mordica Walker	David Smith	Charity Ridgway
David Ross	Jonathan Wright	Eliz'h Balenger	Alice Smith
Henry Likens	John Tremble	Hannah Pickering	John Smith
	William Lupton	Rebecca Beaumount	William Smith
	Joseph Hackney	Mary Rees	Mary Smith
	Frances Townsend	Miriam Brown	Martha Mendenhall
	Lewis Walker	Catharine Ross	Sarah Smith
	Abijah Richards	Esther Roberts	Abel Walker
	Abraham Branson	Martha Beeson	Martha Walker
	Richard Barrett	David Ridgway	Rachel Ridgway
	Isaac Steer	Anna Williams	Joseph Smith
	Moses Embree	Abigail Steer	Josiah Ridgway
	Nathan Littler	Grace Steer	Patience Ridgway
	Jonathan Barrett	Martha Dingee	George Smith
	Bathsheba Lupton	Elizabeth Nevitt	
	Mary Smith	Richard Ridgway	

FAULKNERE—HASTINGS

Jesse Faulknere, Senior, of the County of Berkeley and State of Virginia, and *Mary Hastings,* of the same Place (having Declared their Intentions of taking Each Other in Marriage); 8th day of 11th month, 1786; at Middle Creek.

Jesse Faulkner
Mary Faulkner

Witnesses who signed this Marriage Certificate:

Angness Mendenhall	Jesse Faulkner Junr.
Hannah Danel	James Mendenhall
John Hais	Anthony Lee
Thomas Brabson	James Miller
James McCallister	Martha Mendenhall
Archabald Fleming	Jane Beeson
Samuel Park Junr.	Abegail Lee
	Sarah Thornbrugh

WHITE—BEVAN

John White, Son of William White and Sarah his wife, Deceased, of Frederick County in Virginia, and *Susannah Bevan,* Daughter of Samuel and Susannah Bevan, Deceased, of the same place; 15th day of 3rd month, 1787; at Hopewell.

John White
Susannah White

Witnesses who signed this Marriage Certificate:

Nathan White	Jno. Tremble	Margret Ridgway	Eliz'h Ballenger
Isaac Brown	David Ross	Mary Lupton	Stacy Beven
David Lupton	Judith Faulkner	Rachel Nevitt	Susannah Ogan
William Lupton	Sarah Roberds	Lydia Woodrow	Margaret White
Thos. Brown	Elizabeth Woodrow	Charity Ridgway	William White
Daniel Brown	Martha Dingee	Bathsheba Lupton	Jane White
Isaac Steer	Rebekah Pickering	Sarah Lupton	Sarah Ewan
Lewis Walker	Ezek'l Stanbrough	Hannah Pickering	Mary Smith
Levy Smith	Richard Barrett	Rachel Walker	Mary White
	Sarah Barrett	Abel Walker	Patience Smith
	John Barrett Jr.	Mordecai Walker	
	Chs. Dingee	Jonathan Wright	
		James Steer	

JENKINS—PUGH

Michael Jenkins, of Hampshire County and State of Virginia, and *Rachel Pugh,* Daughter of Thomas and Ann Pugh of Frederick County; 11th day of 4th month, 1787; at Back-creek.

Michael Jenkins
Rachel Jenkins

Witnesses who signed this Marriage Certificate:

John Pickering	Mary Rogers	Jane Denny	Jacob Jenkins
Jane Pickering	Sarah Pickering	James M'Coole	Ann Pugh
Josiah Rogers	Jacob Jenkins	William Denny	Eliz'h Jenkins
Jonathan Pickering	Robert Rogers	Alice McGrew	Alice Pugh
Phebe Pickering	Evan Rogers	Evan Jenkins	John Hoge
Jacob Pickering	Jesse Beeson	Eliz'h Jenkins	Mary Hoge
Elizabeth Rogers	John Lewis	Joseph Hackney	Sarah Rogers
Sidney Rogers	Ebenezar John	Evan Rogers Junr.	Job Pugh
Hannah Berry	John Rogers	John Wright	John McCoole
Joseph Fisher	Sarah Pugh	Phebe Wright	Lydia Pugh
William Lewis	Charity Hackney	Elenor McCoole	John McGrew
Owen Rogers	Martha Beeson	William Pickering	
John Brock	Mary Rinker	Eliz'h Jenkens	
	Charlotta Davis		

LUPTON—HANK

Asa Lupton, Son of William Lupton, Deceased, and Grace Lupton in the County of Frederick in Virginia, and *Hannah Hank,* of the same place, Daughter of John Hank, Deceased, and Margaret Hank of Rockingham County; 17th day of 5th month, 1787; at Hopewell.

Asa Lupton
Hannah Lupton

Witnesses who signed this Marriage Certificate:

Lydia Rees	Joseph Steer Junr.	Joshua Lupton	Grace Lupton
Isaac Steer Junr.	James Steer	Nathan Lupton	Samuel Lupton
Grace Jackson	Isaac Steer	Mary Lupton Jr.	Jesse Lupton
Joseph Steer 3d	Phebe Steer	Rachel Lupton	David Lupton
Richard Ridgway	Eliz'h Woodrow	Betty Lupton	John Lupton
Lewis Walker	Abigail Steer	Ruth Lupton	Ann Lupton
Nath'l White Junr.	Samuel Jackson	Joseph Lupton	William Lupton
Chas. Dingee	Hannah Steer	Lydia Woodrow	Bathsheba Lupton
Richard Barrett	Grace Steer Jun.	John Woodrow	Mary Lupton
Joseph Hackney	Rachel Steer	Jonathan Pickering	Rebekah Lupton

[Additional names on this marriage certificate appear on page 239.]

PICKERING—FISHER

Jonathan Pickering, Son of Samuel and Grace Pickering of the County of Frederick and State of Virginia, and *Sarah Fisher*, Daughter of Barak and Mary Fisher of the same place; 7th day of 11th month, 1787; at Back Creek.

Jonathan Pickering
Sarah Pickering

Witnesses who signed this Marriage Certificate:

John Pickering	Hannah Berry	John Fisher	Sam'l Pickering
Phebe Pickering	Jacob Pickering	Elias Fisher	Mary Fisher
Rebekah Fisher	Jonathan Pick'g.	Mary Fisher	Wm. Pickering
John Berry	Elizabeth Grigg	Thomas Fisher	Sarah Pickering
Susannah Lewis	Evan Rogers	Barak Fisher	Jacob Pickering
Sarah Pickering	Jane Pickering	Eliz'h Fisher	Hannah Pickering
Ann Pugh	Jane Brock	Hannah Fisher	Samuel Pickering
Deborah McCool	John Hodgson	Eliz'h Fisher	Phebe Pickering
Josiah Rogers	James Raley	David Berry	Rachel Pickering
			Marcy Pickering

WOOD—GRUBB

Isaac Wood, of the County of Frederick, and *Lydia Grubb*, of the County of Berkeley, both in Virginia; 9th day of 1st month, 1788; at Bulskin.

Isaac Wood
Lydia Wood

Witnesses who signed this Marriage Certificate:

John Haynie	Patience Ridgway	William Grubb
Samuel Patterson	George McMunn	Susannah Grubb
William Figg	Adam Grubb	Sarah Grubb
Rachel Simmons	Nathan Wood	William Grubb Jr.
David Ridgway	Hannah McPherson	Curtis Grubb
Jno. Cowgill	Hannah Grubb	Daniel McPherson
Augustine Pasmore	Jonas Chamberlain	Mary McPherson
Joseph Pyle	Wm. McPherson	Jane McPherson
Nathan Hains	John Wood	Mary Hains
John McPherson	Mercy McCormack	Jane McPherson
Philip Nolan	Samuel Love	Ann McPherson
Abigail Steer	Abner Bane	Elizabeth Passmore
James Steer	Joseph Hackney	
Joseph Parkins		

TOWNSEND—WALKER

Joseph Townsend, Son of Francis Townsend of Bethleham Township, Washington County, Pensylvania, and *Sinah Walker*, Daughter of Abel Walker of Frederick County, Virginia; 10th day of 4th month, 1788; at Hopewell.

Joseph Townsend
Sinah Townsend

Witnesses who signed this Marriage Certificate:

Ruth Cowgill	Richard Ridgway	Amos Jolliffe	Abel Walker
Phebe Steer	John Tremble	Edward Walker	Martha Mendenhall
Mary Lupton	James Steer	Abel Walker Jr.	Charity Ridgway
Henry Cowgill	Thomas Smith	Isaac Walker	Lewis Walker
Charles Dingee	Mary Ridgway	Lydia Bruce	Mordicai Walker
Katharine Ross	Jonathan Wright	Elizabeth Jolliffe	Margret Ridgway
Lydia Rees	Rachel Neill	Lydia Walker	Martha Walker
Mary Rees	Sarah Brown	Ann Grisell	Sarah Walker
David Ross	Phebe White	Sinah Walker	Mary Walker
	Martha Hackney		Martha Beeson

TRIMBLE—RIDGWAY

John Trimble, Son of Joseph and Sarah Tremble, Deceased, and *Rachel Ridgway*, Daughter of Richard Ridgway, deceas'd, and Charity his Wife, Both of the County of Frederick in Virginia; 10th day of 4th month, 1788; at their Publick Meeting house.

John Trimble
Rachel Trimble

Witnesses who signed this Marriage Certificate:

William Lupton	Rachel Steer	Charity Ridgway
Thomas Brown	Joseph Steer	Martha Mendenhall
Isaac Brown	Richard Ridgway	Josiah Ridgway
Jacob Pickering	Mord'i Walker	Martha Smith Jr.
Richard Barrett	Jonathan Wright	Mary Ridgway
Nathan Littler	Joseph Hackney	Abel Walker
Abraham Branson	Lewis Walker	Patience Ridgway
Edward Walker	Josiah Jackson	David Ridgway
Sarah Branson	Isaac Smith	Abel Walker Jun.
Rachel Neell	David Lupton	Grace Steer
Sarah Brown		

ROGERS—BROCK

Josiah Rogers, Son of Evan Rogers and Sarah Rogers, Dec'd, of Back Creek in Frederick County and State of Virginia, and *Alice Brock*, Daughter of John and Jane Brock; 7th day of 5th month, 1788; at Back Creek.

Josiah Rogers
Alice Rogers

Witnesses who signed this Marriage Certificate:

Odday Brock	Mary Rogers	Evan Rogers Senr.
John Wright	James Rogers	John Brock
Jane Parkins	Nathan Brock	Jane Brock
Walter Denny	Wm. Pickering	Sidney Rogers
Jonathan Pickering	Ann Pugh	Elizabeth Rogers
Sarah Pickering	Sarah Pickering	Mary Rogers
John Fisher	Phebe Wright	Sarah Rogers Junr.
Mary Fisher	Esther Hoge	John Rogers
Deborah Smith	Stephen Brock	Evan Rogers Junr.
William Lewis	Jacob Pickering	Jonathan Pickering
Josiah Jackson	John Pickering	Sarah Rogers
Ruth Jackson	Grace Jackson	
	Samuel Jackson	

ELLIS—WORREL

Samuel Ellis, Son of Mordecai and Mary Ellis, Deceased, of the County of Berkeley and State of Virginia, and *Keziah Worrel*, of the same place, Daughter of Jonathan and Elizabeth Worrel of Pensylvania; 21st day of 5th month, 1788; at Middlecreek.

Samuel Ellis
Keziah Ellis

Witnesses who signed this Marriage Certificate:

Jacob Ong	Jacob Moon	Anthony Lee
Thomas Lee	Robert Miller	Abigail Lee
Thomas Houlten	Amy Sidwell	Susannah Ellis
Ann Eyre	Martha Beeson	Elleanor Ellis
Jonathan Ellis	Alice Beeson	Edward Morris
Mary Rees	Mary Falknier	Hannah Morris
Hannah Rees	Cassandra Miller	James Mendenhall
Rebekah Rees	Deborah White	Martha Mendenhall Jr.
Enos Ellis	Tace Beeson	Martha Mendenhall
Enoch Rees	Sarah Lee	
Jacob Rees	Jane Miller	
Phebe Rees		

PICKERING—ADAMS

Jacob Pickering, Son of William Pickering and Sarah his Wife of Frederick County and State of Virginia, and *Lydia Adams*, Daughter of John and Hannah Adams; 10th day of 12th month, 1788; at Back Creek.

Jacob Pickering
Lydia Pickering

Witnesses who signed this Marriage Certificate:

Ruth Jackson	Elizabeth Rogers	David Berry	Wm. Pickering
Ann Jackson	Grace Jackson	Joseph Adams	Hannah Berry
Josiah Jackson Jr.	William Lewis	William Hoge	Mary Adams
Isaac Jackson	David Adams	Henry Adams	John Pickering
Sidney Rogers	Barak Fisher	Jane Brock	Jane Pickering
	James Wickersham	Josiah Rogers	Jonathan Pickering
	Thos. Brownfield	Alice Rogers	Phebe Pickering
	Josiah Jackson	Mary Stonbridge	William Adams
		Mary Hoge	

SMITH—WALKER

Joseph Smith, of the County of Frederick in Virginia, Son of Samuel Smith of Harrison County in Virginia and Mary Smith, Deceased, and *Lydia Walker*, Daughter of Mordecai and Rachel Walker of the County of Frederick in Virginia; 16th day of 4th month, 1789; at Hopewell.

Joseph Smith
Lydia Smith

Witnesses who signed this Marriage Certificate:

Isaac Brown	Martha Walker	Elizabeth Jolliffe	Mordecai Walker
Nathan Littler	Abel Walker	Mary Walker	Rachel Walker
Michael Shihon	Isaac Walker	Sarah Walker	Elizabeth Smith
Abraham Branson	Lydia Barrett	Jonathan Wright	Elizabeth Smith
Edward Walker	Ruth Lupton	Chas. Dingee	Martha Mendenhall
Rebecca Walker	William Walker	Joseph Hackney	Rachel Neill
David Lupton	Nath'l White Jr.	Phebe White	Eliz'h Woodrow
Jacob Pickering	Richard Barrett	Hannah Pickering	Charity Ridgway
Isaac Woodrow	David Ross	Rachel Walker	Hannah Wright
Sinah Thompson	William Lupton	Sinah Walker	William Lewis
Rachel Lewis	John Cowgill	Ann Trimble	Lewis Walker
	Amos Jolliffe	Rachel Ross	Lydia Bruce

SMITH—PAYNE

Levi Smith, Son of Joseph Smith, Deceased, and Rachel Smith of Frederick County in Virginia, and *Alice Payne*, Daughter of George Payne and Rachel his Wife of Berkley County in Virginia; 4th day of 6th month, 1789; at Hopewell.

Levi Smith
Alice Smith

Witnesses who signed this Marriage Certificate:

Jonathan Wright	Richard Ridgway	Elizabeth Smith	George Payne
James Steer	Abel Walker	Mary Griffith	Rachel Payne
John Antram	Mordecai Walker	Martha Griffith	Rachel Smith
David Ross	Joseph Hackney	Martha Mendinghall	Jacob Smith
William Lupton	Lewis Walker	Chas. Dingee	Isaac Smith
David Lupton	Nathan Littler	Mary Worral	Mary Smith
Amos Jolliffe	Joseph Smith	Hannah Pickering	Sarah Squibb
John Woodrow	Mary Lupton	Margaret Ridgway	Martha Smith
Edward Walker	Judith Falkner	Eliz'h Nicolin	John Cowgill
John Griffith	Grace Steer Junr.	Rachel Garrett	Joseph Haire
Henry Cowgill	Ann Eyre	Mary Griffith	Henry Haire
	James Cowgill	Elizabeth Walker	Rachel Cowgill
		Frederick Smith	Henry Payne
		Rebekah Bruce	George Payne Jr.
			Mary Smith

MORGAN—GRIFFITH

Joseph Morgan, son of John Morgan, Dec'd, and Mary Morgan of Frederick County in Virginia, and *Martha Griffith*, Daughter of John Griffith and Mary his wife, Dec'd, of the County aforesaid; 12th day of 11th month, 1789; at Hopewell.

Joseph Morgan
Martha Morgan

Witnesses who signed this Marriage Certificate:

Jacob Smith	Charles Dingee	Elizabeth Walker	John Griffeth
Curtis Langley	Joseph Mooney	Hannah Falkner	Mary Griffeth
Sibbell Griffeth	John Griffeth Jr.	Andrew Daniel	Mary Morgan
Nathaniel White	John Griffeth	Hannah Daniel	Mary Griffeth
Lewis Walker	Abel Walker	Margret Daniel	Deborah Morgan
Joseph Hackney	Mord Walker	Mary Butterfield	Rob't Dunn
Joseph Steer Jun.	Rachel Walker	Abigail Steere	John Morgan
Goldsmith Chandlee	Rachel Neill	Sarah Brown	Jesse Faulkner
John Rees	Martha Dingee	Rachel Ross	Ruth Faulkner
Isaac Steer	John Wood	Eliz'h Woodrow	Ann Hackney
Evan Griffeth	Nathan Littler	Rebecca Pickering	
Mary Dilwin			

McPHERSON—BEESON

Daniel McPherson, of the County of Fairfax and State of Virginia, son of Daniel McPherson Deceased and Mary his Wife, and *Martha Beeson*, Daughter of Edward and Jean Beeson of the County of Berkley and state aforesaid; 7th day of 1st month, 1790; at Tuscaroah.

Daniel McPherson
Martha McPherson

Witnesses who signed this Marriage Certificate:

Micaiah Beeson	Ann McPherson	Edward Beeson
Edward Beeson	Matha Mendinghall	Jane Beeson
Anthony Lee	Jr.	William McPherson
Jacob Ong	Alice Beeson	James Mendinghall
Robert Miller	Mary Mendinghall	Martha Mendinghall
Bernard Gilpin	Jane McPherson	John McPherson
Jas. Maxwell	Mary Ong	Aquila Jenney
J. Riddle	Tace Beeson	Rebecca McPherson
James Anderson	Jane Beeson	
Abigal Lee	Nathan Haines	
Cassandra Miller	Jesse Beeson	

NEILL—M'PHERSON

Joseph Neill, of the County of Frederick, and *Rebekah M'Pherson*, daughter of Daniel M'Pherson deceased of the County of Berkely, Both of the State of Virginia; 7th day of 4th month, 1790; at Bullskin.

Joseph Neill
Rebekah Neill

Witnesses who signed this Marriage Certificate:

Elijah Chamberlin	Zillah Chamberlin	Ann M'Pherson	Mary M'Pherson
Lydia Neill	Ruth Jenney	Lewis Neill	John Neill
Sarah Neill	Nathan Haines	Thomas Neill	Wm. M'Pherson
Abigail Chamberlin	Jonah Chamberlin	Mary Neill	
William Grubb	John M'Pherson	Rachel Neill	

And 13 names more, not recorded.

COPE—STEER

George Cope, of Joshua Cope of Frederick County and State of Virginia, and *Abigail Steer*, Daughter of James Steer of the County and State Afforesaid; 15th day of 4th month, 1790; at Hopewell.

George Cope
Abigail Cope

Witnesses who signed this Marriage Certificate:

David Lupton	Grace Jackson	John Cope	Joshua Cope
Wm. Lupton	Catherine Sexton	Mary Cope	James Steer
Isaac Smith	Martha Dingee	Charity Cope	Abigail Steer
Abel Walker Jr.	William Likins	Samuel Cope	Isaac Steer
Thos. Bailiss	Mary Johnson	Abigail Steer	Phebe Steer
Lewis Niell	Rich. Ridgway	Eliz'h Woodrow	James Reiley
Abra. Branson	Abel Walker	Mary Lupton	Rachel Reiley
Joseph Smith	Mord. Walker	Rachel Walker	Hannah Steer
Rich'd Barrett	Jonathan Wright	Hannah Pickering	Grace Steer
Lewis Walker	John Trimble	Rachel Neill	Joseph Steer
Wm. Wickersham	David Ross	Sarah Brown	Ruth Steer
Enoch Wickersham	Charles Dingee	Mary Walker	
	Wm. M'Pherson	Phebe White	
	Samuel Jackson	Charity Ridgway	
	Isaac Brown		

SMITH—THOMPSON

William Smith, son of Joseph Smith (Dec'd) and Rachel Smith in the County of Frederick and State of Virginia, and *Hannah Thompson*, Daughter of William and Elizabeth Thompson of the County Afforesaid; 17th day of 2nd month, 1791; at Hopewell.

William Smith
Hannah Smith

Witnesses who signed this Marriage Certificate:

Isaac Walker	Levi Keeran	Rachel Smith
Nath'l White	John Griffeth Jur.	Eliz'h Thompson Sen.
John Griffeth	Charls Dingee	Jacob Smith
Mary Griffeth	James Steer	Levi Smith
Rich. Barrett	Rich'd Ridgway	Alice Smith
Rich'd Sidwell	Abel Walker	Mary Smith
George Pain Jr.	Mord Walker	Mary Smith Jun.
David Falkner	John Cowgill	John Thompson
Judith Falkner	Nathan Littler	Eliz'h Thompson Jr.
	James Raley	Jame Thompson
	John Wood	Mary Griffeth Jun.
	Rachel Ross	

SIDWEL—HACKNEY

Richard Sidwel, of Frederick County and State of Virginia, Son of Hugh and Ann Sidwel (Dec'd), and *Charity Hackney*, Daughter of Joseph and Martha Hackney his wife of the County Afforesaid; 14th day of 4th month, 1791; at Hopewell.

Richard Sidwell
Charity Sidwell

Witnesses who signed this Marriage Certificate:

John Antrim	Mary Griffeth	Rich'd Fallise	Joseph Hackney
Mary Griffeth	Rachel Fallis	Sarah Antrim	Martha Hackney
Lydia Dellen	Ann Moon	Catharine Lewis	Samuel Sidwell
John Antrim Jr.	James Reiley	Wulliam Lewis	Ann Pugh
Rich'd Ridgway	Nathan Littler	Samuel Boyd	Jean Denny
Abel Walker	James Steer	Katharine Ross	Ann Hackney
Mord Walker	Mary Lupton	Phebe Rees	Jos. Hackney Jr.
Lewis Walker	Rachel Ross	Margaret Ridgway	Walter Denny
Samuel Bond	Rebekah Long	Mary Walker	Jon. McCoole
Nathan White Sr.	Lewis Walker Jr.	Rachel Neill	Mary M'Coole
Isaac Brown	John Griffeth	Joseph Gorden	Sarah Sidwell
			Abner Wells
			Deborah Wells

And 5 names more, not transcribed into the record book.

BARRETT—BALEY

David Barrett, Son of Benjamin Barrett, De'd, and Eleanor his wife of Frederick County in Virginia, and *Rachel Baley*, Daughter of John Baley and Rachel his wife, Deceased, of the same place; 12th day of 5th month, 1791; at Hopewell.

David Barrett
Rachel Barrett

Witnesses who signed this Marriage Certificate:

Rebekah Littler	Rachel Barrett	Richard Barrett
Rachel Neill	Sarah Barrett	Jona. Barrett
Eliza Woodrow	Sam'l Lewis	John Mercer
Martha Dingee	Sarah Lewis	Benj. Barrett
Katharine Ross	Martha Bailey	Lydia Mercer
Mary Walker	Lydia Dillon	Wm. Bailey
Charity Ridgway	John Dillon	
Rebk. Wickersham	Charles Dingee	
Sinah Walker	Joseph Hackney	
	Chatherine Lewis	

And 31 names more, not transcribed into the record book.

WOOD—LITTLER

John Wood, of Frederick County and State of Virginia, Son of Cornelius Wood of the County of Chester and State of Pennsylvania, and *Catharine Littler*, Daughter of Nathan Littler of the County of Frederick and State of Virginia Afforesaid; 14th day of 7th month, 1791; at Hopewell.

John Wood
Catherine Wood

Witnesses who signed this Marriage Certificate:

James Steer	Adam Grubb	Charles Dingee	Nathan Littler
Isaac Smith	Rachel Walker	Abel Walker	Rebecca Littler
Isaac Brown	Rachel Neill	Jacob Rees	Isaac Wood
Lewis Niell	Mary Rees	Amos Jolliffe	Sam'l Littler Sr.
John Talbot	Martha Dingee	Cuth. Hayhurst	John Littler
Isaac Nevitt	Lydia Neill	George Coope	Samuel Littler
James Raley	Richard Ridgway	Jacob Talbot	Rachel Ross
John Littler Jr.	Mord. Walker	Joseph Hackney	

BEVAN—ROGERS

Stacy Bevan, of Hampshire county in the Colony of Virginia, Son of Samuel and Suvanna Bevan Deceast, and *Lydia Rogers*, Daughter of Owen and Lydia Rogers of the county afforesaid; 12th day of 4th month, 1792; at Beargarden.

Stacy Bevan
Lydia Bevan

Witnesses who signed this Marriage Certificate:

Mordi'a Rogers	Josiah Jackson	Susanna Ougan	Owen Rogers
Mary Rogers	Rebeckah Wickersham	Peter Ougan	Mary Rogers
Lydia Berry	Elizabeth White	Jesse Hoge	Robert Rogers
	Walter Denny	James Rogers	Ann Pugh
	David Berry	Martha Bonsel	Evan Rogers Sen.
	Hannah Berry	Asa Hoge	Jacob Jinkins
	Jesse White	James Wright	Evan Rogers Jun.
	John Mauzy	Deborah Smith	Eliz'h Jinkins
		Evan Jinkins	Mary Lewis
		Uriah White	William Hoge
			Misheal Jinkins
			Chamy Owgan

ALLEN—LUPTON

Thomas Allen, son of Joseph Allen and Ruth his wife, Dec'd, of Shanandoah County and state of Virginia, and *Betty Lupton*, Daughter of Samuel and Sarah Lupton of Frederick County and State afforesaid; 9th of the 5th month, 1792; at their usual meeting house, the Ridge school house.

Thomas Allen
Betty Allen

Witnesses who signed this Marriage Certificate:

Mary M'Clun	Phebe Steer	Ann Updegraff	Samuel Lupton
Isaac Walker	Sarah Brown	Cuthbert Hayhurst	Sarah Lupton
Mildred Flenton	Sarah Steer	Ruth Lupton	Rachel Lupton
John Woodrow	Sarah Walker	Sarah Steer	Sarah Lupton Jr.
James Raley	James Miller	Grace Lupton	Susanna Allen
Samuel Finch	William Brown	Isaac Steer	William Allen
	Isaac Brown Jun.	Joshua Bailiss	William Lupton
	Joshua Steer	Sam'l Lupton Jr.	Bathsheba Lupton
	David Steer	Isaac Steer Jr.	David Lupton
	Lydia Case	Jos. Steer Jr.	Isaac Smith
	Rachel Walker	Sarah Brown	Nathan Updegraff
	Eliz'h Parkins	Hannah Wright	Mary Lupton
		Isaac Brown	
		Jonathan Wright	

LUPTON—CASE

John Lupton, son of Jonathan and Sarah Lupton of the County of Frederick and State of Virginia, and *Lydia Case*, daughter of Reuben and Mary Case of Nelson County in Kentucky; 16th day of 5th month, 1792; at the Ridge.

John Lupton
Lydia Lupton

Witnesses who signed this Marriage Certificate:

Sarah Steer Jr.	Elizabeth Walker	Mary Lupton	Jonathan Lupton
Sinah Walker	Rachel Walker	Joseph Smith	Sarah Lupton
Ruth Lupton	Isaac Brown	Nathan Updegraff	John Lupton
Mary Steer	Sarah Brown	Jos. Longacre Jr.	Mord. Walker
Sarah Steer	Mildred Fenton	Rebecah Lupton	Rachel Walker
Joseph Guthrey	Sarah Brown Jur.	Lydia Smith	William Lupton
Mary Guthrey			David Lupton
			Rachel Hollinsworth
			Grace Steer
			Rachel Lupton

And 44 names more, not transcribed into the record book.

ANTRIM—HACKNEY

John Antrim, of Frederick county and State of Virginia, son of John and Elizabeth Antrim of the county and state afforesaid, and *Ann Hackney*, Daughter of Joseph and Martha Hackney his wife of the county and state afforesaid; 17th day of the 5th month, 1792; at Hopewel.

John Antrim
Ann Antrim

Witnesses who signed this Marriage Certificate:

Sarah Rogers	David Barrett	Nathaniel White	John Antrim
Jane Denny	Rache Walker	Chas. Dingee	Joseph Hackney
Charity Sidwell	Martha Dingee	Abraham Branson	Martha Hackney
Edwd Morris	Mary Walker	Abel Walker	Eliz'h Antrim
Hannah Morris	Mary Rees	Lewis Walker	Ann Pugh
Polly Griffeth	Rachel Ross	Richard Barrett	Lydia Pugh
Hannah Mooney	Eliz'h Walker	Nathan Littler	Edward Walker
Mary Mooney	John Griffeth	Morde Walker	Aaron Hackney
John Thompson	Mary Griffeth Sr.	David Ross	Phebe Rees
James Mooney	Richard Sidwell	James Steer	Meriam Fallis
James Davis	Elizabeth Allon	Walter Denny	Sarah Antrim
David Rees			

LONGSTRETH—REES

Jonathan Longstreth, son of Daniel Longstreth of Bucks County and State of Pennsylvania and Grace his wife, Dece'd, and *Phebe Rees*, Daughter of Morris Rees and Sarah his wife of Berkley County and State of Virginia; 16th day of 8th month, 1792; at Hopewel.

Jonathan Longstreth
Phebe Longstreth

Witnesses who signed this Marriage Certificate:

Abel Walker Jr.	Sarah Bond	Jacob Rees	Sarah Rees
Evan Lewis	Mary Walker	David Rees	David Rees
Rich'd Ridgway	Alice Smith	Abel Walker	Morris Rees
John Griffeth	Marg't Ridgway	James Steer	Mary Rees
Evan Rees	Ann Eyre	Charles Dingee	Lydia Rees
Thos. Matlock	Lydia Booth	Lewis Walker	Abigail Steer
Greg Chew	Hannah Rees	Abraham Branson	Mary Butterfield
Thos. Brabson	Katherine Ross	David Ross	Ruth Butterfield
	Eliza Walker	Nathan Littler	Rachel Ross
	Amos Jolliffe	Eliza Jolliffe	Charity Ridgway
	David Ridgway	Thos. Butterfield	Martha Dingee
		Mary Jolliffe	Mary Binnegar
			Martha Rees

GRIFFETH—BUTTERFIELD

David Griffeth, Son of William and Esther Griffeth Dec'd, and *Ruth Butterfield*, Daughter of John and Hannah Butterfield Dec'd, Both of Berkley County and state of Virginia; 15th day of 11th month, 1792; at Hopewell.

David Griffeth
Ruth Griffeth

Witnesses who signed this Marriage Certificate:

Joseph Bond	Charles Dingee	John Griffeth Jr.
Jacob Talbot	Abraham Branson	Thos. Butterfield Jr.
Rich'd Ridgway	Richard Barrett	Thomas Butterfield
James Steer	Wm. Hancher	Ann Butterfield
Lewis Walker	Abel Walker	Sarah Johnston
Rachel Niell	Joseph Hackney	Amy Sidwell
Rachel Walker	Mord' Walker	Mary Butterfield
Ann Antrim	John Talbot	Rebekah Long
Lydia Rees	Evan Rees	Ruhamah Hanshaw
Rachel Ross	Hiram Hanshaw	Sarah Clark
Eliza Walker	Amos Jolliffe	Rachel Butterfield
Salla Ridgway	Sarah Bond	Sarah Cowgill
Lydia Neill	Eliza Jolliffe	Jane Rees
Hannah Rees	Barnard Gilpin	Hannah Jacobs
Mary Griffeth	Sinah Walker	Natha. White
Mary Smith	John Griffeth	
Elijah Littler	Martha Hackney	

MOORE—BOND

Asa Moore, son of Thomas Moore and Elizabeth his wife of the County of Loudoun and State of Virginia, and *Sarah Bond*, Daughter of Samuel Bond Dec'd and Tamson his wife Dec'd; 16th day of 5th month, 1793; at Hopewell.

Asa Moore
Sarah Moore

Witnesses who signed this Marriage Certificate:

Richard Ridgway	Mary Smith	Mahlon Janney	Joseph Bond
Abel Walker	Lydia Bruce	Jas. M'Cormack	Hannah M'pherson
Mord Walker	Miriam Brown	Jane M'pherson	John M'pherson
James Steer	Margaret Ridgway	Lydia Neill	Elizabeth Moore
Isaac Smith	Alice Smith	Lewis Neill	Ann Oliver
Mary White	Mary Walker	Amos Jolliffe	Mankin James
Rache. Walker		Mary Jolliffe	James Bruce
Mary Griffeth			Thomas Gheen
Katherine Ross			Margaret Gheen
Eliz'h Jolliffe			Rachel Neill
Ann Hily			
Sarah Walker			
Eliz'h Walker			
Lydia Rees			
Rachel Carter			

And 8 names more, not transcribed into the record book.

LEWIS—ANTRIM

William Lewis, of Frederick County and Common Wealth of Virginia, and *Sarah Antrim*, Daughter of John and Elizabeth Antrim; 13th day of 6th month, 1793; at Hopewel.

William Lewis
Sarah Lewis

Witnesses who signed this Marriage Certificate:

John Griffeth	George Miles	David Rees	Henry Lewis
Mary Griffeth	Hannah Miles	David Parkins	John Antrim
Mary Griffeth Jr.	Evan Rees	Mary Rees	Eliz'h Antrim
	Isaac Eaton	Evan Griffeth	Rachel Lewis
	Lewis Walker	John Poyle	Catherine Lewis
	James Steere	Thomas Barrett	John Lewis
	Daniel Brown	John Antrim	Azel Walker
	Richard Barrett	Miriam Fallis	Joshua Antrim
	Isaac Walker	Rachel Thompson	Ann Antrim
	David Ross	Abel Walker	Mary McCoole
	Willm. Hiett	Mord Walker	Elizabeth Babb
	Charity Ridgway	Joseph Hackney	Ann M'Coole
	Rebecah Littler	Mary Jolliffe	James M'Coole
	Rachel Ross	Rachel Walker	Robert Rogers
		Sarah Neill	Abraham Branson
		Rachel Neill	Rachel Walker
			Joseph Smith
			Lydia Smith
			Jacob Jenkins

PENNELL—GRUBB

Jesse Pennell and *Hannah Grubb*, Both of the County of Berkeley and State of Virginia; 3d day of 7th month, 1793; at Bullskin.

Jesse Pennell
Hannah Pennell

Witnesses who signed this Marriage Certificate:

Martha Withrow	John Gooding	William Grubb
William Grubb	Mary Haines	Susannah Grubb
Hannah Wood	Eliza. M'Cormach	Lydia Wood
Susannah Wood	Sarah M'Cormach	Sarah Grubb
	Ann McClay	Zillah Chamberlin
	John M'pherson	Curtis Grubb
	Charity Ridgway	Adam Grubb
	Abigil Steere	Thomas obWilliams
	Rachel Bane	James Moseley
	Jane McPherson	Sam'l Horsell
	Sarah Haines	David Timberlake
	Abigail Chamberlain	Thomas Peterkin
	George Matthew Jr.	John Gaunt
		Jonas Mcpherson
		Aquila Jenney

LUKENS—CLEAVER

Levi Lukens, of Fauquire County and State of Virginia, son of John Lukens of the State of Pennsylvania, and *Elizabeth Cleaver*, of Berkely County of Virginia, Daughter of Ezekiel Cleaver, Deceased, of the State of Pennsylvania; 8th day of 8th month, 1793; at Tuscorora.

Levi Luckens
Elizabeth Luckens

Witnesses who signed this Marriage Certificate:

Banjamin Bates Jr.	Eph'm Gaither	Ezekiel Cleaver
Rich'd Ridgway	Edmond Graham	Abigail Cleaver
James Mendinhall	Ann Graham	Peter Cleaver
Edw'd Beeson	Nathaniel Dillhorn	
Stephen Thatcher	Martha M'Pherson	
David Shinn	Jane Beeson	
Robert Miller	Tace Beeson	
Jesse Beeson	Juliam Beeson	
Joshua Riddle	Sarah Ridgway	
John Graham	Bulah Ridgway	
Micajah Beeson	Mary Ann Graham	
David Ridgway	Martha Mendenhall	
Jacob Muers	Casandra Miller	

RIDGWAY—M'PHERSON

David Ridgway, son of Richard Ridgway and Margaret Ridgway of the county of Berkley and State of Virginia, and *Martha M'Pherson*, Widow, Daughter of Edward and Jean Beeson, of the same place; 3rd day of 10th month, 1793; at Tuscarorah.

David Ridgway
Martha Ridgway

Witnesses who signed this Marriage Certificate:

Ephriam Gaither	James Mendenhall	Richard Ridgway
Robert Miller	Jonathan Wright	Edward Beeson
Stephen Thatcher	Micajah Beeson	Jane Beeson
Joseph Harris	Edward Beeson Jr.	Alice Beeson
Jonas McPherson	Agnes Mendenhall	Bulah Ridgway
Peter Cleaver	Juliam Beeson	Patience Ridgway
Samuel Mcpherson	Abigail Lee	Hannah Wright
Wm. Bailey	Elizabeth Frame	Jane McPherson
David Berry	Martha Mendenhall Jr.	Sarah Haines
David Shinn	Lydia Mendenhall	Mary Haines
Moses Harlin	Mary Chaplane	Martha Mendenhall
Benjamin Frame		Jesse Beeson

PIGGOTT—STEER

Moses Piggott, son of Henry Piggott, Dec'd, and Hannah his wife of Frederick County in Virginia, and *Hannah Steer*, Daughter of James Steer and Abgail his wife of the same place; 10th day of 10th month, 1793; at Hopewell.

Moses Piggot
Hannah Piggot

Witnesses who signed this Marriage Certificate:

Katherine Ross	Joseph Bond	Lydia Piggott	James Steer
Katherine Lewis	Abrah'm Branson	John Piggott	Abigail Steer
Katherine Cowgill	Lewis Walker	Isaac Nevitt	Hannah Piggott
John Cowgill	David Ridgway	Henry Brock	Grace Steer
Charity Ridgway	Jacob Talbot	Mary Milton	Ruth Steer
Mord'i Walker	Cuthbert Hayhurst	Thos. Milton Sr.	George Cope
David Ross	John Griffeth	Thos. Milton Jr.	Abigail Cope
Mary Griffeth Sr.	Eliza Jolliffe	Lydia Miles	Grace Jackson
Azel Walker	Mary Jolliffe	Rich'd Ridgway	John Cope
Ann Highlee	Margery Perry	Abel Walker	Charity Cope
	Jenney Ferguson	B. Page. Clk	Enoch Wickershame
	Ann McGill	Isaac Smith	Daniel Brock
	Rachel Walker	Rich'd Barrett	Rachel Brock
	Lydia Cowgill	John Antrim	Hannah Miles
	Rachel Perry		George Miles
	Mary Rees		

BEESON—RIDGWAY

Micajah Beeson, son of Edward Beeson and Jean his wife of the county of Berkely and state of Virginia, and *Patience Ridgway*, Daughter of Richard and Margaret Ridgway of the County and state afforesaid; 14th day of 11th month, 1793; at Hopewel.

Micajah Beeson
Patience Beeson

Witnesses who signed this Marriage Certificate:

Peggy Wright	Baldwin Johnson	Peter Cleaver	Edward Beeson
Mary Rees	Lewis Walker Jr.	Charles Dingee	Richard Ridgway
Eliz'h Walker	Elice Beeson	William Hiett	Ann Trimble
Mary Jolliffe	Juliam Beeson	Mord. Walker	Margaret Ridgway
Margaret M'Kay	Mary Walker	Nath'l White Sr.	David Ridgway
Rachel Ross	Mary Hackney	Lewis Walker	Jesse Beeson
Charity Ridgway	Rachel Walker	Rich'd Barrett	Edw'd Beeson Jr.
Catherine Ross	Eliz. Jolliffe	Abrah. Branson	Jacob M'Cay
David Ross	Lydia Rees	Isaac Smith	Martha Ridgway
Joseph Hackney	Hannah Lloyd	Thomas Lloyd	Tace Beeson
Samuel Cleaver	Mary Griffeth	Edward Walker	Jona Wright
		Esther Wright	Hannah Wright
		Bulah Ridgway	
		Sarah Ridgway	

HOPEWELL MEETING HOUSE
Prior to remodeling in 1910
Looking Northeast

Lefthand half built 1789

Righthand half built 1759

HARVEY—ELLIS

Job Harvey, of Berkely county and state of Virginia, son of Amos and Kissiah Harvey (both Dec'd), and *Eleanor Ellis*, of the County and State Affores'd, Daughter of Mordicai and Mary Ellis (both Dec'd); 5th day of 2nd month, 1794; at Middle Creek.

Job Harvey
Eleanor Harvey

Witnesses who signed this Marriage Certificate:

John Newberry	Mary Campbell	Anthony Lee
J—— Wilson	Ann Campbell	Abigail Lee
Joseph Park	Anthony Lee Jun.	Deborah White
Ruth Falkner	Samuel Lee	Susannah Carter
James Mayers	John White	Sarah Lee
Alex. Miller	Eleanor Lee	Elisabeth Ellis
Joseph Brown	Ealin Lee	Thomas Lee
Jesse Faulker	Abigail Lee Jun.	Mary Ellis
Mary Faulkner	Cassandra Miller	John Steel
Jacob Moon	Esther Miller	John Lee
Wm. Donning	Thomas Houlton	Jonathan Ellis
Jesse Faulkner Jr.	Robert Miller	Enos Ellis
William Denham		
Elizabeth Frame		

HOGE—FISHER

Solomon Hoge, of Frederick County and State of Virginia, son of Wm. and Esther Hoge, Dec'd, and *Mary Fisher*, Daughter of Barak Fisher, Dec'd, and Mary his wife, of the County affores'd; 5th day of 3rd month, 1794; at Back Creek.

Solomon Hoge
Mary Hoge

Witnesses who signed this Marriage Certificate:

Thomas Fisher	Zillah Pugh	William Hoge
David Adams	Hannah Jinkins	Mary Fisher
Ruth Fenton	William Hoge Sen.	Barak Fisher
John Fenton	Joseph Fisher	William Malin
Deborah McKool	Jesse Hoge	Thomas Brownfield
Gabriel McKool	Asa Hoge	Sarah Fisher
	John Fisher	Anne Jinkins
	Richard Sidwell	Esther Hoge
	James Crumly	Rebekah Fisher
	William Farmer	Alice M'Grew
	Richard Barrett	Mary Crumley
	Evan Rogers	Mary Jinkins
	Susannah Adams	Ann McKool
	Martha Hoge	Katharine Lewis
	Hannah Fisher	Mary Adams
		Mary M'Kool

BARRETT—BUTTERFIELD

David Barrett, son of James Barrett and Sarah his wife of Frederick county in the State of Virginia; and *Rachel Butterfield,* Daughter of Thomas Butterfield and Mary his wife, Decd, of the same place; 14th day of 8th month, 1794; at Hopewell.

David Barrett
Rachel Barrett

Witnesses who signed this Marriage Certificate:

Lydia Dillon	Hannah Morris	James Barrett
John Dillon	Mary Hackney	Tho. Butterfield
John Griffeth	Mary Rees	Sarah Barrett
Richard Ridgway	Mary Jolliffe	Ann Butterfield
Mord. Walker	Mary Walker	Rachel Nevitt
Joseph Hackney	Lydia Rees	Nathan Barrett
Nathaniel White Sen.	Lydia Neill	Isaac Nevitt
Lewis Walker	Rachel Walker	Arthur Barrett
Abraham Branson	Sarah Ridgway	Sarah Johnson
Joseph Bond	Sinah Walker	Jas. Butterfield
David Ross	Sarah Steer	David Faulkner
David Lupton	Rachel Ross	Judith Faulkner
Isaac Smith	Lydia Ross	George Hartman
Lewis Neill	Rebeccah Long	Charity Ridgway
Joseph Steer Jr.		Rachel Walker
Michael Shihon		Rachel Neill
Thomas Bailiss		Hannah Miles
James Steer		
Richard Barrett		

TALBOTT—LITTLER

Samuel Talbott, of Loudon County and State of Virginia, son of Joseph Talbott of Loudoun County affores'd, and *Rachel Littler,* Daughter of Nathan Littler of Frederick County and State of Virginia affores'd; 6th day of 11th month, 1794; at Hopewel.

Samuel Talbott
Rachel Talbott

Witnesses who signed this Marriage Certificate:

Rachel Walker	Abigail Steer	Joseph Hackney	Nathan Littler
Sinah Walker	Margat Ridgway	Thomas Wilson	Joseph Talbott
Lydia Neill	David Wilson	Sarah Walker	Rebeckah Littler
Lydia Neill Jr.	Jno. Griffeth	Amos Janney	Ann Trimble
	John Cowgill	Hannah Rees	John Littler
	Edw'd Walker	Thomas Hirst	Samuel Littler
	Rachel Niell	Samuel Rees	Mary Talbott
	Mary Fallis	David Ross	Sarah Talbott
	Cathe'n Ross	Joseph Bond	John Littler
	Mary Griffeth	Abra. Branson	Joseph Talbott
	Sarah Branson	Isaac Smith	David Trimble
	Mary White	Rachel Walker	Elisha Littler
	Mary Walker	Isaac Davis	Sarah Littler
	Mary Rees	James Steere	Nath'l White Sr.
	Mary Jolliffe	Lewis Walker	Abel Walker
			Mord Walker
			Rich'd Barrett

HUNT—ROSS

Joshua Hunt, son of Robert Hunt and Abigail his wife of the County of Frederick and State of Virginia, and *Rachel Ross*, Daut. of David and Catherine Ross of County and State afforesaid; 13th day of 11th month, 1794; at Hopewell.

Joshua Hunt
Rachel Hunt

Witnesses who signed this Marriage Certificate:

Edw'd Walker	Rachel Neill	Robert Hunt
Jesse Mosley	Lydia Ross	David Ross
Isaac Walker	Rachel Walker	Abigail Hunt
Mary Chandlee	Ann Neill	Catherine Ross
Anna Williams	Eliza Jolliffe	Mary Painter
Abra Branson	Eliza Walker	Abigail Hunt Jr.
Sarah Branson	Ann Trimble	Jacob Painter
Lydia Ross Jr.	Lewis Rees	Joseph Steer
Mary Ross	Evan Griffeth	John Cowgill
Phebe Ross	Lewis Walker	John Barrett
Martha Faulkner	James Steer	Judith Faulkner
Eliza King	Joseph Bond	Rebeckah Long
	Joseph Hackney	David Ross Jr.
	Richard Barrett	Jonathan Ross
	Caleb Antram	Samuel Hunt
		Joseph Hunt

COWGILL—BARRETT

Henry Cowgill, son of Henry Cowgill and Ruth his wife of Culpeper County in the State of Virginia, and *Eleanor Barrett*, Daughter of Benj'a Barrett dec'd and Eleanor his wife of Frederic County and State affores'd; 13th day of 11th month, 1794; at Hopewell.

Henry Cowgill
Eleanor Cowgill

Witnesses who signed this Marriage Certificate:

Rachel Walker	Abel Walker	Jesse Lupton	Henry Cowgill
Rob't Hunt	Mord Walker	John Barrett	John Cowgill
Jno. Griffeth	Abraham Branson	Rhoda Barrett	Jona Barrett
Jos. Hackney	Lewis Walker	Abigail Hunt	Thomas Barrett
John Pyle	James Steere	Catherine Ross	Eliza Barrett
	Joseph Bond	Rebekah Long	Rich'd Barrett
	Evan Griffeth	Judith Falkner	Sarah Barrett
	Lewis Rees	Jacob Painter	Sudny Barrett
	Isaac Walker	David Ross	Ruth Girce
	David Faulkner	Abigail Hunt Jr.	Sarah Cowgill
	Jesse Mosley	Lydia Neill	Benj. Barrett
	Isaac Nevitt	Rachel Walker	David Barrett
	Caleb Antram	Lydia Dillon	John Mercer
			Jona Pickering

JEFFERIS—LONG

Job Jefferis of Berkely county Virginia, son of William Jefferis Dec'd and Hannah his wife, and *Rebekah Long*, of Frederick county, Virginia, Daughter of Owen Long and Lydia his Wife dec'd; 10th day of 12th month, 1794; at Middle Creek.

Job Jefferis
Rebekah Jefferis

Witnesses who signed this Marriage Certificate:

John Lee	Mary Brady	John Butterfield
Samuel Lee	Phebe Downing	Mary Butterfield
David Ross	Enos Ellis	Thomas Butterfield
Catharine Ross	George Smith	Ann Butterfield
Ruth Wood	George Hill	Amy Sidwell
Jane Crumly	William Fleming	Abigail Lee
Elice Seaburn	Daniel Seaburn	Jane Wright
Henry Fleming	Griffeth Roberts	Hannah Babard
Mary Faulkner	Jacob Moon	Jacob Edge
Thesdores Seaburn	Thomas Lee	Lydia Edge
		Margaret Sidwel

ELLIS—ROGERS

Elisha Ellis, of Frederick County, Virginia, son of Theoder Ellis and Elizabeth his wife, and *Sarah Rogers*, Daughter of Evan Rogers and Sarah his wife, dec'd, of the County affores'd; 10th day of 12th month, 1794; at Back Creek.

Elisha Ellis
Sarah Ellis

Witnesses who signed this Marriage Certificate:

John Darby	John Fenton	Benj. Fenton	Theoder Ellis
John Wright	Joseph Fenton	Thomas Adams	Eliz'h Ellis
Phebe Wright	Stacy Bevan	Josiah Jackson	Evan Rogers
Isaac Steer	Owen Roger Jur.	Rich. Sidwell	Ann Pugh
Jno. Pickering	Jona. Pickering	John Adams	Owen Rogers
Josiah Ballenger	Ruth Fenton	Lydia Adams	Mary Rogers
Mary Jackson	Anne Jinkins	Mary Campbell	Josiah Rogers
	Nathan Wright	Ann Jackson	Rees Cadwolader
	Lydia Bevan	Rebckah Fenton	Eliz'h Rogers
	Jos. Fisher	Sarah Fenton	James Rogers
	Eliza Fisher	Jacob Jinkins Jr.	Jonathan Ellis
	Thomas Edwards	John Rogers	Jacob Pickering
	Barak Fisher	Jacob Smith	Sidney Rogers
	Jesse Hoge		Charity Sidwell
			Mary Adams

GEORGE—LUPTON

Jesse George, son of Elis George and Lydia his Wife of the County of Hamshire and State of Virginia, and *Mercy Lupton*, Daughter of Isaac Lupton and Eliza. his wife, of the same place; 14th day of the 1st month, 1795; at a Meeting appointed in Hampshire county.

Jesse George
Mercy George

Witnesses who signed this Marriage Certificate:

Amos Park	James George	Ellis George
Anne Park	Rachel Lupton	Isaac Lupton
Hesther Dilliplain	David Lupton	Lydia George
Rachel Perrel	Mary Lupton	Richard George
Thomas Hughs	Joseph Hackney	Rebekah Lupton
	Ann Pugh	Mary Lupton
	Jonathan Wright	Amy Griffeth
	Joseph Steer	Asa Lupton
	James Raley	Samuel Lupton
	Georg Park	Sarah Lupton
	John Park	Jesse Lupton
		William Lupton

TAYLOR—JENKINS

Ambrose Taylor, of Frederick County and State of Virginia, and *Amy Jenkins*, of the same place; 11th day of the 5th month, 1796; at Back Creek.

Ambrose Taylor
Ann Taylor

Witnesses who signed this Marriage Certificate:

Mary Adams	Jonathan Pickering	Stephen Taylor
Ann Pugh	Phebe Pickering	Isreal Jenkins
Ruth Fenton	Richard Sidwell	Jacob Jenkins
	John Fenton	Peter Taylor
	Charity Sidwell	Susanna Jenkins
	Elizabeth Rogers	Mary Taylor
	William Hoge	Walter Denny
	Jacob Taylor	Stephen McBride
	Mordecai Taylor	
	Hannah Jenkins	

ANTRIM—CONNER

Caleb Antrim, Son of John Antrim and Elizabeth his wife of Frederick county and State of Virginia, and *Martha Conner*, Daughter of John Morgan, Dec'd, and Mary his wife of the same place; 10th day of 11th month, 1796; at Hopewell.

Caleb Antrim
Martha Antrim

Witnesses who signed this Marriage Certificate:

Abraham Branson	John Griffeth	John Antram
Nath. White Jur.	Eliza Bruce	Elizabeth Antram
David Ross	Lydia Littler	Mary Morgan
Isaac Smith	Mary Griffeth	John Antram Jur.
Rachel Walker	Martha Hackney	William Lewis
Sarah Neill	John Fergason	Curtis Langly
Lydia Rees	Rachel Walker	Sarah Lewis
Ann Neill	Abigail Steer	Martha Morgan
Sarah Janney	Sarah Branson	Cuthbert Hayhurst
Mary Jolliffe	Elizabeth Walker	Eliza. Jolliffe
Richard Ridgway	Mary Hackney	Mary Griffith Sen.
Abel Walker	Martha Fergason	
Mordecai Walker		
Lewis Walker		
Joseph Hackney		

FAULKNER—PICKETT

Jesse Faulkner, of Berkly County in the state of Virginia, and *Hannah Pickett*, of Frederick County and State afforesaid; 5th day of 7th month, 1797; in the County of Berkely.

Jess Faulkner
Hannah Faulkner

Witnesses who signed this Marriage Certificate:

Jesse Faulkner Jr.	Amos Allison	Hannah Miles
Jno. Wright	Abraham Millar	Lydia Woodrow
Anthony Lee	Sam'l Chenoworth	Ruth Thatcher
John Griffith	Martha Faulkner	James Mendenhall
William Downing	Phebe Eaches	Margaret Cambell
Jacob Moon	Mary Baliff	Elizabeth Black
William Newland		Elizabeth Millar
William Newland Jr.		Catherine Sexton
		Martha Mendenhall
		Tace Beeson
		Alex'd. Millar
		Deborah White

PICKERING—ROGERS

Jonathan Pickering, son of Samuel Pickering and Grace his wife, deceased, of Frederick County and State of Virginia, and *Elizabeth Rogers*, Daughter of Evan Rogers (and Sarah his wife dec'd) of the county and State aforesaid; 10th day of 1st month, 1798; at Back Creek.

Jonathan Pickering
Elizabeth Pickering

Witnesses who signed this Marriage Certificate:

Gabriel Davis	Zadok Rogers	Samuel Pickering
Jacob Pickering	Isaac Jackson	Evan Rogers
Mary McCoole	Jane Pickering	Josiah Rogers
Henry Lewis	R. Holliday	Phebe Pickering
James Campbell	Jonathan Pickering	Mary Fisher
Jacob Smith	Mary Rogers	Sidney Rogers
Mary Adams	John Rogers	Sarah Elliss
Ambrose Taylor	Joseph Adams	Phebe Pickering
Joseph Hackney	Elisha Elliss	Ann McCoole
Stephen McBride	Jonathan Marsh Ellis	Hannah Pickering
William Lupton	Ann Taylor	James Rogers
Matha Hackney	Mary Pickering	Mary Jinkens
Charity Sidwell	Robert Rogers	Samuel Pickering
Jane Denney	Richard Sidwell	James Russell
Ruth Jackson	Josiah Jackson	Lydia Adams
Phebe Wright	James Wright	Sarah Pickering
James McCoole	Hannah Jackson	

HIBBERD—MENDENHALL

Aaron Hibberd, of Frederick county in the state of Maryland, son of Joseph Hibberd and Jane his wife, of the same place, and *Martha Mendenhall*, Daughter of James Mendenhall of Berkely county in the common Wealth of Virginia and Agnes his Wife; 7th day of 2nd month, 1798; at Middle Creek.

Aaron Hibberd
Martha Hibberd

Witnesses who signed this Marriage Certificate:

Deborah White	Abel Walker Jr.	James Mendenhall
Edy Mendenhall	William Paterson	Lydia Mendenhall
Ruth Piggott	William Riddle	Jane Hibberd
Anthony Lee	Edward Walker	Sarah Hibberd
Jacob Mendenhall	John Lee	Tace Beeson
Samuel Lee	Amos Mendenhall	Hannah Farquhar
Lewis Walker Jr.	Benj. Fram	Mary Walker
Ann Mendenhall	William Newlon	Edward Beeson
Hannah Faulknere	Miajah Beeson	Alen Hibberd
Phebe Downing		William Farquhar
Betty Mendinhall		
Elizabeth Frame		

ROSS—REES

Enos Ross, son of David Ross of Frederick county and state of Virginia and Katherine his Wife, and *Lydia Rees,* Daughter of David Rees of Berkly county and State afores'd and Martha his Wife dec'd; 15th day of 2nd month, 1798; at Hopewell.

Enos Ross
Lydia Ross

Witnesses who signed this Marriage Certificate:

James Steere	Rachel Walker	David Ross
Joshua Cope	Elizabeth Bond	David Rees
David Rees	Jacob Rees	Katherine Ross
William Daniel	William Jolliffe	Rebekah Littler
William Walker	David Rees Jr.	Leah Rees
Isaac Walker	Nathan Littler	Jane Rees
Cuthbert Hayhurst	Samuel Bond	Jane Wilson
Ann Highly	Edward Walker	Mary Rees
Elizabeth Risler	Thomas Wilson	Hannah Rees
Rob't Bond	Ellis Rees	Phebe Ross
Isaac Walker Jr.	Jesse Brown	Rachel Ross
Rich. Ridgway	Jonathan Ross	Sarah Lupton
Abel Walker	Jacob Rees	Sarah Janney
Abra. Branson		
Lewis Walker		
Lewis Neill		
Isaac Smith		

TAYLOR—JINKINS

Stephen Taylor, son of Ambrose Taylor and Mary his Wife Dec'd, and *Mary Jinkins,* Daughter of Jonathan Jinkins, Dec'd, and Anne his Wife; 14th day of 3d month, 1798; at Back Creek.

Stephen Taylor
Mary Taylor

Witnesses who signed this Marriage Certificate:

Ann McCoole	Phebe Wright	Ambrose Taylor
Mary McCoole	Elizabeth Ellis	Anne Taylor
Hannah McBride	Cathern Lewis	Susannah Jenkins
John Jinkins	Barak Fisher	Asa Hoge
Joseph Hackney	Evan Rogers	Jesse Pugh
John Thompson	Stephen McBride	Theoder Ellis
Sarah Ellis	John Fenton	Israel Jinkins
Lydia Adams	Jonathan Pickering	Peter Taylor
Sudney Rogers	Joseph Adams	Ezra Grover
Ruth Fenton	Samuel Jackson	Mary Taylor
Rachel Gordon		
Mary Adams		
Grace Jackson		

FOLLIS—DILLON

Richard Follis, of Frederick County, son of George Follis late of Stafford County in Virginia, decd., and Mary his wife, and *Phebe Dillon*, daughter of John Dillon and Lydia his wife of Frederick County in the State afforesaid; 16th day of 5th month, 1798; at their meeting house on the Ridge.

Richard Fallis
Phebe Fallis

Witnesses who signed this Marriage Certificate:

Martha Antrim	Sampson Gainer	Jane Elmore	John Dillon
Rhoda Barrett	Jona. Morris	Han. Sanders	Mary Fallis
Abner Wells	Caleb Antrim	Catherine Bridges	Lydia Dillon
Saml. Talbott	Jona. Barrett	Lydia Dillon	Rachel Gordon
Ann Antrim	Tho. Barrett	David Falkner	Joseph Gordon
Mary Hackney	Edw'd Morris	David Barrett	Rich. Ridgway
Mary McDonald	John Barrett	Nath'l White Jr.	David Ridgway
Sarah Barrett	Martha Hackney	Rich'd Barrett	Sarah Rees
Marth Faulkner	Eliz. Antrim	Jno. Antrim	Jona Wright
Phebe Mooney	Mary Griffith		
Mary Griffith Jr.	Judith Faulkner		
John Boyd	Ann Eyre		

BEAL—M'CLUN

William Beal, of Frederic county and State of Virginia, and *Mary M'Clun*, Daughter of Thomas and Hannah McClun of the county and state affores'd; 15th day of 8th month, 1798; at a public meeting for worship in said county.

William Beal
Mary Beal

Witnesses who signed this Marriage Certificate:

Joseph Steer	Esther Wright	Joseph Beal
Mary Lupton	Samuel Lupton	Phebe Steer
Sarah Lupton	David Lupton	Sarah Brown
Rachel Raley	Jona. Wright	Grace Parkins
Peninah Finch	William Lupton	Philip Beal
Hannah Wright	Sam'l Finch	Rachel McClun
Joseph Steer Jr.	John Cooper	Lydia McClun
Lydia Steer	Sam'l Lupton Jur.	Mercy Rogers
Ann Steer	Joseph Lupton	Mary Steer
James Rayley	David Finch	Mary Parkins
Charles Chapman	Isaac Lupton	Isaac Steer
Isaac Brown	David Lupton Jur.	Robert Rogers
Casandra Brown	Joshua Steer	Elizabeth Parkins
Sam'l Brown	David Steer	Betsy Parkins
Isaac Brown Jur.	Richd. Wright	Mary McClun
	Sarah Steer	Polly Parkins
		Jonah Steer

JANNEY—McPHERSON

Abijah Janney, of the County of Loudon and State of Virginia, son of Israel Janney and Pleasant his wife of the same place, and *Jane McPherson*, Daughter of John McPherson and Hannah his wife of the county of Berkley and State afforesaid; 15th day of 8th month, 1798; at Berkley.

Abijah Janney
Jane Janney

Witnesses who signed this Marriage Certificate:

Hannah Bond	Mary Chamberlin	Israel Janney
Ruth Lupton	Mary McPherson	John McPherson
Jane Janney Jr.	Ann McPherson	Hannah McPherson
Cosmelia Janney	Rebekah McPherson	Hannah Janney
Marg McPherson	Sam'l Valentine	Wm. McPherson
Rebekah Haines	Sam'l Bond	Nathan Haines
Wythe Baylos	Sam'l McPherson	Joseph Bond
William Grubb	Phineas Janney	Samuel Howall
Abra. Branson	Aron Hackney	Daniel McPherson
James Steer	Daniel McPherson	Aquila Janney
Abigail Steer	Redwood Fisher	Ruth Janney
Elisa Chamberlin	Mary Haines	Sarah Howell
Geo Cope	Ruth Haines	Rebecah Neill
Abigail Cope	Lydia Neill	
Abijah Chamberlin	Rebeccah Neill Jr.	
Joseph Steer Jr.	Sarah Neill	
Abel Neill	Zillah Chamberlin	
	Rebecca Grubb	
	Ruth Steer	

HACKNEY—BOND

Aaron Hackney, of Frederick county and State of Virginia, son of Joseph Hackney and Martha his wife, and *Hannah Bond*, Daughter of Joseph Bond of the county and state Affores'd and Eleanor his wife, dec'd; 13th day of 9th month, 1798; at Hopewell.

Aaron Hackney
Hannah Hackney

Witnesses who signed this Marriage Certificate:

James Steer	Rachel Hackney	Joseph Hackney
Abigail Steer	Richard Sidwell	Martha Hackney
Sinah Walker	Martha Hackney	Joseph Bond
Phebe Jones	John Antrim	Elizabeth Bond
Mary Griffeth	Sam'l Bond	John McCoole
Lydia Neill	Ann McCoole	Joseph Hackney Jur.
Ruth Lupton	Katherine McCloole	John McPherson
Sarah Neill	Robert Bond	Daniel Mcpherson
Lewis Walker	Sam'l Valentine	Samuel Mcpherson
Isaac Walker	Jon'a Wright	Charity Sidwell
Mary Steer	Jon'a Taylor	Ann Antrim
David Lupton	Ann Taylor	Mary Hackney
Mary Lupton	Nathan Littler	Rachel Walker Jur.
Ann Neill	David Ross	Rachel McCanless
Lewis Walker Jur.	Jesse Wright	Mary Smith
Mary Brown	William Hiatt	Isaac Smith
Thomas Brown	Margaret Ridgway	Edward Walker
Igs. Perry	Margery Perry	Jesse Faulkner
Mord'a Walker	Rachel Walker	Ruth Faulkner
Abraham Branson	Hannah Miles	Mary Walker
Rebecca Neill	Ann Neill Jur.	Abel Walker Jur.

SMITH—WRIGHT

David Smith, of Loudon County and state of Virginia, son of Henry Smith and Alice his wife, and *Ruth Wright*, Daughter of James Wright and Phebe his wife of Hampshire County and State afforesaid; 8th day of 11th month, 1798; at Bear Garden in the county of Hampshire.

David Smith
Ruth Smith

Witnesses who signed this Marriage Certificate:

Stephen McBride	Sarah Fenton	James Wright
John Lewis	Sarah Rogers	Phebe Wright
Mercy Rogers	Barnard Taylor	Owen Rogers
Lydia Bevan	Joseph Smith Jur.	Joseph Adams
Robert Rogers	Asa Hoge	Stacy Bevan
Ann Taylor	Evan Hiett	Jonathan Wright
Sarah Beale	Hannah McBride	Rachel Wright
Sidney Fenton	Susanna Quantane	Mary Rogers
Joseph Quantane	William Beale	Mary Beale

HYATT—THOMPSON

William Hyatt, of Berkely County and State of Virginia, and *Elizabeth Thompson*, of Frederick County and State afforesaid; 12th day of 12th month, 1798; at a Public Meeting of the afforesaid People held by indulgence in the County of Frederick.

his
William X Hyatt
mark
her
Elizabeth X Hyatt
mark

Witnesses who signed this Marriage Certificate:

Polly White	Mary Griffith	Nathaniel White
Hannah Butterfield	Phebe Mooney	John Antrim
Joseph Hackney	Thomas Barrett	Isaac Smith
Martha Hackney	Edward Morris	Richard Barrett
Mary Smith Jr.	John Griffith Jr.	David Faulkner
Mary Smith	James Hackney	Judith Faulkner
Ann Mayhugh	Caleb Antrim	Ann Eyer
John Wright	George Suhier	Mary Griffith
Susannah Wright	Sarah Sidwell	Hannah Miles
John Thompson	Patty Hackney	Elizabeth Antrim
Jane Thompson		Jesse Wright

JOLLIFFE—NEILL

William Jolliffe, son of John Jolliffe (dec'd) and Mary his wife of Frederick County and State of Virginia; and *Rebecca Neill*, Daughter of Lewis Neill and Rachel his wife of the same place; 12th day of 9th month, 1799; at Hopewell.

William Jolliffe
Rebecca Jolliffe

Witnesses who signed this Marriage Certificate:

Samuel Jones	Ruth Lupton	Lewis Neill
Abel Walker Jr.	Mary Steer	Rachel Neill
Isaac Walker Jr.	Lydia Neill	Ann Lupton
Robert Bond	Ruth Neill	Phebe Yarnall
David Ross	Cassandra Brown	John Jolliffe
Joseph Bond	Eliza J. Bruce	Lydia Bruce
Elizabeth Bond	Richd. Ridgway	Sarah Neill
Samuel McPherson	James Steere	Rebecca Neill
Samuel Miller	Lewis Neill	Lydia Neill Jur.
Lewis Neill	Abel Walker	Eliza Mcalester
Wm. H. Brown	Morda. Walker	Ann Neill
Daniel McPherson	Abraham Branson	Mary Yarnall
Joseph Lupton	Isaac Smith	Thamzon McPherson
Isaac Neill	David Ross Jr.	Mary McPherson
Joseph Steere	Isaac Nevitt	John Mcalester
Cuth. Hayhurst	Edward Walker	Rachel Hollingsworth
Thomas Neill	Joseph Steer Jr.	Charity Ridgway
Mary Neill	John Cowgill	Mary Walker
Thomas Neill Jr.	Nathan Littler	Hannah Lamborn
Joseph Neill	John Lupton	Mary Rees
	Saml Bond	Permenas Lamborn
		Hester Spackman

JANNEY—LUPTON

Phineas Janney, of the county of Loudoun and State of Virginia, son of Israel Janney and Pleasant his Wife of the same place, and *Ruth Lupton*, Daughter of David Lupton and Mary his Wife of the County of Frederic and State aforesaid; 13th day of 11th month, 1799; at Upper Ridge.

Phineas Janney
Ruth Janney

Witnesses who signed this Marriage Certificate:

Bathsheba Lupton	Joseph Steer	Israel Janney
Joseph Bond	Grace Steer	David Lupton
Jonathan Wright	Isaac Brown	Mary Lupton
Hannah Wright	Sarah Brown	Rachel Lupton
Mary McPherson	William Lupton	Rachel Hollingsworth
Sarah Steer	Samuel Lupton	John Lupton
Cassandra Brown	David Updegraff	Pleasant Janney
William H. Brown	Aaron Hackney	Joseph Lupton
Lewis Neill 3d	Joshua Lupton	Isaac Lupton
Betty Lupton	Nathan Lupton	David Lupton Jur.
Esther Wright	Ruth Neill	Rachel Lupton Jur.
Elizabeth Lupton	Lydia Neill	Jane Janney Jur.
Sarah Neill	Sarah Hollingworth	Jane Janney
Martha Canon	Isaac Hollingworth	David Janney
Rachel Lupton	Samuel Finch	Ann Updegraff
Hannah Finch	Samuel McPherson	Nathan Updegraff
Grace Lupton	Redwood Fisher	Isaac Steer
Samuel Lupton Jr.	Isaac Walker	Phebe Steer
William Lupton Jur.	Abel Neill	Rachel Updegraff
Hannah Yonally	Isaac Brown Jr.	Joseph Steer Jur.
Rachel Walker	Joshua Steer	Isaac Neill
Rachel Wood	Cuthbert Hayhurst	Thom. Neill
Ann Neill Iur.	Solomon Lupton	Rachel Carter
Sinah Walker	James Baily	James Carter
Peninah Finch	Rachel Baily	Hannah Evans
Charles Chapman		Mary Steer
		Ann Steer

HOGE—GRIFFITH

Asa Hoge, of Frederick county and State of Virginia, son of William Hoge of the same place and Esther his wife, deceased, and *Mary Griffith,* daughter of John Griffith of the County and State afforesaid and Mary his wife, deceased; 11th day of 12th month, 1799; at Lower Ridge.

Asa Hoge
Mary Hoge

Witnesses who signed this Marriage Certificate:

Elizabeth Antrim	Henry Crumley	William Hoge Sen.
Ann Eyre	Martha Faulkner	John Griffith
Nathan White Jr.	Susanna Wright	Mary Griffith
Richard Ridgway	Mary Dillon	Israel Hoge
Mary Hackney	Jesse Faulkner	Ambrose Taylor
Bulah Ridgway	Martha Thatcher	Anne Taylor
Rachel Hackney	Sarah Crumley	Martha Fisher
Martha Hackney	Mary Crumley	Israel Jenkins
Joseph Hackney	Mary Brown	Susannah Jenkins
Jno. Boyd	Lydia Dillon	John Griffith Jun.
Jna. Thompson	Mary Davis	William Thatcher
William Davis	John Antrim	Hannah Griffith
Sampson Gainer	Richard Barrett	Sarah Sidwell
Lydia Dillon	Edward Morris	Phebe Fallis
Martha Hackney	Elex. Fleming	Sarah Eyre
Robert Dunn	Thomas Crumley	
William Dillon	Jonathan Morris	

WALKER—FAULKNER

William Walker, of Frederick county and State of Virginia, son of Mordicai Walker and Rachel his wife, and *Martha Faulkner,* Daughter of David Faulkner and Judith his wife, of the county and State afforesaid; 5th day of 3d month, 1800; at a public assembly of the aforesaid people held by indulgence of the monthly meeting aforesaid at a schoolhouse near Joseph Hackney's.

William Walker
Martha Walker

Witnesses who signed this Marriage Certificate:

Azel Walker	Thomas Berrett	Mord. Walker
Elizabeth Babb	Abel Walker	David Faulkner
Jesse Faulkner Jr.	Isaac Walker Jr.	Judith Faulkner
David Painter	Lewis Walker Jr.	Rachel Walker
Phebe Faulkner	Abel Thompson	Jesse Faulkner
Natha White	Sarah Barrett	Lydia Smith
Ann Eyre	Rachel Barrett	Joseph Smith
Mary Griffith	Abraham Branson	John Thompson
Ann Antrim	John Antrim	Jonathan Morris
Hannah Hackney	Lydia Hackney	Steward Thompson
Mary Melton	Rachel Rees	William Davis
Ann Davis	Lydia Dillon	David Rees
Sarah Sidwell	Ann Dillon	John Wright
Richard Barrett	Eliza. Barrett	Susannah Wright
Edw. Morris	William Faulkner	Sinah Thompson
Phebe White		Lydia Walker
		Joseph Hackney

BOND—LUPTON

John Bond, Son of John and Marg't Bond his wife, dece'd, Shanando county and State of Virginia, and *Rachel Lupton*, Daug't of Samuel and Sarah Lupton his wife of Frederic county and state affores'd; 1st day of 10th month, 1800; in a public meeting of the said people at the Ridge meeting near William Lupton's.

John Bond
Rachel Bond

Witnesses who signed this Marriage Certificate:

Ann Steer	Rachel Hollingsworth	Ann Lupton	Samuel Lupton
Grace Steer	Jona. Wright	Lydia Lupton	Sarah Lupton
Rachel Lupton	Samuel Finch	Betty Lupton	Betty Allen
Martha Cannon	Isaac Lupton	David Lupton	Grace Lupton
Esther Wright	Jas. Lupton	Mary Lupton	Wm. Lupton
Mary Steer	Josh'a Steer	Isaac Brown	Bathsheba Lupton
David Finch	Aaron Grigg	Sarah Brown	Samuel Lupton Jr.
Jno. Steer Jur.	Peggy Brown	Joseph Steer	Solomon Lupton
Sam Talbott	Lydia Steer	Hannah Wright	
Esther Brown	Abner Barrett	Rachel Raley	
Rachel Updegraff	James Raley	Isaac Steer	
Jonah Steer			

HAINES—GRUBB

John Haines, son of Nathan Haines and Mary his wife, and *Rebekah Grubb*, Daughter of William Grubb and Susannah his wife; 1st day of 10th month, 1800; at Berkeley.

John Haines
Rebekah Hains

Witnesses who signed this Marriage Certificate:

Catharine Wager	Sarah Howell	Nathan Hains
Elizabeth Hunter	Sarah Brown	William Hains
Sarah Sinclair	Thamsan McPherson	Susanna Grubb
Daniel Collett	Daniel McPherson	Mary Hains
Jane Hunter	Daniel Hains	Susanna Grubb
Eleanor Hunter	Curtis Grubb	Lydia Wood
Hannah Wager	Ruth Hains	John Grubb Wood
Elizabeth Grigg	Elizabeth Grubb	Isaac Wood
Nicholas Lunsford	Rebekah Hains	William Wood
John Roach	Hannah McPherson	Susannah Wood
Richard Bond	Mary Raley	Hannah Wood
David Smedley	Elizabeth Smedley	John Grubb
Mary Payne	James Steer	Hannah Janney
	John McPherson	Ann McPherson
		Rebecca McPherson
		Jane McPherson
		Daniel McPherson
		Susannah McPherson
		Adam Grubb
		Samuel McPherson

WALKER—BRANSON

Abel Walker, of Frederick county and State of Virginia, son of Abel Walker of the same place and Mary his wife dec'd, and *Mary Branson*, Daughter of William Branson of Stafford County and state afforesaid and Elizabeth his wife, both dece'd; 5th day of 3d month, 1801; at Hopewell.

Abel Walker
Mary Walker

Witnesses who signed this Marriage Certificate:

Richard Ridgway	Ann Neill Jr.	Abel Walker
Nathan Littler	Rachel Neill	James Mendenhall
James Steer	Mary Rees	Edward Walker
Joseph Haire	Hannah Rees	Rachel Hollway
George Hiett	Lydia Neill Jr.	Mary Walker
Lewis Neill	Mary Smith	Elizabeth Walker
Isaac Nevitt	Lydia Neill	Lydia Walker
David Ross	Ruth Neill	Rachel Walker
Joseph Steer	Abigail Cope	Rebecca Littler
James Steer	Azel Walker	Martha Ridgway
Sarah Brown	Rees Branson	Eliza Jolliffe Bruce
Lydia Mendenhall	Thomas Brown Jr.	Charity Ridgway
Sinah Walker	William Brown	Lewis Walker
Rachel Walker	Sinah Thompson	Mord. Walker
Isaiah Littler	Abel Thompson	Isaac Walker
John Littler	William Holloway	Lewis Walker Jur.
	Nathaniel Branson	Isaac Walker
	Cuthbert Hayhurst	Marth Holloway
	Abraham Branson	William Branson
	Mary Branson	Mary Branson

McPHERSON—STEER

Samuel McPherson, son of John McPherson of Berkely county and Hannah his wife, and *Mary Steer*, Daughter of Isaac Steer of the county of Frederick and Phebe his wife; 15th day of 4th month, 1801; at the Ridge.

Samuel McPherson
Mary McPherson

Witnesses who signed this Marriage Certificate:

Rachel Lupton	Joseph Steer Jur.	John McPherson
Rachel Hollingworth	Daniel McPherson	Isaac Steer
Jr.	Solomon	Phebe Steer
Rachel Steer	Hollingworth	Hannah McPherson
Ruth Steer	Thomas Neill	Wm. McPherson
Isaac Hollingworth	David Lupton Jur.	Rachel Hollingworth
John Haines	David Steer	Ann Steer
Jonah Steer	Joseph Steer	Thamzin McPherson
Sarah Lupton	Grace Steer	Mary McPherson
Sarah Steer	David Lupton	Ruth Hains
Sam'l Lupton	Mary Lupton	Lydia Steer
Lydia Neill	Sarah Hollingworth	Mary Hains
Isaac McPherson	Joseph Lupton	Isaac Brown
Bathsheba Lupton	Joshua Steer	Sarah Brown
Cassandra Brown	Isaa Lupton	Samuel Talbott
Grace Lupton	Solo'm Lupton	Hannah Wright
Betty Lupton	David Janney	John Lynn
Peggy Brown	Samuel Lupton Jr.	Esther Wright
Wm. Lupton	Jane Babb	Ruth Neill
Charles Chapman		
Jonathan Wright		
Thomas Babb		

GRIFFETH—HACKNEY

John Griffeth jur., son of John Griffith and Mary his wife, the latter dece'd, in Frederick County in the State of Virginia, and *Rachel Hackney*, daughter of Joseph Hackney and Martha his wife, in the county and State afores'd; 15th day of 4th month, 1801; at the Lower Ridge.

John Griffith
Rachel Griffith

Witnesses who signed this Marriage Certificate:

Mary Smith	Susanna Wright	John Griffith
Ann Eyre	Ruth Downing	Joseph Hackney
Eliza Antrim	Henry Crumbly	Mary Griffith
Mary Crumbly	Thomas Rees	Mary Hackney
John Dillon	Morris Rees	Hannah Hackney
Abraham Woodrow	Cate McCoole	Aaron Hackney
Mary Rees	Marth Morgan	Joseph Hackney Jr.
Enoch Rees	Nathl. White	Ann Antrim
Jona Morris	Isaac Smith	James Hackney
Charles Kidd	John Antrim	Martha Hackney
William Healfer	Richard Barrett	Asa Hoge
Lewis McCoole	Jonathan Barrett	Richard Sidwell
John Thompson	Phebe White	John Antrim
	Hannah Rees	John Wright
	Phebe Baldwin	

BROWN—JACKSON

William Brown, son of Thomas Brown and Mary his Wife, and *Mary Jackson*, Daughter of Josiah Jackson, dec'd, and Ruth his wife in the county of Frederick and State of Virginia; 22d day of 4th month, 1801; at Back Creek.

William Brown
Mary Brown

Witnesses who signed this Marriage Certificate:

Abel Thompson	John Ball	Thomas Brown
Jas. Rogers	William Pickering	Josiah Jackson
Susan Perkins	Azel Walker	Ruth Jackson
Mary Brown	Luther Spencer	Mary Brown
Abigail Perkins	Isaac Walker	Sarah Brown
Mord. Walker	Benj. Chandlee	Grace Jackson
Wm. H. Brown	Jonathan Pickering	Hannah Jackson
David Brown	Ambrose Taylor	Thomas Brown Jr.
Rachel Walker Jr.	Theodor Ellis	David Steer
Sinah Walker	John Fenton	Caleb Brown
Grace Parkins	Jonathan Ellis	Lewis Neill 3d
Polly Ball	Thomas Catter	Elizabeth Neill
Evan Rogers	Stephen McBride	Hannah Hollingworth
Ruth Fenton	Ann Taylor	Sarah Steere
	Hannah McBride	Joshua Steer

WALKER—HAINES

Edward Walker, son of Abel Walker of the county of Frederick and State of Virginia and Mary his wife, dec'd, and *Mary Haines*, Daughter of Nathan Haines of the County of Barkeley and State afores'd; 7th day of 10th month, 1801; at Berkely Meeting house.

Edward Walker
Mary Walker

Witnesses who signed this Marriage Certificate:

Jane M'Pherson	Mary Raley	Wm. Pherson	Abel Walker
Lydia Wood	Lydia Neill	Natha Haines Jur.	Nathan Haines
Isaac Wood	Bulah Grubb	Az. Walker	Mary Haines
Moses Collett	James Steer Jr.	Isaac McPherson	Mary Walker
Abigail Steer	Rebekah McPherson	Jane McPherson Jr.	Eliz'h Walker
Phebe White	Isaac Walker	Rachel Walker Jr.	Eleanor Hunter
Charity Ridgway	David Ridgway	Sinah Walker	Jas. Mendenhall
Sarah Crow	Lewis Walker Jr.	Leah Walker	Mord'a Walker
Eliz. Hunter	Abel Walker Jr.	Joshua Steer	Edward Beeson
Grace Parkins	Mary Walker 2d	Sarah Steer	James Steer
Eliza Bond	Isaac Walker Jr.	Susan Parkins	John McPherson
John Haines	Lydia Walker	Jona. Taylor	Lewis Walker
Martha Ridgway	Samuel McPherson	Hocton Howard	
Charity Beeson	Mary McPherson	William Grubb	
Eliza. J. Bruce	Tamzin McPherson	William Dixon	
Dan'l McPherson	Mary McPherson Jr.	Joseph Bond	
Rebekah Haines	Rebekah Hains	Ann Taylor	
Sarah Howell	Taca Beeson	Ruth Hains	
	Mary Howell		

JANNY—MENDENHALL

Abel Janny, son of Janas and Ruth Janny of the county of Loudon and State of Virginia, and *Lydia Mendenhall*, Daughter of Jame and Agnes Mendenhall of the county of Berkely and State afforesaid; 4th day of 11th month, 1801; at Middle Creek.

Abel Janney
Lydia Janney

Witnesses who signed this Marriage Certificate:

Joseph Grubb	Edward Beeson Jur.	James Mendenhall
John Lee	Micajah Beeson	Agnes Mendenhall
Jacob Mendenhall	Thomas Patterson	Jane Beeson
Sam'l Mendenhall	Elizabeth Walker	Charity Mendenhall
Amos Mendenhall	Mary Walker	Sarah Janney
Edy Mendenhall	Jane McPherson	Tace Beeson
Hant Mendenhall	Jane Beeson Jur.	Edward Beeson
Nancy Patterson	Lydia Neill	Abel Walker Jur.
Charity Beeson	Martha Ridgway Jur.	George Janney
Betty Mendenhall	Susan Riddle	Edward Walker
Abigail Lee	William Riddle	Lewis Walker Jur.
	Abel Neill	Rees Branson
	David Ross Jur.	David Ridgway
		Isaac Walker
		Jesse Beeson

BROWN—NEILL

William H. Brown, son of Isaac and Sarah Brown of the County of Frederick and State of Virginia, and *Sarah Neill*, Daughter of Lewis and Rachel Neill of the county and state afforesaid; 17th day of 12th month, 1801; at Hopewell.

William H. Brown
Sarah Brown

Witnesses who signed this Marriage Certificate:

Rich. Ridgway	Rebekah Neill	Isaac Brown
Abel Walker	Sarah Zane	Lewis Neill
Lewis Walker	Sarah Steer	Rachel Neill
Meredith Helm	Nancy Helm	Lydia Neill 2d
Elijah Littler	Ann Steer	Ann Neill Jur.
Isaac Walker	Mary Walker	Susan Parkins
Abel Walker Ju.	Thamzen McPherson	Sarah Brown Ju.
Aaron Hackney	Mary McPherson	Thomas Brown
Lewis Walker Ju.	Mary Steer	Mary Brown
Isaac Neill	Daniel McPherson	Abel Neill
David Ross Jur.	Isaac Lupton	Lewis Rees
Isaac Walker Jur.	Joseph Lupton	Isaac Brown Jur.
William Brown	Edward Walker	Joseph Neill
Samuel Lupton	Joshua Steer	Wm. Jolliffe
Joseph Steer	Samuel Lupton Jur.	Mary Neill
Franky Helm	Joseph Steer	Thomas Neill
Peggy Littler	Elizabeth Lupton	Thomas Neill Jur.
Elizabeth Walker	Thomas Brown Jr.	Cassandra Brown
Mary Rees	Esther Brown	Grace Steer
Rachel Walker Ju.	Sarah Jannay Ju.	Margaret Brown
Sina Walker	Mary Brown Ju.	Joseph Steer
Hanah Rees	Abigail Steer	Rebecca Jolliffe
Lydia Walker	James Steer	Cuthbert Hayhurst
Grace Lupton		Ruth Neill
Hannah Hackney		

BRANSON—DOWNING

Rees Branson, son of Abraham Branson and Catherine his Wife, the latter dece'd, of the county of Frederick and State of Virginia, and *Ruth Downing,* daughter of William Downing and Phebe his wife of the county of Berkley and State aforesaid; 10th day of 3rd month, 1802; at Middle Creek.

Rees Branson
Ruth Branson

Witnesses who signed this Marriage Certificate:

Sam. Lee	P. Nadenbousch	Abraham Branson
Phebe Dross	James Farr	Sarah Branson
Ruth Humby	Wm. Thatcher	Wm. Downing
Jacob Mendenshall	Mary Lee	Tom Downing
Thomas Rees Jr.	Jane Coethers	Phoebe Downing
Enos Ross	Susanna Crubb	Ruth Faulker
Jane Rees	Henrietta Chinoweth	Jesse Faulker
Edy Mendenhall	Ann Thompson	Elizabeth Freame
Hannah Mendenhall	Betty Mendenhall	Ann Mendenhall
John Lee	Samuel Rees	Anthony Lee
Isaac Walker Jr.	Hannah Rees	Benjamin Freame
Jonathan Ross	Eleanor Downing	Lewis Walker Jr.
Joseph Grubb	John Downing	James Miller
	Eleanor Lee	Philemon Chenoweth
	Mary Branson	Wm. Campbell
	Able Walker	James Campbell
	Wm. Faulker	Ruth Lyle
	Eliz. Holloway	Samuel Mendenhall

BROWN—BONSALL

Isaac Brown, son of Daniel and Miriam Brown of the county of Hampshire and state of Virginia, and *Rebecca Bonsall,* Daughter of Joseph and Martha Bonsall of the county and state aforesaid; 15th day of 4th month, 1802; at Beargarden.

Isaac Brown
Rebecca Brown

Witnesses who signed this Marriage Certificate:

Jonathan Ellis	Ann Taylor	Daniel Brown
Esther Ogan	Susanna Ginkins	Joseph Bonsall
Mary Buzzard	Martha Ellis	Martha Bonsall
Elizabeth Buzzard	Elizabeth Crambell	Miriam Brown
Patience Dicks	Rachel Resley	Miriam Brown Jr.
Ruth Jinkins	Joseph Bonsall Jur.	Susannah Bonsall
Lydia Brown	Samuel Bonsall	Evan Hiett
Misheal Jinkins	David Brown	James Connard
Frederick Buzzard	Joel Brown	Evan Rogers
	Stacy Bevan	Ambrose Taylor
		John Fenton
		Ruth Fenton
		Wm. Brown

WALKER—JACKSON

Azel Walker, son of Mordecai Walker of the County of Frederick and state of Virginia and Rachel his wife, and *Hannah Jackson*, Daughter of Josiah Jackson of the county and state aforesaid and Ruth his wife; 12th day of 5th month, 1802; at Back Creek.

Azel Walker
Hannah Walker

Witnesses who signed this Marriage Certificate:

Isaac Jackson	Abel Thompson	Mordecai Walker
David Jackson	Abigail Parkins	Rachel Walker
James Steer Jur.	Grace Parkins	Ruth Jackson
William Brown	Mary Walker	Grace Jackson
Anna Steer	Edward Walker	Elizabeth Babb
Lydia Walker	Leah Walker	Lydia Smith
Sudney Fenton	Evan Rogers	Eliza Jolliffe Bruce
Grace Fleming	Joseph Hackney	Rachel Bruce
Thornton Fleming	Jona. Lovett	Ann Fenton
Joab Clawson	Jona. Parkins	Eliza B. Holliday
Josiah Jackson	Ambrose Taylor	Abel Walker
David Steer	Joseph Adams	Isaac Parkins
Ruth Fenton	John Fenton	Sinah Thompson
Anne Taylor	Theodor Ellis	Lewis Walker Jur.
	Stephen McBride	Abel Walker Jur.
	Asa Hoge	Rachel Walker Jur.
	Jas. Rogers	Isaac Parkins Jur.
		Isaac Walker Jur.
		Sarah Steer

REESE—DOWNING

Thomas Reese, son of Thomas and Margaret Reese of the County of Berkeley and State of Virginia, and *Ellen Downing*, Daughter of William and Phebe Downing of the same place; 15th day of 12th month, 1802; at Middle-Creek.

Thomas Reese
Ellen Reese

Witnesses who signed this Marriage Certificate:

David Brown	Jesse Brown	Hannah Rees	Thomas Reese
Henry Cromley	Abel Janney	Hannah Rees	Wm. Downing
Amos Mendenhall	John Chenoeth	Ann Gross	Phebe Downing
James Sellers	Jas. Mendenhall	Mary Cromley	Ruth Branson
John Boyd	Joseph Grubb	Leah Rees	Ruth Faulkner
John Sleet	Anthony Lee	Jane Rees	Joseph Mooney
	Edward Beeson	Mary Job	Evan Rees
	Jacob Moon	Isabella Stephenson	Rees Branson
		Mary Downing	Thomas Job
			Mary Rees
			John Downing

LUPTON—WRIGHT

Joseph Lupton, Son of David and Mary Lupton of Frederic County and State of Virginia, and *Esther Wright*, Daughter of Jonathan and Hannah Wright of the County and State aforesaid; 16th day of 3rd month, 1803; in Meeting-House at the Upper Ridge.

Joseph Lupton
Esther Lupton

Witnesses who signed this Marriage Certificate:

Solomon Hollingsworth	Lewis Walker	David Lupton
Rachel Steer	David Ridgway	Jonathan Wright
David Steer	Martha Ridgway	Hannah Wright
Wm. Dooley	Mary McPherson	Mary Lupton
Sarah Brown	Thamzin McPherson	Richard Rigway
Sinah Walker	Mary McPherson	Ruth Janney
Sarah Walker	Ann Steer	Rachel Lupton
Isaac Walker	Daniel McPherson	Isaac Lupton
Aron Greeg	David Janney	David Lupton Jr.
Wm. H. Brown	Isaac McPherson	Jonah Lupton
Leah Walker	Margaret Ridgway	Peggy Wright
Jane B. McPherson	Samuel Lupton Jur.	Rachel Wood
Margaret Brown	David Wood	Joseph Steer Jr.
Isaac Parkins Jur.	Bathsheba Lupton	
Grace Lupton	Sarah Brown	
Nancy Dick	Joseph Steer	
Thomas Rogers	Grace Steer	
Patience Beeson	James Russell	
William Lupton	Sarah Russell	
	Nicholas Scarff	
	Sarah Steer	
	Cassandra Brown	
	Esther Brown	

MILLER—ELLIS

John Miller, Son of John and Jean Miller of the County of Frederick and state of Virginia, and *Margaret Ellis*, Daughter of Thomas Ellis (Deceased) and Margaret his Wife of the County of Berkeley and State aforesaid; 6th day of 4th month, 1803; in Meeting House at Middle Creek.

John Miller
Margaret Miller

Witnesses who signed this Marriage Certificate:

Mary Ellis	Elisabeth Frame	James Mendenhall
Mary Vinegar	Anthony Lee	Enos Ross
Jonas Chamberlin	Abigail Lee	Thomas Rees
Jane Miller	Thomas Lee	John Danel
Elenor Lee	Anthony Lee Jur.	Daniel Rees
Elenor Bennett	Abigail Lee Jur.	William Downing
Jane Reese	John Lee	Phebe Downing
Sarah Miller	Samuel Lee	Betty Mendenhall
Deborah White	Joseph Grubb	
	Wm. Danel	
	Jacob Moon	
	Joshua Miller	
	Anna Ellis	
	John Crother	

JACKSON—WALKER

Josiah Jackson, of Frederic County and State of Virginia, Son of Josiah Jackson (Deceas'd) and Ruth his Wife, and *Rachel Walker*, Daughter of Lewis and Sarah Walker of the same place; 7th day of 7th month, 1803; at Hopewell.

Josiah Jackson
Rachel Jackson

Witnesses who signed this Marriage Certificate:

Isaac Smith	Isaac Walker	Rachel Walker	Lewis Walker
Moses Coates	Joseph Lupton	Leah Walker	Sarah Walker
Hannah Coates	Esther Lupton	Mary Walker	Ruth Jackson
Abel Walker Jur.	Rachel Lupton	Phebe White	Abel Walker
Rachel Bruce	Mary Walker	Rebecca Littler	Mordecai Walker
Isaac Lupton	Rich'd Ridgway	Benj'n Fenton	Nathan Littler
Ruth Steer	Abra'm Branson	Lethe Talbott	Eliz'h Walker
Solomon Lupton	James Steer	Mary Smith	Lydia Bruce
Abel Thompson	Joshua Wood	David Lupton	Martha Ridgway
Isaac Walker Jur.	Ann Neill Jur.	Mary Lupton	Azel Walker
Ann Fenton	Mary Rees	Lewis Walker Jr.	Edward Walker
Grace Jackson	Lydia Neill	Susan Parkins	Hannah Walker
Abigail Parkins	Sarah Janney	Sarah Steer	Mary Walker
Rachel Wood	Elizabeth Brent	Eliza. J. Bruce	Sinah Walker
David Steer	Betty Lupton		
Sam'l Lupton Jr.	Lydia Lupton		
Grace Lupton	Isabella Jene Steel		
Edw'd Talbott			

McPHERSON—LUPTON

Isaac McPherson, Son of William and Jane McPherson of Jefferson County and State of Virginia, and *Betty Lupton*, Daughter of William and Bathsheba Lupton of Frederic County and State aforesaid; 7th day of 9th month, 1803; in Meeting-House at the Upper Ridge.

Isaac McPherson
Betty McPherson

Witnesses who signed this Marriage Certificate:

Rachel Jackson	John Hains	Lydia Lupton	Wm. McPherson
Sinah Walker	Betty Hains	Grace Lupton	Wm. Lupton
Leah Walker	Isaac Lupton	Jonathan Lupton .	Bathsheba Lupton
Lewis Walker	Isaac Smith	David Lupton	Jane McPherson
Sarah Walker	Mary Smith	Mary Lupton	Daniel McPherson
Rachel Walker	Isaiah Lupton	Phineas Janney	Susanna McPherson
Joseph Steer	Ann Lupton	Ruth Janney	Rachel Bond
Grace Steer	Mord'i Walker	Joseph Lupton	Samuel Lupton
Sarah Steer	Isaac Brown	Esther Lupton	Sarah Lupton
David Steer	Sarah Brown	Sam'l McPherson	Solomon Lupton
Rachel Steer	Rachel Lupton	Mary McPherson	
Sam'l Lupton Jr.			

GRUBB—HAINES

John Grubb, son of William Grubb (of Jefferson County and State of Virginia) and Susanna his Wife, and *Ruth Haines*, Daughter of Nathan Haines of the County aforesaid and Mary his Wife; 11th day of 1st month, 1804; at Berkeley Meeting House.

John   Grubb
Ruth   Grubb

Witnesses who signed this Marriage Certificate:

James Harris	Daniel McPherson	William Grubb
John Haines	Betty McPherson	Nathan Haines
Rebecca Haines	Jane McPherson	Mary Haines
Rebecca Haines	Mary McPherson	Susannah Grubb
Sarah Grubb	Isaac McPherson	John McPherson
Lydia Wood	Thamzin McPherson	Wm. McPherson
Hannah Wood	Ann McPherson	Daniel Collett
Susan Wood	Elizabeth Walker	Edward Walker
Daniel Haines	Curtis Grubb	Robert Coborn
Mercy Collett	Moses Collett	Samuel McPherson
Nathan Haines Jr.	Isaac Wood	Eliz'h McPherson
		Mary McPherson

NEILL—McPHERSON

Thomas Neill, son of John Neill Deceased of the County of Frederic and State of Virginia and Ann his Wife, and *Mary McPherson*, daughter of John McPherson of the County of Jefferson and Hannah his Wife; 4th day of 4th month, 1804; at Berkeley Meeting House.

Thomas Neill
Mary Neill

Witnesses who signed this Marriage Certificate:

Sarah Branson	John Kennedy	John McPherson
Joseph Neill	Isaac Wood	Hannah McPherson
John Grubb	William Grubb	Ann Neill
Nathan Haines	Susannah Grubb	Thamzin McPherson
Mary Haines	Mary Figg	Samuel McPherson
Joseph Bond	John Crow	Mary McPherson
Samuel Howell	Sarah Crow	Daniel McPherson
Sarah Howell	John Haines	Rebecca McPherson
Abraham Neill	Isaac Lupton	Wm. McPherson
Abel Walker Jur.	Ann Steer	Hannah McPherson
Samuel Bond	James Carter	John McPherson Jr.
Daniel Haines	Rachel Carter	Susanna McPherson
Rebecca Haines	Ann Neill Jun'r	Lydia Neill
Ruth Grubb	Lewis Neill	Lewis Neill Jur.
Sally Janny	Eliza Neill	Abijah Janney
	Rachel Neill	Phebe Neill

WILLIAMS—NEILL

John Williams, Son of William Williams (Deceased) and Elisabeth his Wife of the County of Loudoun and State of Virginia, and *Lydia Neill*, Daughter of Lewis Neill and Rachel his Wife of the County of Frederic in the State aforesaid; 10th day of 5th month, 1804; at Hopewell.

John Williams
Lydia Williams

Witnesses who signed this Marriage Certificate:

Lydia Ross	Sarah Brown jur.	Lewis Neill
Lewis Walker	Rebecca Jolliffe	Rachel Neill
Edward Walker	Isaac Brown	Mahlon Janney
Lewis Walker Jur.	Sarah Brown	Abner Williams
Abel Walker jur.	Sam'l Brown	Susanna Janney
Isaac Walker jur.	Sarah Branson	Joseph Neill
George Hiett	Rachel Walker	Ann Neill
Hezekiah Edwards	Mary Rees	Sarah Janney
	Mary Walker	Abel Neill
	Elizabeth Walker	William Jolliffe
	Sinah Walker	Wm. H. Brown
	Jane B. McPherson	Isaac Brown jur.

HAINES—GRUBB

Daniel Haines, son of Nathan Haines and Mary his wife of Jefferson County and State of Virginia, and *Beulah Grubb*, daughter of William and Susannah Grubb of the County and State aforesaid; 13th day of 6th month, 1804; at Berkeley Meeting House.

Daniel Haines
Beulah Haines

Witnesses who signed this Marriage Certificate:

Mary McPherson	Lydia Wood	Nathan Haines
Susanna McPherson	Hannah Wood	William Grubb
Alexander Cleveland	William Wood	Mary Haines
Joshua Cope	Phebe Grubb	Susannah Grubb
Wm. Hyatt	Sarah Howell	John Haines
David Smedley	Wm. McPherson	Nathan Haines Jr
James Steer	Edward Walker	Mary Walker
Lewis Walker Jr.	Thamzin McPherson	Isaac Wood
Isaac Walker Jr.	Rebecca Haines	Curtis Grubb
James Harris	Susan Wood	John Grubb
Samuel Bond	Isaac McPherson	Ruth Grubb
Benj'n Wilson	Betty McPherson	
Alexander Wilson	Rebecca McPherson	
Cassandra Brown	Samuel Howell	
Jane McPherson Jr.	Daniel McPherson	
Sarah Brown	Hannah McPherson	
	Jane McPherson	
	Ann McPherson	

LUPTON—WALKER

Samuel Lupton, Son of Samuel and Sarah Lupton of the County of Frederic and State of Virginia, and *Leah Walker*, Daughter of Lewis and Sarah Walker of the county and state aforesaid; 25th day of 10th month, 1804; at Hopewell.

Samuel Lupton jur.
Leah Lupton

Witnesses who signed this Marriage Certificate:

Isaac Walker jur.	Lewis Walker jur.	Samuel Lupton
Rachel Jackson	Sinah Walker	Lewis Walker
Joseph Lupton	Betty McPherson	Sarah Walker
Esther Lupton	Ann Lupton	Abel Walker
Thomas Wright	Margaret Jackson	Mary Walker
John Gregg	James Steer	Grace Lupton
David Ross	Lewis Neill	Abel Walker jur.
Abel Neill	Charity Ridgway	Edward Walker
Lewis Rees	Rachel Neill	
John Cowgill	Sarah Janney	

LUPTON—McPHERSON

Isaac Lupton, son of David Lupton of the County of Frederic and State of Virginia and Mary his Wife, and *Thamzin McPherson*, Daughter of John McPherson of the County of Jefferson and Hannah his Wife; 16th day of 1st month, 1805; at Berkley Meeting-House.

Isaac Lupton
Thamzin Lupton

Witnesses who signed this Marriage Certificate:

Daniel Haines	Daniel McPherson	David Lupton
Nathan Haines	Rachel Lupton	Mary Lupton
Mary Walker	Ann McPherson	John McPherson
Leah Lupton	Eliz'h G. McPherson	Hannah McPherson
Wm. McPherson	David Lupton jur.	Samuel McPherson
Joseph Lupton	Sam'l Lupton jur.	Mary McPherson
Esther Lupton		

HACKNEY—SIDWELL

Joseph Hackney Jur., of Frederic County and State of Virginia, Son of Joseph Hackney and Martha his Wife, and *Lydia Sidwell*, daughter of Samuel Sidwell and Sarah his Wife (the former deceased); 12th day of 6th month, 1805; at meeting and schoolhouse near Joseph Hackney's.

Joseph Hackney
Lydia Hackney

Witnesses who signed this Marriage Certificate:

John Miller	John Pugh	Joseph Hackney
N. White	Debby Pugh	Martha Hackney
John Griffith	Mary Griffith	Sarah Sidwell
Richard Barrett	Sarah Eyre	Aron Hackney
Jonathan Barrett	David Rees	Richard Sidwell
Levi Job	Ann Eyre	John Griffith Jur.
Joshua Baldwin	Ann White	Rachel Griffith
Wm. Scott	Rachel Larkin	Sarah Miller
Wm. S. Henshaw	Phebe White Jur.	Mary Hackney
John Wright		Martha Hackney
Susannah Wright		

JACKSON—McBRIDE

Isaac Jackson, of Frederic County and State of Virginia, son of Josiah Jackson and Ruth his Wife of the County and State aforesaid, and *Ann McBride*, daughter of Stephen McBride and Hannah his Wife of the same place; 9th day of 10th month, 1805; at Back Creek.

Isaac Jackson
Ann Jackson

Witnesses who signed this Marriage Certificate:

Benjamin Fenton	Anne Taylor	Stephen McBride
Mary Adams	Mary Taylor	Ruth Jackson
George Smith	Sarah Smith	Grace Jackson
Jonathan Smith	Ann Seal	Rachel Jackson
Caleb Seal	Lydia Seal	William Brown
James McBride	Ann McCurter	Josiah Jackson
Jonathan Lovett	Ambrose Taylor	David Jackson
	John Fenton	Jeremiah McBride
		Mary Brown
		Margaret Jackson

BUTCHER—ROSS

Jonathan Butcher, of the Town and County of Alexandria, District of Columbia, Son of Jonathan and Ann Butcher (deceased) of Bucks County, State of Pennsylvania, and *Phebe Ross*, daughter of David and Katherine Ross (the former deceased) of Frederick County, State of Virginia; 4th day of 9th month, 1806; at Hopewell.

Jonathan Butcher
Phebe Butcher

Witnesses who signed this Marriage Certificate:

Lewis Walker jur.	Tacy Beeson	Katherine Ross
John Hirst	Sinah Walker	David Ross
Wm. Jolliffe	Ann Stephenson	Mary Grier
Francis Stribling	John Jolliffe	Lydia Ross
David Ridgway	Rebecca Jolliffe	Jonathan Ross
Lewis Neill	Abel Neill	Enos Ross
L. Janney	Sarah Janney Jur.	Nancy Stribling
Joseph Janney	Rachel Bruce	Francis Stribling Jr.
Rebecca Butcher	Margaret Ridgway	Lydia Ross
Mary Janney	Eliza J. Bruce	Mary Stribling
Martha Ridgway	Rachel Neill	
Phebe Cobourn	Phebe Jones	
Abigail Steer	Maria R. Brown	
Mary Walker	Abel Walker	
Elizabeth Walker	Isaac Walker	
Ann Neill jur.	Edward Walker	
Sarah Brown	W. Dixon	
Jno. B. Paton	Ann Maria Paton	
Lewis Walker	George Bruce	

SCHOLFIELD—NEILL

Mahlon Scholfield, of the town of Alexandria in the District of Columbia, son of John Scholfield deceased and Rachel Scholfield of Prince George's County in Maryland, and *Ann Neill*, daughter of Lewis and Rachel Neill of Frederic County in Virginia; 5th day of 3rd month, 1807; at Hopewell.

Mahlon Scholfield
Ann Scholfield

Witnesses who signed this Marriage Certificate:

Lewis Walker jur.	Martha Ridgway	Lewis Neill
Abel Walker	Ruth Steer	Rachel Neill
Lewis Walker	Phebe White jur.	Abel Neill
James Steer	Maria R. Brown	Joseph Neill
Richard Wright	George Bruce	William Jolliffe
Mary White	Edward Walker	Lydia Neill
Lydia Ross	James Steer Jur.	Rebecca Butcher
Ann McPherson	Sally Thompson	George S. Hough
Mary Walker	Rebecca McPherson	
Hannah Janney	Margaret Brown	
John McPherson	Elizabeth Walker	
Isaac Walker	Cassandra Brown	
Sarah Janney	Eliza Jolliffe Bruce	
Jonathan Ross	Rachel Bruce	
Jacob Janney	Jane B. McPherson	
Joshua Wood	Richard Ridgway	
Robert Coburn		
Phebe Coburn		
Hannah Wood		
David Ross		

JENKINS—GAWTHROP

Jacob Jenkins, of the State of Virginia in the County of Frederick, son of Jonathan Jenkins (Deceased) of the County of Hampshire and state aforesaid and Ann his Wife, and *Hannah Gawthrop*, daughter of James Gawthrop and Patience his Wife; 8th day of 4th month, 1807; "At the upper meeting on appe-pye ridge."

Jacob Jenkins
Hannah Jenkins

Witnesses who signed this Marriage Certificate:

Jonathan Wright	David Lupton Jr.	Ambrose Taylor
Isaac Brown	Joseph Lupton	Anne Taylor
John Roach	Rachel Neill	Rachel Gawthrop
Margaret Wright	Hannah Wright	Edith Taylor
Samuel Lupton	Mary Adams	Mary Taylor
Thomas Norfolk	Rebecca Jolliffe	Sarah Brown
Thomas Bryarly	Grace Lupton	Sarah Lupton
Thomas Wright	Esther Lupton	Mary Lupton
John Bond	Rachel Bond	David Lupton
Isaac Lupton	Rachel McClun	Hannah Adams
Richard Wright	Margaret H. Brown	John Fenton
	Eliza Bill	Hetty Brown
		Sarah Wright

GRIFFITH—SMITH

John Griffith, of the county of Ross and State of Ohio, Son of William Griffith and Joanna his Wife (both deceased), and *Mary Smith*, daughter of Joseph Smith (dec'd) and Rachel his Wife of the county of Frederick and State of Virginia; 9th day of 4th month, 1807; in their public meeting place in Frederick County.

John Griffith
Mary Griffith

Witnesses who signed this Marriage Certificate:

Lewis Walker Jr.	Hannah Cowgill	David Griffith
David Ross	George Harbert	Isaac Smith
Joseph Neill	Mary Butterfield	Mary Smith
Elizabeth Walker	James Steer	Mary Griffith
Mary Walker	Abraham Branson	Levi Smith
Lydia Ross	Edward Walker	George Smith
Sarah Branson	Josiah Harding	Rachel Smith
Sinah Walker	Nathan Littler	John Cowgill
Lydia Hackney	Aaron Hackney	Ann Cowgill
Mary Branson	Isaac Walker	Rachel Payne
John Baker	Phebe Coburn	Elizabeth Payne
Lewis Walker	Hannah Wood	
Joseph Hackney	Mary Walker	
Martin Payne		
Sarah Walker		

BROWN—LUPTON

William Brown, of the County of Hampshire and State of Virginia, Son of Daniel Brown and Miriam his Wife of the aforesaid county, and *Grace Lupton*, daughter of Samuel Lupton and Sarah his Wife of the County of Frederick and State aforesaid; 4th day of 11th month, 1807; at the Upper Ridge Meeting-House.

William Brown
Grace Brown

Witnesses who signed this Marriage Certificate:

David Lupton	Richard Ridgway	Daniel Brown
Mary Lupton	John Fenton	Samuel Lupton
Jonathan Wright	Lewis Walker	Sarah Lupton
Peter Light	Isaac Brown	Miriam Brown
Nathan Lupton	Margaret Brown	Edith Lupton
Jonah Lupton	Rachel Jackson	Hannah Lupton
Mary Fenton	Thamzin Lupton	Elizabeth Brown
John Pugh	Esther Lupton	Jesse Brown
David Brown	Leah Lupton	Catherine Brown
Thomas Wright	David Lupton Jur.	Ruth Wood
William Horseman	Richard Wright	John Bond

MILLER—MENDENHALL

Samuel Miller, son of James Miller of Pennsylvania (deceased) and Phebe his Wife, and *Charity Mendenhall*, daughter of James Mendenhall and Agnes his Wife of Berkeley County and State of Virginia; 4th day of 5th month, 1808; at Middle Creek.

Samuel Miller
Charity Miller

Witnesses who signed this Marriage Certificate:

Lydia Ross	Mary Walker	James Mendenhall
Enos Ross	Agness Nadenbousch	Phebe Coburn
Henrietta M.	Lewis Walker Jur.	Martha Hibberd
Chenoeth	Sarah Miller	Abel Janney
Betsy Wilson	Mary E. Clark	Phip. Nadenbousch
Charlotte Chenoweth	Joseph Grubb	Aron Hibberd
Ann Graham	Margaret Daniel	Robert Coburn
Phe Downing	Abigail Lee	Edward Beeson
Phebe Downing Jur.	Thomas Crawford	Tacy Beeson
		Edward Beeson Jur.
		Jesse Beeson
		James Beeson
		Charity Beeson

LUPTON—McPHERSON

David Lupton Jur., in the County of Frederick and State of Virginia, Son of David Lupton of the same place and Mary his Wife, and *Ann McPherson*, daughter of John McPherson of Jefferson County and State aforesaid and Hannah his Wife; 14th day of 2nd month, 1809; at Berkeley Meeting-House.

David Lupton Jur.
Ann Lupton

Witnesses who signed this Marriage Certificate:

Nathan Haines Jr.	Hannah Bond	David Lupton
Joseph Bond	Rachel Updegraff	Mary Lupton
Lydia Neill	Samuel Howell	John McPherson
Rebecca Janney	Abel Walker	Hannah McPherson
John McPherson Jr.	James Steer	Wm. McPherson
Jonah Lupton	Rebecca Swayne	Abijah Janney
Elizabeth Bond	Samuel Swayne	Joseph Lupton
Daniel Haines	Joseph Neill	Isaac Lupton
Abigail Steer	Ruth Janney	Daniel McPherson
Rebecca Haines	Lewis Neill	Nathan Haines
Lewis Walker Jr.	Rebecca McPherson	Hannah McPherson
John Haines	Daniel McPherson	Jr.
Sarah Janney	Samuel McPherson	Hannah Janney
	Mary McPherson	Jane B. McPherson
		Alex'r M. Briscoe
		Joseph B. Webb
		Daniel Janney
		Jonathan Janney
		Esther Lupton

SWAYNE—BROWN

Samuel Swayne, of the County of Jefferson and State of Virginia, son of Joshua Swayne (deceased) and Rebecca his wife, and *Margaret Brown,* daughter of Isaac Brown and Sarah his wife of the County of Frederic and state aforesaid; 12th day of 4th month, 1809; at Ridge Meeting House.

Samuel Swayne
Margaret Swayne

Witnesses who signed this Marriage Certificate:

Wm. Daingerfield	Lucy Daingerfield	Isaac Brown
Richard Ridgway	Frances Daingerfield	Sarah Brown
Hannah Wright	David Pusey	Thomas Smith
Lewis Walker	Samuel Miller	Rebecca Swayne
Jesse Beeson	Sina Walker	Cassandra Brown
Alex'r White	Sarah Wright	Thomas Swayne
Samuel Lupton	Thomas Wright	Sarah Brown Jur.
Jon'n Wright	Edith Lupton	Amos Haines
Tacy Beeson	Mary Brown Jur.	Samuel Brown
Leah Lupton	James Bryarly	Hannah Brown
Margaret Wright	Robert Haines	Phebe Smith
Sarah Walker	Richard Wright	Thomas Brown Sen.
Sally Janney	James Beeson	David Wilson
Charity Beeson	Goldsmith Chandlee	David Brown
Sarah Lupton	Jr.	Esther Brown
Sarah Hollingsworth	Elizabeth Chandlee	
Jane B. McPherson	Hannah Lupton	
Marth Wilson	Susan Wood	
Goldsmith Chandlee	Benj'n Chandlee	
Hannah Chandlee	Joseph Neill	
	Edward Beeson Jur.	
	Samuel Howell	
	Abel Neill	

REES—SIMMONS

Jacob Rees, of the County of Berkley in the state of Virginia, son of David Rees of the county and state aforesaid and Martha his Wife Dec'd, and *Ruth Simmons,* Daughter of Samuel Simmons Dec'd and Ann his Wife; "Appeared in a public Meeting of the said people held by Indulgence of the Monthly Meeting aforesaid at a School House near Joseph Hackney's Distinguished by the name of Lower Ridge"; 8th day of 11th month, 1809.

Jacob Rees
Ruth Rees

Witnesses who signed this Marriage Certificate:

Thos. Wilson	Joseph Hackney	Ellis Pugh
Jos. Chamberlin	John Griffith	Hugh Sidwell
Mary Rees	Mordecai Taylor	Ann White
Jane Chamberlin	Rich'd Ridgaway	Jos. Chamberlin
Lydia Ross	Martha Hackney	Wm. Dillon
Hannah Bond	Phebe White	Jos. Larkin
Kitty Wilson	Grace Cope	John Gill
Tellithe Coburn	Patience Beeson	Mary Hoge
Mary Chamberlin	N. White	Frances Taylor
Rachel Larkin	Thos. Barrett	Lydia Hackney
Samuel Wilson	Mary Griffith	Jane Hackney
	Sarah Eyre	Rebecca Kerr
	Rachel Rees	Isaac Smith
	James Miller	Massey Jourdan

GREGG—BROWN

John Gregg, of the County of Loudoun and State of Virginia, Son of John Greeg of the County and State aforesaid and Ruth his Wife (both Dec'd), and *Esther Brown,* Daughter of James Allen of West Nottingham hundred, Cecil County and State of Maryland, and Rebecca his Wife, the former deceased; at Berkely; 15th day of 11th month, 1809.

John Gregg
Esther Gregg

Witnesses who signed this Marriage Certificate:

Thomas Wilson	Rebecca Haines	Nathan Haines	Isaac Allen
Rebecca Swayne	Hannah Bond	Hannah McPherson	Susan Gregg
Eliz'h Chamberlin	Beulah Haines	William White	Martha Wilson
Wm. McPherson	Thomas Littler	Ann Bond	
Mary McPherson	Adam Grubb	Ruth Howell	
Joseph Bond	Lydia Neill	Thomasin Haines	
Hannah Janney	Samuel Swayne	Rebecca Janney	
Daniel Haines	Margaret Swavne	Jane McPherson	
David Pusey	Cornelia Janney	Sarah A. Burguoyne	
Nathan Haines	John McPherson		

CHANDLEE—NEILL

Goldsmith Chandlee Jun'r, son of Goldsmith Chandlee and Hannah his wife of the Borough of Winchester, County of Frederick, and State of Virginia, and *Phebe Neill*, daughter of John Neill (deceased) and Ann his wife of the County and State aforesaid; 3rd day of 1st month, 1810; at Centre.

Goldsmith Chandlee Jur.
Phebe N. Chandlee

Witnesses who signed this Marriage Certificate:

Samuel Brown	Jonathan Wright	Abigail Parkins	Ann Neill
Jos. C. Baldwin	Isaac Parkins	Thomas Carter	Hannah Chandlee
Leml. Bent	Amos Miles	Mary Gibson	Mary Neill
Jacob Cooper	Joshua Lupton	Hannah McConnel	Benj'n Chandlee
Wm. Hening	James Carter	Mary Noble	Ann Lupton
C. B. Baldwin	John Lupton	Hannah Miles	Jonah Hollingsworth
Joseph Wood	John Carter	Hannah Miles	Jos. Hollingsworth
John Wright	Nathan Parkins	Hannah Wilson	Saml. Hollingsworth
Susanna Wright	Sarah Hollingsworth	Mary Carter	Solo'n Hollingsworth
Maria J. Beattv	Ann Carter	Unice Fawcett	Elizabeth Lupton
Thos. Brown Jur.	Grace Parkins	Eliz'h Sperry	Margaret Wood
Jona'n Cooper	Rachel McClun	Mary Thompson	Isaac Neill
M. H. McClun	Sarah Gibson	Mary Brown Jur.	Lydia McClun
Eliz'h Hollingsworth	Han'h Hollingsworth	Sarah McClure	Thomas Neill
Mary Hollingsworth	Mary Parkins	Lydia Parkins	Mary Neill
Robt. W. Holloway	Juliet Beatty	Sarah Brown	Ann Carter Junr.

SAUNDERS—McPHERSON

Peter Saunders, of the Town and County of Alexandria and District of Columbia, Son of John Saunders (Dec'd) and Mary his Wife, and *Hannah McPherson*, of Jefferson County, Virginia, Daughter of John McPherson and Hannah his Wife; 7th day of 2nd month, 1810; at Berkley.

Peter Saunders
Hannah Saunders

Witnesses who signed this Marriage Certificate:

Wm. Ginelair	Nathan Haines Jr.	Ruth Janney	John McPherson
Thos. McClanahan	Hetty Turner	Wm. McPherson	Mary Wantan
Wm. H. Tillery	Christian Blackburn	Hannah Bond	Sam'l McPherson
Sam'l Swayne	Cosmelia Janney	Isaac Walker	Sarah Talbott
Rebecca Swayne	Rebecca Janney	Robt. Bond	Isaac Lupton
Nathan Haines	Thomasin Haines	Lewis Neill	David Lupton Jr.
Joseph Bond	Cosmelia Janney Jr.	Sarah S. Hartshorne	John McPherson Jr.
Sam'l Bond	Sam'l Howell	Jonathan Janney	Rebecca McPherson
Abijah Janney	Oliver Wilson	Sarah Janney	Lydia Neill
David Pusey	Aquila Janney	Jane McPherson	

HOWELL—JANNEY

Samuel Howell, of the County of Jefferson and State of Virginia, son of David Howell (dec'd) of the county of Chester and Mary his wife, and *Hannah Janney*, daughter of Aquila Janney (dec'd) of the Town and County of Alexandria and Ruth his Wife; 7th day of 3rd month, 1810; at Berkley Meeting House.

[This meeting was on the Bullskin, near Charles Town, in Jefferson County since 1801, but still called Berkley Meeting.]

Samuel Howell
Hannah Howell

Witnesses who signed this Marriage Certificate:

H. S. Turner	David Pusey	Aquila Janney	Ruth Janney
Beverly Whiting	Joseph Neill	Jane B. McPherson	Nathan Haines
Robt. Bond	Nathan Haines Jr.	Jane McPherson	John McPherson
Saml. Washington	Jonathan Janney	Sarah Janney	Wm. McPherson
Joseph B. Webb	John Haines	Cosmelia Janney	Rebecca Janney
Jno. Humphreys	Mary McPherson	Daniel Janney	Mary Haines
Geo. S. Hough	Sarah McCormac		Ruth Howell
Thos. Wilson	Beulah Haines		Eliz'h Haines
Joseph Bond			Lydia Haines
John D. Brown			Israel Jammey
Elizabeth Bond			Wm. Janney
			Mary Neill
			Lydia Neill
			Mary Ann Janney

[Saml. Washington was the son of Col. Chas. Washington, patron of Charles Town, or a relative of the same name, son of Thornton Washington and grandson of Col. Samuel Washington.]

STEER—LUPTON

Isaac Steer, of Loudoun County and State of Virginia, son of Benjamin Steer and Anne his Wife (Dec'd) of the County aforesaid, and *Leah Lupton*, of Frederick County in the State aforesaid; 12th day of 4th month, 1810; at Hopewell.

Isaac Steer
Leah Steer
(Daughter of Lewis Walker)

Witnesses who signed this Marriage Certificate:

Rich'd Ridgway	Christopher Anthony	Rachel McClun	Benjamin Steer
Thos. Wright	James Steer	Mary Steer	Lewis Walker
Lydia Steer	John Wright	Hannah Lupton	Sarah Walker
Esther Brown	Thos. Brown	David Lupton	William Steer
Mercy Horsman	Isaac Nevitt	Mary Lupton	Abel Walker
Cassandra Brown	Isaac Smith	Hannah Wright	Geo. Bruce Jr.
Sarah Wright	Mary Smith		Nathan Littler
Joseph Lupton	Lydia Ross		Edward Walker
Thos. Littler	Mary Branson		Samuel Lupton
Jonah Steer	Jane B. McPherson		Elizabeth Steer
James Steer Jr.	Phebe White		Mary Walker
George Smith	Susan Steer		Mary Walker
Abraham Branson	Susanna Wright		Josiah Jackson
Peter Davies	Rachel Bruce		Eliz'h Walker
Thos. Rogers	Margaret Wright		Rebecca Littler
Sinah Walker	Richard Wright		Ruth Wright
			Eliz'h Littler
			Rachel Harvey

COWGILL—STEER

John Cowgill, of Frederick County and Commonwealth of Virginia, Son of John Cowgill and Catherine his Wife, and *Susanna Steer*, Daughter of James Steer of County and Commonwealth aforesaid and Abigail his wife (Dec'd); 23rd day of 8th month, 1810; at Hopewell.

John Cowgill
Susanna Cowgill

Witnesses who signed this Marriage Certificate:

Susanna Cloud	Thomas Littler	Abel Walker	John Cowgill
Catherine Nevitt	Mary Strope	Lewis Walker	Catherine Cowgill
Ann Cope	Mary Smith	Isaac Smith	James Steer
Edward Walker	Thomas Ross	Rachel Smith	Joseph Steer
Mary Walker	Mary Walker	Sarah Janney	Grace Cope
Mary Steer	Eliz'h Walker	Mary T. Stribling	William Cowgill
Maryan Cowgill	Marg't Ridgaway	Rachel Neill	Henry Cowgill
George Smith	Eliz'h Littler	Sinah Walker	Mary A. Cowgill
John Collen	Mary Ridgaway	Sarah Walker	James Steer Jr.
John Hays	John Wright	Sarah Brown	Phebe Steer
Aquila Coates	Susanna Wright	Mary Smith	Abigail Parkins
Levi Sheppard	Moses Coates	Eliza Roberts	Ann Cowgill
Thos. Nevitt	Hannah Coates	Ann Stribling	Isaac Steer
Eliza Coates	Benj'n Fenton	Maria Helm	Grace Jackson
Hannah Nevitt	Sarah Jones	Anny Strupe	Grace Parkins
Sarah White	Isaac Nevitt	Ann White	Ann Fenton
Isaac Walker	Charity Ridgaway	Joseph Neill	Sarah Cope
	Abraham Branson	Rebecca Jolliffe	Elisha O. Cowgill

BROWN—WILSON

William H. Brown, of the town of Alexandria and District of Columbia, son of Isaac and Sarah Brown of the County of Frederick in the State of Virginia, and *Martha Wilson*, daughter of Thomas and Jane Wilson, the latter dec'd, of the County of Jefferson and State aforesaid; 3rd day of 10th month, 1810; at Berkley.

Wm. H. Brown
Martha Brown

Witnesses who signed this Marriage Certificate:

Sam'l Williams	Joseph Steer	Nathan Haines	Lydia Ross
John McPherson	Grace Steer	D. Rutherford	Thomas Wilson
Sam'l Howell	Elizabeth Bond	Mary Littler	Isaac Brown
Wm. McPherson	Isaac Steer	Joseph Bond	Sarah Brown
Hannah Howell	Lydia Neill	Ellen Lyles	Esther Brown
Rebecca McPherson	Beulah Haines	Catherine McM.	Rebecca Littler
Rachel Steer	Mary Neill	Moon	Margaret Swayne
Mary McPherson	Hannah McPherson	Sally D. Rutherford	Rebecca Wilson
Sam'l McPherson	Ruth Janney	Jane T. Williams	David Wilson
Ellis Rees	John Littler	Thos. Littler	Joseph Neill
		Sam'l Wilson	Robt. V. Bond

SMITH—WHITE

Thomas Smith, of Saintclair-Township, Bedford County and state of Pennsylvania, son of James Smith and Mary his Wife; and *Phebe White, Junr.*, daughter of Nathaniel White and Phebe his Wife of Berkley County and state of Virginia; 9th day of 3rd month, 1811; at the Lower Ridge Meeting House.

Thomas Smith
Phebe Smith

Witnesses who signed this Marriage Certificate:

Maria R. Brown	Mary Barrett	Abel Walker	N. White
Mary G. Barton	Goldsmith Chandlee	Joseph Hackney	Abraham Branson
Isaac Morgan	John Flower	David Griffith	Sarah Branson
Rachel Griffith	LeRoy Daingerfield	Jonathan Wright	Mary Smith Jr.
Eliz'h Walker	Ellis Pugh	David Lupton	Mary White
Richard Barrett	Jane Thompson	Mary Lupton	Mary Branson
Lydia Hackney	John Griffith	Wm. Abbott	Martha Hackney
Thos. Leright	Mary Griffith	Robert Daniel	Rees Branson
James Dillon	John Wright	Martha Daniel	Thomas White
George Brown	Susanna Wright	Rebecca Kerr	John White
Jane Dinsmore	John Griffith Jr.	Mary Hackney	George White
Sedney Fenton	Aaron H. Griffith	Mary Morgan	Jesse White
Hannah Adams			

WRIGHT—BROWN

Thomas Wright, of the County of Frederick and state of Virginia, Son of Jonathan Wright of the same place and Hannah his Wife, and *Esther Brown*, daughter of Isaac Brown of the County and State aforesaid and Sarah his Wife; 10th day of 4th month, 1811; at Upper Ridge.

Thomas Wright
Esther B. Wright

Witnesses who signed this Marriage Certificate:

Goldsmith Chandlee Jr.	Joel Oxley	Beulah Wright	Jonathan Wright
Joseph Neill	Rachel Neill	Ruth Wright	Isaac Brown
George Smith	Sinah Walker	Tace Wright	Rich'd Ridgwav
John Ball	Sarah Walker	Jane Beeson	Sarah Brown
Rachel Bond	Hannah Lupton	Caleb Brown	Hannah Wright
Robert Holloway	Rachel McClun	Margaret Swayne	Sam'l Brown
Samiel Wilson	John Bond	Juliet Beatty	Richard Wright
David Hollingsworth	Sarah Lupton	Evelina W. Buchanan	Joseph Lupton
Hannah Hollings- worth	Catherine Wilson	Sarah Buchanan	Mary Brown
Rachel H. Brown	David Lupton	Sarah Janney Jr.	Marg't Ridgway
Sarah N. Brown	Mary Lupton	Mary Thompson	David Brown
Richard Brown	Isaac Lupton	Phebe Chandlee	Sarah Wright
Cassandra Brown	Mary Adams	Jane B. McPherson	David Wright
Thomas Brown Junr.	Joseph Adams	Maria Parkins	Margaret Wright
Elizabeth Brown Jr.	Samuel Lupton	Sarah H. Parkins	
Rebecca Brown	David Pusey		
Elizabeth Brown			
Mary Brown			

MENDENHALL—JANNEY

James Mendenhall, of the County of Berkley in the State of Virginia (son of John Mendenhall and Martha his wife deceased), and *Ruth Janney* (daughter of Daniel McPherson and Mary his wife deceased); 15th day of 5th month, 1811; at Berkley.

> *James Mendenhall*
> *Ruth Mendenhall*

Witnesses who signed this Marriage Certificate:

Sarah White	John Cowgill	Jane Beeson	Edward Beeson
Susannah McPherson	Sam'l Swayne Jr.	Jane McPherson	Abel Walker
Rebecca Neill	David Wilson	Nathan Haines	Wm. McPherson
Lydia Neill	Robert V. Bond	Cosmelia Janney	John McPherson
Aquilla Janney	Thomas Wilson	Rebekah Naines	Aron Hibberd
Beulah Haines	Catherine Wilson	Isaac Walker	Daniel Hains
Rebecca Janney	Lucy Jones	Sam'l Howell	Nathan Haines Jr.
Mary Neill	Elizabeth Bond	Sam'l McPherson	Daniel Janney
David Howell	Courtencey S. Jones	Daniel McPherson	Sarah Janney
Nathan Howell	Catherine Cowgill	Phi'p Nadinbousch	Martha Hibberd
			Alice Cleaver

CHANDLEE—ALLEN

Goldsmith Chandlee, of the Borough of Winchester in the County of Frederick and State of Virginia, son of Benjamin and Mary Chandlee deceased of the county of Cecil and State of Maryland, and *Eunice Allen*, daughter of Edward and Hannah Rogers of the county of Frederick, and widow of Joseph Allen of the county of Shanandoah and state of Virginia; 12th day of 6th month, 1811; at a School-house near Smiths-Creek.

> *Goldsmith Chandlee*
> *Eunice Chandlee*

Witnesses who signed this Marriage Certificate:

William Steinbergen	Betty Allen	Betty Allen	Anna Hawkins
Alex'r Pollock	John McPherson	Thomas Allen	Sarah Walton
Christorpher Hickle	Phebe White	S. Walton	Mary Thompson
John Morgan	Samuel Lupton	Moses Allen	Atlantic Ocean
Alexander Doyle	Sarah Lupton	John Walton	Walton
Mary Pollock	Eliza Ann Beal	John Allen	Hannah Allen
Ann Moore	Betsy Ann Stein-	Rhesa Allen	Elizabeth Allen
Jacob Miller	bergen	James Pollock	Eunice Allen
George Hickle	Sally Hingeel	Edward Walton	Ruth Ozburn
Moses Walton	Elizabeth Walton	Wesley Allen	Patience Ozburn
	Samuel Hawkins		Phebe Walton

HIBBERD—BEESON

Benjamin Hibberd, son of Joseph Hibberd and Jane his Wife, and *Charity Beeson,* daughter of Edward Beeson and Jane his Wife of Berkley County, state of Virginia; 13th day of 11th month, 1811; at Middle Creek.

Benjamin Hibberd
Charity Hibberd

Witnesses who signed this Marriage Certificate:

Martha Ridgway	Jane M. Hibberd	Martha Hibberd	Joseph Hibberd
Jane Wickersham	Harriot B. Lyle	Jesse Beeson	Edward Beeson
Alice Cleaver	Nancy C. Miller	James Mendenhall	Jane Beeson
Rebecca Janney	Cath. Oferrall	Abel Walker	Jane Hibberd
Margaret Ridgway	Eliza Reed	Lydia Janney	Jane Hibberd Jr.
Elizabeth Walker	Eliz'h Holloway	Micajah Beeson	Sarah Hibberd
Jane B. McPherson	Wm. Campbell	Joshua Wood	Tacy Beeson
Isaac Walker	Robt. Lyle	William ————	Julia Graham
Mary Ridgway	John McDonald	Jane Downing	Ann S. Graham
Rachel Townsend	Raphael Conn	Jona. Wickersham	Jane B. Kerney
Edward Cleaver	Robert Miller	Edward Beeson	Aron Hibberd
	Ruth Mendenhall	Samuel Beeson	Jos. Hibberd Jr.

WILSON—WALKER

Thomas Wilson, of the county of Jefferson and State of Virginia, Son of Samuel Wilson and Catherine his Wife dec'd, and *Mary Walker,* daughter of Abel Walker of the County of Frederick and State aforesaid (and Mary his Wife dec'd); 12th day of 3rd month, 1812; at Hopewell.

Thomas Wilson
Mary Wilson

Witnesses who signed this Marriage Certificate:

Magnus Stribling	Phebe Cobourn	Mary Ridgway	Abel Walker
Richard Beckwith	Jane B. McPherson	Mary McCandless	Rebecca Littler
George Bruce Jur.	Sarah Walker	Mary Taylor	Sinah Townsend
Henry Parker	Sarah Walker Jur.	Phebe Steer	Sinah Walker
Lewis Neill	Rachel Townsend	David Brown	Elizabeth Walker
Rich'd Daingerfield	Tacy Beeson	James Mendenhall	David Wilson
Thomas Stribling	Ellen Lyles	Lewis Walker	Isaac Walker Jr.
Joel Brown	Kitty Wilson	Ruth Mendenhall	Robert Coburn
Isaac Nevitt	Edward Walker	Isaac Walker	John Cowgill
Jess Beeson	Hester Wright	Alice Cleaver	Rebecca Littler Jr.
Robert V. Bond	Sarah Janney	Rachel Neill	Mary Brown Junr.
Joseph Steer	Rachel Smith	John Wright	Elizabeth Littler
Margaret Ridgway	Mary B. Daingerfield	Susanna Wright	Margaret Stribling

WRIGHT—SMITH

Richard Wright, of Frederick County and State of Virginia, son of Jonathan and Hannah Wright, and *Rachel Smith*, daughter of Levi and Alice Smith (the latter deceased) of the County and State aforesaid; 16th of 4th month, 1812; at Hopewell.

Richard Wright
Rachel Wright

Witnesses who signed this Marriage Certificate:

Abel Walker	Charity Ridgway	Mary Griffith	Jonathan Wright
Abraham Branson	John Cowgill	Eliza S. Reed	Levi Smith
Joseph Neill	Rachel Neill	Mary T. Stribling	Hannah Wright
Strother Helm	James Steer	Marg't E. Alexander	Mary Smith
David Brown	Lydia Hackney	Elizabeth Littler	George Smith
Lewis Walker	Sarah Janney	John Griffith	Esther B. Wright
Sarah Walker	Eliza Littler	Mary White	Isaac Smith
Edward Walker	Marg't P. Stribling	Richard Ridgway	Thomas Wright
Mary Walker	Elizabeth Walker	John Wright	George Payne
Josiah Harding	Rachel Townsend	Cassandra Brown	David Ridgway
Wm. H. Harris	Mary Branson	Lydia Sidwell	Sarah Wright
Amos Mile	Valindia W.	David Wright	Rachel Payne
William Hickman	Magrudre	George Bruce Jr.	Martha Ridgway
George Harbart	Eliza Coates	Margaret Ridgway	Elizabeth Payne
Joseph Hackney	Ann Cowgill	Elizabeth Powell	Mary Payne
James Hamilton	Hannah Miles	Joseph Lupton	Hannah Payne
Rebecca Littler	Elizabeth Harris	Rachel Hamilton	Sarah D. Payne
John Powell	Margaret Harbert	Amy Strupe	Mary Smith
Maria Littler	Mary Ridgway	Margaret Wright	Joseph Smith
	Susanna Wright		Beulah Wright
			Ruth Wright

JOHNSON—GEORGE

Joshua Johnson, of Patapsco Upper Hundred in the county of Baltimore in Maryland, son of Joseph Johnson and Rachel his Wife, and *Lydia George*, of Dillens Run in the county of Hampshire in Virginia, daughter of Richard George and Mary his Wife; 15th day of 7th month, 1812; at Dillons Run.

Joshua Johnson
Lydia Johnson

Witnesses who signed this Marriage Certificate:

William Lupton	Sarah Lupton	Joshua Wood	Richard George
Evan Highett	Ambrose Taylor	William Horsman	Mary George
John Ward	Anne Taylor	Mercy Lupton	Lydia George
John Barrett	Elizabeth Lupton	Rebekah Lupton	Henry George
Joel Ward	Jesse Lupton	Amy Park	Ruth George
Jonathan Barrett	William Lupton	Lydia Horsman	Rachel George
Isaac Lupton	Jonathan Crumpton	Amos Park	Evan George
Mary Barrett			Ellis George
			James George
			Richard George

SMITH—WRIGHT

George Smith, of Frederick County and State of Virginia, son of Levi Smith and Alice his Wife (the latter deceased), and *Sally Wright*, daughter of Jonathan Wright and Hannah his Wife of the County and State aforesaid; 16th day of 9th month, 1812; at the Ridge Meeting House.

George Smith
Sally Smith

Witnesses who signed this Marriage Certificate:

Lewis Walker	Sarah Russell	David Lupton	Levi Smith
Samuel Lupton	Alice Flower	Mary Lupton	Jonathan Wright
Joseph Adams	Hannah Lupton	Isaac Brown	Hannah Wright
Mary Adams	Rachel Townsend	Sarah Brown	Richard Wright
Sarah Lupton	Cassandra Brown	Rachel Payne	Rachel Wright
John Wright	Rachel McClun	Margaret Ridgway	Thomas Wright
Susanna Wright	Amy Strupe	Sarah Griffith	Esther B. Wright
Ruth Wright	Martha Scarff	Henry Payne Jur.	Mary Smith
Sina Walker	Nicholas Scarff	Joseph Smith	Isaac Smith
Sarah Walker			Margaret Wright
			Tacy Wright
			Mary Smith
			Martha Ridgway

TAYLOR—NEILL

Abijah Taylor, of the County of Frederick and State of Virginia, son of Ambrose Taylor and Mary his Wife (the latter deceased), and *Mary Neill*, daughter of John and Ann Neill (the former deceased) of the County and State aforesaid; 11th day of 11th month, 1812; at Center.

Abijah Taylor
Mary Taylor

Witnesses who signed this Marriage Certificate:

Isaac Parkins	Dawson McCormick	Anne Taylor	Ambrose Taylor
Mary Parkins	Joseph Carter	Edith Taylor	Ann Neill
Hannah Hollingsworth	Amos Lupton	Frances Taylor	Lewis Neill
Thomas Smith	Joshua Lupton	Mordecai Taylor	Elizabeth Neill
Eunice Fawcett	Goldsmith Chandlee	Sarah A. Gibson	William Neill
Grace Parkins	Eunice Chandlee	Mary Thompson	Hannah Neill
Elizabeth Fawcett	Lydia Parkins	Hannah Thompson	Abraham Neill Jr.
Juliet Beatty	Sarah H. Parkins	Nancy Thompson	Ann Carter
Harriet Holliday	Eliza Holliday	John Carter	Rachel Carter
Nancy K. Slater	Abigail Parkins	Thomas Carter	Goldsmith Chandlee
		Mariah Carter	Jr.
			Phebe N. Chandlee

PIDGEON—WALKER

Isaac Pidgeon, of Frederick County and State of Virginia, son of William Pidgeon and Rachel his Wife (the latter Deceased), and *Elizabeth Walker,* daughter of Abel Walker and Mary his Wife (the latter Deceased) of the County and State aforesaid; 12th day of 11th month, 1812; at Hopewell.

Isaac Pidgeon
Elizabeth Pidgeon

Witnesses who signed this Marriage Certificate:

Rachel Neill	Abraham Branson	Eliza McAlester	Abel Walker
Jacob Rees	Sarah Branson	Sina Townsend	Edward Walker
Mary Rees	Robert Coburn	Rachel Townsend	Isaac Walker
John Cowgill	Phebe Coburn	Sina Walker	Susan Walker
Catherine Cowgill	John Wright	Jane B. McPherson	Mary Walker
Charles W. Littler	Mary Griffith	George Bruce Jur.	Mary Wilson
Mary White	Moses Coates	Isaac Pidgeon Jur.	Leah Steer
Rachel Chenowith	Hannah Coates	Lewis Walker	Sally Smith
William Branson	Eliza Coates	John McAlester	Rachel Wright
Ann White	Mary Ridgway	Charity Ridgway	Ann Warner
Frances Taylor	Mordecai Taylor		
Joseph Hackney			

SMITH—REES

Levi Smith, son of Joseph Smith and Rachel his Wife Deceased of Frederick County and State of Virginia, and *Mary Rees,* Daughter of David Rees and Martha his Wife Deceased of Berkeley County and State aforesaid; 13th day of 5th month, 1813; at Hopewell.

Levi Smith
Mary Smith

Witnesses who signed this Marriage Certificate:

Frances Taylor	Isaac Pidgeon	Abel Walker	Isaac Smith
Rachel Griffith	Elizabeth Pidgeon	Lewis Neill	Mary Smith
Mary White	Mary Brown	Rachel Neill	Jacob Rees
David Brown	Mary Ridgway	John Griffith	Ruth Rees
Abraham Branson	Margaret Ridgway	Mary Griffith	George Smith
Sarah Branson	Amy Strupe	Joseph Hackney	Sally Smith
Aaron Hackney	Wm. McPherson	Mordecai Taylor	Mary Smith Jur.
Hannah Hackney	Nathan Littler	Thomas Brown	Morris Rees
Lewis Walker	Benjamin Harris	Mary G. Barton	Richard Wright
Edward Walker	John Wright	Nancy Rippey	Jane Rees
Mary Walker	Sina Walker	Mary Malony	Jos. Hackney
Lydia Hackney	Mary T. Crawford	Ann Stribling	
Margaret Littler	Jane J. Harris	Maria Littler	

CATTELL—WRIGHT

David Cattell, Son of Jonas Cattell of Fayatt County, state of Pennsylvania, and Elizabeth his Wife, and *Margaret Wright*, daughter of Jonathan Wright of Frederick County, state of Virginia, and Hannah his Wife; 15th day of 9th month, 1813; at the Ridge Meeting House.

David Cattell
Margaret Cattell

Witnesses who signed this Marriage Certificate:

Isaac Brown	Isaac E. Steer	George Smith	Jonathan Wright
Sarah Brown	Leah Steer	Ruth Wright	Hannah Wright
Ruth Miller	Samuel Lupton	Tacy Wright	Ruth Horsman
Leah Barrett	Sarah Lupton	Beulah Wright	Richard Wright
Eliz'h Barrett	William Yeates Jr.	Richard Lupton	Rachel Wright
Lydia McClun	Rachel McClun	Marg't Ridgway	Thomas Wright
Nicholas Scarf	Jane B. McPherson	Phinehas Lupton	Esther B. Wright
David Lupton	Levi Smith	Cassandra Brown	Hannah Cattell
Lewis Walker	Mary Smith	Jane Beeson	David Wright
	Sina Walker	Mary Smith	Joseph Lupton
	Hannah Hackney	Mary Ridgway	Esther Lupton

LUPTON—BARRETT

William Lupton, son of Jese Lupton and Rebekah his wife of Hampshire County and State of Virginia, and *Mary Barrett*, daughter of John Barrett and Rhoda his wife of the same place; 13th day of 10th month, 1813; at Dillens Run Meeting House.

William Lupton
Mary Lupton

Witnesses who signed this Marriage Certificate:

Evan Hiet	James George	Richard George	Jese Lupton
David Shinn	Jonathan Pickering	Henry George	Rebekah Lupton
Jonathan Compton	Hannah George	Rachel George	John Barrett
John Ward	Evan George	Lydia Horner	Rhoda Barrett
Hannah Ward	Ellis George	Edith Lupton	Lydia George
Joel Ward	Thomas Allen	Margaret Lupton	Jonathan Barrett
John Fenton	Jacob Cannen	Ruth George	Lydia Horsman
George Myers	William F———	Leah Barrett	Rebekah Lupton
Absalom Yonally	Nathaniel Bett	Mary Barrett	Mercy Pickering
	Catherine Myers	Isaac Lupton	William Horsman
		Benj. Pickering	Thomas Barrett
			Richard Barrett

FAWCETT—BRANSON

Joseph Fawcett, son of Thomas Fawcett of Frederick County and State of Virginia and Martha his Wife, and *Mary Branson*, Daughter of Abraham Branson of the County and state aforesaid and Sarah his Wife; 21st day of 10th month, 1813; at Hopewell.

Joseph Fawcett
Mary Fawcett

Witnesses who signed this Marriage Certificate:

Jacob Rees	Elizabeth Pidgeon	Abel Walker	Thomas Fawcett
Ruth Rees	Ann Warner	John Griffith	Martha Fawcett
Amos Lupton	Hannah Hackney	Lewis Neill	Abraham Branson
John Lupton	Mary Griffith	Rachel Neill	Sarah Branson
Thomas P. Monroe	Ann White	Joseph Hackney	William Branson
Amos Pidgeon	Rachel Wright	Isaac Smith	Nathaniel Branson
Elizabeth Holloway	Sina Townsend	Lewis Walker	Isaac Branson
Philadelphia Holloway	Ann Brown	Isaiah Littler	Thomas Branson
Jane R. Beeson	Phebe Coburn	Nathan Parkins	Joseph Branson
Mary Ridgway	Margaret Ridgway	Isaac Pidgeon	Benjamin Branson
John Cowgill	Mary Thompson	Mordecai Taylor	Mary Fawcett
Edward Walker	Hannah Thompson	Frances Taylor	Eunice Fawcett
Rebecca Thomas	Goldsmith Chandlee	Thomas Ross	Thomas Fawcett
Thomas Brown Jur.	Phebe W. Chandlee	Marv Brown	Sarah Fawcett
		Joel Brown	John Fawcett
		Mary Brown Jur.	Josiah Fawcett
			Elizabeth Fawcett

BROWN—WOOD

David Brown, son of Thomas Brown and Mary his Wife, and *Esther Wood*, daughter of Joseph Wood and Ann his Wife in the County of Frederick and State of Virginia; 10th day of 11th month, 1813; at Center.

David Brown
Esther Brown

Witnesses who signed this Marriage Certificate:

Eliza McAlester	Evelina Ball	Mary B. Fawcett	Thomas Brown Sr.
Mary Brown	Goldsmith Chandlee	Isaac Brown	Mary Brown Sen.
Grace Parkins	Jr.	Sarah Hollingsworth	Joseph Wood
Lydia Parkins	John Lupton	Isaac Parkins	Ann Wood
Abigail Parkins	Ann Magill	Mary Parkins	Edward Brookes
Sarah H. Parkins	Amos Lupton	Isaac Wood	Joel Brown
John Fawcett	Hannah C. Dunbar	Mary Brown Jur.	Jesse Wood
Joshua Lupton	Samuel Swayne	Ann Antrim	Sarah Hollingsworth
Hannah Hollingsworth	Ambrose Vasse Jr.	Goldsmith Chandlee	Joshua Wood
Hannah Brown	Mary Vasse	Eunice Chandlee	Deborah Brown
Betsy Hollingsworth	Robert Coburn		
	Levi Smith		

HOLLINGSWORTH—PARKINS

Lewis Hollingsworth, of the County of Frederick and State of Virginia, Son of Robert and Susannah Hollingsworth (the former deceased), and *Abigail Parkins*, daughter of Isaac and Mary Parkins of the County and State aforesaid; 12th day of 1st month, 1814; at Center.

Lewis Hollingsworth
Abigail Hollingsworth

Witnesses who signed this Marriage Certificate:

Samuel Swayne	Solomon	Isaac Parkins
Margaret Swayne	Hollingsworth	Mary Parkins
Jonathan Wright	Amos Lupton	Hannah Hollingsworth
Samuel Lupton	Jonah Fawcett	Grace Parkins
Jonathan Smith	Thomas Fawcett	Mary Brown
Joshua Lupton	Thomas Fawcett	Rachel Mahaney
Isaac Hollingsworth	Hannah Hollingsworth	Elizabeth Neill
Jos. C. Baldwin	Mary Hollingsworth	Sarah H. Parkins
David Brown	Mary L. McCormick	Nathan Parkins
Joshua Wood	Betsy Hollingsworth	Lydia Parkins
Eliza McAlester	Mary Mahaney	Alfred Parkins
Eliza C. Baldwin	Sidney Sowers	Isaiah Littler
	Sally Vance	

THOMAS—HORSEMAN

Ezekiel Thomas, of Frederick County in the State of Virginia, Son of Evan Thomas of Rockingham County and state aforesaid and Rebecca his Wife, and *Ruth Horseman*, of Frederick County and state aforesaid; 13th day of 4th month, 1814; at Upper Ridge in the County of Frederick aforesaid.

Ezekiel Thomas
Ruth Thomas

Witnesses who signed this Marriage Certificate:

Edward Vasse	David Barrett	Mary Adams	Jonathan Wright
Robert Glass	Jonah Lupton	Sarah Russell	Hannah Wright
David Lupton	Isaac Adams	Ann Brown	Beulah Wright
Mary Lupton	Samuel Lupton	Rachel M'Clun	David Wright
Sarah Brown	Thomas Barrett	Lydia M'Clun	Ruth Wright
	Lewis Lupton	Sarah M'Clun	Tacy Wright
	David Lupton	Cassandra Brown	Amos Wright
	Joel Lupton	Sarah Ann Gantt	John Bond
	Phinehas Lupton	Mary S. H. Gantt	Sarah Lupton
	Ruth Adams	Mary Barrett	Joseph Lupton
	Rachel Mahaney	Leah Barrett	Esther Lupton
	Mary Likens	Elizabeth Likens	Hannah Thomas
	Richard Lupton	Margaret Lupton	Mary Thomas
			Isaac Thomas

GEORGE—GRIMES

Henry George, son of Richard George and Mary his Wife of Hampshire County and state of Virginia, and *Tamar Grimes*, daughter of Thomas Grimes and Rachel his Wife of same place; 14th day of 12th month, 1814; at Dillens Run Meeting House in Hampshire County and state aforesaid.

Henry George
Tamar George

Witnesses who signed this Marriage Certificate:

William Horseman	Wm. Lupton Jr.	Evan Hiett	Richard George
Lydia Horsman	Mary Lupton	John Ward	Mary George
Rebekah Lupton	Ellis Lupton	David Shinn	Thomas Grimes
Elizabeth Yonally	Mercy Pickering	Mary Rinehart	Rachel Grimes
George Bethel	Benj. Pickering	Abraham Rinehart	Lydia George
	Jonathan Barrett	Joel Ward	Evan George
		Samuel Lupton	Ellis George
		Sarah Lupton	Rachel George
		Thomas Allen	Richard George
		Amos Park	John George
		Evan Park	Tacy Grimes
		Isaac Lupton	Jesse Lupton
			James George

COFFEE—WARNER

William Coffee, of Belmont County, Ohio State, son of John Coffee and Rachel his wife of the same place, and *Anne Warner*, of Frederick County, Virginia, daughter of Croasdel Warner and Mary his wife of Hartford County, Maryland, Deceased; 12th day of 1st month, 1815; at Hopewell.

William Coffee
Anne Coffee

Witnesses who signed this Marriage Certificate:

Sina Townsend	Rachel Neill	Abel Walker	Isaac Pidgeon
William Pidgeon	Rebekah Littler	Abraham Branson	Elizabeth Pidgeon
Ambrose Vasse Jr.	Sarah Branson	Isaac Smith	Margaret Ridgway
Elisha Easton	Eliza Littler	Jacob Rees	Thomas Swayne
Edward Walker	Mary Brown	Lewis Walker	Ann Clendenon
Nathan Walker	Esther Brown	John Wright	Rachel Townsend
Moses Coates	Sarah Smith	Joseph Hackney	Hannah Townsend
Hannah Coates	Rachel Wright	Robert Coburn	Sina Walker
Rachel Pidgeon	Mary R. Smith	Mordecai Taylor	Sarah Walker
John Hiett	Ruth Rees	Frances Taylor	Mary Walker
Mary A. Ridgway	Martha Ross	Joel Brown	Lydia Walker
Isaac Wood	Sarah Wilken	John Fawcett	Mary Vasse

JACKSON—FENTON

Abel Jackson, son of Josiah Jackson, deceased, of Frederick County and State of Virginia and Ruth his wife, and *Rachel Wilkinson Fenton,* daughter of John Fenton of the County and State aforesaid and Ruth his wife; 11th day of 10th month, 1815; at a public Meeting at Backcreek in the County aforesaid.

Abel Jackson
Rachel W. Jackson

Witnesses who signed this Marriage Certificate:

James Robinson	David Lupton	Anne Darlington	John Fenton
Jonathan Jackson	Jonathan Pickering	William Brown	Ruth Fenton
J. J. Fenton	Joseph Fenton	Merdith Darlington	Ruth Jackson
John Gordon	Anne Taylor	Eleanor Pickering	Grace Jackson
Isaac Vanhorn	Ambrose Taylor	Gabriel H. Davis	Sidney Fenton
Aug. Green	David Barrett	Sarah Davis	Marg't Robinson
Dorcas Sexton	William Pickering	Martha Fenton	Benjamin Fenton
		Rebecca Barnett	Ann Fenton
		Betsy Doster	John Fenton
		Sarah Brown	Ruth Pickering
		Andrew A. Robinson	Priscilla Fenton

JANNEY—HAINES

Daniel Janney, of the County of Loudon and State of Virginia, son of Israel Janney of the County and State aforesaid and Anna his wife (deceased), and *Elizabeth A. Haines,* daughter of Nathan Haines of the County of Jefferson and State aforesaid and Mary his wife (deceased); 12th day of 6th month, 1816; at the Berkly Meeting House.

Daniel Janney
Elizabeth A. Janney

Witnesses who signed this Marriage Certificate:

Charles Jones	John McPherson Jr.	Israel Janney
Rebeckah Jolliffe	Samuel Howel	Nathan Haines
Hannah Coates	Mary Ann Janney	Ruth Mendenhall
Abraham Branson	Hugh Sidwell	James Mendenhall
Isaac Pidgeon	Mary Neill	Abel Walker
William Jolliffe	Sarah Walker	Mary Walker
Moses Coates	Nathan Howell	Jane McPherson
Pleasant Janney	Aqula Haines	Lydia N. Haines
David Howell	Abraham Haines	Thomasin Haines
Mary Haines	Jane McPherson Jr.	David Janney
Mary Neill	Lydia Neill	Elisha Janney
Sally Howell	John Haines	Nathan Haines Jr.
	John McPherson	William Janney
	Ruth Howell	Edward Walker

LUPTON—McCLUN

David Lupton, of Frederick County and State of Virginia, and *Rachel McClun*, of the same County and State; 13th day of 11th month, 1816; at the Ridge.

David Lupton
Rachel Lupton

Witnesses who signed this Marriage Certificate:

Isaac Brown	Mathew Rippey	Isaac Wilson	Joseph Lupton
Lewis Albott	James G. Barton	Margaret Lupton	Esther Lupton
Mahala Albott	David Wright	Joshua Lupton	Lydia McClun
Nancy C. Miller	Jonathan Wright	Lydia Lupton	Eliz. Mahony
Maria B. Miller	John Wright	Samuel Lupton	Nathan Lupton
Tacy Wright	Susanna Wright	Hannah McClun	Jonah Lupton
Cassandra Brown	John Bond	Sarah McClun	Isaac Lupton
Dilly Bryarly	Hanna Wright	Rachel Ann Hackney	Lewis Lupton
Hannah Bryerly	Ezekiel Thomas	Elizabeth McClun	John McPherson Jr.
Ruth Wright	Susan B. Compton	Robert McClun	John Mcpherson
Sarah Brown	Ann White	Jane Lupton	Ann Lupton
		Mary Lupton	Joel Lupton
		Hannah Lupton	Richard Lupton
			Phinehas Lupton

[David Lupton was a son of Joseph and Rachel Lupton, and this was his second marriage.]

FAWCETT—THOMPSON

Josiah Fawcett, of the County of Frederick and state of Virginia, Son of Thomas Fawcett and Sarah his wife (deceased), and *Ann Thompson*, Daughter of William Thompson and Mary his Wife (the former deceased); 12th day of second month, 1817; at Center.

Josiah Fawcett
Ann T. Fawcett

Witnesses who signed this Marriage Certificate:

Joshua Lupton	Grace Parkins	Ann Neill	Mary Thompson
Lydia Lupton	Susannah Fawcett	Phebe N. Chandlee	John Fawcett
Samuel Brown	Natn Parkins	Eliz. B. Fawcett	Goldsmh. Chandlee Jr.
Yardley Taylor	Hannah Brown	Abraham Branson	Goldsmh. Chandlee
Ann White	Elisha Fawcett	Sarah Branson	Eunice Chandlee
Amos Lupton	Lydia Fawcett	Ludia Parkins	

LUPTON—SIDWELL

Jonah Lupton, Son of David Lupton of Frederick County and state of Virginia and Mary his Wife, Deceased, and *Martha Ann Sidwell*, Daughter of Richard Sidwell and Charity his Wife of the same county and state both named afore; 14th day of 4th month, 1817; at Hopewell.

Jonah Lupton
Martha Ann Lupton

Witnesses who signed this Marriage Certificate:

Nathan Lupton	Margaret Lupton	David Lupton
Abel Walker	James Antrim	Martha Hackney
Eleanor Hackney	Aaron Hackney	Rachel Lupton
Mary R. Smith	Robert Daniel	Joseph Hackney Jr.
John Bond	Martha Daniel	Lydia Hackney
John Griffith	James Hackney	John Griffith Jr.
John Wright	John McCoole	Rachel Griffith
Susanna Wright	Joseph W. Hackney	Joseph Lupton
Benjamin Sidwell	Joel Lupton	Hugh Sidwell
Richard Sidwell	AAron H. Griffith	Esther Lupton
Levi Smith	Mary Griffith	Isaac Lupton
Jane Lynn	Charity Hackney	Lewis Lupton
	Mary Lynn	

HAINES—BEESON

Nathan Haines, son of Nathan Haines of the County of Jefferson in the state of Virginia and Mary his wife, and *Jane R. Beeson*, Daughter of Micajah Beeson of the County of Berkeley and the state afoersaid and Patience his wife; 24th day of 9th month, 1818; at Hopewell.

Nathan Haines
Jane R. Haines

Witnesses who signed this Marriage Certificate:

Wm. Hiett	Sinah Walker	Micajah Beeson
Jeremiah Coopers	Mary Joliffe	Patience Beeson
Edward Walker	David Ridgway	Nathan Haines
Thomas Wright	Sarah Smith	Mary Walker
Joseph Lupton	Lydia H. Haines	Hugh Sidwell
David Wright	Thamasin Haines	Wm. Jolliffe
Jonah Lupton	Martha Ridgway	Jos. Hackney
Edward S. Beeson	Sarah Branson	Wm. Hays
Richard Ridgway	Martha B. Clever	Levi Smith
Joseph Branson	Julian Ridgway	John Haines
Abel Walker	Tacy B. Ridgway	Thomas Brown
Daniel Walker	Ruth Wright	Robert Coburn
Nathan Walker	Tacy Wright	Isaac Pidgeon
Mary F. Ridgway	Lydia Walker	Benjamin Branson
Rebecca Jolliffe	Sally Ridgway	Abraham Branson
		Mary Hackney

SIDWELL—HAINES

Hugh Sidwell, son of Richard Sidwell of the County of Frederick and state of Virginia and Charity his wife, and *Thamasin Haines*, Daughter of Nathan Haines and Mary his wife of the County of Jefferson and State afforesaid; 10th day of 3rd month, 1819; at the Bercley meeting house.

Hugh Sidwell
Thamasin Sidwell

Witnesses who signed this Marriage Certificate:

Nathan Haines	Sally Howell	Jonah Lupton
Joseph Hackney	Jane R. Haines	Nathan Walker
John Haines	Martha A. Lupton	Israel Janney
William McPherson	Daniel Janney	David Howell
Edward Walker	John A. McPherson	Ruth Howell
Mary Walker	Nathan Howell	Elizabeth Haines
Susan McPherson	Elizabeth Janney	Sarah R. Beeson
Mary Haines	Lidia H. Hain:s	Nathan Haines Jr.
Robert Coburn	Hannah Coates	Isaac McPherson
Isaac Pidgeon	Elizabeth Pidgeon	James Antrim
Moses Coates	John Myers	William Jolliffe
		Rebecca Janney
		Lydia Walker
		Aquila J. Haines

LUKINS—THOMPSON

Peter Lukins, in the County of Frederick and State of Virginia, son of Jonathan and Lydia Lukens of County and State aforesaid, and *Hannah Thompson*, daughter of William and Mary Thompson (the former deceased); 10th day of 3rd month, 1819; at Center.

Peter Lukens
Hannah Lukens

Witnesses who signed this Marriage Certificate:

M. W. Brown	Eliz'h H. Thompson	Jonathan Lukens
O. M. Brown	Grace Parkins	Mary Thompson
S. A. E. Brown	John Lapher	Josiah Faucett
Margaret Swayne	Mary R. Brown	Joseph F. Lukens
Rebecca L. Sperry	John Lupton	Goldsmith Chandlee
Catherine Crockwell	Abigail Hollingsworth	Eunice Chandlee
Eliza. Campbell	Alfred Parkins	John Faucett
Amos Lupton	Sarah Anderson	Jesse Lukens
Sarah Lupton	Eliz'h A. Baker	Rachel Lukens
Joshua Lupton	Mary O. Anderson	Ann. T. Faucett
Joel Brown	George Brent	Lydia F. Brown
Benjamin Branson	Andw. Billmeyer	Thomas Brown Jr.
Joseph Branson	Elizabeth Anderson	Sarah Branson
Ann B. Fawcett	Mary Grove	Ann White
John Fawcett	Joseph Snapp Jr.	Mary Ann Thompson
Lydia T. Faucett	Abraham Branson	Martha Lukens
Elisha Fawcett	Elizabeth Brown	Hannah Brown
Samuel Brown	Eliz'h M. Brown	Jonathan Taylor Jr.
		Eliz'h B. Fawcett

SMITH—ROSS

Isaac Smith, son of William Smith and Hannah his Wife of Saliran County and State of Tennese, and *Martha Ross,* daughter of Enos Ross and Lydia his Wife (the latter deceased) of Frederick County and State of Virginia; 16th day of 9th month, 1819; at Hopewell.

Isaac Smith
Martha Smith

Witnesses who signed this Marriage Certificate:

Phebe Owen	Sarah Smith	Isaac Smith
Jos. Hackney	Margaret P. Stribling	Mary Smith
Lydia Hackney	Elizabeth B. Tate	Levi Smith
Rebecca Jolliffe	Mary Stribling	Mary R. Smith
Eleanor W. Hackney	Elizabeth Janney	Jos. T. Smith
Mary Griffith	Eliza W. Littler	Jane Thompson
Charity Hackney	Elizabeth Shreve	Elizabeth Scott
Chs. W. Littler	Esther Wright	Isaac Scott
Wm. Jolliffe	Lydia Walker	Mary Jolliffe
Josiah J. Fenton	Edward Walker	Sinah Walker
Jgs. P. McCandless	Jgs. P. Lyles	Jacob Rees
Thos. P. Cope	Jos. Branson	Jane Rees
Nathan Walker	Martha Lynn	Lydia Ross
Mary Walker	Aaron Hackney	Jane Rees Jr.
Alfred Ross	Aaron H. Griffith	Isaac Pidgeon
Joseph W. Hackney	Martha Ann Griffith	Josiah Faucett
		Lydia Brown
		Richard Sidwell

["Saliran County" is probably Sullivan County, Tenn., which was created in 1799.]

SHARP—BROWN

George Sharp, of Winchester in the County of Frederick in Virginia, Son of Samuel Sharp of Farquier County and Martha his Wife; and *Elizazeth Brown,* daughter of John Brown of Winchester and Elizabeth his Wife; 4th day of 10th month, 1820; at Winchester.

George Sharp
Elizabeth Sharp

Witnesses who signed this Marriage Certificate:

John Brown	Susan Bernt	Jeremiah Datson
Eliz. Brown	Mary C. Harry	Amos Lupton
Isaac Brown	Lydia H. Baker	Elisha Fawcett
Abm. Hollingsworth	J. B. Cooper	James Reeman
Joseph R. Coames	Cas. Litle	Lydia Lupton
Nathan Parkins	Elizh. Sperry	Josiah Fawcett
Jane C. Carr	Elizh. Carlile	Nathan John
N. W. Baker	Sidney S. Parkins	Jacob Cooper
Nancey A. Carr	Elizh. George	Mary C. Cooper
Frances Coalter	Jno. Coalter	Robert Coburn
Sarah Lupton	Jno. M. Bale	John Bell
Elizh. Coalter	Jesse Sharp	Isaac Parkins
Hanna Thomas	B. Carson	Mary Parkins
Rebecca Smith	E. H. Pendleton	Eunice Chandlee
Catherine Haas	Wm. L. Clark	John R. Pierpoint
William Thompson	Jas. Hackney	Phineas T. Sharp
Rebecca R. Brown	Wm. Sickles	Oliver M. Brown
Isaac Brown Jr.	Samuel Brown	Nancy Clark
Eliza Cookus	Mary M. Brown	Elizh. B. Fawcett
Sarah Brown	Betsy Hollingsworth	
	Nancy Brown	

STEER—BROWN

William B. Steer, of Loudon County and State of Virginia, son of Isaac Steer of the same County and state and Phebe his wife, and *Louesia Brown,* daughter of Divid Brown of Frederick County and state aforsaid and Mary his wife; 20th day of 3rd month, 1822; at Centre.

William B. Steer
Louesia Steer

Witnesses who signed this Marriage Certificate:

Ann Neill	Alfd. Parkins	Mary Brown
Harriet B. Holliday	William Clark	Isaac Parkins
Charles Litle	Amos Lupton	Mary Parkins
George Sharp	Sarah Lupton	Jonah Steer
John Janney	John Lupton	Rebecca R. Brown
Lewis Neill	Sarah Lupton	Ann M. How
Lewis Hollingsworth	Joshua Lupton	Mary R. Brown
Lewis Coale	Abraham Branson	Elizabeth Sharp
Thos. L. Mahaney	Sarah Branson	Franklin Brown
	Nathan Parkins	Lydia Parkins
	Eliza Parkins	Eliza Brown
	Elizabeth Neill	

TAYLOR—SIDWELL

Benjamin Taylor, of the County of Frederick and State of Virginia, son of Mordecai Taylor of the same county and state and Frances his wife, and *Rebecca Sidwell,* daughter of Samuel (dec'd) and Sarah Sidwell of the County and State aforesaid; 11th day of 4th month, 1822; at Hopewell.

Benjamin Taylor
Rebecca Taylor

Witnesses who signed this Marriage Certificate:

William Abbott	Jonah Lupton	Stephen Taylor
Thomas Barrett Jr.	Lewis Lupton	Jas. Hackney
Levi Cain	Joel Lupton	Lydia Hackney
Thomas Russell	Aaron H. Griffith	Abraham Branson
Wm. Jolliffe	Sarah Taylor	Mary A. Hackney
Mary Walker	Lydia Walker	Sarah Hackney
Rachel Griffith	Phebe Coburn	Benjamin Sidwell
Maria Taylor	John Griffith Jr.	Thomasin Sidwell
Mary Griffith	Deberah L. Morgan	Ann Sidwell
Rachel A. Mahaney	Charity S. Hackney	Mary Hackney
Martha Griffith	Mary R. Smith	Richard Sidwell
Eleanor W. Hackney	Levi Smith	Samuel S. Hackney
Robert Bond	Edward Walker	Jonathan Taylor
		Hugh Sidwell

LITLE—PARKINS

Charles Litle, of Winchester in the County of Frederick in Virginia, son of John and Hannah Litle (both Deceased), and *Lydia Parkins*, daughter of Isaac and Mary Parkins of the County and State aforsaid; 24th of 4th month, 1822; at Centre.

Charles Litle
Lydia P. Litle

Witnesses who signed this Marriage Certificate:

George Sharp	Harriet B. Holiday	Jos. V. Hollings-
A. C. Smith	Susan Strait	worth
Joshua Lupton	Evelina Strait	Nathan Parkins
Mary Brown	Robert Coburn	Lewis Hollingsworth
Wm. V. Star	Phebe Coburn	Lewis Neill
Edward Walker	Nancy Powell	Robert Litle
Louesia C. Holliday	Lucy Powell	Abdl. Hollingsworth
Eliza N. Brown	Milliunt McGuire	Susanna Boll
Mary P. Hol-	John Reed	Louesia Steer
lingsworth	E. B. Fawcett	Thos. S. Mahaney
Isabella Mahaney	Margaret Ransdell	Grace Parkins
Hannah P. Hol-	Wm. L. Clark	Eliza Parkins
lingsworth	Samuel H. Davis	Isaac Parkins
Eleanor Hollingsworth	Elisha Fawcett	Mary Parkins
Mary Brown		

LITTLER—RIDGWAY

Thomas Littler, of the County of Cleark in the state of Ohio, son of Nathan and Rebecca Littler, both now deceased, late of the County of Frederick in the state of Virginia, and *Mary Ridgway*, daughter of David and Martha Ridgway of the County of Frederick in the state of Virginia; 12th day of 9th month, 1822; at Hopewell.

Thomas Littler
Mary Littler

Witnesses who signed this Marriage Certificate:

J. P. McCandless	Martha Ridgway	David Ridgway
Thomas Stribling	Sally Smith	Martha Ridgway
Isaac Pidgeon	Algernon S. Ridgway	Tacy B. Ridgway
Edward Walker	Tacy Wright	Rebecca Littler
Nathan Walker	Margaret R. Wood	Richard Ridgway
John Jolliffe	Sally R. Beeson	Chs. W. Littler
Hannah Wilson	Margaret Clevenger	Micajah Beeson
Mary Walker	Lydia Walker	David Wright
Phebe Cabourn	Elizabeth Jolliffe	John Littler
Mary J. Brown	Mary Ann Kinlin	Amos Wright
Margaret Wood	Rachel Ann Littler	Thos. Wright
Rachel Ward	Sally Ridgway	Esther Wright
Sinah Walker	Nancy Littler	Juliann Ridgway
Sarah Walker	Joel Brown	Jane Beeson
Jos. Hackney	Henry S. Taylor	Hannah Coats
Robert Cabourn	Wm. Branson	
Moses Coats	John R. Pierpoint	
Wm. Jolliffe	James R. Coburn	

WRIGHT—GRIFFITH

David Wright, of Frederick County in the State of Virginia, son of Jonathan and Hannah Wright (the former deceased) of the County and State aforesaid, and *Mary Griffith*, daughter of John and Rachel Griffith of the same County and State; 12th day of 12th month, 1822; at Hopewell.

David Wright
Mary Wright

Witnesses who signed this Marriage Certificate:

Mary Walker	Rebecca Jolliffe	John Griffith
Rebecca Littler	Edward Walker	Rachel Griffith
Nancy Littler	John Lupton	Hannah Wright
Rachel Ann Littler	James G. Bell	Joseph Lupton
Mary Brown	Daniel Taggart	Jos. Hackney
Asa H. Hoge	Margaret R. Wood	Thos. Wright
Eliza Cowgill	Esther Lupton	David Ridgway
Martha R. Smith	Tacy Wright	Levi Cain
Israel Hoge	Martha A. Lupton	John Hiett
Michael S. Hansicker	Mary R. Smith	Wm. Maston
Thomas Roberts	Mary Samples	
Joel Lupton	Hannah Coates	
Nathan Walker	Robert Coburn	
Richard Lupton	James R. Coburn	
Joseph W. Branson	Isaac Pidgeon	
Josiah Fawcett		

THATCHER—THOMAS

Mark Thatcher, Son of Jonathan and Hannah Thatcher of Berkley County in the State of Virginia, and *Hannah Thomas*, Daughter of Ezekiel and Rebecca Thomas, the latter deceased, of Frederick County and State aforesaid; 16th day of 4th month, 1823; at the Upper Ridge Meeting House.

Mark Thatcher
Hannah Thatcher

Witnesses who signed this Marriage Certificate:

Joseph Lupton	Lewis Lupton	Jonathan Thatcher
Esther Lupton	William H. Brown	Hannah Thatcher
Jonah Lupton	Ruth Lupton	Ruth Thomas
Martha Ann Lupton	Mary A. Lupton	Thos. Wright
Abner Bond	Leah Bond	David Wright
Mary Kiter	Hannah Lupton	John Bond
Joseph W. Branson	Anna Janney	Sarah Lupton
Richard Lupton	Anthony Lee	Amos Wright
Ann Lupton	James M. Hibberd	Samuel Lupton
Rebecca Lupton	Tacy Wright	Esther Wright
Sarah E. Wright	Levi Cain	Nancy Thatcher
Margaret Swayne	Thomasin M. Lupton	Hannah Thatcher Jr.
Hannah Wright	Susanna Pierson	Mary Wright
Isaac Brown	Sarah Brown	Thos. Bryarly
Jacob Kiter	John George	Mary Lupton
Jane Lupton	Sally Williams	

COATS—PIDGEON

Aquila Coats, of the county of Frederic in the state of Virginia, son of John and Hannah Coats (the former deceased) of the county of Chester in the state of Pennsylvania, and *Rachel Pidgeon*, daughter of Isaac and Elizabeth Pidgeon (the latter deceased) of the county of Frederic in the state of Virginia; 15th day of 5th month, 1823; at Hopewell.

Aquila Coats
Rachel Coats

Witnesses who signed this Marriage Certificate:

Mary J. Brown	John R. Pierpoint	Isaac Pidgeon
David Brown	William Clark	Elizabeth Pidgeon
John Lock	John Wood	Moses Coats
Isaac Wood	Abel Walker	Hannah Coats
Joseph Caldwell	Israel Coburn Jr.	Mary Pidgeon
Isaac Smith Jr.	Robert Coburn	Lydia Walker
Isaac Smith	William Cowgill	Eliza Cowgill
Thos. Wright	Joseph W. Branson	Mary Pidgeon
Wm. Thomas	Daniel Walker	Elizabeth Baldwin
Wm. Watson	Lewis W. Jackson	Rachel Payne
Nathan Walker	Daniel Haines	Sarah Paul
Joseph W. Hackney	Mary Walker	Thamasin Walker
		Rebecca Walker

On page 191 of Hopewell Book 4, under date of 1-7-1823, the following minute is recorded:

"It appearing necessary that the marriages amongst us shall be certified to the County office in the county in which they are solemnized the clerk of the monthly meeting is appointed to give certificates of such as latterly have been and such as may be hereafter consumated in our meetings."

Prior to this period Friends' marriages were not, as a rule, entered upon the county records.

TATE—FENTON

William Tate, of Goose creek in the county of Loudon and state of Virginia, son of Levi and Edith Tate of the county and state aforesaid, and *Priscilla Fenton*, daughter of Benjamin and Ann Fenton of Frederick county and state aforesaid; 15th day of 10th month, 1823; at Upper Ridge.

William Tate
Priscilla Tate

Witnesses who signed this Marriage Certificate:

Jos. Hackney	Mary Lupton	Benjamin Fenton
Isaac Brown	Tacy Wright	Ann Fenton
Wm. H. Brown	Sarah Sexton	Sarah Tate
John Griffith Jr.	Stephen Taylor	Ann Tate
Joseph Lupton	Esther Lupton	Benjamin Fenton Jr.
Joshua Lupton	Ann Lupton	Jonathan Jackson
Thos. Bryarly	Martha Brown	Josiah J. Fenton
Lewis Lupton	Cassandra Brown	Enoch Fenton
Jonas Janney	Sally Smith	John Fenton
Jonah Lupton	Sarah Brown	Abel Jackson
Martha Ann Lupton	Sinah Walker	John Fenton
Samuel Swayne	David Wright	Hannah Wright
Beulah Wright	Mary Wright	Rachel Lupton
Sarah Lupton	Elizabeth Sexton	
Martha A. Griffith	Aaron H. Griffith	

SCHOOLEY—BROWN

Enoch Schooley, of Loudon County and State of Virginia, son of Reuben Schooley and Esther his wife (the latter decs'd) of the same place, and *Sarah Brown*, daughter of William Brown and Mary his wife (the latter decs'd) of Frederick County in the state aforesaid; 14th day of 4th month, 1824; at Back Creek.

Enoch Schooley
Sarah Schooley

Witnesses who signed this Marriage Certificate:

Margaret R. Wood	Mary Brown Jr.	William Brown
Mary Payton	Mary J. Brown	Josiah Brown
Sarah Taylor	Rachel W. Jackson	Eli. L. Schooley
Maria Taylor	John Fenton	Thomas Brown
Valentine Payton	Sarah Sexton	Hannah Brown
J. Hironimus	Margaret Sexton	Enoch Fenton
Jonathan Taylor	Julia A. Sexton	Caleb J. Brown
Banjamin F. Davis	Charles Sexton	John Schooley
Rachel Gorden	Eliza. Hironimus	Esther Lupton
Joseph Lupton	Dorcas Sexton	Ruth Fenton
Stephen Taylor	Mary D. Mitchell	
Jos. Hackney		

GEORGE—BOND

Evan George, of the County of Hampshire and State of Virginia, son of Richard and Mary George (the former Deceased) of the same county and state, and *Hannah Bond*, Daughter of John and Rachel Bond of the county of Frederick and state aforesaid; 12th day of 1st month, 1825; at Upper Ridge.

Evan George
Hannah George

Witnesses who signed this Marriage Certificate:

David Barrett	Ann Lupton	Mary Barrett	John Bond
John George	Jane C. Brown	Mary Lupton	Rachel Bond
Isaac Thomas	Sarah A. Swayne	Rebecca N. Lupton	Leah Bond
Joel George	Mary Thomas	Rachel Lupton	Samuel Lupton
Jos. W. Branson	Ann Lupton	Ruth Lupton	Rachel George
Sarah Bond	Mary Ann Lupton	Anna Janney	Abner Bond
Martha Brown	Hannah W. Lupton	Sarah N. Brown	Thos. Bryarly
Tacy Wright	Wm. H. Brown	Maria George	Mary Beal
Jonah Lupton	David Wright	Leah Barrett	Sarah Brown
Lewis Lupton	Joseph Adams	Sarah George	Samuel Swayne
Thomas Barrett	Josiah J. Fenton	Jane Lupton	Joel Lupton
	Thos. Barrett Jr.	Rachel Lupton	
	Joseph Lupton	Martha A. Lupton	
	Hannah Wright	Cassandra Brown	

On page 231 of Hopewell Book 5, under date of 10-3-1825, appears the following minute:

"Centre Preparative proposes for the consideration of this meeting the propriety of having the discipline so changed that marriages may be allowed to be accomplished at friends' homes, instead of being at public meetings."

GEORGE—BARRETT

James George, of Hampshire County and state of Virginia, son of Ellis and Lydia George (both deceased) of the same place, and *Mary Barrett*, daughter of Thomas and Elizabeth Barrett of Frederick County and state aforesaid; 13th day of 4th month, 1825; at Upper Ridge.

James George
Mary George

Witnesses who signed this Marriage Certificate:

Isaac Brown	Wm. H. Brown	Thomas Barrett
Samuel Lupton	Nathan Lupton	Elizabeth Barrett
Sarah Brown	Jonah Lupton	John Barrett
Ruth Thomas	Lewis Lupton	Lewis George
Hannah Wright	Joel Lupton	Jonathan Barrett
Lydia McClun	Evan George	Thomas Barrett Jr.
Sarah N. Brown	James M. Glass	Leah Barrett
Joseph Lupton	Richard Lupton	Eleanor Barrett
Esther Lupton	David Lupton	Rebecca George
Beulah Wright	Mary Lupton	Lydia Horner
Mary Wright	Martha A. Lupton	Martha Brown
Rachel Lupton	Samuel Swayne	Margaret Swayne
Tacy Wright	Peter Thomas	
Martha A. Griffith	John Griffith Jr.	
Hannah Ross	John Bond	
Elizabeth Jolliffe		

FAWCETT—TAYLOR

Josiah Fawcett, of Winchester in the county of Frederick in Virginia, son of Thomas and Sarah Fawcett (both deceased), and *Sarah Taylor*, daughter of Stephen and Mary Taylor (the latter deceased) of the county and state aforesaid; 22nd day of 3rd month, 1826; at Back Creek.

Josiah Fawcett
Sarah T. Fawcett

Witnesses who signed this Marriage Certificate:

Isaac Lamborn	Lewis Fisher	Mary Thompson
Josiah Jackson	Thomas E. Dent	Lydia Brown
Benj'n Fenton	Isaac Smith	Maria Taylor
John Fenton	Thomas Brown	Stephen Taylor
Thomas Fisher	Hannah Ross	Ezra Taylor
Andrew Robinson	Eliz'h M. Thompson	Elisha Fawcett
William Brown	Ann Chandlee	Joseph Branson
John Rogers	Asa H. Hoge	Israel Hoge
John Davis	Ruth Fenton	Joseph Darlington
Grace Mitchell	Ann Fenton	
Margaret Davis	E. A. Mitchell	
Eleanor Darlington	Wm. Campbell	

PIGEON—HOLLINGSWORTH

Isaac Pigeon, of Frederick county in the State of Virginia, son of William and Rachel Pigeon late of Belmont County, state of Ohio (now deceased), and *Sarah Hollingsworth*, Daughter of Thomas and Mary Brown late of Frederick county, state of Virginia (now deceased); 17th day of 8th month, 1826; at Hopewell.

Isaac Pidgeon
Sarah Pidgeon

Witnesses who signed this Marriage Certificate:

Jos Hackney	Phebe Cobourn	David Brown
Isaac Smith Jr.	Eliza Cowgill	Joel Brown
Aaron Hackney	Abel Walker	Wm. H. Brown
Isaac B. Beale	Margaret Wood	Abraham Branson
Thamasin Sidwell	Rebecca Brown	Sarah Branson
Sally Smith	Sarah N. Brown	Esther Wright
Ann C. McCandless	Mary Thompson	Mary Brown
Sinah Ann Newton	Elizabeth Sharp	Hannah Brown
Elizabeth Jolliffe	James R. Cobourn	Edward W. Pidgeon
Eliz'h Scholfield	Lydia Walker	Caleb S. Brown
Hannah Ross	Rebecca H. Walker	Thomas Brown
Thamasin H. Walker	Isaac Lamborn	Joseph W. Branson
Israel Hoge	John J. Higgins	Nathan Walker
Thos. Wright	Rebecca W. Brown	Lydia Brown
Daniel Walker	John R. Pierpoint	Cath. K. Hol-
John Hodgson	Mary L. Brown	lingsworth
Mary Walker	Sarah E. Wright	Abraham
Edward Walker		Hollingsworth
Wm. Jolliffe		Elizabeth M.
Rebecca Jolliffe		Thompson
		Levi Smith

SMITH—HACKNEY

Levi Smith, of the county of Frederick and State of Virginia, son of Joseph and Rachel Smith deceased, and *Mary Hackney,* daughter of Joseph and Martha Hackney (the former deceased) of the county and state aforesaid; 21st day of 9th month, 1826; at Hopewell.

Levi Smith

Mary H. Smith

Witnesses who signed this Marriage Certificate:

Sarah Smith	Isaac Smith	Aaron Hackney
Martha Daniel	Edward Walker	Jos. Hackney
Thamasin Sidwell	Robt. Daniel	Rachel Griffith
Jos. W. Hackney	[of Andrew]	John Griffith Jr.
Mary Ann Hackney	Benj'n Tanquary	Susanna Wright
	David Wright	
	Ruth Rees	

Joseph H. Daniel	L. B. Gardener
Andrew Daniel	J. F. Dangerfield
Hannah W. Smith	John Jolliffe Jr.
Mahlon Scholfield	Lewis Scholfield
Robert Bond	Isaac B. Beale
James W. Trimble	Morgan Morgan
Ezra Taylor	Alfred Ross
Mary Wright	Thomas Wright
Eleanor W. Hackney	Martha Smith
Aaron H. Griffith	Martha Ann Griffith
James H. Griffith	Ann Scholfield
Aaron H. Hackney	Mary Walker
Martha Morgan	Thomas Barrett
Elizabeth F. Heterick	Isaac Smith Jr.
Martha C. Heterick	Hannah Ross
Ann C. McCandless	Rebecca M. Lupton
Esther Wright	Jane Rees
Lydia Walker	Rachel Smith
Lavenia Jolliffe	Joseph T. Smith
Rebecca H. Walker	Jess Wright Jr.
Thamasin H. Walker	Jonah Lupton
Deborah L. Morgan	Mary S. Hackney
Lydia Ross	Lydia Hackney
Harriet Hackney	
Mary Ann Daniel	

JANNEY—HAINES

Asa M. Janney, of Loudon County in the State of Virginia, son of Abijah Janney of Alexandria in the District of Columbia and Jane his wife deceased, and *Lydia N. Haines*, daughter of Nathan Haines deceased of Jefferson County Virginia and Mary his wife also deceased; 12th day of 10th month, 1826; at Hopewell.

Asa M. Janney
Lydia N. Janney

Witnesses who signed this Marriage Certificate:

John Griffith	Edward Walker	Daniel Janney
Aaron Hackney	Mary Walker	Sam'l M. Janney
Levi Smith	Thomasin Sidwell	Hetty Ficklin
Jane R. Haines	Thirza Wood	Ann Scholfield
Nathan F. Walker	Jos. Hackney	Ann M. Caldwell
Lydia Walker	Robt. Sanford	Ann C. McCandless
Nathan Haines	Jos. R. Richards	Levenia Jolliffe
Daniel H. Walker	Abraham Branson	Sam'l Janney
Mary Lupton	Isaac Lamborn	Lewis W. Jackson
Elizabeth Jolliffe	Isaac Smith Jr.	Eliza Cowgill
John J. Higgins	Edward S. Beeson	Hannah Coates
Elizabeth Scholfield	Lewis Scholfield	Richard R. Lupton
Martha Ridgway	Sam'l McPherson	Wm. Jolliffe
Maria R. Branson	Samuel Haines	Thomas Russell
Rebecca M. Lupton	Sally Ridgway	Eliza E. Russell
Jane J. Lupton	Hannah M. Janney	Hugh Sidwell
Ruth Lupton	Tamzin Janney	Hannah W. Lupton
Rachel Lupton	Thamasin H. Walker	Thomas M. Bond
Abel Walker	Rebecca H. Walker	
Joseph W. Branson	Sarah Howell	
	John Jolliffe Jr.	

TRIMBLE—HACKNEY

James W. Trimble, of the county of Frederick, state of Virginia, son of Elisha and Ann Trimble of Ceocil County, state of Maryland, and *Mary Ann Hackney*, daughter of Joseph and Lydia Hackney of Frederick county, state of Virginia; 14th day of 12th month, 1826; at Hopewell.

James W. Trimble
Mary Ann Trimble

Witnesses who signed this Marriage Certificate:

Martha Ridgway	Mary Walker	Jos. Hackney
Hannah Ridgway	Eliza Cowgill	Aaron Hackney
Maria N. Curl	Martha Smith	John Griffith Jr.
Rebecca Mc. Lupton	Ann C. McCandless	Rachel Griffith
Thurza M. Wood	Levenia Jolliffe	Deborah L Morgan
Sally Ridgway	Rebecca H. Walker	Richard Sidwell
Aaron H. Griffith	Wm. Jolliffe	Martha Ann Griffith
David Wright	Isaac Pidgeon	Mary C. Henshaw
Joseph P. Wood	Robert P. McCandless	Charity S. Hackney
Edward S. Beeson	George Hiett	Wm. Janney
Richard Ridgway	Joseph W. Branson	H'h Sidwell
David Barrett	Abel Walker	Rachel Ann Kerr
Joseph Hackney	Lewis Scholfield	Robt. Sanford Jr.
Jos. H. Daniel	John W. Chenworth	Jesse Wright
William D. Kerr	Daniel H. Walker	Thomas Trimble
Jos. W. Hackney	Nathan Walker	Robt. Daniel
Joseph Lynn	Isaac B. Beale	[of Andrew]
Robert Bond	Israel Hoge	William Dillon
Andrew Daniel	James Hackney	Sarah Hackney
	Martha Ann Lupton	Harriet Hackney
		Mary Ann Daniel
		Gabriel C. Harris

BRANSON—WRIGHT

Joseph Branson, of Hopewell in the county of Frederick and state of Virginia, son of Abraham and Sarah Branson of the same place, and *Tacy Wright*, daughter of Jonathan and Hannah Wright (the former deceased) of the county and state aforsaid; 11th day of 4th month, 1827; at Upper Ridge.

Joseph W. Branson
Tacy Branson

Witnesses who signed this Marriage Certificate:

Cassandra Brown	Jos. W. Hackney	Abraham Branson
Lydia Brown	Evan George	Sarah Branson
Isaac Brown	James Ridd	Hannah Wright
Mary Brown	Wm. G. Thompson	Esther Lupton
Sarah Ann Lupton	AAran H. Griffith	Elisha Fawcett
Sarah Brown	Daniel H. Walker	Sally Smith
Ann Lupton	Edward S. Beeson	David Wright
Lydia McClun	Nathan Lupton	Levi Smith
Lydia Walker	John Griffith Jr.	William Branson
Rebecca H. Walker	Rachel Griffith	Abner Bond
Deborah L. Morgan	Richard Ridgway	Thomas Brown
Maria Branson	Wm. H. Brown	Asa H. Hoge
Eliz'h M. Thompson	Jos. H. Griffith	Jane Lupton
Martha Lukens	David Lupton	Ruth Lupton
Isaac Lamborn	Jonathan W. Lupton	Mary Thomas
Sally Ridgway	Jonathan G. Smith	Sarah Bond
Wm. P. Branson	Abel Walker	Ann Lupton
Lewis Lupton	Rebecca M. Lupton	Tacy B. Ridgway
Richard R. Lupton	Benjamin Fenton	Thamasin Mary Lupton
Hannah W. Lupton	Leah Bond	John Bond
Thamasin H. Walker	Rachel Lupton	
Isreal Hoge	Micajah Beeson	
Enoch Fenton	Jonah Lupton	
Narina Wickersham	Martha Ann Lupton	
S. Emeline Wright		

SMITH—ROSS

Joseph T. Smith, of the county of Frederick and state of Virginia, son of William and Hannah Smith of the county of Washington and state of Tenessee, and *Hannah Ross*, of the county of Frederick of state of Virginia, daughter of Enos and Lydia Ross (the Latter dec'd) late of the county and state aforesaid; 11th day of 10th month, 1827; at Hopewell.

Joseph T. Smith
Hannah R. Smith

Witnesses who signed this Marriage Certificate:

Ann C. McCandless	Eliza Cowgill	Phebe Butcher
Elizabeth Jolliffe	Sarah Smith	Ruth Rees
Levenia Jolliffe	Levi Smith	Mary Smith
William Jolliffe Jr.	Isaac Smith	Joseph W. Hackney
Jos. Hackney	Martha C. Heterick	Jane C. Brown
Meredith Jolliffe	John Griffith Jr.	Lydia Ross
Thos Stribling	Isaac Pidgeon	Charity S. Hackney
Abel Walker	Isaac B. Beall	Eleanor W. Hackney
Joseph Walker	Daniel Walker	Martha Brown
Joseph Branson	Eliz'h H. Heterick	Lewis Scholfield
Nathan Walker	Ann Scholfield	Andrew Hyatt
Henry A. Byrne	Martha Ann Griffith	Jacob R. Nicklin
Isaac Smith Jr.	Deborah L. Morgan	Jonathan Butcher jr.
Alfred Ross	Sarah N. Brown	James Hackney
Enos Ross	Cassandra Brown	Thomas Wright
	Ellis Rees	
	Tacy Branson	
	Samuel Hackney	
	Zepheniah Silvers	

WALKER—LUPTON

Abel Walker, of the County of Frederick in the state of Virginia, son of Edward and Mary Walker of the same county and state, and *Hannah W. Lupton*, daughter of Joseph and Esther Lupton (the former deceased) of the county and state aforesaid; 16th day of 4th month, 1828; at Upper Ridge.

Abel Walker
Hannah W. Walker

Witnesses who signed this Marriage Certificate:

Esther Lupton	Daniel Janney	Edward Walker
Sarah Ann Brown	Thos Wright	Mary Walker
Daniel H. Walker	Nathan Haines	Levi Smith
Hugh Sidwell	Nathan Walker	John Bond
Lydia Walker	Asa M. Janney	Lewis W. Jackson
Mary H. Smith	David Lupton	Anna Lupton
Deborah L. Morgan	Israel Hoges	Rachel Lupton
Rebecca McLupton	Abraham Branson	Martha Ann Lupton
Martha Ann Griffith	Enoch Fenton	Thamazin Mary
David Wright	Asa H. Hoge	Lupton
Rebecca H. Walker	Joseph H. Griffith	Jonah Lupton
Thamasin H. Walker	Mary Wright	Isaac Brown
Maria R. Branson	Elizabeth Bryarly	Leah Bond
Richard R. Lupton	Clarissa H. Baker	Joseph L. Jackson
Mary Lupton	Isaac B. Thomas	Jonathan W. Lupton
Ruth Lupton	Rachel Lupton	James Marrow
Jane Lupton	Thomas Bryarly	Evan George
Nathan Lupton	Mary Lupton	Wm. H. Brown
Abner Bond	Emeline Wright	Elisha H. Jordan
	Eliz'h L. Bryarly	Willys Buele
	Ann Lupton	Robt. L. Baker
		Stevn Baker
		B. Bushnell
		Thomas Clark
		Isaac B. Swayne

GEORGE—BOND

John George, of the County of Hampshire in the state of Virginia, son of Richard and Mary George of the same County and state, and *Leah Bond,* daughter of John and Rachel Bond of Frederick County and state aforesaid; 24th day of 12th month, 1828; at Upper-Ridge.

John George
Leah George

Witnesses who signed this Marriage Certificate:

Isaac Brown	Martha Ann Lupton	John Bond
Lewis Lupton	Jane Lupton	Rachel Bond
Joel Lupton	Rebecca Mc Lupton	Abner Bond
Isaac B. Swayne	Cassandra Brown	Sarah E. Wright
David Wright	Hannah Barrett	Rebecca Brown
Enoch Fenton	Hannah McClun	Jonathan W. Lupton
Richard R. Lupton	Eliza Brown	Isaac B. Thomas
G. M. Bryarly	Rachel Lupton	Thomas Barrett
Asa Allen	Wm. H. Brown	Martha Brown
Betty Allen	David B. Barrett	Esther Lupton
Thomas N. Wood	Thomas Barrett Jr.	Tho's Wright
Lydia McClun	Nathan Lupton	Mary George
Hannah George	James Allen	Sarah George
	Evan George	

THOMAS—LUPTON

Isaac B. Thomas, of Frederick County in the state of Virginia, Son of Ezekiel and Rebecca Thomas (both deceased), and *Jane Lupton,* daughter of Isaac and Tamson Lupton (both deceased); 14th day of 4th month, 1830; at Upper Ridge.

Isaac B. Thomas
Jane Thomas

Witnesses who signed this Marriage Certificate:

Ann Lupton	Esther Lupton	Hannah W. Walker
Rachel Lupton	Rebecca H. Walker	Mary Ann Lupton
John McPherson	Rebecca Mc Lupton	Eliz'h L. G. Bryarly
Isaac Brown	Thamasin H. Walker	Margaret Bond
Sarah Brown	Hannah Wright	Abner Bond
Nathan Lupton	Thomas Wright	Sarah Bond
Richard R. Lupton	Mary Lupton	Ann Lupton
Lewis Lupton	Jane R. Lupton	John McLupton
Stevn Baker	Mary D. Lupton	John Davis
Lewis W. Jackson	Thos. Bryarly	Joel Lupton
Willys Buell	Lydia Walker	Enoch Fenton
Robert L. Baker	Elizabeth Bryarly	Asa H. Hoge
Isaac B. Swayne	Caroline E. Baker	Abel Walker
David B. Barrett	Clarissa H. Baker	Jonathan Lupton
Jonah Lupton	Ruth Lupton	Daniel H. Walker
Martha Ann Lupton	Thamasin Mary Lupton	Nathan Walker

SUPPLEMENTARY MARRIAGE LIST

Marriages taken from the Hopewell minutes, and not recorded in the marriage record book.

The dates indicate the times that the marriages were reported to the meeting by the committee, except in those instances when certificates were requested. All the grooms named herein were members of Hopewell.

Day	Mo.	Year	
22	10	1759	Benjamin Thornburg and Mary Brooks
24	12	1759	David Brooks asks for a certificate to Cedar Creek in order to marry Sarah Sanders
5	1	1761	David Rees and Elizabeth Babb
1	6	1761	Richard Ridgeway and Charity Beeson
6	7	1761	William Neall and Mary Frost
3	5	1762	James Ballinger and Lydia Taylor
5	8	1763	William Rees and Charity Dillon Ebenezer Walker and Mary married by an hireling teacher and after being dealt with were retained as members when their acknowledgement was read at the Monthly Meeting 6-5-1771
2	3	1772	William McPherson to marry Jean Chamberlin of Sadsbury Mo. Mtg.
2	11	1772	Thomas Ellis and Margaret Reese
3	3	1777	Isaac Brown was given a certificate to Pipe Creek in order to marry Sarah Ballinger
3	3	1777	John Thomas and Alice his wife gave satisfaction (for being married by an hireling teacher)
6	1	1778	Jonah Hollingsworth was given a certificate to Pipe Creek in order to marry Hannah Miller
1	6	1778	Jacob Pickering and Mary Dillons
5	4	1779	Owen Long and Charity Thornburg
7	2	1780	Jonathan Ross and Martha Brown
2	10	1780	Owen Rogers was given a certificate to Fairfax in order to marry Mary Roach
5	11	1780	Walter Denny and Jane Pugh
5	1	1784	Henry Mills was given a certificate to Monallen in order to marry Elizabeth John

Day	Mo.	Year	
2	2	1784	Nathaniel White Jr. was granted a certificate to Goshan Mo. Mtg. in order to marry Phebe Smeedly
1	3	1784	Robert Faulkner was granted a certificate to Crooked Run in order to marry Elizabeth Painter
30	11	1786	Israel Hogge and Ruth Jinkens—by hireling teacher
5	3	1787	Abijah Richard was given a certificate to Goose Creek in order to marry Esther Daniel
1	12	1794	Joseph Bond and Elizabeth Moore of Fairfax Mo. Mtg.
1	9	1800	James Wright—certificate to Crooked Run for marriage with Hannah Pickering
3	5	1802	Isaac Walker to Radnor Mo. Mtg. to marry Mary Rankin
5	9	1803	Daniel McPherson requests a certificate for marriage to Elizabeth Grubb, a member of Wilmington Mo. Mtg.
2	12	1805	Samuel Brown to Hannah Matthews of Baltimore Mo. Mtg.
7	11	1808	David Ross—certificate to Fairfax to marry Mary Janney

CERTIFICATES TO MARRY GIVEN AT HOPEWELL
(1811-1851)
From Book 4

Day	Mo.	Year	
5	3	1812	Isaac Walker to Susanna Talbert of Fairfax Mo. Mtg.
7	1	1819	Elisha Fawcett to Lydia Taylor of Goose Creek Mo. Mtg.
4	8	1825	Richard R. Lupton to Anna Janney of Alexandria Mo. Mtg.
5	1	1826	Amos Lupton to Hannah Janney of Goose Creek Mo. Mtg.
6	3	1827	James N. Hibbard to Mary Nixon of Waynsville, Ohio
10	4	1828	David Howell to Hannah N. Janney of Alexandria Mo. Mtg.
7	5	1829	Elisha Fawcett to Rebecca Janney of Goose Creek Mo. Mtg.

CROOKED RUN MARRIAGE CERTIFICATES
1783-1803
As Recorded in Book A
JONA LUPTON, *Clerk*

SAUNDERS—PANCOAST

WHEREAS, *John Saunders* of the Town of Alexandria and County of Fairfax in Virginia, Son of Joseph & Hannah Saunders of the City of Philadelphia in Pennsylvania, and *Mary Pancoast*, Daughter of David and Sarah Pancoast of the Borough of Winchester, & County of Frederick in Virginia, Having declared their intentions of Marriage before Several Monthly Meetings of the People Called Quakers at Crooked Run in the County of Frederick afforesaid, According to the good order used Amongst them: And having consent of Parents, Their said Proposals of Marriage was allowed of by the said Meeting:

NOW these are to Certifie whom it may concern, that for the full Accomplishing their said Intentions this Ninth day of the fourth Month in the Year of our Lord one Thousand Seven Hundred and Eighty Three; They the Said John Saunders & Mary Pancoast appeared in a Publick Meeting of the said people at Center in the County of Frederick afforesaid. And the said John Saunders, takeing the said Mary Pancoast by the hand did in a Solemn manner openly declare: That he took her the said Mary Pancoast to be his Wife Promising Through divine Assistance to be unto her a loving and faithful Husband untill death Should Separate them. And then and there in the Same Assembly, the Said Mary Pancoast did in like manner, declare that she took him the said John Saunders to be her Husband, Promissing Through divine Assistance to be unto him a loving and faithful Wife untill death should Separate them. AND MOREOVER They the said John Saunders and Mary Pancoast (She According to the custom of Marriage assumeing the Name of her Husband) as a further Confirmation theirof did then and There to these Presents set their hands; And we whose names are here under also Subscribed being Present at the Solemnization of the said Marriage & Subscription, have as Witnesses thereunto set our hands The day and Year above Written.

John Saunders
Mary Saunders

Joseph Lupton	Henry Bush	Gold Chandlee	David Pancoast
John Lupton	Ellis Chandlee	Susanna Brown	Sarah Pancoast
Daniel Brown	Isaac Parkins	Sally Brown	Elisabeth Pancoast
Daniel Brown Sr.	Jane Brock	John Brock	Mary Lownes
Sam'l Pickering	Ann Parkins	David Brown	Sally Lownes
Joseph Steer	Catharine Bush	George Ormand	Sarah Lownes
Mary Lupton	Amy Long	Jona Pickering	Rachel Hollingsworth
Grace Steer Junr.	Leah Parkins	James Wright	Susanna Brown
Catharine Sexton	Meshec Sexton	Joshua Lupton	Sarah Brown

FAWCCETT—BRANSON

WHEREAS *Thomas Fawccett* son of John and Rebeekah Fawccett of Frederick County in Virginia and *Sarah Branson* of the County afforesaid Daughter of William Branson (and Elisabeth his wife deceased) of Stafford County in Virginia having declared their intentions of Marriage with each other before several Monthly Meetings of the people called Quakers at Crooked Run in the County afforesaid According to the good order used amongst them. And nothing appearing to Obstruct their further Proceedings. Therefore they are left to their liberty to Consummate their said intentions according to Discipline.

NOW These are to Certifie all whome it may concern that for the full accomplishment of their said intentions this Eighth Day of the Tenth Month in the Year of our Lord one Thousand Seven hundred and Eighty Three. They the Said Thomas Fawccett and Sarah Branson appeared in a Publick Meeting of the people called Quakers at Crooked Run Meeting House. And the said Thomas Fawccett, taking the said Sarah Branson by the hand did in a Solemn manner openly declare that he took her to be his Wife. promising through divine assistance to be unto her a loving & faithful Husband untill death separate them or words to that that purport. And then & there she the said Sarah Branson did in like manner openly declare that she took the said Thomas Fawccett to be her Husband promising through divine assistance to be unto him a loving & Faithful Wife untill death separate them or words to that purport. AND MOREOVER The said Thomas Fawccett & Sarah Branson (she according to the Custom of Marriage assumeing the Name of the husband) as a further confirmation thereof did then & there to these presents set there hands and we whose Names are here under subscribed, being present at the soleminzation of the said Marriage and Subscription as Witnesses Thereunto have set our hands, the Day & Year first above written.

Thomas Fawcett
Sarah Fawccett

Jesse Holloway	John Painter	Rebeckah Fawccett
Anthony Moore	John Smith	Thomas Fawceett
Nathan Pusey	Roland Richard	Abraham Branson
James Swayne	Margery Ellis	Catharine Branson
Mary Ellis	Isaac Painter	William Branson
Mary Clevenger	John Wright	Caleb Antram
Robert Rea	Martha Fernly	Jonathan Lupton
Phebe Painter	Ann Smith	Hannah Smith
Ann Jones	Samuel Chew	Beulah Painter
Elisabeth Painter	Jacob Painter	David Painter

HOLLOWAY—SHINN

John Holloway, son of John & Margaret Holloway in the County of Stafford in the State of Virginia, and *Mary Shinn*, Daughter of George and Rachel Shinn of the County and State aforesaid; 17th day of 12th month, 1783; at Stafford.

Witnesses who signed this Marriage Certificate:

Amos Holloway	Abigail Green	Isaac Branson	John Holloway
Rachel Shinn	Edith Antram	Isaac James	Margarett Holloway
George Shinn	Rachel Branson	Mary Godley	Rachel Shinn
Epheram Holloway	Eunice Wright	Robert Painter	Ann Shinn
	Eunice Painter	Daniel Antram	Abigail Holloway
	Rachel Antram	Jacob McKay	William Wright
	Susanna Antram	Samuel Chew	David Holloway
	Hannah Godley	James Holloway	William Holloway
	Mary Green	Assa Holloway	Thomas Holloway
	William Garred Jr.	Joseph Taylor	Isaac Holloway
	Edward Godley	Robert Green	

HOLLOWAY—BRANSON

Abel Holloway, son of Isaac & Mary Holloway of the County of Stafford in Commonwelth of Virginia, and *Rachel Branson*, Daughter of William Branson & Elisabeth his Wife Deceased; 11th day of 2nd Month, 1784; at their Meeting House in Stafford.

Witnesses who signed this Marriage Certificate:

Shody Skidmore	Isaac James	Daniel Antram	Isaac Holloway
Jane Smith	Robert Green	Scholy Wright	Mary Holloway
Levi Antram	Charles Geo. Martin	John Green	William Branson
Isaac Branson	Joseph Taylor	Robert Painter	Amos Holloway
	Rachel Antram	Enice Painter	John Holloway
	Martha Branson	Rachel Shinn	Margaret Holloway
	Edith Antram	Sasannah Antram	Abigail Holloway
	Mary James	John Holloway	Enice Wright
	Margaret Primm	Mary Holloway	Asa Holloway
	William Holloway	Isaac Green	James Holloway
	Alice Green	Mary Green	Mary Holloway

GRIFFITH—ELLIS

John Griffith, of Frederick County in Virginia, & *Mary Ellis* of the County aforesaid; 10th day of 3rd month, 1784; in Crooked Run Meeting House.

Witnesses who signed this Marriage Certificate:

Robert Moore	Rowland Richard	Margery Ellis
Joseph Tuley	Andrew McKay	Martha Griffith
David Painter	John Painter	David Faulkner
Isaac Painter	Robert Hains	Robert Faulkner
Jacob Painter	Thomas Fernley	Jesse Holloway
Sarah Beckett	Thomas Fawceett	Sarah Holloway
Hannah Smith	Anthony Moore	Elisabeth Painter
Hannah McKay	Margaret Hains	Robert Hanna
Jane McKay	McKay	Nathan Pusey
Martha Fernley	Ann Rea	Martha Fawceett
Martha Branson	Hannah Sharp	Hannah Antram
Lydia Richard	Phebe Painter	Daniel McLean
John Wright	Elias Earle	Joel Browne
Mary Clevenger	Beulah Hains	
William Branson	Joshua Swayne	

FAULKNER—PAINTER

Robert Faulkner, son of Jesse Faulkner and Martha his Wife of Berckley County in Virginia, & *Elisabeth Painter*, Daughter of John Painter & Susannah his Wife of Frederick County in Virginia; 14th day of 4th month, 1784; in Crooked Run Meeting House.

Witnesses who signed this Marriage Certificate:

David Faulkner	Rowland Richard	Hannah Smith	John Painter
Jesse Faulkner	Andrew McKay	Mary Clevenger	Susannah Painter
David Painter	Caleb Antram	Martha Branson	Martha Faulkner
	Thomas Fernley	Sarah Beckett	Hannah Painter
	Joshua Swayne	Mary Greenway	Jane Faulkner
	James Swaune	Ann Rea	Judith Faulkner
	Robert Rea	Hannah Swayne	Phebe Painter
	Kames Moore	Mary Pusey	Martha Faulkner
	John Smith	Rebeckah Branson	Jacob Painter
	Robert Hains	Margaret Hains	Jesse Holloway
	Levi Hains	Lydia Richard	Sarah Holloway
	Thomas Faulkner	Jane McKay	

CHEW—GREEN

Samuel Chew, of the County of Frederick, & *Abigail Green*, of the County of Stafford, both in Virginia; 21st day of 4th month, 1784; at the publick Meeting House in Stafford.

Witnesses who signed this Marriage Certificate:

Abigail Golloway	Ann Shinn	Lydia Green	Mary Green
Mary Fablis	Elisabeth Allen	Robert Green	John Paxson
Mary Holloway	Sally Mountjoy	Ruben Green	Lydia Gray
Enice Wright	Mary Gregg	Mary Paxson	Daniel Antram
Edith Antram	Thomas Pall	Robert Painter	John Green
Katharine Benson	Isaac James	Asa Holloway	Alice Green
Jane Fablis	Rachel Shinn	John Gregg	Garret Grey
Mary Fablis	Lewis Antram	William Garrard Jr.	Susannah Antram
Rachel Fablis	Charles Barn	Jacob McKay	
Sarah Thomas	Charles Martin	William Wright	
Elisabeth Samuel	Enoch Herton	Amos Holloway	
N. Tho. Mullen			

McKAY—SHINN

Jacob McKay, in the County of Frederick and State of Virginia, and *Rachel Shinn*, of the County of Stafford and State Aforesaid; 7th day of 7th month, 1784; at Stafford.

Witnesses who signed this Marriage Certificate:

Elisath _____?	Charles Carter	James Brown	Hannah McKay
Susannah Fuklin	Wm Mullen	Samuel Ridgway	Mary Holloway
Susannah Fulkner	Gabriel Jones	Rachel Holloway	Abigail Holloway
John Paxson	Thomas West	Rachel Hob	Mary Fallis
Mary Green	John Stern	Walker Randolph	William Wright
Alice Green	Charles Carter	Carter	Jane Fallis
Shody Skidmore	Edward Mullin	Levi Antram	John Fallis
Asa Holloway	Abel Holloway	Isaac James	Patience Mc Kay
Frances Fuklin	Thomas Pall	Isaac Green	John Holloway Jr.
	Joshua Antram	Joshua Swayne	Ann Shinn
	Isaac Branson	Wm. Holloway	Rachel Fallis
	Amos Holloway	Daniel Antram	Eunice Wright
	John Green	Robert Painter	Mary Fallis Jr.
	Edward Godley	Thomas Fawceett	
		Susannah Antram	

ALLEN—BOND

Joseph Allen, son of Joseph Allen and Ruth his Wife of the County of Shannandoe in the State of Virginia, and *Susanna Bond*, Daughter of Edward Bond and Mary his Wife in the same County; 14th day of 12th month, 1784; at Smiths Creek in the County of Shannandoe.

Witnesses who signed this Marriage Certificate:

Mary Moore	Hugh Judge	Joseph Cadwalader	Joseph Allen
Ann Moore	Isaac Jacobs	John Hank	Edward Bond
Mary Cadwalader	Richard Ridgway	John Antram	Mary Bond
Dorcas Moore	John Bond	John O'Neall	Mary Moore
Rebeckah Bond	Andrew McKay	Griffin Dobyns	Deborah Rambo
Mary Brinker	John Moore	William Moore	Benjamin Allen
Hannah Allen	Ruben Moore	Betty Allen Junior	Jackson Allen
Hannah Bond	Joseph Moore	Mary Smith	Susanna Allen
Sarah Bond	Jacob Rambow	Ann Moore	Davice Allen
Sarah Allen	Caleb Antram	Elisabeth Antram	Catharine Hank
Sarah Dobyns	John Taylor	Mary Ann Dobyns	Lydia Allen

[Smith Creek meeting house was in Shenandoah County, near New Market; probably between New Market and Mt. Jackson. In 1784 Margaret Hank was head of a family of 4 near the site of Broadway, Rockingham County. In 1785 John Hank was head of a family of 6 near the site of Edinburg, Shenandoah County. See U. S. census report of 1790.]

HOLLOWAY—GARWOOD

Daten Holloway, son of John Holloway and Margaret Holloway of the County of Stafford in the State of Virginia, and *Hope Garwood*, Daughter of John Garwood and Esther Garwood of Culpeper County & State aforesaid; 12th day of 10th month, 1785; at a Publick Meeting appointed at Culpeper.

Witnesses who signed this Marriage Certificate:

Mary Garwood	Thomas Branson	Sarah Painter	John Garwood
Mary Stratton	Henry Miller	Mary Hains	Esther Garwood
Ann Moore	Alehsiah Miller	Mary Moore	Sarah Garwood
Levi Hains	Robert Moore	Levi Garwood	Daniel Garwood
Ann Smith	Zilph Moore	Enice Walton	Jesse Holloway
Jane Branson	Job Sharp	Susana Painter	Isaac Hains
Sarah Moore	Benjamin Moore	Naome Stratton	
Anthony Moore	Jacob McKay	Joseph Straten	
Sarah Stratten			
Berry Duff			
Susana Garwood			

O'NEAL—RAMBO

John O'Neal, son of Robert O'Neal of the County of Shannandoah in the State of Virginia, and *Rebeckah Rambo,* Daughter of Jacob Rambo of the same County; 8th day of 12 month, 1785; at the Meeting House at Smiths Creek.

Witnesses who signed this Marriage Certificate:

Aaron Solomon	Agnes Mathews	Thomas Embree	Jacob Rambo
William Cathey	Esther Antram	Griffith Dobyns	Deboraugh Rambo
John Tayler	Turner Coulson	Benjamin Allen	Lydia Rambo
Davis Allen	Betty Allen	John Hank	Jackson Allen
Joseph Asband	Susanna Allen	Jackson Allen	Betty Allen
William Allen	Hannah Moore	Sarah Hawkins	Elisabeth Antram
George Moore	Ann Penewitt	Mary Bond	John Bond
Solomon Kingree	Hannah Allen	Margret Cathey	John Antram
	Sarah Allen		John Moore

SWAYNE—SMITH

Joshua Swayne, of Frederick County and State of Virginia, son of Joshua Swayne late of Chester County and Province of Pennsylvania, Deceased, & *Rebeckah Smith,* Daughter of John Smith of Frederick County in Virginia; 11th day of 1st month, 1786; at Crooked Run.

Witnesses who signed this Marriage Certificate:

Joel Brown	Thomas Fawccett	Susanna Smith	James Sinkler
Thomas Farnly	Jesse Holloway	Isaac Taylor	John Smith
David Painter	Sarah Holloway	Job McKay	Ann Smith
Joshua Antram	Jane M'Kay	Ann McKay	Margaret Hains
James MConnel	Margery Ellis	Hannah Smith	Mary Clevenger
Gidion Rees	Caleb Antram	John Smith	Phebe Sinkler
Nancy Stephens	Martha Fawccett	Andrew McKay	Thomas Smith
Patience Hains	Ann Collins	Thomas Branson	Evan Evens
Esther Tharp	Sarah Painter	Mary Pusey	
John Meade	Eunice Walton	Robert Rea	
John Hains	Joseph Hains	Robert Hanna	
Mary Hains	Tunis Jones	Rachel McKay	
Mary Meade	Shackelford	Catherine Hanna	
Hannah Greenaway	Martha Farnly		
Isaac Painter	Roland Richard		
	Nathan Pusey		

ANTRAM—GARWOOD

Caleb Antram, son of John and Elisabeth Antram of Shanandoah County in the State of Virginia, & *Sarah Garwood,* daughter of John and Esther Garwood of Culpepper County and State aforesaid; 21st day of 9th month, 1786; at Culpepper.

Witnesses who signed this Marriage Certificate:

Abigail Hains	David Moore	John Garwood
Mary Hunt	Reubin Moore	Esther Garwood
Mary Garwood	Daten Holloway	Daniel Garwood
Robert Hunt	Anthony Moore	Susannaa Garwood
Abigail Hunt	Elisabeth Hains	Levi Garwood
Eunice Walton	Zilpha Moore	Robert Hains
Joshua Hunt		Isaac Hains
William Hunt		Mary Hains

BOND—DOBYNE

Allen Bond, of Shannandoah County in the State of Virginia, son of John Bond, and *Sarah Dobyne,* of the same place, daughter of Griffith Dobyne; 14th day of 12th month, 1786; at Smiths Creek Meeting House.

Witnesses who signed this Marriage Certificate:

William Allen	Hannah Allen	John Bond
Mary Bond	Susanna Allen	Griffith Dobyne
Mary Bond	Mary Brinker	Mary Ann Dobyne
Hannah Bond	Sarah Allen	Rebeckah Bond
Sarah Bond	Benjamin Bond	Mary Bond
Reubin Moore	Joseph Allen	Edward Bond
Ann Moore	Joseph Methany	Joseph Allen
Jackson Allen	Jackson Rambo	Isaac Bond
Joseph Moore	Samuel Smith	Ann Moore
John Bonnet		

[Dobyne, Dobin, &c., was a French name, the original spelling of which was D'Aubigne. Note by R. E. Griffith.]

NEILL—BROWN

Joseph Neill, son of Lewis and Lydia Neill in the County of Frederick in Virginia, deceased, and *Sarah Brown*, Daughter of David and Sarah Brown in said County in Virginia; 9th day of 5th month, 1787. "At or near Center Meeting."

Witnesses who signed this Marriage Certificate:

Isaac Parkins	Nathan Pusey	Jonah Hollingsworth	Lewis Neill
Mary Parkins	Mary Pusey	Hannah Hollingsworth	Daniel Brown
Lydia Miller	Rachel Parkins	Elisabeth Hughs	Sarah Brown
Amos Janney	Margaret Rees	Phebe Steer	Daniel Brown Jr.
Abel Janney	Joseph Parkins	Elisabeth Hodgson	Abraham Neill
William Hughes	Jeremiah Cooper	Deberough Hodgson	Susanna Brown
John Hough 3d	Sarah Hughs	Sarah Brown	John Neill
Mary ann Taylor	Phebe Brown	Rachel Hollingsworth	Jonathan Brown
Joshua Wood	Samuel Berry	Rachel Neill	Elisabeth Brown
Joseph Lupton	Charles Horsman	Mary Janney	Ann Lupton
Rachel Lupton	Lewis Rees	Rachel Neill	Ann Neill
Goldsmith Chandlee	Joseph Steer Jr.	Mary Lupton	Susanna Brown
Hannah Chandlee	Grace Steer Jr.	Ann Lupton	Eleanor Hough
Nathan Updegraff	John Lupton	Hannah Lupton	Lydia Hough
Mahlon Smith			
Mary Smith			
Joshua Lupton			
Nathan Lupton			

BOND—ALLEN

Isaac Bond, of Shanandoah County in the State of Virginia, and *Lydia Allen*, daughter of Jackson Allen deceased; 14th day of 6th month, 1787; at Smiths Creek Meeting House.

Witnesses who signed the Marriage Certificate:

Jackson Allen	John O'Neal	Betty Allen
Israel Allen	Griffith Dobyne	Joseph Allen Elder
Wesley Allen	Ruben Allen	Bathsheba Lupton
Elisabeth Allen	Thomas Embree	Benjamin Allen
Susannah Allen	Daniel Dieckinson	John Bond
Deberough Allen	Rebeckah Dieckinson	Edward Bond
Mary Allen	Davis Allen	Jacob Rambo
Sisley Allen	Rebeckah Bond	John Moore
Mary Bond	Sarah Bond	Joseph Allen Jr.
Ann Gordan	Sarah Branum	
Esther Antram	Betty Allen	
John Woodrow	Mary Bond	
	Richard Branham	

CLEAVER—RICHARDS

Ezekial Cleaver, of the County of Frederick in the State of Virginia, son of Ezekial and Mary Cleaver late of the Township of Gwynedd and the County of Montgomery in the state of Pennsulvania, deceased, and *Abigail Richards*, daughter of Rowland and Lydia Richards of the said County and State aforesaid; 4th day of 7th month, 1787; at Crooked Run.

Witnesses who signed this Marriage Certificate:

Joseph Taylor	Andrew McKay	Rowland Richards
Jane Taylor	Jane McKay	Lydia Richards
John Painter	John Hurford	Abjah Richards
Susannah Painter	Rachel Shinn	Esther Richards
Martha Painter	Hannah McKay	Samuel Richards
Thomas Fawcett	Abigail Wickersham	Elijah Richards
Martha Fawcett	Elisabeth Lewis	Catharine Lewis
Martha Branson	Rachel McKay	Jacob Lewis
Moses McKay	Patience McKay	Hannah Richards
Hannah Hurford	Jonathan Lupton	Eli Richards
Naomi Hurford	Isaac Woodrow	Towndsend Richards
Nathan Pusey	David Russell	Robert Hains
Mary Pusey	Isaac Painter	Margret Hains
John Roberts	James M'Connal	Thomas Fernly

M'CONNELL—ANTRAM

James M'Connel, of Frederick County Virginia, son of Morris and Elisabeth M'Connel of Tirone County, Ireland, and *Rachel Antram*, Daughter of Daniel Antram and Susannah his Wife of Stafford County in Virginia; 3d day of 10th month, 1787; at Stafford.

Witnesses who signed this Marriage Certificate:

Abigail Holloway	Eunice Painter	Daniel Antram
Susanna Fricklin Jr.	Rachel Holloway	Robert Painter
Frances Fricklin	Mary Holloway	Wright William
Milly Fricklin	Eunic Wright	George Roack
Mary Paxson	Martha Branson	Lewis Fricklin
David Rogers	Gabriel Jones	William Branson
Asa Holloway	Jacob Allintharp	
Fielding Fricklin	John Green	
John Paxson	Thomas Ederington	

ALLEN—WALTON

Joseph Allen, of Shanandoah County in the State of Virginia, and *Unice Walton*, in the State aforesaid; 9th day of 4th month, 1788; at Crooked Run.

Witnesses who signed this Marriage Certificate:

Hannah Hurford	Andrew M'Kay	Thomas Fawcett	Benjamin Allen
Ann Hurford	Roland Richards	Martha Fernley	Thomas Fernley
Tabith Earle	Lydia Richards	Margaret Hains	Mary Walton
Nancy Williams	Thomas Branson	Martha Branson	James M'Connel
Samuel Walton	Josaph Tayler	Rachel M'Kay	Robert Rea
Jeremiah Dunkan	Jane Tayler	Mary Hains	Jesse Penrose
Hannah Walton	Joshua Swayne	Unice Walton	Rebeckah Dunken
Mary Dunkan	John Smith	David Painter	
Isaac Painter	Arch'd Brounley	Mary Clevenger	
Joshua Antram	Robt. J. Leewright	William Fernly	
Unice Walton	Joseph Pollard	Eunice Fernley	

ALLEN—BOND

Jackson Allen, of Shanandoah County in the State of Virginia, son of Joseph Allen, and *Sarah Bond*, of the same place, daughter of Edward Bond; 10th day of 4th month, 1788; at Smiths Creek Meeting House.

Witnesses who signed this Marriage Certificate:

Betty Allen	Margaret Moore	Edward Bond
Elisabeth Moore	Hannah Bond	Mary Bond
Abigail Ellioss	Sarah Bond	Susanna Bond
Hannah Bird	Mary Bond	Lydia Allen
Ann Brannum	Susanna Allen	Mary Moore
Martha Bond	Joseph Allen	Mary Bond
Mary Allen	William Allen	Isaac Bond
Allen Bond	Mary Patton	Ann Pennywitt
A. Moffett	John O'Neal	Joseph Methany
Agnes Mathews	Jacob Falliss	Gaydon Brayham
Mary Moore	Esther Embree	Jacob Rambo
Sisley Allen	Ann Moore	Westley White
Westley Allen	John Bond	
Benjamin Bond		

["Ellioss" should probably be Elliss or Elless. Under date of 12th day of 12th month, 1770, at Crooked Run, the name Abigail Elles appears.]

UPDEGRAFF—LUPTON

Nathan Updegraff, of Winchester in the County of Frederick in Virginia, son of Joseph Updegraff of York Town in the County of York in Pennsylvania and Susanna his Wife, Deceased, and *Ann Lupton*, Daughter of Joseph and Rachel Lupton in Virginia and County aforesaid; 14th day of 5th month, 1788; at Center Meeting.

Witnesses who signed this Marriage Certificate:

Joseph Steer Jr.	Jonathan Brown	Rachel Hollingsworth	Joseph Lupton
Isaac Woodrow	Samuel Pickering	Sarah Brown	Rachel Lupton
David Horsman	Joshua Baker	Susanna Brown	David Lupton
Rachel Steer	Gidion Rees	Rachel Parkins	John Lupton
Elisabeth Parkins	Lewis Rees	Catherine Lewis	Ann Lupton
Isaac Parkins	Samuel Love	Mahlon Smith	Hannah Lupton
Rebeckah Lupton	James Raley	Mary Smith	Mary Lupton
Ann Parkins	Jonah Hollingsworth	Francis Raley	Mary Lupton Jr.
Isaac Wood	Amos Janney	Mary Gibson	Grace Steer Jr.
John Murrell	Daniel Brown 3d	Phebe Brown	Sarah Lupton
Robert M. 'Munn	George M. 'Munn	Grace Parkins	Joshua Lupton
Isaac Steer	Joseph Parkins	Goldsmith Chandlee	Nathan Lupton
William Bailey	Ann Wood	Ann Smith	Joseph Wood
Joseph Lupton	Sarah Steer	John Smith	John Lupton
	Isaac Steer	Ann Smith	
	Hannah Chandlee	Lydia Wood	
	Ione M'Munn	Robert Miller	

RALEY—STEER

James Raley, of the County of Frederick in Virginia, son of Robert and Ann Raley, and *Rachel Steer*, of the County aforesaid in Virginia, daughter of James and Abigail Steer; 4th day of 6th month, 1788; at Center.

Witnesses who signed this Marriage Certificate:

Asa Lupton	Mahlon Smith	Rachel Hollingsworth	James Steer
Hannah Lupton	Deborah Hodgson	Ann Lupton	Hannah Steer
John Lupton	Samuel Berry	Samuel Lupton	Grace Steer
John Griffith	Robert M'Munn	Eli Raley	Joseph Steer 3d
Samuel Pickering	Joseph Lupton	Grace Parkins	Frances Raley
Phebe Pickering	Jonathan Brown	Mary Lupton	Grace Jackson
Joshua Lupton	Elisabeth Brown	Mary M'Munn	Katharine Sexton
Nathan Lupton	Goldsmith Chandlee	Isaac Steer Jr.	Rachel Parkins
Josiah Jackson	Hannah Chandlee	Isaac Steer Sr.	Mary Parkins
Samuel Jackson	Marcy Pickering	Sarah Steer	Joseph Steer Jr.
Charles Horsman	Phebe Wright	Betty Lupton	Grace Steer Jr.
	Isaac Parkins	Jonah Hollingsworth	
	Mary Parkins	Sarah Brown	
	Joseph Parkins	Isaac Woodrow	

STANTON—HOLLOWAY

William Stanton, son of William and Phebe Stanton of the County of Campbell and State of Virginia, and *Katharine Holloway*, daughter of George and Elisabeth Holloway of the County of Stafford and State of Virginia; 12th day of 11th month, 1788; at the public Meeting House in Stafford.

Witnesses who signed this Marriage Certificate:

Jane Lauron	John Paxson	Mary Holloway
Polly Allason	Robert Painter	Thomas Holloway
Anna Lauron	Daniel Antram	Abigail Holloway
Achsah Paxson	William Wright	Mary Holloway
P. Benson	Scholey Wright	Rachel Holloway
Feiling Fickling	Levi Antram	Asa Holloway
Masey Arrasmith	Isaac Branson	John Holloway
	Joseph Benson	

LUPTON—REES

Nathan Lupton, of the County of Frederick in Virginia, son of John Lupton and Sarah his Wife, deceased, and *Margaret Rees*, of the County aforesaid in Virginia, daughter of Henry Rees (deceased) and Ann his wife; 12th day of 11th month, 1788; at Center Meeting House.

Witnesses who signed this Marriage Certificate:

John Hodgson	Rachel Hollingsworth	Rachel Raley	John Lupton
John Pickering	Daniel Brown Sr.	Rachel Neill	Ann Lupton
James M'Cormick	Samuel Pickering	Lydia Neill	Joseph Lupton
Samuel Pickering Jr.	Aaron Mercer	Sarah Mercer	Jonathan Lupton
Phebe Pickering	Mahlon Smith	Samuel Lupton	Joshua Lupton
John Hambleton	Isaac Parkins	David Lupton	John Lupton Jr.
Susanna Brown Jr.	Lewis Neill	John Lupton Jr.	Mary Lupton Jr.
Hannah Steer	Joseph Neill	Rachel Lupton	Sarah Lupton
Joseph Steer Jr.	John Neill	William Lupton	Grace Steer Jr.
Isaac Steer	Elis'h M'Cormack	Hannah Lupton	Gidion Rees
Susanna Brown	Mary Parkins	Mary Lupton	Joseph Lupton Jr.
Phebe Brown	Joseph Parkins	Rebeckah Lupton	Elisabeth Lupton
Goldsmith Chandlee	Elis. Jolliffe	Jonah Lupton	Lewis Rees
William Horsman	Deberough Hodgson	Bathsheba Lupton	
John Brown	William Hodgson	Betty Lupton	
Samuel Berry	Rachel Pickering	Rachel Lupton	
Isaac Steer	Elisabeth Hodgson		
Phebe Steer	James Raley		

RALEY—LUPTON

Eli Raley, of the County of Frederick in Virginia, son of Robert Raley and Ann his Wife of Washington County in Pennsylvania, and *Mary Lupton*, of the County aforesaid in Virginia, Daughter of John Lupton and Sarah his wife, deceased; 18th day of 3d month, 1789; at Center.

Witnesses who signed this Marriage Certificate:

Isaac Parkins	Hannah Chandlee	Margaret Lupton	John Lupton
Mary Parkins	Sarah Brown	Joseph Steer Jr.	Ann Lupton
David Horsman	Phebe Brown	Grace Steer Jr.	Frances Raley
John Hamilton	Susanna Brown	Mary Lupton	Joshua Lupton
John Wilson	Elisabeth Hamiton	Sarah Steer	James Raley
Nathan Updegraff	Elisabeth Parkins	Elis'h M'Cormick	Joseph Lupton
	John Pickering	Elisabeth Hodgson	Rachel Lupton
	Rachel Pickering	Deborah Hodgson	Samuel Lupton
	Hannah Pickering	Sarah Mercer	Hannah Lupton
	Marcy Pickering	Gidion Rees	John Lupton Jr.
	Edward Mercer	Sarah Lupton	Lewis Rees
	Jas. M'Cormick Jr.	Mary Lupton	Ann Updegraff
	Mashack Sexton	Samuel Pickering	John Lupton
	Jonathan Brown	Sam'l Pickering Jr.	Lydia Rees
	Elisabeth Brown	Goldsmith Chandlee	Sarah Lupton
			Nathan Lupton

WRIGHT—HOLLOWAY

Scholey Wright, in the County of Frederick and State of Virginia, and *Levina Holloway*, of the County of Stafford and State aforesaid; 8th day of 4th month, 1789; at Crooked Run Meeting House.

Witnesses who signed this Marriage Certificate:

Martha Fawcett	Roland Richard	Rachel M'Kay
Mary Haines	William Branson	Jacob M'Kay
Jane Taylor	Robert Hains	Patience M'Kay
Ann Antram	Robert Rea	Nathan Pusey
Eunice Fernley	Joshua Swayne	Mary Pusey
David Painter	John Painter	Jane M'Kay
Ann M'Kay	Thomas Fawcett	Rachel Shinn
Ann Horsley	Samuel Hurford	Ann Duffy
Thomas Webb	Thomas Fernley	Hannah M'Kay
Asa M'Kay	William Fernley	John M'Kay
George Harris	Isaac Painter	Sarah M'Kay
Elijah Wlaken	Joshua Antram	Margret M'Kay
Barnay Duffy	Catharine Phillips	Martha Branson
Anthony Hite	Margery Ellace	Martha Fernley
	John Chambel	Ann Salsburey

POOL—HURFORD

Joseph Pool, of the County of Loudoun in Virginia, son of Benjamin Pool, late of the said County, deceased, and Rebeckah his wife, and *Hannah Hurford*, daughter of Joseph Hurford of the County of Frederick in Virginia, deceased, and Naomi his wife; 15th day of 4th month, 1789; at Center.

Witnesses who signed this Marriage Certificate:

Nathan Lupton	John Brown	Rachel Hollingsworth	Naomi Hurford
Benjamin Meade	Jonathan Brown	John Lupton	Iohn Hurford
Robert Whitacre	Isaac Parkins	Robert M'Munn	William Hurford
Mahlon Smith	Jane Taylor	John Lupton Jr.	Ann Hurford
Mary Smith	Goldsmith Chandlee	Lewis Rees	Hannah Hurford
Susanna Brown	Hannah Chandlee	Samuel Pickering	Elisabeth Poole
Sarah Brown	Susanna Brown	Daniel Brown	Catharine Hurford
Margaret Hains	Isaac Woodrow	Phebe Brown	
Rach M'Kay	Ellis Chandlee		
Robert Hains	Hannah M'Kay		
Mary Hains	Patience Ridgway		

PAINTER—HUNT

Jacob Painter, son of John and Susannah Painter of the County of Frederick and State of Virginia, and *Mary Hunt*, daughter of Robert and Abigail Hunt of the County of Culpepper and state Aforesaid; 16th of 4th month, 1789; at Culpepper in the State aforesaid.

Witnesses who signed this Marriage Certificate:

John Garwood	Rebeckah Wilks	John Painter
Esther Garwood	Elisabeth Keyce	Robert Hunt
Caleb Antram	Nancy Cunningham	Abigail Hunt
Robert Moore	Anthony Moore	David Painter
Hope Holloway	Zilpha Moore	Joshua Hunt
Sarah Moore	Abigail Hunt	Mary Painter
Sarah Antram	John Hunt	William Hunt
James Wheeler	Seth Hunt	Samuel Hunt
Stephen Lupton	John Cunningham	Joseph Hunt
John Wily	Ruben Payn	

WHITACRE—M'KAY

Robert Whitacre, of the County of Louden and State of Virginia, son of John Whitacre, deceased, and Naomi his Wife of the County and State aforesaid, and *Patience M'Kay*, daughter of Andrew M'Kay and Jane his Wife of the County of Frederick and State aforesaid; 11th day of 11th month, 1789; at Crooked Run.

Witnesses who signed this Marriage Certificate:

Ann Smith	Joseph Taylor	Rachel M'Kay	Andrew M'kay
Martha Fawcett	Jane Taylor	Rachel Shinne	Jane M'Kay
Ann Hurford	Stephen Grigg	Shedy Ridgway	Moses M'Kay
Hannah Hurford	Thomas Farnley	Asa M'Kay	Jacob M'Kay
Hannah Lupton	Jacob Gregge	John M'Kay	David Ridgwav
Scholey Wright	George Redd	Robert Rea	Benj. Whitacre
Sarah Gregg	Martha Fernley	Isaac Painter	Caleb Whitacre
Mary Painter	Rachel Hurford	Robert Hains	Phebe Whitacre
Lydia Richards	John Smith	Joshua Swayne	Hannah M'Kay
Joshua Wood	Margery Ellas	Nathan Pusey	Patience Ridgway
Mary Clevenger	Martha Branson	Mary Pusey	Rachel Rattis
	Susannah Painter	Mary Hains	Alice M'Kay

LUPTON—REES

Joshua Lupton, of the County of Frederick in Virginia, son of John Lupton and Sarah his Wife, deceased, and *Lydia Rees*, of the County aforesaid in Virginia, daughter of Henry Rees (deceased) and Ann his Wife; 3d day of 3d month, 1790; at Center Meeting House.

Witnesses who signed this Marriage Certificate:

Goldsmith Chandlee	Isaac Parkins	John Lupton
Jonathan Brown	John Brown	Ann Lupton
James M'Cormick Jr.	Daniel Brown Sr.	Grace Steer Jr.
Sarah Hamilton	Susanna Brown	Mary Raley
Eli Raley	Rachel Hollingsworth	Sarah Lupton
	Joseph Steer Jr.	John Lupton Jr.
	Mary Lupton	Lewis Rees
	Rebeckah Lupton	John Neill
	Elizabeth M'Cormick	Ann Neill
		Rachel Neill
		Lydia Neill
		Jona Lupton
		Nathan Lupton
		Isaac Steer
		John Lupton
		Joseph Lupton

HAGUE—BISHOP

Samuel Hague, of the County of Culpeper and State of Virginia, and *Hannah Bishop*, of the County and State aforesaid; 15th day of 12th month, 1790; at Southland.

Witnesses who signed this Marriage Certificate:

William Stokes	Nathan Pusey	Jonathan Bishop
Hebe Stokes	Mary Janney	Patience Bishop
Mary Gibson	Hope Inskip	Joseph Bishop
Deborah Hains	Jake Holloway	Josiah Bishop
Roadham Ramy	Sarah Holloway	Mary Bishop
James Inskip	Esther Mattock	Thomas Bishop
James M'Connal	Martha Eldridge	John Bishop
Joshua Inskip	Rachel Inskip	Mary Pusey
Amos Janny	Timothy Mattock	
Rachel Pusey	Edward Lightfoot	

LUKENS—FAWCETT

Jonathan Lukens, of Frederick County and State of Virginia (son of Peter and Martha Lukens of Mountgomery County and State of Pennsylvania), and *Lydia Fawcett*, daughter of Richard Fawcett (deceased) and Rachel his Wife; 13th day of 1st month, 1791; at Mount Pleasant Meeting in the County aforesaid.

Witnesses who signed this Marriage Certificate:

Samuel Fawcett	John Longacre	Richard Fawcett
Elisabeth Longacre	Mary Lupton	Thomas Fawcett
Elisabeth Longacre Jr.	Rebeckah Lupton	Sarah Fawcett
William Spencer	Phebe Lupton	Levi Lukens
Mary Clark	Ezekiel Cleaver	Jonathan Lupton
William Clerk	Abigail Clever	Mary Clevenger
Joseph Wattson	John Fawcett Jr.	Sarah Lupton
Rachel Fawcett	Richard Fawcett Jr.	Andrew Longacre
John Lupton	John Longacre Jr.	Joseph Longacre
	Patrick Smith	George Redd
	George Clevenger	Joseph Longacre Jr.
		John Jones

ALLEN—WALTON

Benjamin Allen, son of Joseph Allen of the County of Shannandoah in the State of Virginia, and *Hannah Walton*, daughter of Moses Walton (deceased) of the same County; 13th day of 1st month, 1791; at Smiths Creek Meeting House.

Witnesses who signed this Marriage Certificate:

Jacob Rambo	John Walton	Joseph Allen
Joseph Rambo	Wesley Allen	Eunice Allen
Joseph Allen Jr.	Jackson Allen	Mary Walton
Moses Walten	Isaac Bond	Susanna Allen
Edward Walten	Mary Moore	Eunice Walton
John O'Neal	Elisabeth Bond	Betty Allen
Rebeckah O'Neil	Lydia Bond	Sarah Alen
Margret Bond	Hannah Bond	Mary Allen
George Moore	Joseph Moore	Samuel Walton
Adam Reader	Margaret Moore	Thomas Allen
Brittain White	Ruth Jones	
Samuel Hup	Jackson Rambo	

FISHER—FAWCETT

John Fisher, son of Barak Fisher (deceased) and Mary his Wife of Frederick County and State of Virginia, and *Sarah Fawcett*, daughter of Richard Fawcett and Mary his Wife of the County and State of aforesaid; 7th day of 4th month, 1791; at Mount Pleasant Meeting House in the County aforesaid.

Witnesses who signed this Marriage Certificate:

Joseph Fawcett	Richard Fawcett
Grace Fawcett	Mary Fawcett
Marcy Pickering	Mary Fisher
Andrew Longacre	Rachel Fawcett
George Redd	Elisabeth Fisher
Rachel Redd	Barak Fisher
Thomas Fawcett	Joseph Fisher
Sarah Fawcett	Elisabeth Fisher
Rebeckah Fawcett	Samuel Pickering
Jona Lupton	Samuel Pickering Jr.
Sarah Lupton	Jonathan Pickering
	Sarah Pickering

BROWN—HURFORD

Daniel Brown, son of Jonathan Brown of Frederick County in the State of Virginia, and *Hannah Hurford*, daughter of Samuel Hurford of the County and State aforesaid; 3d day of 8th month, 1791; at Crooked Run.

Witnesses who signed this Marriage Certificate:

Jeremiah ——?	Joshua Swayne	Jonathan Brown
John Hains	Andrew M'Kaye	Samuel Hurford
Joshua Wood	Robert Hains	Elisabeth Brown
Thomas Smith	John Hurford	Rachel Hurford
Jacob M'Kaye	William Hurford	Naomi Hurford
Rachel M'Kaye	Ann Hurford	Rachel Hurford
John Painter Sr.	Susanna Brown	Sarah Hurford
Susannah Painter	Phebe Brown	Joseph Hurford
Jane Taylor	Margery Ellis	Jonathan Brown Jr.
Rowland Richards	Martha Fernley	
Lydia Richards	Ruth Rea	
Hannah Jones	Rachel Moore	
	Ruben Moore	
	Joseph Taylor	
	Thomas Fernley	

PARKINS—BROWN

Joseph Parkins, son of Isaac and Mary Parkins of the County of Frederick and State of Virginia, and *Susannah Brown*, daughter of David and Sarah Brown of the County and State aforesaid; 7th day of 12th month, 1791; at Center.

Witnesses who signed this Marriage Certificate:

Hannah Pool	Samuel Love	Sarah Brown
Ann Hurford	George M'Munn	Isaac Parkins
Naomi Hurford	John Brown	Mary Parkins
Benjamin Hurford	William Hurford	Susannah Brown
Charles Foreman	Elisabeth Brown	Grace Parkins
John Lupton Sr.	Samuel Murry	Rachel Mahaney
Joshua Lupton	Peter Miller	Mary Parkins
Joseph Pooll	Joseph Steer Jr.	Sarah Brown Jr.
	Grace Steer	Daniel Brown Jr.
	Goldsmith Chandlee	Elisabeth Parkins
	Hannah Chandlee	Jonathan Brown
	Hannah Lupton	Josiah Jackson

HARRIS—HOLLOWAY

George Harris, son of Samuel and Martha Harris of Faquer County in the State of Virginia, and *Hope Holloway*, daughter of John and Esther Garwood of the County of Culpepper and State aforesaid; 8th day of 12th month, 1791; at Culpepper.

Witnesses who signed this Marriage Certificate:

Sarah Hurford	Nancy Neader	John Garwood
James Wheler	Thomas Harford	Samuel Harris
John Jett	Joshua Inskeep	Esther Garwood
William Heaton	Sally Inskeep	Caleb Antram
Robert Hunt	Catharine Harris	Sarah Antram
Barne Duffee	Sarah Penrose	Levi Garwood
Margaret Meather	Abigail Hunt	Susanna Garwood
Azall Heaton	Merrick Star	Daniel Garwood
		Margaret Garwood

MIDDLETON—HAINS

Hudson Middleton, son of Nathaniel and Sarah Middleton of Burlington County in the State of West New Jersey, and *Deborah Hains*, daughter of Levi and Elisabeth Hains of the County of Culpepper and State of Virginia; 14th of 12th month, 1791; at Southland.

Witnesses who signed this Marriage Certificate:

Joshua Woodrow	Nathan Pusey	Levi Hains
Daniel Garwood	Samuel Coles	Elisabeth Hains
James Cowgall	Joel Brown 3d	Hope Harris
Lightfoot Janney	Mary Pusey	Patience Hains
James M'Connal	Elizabeth Woodrow	Enoch Hains
Evan Evans	John B. Norman	Lydia Hains
Mary Jannye	Kizea Norman	Eunice Hains
Ruth Cowgill	Isaac Woodrow	Rachel Inskeep
Mary Gibson	Isaac Cowgill	Rebeckah Smith
Jesse Holloway	Lewis Japp [?]	Nathan Hains
Sarah Holloway	James Stout	Sarah Janney
Richard Janny	Phillip Brooks	Hannah Hains
Sarah Cowgill	Jacob Steel	Mary Bishop
Attlantick Evans	Henry Woodrow	John Bishop
Darling Conrow	Semeon Woodrow	
	Amos Janney	

FAWCETT—PAINTER

John Fawcett, son of Thomas and Martha Fawcett of Frederick County in the State of Virginia, and *Mary Painter*, daughter of John and Susannah Painter of the County and State aforesaid; 11th day of 4th month, 1792; at Crooked Run.

Witnesses who signed this Marriage Certificate:

Hannah M'Kay	Keziah Straton	Martha Fawcett
David Stratton	Rebeckah Smith	Susannah Painter
Shady Stratton	David Fawcett	David Painter
Phebe Clevenger	Robert Painter	Jacob Painter
Hannah Richards	Mary Garwood	Mary Painter
Thomas Fearnly	John Garwood	Rachel Fawcett
Robert Harris	Mahlon Stratton	Martha Fawcett
John Harris	Andrew M'Kay	Rachel Painter
Rachel M'kay	John Smith	Richard Fawcett
Roland Richards	Thomas Smith	Hannah Fawcett
Lydia Richards	Joshua Swayne	Rebeckah Painter
Samuel Berry	Scholy Wright	John Painter
Jacob Branson	Joshua Wood	
Seth Stratton	Moses M'Kay	
David Devo		

WOOD—M'KAY

Joshua Wood, of Frederick County in the State of Virginia, son of William and Margret Wood, late of Londongrove, Chester County in Pennsylvania, deceased, and *Hannah M'Kay*, daughter of Jacob M'Kay and his Wife Rachel M'Kay, deceased, of the County of Frederick and State aforesaid; 16th day of 5th month, 1792; at Crooked Run.

Witnesses who signed this Marriage Certificate.

Hannah Pool	Thomas Fernly	Richard Ridgway	Jacob M'Kay
Rachel Painter	Joshua Swayne	Joseph Wood	Rachel M'Kay
Rachel Fawcett	Martha Fernly	Robert Whitacre	Moses M'Kay
John Gregory	Samuel Hurford	Patience Whitacre	John M'Kay
Margret Hains	Robert Hains	Jacob M'Kay	Bulah Ridgway
Joseph Pool	Thomas Smith	Richard Bryerly	Patience Hume
Samuel Walton	Phebe Smith	Abigail Shinn	Sarah M'Kay
Sarah Cooper	Samuel Schooly	Asa M'Kay	Patience Ridgway
Phebe Clevenger 3d	John Hains	Jesse M'Kay	Enoch Hume
John Weaver	Mary Hains	Joshua Antram	Margaret M'Kay
Elisabeth Alder	John Fawcett	Ann Antram	Ann Wood
Hannah Fawcett	Mary Fawcett	Mary Wood	Andrew M'Kay
Ann Hands	Jeremiah Cooper	Martha Branson	Jane M'Kay
Ann Gibson	Hannah Richards	Thomas Fawcett	
Caty Hurford	Thos. Lathan Jr.		

REA—GARWOOD

Joseph Rea, son of Robert and Rebeckah Rea of the County of Frederick and State of Virginia, and *Susannah Garwood,* daughter of John and Esther Garwood of the County of Culpepper and State aforesaid; 17th day of 5th month, 1792; at Culpepper.

Witnesses who signed this Marriage Certificate:

Henry Harford	Isaac Painter	John Garwood
Thomas Deathrege	Joseph Hains	Esther Garwood
Hannah Clevert	Merrick Starr	Daniel Garwood
Elisabeth Calvert	Ann Starr	Ruth Rea
Sarah Painter	Isaac Hains	Levi Garwood
Mary Smith	Christopher Smith	John Hains
Sarah Penrose	Mary Hains	George Harris
Asa M'kay	Samuel Wilks	Hope Harris
William Cunhan	George Calvert	Margaret Garwood
Ruben Moore	Joshua Hopper	
	John Wilks	
	Anna Calvert	

HAINS—ALLEN

John Hains, son of Robert Hains of the County of Frederick in the State of Virginia, and *Betty Allen,* daughter of Jackson Allen of the County of Shannandoah and State aforesaid; 6th day of 12th month, 1792; at Smiths Creek in the County aforesaid.

Witnesses who signed this Marriage Certificate:

Sarah Moore	Mary Seiglae	Betty Allen
Sarah Allen	Henry Taylor	Robert Hains
Mary Bond	John O'Neil	Ruben Allen
Alse Bond	Rebeckah O'Neil	Davis Allen
Margaret Bond	Lydia Bond	Jackson Allen
Mary Kingery	Magdalen Allen	Noah Hains
Mary Moffett	Susanna Allen	Jackson Rambo
Rubin Moore	David Harned	Israel Allen
Asa M'Kay	George Moore	Sarah Lupton
Hannah Bird	Daniel Moffett	Isaac Smith
Susanna Allen	Charles Moore	Mary Smith
Hannah Bond	Ezekiel Thomas	Wann Rambo
Mary Kingree	Aaron Thomas	Ann Penyweight
Joseph Allen	Samuel Schooly	Hannah Penyweight
Mary Allen	Sislee Allen	

GARWOOD—BISHOP

Daniel Garwood, son of John and Esther Garwood of Culpeper County in the State of Virginia, and *Mary Bishop*, daughter of Jonathan and Patience Bishop of the County and State aforesaid; 14th day of 11th month, 1792; at a Publick Meeting in Southland.

Witnesses who signed this Marriage Certificate:

John Hunt	Hudson Middleton	Jonathan Bishop
Samuel Cole	Enos Hains	Patience Bishop
Nathan Pusey	Lydia Hains	Caleb Antram
Mary Pusey	Atlantic Evans	Levi Garwood
Abraham Hains	Jesse Holloway	Margret Garwood
James Inskeep	Stephen Syms	Samuel Garwood
Joshua Woodros	Sarah Evans	Hannah Hague
Henry Woodrow	Evan Evans	Martha Eldridge
Jacob Pickering	Rachel Inskeep	Thomas Bishop
Hannah Pickering	Sally Inskeep	Grace Woodrow
Joshua Wood	Hope Inskeep	Henry Jones
Robert Hunt	Rachel Pusey	Sarah Holloway
Ruth Cowgill	Joel Brown	
Hannah Wood	Joshua Hunt	

FAWCETT—FERNLY

Richard Fawcett, son of Thomas and Martha Fawcett of Frederick County in the State of Virginia, and *Eunice Fernly*, daughter of Thomas and Martha Fernly of the County aforesaid; 12th day of 12th month, 1792; at Crooked Run.

Witnesses who signed this Marriage Certificate:

John S. Woodcock	Ann Wright	Thomas Fawcett
Rachel Fawcett	George Larrick	Thomas Fernly
Hannah Richards	Rachel Hurford	Martha Fernly
Jemima Briten	Charity Mastin	Martha Fawcett
Lydia Richards	Frances T. Mastin	Richard Fawcett Sr.
	Samuel Walton	John Fawcett
	Isaac Larrick	David Fawcett
	Peter Madden	Hannah Fawcett
	Moses M'Kay	William Fernly
	David Holloway	Martha Wheelen
	David Devo	
	John Hains	

McKAY—SHINN

Moses McKay, son of Andrew and Jane McKay of Frederick County in the State of Virginia, and *Abigail Shinn*, daughter of George Shinn late of Stafford County in the State aforesaid, deceased, and Rachel his Wife; 6th day of 3d month, 1793; at Crooked Run.

Witnesses who signed this Marriage Certificate:

Joshua Swayne	Samuel Walton	Andrew M'Kay
Robert Hains	Samuel Smith	Jane M'Kay
Reubin Moore	George Smith	Asa M'Kay
Robert Whitacre	Daniel Holloway	Patience Whitacre
Thomas Fernly	Atlantick Hains	Rachel Shinn
Thomas Fawcett	Rachel Painter	Jacob M'Kay
Thomas Anderson	William Conner	John M'Kay
Jacob Painter	Margret Hains	Enos M'Kay
Robert Hunt	Martha Branson	Margaret M'Kay
David Painter	Sarah M'Kay	Jesse M'Kay
Mary Hains	Ann Hurford	Roland Richards
John Hains	Hannah Richards	Lydia Richards
Eli Hains	Rachel Fawcett	

COWGILL—HOLLOWAY

James Cowgill, son of Henry and Ruth Cowgill of Culpeper County in State of Virginia, and *Charlotte Holloway*, Daughter of John and Margaret Holloway of the County of Stafford and State foresaid; 13th of 11th month, 1793; at Stafford.

Witnesses who signed this Marriage Certificate:

Aaron Holloway	Robert Painter	Henry Cowgill
Joseph Holloway	Joshua Wood	Ruth Cowgill
Joseph Wright	William Branson	John Holloway
Ruth Holloway	Eunice Wright	Margaret Holloway
Sarah Wright	William Wright	Jesse Holloway
Abigail Holloway	Eunice Painter	John Holloway Jr.
Sarah Cowgill	Thomas Holloway	Isaac Cowgill
Isaac James	Ephraim Holloway	David Holloway
John James		

HOLLOWAY—RICHARDS

David Holloway, of the County of Frederick and State of Virginia, son of John and Margaret Holloway of the County of Stafford and said State of Virginia, and *Hannah Richards*, daughter of Roland and Lydia Richards of the County of Frederick and State aforesaid; 12th day of 3d month, 1794; at Crooked Run.

Witnesses who signed this Marriage Certificate:

Andrew M'Kay	Martha Fawcett	Roland Richards
Thomas Fernly	Mary Hains	Lydia Richards
Joshua Swayne	Rachel Painter	Ezekiel Clever
Rebeckah Swayne	Rachel Fawcett	Abigail Clever
William Fernly	Rachel Shinn	Eli Richards
John Painter Sr.	Hannah Fawcett	Samuel Walton
Samuel Berry	Mary Branson	Jacob Branson
John M'Kay	Nathaniel Dilhorn	Lydia Richards
Richard Fawcett Jr.	Susannah Painter	Martha Fernly
David Fawcett	Jacob Painter	
Susannah Painter	John Painter	
George Shinn	Rachel M'Kay	

POTTS—BROWN

Jonas Potts, of the County of Loudon and State of Virginia, son of Jonas and Mary Potts of said County and State, deceased, and *Phebe Brown*, daughter of David Brown of the County of Frederick and State aforesaid and Sarah his Wife, deceased; 9th day of 4th month, 1794; at Center.

Witnesses who signed this Marriage Certificate:

Phebe Steer	Grace Parkins	Eleanor Hough
Goldsmith Chandlee	John Lupton	Isaac Brown
Hannah Chandlee	Ezekiel Cleaver	Jonathan Brown
Naomi Hurford	Joshua Lupton	David Brown Sr.
Robert Hunt	Ann Lupton	Joseph Parkins
Rachel Hollingsworth	Abigail Hunt	Susannah Brown
Grace Parkins	Betty Holmes	Sarah Brown
Elisabeth Parkins	Mary Yarnall	Susannah Parkins
Barsheba Oglisby	Hannah Hollingsworth	Sarah Talbutte
Jane Crisman	Mary Parkins	Joseph Hough
	Mary Chandlee	William Hurford
		John Brown
		William Brown

BOND—ALLEN

Benjamin Bond, of Bedford County in the State of Virginia, and *Susannah Allen*, of Shanandoah in State aforesaid; 4th day of 9th month, 1794; at Smiths Creek Meeting House.

Witnesses who signed this Marriage Certificate:

Ezekiel Thomas	Rebeckah Bond	Joseph Allen
John Giger	Elisabeth Allen	Hannah Allen
Mary Scelser	Rachel Lupton	Eunice Allen
Joseph Allen Jr.	Edith Thomas	William Allen
Cornelius O'Neil	Mary Moore	Benjamin Allen
John O'Neil	Isaac Bond	Jackson Allen
Andrew Brinker	Moses Walton	Eunice Walton
John Brinker	Barbara Brinker	Samuel Walton
Adam Giger	Lydia Bond	Edward Walton
James Lohey	Grace Lupton	John Bond
Mary Walton	Evan Thomas	Israel Allen
Hannah Penniwett	Jacob Rambo	Aaron Allen

BROWN—HURFORD

David Brown Sr., of the County of Frederick and State of Virginia, and *Naomi Hurford*, of said County and State, Widow of Joseph Hurford, late of said County and State, deceased; 5th day of 11th month, 1794; at Center.

Witnesses who signed this Marriage Certificate:

Joshua Lupton	Joseph Neill	Jonathan Brown
Sarah Lupton	Rachel Hollingsworth	Isaac Brown
Goldsmith Chandlee	Hannah Chandlee	Susanna Brown
John Lupton	Mary Parkins	Sarah Brown
Robert Hains	Ann Lupton	Rachel Pusey
James Nance	Abigail Hunt	Sarah Brown Jr.
John Lupton Jr.	Grace Steer	Samuel Hurford
William Chipley	Elisabeth Lupton	John Brown
Isaac Hollingsworth	Mary Parkins Jr.	Joseph Steer Jr.
Mary Smith	Grace Parkins	William Brown
Mary Brown	Elisabeth Redd	
Joseph Pool	Mary Nance	

BROWN—INSKEEP

Joel Brown, son of Daniel and Susanna Brown of Frederick County and State of Virginia, and *Rachel Inskeep*, daughter of James and Hope Inskeep in the County of Culpeper and State aforesaid; 10th day of 12th month, 1794; at Southland.

Witnesses who signed this Marriage Certificate:

Jesse Holloway	Mary Janney	Hope Inskeep
Sarah Holloway	Betty Barbour	Margret Inskeep
Deborah Middleton	Polly Bradley	Nathan Pusey
Henry Jones	Lydia Hains	Mary Pusey
Jonathan Bishop	Sarah Evans	William Inskeep
Joshua Woodrow Jr.	Sarah M'Kay	Charlotte Inskeep
Amos Jannay	Lydia Woodrow	Susanna Inskeep
Polly Woodrow	Elisabeth Woodrow	James Inskeep
James M'Connal	Elisabeth Hains	Rachel Pusey
Joshua Wood	Patience Bishop	Ann Stokes
Evan Evans	Grace Woodrow	Hope Inskeep
Jacob Pickering	Mildred Ballenger	Sally Inskeep
Hudson Middleton	Hannah Pickering	John Inskeep
Lydia Woodrow	Isaac Woodrow	

BROWN—HODSON

Jonathan Brown, of Frederick County and State of Virginia, son of Daniel and Susannah Brown, deceased, and *Deborah Hodson*, of said County and State, Daughter of Robert Hodson, late of said County of Frederick, deceased, and Elisabeth his wife; 14th day of 1st month, 1795; at Center.

Witnesses who signed this Marriage Certificate:

Robert Hunt	Grace Parkins	Grace Brown
John Lupton	Rachel Hollingsworth	Daniel Brown
Mahlon Smith	Rachel Johnson	Sarah Brown
Joshua Lupton	Mary Chandlee	Naomi Brown
Abigail Hunt	Joshua Hunt	William Hodgson
Isaac Parkins	Mary Parkins	Hannah Brown
Ann Lupton	Hannah Pool	Rachel Hodgson
John Hurford	Hannah Chandlee	Ruth Hodgson
Samuel Pickering Jr.	Samuel Pickering Sr.	
Hannah Pickering	William Hurford	

NICKOLS—WATERS

Isaac Nickols, son of William Nickols of Loudoun County and Sarah his Wife, and *Lydia Waters*, daughter of George Waters of Culpeper County and Dinah Waters his Wife; 26th day of 11th month, 1795; at Culpeper.

Witnesses who signed this Marriage Certificate:

Hesther Garwood	George Waters
Levi Garwood	Isaac Nickols
Rebeckah Rea	Dianah Waters
George Harris	Sarah Nickols
John Garwood	Thomas Waters
Eli Janney	James Waters
Lydia Janey	Sarah Waters
	Mary Nickols
	Samuel Nickols

BRANSON—HOLLOWAY

Jacob Branson, of Stafford County in Virginia, son of William Branson of the County aforesaid and Elisabeth his wife, and *Rebeckah Holloway,* daughter of Asa Holloway of the same County and Abigail his wife; 16th day of 12th month, 1795; at Stafford.

Witnesses who signed this Marriage Certificate:

Henry K. Mullin	John Holloway	William Branson
Eli Nickols	Evan Evans	Asa Holloway
Thomas Jones	L. A. Mullen	Joseph Holloway
John Brown	Daniel Kirk	Aaron Holloway
Isaac James	Jno. L. Mullin	John Branson
Robert Painter	John Reddish	James Butter
Eunice Painter	Mary Holloway	Sarah Holloway

HAINS—EVANS

Enos Hains, of Culpeper County in the State of Virginia, son of Levi Hains of the County and State aforesaid and Elisabeth his Wife, and *Mary Evans,* of the aforesaid County and daughter of Evan Evans and Sarah his Wife; 23d day of 12th month, 1795; in their Meeting House at Southland.

Witnesses who signed this Marriage Certificate:

Joseph Taylor	James Pickering	Levi Hains
Amos Janney	Isiah Garwood	Elisabeth Hains
Nathan Pusey	Rachel Pusey	Evan Evans
Mary Pusey	Abel Janney	Sarah Evans
Joshua Wood	Sarah Cogall	Mahlon Hains
Hudson Middleton	Sarah Holloway	Lydia Hains
Jesse Holloway	Hannah Woods	Atlantic Evans
Isaac Woodrow	Mary Garwood	Elisabeth Woodrow
James M'Connal	Deborah Middleton	Isaac Cogall
Henry Cogall		

FEARNLEY—FAWCETT

William Fearnley, of Frederick County in the State of Virginia, son of Thomas Fearnley of the County and State aforesaid and Martha his wife, and *Hannah Fawcett,* daughter of Thomas Fawcett of the above said place and Martha his Wife; 16th day of 3d month, 1796; at Crooked Run.

Witnesses who signed this Marriage Certificate:

John Hains	Abraham Branson	Thomas Fearnley
Mary Hains	Sarah Branson	Martha Fearnley
Rachel M'Kay	Sarah Fawcett	Thomas Fawcett
Joshua Swayne	William Branson	Martha Fawcett
Rowland Richards	John Painter	Martha Branson
Moses M'Kay	Patience Whitacre	Rebeckah Branson
Jacob Painter	Jacob M'Kay	John Antram
		Richard Fawcett
		John Fawcett
		Mary Fawcett

CONROW—FAWCETT

Darling Conrow, of Frederick County in the State of Virginia, son of Jacob Conrow of Burlington County, West New Jersey, deceased, and Eunice his wife, and *Rachel Fawcett*, daughter of Thomas Fawcett of the County of Frederick aforesaid and Martha his Wife; 16th day of 3d month, 1796; at their Meeting House at Crooked Run.

Witnesses who signed this Marriage Certificate:

John Hains	Sarah Fawcett	Thomas Fawcett
Mary Hains	Rachel M'Kay	Martha Fawcett
Moses M'Kay	Susannah Painter	Martha Branson
Joshua Swayne	Sarah Branson	Thomas Fernley
Roland Richards	Abram Branson	Martha Fearnley
Thomas Smith	Patience Whitacre	John Antram
Moses Walton	William Branson	Richard Fawcett
Mary Branson	Jacob M'Kay	Mary Fawcett

ELLISS—WOODROW

Jonathan Elliss, of Culpeper County in the State of Virginia, son of Enos Elliss of Berkley County (deceased) and Elisabeth his Wife, and *Lydia Woodrow*, daughter of Joshua Woodrow of the County of Culpeper aforesaid and Elisabeth his Wife; 18th day of 1st month, 1797; at Southland.

Witnesses who signed this Marriage Certificate:

Nathan Pusey	William Gray	Joshua Woodrow
Mary Pusey	Joshua Wood	Elizabeth Woodrow
Hudson Middleton	Hannah Wood	Enos Elliss
Enos Hains	Joel Brown	Hannah Pickering
Levi Hains	Rachel Brown	Jacob Pickering
Elisabeth Hains	Ann Trimble	Elanor Pickering
Jesse Holloway	Evan Evans	Joshua Woodrow Jr.
Sarah Holloway	Merrick Starr	Isaac Woodrow
Levi Lukens	Israel Taylor	Mary Woodrow
John Bishop	Francis Shinn	Elizabeth Woodrow
		Rachel Woodrow
		Abel Janney
		Benjamin Pearson

LUPTON—SHINN

John Lupton, son of Jonathan Lupton and Sarah his Wife of Frederick County and State of Virginia, and *Rachel Shinn*, daughter of George Shinn late of Stafford and State aforesaid (deceased) and Rachel his Wife; 3d day of 5th month, 1797; at Crooked Run.

Witnesses who signed this Marriage Certificate:

Mary Hains	Phebe Lupton	Jonathan Lupton
Eunice Allen	Jane M'Kay	Sarah Lupton
Rachel Longacre	Barna Duffey	Rachel M'Kay
Isaac Woodrow	Simion Woodrow	Jacob M'Kay
Sarah Lupton	Francis Shinn	John Lupton Sr.
Margret M'Kay	Asa M'Kay	John M'Kay
George Shinn	Jacob M'Kay Jr.	Patience Whitacre
Robert Whitacre	Abraham Woodrow	Jesse M'Kay
	Jacob M'Kay 3d	Sally M'Kay
	Moses M'Kav	Ann Duffey
	James Ireland	Rebeckah Lupton
	Mary Parkins	Lydia Lupton

GARWOOD—REA

Thomas Garwood, son of John Garwood of the County of Culpepper and State of Virginia and Esther his Wife, and *Hannah Rea*, daughter of Robert Rea of the County aforesaid and Rebeckah his wife; 16th day of 11th month, 1797; in their Meeting House in the County of Culpepper.

Witnesses who signed this Marriage Certificate:

Mary Garwood	Joseph Hains	John Garwood
Sally Garwood	John Miller	Robert Rea
Mary Estes	Margret Inskeep	Rebeckah Rea
Frederick Irvin	Mary Hains	Esther Garwood
Marstoll Estes	Rachel M'Kay	Joseph Rea
Daniel Updyke	Joshua Swayne	Daniel Garwood
Ezekiel Hains	William Porter	Henry Miller
Thomas Thorn	Bennett Payne	
Roland Richards	Joshua Inskeep	

WALTON—M'KAY

Samuel Walton, of Shanandoah County in the State of Virginia, son of Moses Walton late of Frederick County, deceased, and Eunice his Wife, and *Sarah M'Kay*, daughter of Jacob M'Kay of Frederick County aforesaid and Rachel his Wife, deceased; 6th day of 12th month, 1797; at Crooked Run.

Witnesses who signed this Marriage Certificate:

Mary Hains	Andrew M'Kay	Jacob M'Kay
Roland Richards	Jacob M'Kay Jr. 2d	Rachel McKay
Robert Whitacre	James Ireland Sr.	Eunice Allen
Isaac Painter	Margaret Hains	Hannah Wood
Lydia Richards	James Ireland Jr.	Edward Walton
John Hains	Abraham Woodrow	Eunice Walton
Eli Hains	Moses Walton	Joshua Wood
Sarah Middleton	Isaac Woodrow	Jesse McKay
Westley Allen	John Lupton	Jacob McKay Jr.
Rachel Painter	Jane M'Kay	Peggy McKay
John M'Kay	Moses M'Kay	Asa M'Kay

McKAY—HAINS

Jacob McKay Jr., of Frederick County in the State of Virginia, son of Andrew M'Kay of the same place and Jane his wife, and *Mary Hains*, daughter of Robert Hains late of the County and State above said (deceased) and Margret his wife; 9th day of 1st month, 1799; in Meeting House at Crooked Run.

Witnesses who signed this Marriage Certificate:

Patience Hains	Noah Hains	Andrew M'Kay
Eli Hains	Richard Ridgway	Margret Hains
Ebenezer Hains	Jonathan Wright	Jane M'kay
James M'Kay	Rachel M'Kay	Martha Branson
John Painter	John Hains, Sr.	Martha Fawcett
Isaac Painter	Mary Hains	Patience Whitacre
Darling Conrow	David Ridgway	Abigail M'Kay
Rachel Conrow	Enos M'Kay	John Hains
Abraham Woodrow	Jesse M'Kay	Moses M'Kay

PIGGOTT—FAWCETT

John Piggott, of Frederick County and State of Virginia, son of John Piggott of Louden County and State aforesaid and Phebe his Wife, and *Rachel Fawcett*, daughter of Richard Fawcett of Frederick County and State aforesaid and Mary his Wife; 4th day of 4th month, 1799; at Mount Pleasant Meeting House.

Witnesses who signed this Marriage Certificate:

Jonathan Taylor	Samuel Pickering	Richard Fawcett
Ann Taylor	Jonathan Lukens	Mary Fawcett
Jonah Hollingsworth	George Redd	Joseph Fawcett
Hannah Hollingsworth	Rachel Redd	Samuel Fawcett
Jonathan Fawcett	Rebecka Redd	Thomas Fawcett
Phebe Fawcett	Moses Piggott	Ebenezer Piggott
Hannah Fawcett	John Pickering	Hannah Pickering
	Samuel Pickering Jr.	Thomas Fawcett Jr.
	Phebe Pickering	Jonas Pickering
	Sarah Fisher	John Fisher

MULLIN—RICHARDS

John Mullin, of Frederick County in the State of Virginia, son of John Mullin late of Burlington County, West New Jersey, deceased, and *Lydia Richards*, daughter of Roland Richards of the said County of Frederick; 9th day of 10th month, 1799; at Crooked Run.

Witnesses who signed this Marriage Certificate:

Sarah Painter	Andrew M'Kay	Roland Richards
Thomas Fernley	Jane M'Kay	Lydia Richards
John Painter	Joshua Swayne	Isaac Mullin
Thomas Draper	John Smith Sr.	Catharine Richards
Simion Hains	Eli Hains	Mary Richards
Eunice Allen	Jacob M'Kay Jr.	Sarah Richards
Betty Hains	Moses M'Kay	Jane Mullin
Isaac Painter	Richard Fawcett	David Holloway
	Darling Conrow	William Branson

PAINTER—HAINS

Robert Painter, of Frederick County in the State of Virginia, son of John Painter of the same place and Susannah his Wife, and *Mary Hains*, daughter of Joseph Hains of the County aforesaid and Bulah his Wife; 4th day of 12th month, 1799; at Crooked Run.

Witnesses who signed this Marriage Certificate:

Jesse M'Kay	John Hains	John Painter
Noah Hains	Joshua Swayne	Joseph Hains
Mary Davis	Rebeckah M'Kay	Susannah Painter
Grace Antram	Sarah Middleton	Bulah Hains
Sally Cooper	Nathan Hains	Eli Hains
Levi Cooper	Rebeckah Hains	Susannah Painter
James Dawson	Hannah Wood	Isaac Painter
		Sarah Painter
		Jacob Painter

THOMAS—BOND

Ezekiel Thomas, son of Evan Thomas of Rockingham County in the State of Virginia, and *Rebekah Bond*, daughter of Isaac Bond of the County of Shannandoah; 5th day of 12th month, 1799; at Smiths Creek Meeting House.

Witnesses who signed this Marriage Certificate:

Eunice Allen	Hannah Bond
Hannah Allen	Rebeckah Bond
Evan Thomas	Sarah Allen
Isaac Bond	Deborah Allen
Benjamin Allen	Mary Allen
Joseph Allen	Anna Allen
Jackson Allen	Elisabeth Pennywitt
William Allen	John O'Neil
Joseph Allen Sr.	Moses Thomas

WRIGHT—PICKERING

James Wright, of the County of Frederick and State of Virginia, son of John Wright and Phebe his Wife, and *Hannah Pickering*, daughter of Samuel and Grace Pickering, deceased, of the County and State aforesaid; 8th day of 10th month, 1800; at Center Meeting House.

Witnesses who signed this Marriage Certificate:

Robert Miller	Sidney Rogers	John Wright
Joseph Wood	Hannah Chandlee	Phebe Wright
Jonathan Parkins	Ann Lupton	Samuel Pickering
Mary Parkins	Elizabeth Lupton	Phebe Pickering
Casander Miller	Joshua Lupton	Mary Fawcett
Susannah Wright	Nathan Lupton	John Pickering
Rachel Hollingsworth	Margaret Lupton	Jonathan Pickering
Sarah Hollingsworth	Joseph Lupton	Mary Pickering
Ruth Miller	Joseph Fawcett	
John Lupton		

HAINS—MILLER

Eli Hains, son of John Hains and Mary his Wife of Frederick County and State of Virginia, and *Ruth Miller,* daughter of Robert Miller and Cassander his Wife of the County and State aforesaid; 8th day of 9th month, 1802; at Center Meeting House.

Witnesses who signed this Marriage Certificate:

Joseph Taylor	Sarah Hollingsworth	John Hains
Mary Taylor	Rachel Hollingsworth	Mary Hains
Isaac Parkins	Solomon Hollingsworth	Robert Miller
Mary Parkins	Isaac Hollingsworth	Cassander Miller
Margaret Wood	John Lupton	Solomon Miller
Mary Wood	Joshua Lupton	William Miller
John Wright	Jonathan Brown	Sarah Miller
Thomas Fawcett	Deborah Brown	Hannah Miller

MILLER—NEILL

Solomon Miller, of Luzene Township, Fayatte County, and State of Pennsylvania, son of Robert Miller and Cassander his Wife, and *Ruth Neill,* daughter of John and Ann his Wife (the former deceased) of Frederick County and State of Virginia; 9th day of 11th month, 1803; at their Meeting house in the County of Frederick aforesaid.

Witnesses who signed this Marriage Certificate:

Sarah Hollingsworth	Isaac Parkins	Robert Miller
Thomas Neill	Mary Parkins	Ann Neill
Isaac Hollingsworth	Ann Lupton	William Miller
Mary Neill	Elisabeth Neill	Isaac Neill
Phebe Neill	Abraham Neill	Ruth Hains
William Neill	Josiah Hollingsworth	Solomon Hollingsworth
Ann Carter	Grace Parkins	Rachel Hollingsworth
Rachel Carter	Hannah Hollingsworth	Lewis Neill

HOPEWELL CERTIFICATES OF MEMBERSHIP AND REMOVAL

From Book I
1759-1776

In those instances in which no meeting is named to which or from which the certificate was given, the person certificated was a new member at Hopewell.

Day Mo. Yr.	Meeting	To Meeting	To Meeting	Names
28 4 1736	E. Nottingham	Hopewell		Simeon Taylor & wife
26 3 1759		Hopewell	Fairfax	William Brooks
23 4 1759	E. Nottingham	Hopewell		Thos. Rees, wife, & child Norris
23 4 1759		Hopewell	Fairfax	Jas. Wright, wife, & child
25 6 1759	Richland	Hopewell		Joseph Hoge
20 8 1759	Fairfax	Hopewell		Henry Carter
22 10 1759	Fairfax	Hopewell		Morris Rees Jr., wife, & child
24 12 1759		Hopewell		Edmund Jolliffe
21 1 1760		Hopewell		Robert Bull
21 1 1760	E. Nottingham	Hopewell		Morris Rees, wife, & son Thomas
4 2 1760	Hatenfield	Hopewell		John Painter & wife
3 3 1760	Richland	Hopewell		George Hoge & wife
2 6 1760	Goshen	Hopewell		Hannah Kirk
4 8 1760	Fairfax	Hopewell		Henry Lewis, wife, & family
4 8 1760	Richland	Hopewell		Wm. Hoge Jr., wife, & family
1 9 1760	Sadsbury	Hopewell		Jesse Webb
6 10 1760		Hopewell	Fairfax	Joseph Hoge
6 10 1760	Kennett	Hopewell		Aaron Hackney, Charity, John, & Jos. Hackney
3 11 1760		Hopewell	E. Nottingham	Catharen Ross
3 11 1760		Hopewell	Fairfax	Mary Barrett
1 12 1760	E. Nottingham	Hopewell		Jacob Hastings, wife, & children, also Rachel Metcalf
2 2 1761	E. Nottingham	Hopewell		Thomas Butterfield
5 4 1761	Wilmington, Del.	Hopewell		Owen Williams
4 5 1761	Burlington	Hopewell		Eunice & Amelia Osmond

Day Mo. Yr.	Meeting	To	Meeting	To Meeting	Names
4 5 1761	Burlington		Hopewell		John Branson, wife, & dtrs. Martha & Ann
4 5 1761			Hopewell	Kennet	Aaron Hackney
1 6 1761	Fairfax		Hopewell		Wm. Harris, wife, & children
6 7 1761	New Garden, N. C.		Hopewell		Debborah Morgan
7 9 1761	Sadsbury		Hopewell		John Rees, wife, & ch., Lydia, Jacob, John, Morris, Hannah, Rachel
7 9 1761	Goshen, Pa.		Hopewell		Jeremiah Largent, son of John & Rachel
7 12 1761			Hopewell		Robert Painter
1 2 1762			Hopewell	E. Nottingham	Rachel Metcalf
5 7 1762	Evesham		Hopewell		Samuel Shinn Jr.
6 9 1762	Fairfax		Hopewell		Jas. Wright, w. Lucy, & ch., Ralph, Jas., Ann, Susannah, Micajah
1 11 1762	E. Nottingham		Hopewell		Stephen Ross
3 1 1763			Hopewell		John Painter's minor ch., Thos., Isaac, Hannah
7 3 1763	Warrington		Hopewell		William Boyd
2 5 1763	Burlington		Hopewell		Rachel Ridgway (w. of Josiah) & son Lot
6 6 1763	Buckingham		Hopewell		Barrack Fisher & w. Mary
6 6 1763	Buckingham		Hopewell		Sam'l Pickering, wife, & children
6 6 1763	Exeter		Hopewell		Enos Ellis, w. Elizabeth, & ch., Thos., Hannah, Rebecca, Jane, Dinah, Ellis, Wm.
6 6 1763	Exeter		Hopewell		Elizabeth, w. of Townsend Marthen
2 4 1764			Hopewell	New Garden, N. C.	Simeon Taylor, wife, & ch., John, Ann
7 5 1764			Hopewell	New Garden, N. C.	Mary Taylor & Katharine Eldrig
7 5 1764			Hopewell	Providence, Pa.	Jane Pugh
5 6 1764			Hopewell	Ceeder Creek	David Brooks
6 8 1764			Hopewell		Request of Sam'l Person for ch., Mary, Enoch, Wm., Benj.
6 8 1764			Hopewell	Petersburg	Robt. Bull, wife, & children, & Mary Bull
3 11 1764			Hopewell	Cane Creek, N. C.	Catherine & Lydia Steward, dtrs. of Robt.
3 12 1764	Fairfax		Hopewell		Jacob Beeson & bro. Edward
1 4 1765			Hopewell	Wateree	Wm. O'Neal, wife, & ch., Abijah & Sarah
3 6 1765	Exeter		Hopewell		Isaac Jackson
2 9 1765	Exeter		Hopewell		Thos. Ellis, wife, & ch., Jane, Rowland, Deborah, John

Day Mo. Yr.	Meeting	To	Meeting	To Meeting	Names
7 10 1765			Hopewell	Wateree	Patience Parkins & children
7 10 1765			Hopewell	Wateree	Elizabeth, w. of David Rees
7 10 1765			Hopewell		Rebecca Beeman
3 3 1766	E. Nottingham		Hopewell		Jos. Day, w. Katherine, & son Evan
3 3 1766	Fairfax		Hopewell		Mary Barrett Jr.
5 5 1766	Ruhland		Hopewell		Sam'l Bevar, w. Susannah, & ch., Phemia, John, Martha, Sam'l, Evan
5 5 1766	Providence, Pa.		Hopewell		Jane Pugh
7 7 1766			Hopewell		John Adams, wife, & ch., Wm., Henry, John, Jos., Mary, Susannah
4 8 1766			Hopewell	Wilmington	Jas. Wright, minor son of Isaac & Sidney
6 10 1766			Hopewell	Petersburg	Robt. Bull, wife, & children
6 10 1766			Hopewell	Wateree	Deborrah Morgan
6 10 1766			Hopewell	Fairfax	Phebe Barrett, d. of Jas.
3 11 1766	E. Nottingham		Hopewell		Arthur Barrett
1 12 1766	Fairfax		Hopewell		Peter Beeson
5 1 1767	Worrington		Hopewell		Ruth Neavet
2 2 1767			Hopewell		Sarah Bruce
2 3 1767			Hopewell		Ruth Parkins
2 3 1767			Hopewell	Petersburg	Isaac Hollingsworth (son of Geo.)
2 3 1767			Hopewell	Fairfax	Hannah Harris & children
6 7 1767			Hopewell		Meschach Saxton
3 8 1767	Fairfax		Hopewell		Jas. Steer, w. Abigail, & ch., Hannah, Grace, Rachel; also Isaac Nevitt, under their care
3 8 1767			Hopewell	Nottingham	Arthur Barrett
3 8 1767			Hopewell	Wilmington	Edward Wright, son of Isaac & Sidney
7 12 1767			Hopewell	Fairfax	Ruth Cadwaleder
4 1 1768			Hopewell	Nottingham	Jonathan Ross
4 1 1768			Hopewell	Bush River	Hannah Pugh & children
1 2 1768			Hopewell	Bush River	Jos. Hollingsworth
1 2 1768			Hopewell	Bush River	Sarah Ruble & ch., Jemima, Jas., Geo., Elizabeth
1 2 1768			Hopewell	Bush River	Sarah Haworth
7 3 1768			Hopewell	Bush River	Mary Babb (w. of Jos.)
6 6 1768			Hopewell	Bush River	Lydia Ballinger & children
6 6 1768			Hopewell	Bush River	Jonathan Taylor, wife, & children
6 6 1768	Sadsbury		Hopewell		Josiah Jackson, wife, & small ch., Grace, Sam'l
6 6 1768	Fairfax		Hopewell		Hannah Hackney, w. of Aaron

Day Mo. Yr.	Meeting	To	Meeting	To Meeting	Names
4 7 1768	Warrington		Hopewell		John Berry, w. Patience, & ch., Sam'l, David, Margaret, John, Lydia, Aaron, Thos., Jos.
4 7 1768			Hopewell		Ann Wright, d. of Lydia Rogers, formerly Wright
1 8 1768			Hopewell		Mary & Ann Bruce, dtrs. of Geo. & Rachel
5 9 1768	Gosham		Hopewell		Mary Duyer
3 10 1768			Hopewell		Thomas Feenly
7 11 1768	Warrington		Hopewell		Elizabeth Neavitt
7 11 1768			Hopewell	New Garden, N. C.	Elizabeth Berry, w. of Wm.
7 11 1768	Crooked Run		Hopewell		Mary Ellis, d. of Jos. & Mary
6 3 1769	Middletown, Pa.		Hopewell		Cuthbert Hayhurst
6 3 1769	Gosham		Hopewell		Jacob Jenkins
1 5 1769			Hopewell	Bush River	Thos. Pugh, wife, & ch., Gabriel, Jane, Alice, Elizabeth, Ann, Lydia
7 8 1769	Uwchland		Hopewell		Isaac Brown
2 10 1769			Hopewell		Job Pugh
5 2 1770	Bradford		Hopewell		Mary Wood (w. of Thos.)
7 5 1770	Warrington		Hopewell		Ruth Pugh
7 5 1770	Evesham		Hopewell		Jos. Stratton, w. Naomi, & ch., Sarah, Jos.
7 5 1770	Evesham		Hopewell		Elias Stratton
4 6 1770	Warrington		Hopewell		John Smith, w. Ann, & ch., Mary, Margaret, Hannah, Ann, Thos., Susannah, Rebecca
4 6 1770	Warrington		Hopewell		Jesse Faulkner & ch., David, Jesse, Ruth, Robt., Martha, Hannah
2 7 1770	Bradford		Hopewell		Thomas White
6 8 1770	Evesham		Hopewell		Abigail Rhoads, w. of Adam
6 8 1770	Warrington		Hopewell		Jean Pugh, w. of Thos.
3 9 1770	Kingwood		Hopewell		John Brock, w. Jean, & ch., Mary, Dan'l, Jacob, Jane, Alice, Steven, Nathan
3 9 1770	Kingwood		Hopewell		Mary Green
5 11 1770	Warrington		Hopewell		Jane Faulkner & ch., Wm., Sarah, Ann, Jas.
5 11 1770	Bradford		Hopewell		Nath'l & Mary White & ch., Sarah, Lydia, Nath'l
7 1 1771	Concord, Pa.		Hopewell		Samuel Thatcher
4 3 1771	Burlington		Hopewell		Geo. Shinn, w. Rachel, & ch., Elizabeth, Mary, Israel
4 3 1771			Hopewell		Lewis Neill Jr.

Day Mo. Yr.	Meeting	To	Meeting	To Meeting	Names
1 4 1771	Goshen, Pa.		Hopewell		Thomas Pugh
1 4 1771			Hopewell		Sidney Wright asks for her son Solomon
6 5 1771	Bradford		Hopewell		Jas. Parviance, w. Elizabeth, & ch., Nathan, John
6 5 1771	E. Nottingham		Hopewell		Ebenezer Kirk
6 5 1771	Concord		Hopewell		Ann White & Mary White
6 5 1771			Hopewell		Moses Walton & children
3 6 1771	Bradford		Hopewell		Joshua Swain
5 8 1771			Hopewell	Bush River	Sam'l Pearson & ch., Enock, Wm., Martha, Benj., Hannah, Sam'l, Unice
2 9 1771	Ireland, near Ballendery		Hopewell		Thos. & John Fawcett
2 9 1771	Evesham		Hopewell		John Garwood, w. Esther, & ch., Hope, Sarah
2 9 1771			Hopewell		Mary Pearson
7 10 1771			Hopewell		Dan'l McPherson; Jas. Holloway; Mary Butterfield
4 11 1771			Hopewell	New Garden, N. C.	Rich'd Hayworth & w. Ann
4 11 1771			Hopewell	Bush River	James Ballinger
4 11 1771	Crooked Run		Hopewell		Robert Ray
2 12 1771			Hopewell	Evesham	Elias Stratton
2 3 1772			Hopewell		Rees Cadwalledar, w. Ruth, & ch., Asa, Mary, Edith
6 4 1772			Hopewell	New Garden, N. C.	Wm. Rees, wife, & children
6 4 1772			Hopewell		Sarah Smith
4 5 1772	Warrington		Hopewell		Wm. Wickersham, w. Mary, & d. Lydia
4 5 1772	New Garden		Hopewell		Nathan Pusey
4 5 1772			Hopewell		Esther Colson
1 6 1772	Goshen, Pa.		Hopewell		John Sargen
1 6 1772	Guinedd		Hopewell		Isaac Hughs & ch., Abner, Anne, Edward
1 6 1772	Perguimonto		Hopewell		Andrew McKay
1 6 1772	Fairfax		Hopewell		Phebe Barrot
1 6 1772	Richsquare		Hopewell		Sidney Wright
6 7 1772	Concord, Pa.		Hopewell		William Grubb
3 8 1772	Chesterfield		Hopewell		John Holloway & ch., Jesse, Ruth, John, Baton, Thos., Geo.
3 8 1772	Ireland, near Ballendery		Hopewell		William Bickat
3 8 1772	Chesterfield		Hopewell		Samuel Holloway
3 8 1772			Hopewell		Rachel Longacre
7 9 1772	New Garden, Pa.		Hopewell		Thomas Brown

Day Mo. Yr.	Meeting	To	Meeting	To Meeting	Names
7 9 1772			Hopewell	New Garden, N. C.	Isaac & John Hiatt
7 9 1772			Hopewell		Jacob Jinkens & ch., Mary, Jonathan, Michael, Evan, Anna, Ruth, Eliz'h. Jacob
2 11 1772	E. Nottingham		Hopewell		Thomas Sheppard
2 11 1772	Evesham		Hopewell		Isiah Garwood
2 11 1772			Hopewell		Mary Jay
2 11 1772			Hopewell	Uwchland	Sol. and Jas. Hogue
1 2 1773			Hopewell		Ezekiel Haines, wife, & 6 ch. Sarah, Carlile, Isaac, Jacob, & Sam'l are named
1 3 1773			Hopewell	Buckingham	Wm. Lupton Jr.
5 4 1773	Guinedd		Hopewell		Mary Chilcot
5 4 1773	Sadsbury		Hopewell		Jean McPherson
3 5 1773	Fairfax		Hopewell		David Williams
7 6 1773	E. Nottingham		Hopewell		Dan'l Brown, wife, & ch., Joel, Merium, Eliz'h, Dan'l
7 6 1773	E. Nottingham		Hopewell		Lydia Gregg
7 6 1773	Exeter		Hopewell		Mordecai Ellis, w. Mary, & ch., Susannah, Jean, Nehemiah, Elinor, Sam'l, Mordecai
7 6 1773	Exeter		Hopewell		Anthony Lee, w. Abigail, & ch., Deborah, Thos., John, Sarah, Anthony. Ellen
7 6 1773	Concord		Hopewell		Alice Swango
5 7 1773			Hopewell		Sarah Brown (w. of David)
5 7 1773	New Garden, Pa.		Hopewell		Rachel Johnston
6 9 1773	Dear Creek		Hopewell		Jean White
6 9 1773	E. Nottingham		Hopewell		Rachel White
6 9 1773			Hopewell	Bush River	Jos. Thompson & w. Ann
6 9 1773	Evesham		Hopewell		Eliz'h Haines (w. of Levi) & ch., Abigail, Enos, Deborah
6 12 1773			Hopewell	Bush River	Absolem Haworth
6 12 1773	E. Nottingham		Hopewell		Jas. Gauthrop & w. Patience
3 1 1774	Warrington		Hopewell		Hannah Newland
3 1 1774	Exeter		Hopewell		Sarah Hutton
1 2 1774			Hopewell	New Garden	Mary Dillon
1 3 1774	E. Nottingham		Hopewell		Timothy Brown, w. Rachel, & ch., John, Timothy, Mary, Wm.
1 3 1774	E. Nottingham		Hopewell		Wm. White, w. Sarah, & ch., John, Sarah, Margaret, Wm.
1 3 1774	E. Nottingham		Hopewell		David Wilson
2 5 1774	Warrington		Hopewell		Katharine Harris, w. of John
2 5 1774	Deer Creek		Hopewell		Henry Cougel, w. Ruth, & ch., Jas., Mary, Ruth, Hennery, Rachel, Isaac

Day Mo. Yr.	Meeting	To Meeting	To Meeting	Names
2 5 1774		Hopewell	Fairfax	John Paxton
2 5 1774		Hopewell		Jacob Rambo
2 5 1774		Hopewell		Thomas Painter
6 6 1774	E. Nottingham	Hopewell		David Rees, w. Martha, & ch., Jacob, Jane, Enoch, Mary, David, Ellis
6 6 1774		Hopewell		Thos. Butterfield requests for his ch., Jas. & Rachel
4 7 1774	Wilmington	Hopewell		James Wright
4 7 1774	Burlington	Hopewell		Geo. Holloway & w. Ruth
11 8 1774	E. Nottingham	Hopewell		Jeremiah Cooper
11 8 1774	Concord	Hopewell		Robert Ayre
5 9 1774	Chester	Hopewell		Dan'l Brown, w. Susannah, & ch., Jos., Mary, Marget, Dan'l, John, Joel
5 9 1774	Fairfax	Hopewell		Rachel Neale
5 9 1774		Hopewell		John McPherson
5 9 1774		Hopewell	Evesham	Isaiah Garwood
3 10 1774	Uwchland	Hopewell		Henry Williams
3 10 1774	Exeter	Hopewell		Owen Long, w. Lidia, & ch., Rebecca, Rachel, Aimy, Robt., Mary, Eliz'h
3 10 1774	Evesham	Hopewell		Jos. Haines, w. Beulah, & ch., Patience, Ebenezer, Eliz'h, Jos.
3 10 1774		Hopewell	Bush River	Jos., Benj., Jeremiah, Arthur, Jacob, Lidia, ch., of Jacob Barrett
1 11 1774	New Garden	Hopewell		Solomon Sheppard
1 11 1774	E. Nottingham	Hopewell		Hannah Piggot & ch., Rachel, Moses, Hannah, Thos.
1 11 1774		Hopewell	Bush River	Jas. Hoge & ch., Jacob, Phebe, Wm.
5 12 1774	New Garden	Hopewell		Elizabeth Turtle
2 1 1775	Abington	Hopewell		Marget Bond & ch., Rebecca, Allen, Hannah, Eliz'h
2 1 1775	Warrington	Hopewell		Jean Smith
6 2 1775	Evesham	Hopewell		Jonathan Bishop, w. Patience, & ch., Hannah, Isiah, John, Mary, Jos., Thos.
6 2 1775	Nottingham	Hopewell		Jesse Lacy & ch., Israel, Tacy, Ellis, Uphamey, Mashack
6 2 1775		Hopewell	Deer Creek	Thomas Sheppard
6 3 1775		Hopewell	Crooked Run	Robt. Ray requests for his ch., Ann, John, Jos., Allen
3 4 1775		Hopewell		Ann Eyre & ch., John, Mary, Hannah, Sam'l, Wm.
3 4 1775		Hopewell		Ch. of Jackson Allen: Lidia, Davis, Bette, Sarah, Sirley

Day Mo. Yr.	Meeting	To Meeting	To Meeting	Names
3 4 1775		Hopewell		Ch. of Jos. Allen: Benj., Jos., Wm., Jackson, Sarah, Thos., Susannah, Mary
3 4 1775		Hopewell		Bette Allen, w. of Jackson
1 5 1775		Hopewell		John Trimble, w. Catharine, & d. Ann
5 6 1775	West River	Hopewell		Jos. Smith, w. Rachel & ch.
5 6 1775	Warrington	Hopewell		Rich'd Wickersham & w. Eliz'h; also Sam'l Wickersham
5 6 1775	Nottingham	Hopewell		Goldsmith Chandlee & Edward White
5 6 1775	New Garden	Hopewell		Lydia Woodrow & ch., Mary, Isaac, Lidia, Eliz'h, Rachel, Abraham
5 6 1775		Hopewell	Pipe Creek	Deborah Ellis
5 6 1775	Crooked Run	Hopewell		Sarah Hawkins requests for her ch., Sam'l & Eliz'h
5 6 1775		Hopewell	Chesterfield	Samuel Holloway
3 7 1775	Bradford	Hopewell		Joshua Cope
7 8 1775	Fairfax	Hopewell		Henry Smith Jr.
4 9 1775	Deere Creek	Hopewell		John Cogelle, w. Catharine, & d. Dinah
4 9 1775		Hopewell		Isaac Brown requests for his son John
2 10 1775	Concord	Hopewell		Mary Thatcher
4 12 1775		Hopewell		Albanah Dodd
1 1 1776	Bush Creek	Hopewell		Sarah Bull & ch., John, David, & Robt. Milburn; & Mary, Sarah, Lydia, Hannah, & Jonah Bull
1 1 1776		Hopewell	New Garden	Solomon Shepard
1 1 1776		Hopewell	New Garden	James Hiett
5 2 1776		Hopewell		Levi Hains
5 2 1776		Hopewell	Uwchland	John McPherson
5 2 1776		Hopewell		Dan'l McPherson Jr.
4 3 1776	Fairfax	Hopewell		Jonah Hollingsworth
1 4 1776		Hopewell		Moses Meser
1 4 1776		Hopewell		Eliz'h Branson requests for her ch., Wm., Rachel, Isaac, Charity, Martha, Jacob, Eliz'h, Mary
1 4 1776	Crooked Run	Hopewell		Abraham Branson
6 5 1776		Hopewell		Wm. Brown, w. Martha, & ch., Martha, Jean
6 5 1776	Fairfax	Hopewell		Rachel Hollingsworth & ch., Phebe, Mary
3 6 1776	Fairfax	Hopewell		Stephen Brown
5 6 1776	Fairfax	Hopewell		Benj. Shreve, w. Hannah, & d. Rebecca

Day Mo. Yr.	Meeting	To Meeting	To Meeting	Names
1 7 1776	Nottingham	Hopewell		Aaron Gregg & w. Elizabeth
1 7 1776	Nottingham	Hopewell		Jonathan Rosse
1 7 1776	Nottingham	Hopewell		Meser Sheppard, w. Susannah, & child
5 8 1776	Fairfax	Hopewell		James Conrad Jr.
7 10 1776	Uwchland	Hopewell		Hannah McPherson
4 11 1776	Fairfax	Hopewell		Robert Smith
4 11 1776	New Garden	Hopewell		Solomon Shepard
4 11 1776	New Garden	Hopewell		Mary Dillon
4 11 1776	Fairfax	Hopewell		Jean Conard
2 12 1776		Hopewell		Ann Lupton requests for her ch., Gideon, Lewis, Marget Rees
5 5 1777		Hopewell		Mary, Deborah, Beersheba Allen, dtrs. of Jackson

FROM BOOK TWO
1777-1791

Day Mo. Yr.	Meeting	To Meeting	To Meeting	Names
7 4 1777	Bush River	Hopewell		Sarah Pugh & Deborah McChoole
5 5 1777		Hopewell		Jackson, Lidia, Jacob, Isaac, ch. of Jacob Rambo
2 6 1777	Bush River	Hopewell		Thos. Pugh, w. Ann, & ch., Jean, Ann, Lidia, Rachel
2 6 1777	Guinedd	Hopewell		Margaret Hank & ch., Susannah, Elenor, Hannah, Margaret
7 7 1777	Nottingham	Hopewell		Abner White
1 9 1777	Concord	Hopewell		Mary Booth
1 9 1777	Concord	Hopewell		Aaron Booth
3 11 1777	Uwchland	Hopewell		John Griffith, w. Mary, & dtrs., Martha, Mary, Sybill
3 11 1777	Deer Creek	Hopewell		Geo. Pain, w. Rachel, & ch., Rachel, Martha, Sarah, Alice, Geo.
3 11 1777	Pipe Creek	Hopewell		Sarah Brown, nee Ballinger
3 11 1777		Hopewell	New Garden, N. C.	John Thomas & w. Alice
5 1 1778	Nottingham	Hopewell		Jas. Sidwell & w. Hannah
5 1 1778	Exeter	Hopewell		Rebekah George
6 1 1778		Hopewell	Pipe Creek	Sam'l Ellis, son of Mordecai
2 3 1778	Nottingham	Hopewell		Isaac England
6 4 1778	Abington	Hopewell		Sarah Littlejohn, w. of John, & ch., Wm., Thos., Ann, John, Martha, Jas.
4 5 1778	Pipe Creek	Hopewell		Hannah Hollingsworth
4 5 1778		Hopewell		Unice Branson

Day Mo. Yr.	Meeting	To Meeting	To Meeting	Names
1 6 1778	Fairfax	Hopewell		Jas. Conard Sr.
1 6 1778	Uwchland	Hopewell		Richard Evan, w. Phebe, & ch., Thos., Sarah, Margaret, Mary, Catherine
1 6 1778		Hopewell		Abigail Green
1 6 1778		Hopewell	Fairfax	Aaron Hackney, w. Hannah, & small ch., Geo., Jos. Lydia, Jehu
6 7 1778		Hopewell		John Green
3 8 1778		Hopewell		Samuel Chew
3 8 1778		Hopewell		Abigail, Enos, Deborah, ch. of Levy & Elizabeth Haines
5 10 1778		Hopewell		Deborah, Elizabeth, & Esther Hodgson
2 11 1778		Hopewell		James Hodson
7 12 1778		Hopewell	Pipe Creek	Solomon Shephard
7 12 1778		Hopewell	Bush River	Absalom Hayworth
4 1 1779		Hopewell	Fairfax	John Hoge & w. Mary
1 2 1779	Abington	Hopewell		John Bond
1 2 1779	Pipe Creek	Hopewell		Joseph Wood
1 2 1779		Hopewell		Dan'l, Sarah, Susannah, David, Phebe, Wm., minor ch. of Sarah & David Brown
1 2 1779		Hopewell		Jane Pugh, d. of Jane & Thos.
1 3 1779		Hopewell		Jos. Lacy's children
1 3 1779		Hopewell	Nottingham	Abner White
1 3 1779		Hopewell		Mary & John, ch. of John Bond of Smith Creek
1 3 1779		Hopewell		Benj., Hannah, Jacob, ch. of Jos. Straton of Culpeper
5 4 1779	Fairfax	Hopewell		James Raley
5 4 1779	Pipe Creek	Hopewell		Dan'l Ballinger
5 4 1779	Concord	Hopewell		William Askew
1 5 1779		Hopewell	Fairfax	Israel, Uphamy, Elias, & Meshack Lacey, ch. of Jos.
3 5 1779	Abington	Hopewell		Edward Bond, wife & 7 ch.
3 5 1779	Buckingham	Hopewell		William Lupton
3 5 1779		Hopewell		Wm. Grubbs of Bullskin & ch., Adam, Mary, Lydia, Hannah, Sarah, Curtis
3 5 1779		Hopewell		Lydia Woodrow's ch., Simeon & Phebe
3 5 1779		Hopewell		John Holloway's ch., David, Ephraim, Charlotte, of Stafford
7 6 1779	Evesham	Hopewell		John Hains & w. Mary
7 6 1779	Abington	Hopewell		Agnes Carter

Day Mo. Yr.	Meeting	To	Meeting	To Meeting	Names
7 6 1779			Hopewell		Agnes Mendinghall & ch., Martha, Mary, Lydia
5 7 1779	Worrington		Hopewell		Finley McGrew, w. Dinah, & ch., John, Jas., Mary, Nathan, Finely, Dinah, Rebecca, Margaret
5 7 1779	E. Nottingham		Hopewell		Ann Stroud
2 8 1779			Hopewell		Walter Denny
6 9 1779			Hopewell	Nottingham	Margaret Sidwell
6 9 1779			Hopewell		Elizabeth Woodrow
6 9 1779	Concord		Hopewell		Michael Shion
6 9 1779			Hopewell		James Moore
6 9 1779			Hopewell	New Garden, N. C.	Thomas Branson
4 10 1779	Kennet		Hopewell		George Red
4 10 1779			Hopewell		Rebeccah Rambo
7 2 1780			Hopewell		Joseph Warden
6 3 1780			Hopewell		Robert Hannah
3 4 1780	Worrington		Hopewell		Rowland Richard, w. Lydia, & ch., Abigail, Ely, Hannah, Townsend
3 4 1780	Sadsbury		Hopewell		Hannah Daniel
3 4 1780			Hopewell		Catherine Hannah
3 4 1780			Hopewell		Robt. Hannah's ch., Thos. & Beni.. of Crooked Run
1 5 1780	Philadelphia		Hopewell		Jas. Lowness, w. Sarah, & ch., Mary, Sarah, Hyat, John, Deborah, Jas., Caleb
1 5 1780	Salem		Hopewell		Aaron Hughs, w. Mary, & ch., Lydia & Sarah
14 6 1780	Hadonfield		Hopewell		Isaac Holloway, w. Mary, & ch., Amos, Abel, Wm., Asa, Isaac, Mary, Sam'l, Abner, Sarah
14 6 1780			Hopewell	Northampton	Jos. Wright, w. Rebecca, & ch., Sarah, Mary, Schooly, Jos., Frances, Elizabeth
14 6 1780			Hopewell	Buckingham	Sidney Pickering & husband
14 6 1780			Hopewell		Joel Chesher
7 7 1780	Warrington		Hopewell		John Cook
7 8 1780	Warrington		Hopewell		Wm. Newlin, w. Margaret, & ch., Mary, Wm., Jas., John, Margaret
7 8 1780	Fairfax		Hopewell		Abner Gregg & w. Sarah
7 8 1780			Hopewell		Mary White's ch., Jos. & Nath'l
7 8 1780			Hopewell		Mary White, reinstated
4 9 1780	Fairfax		Hopewell		John Hoge, w. Mary, & son Wm.
4 9 1780			Hopewell		Mary Wickersham & son Jonathan

HOPEWELL GRAVEYARD

View from near the center, looking southwest

Day Mo. Yr.	Meeting	To	Meeting	To Meeting	Names
5 11 1780	Smith Creek		Hopewell		Griffeth Daubin, w. Mary Ann, & ch., Sarah, Elizabeth, Mary Ann, Catherine, Thos., Griffith, Jos.
5 11 1780	Guined		Hopewell		Ezekiel Cleaver
30 11 1780	Redstone		Hopewell		Nathan Hail, Uriah Coleson, Margaret Crawford, Elizabeth Jinkinson
30 11 1780			Hopewell	New Garden, N. C.	Evan Lewis
1 1 1781	Abington		Hopewell		Isaac Bond
1 1 1781	Deer Creek		Hopewell		Jas. Crawford & ch., Ephraim, Sarah, Mary, Rachel, Ruth, Wm., Jos., Margaret
1 1 1781	New Garden		Hopewell		Jos. Allen, w. Deborah, & ch., Eli, John, Sam'l, Ann, Amy, Wm., Deborah, Joshua, Benj.
1 1 1781	Deer Creek		Hopewell		John Jinkenson & ch., Isaac, Ann, Mary
1 1 1781	Fairfax		Hopewell		Jos. Brown, w. Elizabeth, & ch., Ann, Sarah, Isaiah, Rachel, Sam'l, Leah, Mary, Mahlon, Jos.
1 1 1781	New Garden		Hopewell		David England, wife, & ch., John, Eliz'h, Isaac, Israel, Sarah
1 1 1781	Bradford		Hopewell		Elizabeth Fornsten
5 2 1781			Hopewell	Monallen	James Hodgson
5 2 1781	Fairfax		Hopewell		Aaron Hackney, w. Hannah, & ch., Geo., Jos., Lydia, John, Aaron, Eliz'h
5 2 1781	Worrington		Hopewell		David Griffith
5 2 1781	Fairfax		Hopewell		Mary (Roach) Rogers
5 3 1781	Deer Creek		Hopewell		Joseph Tucker
5 3 1781	Nor. Dist. of Phila.		Hopewell		Jos. Rakestraw, w. Sarah, & ch., Justinian, Eliz'h, Hannah
5 3 1781	Sadsbury		Hopewell		Thomas Embree
5 3 1781	Fairfax		Hopewell		Ann Raley
2 4 1781	Deer Creek		Hopewell		Barnabas McNamee, w. Mary, & ch., Jacob, Isaac, Margaret, Gideon, Sarah, Mary, Elias
2 4 1781	Warrington		Hopewell		Wm. Horseman (to marry Mercy Lupton)
2 4 1781	Fairfax		Hopewell		John Raley
7 5 1781	Warrington		Hopewell		David Horseman
7 5 1781	Fairfax		Hopewell		Ruth Smith
7 5 1781	Nottingham		Hopewell		Susanna Clark & ch., Jas., Sarah, John, Jesse

Day Mo. Yr.	Meeting	To	Meeting	To Meeting	Names
7 5 1781	Fairfax		Hopewell		Abraham Smith
7 5 1781	Fairfax		Hopewell		George Smith
7 5 1781	Fairfax		Hopewell		Naomi Smith & ch., Sam'l, Naomi, Benj., Mary
31 5 1781	Deer Creek		Hopewell		John Cousins, w. Sarah, & ch., Susanna, Ann, Mary, Sarah, Hester, Eliz'h
31 5 1781	Deer Creek		Hopewell		Eleazer Brown, w. Sarah, & ch., Thos., Ann, Margaret, Jos.
31 5 1781	Worrington		Hopewell		Robt. Raley Jr.
31 5 1781	Nor. Dist. of Phila.		Hopewell		Sarah Pancast & dtrs., Mary & Elizabeth
2 7 1781	Fairfax		Hopewell		David Brown
2 7 1781			Hopewell		Evan Hiatt
2 7 1781			Hopewell		Henry Jenkinson, by request of parent John
6 8 1781	Nottingham		Hopewell		Sarah Johnson
6 8 1781	Exeter		Hopewell		Elizabeth Matthews
3 9 1781	Nottingham		Hopewell		Nathan Brown & w. Marg't
3 9 1781			Hopewell	Fairfax	Abner Gregg, w. Sarah, & d. Ann
5 11 1781	New Garden		Hopewell		Sam'l Jackson, w. Rebecca, & ch., John, Nathan, Jos., Susanna
5 11 1781	Duck Creek (M. M. held at Little Cr.)		Hopewell		Wm. Wilson, w. Elizabeth, & ch., Isral, Sarah, Jonathan, Wm., Eliz'h, Rachel
5 11 1781	Duck Creek		Hopewell		Martha Smith
5 11 1781	Warrington		Hopewell		Isaac Wickersham, w. Elizabeth, & ch., Jas., Josiah, Rebecca
5 11 1781			Hopewell		Josiah Crawford, w. Cassandra, & ch., Benedick, Jas., Josiah, Able, Levi, Elijah, Ephraim, Cassandra
29 11 1781	Exeter (M. M. held at Maiden Cr.)		Hopewell		Abijah Richards
7 1 1782	Pipe Creek		Hopewell		Samuel Ellis
7 1 1782	Uwchland		Hopewell		William William
7 1 1782			Hopewell		Mary, Lidia, John, ch. of Hannah & Henry Piggott
7 1 1782			Hopewell		Nathan, Arthur, Jos., ch. of Sarah & Jas. Barrett
7 1 1782			Hopewell	Fairfax	Aaron Hughs, w. Mary, & ch., Lvdia, Sarah, David
7 1 1782			Hopewell	Fairfax	Hannah Shreeve, d. Rebecca, & son Isaac
7 1 1782	Fairfax		Hopewell		Wm. Schooly, w. Ann, & ch., Mahlon, Wm., Isaac

Day	Mo.	Yr.	Meeting	To Meeting	To Meeting	Names
7	1	1782	Warrington	Hopewell		Sarah Rigg
7	1	1782		Hopewell	Fairfax	Mary Smith
4	2	1782	Gunpowder	Hopewell		John England
4	2	1782	Fairfax	Hopewell		Silas Young
4	2	1782	Fairfax	Hopewell		John Young
4	2	1782		Hopewell		Henry Mills
4	2	1782	Fairfax	Hopewell		Sarah Young
4	3	1782	Chester	Hopewell		Joseph Booth
6	5	1782	Kennett	Hopewell		Henry & Eliz'h Dixon & ch., Rebecca, Ruth, Emy, Henry
6	5	1782	New Garden	Hopewell		Thomas Cook
6	5	1782		Hopewell	Warrington	David Griffith
6	5	1782		Hopewell	Redstone	Sarah Smith & ch., Ann, Eliz'h, Geo., Henry, Mary, Rebecca
1	7	1782		Hopewell		Henry & Phebe Likens
1	7	1782		Hopewell		Lydia George & ch., Rachel, Jesse, Jas.
1	7	1782	Warrington	Hopewell		Mary Griffith
1	7	1782	Goshen	Hopewell		Sarah Roberts & ch., Esther, Rebecca, Lydia, Thos., Sarah, John, Asseneth
5	8	1782	E. Nottingham	Hopewell		Rebecca Littler
28	11	1782		Hopewell	Westland	Mary Hutton & ch., Mary, Hannah, Jane, Phebe, Thos., Jos.
28	11	1782		Hopewell	Concord	Mary Thatcher
6	1	1783	Crooked Run	Hopewell		Micheal Shihon, w. Mary, & d. Phebe
3	2	1783	Crooked Run	Hopewell		Isaac Steer, w. Phebe, & d. Mary
3	2	1783	Deer Creek	Hopewell		Thos. Bishop's ch., Thos., Eliz'h, Sarah, Job, Stephen
3	2	1783	New Garden	Hopewell		Amos Ailes
3	2	1783		Hopewell	Crooked Run	Phebe Pickering
3	3	1783	New Garden, N. C.	Hopewell		Jacob Rogers
3	3	1783		Hopewell	Westland	Robt. Raley & ch., Jane, Ann, Micheal, Ellis
3	3	1783	Wrightsboro'	Hopewell		Sarah Hutton
7	4	1783		Hopewell		Frances Raley
7	4	1783		Hopewell		Finley McGrew, wife, & ch., Jas., Mary, Jacob, Nathan, Finly, Dinah, Rebecca, Margaret (Living in the verge of Middle Creek Prep. M.)
29	5	1783	Buckingham	Hopewell		Jos. Fisher, w. Ann, & ch., Berry, Jos., Elice, Robt., John, Sarah, Sam'l, Hannah, Ann

Day	Mo.	Yr.	Meeting	To	Meeting	To Meeting	Names
29	5	1783	Concord		Hopewell		John Askew
29	5	1783			Hopewell		John Littler
7	7	1783			Hopewell	Crooked Run	John Brock, w. Jane, & ch., Alice, Stephen, Nathan, Addy, Jonathan
7	7	1783			Hopewell		Stephen McBride
4	8	1783	Sadsbury		Hopewell		Abner Bean
4	8	1783	Worrington		Hopewell		Jacob Lewis
4	8	1783	Sadsbury		Hopewell		John Miller, w. Jane, & ch., Sarah & John
4	8	1783	Fairfax		Hopewell		John Gregg
4	8	1783	Richland		Hopewell		Thos. Blackledge, w. Margaret, & ch., Wm., Thos., Levi, Abraham, Isaac, Martha, Margaret, Jas.
4	8	1783	Fairfax		Hopewell		Thos. Hatfield & son Thos.
4	8	1783	Cane Creek		Hopewell		Geo. Harlen, wife, & ch., Joshua, Aaron, Geo., Eliz'h, Sarah, Sam'l
4	8	1783	Gunpowder		Hopewell		Mary Partrick
4	8	1783	Fairfax		Hopewell		Sarah Townsend & ch., Amos, Mary, John, Rebecca, Sarah, Thos., Phebe, Hannah, Aaron
4	8	1783	Richland		Hopewell		Phebe Busson
4	8	1783	Fairfax		Hopewell		Sarah Hutton
4	8	1783	Kennet		Hopewell		Wife of Chas. Gause & ch., Amy, Mary, Isaac
4	8	1783	Richland		Hopewell		Mary Adamson & ch., Thos., Jas., Sarah
4	8	1783			Hopewell	Crooked Run	Samuel Berry
1	9	1783	Sadsbury		Hopewell		Jos. Chamberlin
1	9	1783			Hopewell		Deborah McCool's ch., Grace, Ann, Jas., Gabriel, Mary
3	11	1783			Hopewell	Chesterfield	Joel Cheshire (Chesher)
1	12	1783			Hopewell	Worrington	Mary Griffeth
1	12	1783			Hopewell	Gunpowder	Jane Wilson
5	1	1784			Hopewell		Nathan Littler's ch., Sam'l, Rachel, John, Catherine, Nathan, David
5	1	1784			Hopewell	Sadsbury	Jos. Chamberlin
2	2	1784	Nottingham		Hopewell		Tamor Colson
1	3	1784	Deer Creek		Hopewell		Aaron Newport
1	3	1784	Concord, Pa.		Hopewell		Augustine Pasmore
1	3	1784	Crooked Run		Hopewell		Hannah Hank
5	4	1784			Hopewell	Fairfax	Amos Jolliffe
5	4	1784			Hopewell	Fairfax	Mary & Eliz'h Jolliffe (sisters)
3	5	1784	Kennet		Hopewell		Joshua Dixon & w. Dinah

Day Mo. Yr.	Meeting To	Meeting To Meeting	Names
3 5 1784		Hopewell Fairfax	Jos. Fisher, w. Ann, & ch., Betty, Jos., Elias, Robt., John, Sarah, Sam'l, Hanna, Ann
3 5 1784		Hopewell Crooked Run	James Raley
3 6 1784	New Garden, N. C.	Hopewell	Evan Lewis, w. Susannah, & d. Mary
3 6 1784	Warrington	Hopewell	Henry Lewis
3 6 1784	Goshan	Hopewell	Phebe White
3 6 1784	Goshan	Hopewell	Mary Briggs
3 6 1784	Menallen	Hopewell	Elizabeth Mills
3 6 1784	Crooked Run	Hopewell	Mary Griffeth
3 6 1784		Hopewell Crooked Run	Joseph Warden
3 6 1784		Hopewell Fairfax	Dan'l McPherson Jr.
3 6 1784		Hopewell Crooked Run	Wm. Horseman, w. Mercy (Lupton), & ch., Wm., Jos.
3 6 1784		Hopewell New Garden, N. C.	Jacob Rogers
5 7 1784		Hopewell Buckingham	Solomon Wright
2 8 1784	Crooked Run	Hopewell	Benj. Pickering, w. Rebeccah, & ch., Eliz'h, Ellis, Enos
2 8 1784		Hopewell	Lydia Dillon
2 8 1784		Hopewell E. Nottingham	Enoch Rees
2 8 1784	Crooked Run	Hopewell	Elizabeth Faulkner
2 8 1784	Crooked Run	Hopewell	Amy Long
6 9 1784	Fairfax	Hopewell	Jos. Cadwalader & w. Mary
6 9 1784		Hopewell Crooked Run	Michael Shion, w. Mary, & ch., Deborah, Phebe
2 11 1784		Hopewell Bush River	Sarah Buffington, w. of Peter, & Lydia Pugh
2 12 1784		Hopewell Crooked Run	Mary Clevenger (Reinstated 4-10-1784?)
2 12 1784		Hopewell Haverford	Mary Briggs
3 1 1785		Hopewell	Ruth McPherson
3 1 1785	Warrington	Hopewell	Ebenezer John
7 2 1785	Crooked Run	Hopewell	John Brock, w. Jane, & ch., Stephen, Nathan, Oddy (Addy?), Jonathan
7 2 1785	Menallen	Hopewell	John Squibb
4 4 1785	Warrington	Hopewell	Catherine Lewis
2 5 1785	Warrington	Hopewell	Sam'l Lewis Jr.
2 5 1785	Warrington	Hopewell	Sam'l Lewis Sr., w. Catherine, & ch., Eliz'h, Mary, John, Isaac, Bulah, Jehu
2 5 1785	Concord, Pa.	Hopewell	Jacob Tolbot, w. Susannah, & ch., John, Sam'l, Hannah, Rachel, Lydia
2 5 1785	Menallen	Hopewell	John Oldham

Day Mo. Yr.	Meeting	To	Meeting	To Meeting	Names
2 6 1785			Hopewell		Rebecca Heild & ch., John, Wm., Eliz'h, Hannah, Mary, Nathan, Sarah, Richard, Rachel
4 7 1785	Sadsbury		Hopewell		Jonas Chamberlain, w. Eliz'h, & ch., Elijah, Zillah, Abigail, Mary, John, Gersham
1 8 1785	Nottingham		Hopewell		Enoch Rees
1 8 1785			Hopewell	Crooked Run	Eli Raley (apprentice)
1 8 1785	Alexandria		Hopewell		Benj. Shreeve
5 9 1785			Hopewell	Fairfax	Benj. Shreeve
5 9 1785			Hopewell		Elizabeth Moony
5 9 1785			Hopewell	Fairfax	Ruth Jenny
5 9 1785			Hopewell		Sarah Coulson
3 10 1785	Crooked Run		Hopewell		Isaac Lupton, w. Eliz'h, & ch., Mercy, Wm., Mary, Isaiah
3 10 1785	Sadsbury		Hopewell		John Cope, w. Mary, & ch., Isaac, John, Caleb, Joshua, Jesse, Jos., Jas., Israel
3 10 1785	Warrington		Hopewell		Isaac Paden, w. Rebecca, & ch., Jacob, Hannah
3 10 1785	New Garden, N. C.		Hopewell		Thedore Ellis, w. Eliz'h, & ch., Alisha, Jonathan, Sarah, Amos
3 10 1785			Hopewell	Crooked Run	Isaac Painter, & w. Sarah
3 10 1785			Hopewell	Crooked Run	Martha Fawcett
3 10 1785			Hopewell		Eliz'h Woodrow's ch., John, Isaac, Lydia, Joshua, Simeon, Eliz'h, Mary
3 10 1785	Sadsbury		Hopewell		Samuel Cope
7 11 1785			Hopewell	Crooked Run	Naomi Stratton
7 11 1785	Fairfax		Hopewell		Thomas Gregg
7 11 1785	Worrington		Hopewell		Obed Garwood, wife, & ch., Jos., Obed, Eliz'h, Mary, Tacy
7 11 1785	Worrington		Hopewell		Samuel Garwood
7 11 1785	Burlington		Hopewell		Henry Clark & w. Sarah
7 11 1785	Sadsbury		Hopewell		Elizabeth Cope
19 11 1785	Bush River		Hopewell		Lydia Pugh
19 11 1785	Crooked Run		Hopewell		Rebeccah Beaumont
2 1 1786	Concord		Hopewell		Chas. Dingee, w. Martha, & ch., Rachel, Hannah, John
2 1 1786	Concord		Hopewell		Jesse Townsend
2 1 1786			Hopewell		Wm. Grubb's ch., Wm., John, Rebeccah
6 2 1786	Concord, Pa.		Hopewell		Joseph Palmore
6 3 1786			Hopewell		Susannah Grubb

Day Mo. Yr.	Meeting	To	Meeting	To Meeting	Names
6 3 1786			Hopewell	Crooked Run	Samuel Ellis
6 3 1786			Hopewell	Westland	Robt. Faulkner, w. Eliz'h, & d. Susannah
3 4 1786	Nottingham		Hopewell		Hugh Sidwell
3 4 1786			Hopewell	Crooked Run	Martha Painter
3 4 1786	Menallen		Hopewell		William Oldham
1 5 1786	Crooked Run		Hopewell		Schooly Wright
1 5 1786	Exeter		Hopewell		Edward Morris, w. Hannah, & ch., Hannah, David, Elizabeth
1 5 1786			Hopewell	Westland	Jas. Purviance, w. Eliz'h, & ch., Nath'l, John, Jas., David, Thos., Jos., Geo., Wm., Richard
1 5 1786	Exeter		Hopewell		Kezia Warrell
1 6 1786	Nottingham		Hopewell		Richard Sidwell
1 6 1786			Hopewell	Warrington	Hannah Thornbrough
3 7 1786	New Garden		Hopewell		Abigail Wickersham
3 7 1786	New Garden		Hopewell		Jane Taylor & ch., Jesse, Jane, Jos., Isreal, Sarah
7 8 1786	Exeter		Hopewell		Moses Embre, w. Mary, & ch., Moses, Rachel, John
7 8 1786	Crooked Run		Hopewell		Isaac Smith & wife Mary
7 8 1786			Hopewell		Jacob Ong
4 9 1786	Fairfax		Hopewell		Amos Jolliffe
4 9 1786	New Garden, Pa.		Hopewell		Jonathan Bernard
4 9 1786	New Garden, Pa.		Hopewell		Deborah Barnard
4 9 1786			Hopewell	Westland	Anthony Blackburn
4 9 1786			Hopewell	Westland	Jos. Blackburn, w. Deborah, & ch., Jas., Thos., Anthony, Jos., Zacheriah, Deborah, Phinly, Rachel
4 9 1786			Hopewell	Westland	Susannah Mitchel & ch., Thos., Mary, Sam'l
4 9 1786			Hopewell	Westland	Mary Brannen
4 9 1786			Hopewell	Westland	Solomon Shepherd, w. Marg't, & ch., Jane, John, Solomon, Eliz'h, Mary, Benj., Jos., Sarah, Thos.
4 9 1786			Hopewell	Westland	Elizabeth Main
4 9 1786			Hopewell	Westland	Jas. McGrew & w. Jane
4 9 1786			Hopewell	Westland	Andrew Dennin, w. Rachel, & ch., Wm., Susannah, Eleanor, Rachel, John, Anthony, Jos.
4 9 1786			Hopewell	Westland	Thos. Gregg, w. Amy, & ch. not named
4 9 1786			Hopewell	Westland	Ann Lewillen
4 9 1786			Hopewell	Westland	Margaret Lewillen
4 9 1786			Hopewell	Westland	Phebe Mipis

Day Mo. Yr.	Meeting	To	Meeting	To Meeting	Names
4 9 1786			Hopewell	Westland	Marrah Cadwaller
4 9 1786			Hopewell	Westland	Hannah Pik
4 9 1786			Hopewell	Westland	Tamer Coulson (widow)
4 9 1786			Hopewell	Westland	Margaret Anderson
6 11 1786			Hopewell	South River	Sarah Moreland & husband
30 11 1786	Chester		Hopewell		Isaac Wood
30 11 1786			Hopewell	Crooked Run	John Painter
30 11 1786			Hopewell	New Garden, N. C.	Evan Lewis, w. Susannah, & ch., Mary, Richard
30 11 1786			Hopewell	Goose Creek	Martha Smith, w. of Thos.
30 11 1786			Hopewell		Lydia Dillon's ch., Mary, Lydia, Phebe, Jas.
1 1 1787			Hopewell	Crooked Run	Jane Taylor & Abigail Wickersham
5 2 1787	Kennet		Hopewell		John Morgan
5 2 1787	Kennet		Hopewell		Mary Morgan & d. Deborah
5 3 1787	Crooked Run		Hopewell		Samuel Ellis
5 3 1787	Concord		Hopewell		Joseph Piles
12 3 1787			Hopewell	Wrightsboro'	Henry Williams
2 4 1787	Indian Spring		Hopewell		Ann Gill & ch., Thos., John, Sam'l
7 5 1787	Burlington		Hopewell		Jonathan Shinn
7 5 1787			Hopewell	Crooked Run	John & Jesse Brown (bros.)
7 5 1787	Philadelphia		Hopewell		Mary Woodrow
4 6 1787	Haverford		Hopewell		Samuel Richard
4 6 1787	Crooked Run		Hopewell		John Antrim, w. Elizabeth, & ch., John, Sarah
4 6 1787			Hopewell	South River	Moses Embree, w. Mary, & ch., Rachel, Moses, John
4 6 1787	Burlington		Hopewell		Hannah Rancer
2 7 1787	Goose Creek		Hopewell		David Smith
2 7 1787	Exeter		Hopewell		Moses Star
2 7 1787			Hopewell	Westland	Lydia Long (minor)
6 8 1787			Hopewell	Goose Creek	Phebe Evans & ch., Thos., Sarah, Margaret, Mary, Catherine, Phebe, Evan, Wheelon, Martha
3 9 1787			Hopewell	Westland	Hugh Sidwell, w. Mary, & d. Charity
3 9 1787	Sadsbury		Hopewell		Rachel Sammow
3 9 1787	Menallen		Hopewell		Mary Ong
11 9 1787			Hopewell	Fairfax	Joseph Palmer
1 10 1787	Crooked Run		Hopewell		Jonathan Pickering
1 10 1787			Hopewell	Bush River	James Barrett
1 10 1787			Hopewell	Goose Creek	Abijah Richards (to marry)
1 10 1787	Menallen		Hopewell		Catherine Newlan
5 11 1787	New Garden, Pa.		Hopewell		Barnard Gilpin
5 11 1787	Concord		Hopewell		Richard Thatcher

Day Mo. Yr.	Meeting	To	Meeting	To Meeting	Names
5 11 1787	Gunpowder		Hopewell		John Maulsby, w. Lydia, & ch., Susannah, Ann, Wm., Sarah, Eleanor, John, Lydia
5 11 1787			Hopewell	Westland	Henry Mills, w. Elizabeth, & d. Mary
5 11 1787			Hopewell		Rebeccah Curl & ch., Hannah, Amy, Chas., Rebeccah, Eliz'h, Susannah
5 11 1787	Fairfax		Hopewell		Elizabeth Jolliffe
5 12 1787	Concord		Hopewell		Ann Hayes & son Nathan
5 12 1787	Concord		Hopewell		David Hayes
5 12 1787			Hopewell	Wrightsburgh	Henry Williams
5 12 1787			Hopewell	Pipe Creek	Dan'l Ballenger
7 1 1788			Hopewell	Crooked Run	Isaac Woodrow
7 1 1788			Hopewell		Jonathan Pickering's ch., Benj. & Wm.
4 2 1788			Hopewell	Menallen	William Oldham
4 2 1788			Hopewell	Westland	Hannah Faulkner
3 3 1788	Worrington		Hopewell		Ezekiel Fraisher, w. Rebeccah, & ch., Phebe, Rebeccah, John, Alexandria, Hannah
3 3 1788			Hopewell	Bush River	Sarah Roberts, John Roberts, & ch., Rebeccah, Lydia, Thos., John, Assenah, Sarah
3 3 1788			Hopewell	Crooked Run	Lydia Woodrow Jr.
7 4 1788			Hopewell	Goose Creek	Thos. & Sarah Gregg & son Uriah
7 4 1788			Hopewell	Crooked Run	Isaac & Lydia Wood
7 4 1788			Hopewell	Westland	Jesse Townsend
7 4 1788	Crooked Run		Hopewell		Alice Brock
5 5 1788	Crooked Run		Hopewell		Mary Fallis & son Richard
2 6 1788	Pipe Creek		Hopewell		Robt. Miller, w. Cassandra, & ch., Solomon, Ruth, Wm., Jos., Sarah, Hannah
2 6 1788			Hopewell	Westland	Sinah Townsend
2 6 1788			Hopewell	Fairfax	Jos. Kurl (Curl), w. Rebeccah, & ch., Hannah, Amy, Chas., Rebeccah, Eliz'h, Susannah
2 6 1788	Crooked Run		Hopewell		Rachel Fallis, d. of Mary
2 6 1788	Worrington		Hopewell		Hannah Thornbrough
7 7 1788	Crooked Run		Hopewell		Thos. Smith, w. Deborah, & ch., David, Ann, Lydia, Copperthwaite, John
7 7 1788	Crooked Run		Hopewell		Jos. Steer, w. Grace, & ch., Isaac, Sarah, Joshua, David
7 7 1788	New Garden, Pa.		Hopewell		Jas. & Jos. Davis
7 7 1788			Hopewell	Nottingham	Deborah Barnett
4 8 1788	Nottingham		Hopewell		Thos. Butterfield
4 8 1788	Sadsbury		Hopewell		Joseph Moony

Day Mo. Yr.	Meeting To	Meeting To Meeting	Names
4 8 1788	Crooked Run	Hopewell	Thos. Allen (apprentice), son of Jos.
1 9 1788		Hopewell Goose Creek	David Smith
1 9 1788		Hopewell	Mary Crumpton
6 10 1788		Hopewell	Mary Woodrow's ch., Henry, Mary, Lydia, Grace
3 11 1788		Hopewell Crooked Run	Rachel Woodrow
3 11 1788		Hopewell Westland	John Hoge, w. Mary, & ch., Wm., Jonathan, Jacob
1 12 1788	Indian Spring	Hopewell	John Gill
5 1 1789	Crooked Run	Hopewell	Micheal Shihon, w. Mary, & ch., Phebe, Deborah, Ebenezer, Jonah
5 1 1789	Nottingham	Hopewell	Sam'l Sidwell, w. Sarah, & d. Lydia
5 1 1789		Hopewell Crooked Run	Phebe Yarnel
5 1 1789		Hopewell Crooked Run	Jacob Ong's ch., Rebeccah & Finley
2 2 1789		Hopewell Crooked Run	Schooly Wright (to marry)
2 3 1789		Hopewell Exeter	Moses Starr
4 5 1789		Hopewell Fairfax	Ann Strode
23 4 1789		Hopewell	Rebecca & Ann McPherson
6 7 1789	Sadsbury	Hopewell	Benj. Frame, w. Elizabeth, & son Geo.
3 8 1789	Crooked Run	Hopewell	Jas. Reiley & w. Rachel
3 8 1789	Sadsbury	Hopewell	Michel Williams
7 9 1789	Crooked Run	Hopewell	Eli Reily & wife
7 9 1789	Crooked Run	Hopewell	Joseph Morgan
7 9 1789	Sadsbury	Hopewell	Susannah Pearce
5 10 1789	Crooked Run	Hopewell	John Fallis, w. Mary, & ch., Miriam, Rachel, Eliz'h, Mary
5 10 1789	Sadsbury	Hopewell	Caleb Mercer
5 10 1789		Hopewell	Thomas Bailiff
5 10 1789		Hopewell	George Cope
5 10 1789		Hopewell	Eliz'h Parkins & Lydia Case
5 10 1789		Hopewell New Garden, N. C.	John Molsby, w. Lydia, & ch., Ann, Wm., Sarah, John, Lydia, Ebenezer, Eleanor
5 10 1789		Hopewell New Garden, N. C.	Ebenezer John
5 10 1789		Hopewell South River	Sam'l Ellis, w. Kezia, & d. Mary
5 10 1789		Hopewell Sadsbury	Susannah Pierce
2 11 1789	Westland	Hopewell	Hannah Faulkner
7 12 1789	Menallen	Hopewell	Esther Hodgson
4 1 1790		Hopewell Bush River	John Barrett
1 2 1790	Crooked Run	Hopewell	Isaac Wood & w. Lydia
1 2 1790	Crooked Run	Hopewell	John Wood

Day Mo. Yr.	Meeting To	Meeting	To Meeting	Names
1 2 1790	Crooked Run	Hopewell		Jacob Branson
1 2 1790		Hopewell	Bush River	Nathan Wright
1 2 1790	Fairfax	Hopewell		Mary Jolliffe
1 3 1790		Hopewell	Fairfax	Martha McPherson
5 4 1790	Gwvnard	Hopewell		Peter Cleaver
5 4 1790		Hopewell		Samuel Finch
5 4 1790	New Garden, Pa.	Hopewell		Betty Mendinhall
3 5 1790		Hopewell	Fairfax	John Schooly Jr.
3 5 1790		Hopewell	Sadsbury	Caleb Mercer
7 6 1790		Hopewell	Westfield	Abraham Smith, w. Martha, & ch., Rachel, Hannah, Isaac, Geo.
7 6 1790		Hopewell	Concord	Richard Thatcher
5 7 1790		Hopewell	Westfield	Ellis Ellis, w. Mary, & ch., Wm., Enos, Sarah
5 7 1790		Hopewell	Gunpowder	Ann Trimble, d. of John
2 8 1790		Hopewell	Crooked Run	Jonathan Wickersham
6 9 1790	Crooked Run	Hopewell		Jas. Wright, w. Phebe, & ch., Ruth, Jonathan, Rachel, Isaac, David
6 9 1790	Sadsbury	Hopewell		Susannah Pierce
6 9 1790		Hopewell	Crooked Run	Sarah Clerk (Clark)
6 9 1790		Hopewell	Crooked Run	Rebecca Neill
4 10 1790		Hopewell	Westfield	John White, w. Susannah, & son Wm.
4 10 1790		Hopewell		Peninah Finch
4 10 1790		Hopewell		Rachel Baley (Bailey)
6 12 1790		Hopewell		Hannah Thompson
3 1 1791	Mt. Holly	Hopewell		David Shin
3 1 1791		Hopewell	Sadsbury	Mincher William
7 2 1791		Hopewell		Sam'l Finch's ch., David, Hannah, Eliz'h, Lydia, Rachel
7 3 1791	York	Hopewell		Joseph Miller
7 3 1791		Hopewell		David Shin's ch., Sam'l, David, John
7 3 1791		Hopewell		Ann Jinken's ch., Mary, Israel, Jacob, Susannah
4 4 1791	Warrington	Hopewell		Jas. Fisher, wife, & ch., Hannah, Alice, Caphas, Mary, Thos., Jas., John
4 4 1791	E. Nottingham	Hopewell		Ruth Butterfield
4 4 1791	E. Nottingham	Hopewell		Hannah Jacob
4 4 1791		Hopewell		Phebe Eachus's d. Mary
2 5 1791		Hopewell	Westfield	Samuel Lewis
2 5 1791		Hopewell	Crooked Run	Henry Cowgal, w. Ruth, & ch., Isaac, John, Thos., Sarah, Caleb
2 5 1791	Uwchland	Hopewell		Sarah Bond

Day Mo. Yr.	Meeting	To	Meeting	To Meeting	Names
2 5 1791	Uwchland		Hopewell		Susannah Spencer
2 5 1791			Hopewell	Crooked Run	Jas., Henry, & Rachel Cowgill
2 5 1791	Uwchland		Hopewell		Jos. Bond & ch., Sam'l, Hannah, Robt.
6 6 1791	Uwchland		Hopewell		Samuel Bond
6 6 1791	Crooked Run		Hopewell		Jonathan Parkins Jr., w. Jane, & ch., John, Jonathan, David, Nathan, Stephen
6 6 1791			Hopewell	Fairfax	Jonas McPherson
6 6 1791			Hopewell	Crooked Run	Grace Woodrow
6 6 1791			Hopewell	Crooked Run	Mary Woodrow & minor ch., Henry, Lydia, Mary
6 6 1791			Hopewell	Crooked Run	Thomas Wright
6 6 1791			Hopewell		Margaret Daniel
6 6 1791			Hopewell	Westland	Jacob Ong, w. Mary, & ch., Rebecca, Finley, Jacob
6 6 1791			Hopewell	Concord	Thos. Bailiff
6 6 1791			Hopewell		Jos. Moony's ch., Phebe, Elizabeth, Esther
1 8 1791			Hopewell		Elizabeth Woodrow's ch., Rachel, Jos.
1 8 1791			Hopewell	Westfield	Magdalen, Thos. Jr., & Susanah Ellis
1 8 1791			Hopewell	Westfield	Sam'l Ellis, wife, & child
5 9 1791	Westland		Hopewell		Agnes Grisel

FROM BOOK THREE
1791-1811

26 9 1791			Hopewell	Crooked Run	Eliza'h Woodrow & ch., Joshua, Simeon, Eliz'h, Mary, Rachel, Jos.
26 9 1791			Hopewell	Crooked Run	Lydia & Isaac Woodrow
26 9 1791	Middle Creek		Hopewell	Westfield	Thomas Ellis Sr.
7 11 1791			Hopewell	Westfield	Roland Ellis
7 11 1791	Sadsbury		Hopewell		Wm. & Phoebe Downing & ch., Ruth, Eleanor, Mary, John, Sarah, Phebe
7 11 1791			Hopewell		Stephen McBride's minor ch., John, Stephen, Ann, Jas., Jeremiah, Evan
5 12 1791			Hopewell	Crooked Run	Jacob Branson
5 12 1791			Hopewell	Crooked Run	Sarah Littlejohn & ch., Mary, Eliz'h, Sarah
5 12 1791			Hopewell	Westland	Sam'l & Cath. Lewis & ch., Beulah, Isaac, John
5 12 1791			Hopewell		Hannah McBride
2 1 1792	Crooked Run		Hopewell		Job Fallis

Day Mo. Yr.	Meeting	To	Meeting	To Meeting	Names
6 2 1792	Concord		Hopewell		Job Jeffries
5 3 1792			Hopewell	Crooked Run	John Brown, son of Isaac
2 4 1792	Crooked Run		Hopewell		Stacy Bevan
2 4 1792	Fairfax		Hopewell		Esther Conard
7 5 1792	Crooked Run		Hopewell		Nathan & Ann Updegraff & ch., Jas., Jos., David, Rachel
7 5 1792	Sadsbury		Hopewell		John & Margaret Whitson
7 5 1792	New Garden		Hopewell		Abraham Sinclear
7 5 1792	Crooked Run		Hopewell		John Griffith
7 5 1792	Fairfax		Hopewell		Martha McPherson & d. Jane
7 5 1792			Hopewell	Crooked Run	Jacob & Hannah Pickering & ch., Eleanor, Enos, Hannah, David, Jacob, Jonathan
7 5 1792			Hopewell	Crooked Run	Abraham Woodrow
7 5 1792			Hopewell	Westland	Elizabeth Lewis
7 5 1792			Hopewell	Westland	Jacob Lewis
4 6 1792	Crooked Run		Hopewell		Thomas Hurst
4 6 1792	Sadsbury		Hopewell		William Moore
4 6 1792	Gwyned		Hopewell		Jonathan Longstreth
2 7 1792			Hopewell	Crooked Run	Thos. Allen & Betty
6 8 1792			Hopewell	Crooked Run	Lydia Lupton & Rachel Butterfield
3 9 1792			Hopewell		Ruth Fenton's ch., Sarah, Sidney, Jos., Mary, Joshua
3 9 1792			Hopewell	Crooked Run	Elizabeth Parkins
1 10 1792			Hopewell	Westfield	Ezekiel & Rebekah Fraezure & ch., Phebe, Rebekah, John, Alex., Hannah, Ezekiel, Moses
1 10 1792	Warrington		Hopewell		David Griffith
1 10 1792			Hopewell		Henry Lewis's ch., Wm., Mary, Lewis
1 10 1792	Chester		Hopewell		Jesse Pennel
1 10 1792	Haverford		Hopewell		George Matlock
1 10 1792	Gwyned		Hopewell		Elizabeth Cleaver
5 11 1792			Hopewell	Sadsbury	William Moore
5 11 1792	Kennett		Hopewell		Charity Jordan Sr.
5 11 1792	New Garden		Hopewell		Mercy Jordan
5 11 1792	Sadsbury		Hopewell		Gainor Pierce
5 11 1792	Crooked Run		Hopewell		Sarah Fisher
3 12 1792	Nottingham		Hopewell		Patience Pugh
3 12 1792	Fairfax		Hopewell		Ann Neill
3 12 1792			Hopewell	Westfield	Jas. & Jane Fisher & ch., Hannah, Alice, Caiphas, Mary, Thos., Jas., John, Hiram, Jane
3 12 1792			Hopewell	Westland	Hannah Allmon

Day Mo. Yr.	Meeting	To	Meeting	To Meeting	Names
3 12 1792			Hopewell	Westfield	Susannah Hayworth
7 1 1793			Hopewell	Westfield	Nehemiah Ellis, w. Sarah, & ch., John, Mary, Charity
4 3 1793			Hopewell		Ann Mendenhall
4 3 1793			Hopewell	Concord	Chas. & Martha Dingee & ch., Rachel, John, Hannah, Martha, Sarah, Ann; also for Agnes Grizzet
6 5 1793	Concord		Hopewell		Mary Steer
6 5 1793			Hopewell	Westfield	Benj. & Rebekah Pickering & ch., Sam'l, Ellis, Enos, Rebekah, Mary, Benj., Eliz'h
3 6 1793	Crooked Run		Hopewell		Henry Cowgill Jr.
3 6 1793	Evesham		Hopewell		Nathan Haines
3 6 1793	Bush River		Hopewell		John & Rhoda Barrett & son Jonathan
3 6 1793	Goose Creek		Hopewell		Mary White (w. of Jesse) & ch., Uriah, Eliz'h, Jane, Jas., Rachel, Jesse
1 7 1793			Hopewell	Fairfax	Sarah Moore
1 7 1793			Hopewell	Indian Spring	Bernard Gilpin & Jos. White (apprentices)
5 8 1793	Bush River		Hopewell		Nathan Wright
5 8 1793	Nottingham		Hopewell		Benjamin Pugh
2 9 1793			Hopewell	Sadsbury	Susanna Pierce
30 9 1793			Hopewell	Goose Creek	Elizabeth Lukens
4 11 1793	Goose Creek		Hopewell		Aquilla & Ruth Jenney & ch., Isaac, Hannah, David
4 11 1793			Hopewell	Sadsbury	Enos Ellis
2 12 1793	Concord		Hopewell		Thomas Bailiff
6 1 1794	Westland		Hopewell		Job Harvey
6 1 1794			Hopewell	Westfield	Margaret Ellis & ch., Phebe, Rebekah, Margaret, Mary, Thos., David
6 1 1794			Hopewell	Westland	Henry & Susanna Lewis & ch., Wm., Mary, Lewis, Esther
6 1 1794			Hopewell	Bush River	Sarah & Esther Roberts
3 2 1794	Crooked Run		Hopewell		Lewis Rees
3 2 1794	Sadsbury		Hopewell		Mary Ellis
3 2 1794	Crooked Run		Hopewell		Jonathan Wickersham (minor)
3 3 1794			Hopewell		Mary Haines, w. of Nathan, & ch., John, Sarah, Dan'l, Mary, Ruth, Rebecca, Nathan
7 4 1794			Hopewell	Westfield	John Ellis
7 4 1794			Hopewell	Crooked Run	Jesse & Hannah Pennal
7 4 1794	Sadsbury		Hopewell		Caleb Mercer & Wm. Moore

Day Mo. Yr.	Meeting	To	Meeting	To Meeting	Names
7 4 1794	Kennet		Hopewell		Griffith & Rachel Roberts & ch., Hannah, Rebecca, Lydia, Abraham
7 4 1794	Sadsbury		Hopewell		Ruth Faulkner
2 6 1794			Hopewell		Ann Highley (Hily)
2 6 1794			Hopewell		John Ward
7 7 1794	Sadsbury		Hopewell		Elias Simmons
7 7 1794	Crooked Run		Hopewell		Rachel Butterfield
7 7 1794	Goose Creek		Hopewell		Levi Lukens & w. Eliz'h
7 7 1794			Hopewell	Herford	George Matlack
7 7 1794			Hopewell	Redstone	Job & Eleanor Harvey
4 8 1794			Hopewell	Redstone	Samuel Smith
4 8 1794			Hopewell	Westfield	Hannah Wright, w. of Edward
1 9 1794			Hopewell	Sadsbury	Hannah & Margaret Daniel
1 9 1794			Hopewell	Westfield	Mordecai & Sarah Ellis
1 9 1794			Hopewell		Deborah White's ch., Abigail, Rebecca, Sarah, Thos., Mary
3 11 1794			Hopewell		John Ward's ch., John, Sarah, Joel, Mary, Lydia, Hannah
3 11 1794			Hopewell	Bush River	John & Rhoda Barrett & sons, Jonathan, Benj.
1 12 1794			Hopewell	Horsham	Jonathan Longstreth
1 12 1794	Nottingham		Hopewell		Isaac Davis
5 1 1795	Pipe Creek		Hopewell		James Moseley
5 1 1795			Hopewell	Westfield	Jacob & Susannah Talbott (Tolbot) & ch., Rachel, Lydia, Mary, Susanna, Sarah, Rebecca
5 1 1795			Hopewell	Westfield	John & Sam'l Talbott (Tolbot)
5 1 1795			Hopewell	Goose Creek	Rachel Talbert (Tolbert, Tobott)
5 1 1795			Hopewell	Deep River	Hannah Sanders
5 1 1795			Hopewell		John Fenton
2 2 1795			Hopewell	Monallen	John & Margaret Whitson & d. Thomzan
2 2 1795			Hopewell		Elizabeth & Rachel Ward
2 2 1795			Hopewell	Monallen	Susanna Spencer
2 3 1795			Hopewell		Jesse Faulkner's junior ch., Wm., Martha, Thos., Eleanor
6 4 1795			Hopewell	Westland	Solomon & Mary Hoge
4 5 1795	Fairfax		Hopewell		Elizabeth Bond
4 5 1795			Hopewell	Crooked Run	Rachel Hunt
4 5 1795			Hopewell	Fairfax	Thomas Hirst (Hurst)
4 5 1795			Hopewell	Sadsbury	Wm. Moore & Caleb Mercer

Day Mo. Yr.	Meeting	To	Meeting	To Meeting	Names
4 5 1795			Hopewell	Gunpowder	Nathan Littler Jr.
1 6 1795			Hopewell	Crooked Run	Robt. & Cassandra Miller & ch., Solomon, Ruth, Wm., Sarah, Hannah, Caleb, Mary, David
6 7 1795			Hopewell	Warrington	Hannah Nevitt
6 7 1795	Goose Creek		Hopewell		Sam'l & Rachel Talbert (Tabbert)
6 7 1795	Westland		Hopewell		Ambrose Taylor & ch., Jacob, Mordecai, Stephen, Abijah, Peter, Mary
6 7 1795	Crooked Run		Hopewell		Catherine Saxton
3 8 1795			Hopewell	Westland	John & Jane Brock
3 8 1795			Hopewell		Hannah Miles's ch., Amos, Hannah, Lydia, Sarah
1 9 1795			Hopewell		Ch. of Betty Mendenhall, Jacob, Hannah, Sam'l, Betty, Amos, Mary, Phebe
28 9 1795			Hopewell		Edith Mendenhall (d. of Betty)
7 12 1795	Crooked Run		Hopewell		Hannah Saxton & dtrs., Hannah, Mary
7 12 1795			Hopewell	New Hope	Wm. & Hannah Smith & ch., Jos. & Isaac
4 1 1796			Hopewell	Westland	Esther Hoge
4 1 1796	Fairfax		Hopewell		Jos. Smith (s. of Thos.)
4 1 1796	Nottingham		Hopewell		Samuel Jones
1 2 1796			Hopewell	Westland	Mary White & minor ch., Jane, Jas., Rachel, Jesse, Israel; also Uriah & Eliz'h, on their own request
7 3 1796			Hopewell	Redstone	Thos. & Deborah Smith & ch., David, Ann, Lydia, Copathwait, John, Marg't, Eliz'h, Jude
7 3 1796	Goose Creek		Hopewell		John Piggott Jr.
4 4 1796	Crooked Run		Hopewell		Caleb Antram & small ch., Jesse, Eliz'h, Esther
4 4 1796	Bradford		Hopewell		Jos. & Susanna Quaintance & ch., Sam'l, Wm., Eli, Ann, Susanna, Fisher
4 4 1796	Chester (Radford?)		Hopewell		Cornelius & Mary Wood
4 4 1796			Hopewell	Crooked Run	Nathan Updegraff, wife, & ch., Jas., Jos., David, Rachel, Hanna, Nathan
2 5 1796			Hopewell	Redstone	John & Mary Fallis & ch., Miriam, Rachel, Eliz'h, Mary, Jonathan, Isaiah
2 5 1796			Hopewell	Fairfax	Abijah Taylor
2 5 1796			Hopewell	Crooked Run	Levi & Eliz'h Lukens

Day Mo. Yr.	Meeting	To	Meeting	To Meeting	Names
2 5 1796	Fairfax		Hopewell		Wm. & Rachel Beale & ch., Philip, Sarah, Jos., Wm., Hannah
2 5 1796	Fairfax		Hopewell		Mercy Beale
1 6 1796	Nottingham		Hopewell		Sarah Jacobs
6 6 1796			Hopewell	Crooked Run	Moses & Hannah Piggott & d. Rachel
6 6 1796			Hopewell	Crooked Run	Mary Shihon & ch., Phebe, Ebenezer, Jonah, Abel, John
4 7 1796			Hopewell	Redstone	Jas. & Mary Sidwell & ch., Margaret, Lydia
4 7 1796			Hopewell	Crooked Run	Enos & Mary Ellis & son Gainor
4 7 1796			Hopewell	Crooked Run	Rees Branson
4 7 1796	Crooked Run		Hopewell		Rebekah Neil & ch., Lydia, Lewis, Mary
4 7 1796	Kennett		Hopewell		Martha Conner
1 8 1796			Hopewell	Crooked Run	Hannah Piggott Jr.
1 8 1796			Hopewell	Crooked Run	Schooly Wright
1 8 1796			Hopewell	Crooked Run	Henry & Eleanor Cowgill Jr. & d. Sydney
1 8 1796			Hopewell	Goose Creek	Lydia Piggott
7 11 1796	Gunpowder		Hopewell		Thos. & Jane Wilson & ch., David, Martha, Cath., Sam'l, Mary, Thos.
7 11 1796	Chester		Hopewell		Jane Wood
7 11 1796	Little Falls		Hopewell		Nathan Littler Jr.
5 12 1796			Hopewell	New Hope	Isaac Tedhunter (?)
5 12 1796			Hopewell	Crooked Run	Jonathan Ellis
5 12 1796			Hopewell		Jos. & Mary Adams's ch., Hannah, Phebe, Isaac, John, Jos.
2 1 1797	Bush River		Hopewell		John & Rhoda Barrett & ch., Jonathan, Mary
6 2 1797			Hopewell	Chester	Thomas Baliff
6 2 1797			Hopewell	Westland	Jesse Hoge
6 3 1797	Philadelphia		Hopewell	Crooked Run	Sarah Zane
3 4 1797	Monallen		Hopewell		John & Susanna Wright
3 4 1797			Hopewell	Sadsbury	Gainer Pierce
1 5 1797	Deep River		Hopewell		Joseph Saunders
1 5 1797	Crooked Run		Hopewell		Hannah Piggott (Pickett)
5 6 1797			Hopewell	Crooked Run	John & Rachel Trimble & ch., Catherine, John, Wm., David, Charity
5 6 1797			Hopewell	Crooked Run	John Parkins
5 6 1797			Hopewell	Crooked Run	John Piggott (son of Henry)
5 6 1797			Hopewell		Elizabeth Thompson
25 9 1797	Deep River		Hopewell		Jane Elmore

Day Mo. Yr.	Meeting	To	Meeting	To Meeting	Names
25 9 1797	Chester		Hopewell		Mary Wood
25 9 1797	Evesham		Hopewell		Sarah Cattle
6 11 1797			Hopewell		Jesse, Benj., & Ellis Barrett (sons of Jonathan)
1 1 1798	Sadsbury		Hopewell		Jonas Chamberlin
1 1 1798	Sadsbury		Hopewell		Powel Semmonds
1 1 1798			Hopewell	Goose Creek	Wm. Newland Jr.
1 1 1798			Hopewell	Bradford	Hannah Roberts
5 2 1798			Hopewell	New Hope	Phebe Echus & d. Mary
5 3 1798	Sadsbury		Hopewell		Ann Simmonds & d. Ruth
2 4 1798	Westland		Hopewell		Thos. & Susanna Faulkner
2 4 1798			Hopewell	Crooked Run	John Piggott
2 4 1798			Hopewell	Goose Creek	Wm. & Marg't Newland & ch., Jas., Deborah, Jesse, David, Sarah, Elijah
2 4 1798			Hopewell	Goose Creek	John, Tamar, & Marg't Newland (ch. of Wm. & Marg't) request for themselves
2 4 1798			Hopewell	Sadsbury	John Chamberlain (son of Elizabeth)
2 4 1798			Hopewell	New Garden	Ann Dillon
2 4 1798			Hopewell	Pipe Creek	Martha Hibbert
7 5 1798	Sadsbury		Hopewell		Robt. & Phebe Couburn
7 5 1798	Sadsbury		Hopewell		Samuel Miller
7 5 1798			Hopewell	Fairfax	Jacob Jenkins
7 5 1798			Hopewell	Crooked Run	Jonathan & Eliz'h Pickering & ch., Mary, Elias
4 6 1798	Crooked Run		Hopewell		Mary McClunn
6 8 1798	Bradford		Hopewell		Samuel Valentine
6 8 1798			Hopewell	Westland	Josiah & Alice Rogers & ch., Jane, Evan, John, Josiah
6 8 1798			Hopewell	Southland	John Woodrow
3 9 1798	Crooked Run		Hopewell		Mary Branson
1 10 1798			Hopewell	Goose Creek	Jane Janney
1 10 1798	Nottingham		Hopewell		Susannah Wells
5 11 1798			Hopewell	Gunpowder	Patience Pugh
4 2 1799			Hopewell	Redstone	Griffith & Rachel Roberts & son Abraham
4 2 1799			Hopewell	Redstone	Rebeckah & Lydia Roberts (ask for themselves)
4 2 1799			Hopewell	Bradford	Samuel Valentine
4 3 1799			Hopewell	Crooked Run	David Wood (s. of Jos.)
4 3 1799			Hopewell	Westland	Phebe Berry (d. of David)
1 4 1799	New Hope		Hopewell		Marg't Ellis & ch., Marg't, Mary, Thos., David, Rees
6 5 1799			Hopewell	Crooked Run	John & Susanna Wright & ch., Dan'l, Benj.

Day Mo. Yr.	Meeting	To	Meeting	To Meeting	Names
6 5 1799			Hopewell	Westland	Sarah Johnson
3 6 1799			Hopewell		William Jolliffe
3 6 1799			Hopewell	Redstone	Caleb & Martha Antram & ch., Jesse, Mary
1 7 1799			Hopewell		Jas. Conrad, wife, & ch., Jos., Hannah, Eliz'h, Geo., Jas.
1 7 1799			Hopewell	Goshen	Ann Mendinhall
1 7 1799			Hopewell	Southland	Alice Clever
1 7 1799			Hopewell	Goose Creek	Ruth Piggott
5 8 1799			Hopewell		Joseph Grubb
5 8 1799			Hopewell		Jane & Sarah Conrad (dtrs. of Jas.)
5 8 1799			Hopewell		Anthony & Eliza Lee (minor ch. of John)
5 8 1799	Fairfax		Hopewell		Parmenas & Hannah Lamborn
5 8 1799	Crooked Run		Hopewell		David & Martha Painter & ch., Hannah, Jesse, Jacob, Thos.
5 8 1799	Chester		Hopewell		Leah Farr
30 9 1799			Hopewell	New Hope	Joseph Booth
30 9 1799			Hopewell	Deep River	Jane Ellmore
4 11 1799			Hopewell	Redstone	John & Catherine Wood & ch., Nathan, Rebekah, Sarah, Katherine
4 11 1799			Hopewell	Westland	David & Hannah Berry & ch., Thos., Sam'l, Hannah, Beulah
4 11 1799	Baltimore		Hopewell		Jesse Mitcalf
6 1 1800	Crooked Run		Hopewell		Jonathan & Ann Lovett & ch., Nancy, Sarah, Jonathan
6 1 1800			Hopewell	Fairfax	Ruth Janney
6 1 1800	Southland		Hopewell		Rachel Halloway & ch., Levi, Robt. Eliz'h, Phebe, Wm., Philadelphia, Tacy
3 2 1800			Hopewell	Southland	Sidney Crumpton
3 3 1800			Hopewell	Westland	David & Judith Faulkner & ch., Jane, Phebe, Thos., Mary, Judith, Solomon; d. Martha did not accompany them.
3 3 1800			Hopewell	Westland	David & Marg't Painter & ch., Hannah, Jesse, Jacob, Thos.
3 3 1800			Hopewell	Redstone	Hannah Jacobs
3 3 1800			Hopewell		John & Mary Hiett
7 4 1800	Fairfax		Hopewell		David & Ruth Smith & d. Rachel
7 4 1800	Concord		Hopewell		Moses Mendinhall

Day Mo. Yr.	Meeting	To	Meeting	To Meeting	Names
5 5 1800			Hopewell	Fairfax	Parmenus & Hannah Lamborn & son Isaac
2 6 1800			Hopewell	Redstone	Susanna Wells
2 6 1800			Hopewell		George Hiett
29 9 1800	Sadsbury		Hopewell		John Chamberlin
29 9 1800	Goshen		Hopewell		Ann Mendinhall
1 12 1800			Hopewell	Fairfax	Aquilla & Ruth Jannev & ch., Isaac, Hannah, Dan'l, Wm., Rebekah, Aquilla, Israel
2 3 1801			Hopewell	Redstone	Edward Morris & ch., David, Eliz'h, Jane, Hannah, Lydia, Edward
6 4 1801	Goose Creek		Hopewell		Ruth Piggott
4 5 1801			Hopewell	Westland	Hannah Sexton & dtrs., Cath., Hannah, Mary
4 5 1801			Hopewell	Westland	Jas. & Rachel Raley & ch., Joshua, Hannah, Abigail, Asa, Ann
4 5 1801			Hopewell		Martha Ellis
1 6 1801			Hopewell		Isaac Neill
1 6 1801			Hopewell	Crooked Run	Rachel Bond
6 7 1801			Hopewell	Redstone	John Antram, w. Elizabeth, & grandd. Esther Antram
6 7 1801	Concord		Hopewell		Sarah Eyre
3 8 1801			Hopewell		Ellis George
3 8 1801			Hopewell		Naomi Ellis (minor d. of Jonathan)
3 8 1801	Southland		Hopewell		Alice Clever & ch., Ezekiel, Edward, Martha
7 9 1801			Hopewell	Crooked Run	Hannah Mills & ch., Amos, Hannah, Lydia
7 9 1801			Hopewell	Westland	Samuel Lewis
5 10 1801			Hopewell		Rhoda Rogers & son John
2 11 1801	Crooked Run		Hopewell		John & Susanna Wright & ch., Dan'l, Benj.
2 11 1801	Crooked Run		Hopewell		Rees Branson
2 11 1801	Philadelphia		Hopewell		Sarah Zane
2 11 1801			Hopewell	Westland	Wm. & Martha Walker & son Mordecai
2 11 1801			Hopewell	Kennett	Moses Mendenhall
7 12 1801			Hopewell	Redstone	David & Rachel Barrett & dtrs., Marv. Hannah
7 12 1801	Chester		Hopewell		Lydia Wood
4 1 1802			Hopewell	Redstone	Sam'l & Peninah Finch & ch., Lydia, Rachel, Sarah, Ruth, Mary
4 1 1802			Hopewell	Redstone	David Finch
1 2 1802			Hopewell	Redstone	Hannah & Elizabeth Finch

Day Mo. Yr.	Meeting	To	Meeting	To Meeting	Names
1 2 1802			Hopewell	Westland	Eli & Mary Raley & ch., John, Sarah, David, Jos., Ann
1 2 1802			Hopewell		Ebenezer Williams
1 2 1802			Hopewell		Rebekah Bonsall
1 3 1802	Goose Creek		Hopewell		Abel Janney
1 3 1802			Hopewell	Westland	Isaac & Eliz'h Wickersham
5 4 1802			Hopewell		Abraham, Phebe, Wm., & Mary Neill (ch. of Ann)
5 4 1802			Hopewell	Redstone	Amy (or Emmy) Jones
5 4 1802	Crooked Run		Hopewell		Jonathan & Eliz'h Pickering & ch., Mary, Elias, Evan, Isaac
3 5 1802			Hopewell	Fairfax	Isaac & Phebe Steer & ch., Jos., Ann, Jonah, Lydia, Wm., Rachel, Phebe
7 6 1802			Hopewell		David Smedley
7 6 1802	Crooked Run		Hopewell		Moses & Hannah Piggott & ch., Rachel, Thos., Jane, Hannah
7 6 1802	Crooked Run		Hopewell		Joshua & Hannah Wood & ch., Jacob, Rachel, Jesse, Arbinah
5 7 1802	Southland		Hopewell		Sarah Janney
2 8 1802	Fairfax (Endorsed by Gwined)		Hopewell		Aquilla Coates
2 8 1802			Hopewell	Crooked Run	John & Susanna Wright & sons, Dan'l, Benj.
6 9 1802			Hopewell	Redstone	Isaac & Rebeckah Brown
6 9 1802			Hopewell	Redstone	Patience Berry
6 9 1802			Hopewell	Concord	Mishael & Rachel Jinkins & ch., Ann, Jacob, Lydia, Betty, Jane, Caty, Pugh, John
6 9 1802			Hopewell	Crooked Run	Jas. Wright (son of John)
4 10 1802			Hopewell	Philadelphia	Sarah Zane
4 10 1802	Radnor		Hopewell		Mary Walker
6 12 1802	Crooked Run		Hopewell		John Piggott
6 12 1802	Chester		Hopewell		Rachel Matson (w. of Nehemiah)
6 12 1802			Hopewell	Fairfax	David Smith
6 12 1802			Hopewell	Goose Creek	Rachel Smith (d. of David)
3 1 1803	Westland		Hopewell		Elizabeth Lewis (minor)
3 1 1803			Hopewell	Sadsbury	Elias Simmonds
7 3 1803			Hopewell	Chester	Mordecai Taylor
4 4 1803			Hopewell	Alexandria	David Smedley
4 4 1803	Warrington		Hopewell		Hannah Nevitt
4 4 1803	Fairfax		Hopewell		Ann Strode

Day Mo. Yr.	Meeting	To	Meeting	To Meeting	Names
2 5 1803			Hopewell		Ruth Neill
2 5 1803			Hopewell		Thomas Neill
6 6 1803	Radnor		Hopewell		Mordecai Moon
6 6 1803	Nottingham		Hopewell		Abner & Esther Brown & son James
4 7 1803			Hopewell	Crooked Run	Ann Neill & ch., Phebe, Abraham, Wm., Mary
4 7 1803			Hopewell	Pipe Creek	Robt. Bond (minor son of Jos.)
1 8 1803			Hopewell	Westland	Isaac & Mary Walker & d. Jane
1 8 1803	Chester		Hopewell		Enoch Pugh
5 9 1803			Hopewell	Concord, O.	Solomon Lupton
5 9 1803			Hopewell	Concord, O.	Moses & Hannah Piggott & ch., Rachel, Thos., Jas., Hannah
3 10 1803			Hopewell	Concord, O.	Wm. & Barthsheba Lupton & ch., Grace, Jonathan, Allen, Isaac, Mary, Wm., David, Mahlon
3 10 1803			Hopewell	Concord, O.	Jacob & Lydia Pickering & ch., Sarah, Abel, Rhoda, Mary, Jos., Hannah
7 11 1803			Hopewell	Concord, O.	Jonathan & Martha Ellis & ch., Naomi, Elisha, Eliz'h
7 11 1803			Hopewell	Concord, O.	John Miller Jr. & w. Margaret
7 11 1803			Hopewell	Concord, O.	Eliz'h Jenkins (w. of Evan) & ch., Ruth, Eliz'h, Evan, Jas.
7 11 1803			Hopewell		David Dutton & w. Hannah
2 1 1804			Hopewell	Crooked Run	Phebe Wright (w. of Jas.) & ch., John, Hannah, Nathan, Jas., Solomon
2 1 1804			Hopewell	Crooked Run	Jonathan & Rachel Wright, ch. of Jas. & Phebe
2 1 1804			Hopewell	Fairfax	Jos. & Eliz'h Bond & ch., Jos., Ann, Thos.
5 3 1804			Hopewell	Concord, O.	Jos. & Grace Steer & ch., David, Rachel, Sam'l, Amos
5 3 1804			Hopewell	Concord, O.	Sarah Steer (d. of Jos.)
5 3 1804			Hopewell	Concord, O.	Elizabeth Pickering
2 4 1804			Hopewell	Concord, O.	Michael Jenkins (son of Evan)
2 4 1804	Wilmington		Hopewell		Elizabeth McPherson
4 6 1804	Nottingham		Hopewell		Isaac Allen
4 6 1804			Hopewell	Concord, O.	John Piggott
2 7 1804			Hopewell	Fairfax	Lydia Williams (d. of Lewis & Rachel Neill)
3 9 1804			Hopewell	Miami	Asahel & Hannah Walker & son Wm.

Day Mo. Yr.	Meeting	To	Meeting	To Meeting	Names
3 9 1804			Hopewell	Miami	Mordecai & Rachel Walker
3 9 1804			Hopewell	Miami	Jesse & Mary George & ch., Isaac, Enos, Jas., Phebe, Jesse
3 9 1804	Crooked Run		Hopewell		John & Susannah Wright & ch., Dan'l, Benj., Ann
3 12 1804			Hopewell	Short Creek	Israel Jenkins
4 3 1805			Hopewell	Concord	Stacy & Lydia Bevan & ch., Susanna, Eleanor, John, Owen
4 3 1805			Hopewell	Redstone	Richard & Phebe Fallis & ch., Mary, Lydia, Rachel
1 4 1805			Hopewell	Concord, O.	John & Sarah Fisher & ch., Mary, Richard, Rachel, Baruch, Jos.
1 4 1805			Hopewell	Concord, O.	Theodore Ellis, w. Sarah, & ch., Amos, Mary; & grandson, Elisha Ellis
1 7 1805			Hopewell	Warrington	Hannah Nevitt
1 7 1805			Hopewell	Goose Creek	Ruth Nevitt
1 7 1805			Hopewell	Redstone	Mary Pickering (grandd. of Mary Fisher)
1 7 1805			Hopewell	Concord, O.	Jane Parkins (w. of Jonathan) & ch., David, Stephen, Nathan, Jane, Eliz'h, Isaac, Hannah, Ann, Lydia
5 8 1805			Hopewell	Short Creek	Samuel Miller
5 8 1805			Hopewell	Crooked Run	Hannah Faulkner
2 9 1805			Hopewell	New Hope	Rachel Payne
2 9 1805			Hopewell	Miami	Jonathan & Rachel Barrett & ch., Jesse, Benj., Ellis, Levi, Lydia
7 10 1805			Hopewell	Short Creek	George & Abigail Cope & ch., Mary, Joshua, Jas., Geo., Abigail, Jane
7 10 1805	New York		Hopewell		Elizabeth Gray & ch., Robt., Jas.
7 10 1805			Hopewell	Concord, O.	Ruth Piggott
4 11 1805			Hopewell	Middletown, O.	Abel & Mary Walker Jr. & ch., Martha, Jos., Lewis
2 12 1805			Hopewell	Redstone	Mary Fallis
2 12 1805			Hopewell	Concord, O.	Elias Pickering (minor)
6 1 1806			Hopewell	Crooked Run	Elizabeth Antram
6 1 1806			Hopewell	Concord, O.	Isaac Pickering
3 2 1806			Hopewell	Concord, O.	Elizabeth Deselm
3 3 1806			Hopewell		Geo., Mary, & Eliz'h Hiett, minor ch. of John & Mary
3 3 1806			Hopewell	Miami	Lewis Rees
3 3 1806			Hopewell	Salem, O.	Stephen & Hannah McBride & ch., Jas., Jeremiah, Evan, Hannah, Sam'l, Andrew, Betty, Abraham

Day Mo. Yr.	Meeting	To	Meeting	To Meeting	Names
3 3 1806			Hopewell	Salem, O.	Isaac & Ann Jackson
5 5 1806			Hopewell	Miami	Lydia Huffman
2 6 1806	Crooked Run		Hopewell		John & Rachel Bond & ch., Abner, Hannah
7 7 1806			Hopewell		Marg't Fisher (w. of Thos.)
7 7 1806	Pipe Creek		Hopewell		Aaron & Martha Hibbert & ch., Jane, Lydia, Jas.
7 7 1806	Baltimore		Hopewell		Hannah Brown
4 8 1806			Hopewell	Miami	Thomas Thatcher
4 8 1806	Alexandria		Hopewell		Ruth Janney & ch., Hannah, Dan'l, Rebekah, Wm., Aquilla, Israel, Mary Ann
4 8 1806			Hopewell	Miami	Martha Faulkner
4 8 1806			Hopewell	Short Creek	Jos. & Susanna Quaintance & ch., Wm., Eli, Ann, Susanna, Fisher
4 8 1806			Hopewell	Redstone	Susanna Harris (Jenkins)
1 9 1806	Redstone		Hopewell		Ruth Wood
1 9 1806			Hopewell	Miami	Ellen Faulkner
6 10 1806			Hopewell	Baltimore	Isaiah Litler (s. of Nathan)
3 11 1806			Hopewell	Miami	Thos., Hannah, & Jane Faulkner, ch. of Jesse
3 11 1806			Hopewell	Miami	Thos. Faulkner (s. of Robt.)
3 11 1806	Fairfax		Hopewell		Jacob Jenkins
3 11 1806	Warrington		Hopewell		Hannah Nevitt
1 12 1806			Hopewell	Baltimore	James Moseley
1 12 1806			Hopewell	Miami	Ruth Thatcher's ch., Thos., Mary, David, Jos., Ruth
1 12 1806			Hopewell	Miami	Jesse Thatcher
1 12 1806			Hopewell	Miami	Isaac & Betty McPherson & d. Ann
2 2 1807			Hopewell	Alexandria	Phebe Butcher
5 1 1807	London Grove		Hopewell		William Common
5 1 1807			Hopewell	Alexandria	William H. Brown
5 1 1807			Hopewell		Baruch, Eliz'h, Robt., John, Thos., Elias, Mary, & Jos. (ch. of Thos. Fisher)
2 2 1807			Hopewell		Hannah George
2 2 1807	Sadsbury		Hopewell		Margaret Daniel
2 2 1807			Hopewell	Miami	Jacob Smith & ch., Rachel, John, Ann, Mary, Josiah, Jacob, Lydia, Sarah, Hannah, Isaac, Seth
2 2 1807			Hopewell	Salem, O.	Jonathan Perkins Jr., son of Jonathan Sr. & Jane
2 3 1807			Hopewell	Salem, O. (?)	Ruth Faulkner
2 3 1807			Hopewell	Miami	Richard & Sarah Barrett & ch., Lydia, Sarah, Sydney, Amy, Richard, Lewis
2 3 1807			Hopewell	Goshen	Peter (or Richard?) Taylor

Day Mo. Yr.	Meeting	To	Meeting	To Meeting	Names
6 4 1807			Hopewell	Miami	Wm. & Sarah Lewis & d. Elizabeth
4 5 1807			Hopewell	Miami (?)	Ann Schofield
6 8 1807			Hopewell	Miami	Hannah Faulkner
6 8 1807			Hopewell	Miami	Rebekah Callett (Haines)
6 9 1807			Hopewell	Salem	Isaac & Hannah Davis
6 9 1807			Hopewell	Salem	Stephen McBride Jr.
6 9 1807			Hopewell	Alexandria	Wm. & Rebekah Jolliffe & ch., Mary, John, Elizabeth
6 9 1807			Hopewell	Concord	Joseph Wright
5 10 1807			Hopewell	Concord	Jonathan Pickering (s. of Jane)
5 10 1807			Hopewell	Salem	Richard & Eunice Fawcett & ch., David, Jonathan, Anna, Wm., Esther, Druzilla
5 10 1807			Hopewell	Concord	Jane Nichols & ch., Eli, Mary
2 11 1807			Hopewell	Redstone	Wm. Neill (son of Ann)
2 11 1807			Hopewell	Concord	Margaret Baldwin
7 12 1807			Hopewell	Miami	Levi & Eliz'h Lukens & ch., Rachel, Jos., Benj., John, Salathiel
7 12 1807			Hopewell	Redstone	Isaac Hollingsworth
7 12 1807			Hopewell		Susanna & Mary Dutton
4 1 1808			Hopewell	Salem	John McBride
4 1 1808			Hopewell	Fairfield	John & Mary Griffith
4 1 1808			Hopewell	Fairfield	Eleanor Cowgill & ch., Sarah, Benj., Henry
4 1 1808			Hopewell	Concord	Martha McNichols
4 1 1808			Hopewell	Indian Spring	Mary Taylor
4 1 1808			Hopewell	Fairfield	Ann Rees
1 2 1808			Hopewell	Fairfield	John Wright
1 2 1808			Hopewell	Concord	Marg't Baldwin's 4 ch., Thos., Mary, David, Rees Ellis
1 2 1808			Hopewell	Salem	Abel Jackson
7 3 1808			Hopewell	Short Creek	Martha Bonsall
4 4 1808			Hopewell	Center	Elizabeth Faulkner
2 5 1808			Hopewell	Miami	Mary Allen
6 6 1808			Hopewell	Center	David Faulkner (son of Robt.)
6 6 1808	Goose Creek		Hopewell		Asa Frehorn
6 6 1808			Hopewell	Baltimore	Sam'l Parkins (son of Isaac)
4 7 1808	Fairfax		Hopewell		Jos. & Elizabeth Bond & ch., Ann, Thos., Asa
4 7 1808				Hopewell	Short Creek	John & Rachel Lupton & ch., David, Jonathan, Lydia, Francis, Geo.

Day Mo. Yr.	Meeting	To	Meeting	To Meeting	Names
1 8 1808			Hopewell	Fairfield	Elizabeth Halloway
5 9 1808			Hopewell	Salem	Thos. & Martha Fearnley
5 9 1808	Nottingham		Hopewell		Ellis Pugh
3 10 1808	Monallen		Hopewell		Thomas Wright
3 10 1808			Hopewell	Fairfield	Geo. & Elizabeth Shinn & son Francis
3 10 1808			Hopewell	Fairfield	Joshua & Ann Woodrow Jr. & ch., Elizabeth, Rachel, Joshua
3 10 1808			Hopewell	Fairfield	Elizabeth Woodrow & ch., Jos. & Rachel
7 11 1808			Hopewell	Fairfield	John Morgan
7 11 1808			Hopewell	Redstone	Isaac Wickersham
7 11 1808			Hopewell	Plainfield	Lydia Adams
7 11 1808			Hopewell	Westland	Ruth Wood
5 12 1808			Hopewell	Plainfield	William Fawcett
2 1 1809	Radnor		Hopewell		Hannah Coats
2 1 1809			Hopewell	Redstone	Eli & Ruth Haines & ch., Chalkley, Miller, Atlantic, Hiram, Mary
6 2 1809			Hopewell	Sadsbury	Margaret Daniel
6 3 1809			Hopewell	Fairfield	Thomas Holloway
6 3 1809			Hopewell	Westland	Sam'l & Rachel Talbot & ch., Jos., Nathan, John, Rebekah, Sam'l
6 3 1809			Hopewell		Eliza Coats (d. of Hannah)
3 4 1809			Hopewell		Sam'l Howell & ch., Ruth, David, Nathan, Sarah
3 4 1809			Hopewell	Miami	James Miller
3 4 1809			Hopewell	Fairfield	George Holloway
1 5 1809			Hopewell	Salem	John Fawcett Jr.
1 5 1809			Hopewell	Alexandria	David Ross
5 6 1809			Hopewell		Hannah, John, & Deborah White (ch. of Deborah)
3 7 1809			Hopewell	Monallen	Thomas Wright
3 7 1809	Fairfax		Hopewell		David Pusey
3 7 1809	Middletown		Hopewell		Lewis Townsend (minor)
7 8 1809			Hopewell	Chester	Leah Farr
4 9 1809			Hopewell	Plainfield	Jacob & Rebekah McKay
4 9 1809			Hopewell	Miami	Margaret Hains & d. Margaret
4 9 1809			Hopewell	Plainfield	Sarah Dillon
2 10 1809	Deer Creek		Hopewell		John Webb
2 10 1809			Hopewell	Miami	Enoch Pugh
2 10 1809			Hopewell	Miami	Edward & Deborah Walton & ch., Sam'l, Betty, Mary
2 10 1809			Hopewell	Plainfield	Mary Fawcett & ch., Robt., Atlantic, Joshua, Susanna, John, Mahlon, Dorcas, Nancy, Washington

Day Mo. Yr.	Meeting	To	Meeting	To Meeting	Names
6 11 1809			Hopewell	Miami	Daniel Antram
6 11 1809			Hopewell	Plainfield	Joshua & Hannah Wood & ch., Jacob, Rachel, Jesse, Sarah, Aseneth
6 11 1809			Hopewell	Pipe Creek	Ezekial Clever (son of Alice)
6 11 1809	Chester		Hopewell		Mordecai & Frances Taylor & ch., Mary, Benj., Ann, Frances, Ambrose
6 11 1809	Baltimore		Hopewell		Sam'l Parkins (certificate returned)
4 12 1809			Hopewell	Upper Evesham	Isaac Garwood
4 12 1809			Hopewell	Short Creek	Dan'l & Miriam Brown
4 12 1809			Hopewell	Alexandria	Dan'l & Eliz'h McPherson & ch., Rebekah, Mary, Ann, Sam'l
1 1 1810			Hopewell	Short Creek	Jos. & Hannah Saunders & ch., Ann, Susanna, Mary, Martha, John, Jane
1 1 1810			Hopewell	Short Creek	Elizabeth & Miriam Brown
1 1 1810			Hopewell	Goose Creek	Esther (Brown) Gregg & sons, Jas., Sam'l Brown
5 2 1810			Hopewell	Plainfield	Rebekah Pickering
5 3 1810			Hopewell	Short Creek	Sarah Eyre
2 4 1810			Hopewell	Short Creek	Rachel Matson
2 4 1810			Hopewell	Alexandria	Hannah Saunders (McPherson)
2 4 1810			Hopewell	Miami	Hannah Bond
2 4 1810	Goose Creek		Hopewell		William Frayhorn
7 5 1810			Hopewell		Lewis, Silas, & Joel George, ch. of Jas. & Hannah
4 6 1810			Hopewell	Fairfax	Leah, w. of Isaac Steer (2d marriage), & d. Sarah Ann Lupton
4 6 1810			Hopewell	Short Creek	David Brown
2 7 1810			Hopewell	Fairfax	Samuel Miller
2 7 1810			Hopewell	Westland	Lewis Walker Jr.
5 10 1810			Hopewell		Hannah Lloyd
5 10 1810			Hopewell	Short Creek	Eliz'h Gray & ch., Robt. H., Jas. D., John F., Wm., Phebe F., Geo. K.
5 10 1810			Hopewell	Miami	Mary Allen
3 11 1810			Hopewell	Redstone	John & Mary Hains
3 12 1810			Hopewell	Short Creek	Ann Gill
10 1 1811	Pipe Creek		Hopewell		Benj. Hibbert
10 1 1811			Hopewell	Short Creek	Robert Eyre Jr.
10 1 1811			Hopewell	Short Creek	Robert Eyre Sr. & w. Ann
10 1 1811			Hopewell	Redstone	Susanna. Grubb
7 2 1811			Hopewell	?	Massey Jourdan
7 3 1811			Hopewell	?	Ann Hains
7 3 1811			Hopewell	Goose Creek	Asa Fehorn

FROM BOOK FOUR
1811-1851

Day Mo. Yr.	Meeting	To	Meeting	To Meeting	Names
4 4 1811			Hopewell	Alexandria	Martha Brown
4 4 1811	Redstone		Hopewell		William Neill
9 5 1811			Hopewell	Alexandria	David Lupton Jr., w. Ann, & d. Rachel
9 5 1811	Short Creek		Hopewell		Joel Oxley
9 5 1811			Hopewell	Miami	Jackson Allen, w. Sarah, & ch., Edward, Mary, Jos., Solomon, Rebekah, Alice, Sarah, Ann, Harmony, Westley
9 5 1811			Hopewell	Miami	Ruth Allen
9 5 1811			Hopewell	Dunnings Creek	Phebe Smith
6 6 1811			Hopewell	Goose Creek	Abel Janney, w. Lydia, & ch., Nancy, Jas., Jonas
5 9 1811	Westland		Hopewell		Sina Townsend, Rachel Townsend
7 10 1811			Hopewell	Pipe Creek	Jacob R. Thomas
7 10 1811			Hopewell	Miami	Edward Walton, wife, & children
7 10 1811			Hopewell	Plainfield	Benj. Allen, w. Hannah, & ch., Moses, Unice, Dan'l, Mary, John, Hannah, Benj.
7 10 1811			Hopewell	Short Creek	Grace Cope
7 10 1811			Hopewell	Plainfield	Ruth Allen
7 10 1811			Hopewell	Miami	Sam'l Crampton, w. Rachel, & ch., Jeremiah, Rachel, Merrick, Mary, Joshua, Eliz'h
7 11 1811			Hopewell	Miami	Ann Branson & children
5 12 1811			Hopewell	Fairfax	Thos. White, son of Nathaniel
5 12 1811	Plainfield		Hopewell		Rebekah Pickering
5 12 1811			Hopewell		Mary Allen
5 3 1812	Indian Springs		Hopewell		Abijah Taylor
9 4 1812	Fairfax		Hopewell		Robert Bond
9 4 1812	Fairfax		Hopewell		Abel Jackson
9 4 1812			Hopewell	Plainfield	Hannah Ferneley & d. Unice
14 5 1812			Hopewell	Short Creek	Jas. Steer & sons, Jos., Jas.
14 5 1812			Hopewell	Center Mtg., O.	John Cowgill Jr., w. Susanna, & son Jas.
14 5 1812			Hopewell	Alexandria	Lewis Neill Jr., son of Rebekah
14 5 1812			Hopewell	Miami	Susanna Shepherd & d. Susanna
14 5 1812			Hopewell	Short Creek	Hannah McCarta
14 5 1812			Hopewell	Short Creek	Ruth Steer
14 5 1812			Hopewell	Short Creek	Mary Steer

Day Mo. Yr.	Meeting	To Meeting	To Meeting	Names
14 5 1812		Hopewell	Short Creek	Phoebe Steer
4 6 1812		Hopewell	Fairfax	Isaac Walker
4 6 1812		Hopewell	Baltimore	Benj. Chandlee, w. Elizabeth, & d. Ann
9 7 1812	South River	Hopewell		Isaac Pigeon & ch., Wm., Isaac, Rachel, Mary
9 7 1812		Hopewell	Fairfax	Josiah & Jonathan Jackson
6 8 1812		Hopewell	Short Creek	Evan Pickering, a minor
6 8 1812		Hopewell	Short Creek	Wm. Brown & w. Grace
6 8 1812		Hopewell	Fairfax	Grace Jackson
10 9 1812		Hopewell	Dunnings Creek	Joshua Pickering (Cert. returned saying he did not reside there)
10 9 1812		Hopewell		Lydia (George) Johnson, w. of Joshua
5 10 1812		Hopewell	Plainfield	Rebekah Pickering
5 10 1812		Hopewell	Miami	Mary Collett, w. of Dan'l
5 10 1812	Goose Creek	Hopewell		Ruth Nevitt
7 1 1813		Hopewell	Fairfax	Isaac Morgan
4 2 1813		Hopewell	Alexandria	Thos. Wilson, w. Mary, & ch., Rebekah, Enoch, Thos.
4 2 1813		Hopewell	Alexandria	Katherine Wilson
4 3 1813		Hopewell	Darby Creek	Jos. Rhea, w. Susanna, & ch., Robt., Sarah, Allen, Marg't, Rebekah, Deborah, Thos.
4 3 1813		Hopewell	Gunpowder	Patience Pugh
8 4 1813	Alexandria	Hopewell		Mary Buckannan
6 5 1813		Hopewell	Plainfield	Rees Branson, w. Ruth, & ch., Abraham, Mariah
6 5 1813		Hopewell	Short Creek	William Frame
6 5 1813		Hopewell	Short Creek	Benj. Frame, w. Elizabeth, & ch., Jas., Rachel
6 5 1813		Hopewell	Pipe Creek	Benj. Hibberd, w. Charity, and d. Jane
6 5 1813		Hopewell	Pipe Creek	Isaac Branson
6 5 1813		Hopewell	Short Creek	Jane Frame
6 5 1813		Hopewell	Miami	Isaac Wickersham
4 10 1813		Hopewell	Plainfield	Moses Miles (minor), son of Hannah
4 10 1813		Hopewell	Cæsar's Creek	Nathaniel White & sons, John, Jesse
4 10 1813		Hopewell	Cæsar's Creek	Mary & Sarah White
4 10 1813		Hopewell	Plainfield	Hannah & Lydia Miles
4 10 1813		Hopewell	Short Creek	Charity Redd
4 11 1813	Gunpowder	Hopewell		John Price
4 11 1813		Hopewell	Cæsar's Creek	Deborah & Ruth Allen
4 11 1813		Hopewell	Clear Creek	William Cowgill
4 11 1813		Hopewell	Miami	Levi & Jesse Sheppard

Day Mo. Yr.	Meeting	To	Meeting	To Meeting	Names
4 11 1813			Hopewell	Cæsar's Creek	Jos. Allen Jr.
4 11 1813			Hopewell		Lewis Hollingsworth
9 12 1813			Hopewell	Redstone	Margaret Cattell (Wright), w. of David
10 3 1814	Deer Creek		Hopewell		Anne Warner
10 3 1814			Hopewell		Charity McCool
5 5 1814			Hopewell	Salem	Lewis Townsend
5 5 1814			Hopewell	Salem	Eli Fawcett (minor)
5 5 1814			Hopewell	Sadsbury	Elias Simmonds
5 5 1814			Hopewell	Short Creek	Elizabeth Mooney
9 6 1814			Hopewell	Short Creek	Thos. Smith, w. Phebe, & sons, John S., Jonah, Wm., Robert H.
9 6 1814			Hopewell	Alexandria	Sam'l McPherson & w. Mary
9 6 1814			Hopewell	Alexandria	Thos. Neill & w. Mary
7 7 1814			Hopewell	Baltimore	Jos. Hollingsworth
4 8 1814			Hopewell	Fairfax	John Swayne
4 8 1814			Hopewell		Tamar Grimes
4 8 1814			Hopewell		Edward Farr & ch., Isaac, Marg't, Mar·· Tamar; & Aseneth N. Farr
8 9 1814	Abington		Hopewell		Ann Clendenning
8 9 1814			Hopewell	Clear Creek	John Cowgill, w. Katharine, & ch., Asa, Amos, Elisha
8 9 1814			Hopewell	Clear Creek	Ann Cowgill
3 10 1814			Hopewell	Plainfield	Thos. Fawcett, w. Martha, & son Thos.
3 10 1814			Hopewell	Goose Creek	Aaron Holliway, w. Rachel, & ch., Robert S., Aaron S., Asa, Mary S.
3 10 1814			Hopewell	Goose Creek	Ann Lovett & minor ch., Sarah, Jonathan, Joshua, Mahlon, Mary Ann
3 10 1814			Hopewell	Plainfield	Unice & Mary Fawcett
3 10 1814			Hopewell	Plainfield	Unice Painter
3 10 1814			Hopewell	Clear Creek	Hannah Cowgill
3 10 1814			Hopewell	Goose Creek	Nancy Lovett
10 11 1814	Salem, O.		Hopewell		John Fawcett
8 12 1814			Hopewell	Fairfax	Deborah Morgan (minor)
8 12 1814			Hopewell	Plainfield	John Branson, w. Abigail, & ch., Miriam, Nancy, Asa, Elisha
8 12 1814	New Hope		Hopewell		Jesse Smith & John Powell
5 1 1815			Hopewell	Short Creek	Isaac Nevitt, w. Rachel, & minor ch., Isaac, John, Grace, Eliza, Rachel
9 2 1815			Hopewell	Short Creek	George Frame
9 3 1815			Hopewell	Indian Spring	Edward Farr, w. Mary, & ch., Isaac, Marg't, Mary, Tamar, Asenah Newlin

Day	Mo.	Yr.	Meeting	To	Meeting	To Meeting	Names
9	3	1815			Hopewell	Cæsar's Creek	John Miller, w. Jane, & ch., Jonas, Elizabeth
9	3	1815			Hopewell	Short Creek	Hannah Miles & d. Susanna
9	3	1815			Hopewell	Plainfield	Ann Coffee
9	3	1815			Hopewell	Cæsar's Creek	Sarah Miller
6	4	1815	Baltimore		Hopewell		Rachel Johnson
6	4	1815	Baltimore		Hopewell		Joshua Johnson, w. Lydia, & d. Mary R.
4	5	1815			Hopewell	Baltimore	Aquilla Janney
8	6	1815			Hopewell	Short Creek	Adam Eyre
8	6	1815			Hopewell	Fairfax	Isaac Pigeon Jr.
10	8	1815	Plainfield		Hopewell		Sam'l Sharp, w. Martha, & ch., Lydia, Phinehas
7	9	1815			Hopewell	Red Stone	Joel Oxley
7	9	1815	New Hope		Hopewell		Joseph Smith
9	11	1815			Hopewell	Red Stone	Joshua Wood
1	1	1816	Alexandria		Hopewell		Wm. Jolliffe, w. Rebekah, & ch., Mary, John, Eliz'h, Jos., Wm.
1	1	1816			Hopewell		Washington Hough
8	2	1816			Hopewell	Middletown	Rachel Townsend
7	3	1816			Hopewell		Ann Thompson
4	4	1816			Hopewell	Alexandria	Sarah Janney
4	4	1816			Hopewell	Still Water	Hannah Rommins
6	6	1816			Hopewell	Middletown, O.	Sina Townsend
8	8	1816			Hopewell	Fairfield	Joseph Horseman
5	9	1816			Hopewell	Goose Creek	Elizabeth A. Janney
7	10	1816			Hopewell		Ruth Pickering
7	11	1816			Hopewell	Fairfield	Isaac Pickering (minor)
5	12	1816			Hopewell	Baltimore	Robert Bond
5	12	1816			Hopewell	Baltimore	Sam'l McPherson, son of Wm.
5	12	1816			Hopewell		Grace & Jonathan Pickering (minors of Benj.)
9	1	1817			Hopewell	Alexandria	Thomas Swayne
6	2	1817	Goose Creek		Hopewell		Isaac Wilson
6	3	1817			Hopewell	Salem	Simeon & Levi Fawcett (minors)
6	3	1817			Hopewell	Alexandria	Rebekah Swayne & ch., Joshua, Noah
10	4	1817			Hopewell	Alexandria	Margaret Wood
10	4	1817			Hopewell	Goose Creek	Sidney Daniel
10	4	1817			Hopewell		Hannah Dunn
5	6	1817			Hopewell	Alexandria	Dan'l Haines, w. Bulah, & ch., Mariah, Rebekah, Susan
7	8	1817			Hopewell	Derby Creek	Joseph Conrad
7	8	1817			Hopewell		Ann Neill
7	8	1817			Hopewell	Miami	Abijah Taylor, w. Mary, & ch., Jos. Neill, & John Ambrose

Day	Mo.	Yr.	Meeting	To	Meeting	To Meeting	Names
4	9	1817			Hopewell	Middletown, O.	Henry George, w. Tamar, & ch., Caleb, Mary
4	9	1817	Clear Creek		Hopewell		George Pusey
4	9	1817			Hopewell	Fall Creek	Elizabeth Lupton
6	10	1817	New Hope		Hopewell		Isaac Smith
6	11	1817			Hopewell	Alexandria	John McPherson & w. Hannah
6	11	1817			Hopewell	Alexandria	John McPherson Jr.
6	11	1817			Hopewell	Fairfax	Washington Hough
6	11	1817			Hopewell		Rebekah McPherson
4	12	1817			Hopewell	Miami	Solomon Hollingsworth & w. Sarah
4	12	1817			Hopewell	Derby Creek	Jas. Conrad, w. Esther, & d. Esther; also Jas. Conrad Jr., George, Rachel, Ruth, Eliz'h
4	12	1817			Hopewell		Ruth Lupton
8	1	1818			Hopewell	Flushing, O.	Mary Rogers
5	2	1818			Hopewell	Miami	Goldsmith Chandlee Jr., w. Phebe, & ch., Mary, Eliz'h, John
9	4	1818			Hopewell	Philadelphia	Isaac Wilson
9	4	1818			Hopewell	Fairfax	George Pusey
9	7	1818			Hopewell	Elexander (Alexandria)	Hannah Ross
10	9	1818			Hopewell	Plainfield, O.	Ruth Lupton
5	10	1818			Hopewell	Plainfield, O.	Hannah Oneil & ch., Ann, Rebekah, John
5	10	1818			Hopewell		Hannah Thompson
5	11	1818			Hopewell	Redstone	Jesse Wood
10	12	1818	Plainfield		Hopewell		Abraham & Mariah Branson & 2 minor ch.
10	12	1818			Hopewell	Center, O.	Phebe Oglesby
7	1	1819			Hopewell	Cæesar's Creek	Richard Wright, w. Rachel, & ch., Mary Jane, Jonathan, Levi
4	2	1819			Hopewell	Fairfield, O.	Hannah & Rachel Beall
4	2	1819			Hopewell	Westland	George Pusey
4	2	1819			Hopewell	Fairfield	William Beall
4	2	1819			Hopewell	Mill Creek	Jas. McCool, w. Charity, & ch., Eliza, Rachel
4	3	1819			Hopewell	Baltimore	Robert Holliway
8	4	1819	Clear Creek		Hopewell		William Cogill
8	4	1819			Hopewell	Fairfield	Margaret Lupton
8	4	1819			Hopewell		Robt. Daniel, son of Andrew
6	5	1819			Hopewell	Short Creek	Thomas Ross
6	5	1819			Hopewell	Cezar's Creek	Abigail McCoy & ch., Sarah, Geo., Frances, Marg't, Va., Mariah, Tildon, Levi

Day Mo. Yr.	Meeting	To Meeting	To Meeting	Names
6 5 1819		Hopewell	Fairfax	Ruth Mendenhall & d. Mary Ann Janney; also one for Rebekah Janney
6 5 1819		Hopewell	Fairfax	William Janney
10 6 1819	Sadsbury	Hopewell		Sam'l Downing Jr.
5 8 1819	Baltimore	Hopewell		Robert Bond
5 8 1819	Goose Creek	Hopewell		Lydia Fawcett
9 9 1819		Hopewell	Concord, O.	Thomas Branson
4 11 1819	Alexander	Hopewell		Margaret Wood
9 12 1819		Hopewell	Salem, O.	John Fawcett
9 12 1819	Fairfax	Hopewell		John Pairpoint
10 2 1820	Goose Creek	Hopewell		George Sharp
6 4 1820		Hopewell	Fairfax	David Jackson
6 4 1820		Hopewell	Baltimore	Isaac Wilson
8 6 1820		Hopewell	Flushing	Jos. & Thos. Nevitt
6 7 1820		Hopewell		Jacob Keefer
6 7 1820		Hopewell		Ann Dunn
10 8 1820	New Garden	Hopewell		Andrew McBride
10 8 1820		Hopewell		Andrew, Jos. H., Maryann, Hannah, Rachel, ch. of Robt. & Martha Daniel
7 9 1820		Hopewell		Josiah Jackson Fenton
9 11 1820		Hopewell	Pipe Creek	Edward B. Cleaver
7 12 1820		Hopewell	Cæsar's Creek	Thomas Littler
8 3 1821		Hopewell		Sidney Parkins & d. Elizabeth
5 4 1821		Hopewell	Goose Creek	Mary Flower
5 4 1821		Hopewell		Isaac Pidgeon
5 4 1821		Hopewell		Louisa Brown
10 5 1821	Miami	Hopewell		Sarah Hollingsworth
7 6 1821	Philadelphia	Hopewell		Elizabeth R. Byrd
7 6 1821	Alexandria	Hopewell		Dan'l Haines & minor ch., Maria, Rebecca, Susan
5 9 1821	Alexandria	Hopewell		Wm. Brown, w. Martha, & ch., Jane, Rebecca, Eliza
8 11 1821		Hopewell	Sandy Spring	Andrew McBride
6 12 1821		Hopewell	Pipe Creek	Alice Cleaver
6 12 1821		Hopewell	Goose Creek	Rachel Smith
10 1 1822		Hopewell	Miamee	Mordecai Taylor, w. Frances, & ch., Frances, Ambrose, Mordecai, Jacob, Gulielma
10 1 1822		Hopewell	Concord	Abraham D. Branson
10 1 1822	Fairfax	Hopewell		Isaac Lambourn
10 1 1822		Hopewell	Miamee	Mary Taylor
10 1 1822		Hopewell	Miamee	Ann Taylor
7 3 1822	Baltimore	Hopewell		Charles Little
4 7 1822		Hopewell	Goose Creek	Josiah Brown
4 7 1822	Redstone	Hopewell		Isaac Hollingsworth

Day Mo. Yr.	Meeting	To	Meeting	To Meeting	Names
10 10 1822			Hopewell		Mark Thatcher
7 1 1823	Alexandria		Hopewell		Susanna Ball & ch., Eliza H., Jos. P., Wm., Jas.
7 1 1823			Hopewell	Green Plain	Mary Littler
6 2 1823			Hopewell	Indian Spring	Isaac Lambourn
6 3 1823			Hopewell	Miami	Haines McKay
6 3 1823	Plainsfield		Hopewell		Jesse Sharp
10 4 1823			Hopewell	Salem, O.	Elizabeth Fawcett
10 4 1823	Alexandria		Hopewell		David Wilson, w. Hannah, & ch., John Warden, Thos. Irvin
10 7 1823			Hopewell		Priscilla Fenton
7 8 1823			Hopewell	Fairfax	Louisa Steer
4 9 1823	Fairfax		Hopewell		Josiah Jackson
8 1 1824			Hopewell	Goose Creek	Priscilla Tate (Fenton), w. of Wm.
8 1 1824			Hopewell	Falls Creek	Eleanor Pickering
8 1 1824			Hopewell	Falls Creek	Lydia Pickering
5 2 1824			Hopewell	Falls Creek	Jonathan Pickering Sr. & Jonathan Jr.
5 2 1824			Hopewell	Falls Creek	Wm. Pickering, w. Ruth, & ch., David, Sarah, Eleanor
5 2 1824			Hopewell	Falls Creek	David Pickering
5 2 1824			Hopewell	Alexandria	David Wilson, w. Hannah, & ch., John Harder & Thos. Erwin
4 3 1824	Fairfax		Hopewell		Rebecca Janney
4 3 1824	Fairfax		Hopewell		Mary Ann Janney
6 5 1824			Hopewell	Center, O.	Aquilla Coates, w. Rachel, & son Isaac Lewis
6 5 1824			Hopewell	Cæsar's Creek	George White
10 6 1824	Redstone		Hopewell		Jesse Wood
10 6 1824	Indian Spring		Hopewell		Isaac Lambourn
10 6 1824			Hopewell	Fairfax	Isaac Lambourn
9 9 1824	Alexandria		Hopewell		Hannah Ross
9 9 1824	Alexandria		Hopewell		Mahlon Schofield, w. Ann, & ch., Lewis, Eliz'h, Rachel, Ann, Jos., Wm.
9 9 1824			Hopewell	Fairfield	Rebecca Simons
7 10 1824	Baltimore		Hopewell		Sam'l McPherson
9 12 1824	Alexandria		Hopewell		Ann Lupton & ch., Rachel, John, Jane, Mary
9 12 1824	Fairfax		Hopewell		Isaac B. Beall
6 1 1825			Hopewell	Alexandria	John Pierpoint
6 1 1825			Hopewell	Fairfax	Sarah Schooley
7 4 1825			Hopewell	Springborough	Benj. Taylor
7 4 1825			Hopewell	Center, O.	Albon Fawcett
5 5 1825	Alexandria		Hopewell		Asa M. Janney

Day Mo. Yr.	Meeting	To Meeting	To Meeting	Names
5 5 1825	Alexandria	Hopewell		Benj. W. Powel
5 5 1825	Pipe Creek	Hopewell		Alice Cleaver
8 9 1825	Fairfax	Hopewell		Grace Jackson
6 10 1825		Hopewell	Fairfield	Isaac Adams
10 11 1825		Hopewell	Fairfield	Jos. Adams & w. Mary
8 12 1825		Hopewell	Plainfield	Samuel Sharp
8 12 1825	Alexandria	Hopewell		Deborah Morgan
9 2 1826	Goose Creek	Hopewell		Sidney Daniel & ch., Ruth Wright, Sarah Jane
6 4 1826		Hopewell	Stillwater	Sam'l Swayne, w. Margaret (Brown), & ch., Isaac B., Mary B., Sarah Ann, Joshua W., Rachel, Sam'l F., John Thomas, Noah
6 4 1826	Fairfax	Hopewell		Jonathan Jackson
6 4 1826	Fairfax	Hopewell		Isaac Lambourn
8 6 1826	Nottingham	Hopewell		Jas. W. Trimble
10 8 1826	Alexandria	Hopewell		Anna Lupton
7 9 1826		Hopewell	Fairfield	Jonathan Adams
7 9 1826		Hopewell	White Water	Alice Cleaver
7 9 1826		Hopewell	Chesterfield	Israel Taylor
5 10 1826		Hopewell	Alexandria	Chas. Little, w. Lydia, & ch., Wm., Isaac P.
5 10 1826		Hopewell	Spring Boro'	Jonathan Taylor
5 10 1826		Hopewell	White Water	Tacy Beeson
9 11 1826	Alexandria	Hopewell		Thos. V. Huck, w. Mary, & ch., Richard, Rebecca Neil
7 12 1826	Goose Creek	Hopewell		Hannah Lupton
7 6 1827	Goose Creek	Hopewell		Ann Lovett & ch., Mahlon Smith, Mary Ann
9 8 1827	Nottingham	Hopewell		Thomas Trimble
9 8 1827	Springboro'	Hopewell		James Hibberd, minor
4 10 1827	Elk	Hopewell		Mary Hibberd
8 11 1827	Miami	Hopewell		Ann Neile
6 3 1828	Fairfield	Hopewell		William Beal
10 4 1828		Hopewell	Fairfax	Asa Janney, w. Lydia, & d. Mary Jane, minor
10 4 1828	Fairfax	Hopewell		John Fenton, w. Mary, & son Jos. S.
10 7 1828		Hopewell	Philadelphia	Isaac Lambourn
10 7 1828	Alexandria	Hopewell		Hannah M. Howell
6 11 1828		Hopewell	Greenplain	John Littler. (This cert. was lost & another sent from Hopewell to Cincinnati, 10-9-1829.)
8 1 1829		Hopewell		Sarah Ann Branson, minor
8 10 1829		Hopewell	Cincinnati	John Littler
5 11 1829		Hopewell	Center, O.	Elizabeth Henilright [Hemilright?]

FROM A SMALL RECORD BOOK

Day Mo. Yr.	Meeting	To	Meeting To Meeting	Names
7 1 1830			Hopewell Springborough	Francis Taylor
8 7 1830			Hopewell Falls Creek	Evan George, w. Hannah, & ch., Richard, John
8 7 1830			Hopewell Falls Creek	John George & wife Leah
9 9 1830			Hopewell Falls Creek	Jas. George, w. Mary, s. David (minor); also Joel & Jesse
5 8 1830			Hopewell Goose Creek	Casandra Nichols
7 10 1830			Hopewell Goose Creek	Isaac B. Beall
9 12 1830			Hopewell Falls Creek	Mary George Sr., Ruth, Rachel, Sarah, Mary Jr., Richard
6 1 1831			Hopewell Short Creek	David Dutton
7 7 1831			Hopewell Fairfax	Thomas Brown
6 10 1831			Hopewell Centre	Louisa Fawcett
7 6 1832			Hopewell Miami	Samuel B. Hackney
7 6 1832			Hopewell Miami	John Lewis Hackney
7 6 1832			Hopewell Miami	Ch. of Aaron Hackney: Aaron, Edward Bond, Amos, Wm. I., Hugh
9 8 1832			Hopewell Miami	Elenor, Charity, & Mary Hackney
4 10 1832			Hopewell Centre	Isaac B. Thomas & wife Jane
6 12 1832			Hopewell White Water	Martha Ridgeway Sr. & Martha Jr.
10 1 1833			Hopewell Goshen, O.	David Brown & ch., Isaac, Mary, Anne, Marg't, Thos., Sarah, Jos., Israel, Eliz'h
7 3 1833			Hopewell Green Plain	Abel Walker, w. Hannah, & ch., Jos. Lupton & Mary
9 5 1833			Hopewell Fall Creek, O.	Benj. Pickering, w. Mary, & ch., Grace, Jonathan, Phebe, Lydia, Rebecca, Rachel, Hannah, Sarah
9 5 1833			Hopewell Fall Creek, O.	James George Jr.
8 8 1833			Hopewell Goshen, O.	David Brown
7 11 1833			Hopewell Centre, O.	Richard Lupton, w. Anna, & ch., Jos., Abijah, Elizabeth Ann
6 12 1833			Hopewell Concord	Elisha Fawcett, w. Rebecca, & ch., Mahlon Taylor, Thos. Wm., Mary Taylor, Franklin, Jos. Janney, & Lydia Ann
6 2 1834			Hopewell Fairfax	Nathan Walker
10 4 1834			Hopewell Springborough	David Lupton
8 5 1834			Hopewell Fairfax	Sinah Walker
8 5 1834			Hopewell Fairfax	Sarah Walker

Day Mo. Yr.	Meeting	To	Meeting	To Meeting	Names
5 6 1834			Hopewell	Fall Creek, O.	Thos. Rees, w. Elenor, & ch., Wm., Marg't, Mary Ellen, Evan, John, Josiah, Matilda, Jane, Elisha, Thos. Jr.
5 6 1834			Hopewell	Fall Creek, O.	Joel Rees
5 6 1834			Hopewell	Fall Creek, O.	Alfred Reed
10 7 1834			Hopewell	Alum Creek	Josiah Fawcett, w. Sarah, & ch., Sarah Eunice, Olivia G., Wm. T., Mary Ellen, Phineas Anderton
10 7 1834			Hopewell	Alum Creek	Isaac B. Swayne & w. Maria
4 9 1834			Hopewell	Green Plain	Sam'l Howell, w. Hannah, & ch., Cornelia, John, Mary, Wm., Ann, Sam'l, Virginia
4 9 1834			Hopewell	Green Plain	Rebecca Jane Howell
5 2 1835			Hopewell	Honey Creek	Isaac Smith, w. Martha, & ch., Wm., Mary Jane, David R., Hannah, John, Lydia Ann
7 5 1835			Hopewell	Centre, O.	Mary Thomas
9 7 1835			Hopewell	Baltimore	Lydia M. Dare
10 9 1835			Hopewell	Goose Creek	Rebecca H. Taylor
8 10 1835			Hopewell	Miami, O.	Sydney Daniel & dtrs., Ruth & Sarah Jane
7 1 1836			Hopewell	Fairfax	Hannah M. Lupton
7 4 1836			Hopewell	Green Plain	Mary Ann Janney
5 5 1836			Hopewell	Fall Creek, O.	Margaret Bond
4 8 1836			Hopewell	Goose Creek	Sarah Thompson
4 8 1836			Hopewell	Radnor, Pa.	Hannah Coates
4 8 1836			Hopewell	Radnor, Pa.	Eliza Cowgill & ch., Hannah Moor, Catherine Ann, Moses Coats
10 11 1836			Hopewell	Alum Creek	John Purcell, w. Mary, & ch., Thos., Lydia Ann, Priscilla H., Rosanna, John, Rebecca Jane, Elias H.
10 11 1836			Hopewell	Centre, O.	Edward H. Pidgeon
6 7 1837			Hopewell	Springboro'	Jas. F. Hibberd
8 9 1837			Hopewell	Centre, O.	Aaron Hackney
15 11 1837	Fairfax		Hopewell		Lydia Ann Robinson
9 12 1837			Hopewell	Baltimore	Alpheus P. Sharp
21 12 1837	Alum Creek		Hopewell		John Purcell, w. Mary, & ch., Lydia Ann, Priscilla Hunt, Rosanna, John, Rebecca Janney, Elias Hicks
5 4 1838			Hopewell	Fairfax	Robert Coburn
5 7 1838			Hopewell	Alum Creek	Peter Lukens, w. Hannah, & ch., Mary Ann, Lydia, Jos., Wm., Martha Elizabeth

Day Mo. Yr.	Meeting	To	Meeting To Meeting	Names
9 5 1839			Hopewell Centre, O.	Robt. Daniel, w. Martha, & ch., Wm. F., Martha Jane, Robt. B., Lydia E., Rebecca Ann
5 12 1839			Hopewell Fairfax	Nathan Walker, w. Jane, & d. Mary Ruth
5 3 1840			Hopewell White Water	Jacob J. Keefer & w. Jane
6 5 1840			Hopewell Alexandria	Rodney Davis
10 9 1840			Hopewell Baltimore	Samuel McPherson
8 10 1840			Hopewell Baltimore	Jane McPherson
6 1 1842			Hopewell White Water	Jas. F. Hibberd, w. Mary, & ch., Aaron Wm., Sarah Jane, Tacy S., Allen
9 3 1843			Hopewell Fairfax	Ann L. Steer & husband
10 10 1844			Hopewell Alum Creek	Stephen Taylor
10 10 1844			Hopewell Centre, O.	Ruth Carman
4 12 1844			Hopewell Baltimore	Richard S. Huck
10 7 1845			Hopewell Fairfax	Beulah W. Steer
6 8 1848			Hopewell Fall Creek, O.	Miller Johnson
7 9 1848			HopewellFall Creek, Ind.	Joshua Johnson & w. Lydia
5 10 1848			Hopewell Goose Creek	Lydia Ann Dillon
6 9 1849			Hopewell Fairfax	Mary Steer
7 3 1850			Hopewell Fairfax	Robt. Isaac Hollingsworth
7 3 1850			Hopewell Fairfax	Chas. L. Hollingsworth
4 4 1850			Hopewell Fairfax	Eliz'h J. Phillip & infant son Thos.
9 1 1851			Hopewell Baltimore	Mary Ann Hibbard
9 1 1851			Hopewell Baltimore	Lydia M. Dare
4 5 1853			Hopewell Baltimore	Sarah Jane Dare
9 3 1854			Hopewell Green Plain	Thamsin H. Branson
5 10 1854			Hopewell Fairfax	Abigail Hollingsworth
5 10 1854			Hopewell Fairfax	Eliz'h P. Hollingsworth
5 10 1854			Hopewell Fairfax	Lydia Jane Hollingsworth
5 4 1855			Hopewell Springboro'	Jesse Wood
5 4 1855			Hopewell Springboro'	Rachel Ann Wood
5 4 1855			Hopewell Springboro'	Lydia V. Wood
5 6 1856			Hopewell Plain Field, O.	Joshua R. Lupton
4 12 1856			Hopewell Fall Creek, Ind.	Sarah L. Johnson
3 5 1857			Hopewell West Field, O.	Jas. M. & Mary R. Hibbard & ch., Allen, Lydia D., Jas. Edward, Henry H.
4 6 1857			Hopewell White Water	Aaron W. Hibbard
8 4 1858			Hopewell Fairfax	Cornelia H. Walker
6 5 1858			Hopewell Alexandria	Samuel Howell
8 7 1858			Hopewell Sandy Spring	Sarah H. Stone & husband
9 2 1860			Hopewell Green Street, Phila.	Tacy S. Dolby
9 8 1860			Hopewell Fairfax	Margaret A. Gover

Day Mo. Yr.	Meeting	To	Meeting	To Meeting	Names
10 1 1861			Hopewell	Pipe Creek	Rebecca H. Haines
9 5 1861			Hopewell	Clear Creek	Thos. Brown, w. Eliz'h, & ch., Esther Ann, Hannah Maria, Yardley T., David Henry, & (Thamia) or (Ruth Anna)
9 5 1861			Hopewell	Baltimore	Ruth Hannah Matthews & husband
9 5 1861			Hopewell	Fairfax	Marg't Rees & ch., Lydia Ann, Jacob Walker, David Newcomer
5 2 1863			Hopewell	Little Falls	Joshua C. Price, w. Phebe, & ch., Jos., Thos., Emily W., Cornelia
8 10 1863			Hopewell	Pipe Creek	Wm. G. Lupton
7 1 1864			Hopewell	Pipe Creek	Eliz'h L. Haines & ch., Sarah Lippencott, Lewis Lupton
4 2 1864			Hopewell	Pipe Creek	Thos. W. Russell
10 8 1865			Hopewell	Baltimore	Henry Perkins
4 4 1866	London Grove		Hopewell		Ann B. Branson & husband David
8 11 1866			Hopewell	Fairfax	Aaron H. Hackney, w. Sarah, & ch., Sam'l S., Mary S., Sarah E.
8 10 1867	Little Falls		Hopewell		E. Caroline Branson
5 3 1868			Hopewell	Sandy Spring	Sarah Ann Chandlee & husband
9 4 1868	Baltimore		Hopewell		Richard S. Huck, w. Sarah, & ch., Harriet S., Lewis N., Lydia N., Charlotte, Francis S., Richard Jr.
7 5 1868			Hopewell	Miami	Rachel G. Snowden
16 12 1868	Fairfax		Hopewell		Aaron H. Hackney, w. Sarah, & ch., Mary S. & Sarah E.
5 4 1871			Hopewell	Fairfax	Lydia Lytle
10 10 1872			Hopewell	Fairfax	Mary W. Irish
5 3 1874			Hopewell	Cincinnati	Thamasin M. Rees & d. Jane Sidwell
5 3 1874			Hopewell	Cincinnati	Jonah L. Rees, w. Annie J., & ch., Mary Alice, Annie Jackson, Sam'l David
8 7 1875			Hopewell	Benjaminville	Martha A. Messinger
6 9 1877			Hopewell	Cincinnati	Samuel D. Rees
8 11 1877			Hopewell	Prairie Grove	Jos. A. Robinson
8 11 1877			Hopewell	Genoa	Mary A. Myers
5 8 1886			Hopewell	Baltimore	Rebecca J. Broomell
13 10 1886	Fairfax		Hopewell		Mary W. Irish & ch., Rachel S., Edward L., Lydia W.
10 7 1890			Hopewell	Goose Creek	Rachel S. (Irish) Smith & husband

CROOKED RUN CERTIFICATES OF
MEMBERSHIP AND REMOVAL

From the 4th day of 1st month 1783 to the 4th day of 4th month 1807; from the records of Crooked Run Monthly Meeting, held alternately at Crooked Run and Center. These items do not appear in the Hopewell Monthly Meeting records.

All the certificates in the following list were from Crooked Run to the several meetings indicated.

Day	Mo.	Year	To	Persons Certificated
30	8	1783	Philadelphia	Jos. Reakstraw, w. Sarah, & ch., Justinian, Elizabeth, Hannah, Jos.
30	8	1783	Fairfax	Jas. Lownes, w. Sarah, & ch., Sarah, Hyett, John, Deborah, Jas., Caleb, Jane, Jos.
3	4	1784	Hopewell	John Chadwalader, w. Sarah, & ch., Mary, Martha, Ruth, John, Isaac
1	12	1784	Kennet	Hannah Swayne & ch., Fransis, Betty, Lydia
30	7	1785	South River	Amos Holloway
3	9	1785	Monallin	Esther Hodgson
30	11	1785	Fairfax	John McClun
29	1	1786	South River	Jos. Stratton, w. Naomi, & ch., Sarah, Jos., Mary, Benj., Hannah, Jacob, Joel
5	8	1786	Fairfax	Jas. Moor, w. Phebe, & ch., Abner, Jos., Thos.
29	11	1786	New Garden, N. C.	Sam'l Chew, w. Abigail, & ch., Alice, Israel
29	11	1786	Baltimore	Mary Horseman
30	12	1786	South River	Robt. Hanna, w. Catharine, & ch., Thos., Benj., Esther, David, Caleb
2	6	1787	Westland	Marra Chadwalader
1	9	1787	Westland	Eli Reyly
5	7	1788	South River	Griffin Dobin, w. Mary Ann, & ch., Eliz'h, Cath., Thos., Griffin, Jos., Jonah, John, Lydia, Abner

Day	Mo.	Year	To	Persons Certificated
5	9	1788	South River	William Holloway
4	10	1788	New Garden, Pa.	Abigail Wickersham
4	10	1788	Goose Creek, Loudoun Co.	Elizabeth Myres
29	11	1788	York	Josiah Jordon
3	1	1789	Goose Creek	Ann Smith
3	1	1789	York	Lydia Miller
3	1	1789	South River	Catharie Stanton
31	2	1789	New Garden, N. C.	Tamer Colston
4	4	1789	New Garden, N. C.	Thos. Embree, w. Esther, & ch., Elihu, Elijah, Rachel
4	4	1789	New Garden, N. C.	Jacob Rambo Jr. (apprentice to Thos. Embree)
2	5	1789	South River	Allen Bond & w. Sarah
30	5	1789	Goose Creek	Hannah Poole
4	7	1789	South River	Edward Bond, w. Mary, & ch., Benj., Martha, Ruth, Hannah
4	7	1789	South River	Mary Bond
31	10	1789	Chester	Nathan Wood
30	1	1790	Westland	Frances Reily
4	9	1790	Warrington	Abraham Griffith, w. Eliz'h, & ch., Wm., Eliz'h, Abraham, Asa, Jonah, Esther
2	10	1790	South River	Alice Bond
30	4	1791	Pipecreek	Wm. Hunt (apprentice)
30	4	1791	South River	John Schofield
29	9	1791	Westfield	John Green, w. Ruth, & ch., Margaret, Mary, Isaac, John, Jesse
29	9	1791	Westfield	John Paxon, w. Mary, & ch., Ruben, Alice, Jacob, Mary, John, Ann
29	9	1791	South River	Asa Holloway Jr.
29	9	1791	South River	Mary Holloway Jr.
5	11	1791	Westfield	Thos. Branson, w. Jane, & ch., Thos., David, Eunice, Jacob, Eliz'h
5	5	1792	Westland	John Hank
3	11	1792	Westland	Esther Russel
1	6	1793	Goose Creek	John Buchannon
29	6	1793	South River	Abner & Sarah Holloway, minor ch. of Isaac
31	8	1793	South River	Mary Richards

Day	Mo.	Year	To	Persons Certificated
4	1	1794	Evesham	Abraham Hains
3	5	1794	Redstone	Nath'l Dillhorn
31	5	1794	South River	Jackson Allen, w. Sarah, & ch., Ruth, Edward, Mary
31	5	1794	South River	Elizabeth Bond
5	7	1794	Fairfax	Phebe Clevenger
2	8	1794	Fairfax	Phebe Potts
5	11	1794	South River	Susannah Bond
31	1	1795	Goose Creek	Mary Gibson
4	4	1795	Redstone	George Dillhorn
4	4	1795	Redstone	Jesse Pennel, w. Hannah, & d. Mary
4	4	1795	Fairfax	Henry Woodrow
4	4	1795	Fairfax	John Bishop
4	4	1795	Fairfax	Mary Woodrow (w. of John) & dtrs., Mary & Lydia
4	4	1795	Fairfax	Grace Woodrow
2	1	1796	Goose Creek	Lydia Nickles
4	2	1796	New Garden, Pa.	Sarah, Ann, Joel, minor ch. of Jos. Taylor
30	4	1796	Goose Creek	Israel Gregg
30	7	1796	Goose Creek	Joshua Gregg
3	9	1796	Goose Creek	Geo. Walters, w. Dinah, & ch., Judith, Isaac, Mahlon, Ann
3	9	1796	Goose Creek	Sarah Walters
3	9	1796	Goose Creek	James Walters
3	9	1796	Goose Creek	Ann Gipson
3	12	1796	New Garden, Pa.	Joseph Taylor
1	4	1797	New Hope	Anthony Moor, w. Zilpah, & ch., David, Rachel, Ruth, Mary
1	4	1797	New Hope	Robt. Moor & w. Sarah
29	4	1797	New Garden, Pa.	Jesse & Jos. Taylor, sons of Jos.
1	7	1797	Philadelphia	Sarah Zean (Zane)
30	12	1797	Redstone	Joshua Hunt, w. Rachel, & ch., Mary, David
31	3	1798	Goose Creek, Bedford Co., Va.	Dan'l Brown, w. Hannah, & ch., Sam'l, Jos., Elizabeth
31	3	1798	Goose Creek, Bedford Co.	Sam'l Hulford Jr.

Day	Mo.	Year	To	Persons Certificated
31	3	1798	Sadsbury	Jos. Dickenson (minor), son of Dan'l
31	3	1798	London Grove	Jemima Dickenson (minor), d. of Dan'l
1	12	1798	Horsham	Sollomon Miller Jr. (apprentice)
1	12	1798	Westland	Mary Smith (w. of Geo.) & ch., Geo., Tamer
1	6	1799	Southland	Peter Cleaver
1	6	1799	Redstone	Jas. Updegraff (apprentice)
1	6	1799	Westland	Samuel Berry
3	8	1799	Redstone	Wm. Hunt & w. Phebe
2	10	1799	Southland	Rachel Inskip
2	11	1799	Westland	Schooly Wright, w. Lavina, & ch., Mary, Eliz'h, Hannah, Amos, Sarah, Aaron
4	1	1800	Westland	Robt. Hunt, w. Abigail, and son Seth
4	1	1800	Baltimore	Mary Helmer
1	3	1800	Redstone	Jonathan Taylor, w. Ann, & d. Rebecca (minor)
5	10	1800	Westland	Mary Richards
5	10	1800	Westland	David Holloway, w. Hannah, & ch., Daten, Lydia, Margaret
1	11	1800	Westland	Rowland Richards, w. Lydia, & ch., Sarah, Catharine, Sitnah (minors)
31	1	1801	Westland	John Mullin, w. Lydia, & ch., Jane, Hannah, Sarah, John, Rachel, Isaiah, Sam'l
28	2	1801	Redstone	Jesse Penrose, wife, & ch., Abraham, Benj., Jos., Phebe, Wm., Sarah
4	4	1801	Evesham	Sarah Middleton
4	4	1801	Goose Creek, Bedford Co.	Isaac Bond, w. Lydia, & ch., Joshua, Israel, Abraham, Sisley
2	5	1801	Westland	Nathan Updegraff, w. Ann (Lupton), & minor ch., Jos., David, Rachel, Hannah, Nathan, Ann
2	5	1801	Westland	Rachel Lupton
2	5	1801	Redstone	Abigail Hunt
2	5	1801	Westland	Abigail Cleaver, w. of Ezekiel, & children
30	5	1801	Westland	Rachel Wood

Day	Mo.	Year	To	Persons Certificated
30	5	1801	Westland	Mary Evans, w. of David
1	8	1801	Westland	Phebe Yarnell
2	1	1802	Pipe Creek	William Miller
4	9	1802	Pipe Creek	Rachel Johnston
2	10	1802	Westland	Jacob Painter, w. Mary, & ch., David, Sam'l, Robt., Abigail, Jos.
2	10	1802	Concord, O.	Sam'l Pickering, w. Phebe, & ch., Jonas, Levi, Sam'l, Rebekah, Mary, Phebe, Joshua
4	12	1802	Westland	John Hunt (apprentice to Jacob Painter)
5	3	1803	Concord, O.	Hannah Wright & d. Phebe (minor); Hannah to join her husband
5	3	1803	Redstone	Robt. Miller, w. Casandra, & minor ch., Hannah, Caleb, Mary, David, Lydia
5	3	1803	Redstone	Sarah Miller
5	3	1803	Redstone	Solomon Miller
2	4	1803	South River	Rachel Schofield, to join her husband
2	4	1803	South River	Jane Schofield, d. of David & Rachel
5	11	1803	Elexander (Alexandria)	Lydia Horner, to join her husband
4	2	1804	Concord, O.	Samuel Fawcett
3	3	1804	Redstone	Ruth Miller
3	3	1804	Middleton, O.	Ann Stratten
3	3	1804	Middleton, O.	Sarah Cogill
5	5	1804	Redstone	David Schofield
2	6	1804	Monallen	Joshua Johnston
29	9	1804	Concord, O.	Phebe Faucett
29	9	1804	Concord, O.	Mary Faucett & ch., Jonathan, Richard, Jacob
29	9	1804	Concord, O.	Joseph Faucett
29	9	1804	Concord, O.	Hannah Faucett
2	2	1805	Concord, O.	John Piggott, w. Rachel, & minor ch., Mary & Rebekah
30	3	1805	Concord, O.	Rebekah Lupton
30	3	1805	Concord, O.	Joseph Lupton

Day	Mo.	Year	To	Persons Certificated
4	5	1805	Middleton, O.	Jesse Halliway, w. Sarah, & minor ch., Joel, Aaron, Margaret, Eunice, David
4	5	1805	Middleton, O.	Hannah Holliway
4	5	1805	Miami	John Garwood, w. Esther, & ch., Deborah, Lott
4	5	1805	Miami	Thos. Garwood, w. Hannah, & ch., John, Robt., Abijah
4	5	1805	Miami	John Garwood Jr.
4	5	1805	Middleton, O.	Susannah Holloway
1	6	1805	Concord, O.	Samuel Holloway
1	6	1805	Miami	John Hains, w. Betty, & ch., Hester, Stacia, Narcissa, Israel, Betty, Ruben
1	6	1805	Miami	Sam'l Schooley, w. Sicily, & ch., Israel, John, Ann, Wm., Betty
29	6	1805	Concord	Jacob Branson, w. Rebekah, & ch., Abigail, Isaiah, Phebe, Lydia
29	6	1805	Redstone	Ebenezer Shion
31	8	1805	Short Creek	Naomi Brown
31	8	1805	Short Creek	Ann Murry
5	10	1805	Miami	Robt. Whitacor, w. Patienc, & ch., Andrew, John, Prissilla, Aquilla, Jane, Rhoda, Moses
5	10	1805	Miami	Jane McKay
5	10	1805	Concord	Ann Taylor, d. of Jos.
2	11	1805	Concord	Darling Conro, w. Rachel, & ch., Jacob, Unice, Thos., Rebekah
2	11	1805	Miami	Mary Smith
2	11	1805	Miami	Martha Cleaver
2	11	1805	Short Creek	Nathan Lupton, w. Margaret, & ch., Henry, Ann, Gideon, Martin
30	11	1805	Concord, O.	Mahlon Smith & w. Mary
30	11	1805	Short Creek	Jonathan Lupton & w. Sarah
30	11	1805	Short Creek	Ruth Lupton
30	11	1805	Fairfax	Elenor Brown
5	4	1806	Concord, O.	Wm. Wright, w. Unice, & ch., John., Wm., Elizabeth, Rebekah
5	4	1806	Concord, O.	Elizabeth Branson
5	4	1806	Concord	Sarah Wright

Day	Mo.	Year	To	Persons Certificated
3	5	1806	Miami	Isaiah Garwood
31	5	1806	Middleton, O.	Sarah Stokesbury, with her husband
31	5	1806	Fairfax	Susannah Ball & minor ch., Sarah, Maria, Alfred, by her former mrge. to Parkins
2	8	1806	Short Creek	Jos. Poole, w. Hannah, & ch., Naomi, Benj., Eliz'h, Jos., John, Maria, Emily
2	8	1806	Miami	Mary Pusey & ch., Nathan, Mary, Joel, Geo., Wm.
2	8	1806	Miami	Lydia Pusey
2	8	1806	Miami	Margaret Pusey
2	8	1806	Miami	Joel Brown, w. Rachel, & ch., Elgar & Wm.
2	8	1806	Miami	Georg Harris, w. Hope, & ch., Esther, Martha, Deborah, Dan'l, Isaiah
30	8	1806	Miami	Jonas Whitacre, with his father
5	10	1806	Concord	Sam'l Sharp, w. Martha, & ch., Abigail, Geo., Jos., Sarah, Jesse, Lydia, Sam'l, Phinehas
5	10	1806	Fairfax	Joshua Pusey
5	10	1806	Concord	Phebe Faucett, with her husband
14	11	1806	Miami	Noah Hains
3	1	1807	Miami	Rebekah Rhea Jr., with her father
3	1	1807	Miami	Robert Rhea & w. Rebekah
4	4	1807	Miami	Dan'l Garwood & ch., Jos., John, Jonathan, Patience, Sarah, Dan'l
4	4	1807	Miami	Levi Garwood

FAMILY RECORDS OF HOPEWELL

Name	*Born*			*Died*			*Buried*
Allen, Joseph							
w. Ruth			1732	15	10	1781	
s. Joseph							
Antram, Daniel							
w. Susanna							
d. Sarah	8	9	1780				
Babb, Philip	26	8	1731				
w. Mary (Perkins)	13	12	1730				
Sarah	9	2	1754				
Joseph	2	2	1756				
Thomas	17	3	1758				
Babb, Thomas							
w. Sarah							
s. Philip	26	8	1731				
Balenger, Josiah					9	1748	
w. Mary				21	10	1800	
Josiah	24	11	1728				
Sarah	27	11	1731				
James	28	7	1735				
Ballinger, William							
wife ——							
d. Sarah Brown	8	11	1752				
Barr, Robert							
w. Sidney (Jackson)	7	8	1828	30	9	1899	Mt. Hebron
(d. of Abel & Rachel)							
Frank							
Robert	4	2	1872				
Lewis							
Barrett, Benjamin							
w. Elenor							
Thomas	11	10	1757				
Phebe	26	5	1759				
Richard	24	11	1760				
Jonathan	5	11	1762				
John	29	12	1764				
David	19	2	1767				
Barrett, Jonas				17	6	1930	Cemetery at White Hall near Hopewell
wife ——				2	8	1925	White Hall
Barrett, Jonathan				25	4	1933	White Hall
(s. of Joel)							
Barrett, Thomas	11	10	1757				
w. Eliz. (Thornbrough)							
Richard	2	9	1784				
Amos	14	9	1786				

Name	Born			Died			Buried
Bason, Edward							
w. Martha							
Edward	4	1	1739				
Charity	18	1	1741				
Mary	18	11	1743				
Micajah	18	12	1745				
Bean, James							
w. Gulielma (Fawcett)	12	12	1814	5	10	1884	Family burial
(d. of Jos. & Mary)							ground at Taylor Furnace
Berry, John							
w. Patience							
Patience	17	2	1770				
Thomas	2	3	1765	2	10	1772	
Berry, E. Willard	24	11	1900				
(s. of E. Willard Sr. & Mary)							
w. Dorothy E. (Pidgeon)	11	2	1899				
(d. of Lewis & Susan T.)							
Mary Susan	9	6	1928				
Edward Lewis	8	5	1931				
Sam'l Stedman	21	6	1933				
Bond, Abner	10	10	1801	11	1	1884	Ridge
(s. of John & Rachel)							
w. Mary (Beal)	4	4	1801	5	7	1890	Indiana
(d. of Wm. & Mary)							
Rachel A.	13	1	1835				
John L.	4	1	1837	6	4	1914	Ridge
Isaac	24	4	1838	11	3	1845	Upper Ridge
Wm. Allen	16	4	1841	11	11	1843	Upper Ridge
Bond, Edward L.	16	6	1881				
(s. of John & Ann)							
w. Hannah (Peaslee)							
John L.	28	12	1908				
Gideon P.	18	8	1910				
Edward L. Jr.	18	7	1913				
Amos P.	19	9	1917				
Bond, John	20	12	1775	24	5	1854	Upper Ridge
(s. of John & Marg't)							
w. (1) Rachel (Lupton)	6	3	1775	11	1	1833	Upper Ridge
(d. of Sam'l & Sarah)							
Abner	10	10	1801	11	1	1884	Ridge
Hannah	20	9	1804				
Leah	4	12	1807				
Sarah	20	3	1810				
Margaret	27	7	1813				
w. (2) Lydia				27	5	1848	Upper Ridge
Bond, John	4	1	1837	6	4	1914	Ridge
(s. of Abner & Mary)							
w. Ann (Lupton)	14	4	1840	12	12	1920	Ridge
(d. of Jonah & Lydia)							
Howell McPherson	22	8	1874				
Walker McClun	12	12	1875				
Allen Beal	9	10	1877				
Edward L.	16	6	1881				
Ann Sidwell	17	9	1882	27	8	1883	Ridge
Mary Emma	9	5	1884	12	10	1884	Ridge

Name	Born			Died			Buried
Bond, Walker McC.	12	12	1875				
(s. of John & Ann)							
w. (1) Grace L. (Wright)	11	6	1876	17	2	1928	Mt. Hebron
(d. of Jonathan & Louisa of Ohio)							
w. (2) Caroline D. (Lupton)							
(d. of Hugh S. & Mary R.)							
(m. 23-11-1935 at Hopewell)							
Bowman, John G.	25	3	1894				
(s. of Leo & Mary)							
w. Virginia P. (Griest)	24	8	1888	22	1	1934	Hopewell
(d. of Frank & Ellen)							
Lincoln Griest	18	8	1922				
Margaret Gardiner	24	2	1924				
Branson, Abraham	12	10	1754	16	6	1827	Hopewell
(s. of Wm. & Eliz'h)							
w. (1) Catherine (Rees)							
(d. of Henry & Martha)							
s. Rees				11	3	1815	
w. (2) Sarah (White)	20	5	1755	21	2	1832	Hopewell
(d. of Nathan & Mary)							
Mary	7	12	1788				
William P.	11	12	1790				
Nathaniel	23	12	1791	25	10	1817	Alexandria, Va.
Isaac	16	3	1793				
Thomas H.	13	7	1794	22	11	1861	Green Plain, O.
Joseph	1	1	1796	12	11	1878	Hopewell
Benjamin	30	4	1797	27	9	1820	Hopewell
Branson, David W.	28	9	1830	14	6	1906	Hopewell
(s. of Jos. & Tacy)							
w. Ann (Bailey)	1	3	1830	24	3	1918	Hopewell
(d. of Wm. & Sarah)							
Wm. E.	24	6	1867				
Elizabeth A.	14	10	1870	18	12	1873	Hopewell
Branson, John	5	4	1777	2	3	1815	
(bro. of Abraham)							
Branson, Jonathan W.	16	5	1841	17	3	1916	Hopewell
(s. of Jos. & Tacy)							
w. E. Caroline (Cunningham)	7	11	1839	2	1	1926	Hopewell
(d. of Edwd. & Eliz'h)							
Tacy	26	2	1868	2	8	1906	Hopewell
Lillian	24	4	1873	2	2	1894	Hopewell
Branson, Joseph	1	1	1796	12	11	1878	Hopewell
(s. of Abraham & Sarah)							
w. Tacy (Wright)	11	4	1799	14	8	1865	Hopewell
(d. of Jonathan & Hannah)							
Nath'l B.	1	5	1828	18	5	1898	Hopewell
David W.	28	9	1830	14	6	1906	Hopewell
Ruth Hannah	24	10	1833				Hopewell
Phineas A.	23	3	1836	15	3	1881	Hopewell
Jonathan W.	16	5	1841	17	3	1916	Hopewell

Name	Born			Died			Buried
Branson, Nathaniel B.	1	5	1828	18	5	1898	Hopewell
(s. of Jos. & Tacy)							
w. Nancy (Holmes)	11	5	1833		5	1911	Hopewell
(d. of Elijah & Eliz'h)							
Joseph H.	28	7	1866				
Mary Eliz'h	26	6	1873				
Branson, Thomas	13	7	1794	22	11	1861	Green Plain, O.
(s. of Abraham & Sarah)							
w. Thamsin H.							
Branson, William E.	24	6	1867				
(s. of David W. & Ann)							
w. Florence Dell Doing	1	10	1874				
(d. of Chas. & Rosa)							
Chas. David	9	4	1902				
Edith	3	11	1903				
Elizabeth	21	9	1905				
Mary	18	11	1906				
Ann Bailey	14	9	1910				
Ruth Doing	2	6	1916				
Brown, Daniel							
w. Miriam							
Jeremiah	17	12	1773				
William	15	12	1775				
Isaac	14	1	1778				
David	14	12	1780				
Brown, Daniel							
wife ———							
s. Isaac	4	3	1746				
Brown, David							
w. Sarah	29	11	1745				
Daniel	20	6	1767				
Sarah	5	7	1769				
Susannah	29	6	1771				
David	1	1	1774				
Phebe	8	1	1776				
William	4	5	1778				
Brown, Isaac	4	3	1746				
(s. of Daniel)							
wife (1) ———							
s. John	11	8	1770				
w. (2) Sarah (Ballinger)	8	11	1752				
Sarah	28	5	1778	27	10	1796	
William Hunt	4	10	1779				
Isaac	5	12	1781				
Samuel	1	11	1783				
Cassandra	11	8	1785				
Margaret	22	2	1787				
Esther	15	10	1788				
Mary	29	8	1790	21	9	1794	
Brown, John							
w. Eliz'h (Richardson)							
Margaret				27	1	1892	Ridge
Sarah				17	7	1900	Ridge
Richard R.	24	7	1807	26	2	1884	Winchester

Name	Born		Died			Buried
Brown, John I.	9	1862	26	12	1932	Winchester
(s. of Rich'd Sr. & Eliz'h)						
w. Mary E. (Fries)						
John I. Jr.	31	1 1896				
Pearl I.	25	6 1897				
Ruth E.	3	10 1899				
William H.	21	4 1902				
Brown, Martha (widow)			26	3	1779	
Brown, Rich'd R. Sr.	24	7 1807	26	2	1884	Winchester
(s. of John & Eliz'h)						
w. Eliz'h T. (Murphy)	25	8 1828	1	3	1903	Winchester
Anna H.		7 1849		7	1863	
Lucy S.		3 1852		6	1864	
Lizzie		4 1854	12	1	1929	Winchester
Rich'd R. Jr.		12 1856	3	10	1930	Winchester
Alice V.		8 1858	16	4	1926	Winchester
John I.		9 1862	26	12	1932	Mt. Hebron
Rebecca M.		6 1864				
Charles M.		6 1867				
Brown, Rich'd R. Jr.		12 1856	3	10	1930	Winchester
(s. of Rich'd & Eliz'h)						
w. Mary E.		3 1859	19	3	1915	Winchester
(d. of Sam'l & Virginia)						
Leslie R.	21	9 1882				
Lily M.	21	6 1884				
Lucy V.	30	6 1886				
Mary E. Jr.	21	9 1888				
Annie S.	11	11 1890	7	8	1891	Winchester
Richard B.	23	6 1893				
Carroll S.	21	12 1896	16	1	1897	Winchester
Russel E.	31	8 1899				
Brown, Samuel						
w. Hannah						
Sarah Ann Eliz'h	17	11 1810				
Mary Matthews	26	3 1813				
Brown, Samuel E.						
(s. of Chas. & Eliz'h)						
w. Mary A. (Robinson)						
(d. of Jos. & Rebecca)						
Leon R.	23	2 1890				
Lois R.	22	6 1892				
Sam'l E. Jr.	9	9 1898				
Hunter Smith	9	11 1900				
Brown, Thomas						
w. Mary (White)						
William	1	10 1775				
Caleb	20	6 1777				
Sarah	15	9 1779				
Thomas	22	1 1782				
David	19	11 1787				Moved to Ohio
Mary	18	9 1791				
Joel	30	1 1794				Moved to Ohio
Brown, William	30	11 1810	3	2	1901	Private ground on
(s. of Wm. & Mary)						his farm

Name	Born			Died			Buried
Brown, William H. [Hunt]							
w. Sarah (Neill)				9	10	1805	
(d. of Lewis & Rachel)							
Rachel N.	26	10	1802	19	11	1811	
Sarah N.	2	9	1805				
Brown, William Hunt	4	10	1779	2	6	1865	
w. Martha (Wilson)	12	1	1787	20	8	1850	
(d. of Thomas)							
Rachel N.	26	10	1802				
Sarah N.	2	9	1805				
Jane C.	6	1	1812				
Rebecca W.	16	5	1814				
Eliza	28	2	1816				
Wilson S.	26	11	1822				
Elisan	8	6	1826	1	9	1913	Ridge
Catherine	1	8	1829	19	2	1915	Ridge
Cadwallader, Rees							
w. Ruth		6	1748				
Asa	2	8	1768				
Mary	15	1	1770				
Edith	20	10	1771				
Jonah	24	3	1774				
A son was born and died unnamed a week after born in 1775							
Ruth	24	8	1776				
John	27	7	1778	9	2	1781	
Rachel	25	2	1780				
Cather, Wilbur E.	18	11	1883				
(s. of Willard & Mary)							
w. Mabel (Robinson)							
Helen G.	12	5	1916				
Mary Gail	27	7	1918				
Chandlee, Albert							
w. Sarah Ann (Branson)	4	10	1823	20	11	1897	Hopewell
(d. of Wm. & Frances)							
Chandlee, Benjamin							
w. Mary							
s. Goldsmith	18	7	1751				
Chandlee, Goldsmith	18	7	1751				
w. Ann (White)				30	8	1781	
(d. of Nathaniel & Mary)							
Mary	1	12	1776				
Sarah	14	10	1778			1779	
Benjamin	5	3	1780				
Childs, Harry B.							Brucetown
w. Mary H. (Clevenger)	20	3	1878				
(d. of B. Franklin & Ann							
d. Grace Evelyn	14	12	1908				
(m. Thos. Sprint)							
Clark, William							
w. Susannah							
d. Mary	15	5	1783	5	5	1790	

Name	Born			Died			Buried
Clevenger, B. Franklin	13	2	1843	2	2	1916	Hopewell
(s. of David & Hannah)							
w. Ann Eliz'h (Jackson)	16	4	1843	22	4	1922	Hopewell
(d. of J. Fenton & Mary)							
Carrie Alice	11	4	1872				
Etha Brown	23	6	1873	5	2	1916	Hopewell
Mary Hannah	20	3	1878				
Hattie	19	3	1880				
Grace E.	10	8	1884				
Clevenger, Chas. E.	9	3	1839	3	3	1920	Hopewell
(s. of David & Hannah)							
w. Susan S. (Childs)	7	1	1843	24	3	1913	Hopewell
(d. of Griffin & Mary)							
Carroll C.	23	5	1873				
Bertha B.	3	6	1875				
Drury D.	25	5	1881				
Clevenger, David							
w. Hannah (Brown)							
(d. of Wm. & Mary)							
Chas. E.	9	3	1839	3	3	1920	Hopewell
B. Franklin	13	2	1843	2	2	1916	Hopewell
Washington	13	2	1843				Hopewell
Sophia B.	30	7	1847	17	8	1915	Hopewell
Clevenger, Drury D.	25	5	1881				
(s. of Chas. & Susan)							
w. Edith M. (Ritenour)							
(d. of S. L. & Annie)							
Genevieve	4	10	1906				
Stanley Chas.	19	7	1909				
Evangeline	12	11	1913				
Cochran, Fred A. Sr.		11	1850	5	9	1919	Hopewell
w. Carrie A. (Clevenger)	11	4	1872				
(d. of B. Franklin & Ann)							
Cochran, Fred. A. Jr., M. D.							
w. Etha B. (Clevenger)	23	6	1873	5	2	1916	Hopewell
(d. of B. Franklin & Ann)							
Gladys Virginia	12	1	1900				
Mary Elizabeth	14	4	1902				
Connell, Mary D.							
widow of David Jackson							
Cowgill, Henry							
w. Ruth							
John	23	9	1775				
Thomas	27	7	1777				
Sarah	19	2	1780				
Caleb	2	4	1783				
Cowgill, John							
w. Katharine							
Dinah	12	10	1773				
Lydia	6	2	1775				
Day, Joseph							
w. Catharine							
Evan	11	9	1763				
George	26	3	1766				
Joseph	1	6	1768				
Lydia	19	7	1770				

Name	Born			Died			Buried
Dodd, Edward							
w. Mary							
Rachel	1	5	1755				
Albenah	24	8	1757				
Mary	28	2	1760				
Doing, James H.	8	6	1872		9	1934	Laurel, Md.
(s. of Chas. & Rosa)							
w. Tacy (Branson)	26	2	1868	2	8	1906	Hopewell
d. Lillian Eliz'h	2	11	1902				
Ellis, Samuel							
w. Kezia							
d. Mary	23	2	1789				
Fallis, John							
w. Mary							
d. Rachel	25	7	1780				
Fawcett, Joseph	26	4	1786	4	3	1864	
w. Mary (Branson)	7	12	1788	13	2	1860	
(d. of Abraham & Sarah)							
Gulielma	12	12	1814	5	10	1884	Private ground near late home at Taylor Furnace
Sarah Edna	2	10	1818				
Elkanah	24	11	1820	18	6	1900	Mt. Pleasant, near his home in Fred. Co., Va.
Martha Hulda	8	6	1824				
Elvira Frances	23	11	1826				
Fawcett, Thomas	24	3	1748				
w. Martha							
John	14	1	1770				
Richard	22	9	1771				
Martha	3	11	1773				
Rachel	24	3	1775				
Fisher, Barak							
w. Mary							
John	1	2	1762				
Thomas	18	11	1763				
Joseph	28	4	1765				
Barak	13	11	1766				
Sarah	25	7	1768				
Mary	19	3	1771				
Elizabeth	17	4	1773				
Hannah	22	5	1775				
Garwood, John	9	4	1740				
w. Esther	5	9	1747				
Hope	18	1	1765				
Sarah	7	6	1766				
Daniel	8	4	1769				
Susannah	25	2	1771				
Levi	1	9	1773				
Margaret	11	10	1776				
Thomas	7	11	1778				
George, Henry							
w. Tamar							
Caleb	14	10	1815				
Mary	21	12	1816				

Name		Born			Died			Buried
George, Richard								
w. Mary								
Lydia	5	3	1784					
Henry	6	2	1786					
Ruth	24	1	1790					
Rachel	6	8	1792					
Evan	4	12	1794					
Ellis	19	4	1797					
Richard	6	8	1799					
John	17	7	1802					
Sarah	19	5	1805					
Mary	28	1	1809					
Griffith, John								
w. Mary			1747		2	12	1781	
Sibbell	18	2	1773		27	1	1790	
John	16	9	1778					
Hackney, Aaron H.	18	12	1816		18	1	1870	Hopewell
(s. of Jos. & Lydia)								
w. Sarah (Heterick)	19	3	1818		30	1	1897	Hopewell
(d. of Robt. & Mary)								
Mary S.	3	2	1848		8	1	1917	Welltown
Robert H.					19	6	1862	Monallen, Pa.
Samuel S.					10	4	1872	Welltown
Sallie E.					1	10	1874	Welltown
Alex. H.					12	11	1854	Welltown
Joseph E.					24	8	1862	Welltown
Hackney, Joseph								
w. Lydia (Sidwell)								
Aaron H.	18	12	1816		18	1	1870	Hopewell
Lydia					19	1	1888	Hopewell
Sarah Ellen					29	12	1891	Hopewell
Rebecca Jane					22	3	1910	Hopewell
Joseph	22	11	1821		8	3	1901	Hopewell
Hackney, Lydia					29	10	1766	
Haines, Bethany								
w. Mary								
s. Robert	3	9	1736					
(Born the last 3d day in the 9th mo., old style, 1736)								
Haines, Ezekiel	25	3	1721					
w. Abigail	1	3	1722					
s. Jacob	4	10	1761					
Haines, Joseph	2	4	1742					
w. Bulah	30	10	1750					
Patience	11	9	1768					
Ebenezer	4	5	1770					
Elizabeth	4	11	1771					
Joseph	24	5	1773					
Mary	1	10	1775					
Nathan	27	12	1780					
Haines, Joshua								
w. Marcy								
Grace	8	10	1753	} Twins				
Mary	8	10	1753					
Joshua	10	12	1754					

Name	Born			Died			Buried
Haines, Nathan							
w. Jane (Beeson)							
(m. Sept. 24, 1818)							
Edward B.				16	4	1889	Friends' burial ground, Jefferson Co., W. Va.
Alvina				24	8	1896	Waterford, Loudoun Co., Va.
Mary				31	3	1884	Friends' burial ground, Jefferson Co., W. Va.
Richard							Friends' burial ground, Jefferson Co., W. Va.
Haines, Robert							
w. Esther							
s. John	22	8	1769				
Haines, Robert							
w. Margaret							
s. Noah	6	2	1781				
Hannah, Robert							
w. Catharine							
Thomas	2	5	1777				
Benjamin	14	6	1779				
Esther	6	9	1781				
Harman, Rachel A.	13	1	1835				
(d. of Abner & Rachel Bond)							
Harris, William							
wife ——							
Esther	7	9	1744				
Martha	29	9	1746				
William Jr.	19	10	1748				
Daniel	14	11	1751				
Hannah	13	2	1753				
Jesse	24	2	1755				
Samuel	22	3	1757				
Mary	7	4	1759				
Hayhurst, Cuthbert							
w. Deliverance							
s. Cuthbert	22	10	1731	12	2	1803	
Hodgson, Hannah W.							
(d. of Amos & Rachel Wright)							Removed to Kansas
Hollingsworth, Betty	27	11	1791	19	9	1884	Mt. Hebron
(d. of Jonah & Hannah)							
Holloway, John	9	9	1732				
wife ——							
Jesse	5	12	1754				
Ruth	9	12	1759				
John	26	3	1762				
Daten	29	12	1763				
Thomas	14	11	1766				
George	11	3	1769				
David	23	6	1771				
Ephraim	21	1	1774				
Charlotte	18	8	1776				

Name	Born			Died			Buried
Horsman, William							
w. Marcy			1762	21	11	1785	
Joseph	14	4	1782				
William	4	9	1783				
Marcy	8	11	1785				
Huyett, William S.	16	11	1881				
(s. of Luther & Ella)							
w. Hattie (Clevenger)	19	3	1880				
(d. of B. Franklin &							
Eliz'h Ann)							
Beatrice	9	20	1907				
Wm. S. Jr.	1	9	1910				
Gwendolin	16	12	1913				
Elizabeth	30	9	1916				
Ellen	31	10	1919				
Jas. Fenton	25	8	1922				
Irish, William L.	7	7	1844	29	7	1882	Waterford, Loudoun Co., Va.
w. Mary W. (Lupton)	25	6	1841	2	1	1890	Ridge
Rachel S.	24	9	1872				Lincoln, Loudoun Co., Va.
Edward L.	21	10	1876	4	10	1904	Hopewell
Lydia W.	19	11	1879				
Jackson, Abel							
w. Rachel (Fenton)							
Josiah				24	3	1896	White Hall
J. Fenton	28	8	1818	6	2	1889	Hopewell
Isaac		6	1820	27	3	1904	Mt. Hebron
Sarah				22	3	1904	Mt. Hebron
Ruth (m. Jones)	3	9	1824	21	3	1890	Mt. Hebron
Joseph	30	9	1826	26	3	1892	Mt. Hebron
Sidney (m. Barr)	7	8	1828	30	9	1899	Mt. Hebron
David			1836	31	5	1898	Mt. Hebron
Jackson, David			1836	31	5	1898	Mt. Hebron
(s. of Abel & Rachel)							
w. Mary (Smith)				9	12	1915	Mt. Hebron
Jackson, Jonathan	27	6	1832	8	4	1915	Hopewell
(s. of Sam'l & Cynthia)							
Jackson, Joseph S.	7	5	1808	5	9	1896	Mt. Hebron
(s. of Josiah & Rachel)							
w. Mary D. (Lupton)	6	1	1815	12	5	1901	Mt. Hebron
(d. of David & Ann)							
Rachel Annie	17	8	1837	1	4	1915	Mt. Hebron
Mary Jane	6	8	1839	11	2	1921	Mt. Hebron
Sarah W.	29	9	1841	3	9	1862	Mt. Hebron
Lewis W.	5	11	1843	27	11	1911	Mt. Hebron
Joseph	16	2	1847	5	4	1919	Mt. Hebron
Jackson, Josiah							
w. Rachel							
s. Lewis Walker	31	3	1806				
Jackson, Mary E.	11	9	1818	28	3	1903	Hopewell
(widow of J. Fenton)							
Jenkins, Jacob							
w. Elizabeth							
Sarah	19	12	1750				
Jonathan	21	9	1753				
Mary	17	2	1756				

Name	Born			Died			Buried
Jenkins, William	8	2	1897				
Jolliffe, William							
w. Lydia				30	12	1759	
John	18	6	1751				
Phebe	15	12	1752	age about 18 mo.			
Gabriel	19	5	1755	23	12	1762	
Phebe II	12	3	1758				
Jolliffe, William				18	4	1770	
w. Elizabeth							
Edmund	15	1	1762	8	5	1778	
Mary	13	5	1763				
Amos	15	8	1764				
Lydia	9	5	1766				
Elizabeth	16	7	1768				
d. Gulealma	14	9	1770	21	1	1773	
Jones, William							
w. Ruth (Jackson)	3	9	1824	21	3	1890	Mt. Hebron
s. James H.	1	1	1849	16	11	1928	Keyser, W. Va.
Lee, Rebecca White	7	1	1815				Middle Creek
d. of Thos. & Debby (Dunn)							
Lewis, Henry							
w. Mary							
Henry	15	3	1744	4	5	1775	
Samuel	8	7	1746				
Sudney	20	3	1748				
Ellinor	18	1	1751				
Evan	24	6	1755				
Elizabeth	19	8	1758				
John	10	4	1761				
Lodge, William							
w. Rebecca (Purcell)		4	1830	20	4	1901	Mt. Hebron
(d. of John & Mary)							
Lupton, Daniel W.	27	11	1881	19	6	1935	Hopewell
(s. of Hugh & Mary)							
w. Victoria (Noel)	12	7	1882				
(d. of John A. & Louisa)							
Virginia Noel	13	6	1912				
Dorothy Taylor	16	12	1913				
Martha Walker	29	4	1919				
Margaret Stone	15	5	1921				
Lupton, David							
w. Mary (Hollingsworth)	3	12	1758				
Ruth	9	11	1778				
Joseph	15	12	1781				
Isaac	15	8	1784				
David	11	9	1786				
Rachel	31	12	1789				
Nathan							
Jonah H.	20	7	1795	25	7	1870	Ridge
Lewis							
Phineas							
Lupton, David Jr.							
w. Ann							
d. Rachel	8	4	1810				

Name	Born			Died			Buried
Lupton, Edward W.	1	12	1843	6	12	1910	Martinsburg,
(s. of Jonah & Lydia)							W. Va.
w. Mary Eva (Janney)	14	4		24	5	1917	Martinsburg,
d. of Israel & Evelina							W. Va.
(Tabb)							
E. Janney S.	23	12	1877	23	3	1907	Martinsburg,
							W. Va.
Wm. Taylor	31	3	1884				Joined Pres. Ch.
(w. Mildred Codwise)							
Jas. McSherry	13	11	1888				Joined Pres. Ch.
(w. Helena Knight)							
Lupton, Hugh S.	20	3	1845	9	12	1919	Hopewell
(s. of Jonah & Lydia)							
w. Mary R. (Speakman)	4	8	1856	19	4	1928	Hopewell
(d. of Wilson & Eliza							
Roberts)							
Daniel W.	27	11	1881	19	6	1935	Hopewell
Carrie D.	5	11	1883				
James R.	16	10	1892				
Hugh S. Jr.	24	12	1895				
Lupton, Hugh S. Jr.	24	12	1895				
(s. of Hugh & Mary)							
w. Mildred (Hathaway)	4	6	1897				
(d. of Thos. & Mary)							
Hugh S. III	7	2	1919	2	7	1922	Hopewell
David Walker	12	10	1934				
Lupton, James R.	16	10	1892				
(s. of Hugh & Mary)							
w. Margaret H. (Roberts)	11	11	1893				
(d. of Alfred & Jean							
Harmon)							
Jas. R. Jr.	5	9	1919				
Edward Irish	27	10	1921				
Alfred Roberts	20	10	1923				
Mary Jean	9	12	1926				
Margaret Helen	25	10	1929				
Lupton, Joel Sr.				10	2	1883	Ridge
(s. of David & Mary)							
w. Sarah (Haines)							
Joel Jr.	24	2	1847	17	2	1884	Ridge
Maria C.	13	12	1849	9	5	1885	Ridge
Sarah Jane							
William G.							
(6 more ch.)							
Lupton, Joel Jr.	24	2	1847	17	2	1884	Ridge
(s. of Joel & Sarah)							
w. Ellen I. (Hough)	10	11	1848				Mt. Hebron
Mary W.	10	12	1869				
(m. Pitzer)							
Chas. L. W.	6	9	1871				
Hugh (m. Roberts)	27	10	1874				
Anna	22	12	1876	6	9	1877	Ridge

Name	Born			Died			Buried
Lupton, John							
(s. of Joseph)							
w. Sarah (Frost)			1735	22	5	1775	
Grace	9	6	1757				
Joshua	12	9	1759				
Nathan	7	8	1761				
Mary	8	6	1764				
John	3	1	1769				
Joseph	3	6	1771				
Sarah	28	4	1773				
Lupton, Jonah H.	20	7	1795	25	7	1870	Ridge
w. (1) Martha Ann							
(Sidwell)	30	4	1797	24	7	1836	
d. Thamsin	4	3	1818	7	10	1897	
w. (2) Lydia (Walker)	20	1	1804	29	1	1889	Ridge
(d. of Edwd. & Mary)							
Ann M.	14	4	1840	12	12	1920	Ridge
(m. Bond)							
Mary W.	25	6	1841				Ridge
Edward W.	1	12	1843	6	12	1910	Martinsburg, W. Va.
Hugh S.	20	4	1845	9	12	1919	Hopewell
David P.	23	11	1846	25	2	1918	Ridge
Rebecca J.	22	9	1848	20	3	1924	Baltimore
Lupton, Jonathan							
w. Sarah							
Mary	18	4	1765				
John	1	2	1767				
Rebekah	25	5	1769				
Sarah	12	12	1771				
Lupton, Joseph Sr.				9	8	1758	
				(In 72d year)			
w. Marcy (Twining)	8	9	1690	25	5	1762	
d. of Stephen &							
Abigail (Young)							
Lupton, Joseph (Jr.)			1718	9	11	1791	
(s. of Jos. & Marcy)							
w. Rachel (Bull)							
(d. of Richard of							
Chester Co., Pa.)							
David	14	9	1757				
Rachel	31	7	1761	29	12	1782	
Ann	9	6	1767				
Hannah	30	6	1770				
Rachel II							
Lewis							
Phineas							
Lupton, William (Sr.)							
w. Grace							
Samuel	22	4	1746				
Isaac	11	7	1748				
Joseph	5	11	1752				
William	9	11	1754				
Asa	16	3	1757				
Jesse	16	1	1760				
Marcy	13	11	1762				

Name		Born		Died			Buried
Lupton, William (Jr.)	9	11	1754				
w. Bathsheba (Allen)	10	4	1760				
(d. of Jackson)							
Soloman	5	11	1780				
Betty	27	6	1783				
Grace and							
Jonathan	10	1	1787				
Allen	15	4	1790				
Marvin, John W.			1812	19	10	1882	Mt. Hebron
w. Rebecca (Brown)							
Mattison, Don Scott	14	8	1861	8	5	1932	Mt. Hebron
(s. of Jesse & Mary Ann)							
w. Nena (Robinson)	15	1	1871				
(d. of Jos. & Rebecca)							
s. Raymond Love	19	1	1896	23	8	1930	Mt. Hebron
McClun, Thomas							
w. Hannah							
Nathan	11	8	1762	26	10	1762	
Mary	26	1	1764				
Elisabeth		1	1766				
Isaac	13	10	1767				
John	29	1	1769				
Thomas		2	1771				
Rachel	12	4	1773				
Lydia	13	5	1775				
McCoole, James				9	2	1751	
w. Ann				(Age 42)			
Mary	27	11	1743				
John	10	8	1745				
James	12	12	1747				
Martha	31	10	1749				
Gabriel	17	8	1751				
McKay, Andrew	29	12	1736				
w. Jane							
Jacob	17	2	1762	28	2	1762	
Patience	9	2	1763				
Rachel	29	12	1764				
Moses	7	10	1766				
David	5	9	1768	30	8	1773	
John	10	12	1770	1	8	1773	
Jacob	28	12	1772				
Enos	1	10	1774				
Esther	11	12	1776				
Margaret	8	5	1779				
M'Kay, Jacob							
w. Rachel							
d. Edith	21	9	1781				
Mendinghal, John							
w. Martha	14	2	1713	28	10	1794	
s. James	10	12	1751				

Name	Born			Died			Buried
Moore, Anthony							
w. Zilphia							
Benjamin	18	8	1759				
Sarah	31	7	1761				
Robert	25	6	1763				
Abigail	25	12	1765				
Ann	10	10	1769				
David	14	3	1772				
Rachel	21	8	1774				
M'Pharson, William							
w. Jane							
Jonas	18	8	1773				
Daniel	17	1	1775				
William	1	1	1778	3	12	1778	
Painter, John							
w. Susannah							
David	11	1	1761				
Sarah	25	8	1762				
Elesebeth	9	10	1764				
Jacob	21	8	1766				
Painter, Robert	21	1	1738				
w. Eunice	5	6	1742				
Parkins, Isaac							
w. Mary							
Rachel	23	3	1724				
Ebenezer	30	12	1724				
Lydia	22	1	1726				
Charles	29	3	1727				
Phebe	14	2	1729				
Amy	23	11	1731				
Jonathan	26	3	1733				
David	31	1	1735				
Thomas		1	1737				
Elizabeth	3	9	1738				
Hannah		9	1740				
Mary		9	1742				
Isaac		11	1746				
Ruth		6	1748				
Parviance, James							
w. Elizabeth							
Nathaniel	17	10	1768				
John	26	11	1770				
Paxon, John							
w. Mary							
d. Alice	19	5	1779				
Pickering, Benjamin							
w. Rebecca							
Elizabeth	28	2	1778				
Ellis	23	1	1780				
Thomas	13	12	1781				
Enos	1	4	1783				
Rebecca	10	3	1785				
Mary	10	4	1787				
Benjamin	21	7	1789				
Elizabeth	7	5	1791				

Name	Born			Died			Buried
Pickering, Jacob							
w. Hannah							
Elizabeth	3	11	1775				
Ealeanor	4	8	1777				
Enos	10	12	1779				
Hannah	27	4	1784				
Jacob	8	5	1786				
Pickering, Samuel							
w. Grace							
Mary	30	10	1748				
Jacob	4	9	1750				
Benjamin	1	7	1752				
Sarah	2	9	1754				
Samuel	5	2	1757				
Isaac	18	5	1759				
Jonathan	28	3	1761				
John	16	7	1763				
Grace	5	11	1765				
Mercy	28	12	1767				
Rachel	4	10	1770				
Hannah	23	2	1773				
Pickering, William							
w. Sarah							
Hannah	30	10	1750				
John	23	2	1752				
Lidia	11	7	1754				
Jacob	10	12	1756				
William	22	2	1759				
Jonathan	14	4	1761				
Mary	25	7	1763				
Pidgeon, Isaac	24	9	1769	30	11	1855	Hopewell
(s. of Wm. & Rachel)							
w. (1) Eliz'h Hammer	17	7	1775				
John Hammer	10	1	1794				
William	5	3	1796				Moved to Ohio
Isaac Jr.	10	3	1798				Moved to Ohio
Rachel	25	2	1801				
(m. Aquilla Coats)							
Mary	6	1	1804				
(m. Desdmane							
Stone)							
w. (2) ———							
w. (3) Eliz'h Walker				15	4	1825	
Edward W.	20	8	1813				Moved to Ohio
Abel Lewis	8	11	1815				
Sam'l Lukens	7	8	1817	6	8	1902	Hopewell
w. (4) Sarah ———							
Pidgeon, Lewis	8	9	1859				
(s. of Sam'l & Sarah)							
w. Susan T. (Williams)	29	3	1860				
(d. of Wm. & Mary)							
Mary Eliz'h	2	8	1890				
Sarah Chandlee	13	12	1892	24	12	1892	Hopewell
Dorothy Everett	11	12	1899				

Name	Born			Died			Buried
Pidgeon, Samuel L.	7	8	1817	6	8	1902	Hopewell
(s. of Isaac & Eliz'h)							
w. Sarah (Chandlee)	14	2	1825	26	1	1886	Hopewell
Edward W.	10	2	1851	9	8	1852	Hopewell
Eliza C.	13	3	1855	23	2	1930	Hopewell
Rebecca Jane	21	9	1857				
Lewis	8	9	1859				
Charles M.	17	12	1862				
Cassie	21	8	1864				
Pugh, Azariah							
w. Hannah (Bailes)	31	1	1729				
Ruth	26	2	1746				
Ellis	21	1	1748				
Jesse	25	1	1751				
Mary	16	12	1754				
David	26	8	1757				
Pugh, Jesse	16	9	1711				
w. Alice	29	9	1711				
Thomas	16	11	1731-2	(old style)			
Elizabeth	22	3	1735				
Job	4	7	1737				
Jane	21	12	1745				
Alice	10	11	1750				
Pugh, Thomas							
w. Ann							
Alice	10	7	1754				
Elizabeth	6	9	1755				
Sarah	8	4	1758				
Jane	21	3	1761				
Ann	26	7	1764				
Lydia	16	3	1767				
Rachel	16	2	1770				
Purcell, Rosanna							
d. of John & Mary				7	3	1902	Ridge
Rees, David							
w. Martha				16	2	1785	
Lydia	26	10	1775				
Hannah	27	11	1778				
Samuel	2	11	1781				
Rees, Henry							
w. Martha							
d. Katharine	4	3	1760				
Rees, Henry							
w. Ann							
Lydia	10	10	1764				
Gideon	30	11	1766				
Lewis	19	11	1768				
Margaret	14	2	1771				
Rees, John							
w. Lydia							
Lydia	16	5	1746				
Sarah	22	10	1747	7	5	1748	
Jacob	30	7	1749				
John	12	2	1752				
Morris	31	8	1754				
Hannah	23	7	1757				
Rachel	28	1	1759				
Enoch	12	7	1764	10	10	1766	

Name		Born			Died		Buried
Rees, John N.	30	7	1843	30	12	1898	Hopewell
(s. of Sam'l & Lydia)							
Rees, Jonah L.	1	4	1837	1	4	1915	Winchester
(s. of Jacob & Thamasin)							
w. Annie (Jackson) Sr.	17	8	1837	16	10	1925	Winchester
Mary (m. Steer)							
Annie J. Jr.	6	7	1871				
Rees, Lewis							
w. Sala							
Mary	23	1	1797				
Hariet	28	11	1798				
Richardson, N. Webster	18	9	1808	27	11	1894	Mt. Hebron
w. Esther Ann							
(d. of Josiah & Priscilla							
Atkinson)							
Robinson, A. Alexander	5	6	1838	27	8	1923	Winchester
(s. of Arch'd & Lydia)							
w. Virginia (Fris)							
(d. of George S.)							
Margaret V.	22	4	1865				
Lewis A.	15	2	1866				
Mary E.	1	5	1868				
Lydia J.	4	1	1870				
Cora M.	29	10	1871				
George N.	8	1	1874				
Leona I.	22	4	1882				
Robinson, Archibald	4	1	1809	8	2	1879	Back Creek
w. Lydia Ann (Steer)	26	2	1818	21	11	1874	
Joseph S.				21	11	1923	
A. Alexander				27	8	1923	Winchester
Phineas S.				18	3	1901	Ozarks Co., Mo.
James L.	18	2	1844	25	2	1915	Mt. Hebron
Robinson, David	24	3	1820	13	7	1889	
w. Hannah E. (Cather)	20	11	1819	14	5	1903	Back Creek
Charles G.	1	6	1846	15	8	1908	Newport News, Va.
Silas Deane	6	6	1848	13	1	1934	Mt. Hebron
Rufus C.	22	9	1859				
Robinson, Jackson	29	11	1810	11	1	1887	Ridge
(s. of Andrew & Marg't)							
w. S. Emeline (Wright)							
Thomas W.	9	12	1839	5	4	1913	Macon City, Mo.
Joseph A.	3	1	1841				
William N.	15	8	1843				
Annie R.	26	3	1845	19	5	1921	Sheridan, Wyo.
James J.		11	1847	13	6	1872	
Margaret C.		11	1849				Joined Episcopal Ch.
Esther S.	8	1	1854				
Edwin J.	8	10	1857				

Name	Born			Died			Buried
Robinson, James L.	18	2	1844	25	2	1915	Mt. Hebron
(s. of Arch'd & Lydia)							
w. Sallie G. Robinson	16	6	1861				
(d. of Josiah & Mary)							
Ray	22	2	1883				
Mabel	10	7	1885				
Clarence J.	18	12	1891				
Mary O.	22	6	1896				
Robinson, James Wm.	24	9	1865	7	8	1934	Hopewell
(s. of Jonathan & Mary)							
w. Clara Piggott							
Wm. Donald	30	4	1907				
Thos. Harold	6	12	1911				
Anna Frances	10	8	1915				
Robinson, Jonathan							
w. Mary Frances							
(Clevenger)	23	1	1835	12	4	1899	Hopewell
(d. of David & Hannah)							
D. Arthur	8	5	1859				
Jas. Wm.	24	9	1865	7	8	1934	Hopewell
Mary Hannah	4	10	1867				
Robinson, Joseph	23	3	1825	10	6	1901	Back Creek
(s. of Andrew & Marg't)							
w. Sarah Ann (Fenton)						1874	Iowa
John F.							
Wm. T.							
Annie							
Mary S.							
Robinson, Joseph S.				21	11	1923	
(s. of Arch'd & Lydia)							
w. Rebecca (Smith)				27	10	1921	Mt. Hebron
Mary A.							
Charles Hunter							
Archibald S.							
Nena	15	1	1871				
Robinson, Josiah	23	8	1822	26	6	1906	Hopewell
(s. of Andrew & Marg't)							
w. Mary Jane (Clevenger)							
Robinson, Phineas S.							
w. Kate (Pelter)							
Bertha Priscilla	10	9	1895				
Effa Steer	21	4	1901				
Robinson, Ray	22	2	1883				
(s. of Jas. L. & Sallie)							
w. Ida Helen (Robinson)	12	8	1884				
d. of Silas & Florence							
(Lauck)							
Jas. Kenneth	16	5	1916				
Ray Jr.	4	3	1921				
Robinson, William T.	22	5	1835	15	2	1926	Hopewell
(s. of Andrew & Marg't)							
w. Sophia B. (Clevenger)	30	7	1847	17	8	1915	Hopewell
Austin	29	10	1870				
Luther H.	13	11	1873	10	9	1904	Hopewell
Laura Alice	12	8	1876	5	14	1911	Hopewell
Charles W.	6	10	1885				

Name	Born			Died			Buried
Rogers, Evan							
w. Sarah				17	2	1770	
John	31	10	1750				
Josiah	7	1	1752				
Robert	16	7	1754	16	9	1755	
Evan	31	8	1756				
Mary	20	2	1759				
Elizabeth	13	11	1761				
Owen	20	12	1763				
Sidney	18	12	1765				
James	19	3	1768				
Sarah and							
Elenor	26	7	1770				
Rogers, Owen							
w. Lydia							
John	25	8	1757	30	6	1778	
Robert	5	7	1760				
David	1	5	1764	20	6	1778	
Evan	5	5	1767				
Owen	1	9	1769				
Lydia	28	5	1773	27	6	1778	
Sarah	1	8	1775				
Ross, David							
w. Katherine							
s. Enos	9	10	1771				
Ross, John							
w. Lidia							
s. David	18	9	1742	23	3	1763	
Schlack, Grover Hauptman	18	7	1888				
(s. of Chas. & Annie)							
w. Nina (Thwait)	4	7	1889				
(d. of John & Ida)							
Helen Louise	29	4	1922				
Charlotte Belle	26	9	1923				
Mary Lou	29	9	1930				
Shihon, Michael		9	1750				
w. Mary							
Phebe	19	9	1781				
Deborah	5	1	1784				

"Michael Shihon was born in the County of Cork, in the Province of Munster in the Kingdom of Ireland and came into America in the year 1769 and was convinced of the Truth in the year 1773 and joined in Membership with Friends in the year 1774."

Name	Born			Died			Buried
Sidwell, James							
w. Hannah							
d. Margaret	9	1	1779				
Sidwell, Mary F.				30	7	1929	Mt. Hebron
(d. of Rich'd & Rebecca)							
(m. Sam'l W. Appleby)							
Smith, Joseph			1728	16	9	1781	
wife ————							
Nathan	20	6	1759	3	9	1781	
Caleb	7	10	1771	5	9	1781	
Smith, Mary R.	1	8	1833	14	9	1922	Mt. Hebron
(d. of Lewis Lupton &							
Rachel Mahoney)							

Name	Born			Died			Buried
Steer, Grace	19	5	1717	14	3	1794	
(Evidently the widow							
of Joseph Edgerton)							
(m. Joseph Steer Sr.)							
Children by Edgerton:							
Abigail	20	8	1743				
Ruth	3	1	1747				
Hannah	25	1	1749				
Sarah	27	11	1751				
Mary	21	2	1752	(New Stiel)			
Joseph	26	12	1754				
Isaac	6	12	1757				
Steer, Isaac							
w. Phebe							
Mary	17	7	1780				
Joseph	2	7	1783				
Ann	11	5	1786				
Steer, Joseph (Edgerton)	26	12	1754				
w. Grace (Lupton)	9	6	1758				
Isaac	31	12	1776	15	6	1798	
Sarah	28	2	1779				
John	3	1	1782	About 8 weeks old			
Joshua	28	8	1783				
David	25	8	1786				
Nathan	18	4	1789	About 14 mo. & 9 da. old			
Rachel	6	5	1791				
Samuel	18	8	1793				
Amos	16	7	1798				
Stephenson, Sarah Edna	2	10	1818	23	3	1905	Mt. Hebron
(d. of Jos. & Mary							
Fawcett)							
Stipe, Irene Maurice							
(Wolford)	6	5	1887				
(d. of Edward & Sarah)							
(m. J. Wm. Stipe)							
s. James Leslie	8	1	1914				
Tate, Magnus							
w. Honour							
d. Rachel Thomas	30	4	1734				
Taylour, Jacob							
w. Ann							
Elizabeth	30	5	1738				
Patience	6	12	1742	13	9	?	
Lydia	29	2	1744				
Isaac	17	9	1746				
Ann	2	1	1751				
Jane	25	6	1758				
Abram	17	9	1759				
Thatcher, Samuel				8	11	1776	
w. Mary							
Thomas	23	8	1774				
Jonathan	9	7	1776				

Name	Born			Died			Buried
Thatcher, Stephen							
w. Ruth							
Martha	19	1	1781				
William	7	3	1783				
Jesse	1	12	1784				
Thomas	22	9	1787				
Mary	19	1	1790				
David	5	7	1792				
Thomas, Enos							
w. Rachel							
Katharine	9	1	1752				
Evan	4	4	1756	30	4	1769	
Phebe	17	9	1758				
Thomas, Evan							
w. Katharine							
s. Enos				23	3	1763	
Throckmorton, Leah H.				29	5	1884	Middle Creek
(d. of Thos. & Debby Dunn)							
(m. Job Throckmorton)							
s. David William	31	12	1840	26	10	1918	Middle Creek
Tomlinson, Hannah	12	7	1894				
d. Jas. & Hannah (Conrow)							
Williams							
(m. Carroll M. Tomlinson of Pa.)							
Robert							
Elizabeth							
Cynthia							
Trimble, John							
w. Catherine							
Ann	15	8	1774				
Samuel	26	2	1777				
David	22	10	1779				
Walker, Abel							
w. Sina							
Mary	3	5	1730				
Elizabeth	8	10	1732				
Abel	13	1	1735				
Sina	14	3	1737				
Lewis	14	3	1739				
Mordecai	16	8	1742				
Ebinazer	7	7	1745				
Sarah	28	10	1749				
Walker, Abel							
w. Mary			1744	13	1	1782	
Martha	14	6	1762	24	10	1792	
Sinah	15	7	1764				
Mary	12	1	1767				
Abel	21	5	1769				
Edward	27	3	1771	31	3	1833	Hopewell
Elizabeth	10	10	1773				
Lewis	27	7	1776				
Lydia	10	10	1778	1	6	1803	
Isaac	22	3	1781				

Name	Born			Died			Buried
Walker, Abel Jr.							
w. Mary							
Martha	4	1	1802				
Joseph	26	2	1803				
Lewis B.	12	9	1804				
Walker, Daniel	18	8	1807				Hopewell
(s. of Edward & Mary)							
w. Mary (Roberts)							Hopewell
d. Mary R.	10	2	1849	15	7	1920	Hopewell
(m. Robt. Wickersham)							
Walker, Edward	27	3	1771	31	3	1833	Hopewell
(s. of Abel & Mary)							
w. Mary (Haines)	20	2	1782	25	1	1845	Hopewell
Nathan	12	12	1802				Moved to Water-ford, Va.
Lydia	2	1	1804				Ridge
Abel	7	11	1805	1	3	1861	Moved to Green Plain, O.
Daniel	18	8	1807				Hopewell
Rebecca	29	4	1809				Moved to Goose Creek, Va.
Thamison H.	3	3	1811				Moved to Green Plain, O.
White, John							
w. Susannah							
s. William	25	2	1788				
White, Nathaniel							
w. Phebe							
Phebe	11	2	1785				
Ann	23	4	1786				
Mary	24	9	1787				
Joel	12	2	1789				
White, Thomas							
w. Mary							
Joseph	14	3	1776				
Nathaniel	19	5	1777				
Wood, Daniel T.	24	8	1824	29	6	1915	Winchester
(s. of Isaac & Maria)							
w. Miriam G. (Nichols)	20	2	1831	17	6	1898	Winchester
(d. of Joshua & Naomi)							
Mary Conrad	19	1	1860				
Maria Nichols	19	2	1861	24	11	1887	Winchester
Lucretia N.	15	3	1863				
(m. Ely)							
Samuel Brown	11	9	1865	10	9	1888	Winchester
Margaret Logan	26	6	1867				
(m. Walter Tolbert)							
Clara Virginia	27	8	1869				
Laura	21	10	1871	1	9	1890	Winchester
Daniel T. Jr.	23	4	1874				Winchester

Name	Born			Died			Buried
Wright, James Sr.			1671				
w. Mary	2	12	1689				
Mary	3	6	1708				
Hannah	24	1	1709				
Martha	14	2	1713				
Elizabeth	23	11	1714				
John	4	11	1716				
James	8	11	1718				
Thomas	14	1	1720				
Isaac	25	3	1723				
Ann	29	1	1725				
Sarah	15	3	1727				
Lydia	31	8	1730				
Wright, James Jr.							
w. Luce							
Ralph	25	5	1746				
Elizabeth	15	10	1747				
James	1	12	1748				
Ann	25	10	1750				
Susanna	19	3	1753				
Boyater	13	9	1755				
Micajah	24	4	1758				
Wright, James							
w. Phebe							
Ruth	4	9	1777				
Jonathan	11	12	1781				
Wright, John							
w. Susanna							
Daniel	26	6	1797				
Benjamin	6	10	1798				
Ann	14	9	1802				
Jesse	18	5	1806				
Wright, Richard							
w. Rachel							
Mary Jane	16	4	1813				
Jonathan	27	10	1815				
Levi S.	17	7	1817				
Wright, Thomas	11	1	1711	18	8	1765	
w. Esther (Hiatt)	1	4	1731				
Martha	15	5	1748				
Jonathan	27	4	1750				
Mary	8	5	1752				
Thomas	1	7	1756				
Hannah	14	2	1758				
Ruth	6	2	1759				
David	14	3	1763				
Wright, William							
w. Eunice							
s. Joseph	27	3	1781				

ORTHODOX BRANCH
(Incomplete)

Name	Born			Died			Buried
Baldwin, Samuel R.						1903	Hopewell
w. Rebecca (Wright)						(In 46th year)	
Elizabeth Hyde							
Mary Alice							
Wm. Wright							
Samuel Wright							
Joseph R.							
Barrett, Jonathan	7	10	1785			1870	Hopewell
Bishop, William	3	1	1857	9	1	1911	Hopewell
w. Martha (Wright)			1850			1926	Hopewell
Louise							
(m. Newboll)							
Lydia Alma							
Maud Wright							
Jessie Brooke							
Cochran, Hiram Sr.							
w. Anna (Wright)							
Hiram	5	6	1838				
Anna	29	11	1843				
(m. John D. Wright)							
Frederick A.							
(m. (1) Susan Wright)							
(m. (2) Carrie A. Clevenger)							
Griffith, Aaron H.	11	3	1802	18	2	1877	Mt. Hebron
w. Mary P. (Hollingsworth)	15	7	1809	23	7	1896	Mt. Hebron
Elizabeth	25	12	1831	13	3	1913	
(m. Hezekiah Bailey)							
Martha	15	8	1833	8	6	1839	
Jos. Clarkson	13	3	1835				
Harriet H.	26	12	1837				
Aaron H.	10	2	1841				
Edward R.	14	4	1847				Mt. Hebron
Mary Anna			1851				
John							
Griffith, Robert Daniel	19	8	1821				Hopewell
Hoge, Isaac							
w. Phebe ———							
Frederica							
James							
William							
Lewis							
Hoge, Lewis							
w. Susan B. (Jolliffe)							
James D.							
Sarah J.							
Lewis N.							
Elizabeth							
(m. Walter Scales)							

Name	Born			Died			Buried
Huffman, Wilber							
w. Nellie S. (Wright)	29	12	1875				
Virginia	6	4	1905				
Pauline	18	6	1910				
Jolliffe, Edward C.							
wife ———							
Lillie			1860				
Frank							
Jolliffe, Joseph J.	30	10	1851	24	2	1933	Hopewell
w. Sarah J. (Lupton)	10	5	1848	17	4	1925	Hopewell
Neill W.	17	7	1876	9	11	1931	Frederick, Md.
(m. Lula V. Burk-holder)							
Joseph L.	28	10	1877				
(m. Laura Alice Robinson)							
Edith M.	2	9	1879				
John W.	9	8	1882				
(m. Lucy Morrison)							
Jolliffe, Joseph N.	10	4	1813	20	4	1894	Hopewell
w. Sarah J. ———	14	2	1821	23	4	1899	Hopewell
Susan B.	7	4	1843	7	2	1933	Fredericksburg, Va.
Rebecca N.	3	7	1846	27	9	1857	Hopewell
Sallie	10	10	1848	25	9	1864	Hopewell
Jos. John	30	10	1851	24	2	1933	Hopewell
Alice B.	9	1	1854	10	10	1854	Hopewell
George J.	16	10	1857	29	6	1932	Winchester
(m. Charlotte Huck)							
Rachel W.	17	2	1860				
(m. Arthur Robinson)							
Townsend	29	11	1864	24	11	1930	Winchester
(m. Marie Jones)							
Robinson, D. Arthur	8	5	1859				
w. Rachel W. (Jolliffe)	17	2	1860				
Sarah Eliz'h J.	9	8	1886				
Albert G.	2	8	1889				
Willa	15	7	1900				Moved to Goose Cr. Mo. Mtg.
(m. Curtis Wilson)							
Portia	2	9	1902				Moved to Wilmington, O.
(m. Edward Haines)							
Thwaith, James				8	6	1887	
wife ———							
James L.							Apple Pie Ridge
John							
Sophia							
Jennie							
Wright, Jesse				12	10	1882	Hopewell
w. Lydia H. (Griffith)				12	5	1857	Hopewell
Rachel A.				17	10	1924	Hopewell
Martha W.							Hopewell
Rebecca S.							
Joseph R.							
Samuel							

Name	Born			Died			Buried
Wright, John D.	12	11	1843	24	11	1925	
w. Anna (Cochran)	29	11	1843				
Alice G. White	18	2	1874				
(m. Ben Byers)							
Nellie S.	29	12	1875				
(m. Wilber Huff-							
man)							
Wright, Samuel	31	3	1859	29	8	1893	
w. Elizabeth				9	1	1888	
Daniel							
Frederick							
Jesse							

BIRTHS AND DEATHS

FROM RECORDS OF CROOKED RUN MONTHLY MEETING

Name	Born			Died		
Allen, Jackson				30	8	1786
Antram, Caleb						
wife Sarah				20	10	1792
Jesse	20	8	1787			
Elizabeth	10	2	1789			
Esther	8	2	1791			
Bond, John				19	11	1787
Chew, Samuel						
wife Abigail						
Alice	21	1	1785			
Cleaver, Ezekiel						
wife Abigail						
Mary	19	6	1789			
Abigail	12	5	1792			
Ezekiel	1	7	1794			
Peter	18	10	1796			
Cleavinger, Joseph	15	9	1750	28	9	1783
wife Mary	18	6	1753			
John	15	8	1775			
Edith	14	7	1777			
Rachel	24	7	1788			
Ann	4	9	1789			
Cogill (Cowgill), Henry						
wife Ruth						
Rachel				26	9	1791
Ellis, Margery				28	9	1798	(at the house of Isaac Painter)
Fallis, John						
wife Mary						
Elizabeth	8	3	1784			
Fawcett, John				22	11	1786	(in his 70th yr.)
wife Rebecca						
Lydia	21	1	1739			
Sarah	24	4	1741			
John	21	5	1749			
Rachel	3	6	1752			
Thomas	3	1	1757			
Fawcett, John						
wife Margaret						
Isaac	25	9	1782			
Elijah	7	1	1784			

Name	Born			Died		
Fawcett, Richard				24	11	1789
wife Rachel						
Richard	7	5	1745	29	5	1801
Thomas	24	1	1748			
Joseph	14	6	1750	3	10	1775
Hannah (Antram)	30	6	1753	25	4	1784
Mary	14	5	1757			
Lydia	17	10	1761			
Fawcett, Richard						
wife Mary						
Rachel	28	7	1769			
Sarah	18	3	1771			
Rebeckah	8	2	1774	14	7	1795
Grace	10	7	1776	10	9	1800
Joseph	12	8	1778			
Samuel	26	8	1780			
Phebe	20	12	1782			
Hannah	17	11	1784			
Jonathan	28	11	1786			
Richard	30	11	1788	20	5	1801
Jacob	26	11	1793			
Fawcett, Thomas						
wife Martha						
John	14	1	1770			
Richard	22	9	1771			
Martha	3	11	1773			
Rachel	6	10	1775			
David	27	11	1776			
Hannah	17	11	1778			
Lydia	13	10	1781			
Thomas	15	11	1783	25	7	1793
Joseph	26	4	1786			
Mary	3	7	1788			
Eunice	19	10	1790	22	6	1791
Eunice 2d	19	5	1792			
Thomas 2d	16	11	1794			
Fawcett, Thomas						
wife Sarah						
William	8	10	1784			
John	22	1	1786			
Lydia	6	11	1787			
Abner	24	8	1789	15	1	1791
Elisha	18	10	1791			
Josiah	19	9	1793			
Eli	6	10	1795			
Fernley, William						
wife Martha	22	5	1774	29	1	1799
Martha	1	1	1797	20	1	1799
Unice	27	12	1798			

Name	Born			Died		
Garwood, John						
wife Esther						
Hope	18	1	1765			
Sarah	7	6	1766			
Daniel	8	4	1769			
Susanna	25	2	1771			
Levi	1	9	1773			
Margaret	11	10	1776			
Thomas	7	11	1778			
John	1	2	1781			
Isaiah	6	4	1783	21	2	1785
Deborah	11	5	1789			
Green, John						
wife Ruth						
Margret	12	3	1782			
Mary	24	12	1783			
Isaac	18	6	1785			
John	15	10	1787			
Jesse	2	2	1790			
Hains, John	27	10	1754			
wife Mary (Middleton)	4	9	1749			
Eli	14	1	1780			
Atlantic	31	12	1783	25	9	1795
Hains, Robert		9	1735			
(1) wife Esther	1	2	1731	3	6	1778
Allen	2	3	1768	24	4	1768
John	15	8	1769			
(2) wife Marg't (Smith)	16	9	1754			
Noah	6	2	1781			
Mary	6	7	1782	2	8	1786
Ann	18	11	1783	13	10	1784
Amos	14	6	1785			
Robert	31	11	1787			
Enos	12	1	1792			
Margaret	31	11	1793			
Holloway, Asa						
wife Abigail						
Jacob	21	9	1785			
Holloway, Daten				9	6	1787
wife Hope						
John	12	9	1786			
Holloway, Isaac						
wife Mary						
Nathan	13	8	1781			
Phebe	22	4	1785			
Holloway, John						
wife Mary						
George	26	9	1784			
Jesse	1	12	1786			
Longacre, Hannah				4	8	1793

Longacre, Hannah: (in her 78th yr.) She was an older sister to Rebekah & Rachel Fawcett.

Name	Born			Died		
Lupton, John						
(1) wife Lydia						
David	1	11	1795			
(2) wife Rachel						
Jonathan	13	3	1798			
Lydia	4	5	1800			
Frances	31	7	1802			
Abigail	25	1	1805			
Lupton, Jonathan						
wife Sarah						
Mary	18	4	1765			
John	1	2	1767			
Rebeckah	25	1	1769			
Sarah	12	12	1771	11	10	1778
Phebe	27	3	1774			
Lydia	25	5	1777			
Jonathan	1	9	1779	3	12	1781
Joseph	1	4	1782			
Ruth	19	2	1786			
M'Connal, James						
wife Rachel						
Jesse	6	7	1788			
Edward	31	10	1789			
Painter, David						
wife Martha						
Hannah	17	11	1786			
Jesse	1	1	1789			
Painter, Isaac Sr.						
wife Sarah						
Beulah	16	6	1772			
Rachel	11	11	1774			
Rebeckah	23	6	1777			
Isaac	14	3	1779			
Abraham	1	4	1781			
Mahlon	18	1	1783			
Hannah	30	11	1787	26	11	1788
Abihail	22	7	1789			
John	24	1	1793			
Painter, John	5	3	1736			
wife Susanna	14	8	1739			
David	11	1	1761			
Sarah	25	8	1762			
Elisabeth	9	10	1764			
Jacob	31	8	1766			
Phebe	30	6	1768			
Mary	21	11	1769			
John	18	7	1775			
Robert	17	7	1778			
Susanna	14	4	1780			
Paxon, John						
wife Mary						
Jacob	29	12	1781			
Mary	8	11	1784			
John	21	2	1787			
Ann	3	10	1789			

Name		Born			Died	
Pusey, Nathan	17	5	1748			
wife Mary	4	10	1756			
Susannah	16	1	1777	25	12	1782
Rachel	13	3	1779			
Margret	20	2	1781			
John	23	1	1783	23	1	1783
Joshua	15	1	1784			
David	11	11	1785			
Lydia	15	12	1787			
Nathan	4	3	1790			
Redd, George						(Children not
wife Rachel						named)
Richards, Roland						
(1) wife Mary						
Abijah	23	5	1753			
Ebenezer	18	7	1754	9	3	1775
(2) wife Lydia						
Abigail	7	10	1764			
Samuel	27	11	1765	29	12	1787
Elizabeth	13	11	1767	17	2	1788
Susannah	16	10	1769	9	2	1788
Eli	16	9	1771			
Hannah	31	1	1774			
Lydia	24	3	1776	28	7	1777
Townsend	25	3	1778	5	3	1788
Mary	12	9	1780			
Lydia 2d	18	10	1782			
Sarah	28	8	1784			
Catharine	30	7	1786			
Sidney	5	10	1789			
Shihon, Michael						
wife Mary						
Phebe	19	9	1781			
Deborah	5	1	1784			
Ebenezer	19	11	1785			
Jonah	12	2	1788			
Shinn, George				23	9	1782
wife Rachel						
Francis	24	12	1781			
George Shinn's daughter				6	10	1782
Swayne, Joshua	19	6	1753			
wife Rebecca	1	8	1765			
Phebe	9	11	1786	15	11	1786
Samuel	17	11	1787			
John	25	11	1789			
Wright, James						
wife Phebe						
Ruth	4	9	1777			
Jonathan	11	12	1781			
Rachel	6	6	1784			
Isaac	6	7	1786			
David	10	9	1788			
Wright, William						
wife Eunice						
Sarah	4	1	1783			
John	6	3	1785			

DISOWNMENTS AT HOPEWELL
1759-1829
From Book 1

Day	Mo.	Yr.	Person Disowned	Reason for Disownment
		1754	James Moon (Reinstated 24-9-1759)	
21	5	1759	Thomas Sharp Jr.	Fighting and training in the Militia
21	5	1759	John Bailey (from Burlington)	Gaming and fighting
20	8	1759	Thomas Taylor	
20	8	1759	Jacob Rees (Reinstated 6-10-1766)	
24	9	1759	Samuel Littler	Married contrary to discipline
24	9	1759	Ann Thomas (wife of Isaac)	Married contrary to discipline
24	9	1759	Mercer Beeson	
22	10	1759	Susannah Roberts (formerly Southwood)	Married contrary to discipline
24	12	1759	Sarah Haworth (widow of James)	
24	12	1759	Mary Hoge (wife of James)	Neglected attending meetings
21	1	1760	James Hoge	
4	8	1760	Abraham Hollingsworth	Driving a military wagon in military service
3	11	1760	Alexander Ross	Married contrary to discipline
3	11	1760	Lydia (Foster) Thomas	Married contrary to discipline
3	11	1760	Mary (Malin) Babb	Married contrary to discipline
3	11	1760	Hannah (Frazer) Sharp	Married contrary to discipline
2	2	1761	Thomas Carter	Fighting
2	3	1761	David Brooks (Reinstated 3-1-1763)	Married contrary to discipline after stealing the young woman
—	—	—	George Ross (Reinstated 5-4-1761)	from her parents
4	5	1761	Andrew Milburn	Attended a marriage accomplished contrary to discipline
1	6	1761	Mary Babb	Quarrelling

Day Mo. Yr.	Person Disowned	Reason for Disownment
3 8 1761	Mary Jones	
3 8 1761	Henry Carter	Attended a marriage accomplished contrary to discipline
7 9 1761	Joseph Babb	Married contrary to discipline
2 11 1761	Peter Babb	Married contrary to discipline
5 4 1762	Hannah Berry (formerly Hancher)	Married contrary to discipline
7 6 1762	George Hiatt	Neglected attending the meetings; married contrary to discipline
2 8 1762	William Hancher	Assisted his sister in accomplishing her marriage contrary to discipline and danced at weddings
6 9 1762	Elenor Brownfield (formerly Archer)	Married contrary to discipline
4 10 1762	David Rees	Bearing arms
7 2 1763	Edward Morgan	Married contrary to discipline
7 3 1763	Rachel Hurst (formerly Morgan)	Married contrary to discipline
4 4 1763	Richard Beeson	Neglected meetings and failed to pay debt
4 4 1763	Richard Merchant	Training in militia and fighting
2 5 1763	Joseph Hollingsworth	Married contrary to discipline
6 6 1763	John Carter	Dancing and singing and neglected attending meetings
6 6 1763	William Milburn	
— — ——	Samuel Pearson (Reinstated 6-6-1763)	Married contrary to discipline
4 7 1763	Jesse Webb	Married contrary to discipline
7 11 1763	Azariah Pugh	Quarreling and fighting
6 2 1764	Josiah & Jas. Ballinger	For killing a mare belonging to Richard Colvirt and concealing it
2 4 1764	Isaac Wright	
7 5 1764	Samuel Shinn and wife	Married contrary to discipline
5 6 1764	Robert Hollingsworth	Singing and dancing; neglected meetings and went scouting after the Indians
2 7 1764	Mary Bridges (Dillon)	Married contrary to discipline
6 8 1764	Abigail Sunderlin, Rosannah Merchant, and Mary Haworth	Danced at a frolic or place of diversion

Day Mo. Yr.	Person Disowned	Reason for Disownment
1 10 1764	Esther Sharp	Dancing
1 10 1764	Joseph Morgan	Bearing arms and scouting after the Indians
1 10 1764	Charles Parkins	
3 11 1764	Amelia Larrick (formerly Ozmond)	Married contrary to discipline
3 12 1764	Henry Rees	
7 1 1765	Elizabeth (Branson) Corder	Married contrary to discipline
4 3 1765	Katharine (Littler) Jones	Married contrary to discipline
1 4 1765	Elizabeth Powel	
1 4 1765	Edward Beeson (Reinstated 6-10-1766)	
6 5 1765	Jonathan Brittan	Married contrary to discipline
3 6 1765	Richard Hayworth	Scouting after the Indians, bearing arms, and training in the militia
7 10 1765	Nathan Littler (Reinstated 29-5-1783)	Moved without a certificate
2 12 1765	Ann Haworth (Dillon) (wife of Richard)	Married by hireling teacher
2 12 1765	Rebekah (Haines) Ray	Married contrary to discipline
3 3 1766	Sarah Brittan (d. of Samuel)	
2 6 1766	Elizabeth Richardson	Married contrary to discipline
7 7 1766	Deborah Barrett	Dancing and denied the charge
5 9 1766	William Hiatt Jr. (Reinstated 2-4-1792)	Married contrary to discipline
6 10 1766	Mary Stonebridge (formerly Hancher)	Married contrary to discipline
6 10 1766	Rebecca (Hiatt) Edwards	Married by hireling teacher
3 11 1766	Thomas Butterfield	Married by hireling teacher
3 11 1766	Nathan Haworth and wife Hannah	Married by hireling teacher
1 12 1766	Stephen Harlin	Married contrary to discipline
2 2 1767	Morris Rees Jr.	Accusing a neighbor unjustly
2 3 1767	Stephen Ross	Struck a man in anger
6 6 1768	Catherine (Hiatt) Edwards	Married contrary to discipline
3 10 1768	Sarah (Jenkins) Gaddis	Married contrary to discipline
5 12 1768	Lott Ridgeway	Fighting and horse-racing
6 2 1769	William Hoge Jr.	

Day Mo. Yr.	Person Disowned	Reason for Disownment
5 6 1769	Enoch McKay	Attended a marriage accomplished contrary to discipline
2 10 1769	Robert McKay Jr.	Married contrary to discipline
5 2 1770	Phame Ogin (formerly Bevin)	Married contrary to discipline
5 2 1770	Ruth (Nevitt) Ellis	Married contrary to discipline
5 2 1770	Mary Brabson	Married contrary to discipline
2 4 1770	Isaac Brown	Married by hireling teacher
2 4 1770	John Thomas	Married contrary to discipline
7 5 1770	Robert Rees and wife Sudney Lewis	Married contrary to discipline
7 5 1770	John Thomas and wife Alyce Hyatt	Married by hireling teacher (Reinstated 5-5-1777)
2 7 1770	Anoch and Moses Job	Married by hireling teacher
2 7 1770	Margaret Corder	Joined Baptists
6 8 1770	John Hackney	Married first cousin; moved to Carolina without advice of Friends
3 9 1770	Leah Campbel and Lydia Allen	
3 9 1770	John Rees	Married contrary to discipline
3 9 1770	Isaac Painter and Hannah Wright	Married contrary to discipline (Reinstated 1-8-1785)
3 9 1770	Martha Sharp (formerly Wright)	Married contrary to discipline
5 11 1770	Philip Bab	Neglected meetings
3 12 1770	Evan Hiatt	Married contrary to discipline
4 2 1771	Sarah (McKay) Hums (Humes)	Married contrary to discipline
5 8 1771	Job McKay	Neglected meetings and attended wedding conducted by hireling teacher
4 11 1771	Isaac & Abraham McKay	Joined Baptists
2 12 1771	James Mendinhall (Reinstated 5-4-1773)	Married contrary to discipline
2 3 1772	John Jolliffe	Fighting and being at horseraces
2 3 1772	George Ross	Married contrary to discipline
6 7 1772	Ann Hogue	
3 8 1772	John Fawcett	Married first cousin contrary to discipline
3 8 1772	Thomas Fawcett	Married contrary to discipline

Day Mo. Yr.	Person Disowned	Reason for Disownment
7 12 1772	James McCool	Singing and dancing
4 1 1773	Isaac Taylor	Married contrary to discipline
4 1 1773	Thomas Branson (Reinstated 6-9-1779)	Neglected meetings
1 2 1773	John Vestal, wife, and d. Elizabeth Bealer	Neglected meetings and consented to their daughter's marriage in their home contrary to discipline
5 4 1773	Jesse McKay	
5 4 1773	Naomi Stratton (Reinstated 7-11-1785)	
5 7 1773	Ann (Thornburgh) Founds	
6 9 1773	William Vestal	Married first cousin contrary to discipline
4 10 1773	Mary Wood	
1 11 1773	George Hoge	
1 11 1773	Susannah Hayworth (formerly Dillon)	Married contrary to discipline
6 12 1773	Thomas Moore	
1 2 1774	John Barrett	
1 3 1774	Rachel White	
4 4 1774	Jonathan Wright	Gaming and dancing
4 4 1774	Ann Pennewite (formerly Moore)	Attended a marriage accomplished contrary to discipline
2 5 1774	Ruben Moore	Attended a marriage accomplished contrary to discipline
4 7 1774	James Holloway	Dancing
11 8 1774	Mary (Vestol) Blare	Married contrary to discipline
11 8 1774	Hannah (Rees) Rogers	Married contrary to discipline
5 9 1774	Edward Southwood	Married contrary to discipline
3 10 1774	Henry Adams	Married contrary to discipline
7 11 1774	Isaac Jackson	Married contrary to discipline
5 12 1774	Sarah Crumly (formerly Dun)	Married contrary to discipline
2 1 1775	Hannah McGille (formerly Haston)	Married contrary to discipline
6 3 1775	Jean Taylor	
6 3 1775	John Adams Jr.	Gaming and consenting to serve in the station of a soldier
6 3 1775	Mary (Smith) Cleavinger (Reinstated 4-10-1784)	Married contrary to discipline
1 5 1775	Joseph More & wife Mary	Married by hireling teacher

Day	Mo.	Yr.	Person Disowned	Reason for Disownment
5	6	1775	Ann Mongomary (formerly Bruce)	Married contrary to discipline
5	6	1775	Jean White	
5	6	1775	Phebe (Jolliffe) Yarnel (Reinstated 2-7-1787)	Married contrary to discipline
5	6	1775	Alice Pugh	Neglected meetings
7	8	1775	Reese Hastings	Married contrary to discipline
4	9	1775	Jeremiah Cooper	Married by hireling teacher
2	10	1775	Joseph Day	Dancing
2	10	1775	Thomas White & wife Mary	Married by hireling teacher
2	10	1775	Sarah Painter	Married contrary to discipline
6	11	1775	Solomon Reese & wife Ann	Married contrary to discipline
1	1	1776	Mary Pope (formerly Hiatt)	Joined Baptists
5	2	1776	Jeremiah McKay	Gone out in marriage with a woman not of our society
5	2	1776	Samuel Lewis	Married contrary to discipline
4	3	1776	Phebe Thomas	Married contrary to discipline
1	7	1776	Jeremiah Serjant	Training in the militia
5	8	1776	Mary Bennit	Married contrary to discipline
2	9	1776	Jean Jones (d. of Thomas Ellis)	Married contrary to discipline
2	9	1776	Ann Horner (Taylor)	Married contrary to discipline
2	12	1776	Thomas Painter	(Reinstated 1-9-1795)
2	12	1776	Martha Fawcett	

From Book 2

Day	Mo.	Yr.	Person Disowned	Reason for Disownment
3	3	1777	John Bevan	Enlisted in order for war
5	5	1777	Jonathan Jinkens	Acted in military service
2	6	1777	William Dun	Neglected attending meetings; married contrary to discipline
7	7	1777	Sarah (Conard) Butcher, d. of Jas. Conard of Fairfax	Married contrary to discipline
4	8	1777	William Hogue Jr.	Enlisted in military service
1	9	1777	Evan Rodgers Jr. and wife Sarah (Pugh)	Married contrary to discipline
6	10	1777	Mary (Draper) Aris	Married contrary to discipline
6	10	1777	Rachel Bruce	Neglected attending meetings; joined the Methodists

Day Mo. Yr.	Person Disowned	Reason for Disownment
3 11 1777	Alice Swango	Neglected attending the meetings
1 12 1777	Lidia (Pickering) Adams	Married contrary to discipline
6 1 1778	Abraham Taylor	Married contrary to discipline
6 1 1778	John Adams Sr.	Married contrary to discipline and connived his son's marriage by hireling teacher
6 1 1778	Samuel Wickersham (Reinstated 6-3-1780)	Married contrary to discipline
6 1 1778	Ann Smith McKay, d. of John Smith	Married contrary to discipline
6 1 1778	Carlile Hains	Married contrary to discipline
2 2 1778	Elizabeth Ruble	Neglected attending meetings and showed an unbecoming disposition in railing against Friends
2 2 1778	Rachel (McKay) Leath	Married contrary to discipline
6 4 1778	Martha (Bevan) Bonsil (Bonsell)	Married contrary to discipline (Reinstated 5-2-1787)
4 5 1778	Joseph Lacy	Neglected attending meetings
4 5 1778	Susannah (Hank) Bryan	Married contrary to discipline
4 5 1778	Eleanor Hank	
3 8 1778	James Connard Jr.	Married contrary to discipline
7 9 1778	Sarah Bull	Neglected attending meetings
7 9 1778	Ann (Dun) Handsher	Married contrary to discipline
5 10 1778	Joseph Moore	
7 12 1778	Isaac Hains	
7 6 1779	Ruth (Wright) Fenton (Reinstated 6-1-1783)	Married contrary to discipline
5 7 1779	John Vestal	Trained in militia service and hired a man as substitute to go in war
2 8 1779	Elizabeth (Hoge) Leonard	Married contrary to discipline
2 8 1779	Jacob Pickering & wife (Reinstated 3-1-1785)	
2 8 1779	John Milburn	Married first cousin contrary to discipline
2 8 1779	Jesse Faulkner Jr. (Reinstated 7-8-1786)	
2 8 1779	Dinah Ellis	
4 10 1779	Mary Babb & d. Phebe	Joined Methodists and turned their backs on Friends
1 11 1779	Margaret (Hank) Charrington	Married contrary to discipline

Day Mo. Yr.	Person Disowned	Reason for Disownment
1 11 1779	Seth Babb	Joined Methodists
6 12 1779	Moses McKay	Neglected meetings and trained in the militia
6 3 1780	Benjamin Shreeves (Reinstated 28-7-1785)	Hired a man to go into military service
6 3 1780	Margaret Jurey	Married contrary to discipline
1 5 1780	Mary Thatcher Sr.	
14 6 1780	Abram Thornbrough	Quarreling
14 6 1780	David Milburn	
7 7 1780	Thomas Moon	Married contrary to discipline
— — ——	Mary White (Reinstated 7-8-1780)	Married contrary to discipline
7 8 1780	Lidia Adams	
4 9 1780	Jonathan Bishop of Mt. Ponia (Pony)	Neglected meetings; took a fidelity test inconsistent with Friends' principles
4 9 1780	George Fallis	Took a fidelity test
4 9 1780	Ezekiel Hains	Took fidelity test and trained in militia
4 9 1780	Samuel Berry	
4 9 1780	Thomas Ellis	Fighting
2 10 1780	Hannah (Dillon) Wright	Married contrary to discipline
2 10 1780	Joseph Brown	Absence from meetings and the stilling of grain
5 11 1780	Mary (Bull) Merchant	Married contrary to discipline
5 3 1781	Edward White	
2 4 1781	Joseph Wood & wife Rachel (Lupton) (Reinstated 7-1-1799)	
2 7 1781	Mary (Hains) Collet (Reinstated 5-6-1797)	Married contrary to discipline
6 8 1781	Benjamin Thornburgh Jr.	Dancing
6 8 1781	Margaret Hank (widow)	Daughter married contrary to discipline in her home
3 9 1781	Joseph Adams (Reinstated 26-9-1796)	
3 9 1781	John Hancher	Fighting and neglect of meeting
3 9 1781	David Wright	Enlisted as a soldier in order for war
1 10 1781	John Rees Sr.	Neglected attending the meetings
7 1 1782	William Askew	Neglected attending the meetings; purchased two negroes

Day Mo. Yr.	Person Disowned	Reason for Disownment
1 4 1782	John Cook	Married contrary to discipline
1 4 1782	Elizabeth Moore	Frolicking and dancing
6 5 1782	Rachel (Payn) McCleary	Married contrary to discipline
1 7 1782	James Dunn	Neglected attending meetings; married contrary to discipline
1 7 1782	Benjamin Thornburgh	Not attending meeting
5 8 1782	Jane Brown	
2 9 1782	James Moore	Gave way to a spirit of passion so far as to kick at a man, likewise to aggravate him in discourse
2 9 1782	Stephen Brown	Neglected meetings; threatened to strike a man with a stick
2 9 1782	Jane (Ellis) Whitenot	Married contrary to discipline
7 10 1782	Mary (Adams) Hoge	Married contrary to discipline
4 11 1782	James Conard Sr.	Took a fidelity test and trained in militia
4 11 1782	Joel Thornburgh	
4 11 1782	John McGrew	Married contrary to discipline
4 11 1782	Ann (Pugh) Dillon (Reinstated 5-2-1798)	Married contrary to discipline
28 11 1782	David Horsman & wife Ruth (Wright) (Ruth reinstated 10-2-1814)	Married contrary to discipline
28 11 1782	Rachel (Rees) Edwards	Married by hireling teacher
6 1 1783	Thomas Rees	Married contrary to discipline
6 1 1783	Mary (Hoge) Phelty	Married contrary to discipline
6 1 1783	Ann (Jinkens) Gettas (Reinstated 6-8-1787)	Married contrary to discipline
6 1 1783	Sarah (Brown) Thomas	Married contrary to discipline
3 2 1783	Elisabeth Lewis	
3 3 1783	Martha Fawcett	
3 3 1783	Jonathan and Phebe (Barrett) Pickering (Reinstated 5-11-1787)	
4 8 1783	Daniel and Rachel (Pickett) Brock	Married contrary to discipline
1 9 1783	Elisabeth (Bishop) Magilton	Married contrary to discipline
3 11 1783	John Allen (s. of Joseph)	Took fidelity test; married contrary to discipline

Day Mo. Yr.	Person Disowned	Reason for Disownment
1 12 1783	Jacob Brock	Assisted his brother in marrying contrary to discipline
1 12 1783	Rachel (Crawford) Miller	Married contrary to discipline
1 12 1783	Sarah (Rees) McKurdy	Married contrary to discipline
5 1 1784	Isaac Todhunter (Reinstated 7-11-1796)	Married contrary to discipline
2 2 1784	William Wickersham	
2 2 1784	Henry Likens	Married contrary to discipline
3 5 1784	Lydia (Jolliffe) Bruce	Married contrary to discipline
3 6 1784	Rebekah (Shepherd) Allen	Married contrary to discipline
3 6 1784	Thomas Adamson	Married contrary to discipline
3 6 1784	Sarah (Adamson) Blackledge	Married contrary to discipline
3 6 1784	John Askew	Neglected meetings of Middle Creek
2 8 1784	Mary Moon	
2 8 1784	George Day	
6 9 1784	Amy (Gause) Jones (Reinstated 1-3-1802)	Married contrary to discipline
4 10 1784	Charles Gause (Reinstated 4-6-1798)	Reproachful conduct and went over the Allegheny Mts.
4 10 1784	Lydia Berry	
2 11 1784	Mary (Townsend) Death	Married contrary to discipline
2 11 1784	John Berry Jr.	Married contrary to discipline
2 12 1784	Job Bishop	Neglected attending meetings and changed his name to defraud his neighbors
7 2 1785	Robert Milburn	Married contrary to discipline
7 2 1785	Susannah Adams	
7 3 1785	Samuel Smith & wife Sarah (Bishop)	Married contrary to discipline (Samuel reinstated 7-7-1794)
7 3 1785	Morris Rees	Married contrary to discipline
7 3 1785	Eli Allen	Neglected meetings and married contrary to discipline
7 3 1785	Samuel Bavan	
4 4 1785	Mary (Wright) Adams (Reinstated 2-3-1795)	Married contrary to discipline
4 4 1785	Simon Moon	Married contrary to discipline
2 5 1785	Ephraim Crawford	Neglected meeting and struck a man
2 6 1785	Thomas Hattfield	Married contrary to discipline
2 6 1785	William Schooly	Hit a man

Day Mo. Yr.	Person Disowned	Reason for Disownment
2 6 1785	Lydia (Wickersham) Harman	Married contrary to discipline
1 8 1785	Morris Rees, son of John	Married contrary to discipline
3 10 1785	Thomas Babb	Neglected attending meetings and married contrary to discipline
3 10 1785	Thomas Bishop Jr.	Married contrary to discipline
1 11 1785	Evan Day	Frequented places of diversion and dancing
7 11 1785	Joseph Day Jr.	Frequented places of diversion and dancing
19 11 1785	Charity (Long) Hattfield	Married contrary to discipline
6 2 1786	William Littlejohn	Fighting and dancing
6 2 1786	James Crawford Jr.	Married contrary to discipline
6 3 1786	Jane Pugh	Singing and dancing
6 3 1786	Thomas Littlejohn	Dancing and fighting
1 6 1786	Samuel Lewis (Reinstated 3-8-1801)	Married contrary to discipline
3 7 1786	Mordecai Ellis	Attended a marriage accomplished contrary to discipline
3 7 1786	Sarah (Bull) Merchant	Married contrary to discipline
7 8 1786	Thomas Ellis	
4 9 1786	Hannah (Piggott) Miles	Married contrary to discipline
4 9 1786	Charity (Rees) Job	Married first cousin contrary to discipline
4 9 1786	David Vestal	Neglected attending meetings
2 10 1786	Deborah (Lee) White (Reinstated 7-7-1794)	Married contrary to discipline
2 10 1786	Sarah (Hastings) Ellis	Attended a marriage accomplished contrary to discipline and married contrary to discipline
6 11 1786	Aaron Berry	Married contrary to discipline
1 1 1787	Henry Lewis Jr. (Reinstated 3-9-1792)	
1 1 1787	Margaret Berry	
1 1 1787	Rachel (Brown) Berry	Married contrary to discipline
5 2 1787	Rowland Ellis (Reinstated 5-9-1791)	Neglected meetings and married contrary to discipline
5 2 1787	Ann Littlejohn	Dancing and speaking falsely
5 2 1787	Susannah (Hogge) Lewis, wife of Henry (Reinstated 3-9-1792)	Married contrary to discipline

Day	Mo.	Yr.	Person Disowned	Reason for Disownment
5	3	1787	Israel Hoge & wife Ruth (Jinkens)	Married contrary to discipline
2	4	1787	Abigail Rhoads	Joined Baptists
7	5	1787	Joseph Tucker	
7	5	1787	John Squib & wife Sarah (Payn)	Married contrary to discipline
2	7	1787	Seth Smith	Married contrary to discipline
1	10	1787	Martha Littlejohn	Attended a marriage accomplished contrary to discipline
5	12	1787	Lydia (Day) Lashell	Married contrary to discipline
5	12	1787	Joel Brown	Married contrary to discipline
3	3	1788	John Rogers	Married contrary to discipline
3	3	1788	Mary (Wickersham) Davis	Married by hireling teacher
3	3	1788	Jonathan Barnett	Married by hireling teacher
7	4	1788	Joseph Fisher	
5	5	1788	Jonathan Barrett & wife Rachel (George)	Married contrary to discipline (Jonathan reinstated 7-8-1797)
6	10	1788	Lydia Davis	Neglected meetings; attended a marriage accomplished contrary to discipline
6	10	1788	Margaret Rees	
1	12	1788	Mary (Long) Butterfield	Married contrary to discipline
5	1	1789	Thomas Butterfield	Married first cousin contrary to discipline; attended a marriage accomplished contrary to discipline
5	1	1789	Catharine (Lewis) Bogan	Married contrary to discipline
2	2	1789	Augustine Pasmore	Permitted fiddling and dancing in his house; moved away contrary to advice of Friends
2	3	1789	Patience Smith	
6	4	1789	Abner Bane & wife Rachel (Simons)	Married contrary to discipline
4	5	1789	Ruth (Cowgill) Grist	Married contrary to discipline
4	5	1789	Phebe (Thornburgh) Eaches (Reinstated 6-12-1790)	Married contrary to discipline
4	5	1789	James Butterfield	Fighting
6	7	1789	Jonathan Shinn	Married contrary to discipline
6	7	1789	Susannah (Ellis) Carter	Married contrary to discipline
3	8	1789	Rebecca (Rees) Chew	Married contrary to discipline
3	8	1789	Lydia Squib	Joined the Methodists
2	11	1789	Mary (Ridgway) Lee	Married contrary to discipline

Day Mo. Yr.	Person Disowned	Reason for Disownment
7 12 1789	Lydia (Barrett) Mercer	Married contrary to discipline
7 12 1789	Josiah Ridgway	Married contrary to discipline
1 2 1790	Ann (Moon) Wright	Married contrary to discipline
1 3 1790	Henry Clark	Joined the Methodists
5 4 1790	Hannah (Rees) Todhunter	Married contrary to discipline
3 5 1790	Joseph Waln (of Goshen, Pa.)	Married contrary to discipline
7 6 1790	Thomas Fisher (Reinstated 7-7-1806)	Married contrary to discipline
5 7 1790	James Wickersham	Dancing and neglecting meetings
5 7 1790	Mary Eyres	
6 12 1790	Sarah Pugh	
4 4 1791	Hannah (Faulkner) Griffith	Married contrary to discipline
5 9 1791	Mary (Picket) Melton	Married contrary to discipline
5 9 1791	Jacob Jinkens Jr.	

From Book 3

26 9 1791	Elizabeth (Ellis) Stinson	Married by hireling teacher
7 11 1791	Margaret (White) McCabe	Married by hireling teacher
2 1 1792	Elizabeth (Pickering) Deselm	Married by hireling teacher (Reinstated 4-11-1805)
— — ——	Mary Shin (Reinstated 6-2-1792)	
2 4 1792	Ann (McPherson) Moore	Married by hireling teacher
7 5 1792	James Clark	
4 6 1792	Stephen Brock	Attending singing school; married contrary to discipline
6 8 1792	Rachel (Jinkens) Manker	Married by hireling teacher
3 12 1792	John & Elizabeth Lewis	First cousins and married by hireling teacher
3 12 1792	Phebe (Ridgeway) Baley	Married by hireling teacher
7 1 1793	Jesse Beeson	Married by a hireling minister
7 1 1793	Samuel Littler	
4 2 1793	Phebe (Woodrow) Coleman	Married a man not in membership with Friends
4 2 1793	Charity Ridgway Jr.	
4 3 1793	Hannah (Eyre) Sanders	Married out of unity of Friends
1 4 1793	John Pyles	Fighting
3 6 1793	Nathan Brock	Fighting
3 6 1793	Josiah Wickersham	Striking in a quarrelsome way; married contrary to discipline

Day Mo. Yr.	Person Disowned	Reason for Disownment
1 7 1793	Joseph Pyle	Married contrary to discipline
5 8 1793	Deborah (Morgan) Lynn	Married by Methodist teacher contrary to discipline
5 8 1793	John Eyre	Married by hireling teacher
4 11 1793	Martha (Rees) Matlock	Married by hireling teacher
4 11 1793	Elizabeth (Walker) Babb	Married by hireling teacher
4 11 1793	Rebecca (Wickersham) McKee	Married by hireling teacher
2 12 1793	James Littlejohn	
3 2 1794	Jonathan Parkins Jr.	Neglected meetings
3 3 1794	Mishal Pugh	
7 4 1794	Mary (Brown) Ducker	Married by hireling teacher
7 4 1794	Rebecca (Wickersham) Dunn	Married by hireling minister
5 5 1794	Elizabeth (Fisher) Brownfield	Married by hireling minister
4 8 1794	Grace (Steer) Cope	Married contrary to discipline (Reinstated 6-8-1798)
4 8 1794	John & Eleanor (Ellis) Lee	First cousins once removed married contrary to discipline
29 9 1794	David Adams	Neglected meetings; married contrary to discipline
29 9 1794	Daniel & Lydia (Bull) Brown	Married contrary to discipline
1 12 1794	James Davis	Married out of unity of Friends
1 12 1794	Michael Shihon	Neglected attending the meetings
5 1 1795	Thomas Pugh	Neglected meeting and continued disputing with his neighbors
5 1 1795	Job Fallis	Neglected meetings
5 1 1795	Barak Fisher	Fighting, gaming, & attending a marriage consumated contrary to discipline
5 1 1795	James McCool	Attending places of diversion, gaming, & horse-racing
2 3 1795	Enoch Wickersham	Dancing and neglected meetings
6 4 1795	Rachel (Jordan) Yewen	Married by hireling teacher
6 4 1795	Jacob Shepherd	Enlisted in military service
6 4 1795	Sarah Clark	
6 4 1795	Moses Mercer	Not attending meetings
6 4 1795	James Pickering	
4 5 1795	Amos Jolliffe	Married by hireling teacher
4 5 1795	Nathan Barrett	Married by Methodist teacher

Day Mo. Yr.	Person Disowned	Reason for Disownment
6 7 1795	Benjamin Pugh	Married by Baptist teacher
1 9 1795	Joseph Barrett	Hired a substitute in military service
1 9 1795	Owen Rogers Jr.	Attending places of diversion
28 9 1795	Lewis Rees & Wife Salla (Ridgway)	Married by hireling teacher (Lewis reinstated 2-3-1801)
28 9 1795	Jane Ridgway	
28 9 1795	Rachel (Lewis) Eaton	Married contrary to discipline
7 12 1795	Elizabeth Nevitt	Neglected meetings and preached among other societies contrary to Friends' principles
4 1 1796	Thomas Butterfield	
7 3 1796	Hannah (Thornburgh) Griffith	Married by hireling teacher
7 3 1796	Timothy Brown	
7 3 1796	Joseph Miller	Married by hireling teacher
7 3 1796	William White	Married contrary to discipline
4 4 1796	Messer Sheppard	Neglected meetings
4 4 1796	Ann Fenton (formerly Jackson)	Married by hireling teacher (Reinstated 7-8-1823)
4 4 1796	Sarah (Hains) Howell	Married by hireling teacher
2 5 1796	Jobe Pugh	Neglected meetings
2 5 1796	William Adams	
4 7 1796	Thomas Gill	Neglect of meetings; attended muster; married by hireling teacher
4 7 1796	Jesse Pugh	Engaged in military service
26 9 1796	Martha (Hoge) Fisher	Married by hireling teacher
5 6 1797	Lydia Piggott	Married contrary to discipline
5 6 1797	Thomas Thatcher (Reinstated 7-6-1802)	Frolicking and dancing
5 6 1797	Hannah (Adams) Farmer	Married contrary to discipline
5 6 1797	Nathan Hayes	Neglected meetings and fighting
7 8 1797	Edward Beeson Jr.	Dancing
4 9 1797	Joseph Smith	
4 9 1797	Jonah Bull	Neglected meetings; attended muster; married by hireling teacher
6 11 1797	David Hayes	Struck a man in anger
6 11 1797	Elizabeth Brown (Reinstated 1-3-1802)	

Day	Mo.	Yr.	Person Disowned	Reason for Disownment
4	12	1797	Daniel McPherson	Married contrary to discipline
5	3	1798	Robert Rogers	
5	3	1798	Grace (McCool) Babb	Married contrary to discipline
2	7	1798	Sarah (Jenkins) Berry	Married by hireling teacher
2	7	1798	Elizabeth (Smith) Dalby	Married contrary to discipline
6	8	1798	John Clark & wife Sarah (Jacobs)	Married contrary to discipline
6	8	1798	Adam Grubb (Reinstated 7-6-1802)	Married contrary to discipline
3	9	1798	Joseph Davis	
3	9	1798	Enoch Smith	
3	9	1798	Sarah (Steer) Cope	Married contrary to discipline
1	10	1798	Joseph Farr	Married contrary to discipline
1	10	1798	Mary Farr (Reinstated 4-8-1814)	Married contrary to discipline
1	10	1798	Nathan Bull	Attended muster and married out
1	10	1798	Adam Eyre	Married contrary to discipline
5	11	1798	Benjamin Barrett	Fighting
5	11	1798	Jonathan Thatcher (Reinstated 3-7-1809)	Attended muster & shooting matches
3	12	1798	Elizabeth (Jolliffe) McAlister	Married contrary to discipline
7	1	1799	Mary Dillon	
4	2	1799	Abigail (Chamberlin) Farr	Married contrary to discipline
4	2	1799	Thomas Gauthrop	Married contrary to discipline
4	3	1799	William Pickering	Playing cards
4	3	1799	Hannah (Fisher) Farmer	Married contrary to discipline
1	4	1799	John Lewis	
1	4	1799	Mary (Jolliffe) Higgins	Married contrary to discipline
6	5	1799	Lydia (Cowgill) Patterson	Married contrary to discipline
5	8	1799	Rebekah (Fisher) Price	Married contrary to discipline
4	11	1799	Phebe (Mooney) Baldwin	Married contrary to discipline
4	11	1799	Rachel Ward	
3	2	1800	John Jinkens	Gambling
3	3	1800	Ann (McCool) Lewis	Married contrary to discipline
7	4	1800	Moses Harland	Preaching contrary to Friends
5	5	1800	Miriam Sheppards	Dancing
4	8	1800	Jane Conrad	
1	9	1800	Elizabeth (Wickersham) Binnegar	Married contrary to discipline
3	11	1800	Nathan Littler Jr.	Dancing and fighting

Day Mo. Yr.	Person Disowned	Reason for Disownment
1 12 1800	Enos & Sarah (Conard) Pickering	Married by hireling teacher (Sarah reinstated 10-4-1828) (Of Flushing, O.)
1 12 1800	Sarah (Fenton) Davis	Married contrary to discipline
1 12 1800	James Moon	Married contrary to discipline
1 6 1801	Jacob Taylor	
3 8 1801	Gabriel McCool	Fighting
3 8 1801	Joseph Morgan	
7 9 1801	John Wright	Fighting
7 9 1801	Catharine (Lewis) Farmer (Reinstated 1-6-1801)	Married contrary to discipline
5 10 1801	David Wright	Fighting
5 10 1801	Samuel Bond	
5 10 1801	James George (Reinstated 2-2-1807)	Married contrary to discipline
2 11 1801	Evan Jinkins	
2 11 1801	Philip Beale	
2 11 1801	Mary Wood Jr.	
2 11 1801	Rachel Adams	Married contrary to discipline
2 11 1801	Ann (Simmonds) Bennett	Married contrary to discipline
7 12 1801	Mary (Wichersham) Alloway	Married contrary to discipline
1 3 1802	George Payne	
1 3 1802	John Chamberlin	Married first cousin contrary to discipline
5 4 1802	John Griffith Jr. (Reinstated 4-2-1819)	
5 4 1802	Jacob Jinkens	
3 5 1802	David Rees Jr. (s. of David)	
7 6 1802	David Lewis	
7 6 1802	Elijah Chamberlin & wife Mary (McPherson)	Married contrary to discipline
5 7 1802	Samuel Quaintance	
5 7 1802	Catharine (Wickersham) Dunn	Married contrary to discipline
5 7 1802	John Clevenger	Married contrary to discipline
5 7 1802	Rebekah (Ellis) Daniel, New Hope, Tenn.	Married contrary to discipline
6 9 1802	Sarah (Ward) Barrett	Married contrary to discipline
6 9 1802	Jane (Jinkens) Ogen	Married contrary to discipline
6 9 1802	Sarah (Adams) File	Married contrary to discipline

HOPEWELL HISTORICAL MONUMENT
At Clearbrook

Day	Mo.	Yr.	Person Disowned	Reason for Disownment
4	10	1802	James Wright Sr.	
4	10	1802	Sidney (Rogers) Spencer	Married contrary to discipline
1	11	1802	Catharine (McCool) Darlington	Married contrary to discipline
3	1	1803	Curtis Grubb	Married contrary to discipline
7	2	1803	Agnes (Mendinhall) Nadenbousch	Married contrary to discipline
7	2	1803	Thomas Lee	Married contrary to discipline
7	2	1803	Mary Clark of Sadsbury M. M.	
7	3	1803	Mary (Lupton) Bower	Married contrary to discipline
7	3	1803	William Lupton (s. of Isaac)	Married contrary to discipline
7	3	1803	William Powell Simmonds	Married contrary to discipline
7	3	1803	Mary Ward	
4	4	1803	Margaret (Ellis) Baldwin	Married contrary to discipline
4	4	1803	Mary (Rees) Crumley	Married contrary to discipline
2	5	1803	Thomas Brown Jr.	Married contrary to discipline
6	6	1803	Henry Cowgill	Married contrary to discipline
6	6	1803	Samuel Jackson	
3	10	1803	Walter Denny	Neglected meeting and brought suit against a member
7	11	1803	Lydia Ridgway	
2	1	1804	Lewis McCool	Neglected meetings
2	1	1804	William Pickering (s. of Jacob)	Married out and attending muster
2	4	1804	Ann (McCool) Darlington (Reinstated 3-3-1806)	Married contrary to discipline
7	5	1804	John McBride	Attended muster and married contrary to discipline
2	7	1804	James Dillon	Fighting
3	9	1804	Jesse Clark	Married contrary to discipline
7	1	1805	Martha Thatcher	
4	2	1805	John Ward	Striking a man
4	3	1805	Micajah Beeson	
1	4	1805	Jacob Mendinhall	Married contrary to discipline
6	5	1805	William Grubb	Married contrary to discipline
3	6	1805	Arthur Barrett	
3	6	1805	Jonathan Wickersham & Jane Beeson	Married contrary to discipline
3	6	1805	Jane Denny	Neglect of meeting

Day Mo. Yr.	Person Disowned	Reason for Disownment
7 10 1805	Lydia (Dillon) Babb	Married contrary to discipline
2 12 1805	Mary (Downing) Boak	Married contrary to discipline
2 12 1805	John Gawthrop	
3 2 1806	James Gawthrop	Fighting
2 6 1806	John Grubb	Married contrary to discipline
4 8 1806	Jesse Faulkner (Reinstated 7-12-1826)	Altered a note and left the state in an armed manner
6 10 1806	Sarah (Ellis) Williams	Married former husband's half-uncle
6 10 1806	Levi Holloway	
6 10 1806	Phebe (Adams) Bonsell	Married contrary to discipline
2 2 1807	Dan Rees	Married contrary to discipline
2 2 1807	David Littler	Married contrary to discipline
2 2 1807	James Hackney	Married contrary to discipline
2 3 1807	David Rees (s. of Morris)	Married contrary to discipline
2 3 1807	Edith (Gawthrop) Taylor	Married contrary to discipline
2 3 1807	John Pickering (s. of Jane)	
6 4 1807	Nathan Wood	Attended a marriage accomplished contrary to discipline
6 4 1807	Martha Morgan	Encouraged gambling by lending money (Reinstated 4-1-1821)
1 6 1807	Leah (Rees) Moon	Married contrary to discipline
6 7 1807	Mary Selster	Joined the Methodists
6 7 1807	Margaret ONeill	Joined the Methodists
6 8 1807	Rachel (Ray) Ode	Married contrary to discipline
5 10 1807	Moses McKay	
2 11 1807	Sarah (Nevitt) Jones	Married contrary to discipline
7 12 1807	Phebe (Wright) Bonecutter & Eleanor (McCool) Mc-Curty	Both married contrary to discipline
4 1 1808	Hannah Conrad	
4 1 1808	Margaret ONeill	Joined Methodists
4 1 1808	Isaac Brown Jr.	Fighting
1 2 1808	John Downing and Abigail (White)	Married contrary to discipline
1 2 1808	Samuel Haines	Attending muster
1 2 1808	Jesse Haines	Attending muster
4 4 1808	John ONeill	
6 6 1808	Elizabeth (Lewis) Loy	Married contrary to discipline
6 6 1808	Jacob McKay	

Day Mo. Yr.	Person Disowned	Reason for Disownment
5 9 1808	Micajah Beeson	
5 9 1808	Hannah (Ward) McBride	Married contrary to discipline
5 9 1808	Jonathan McClun	Married contrary to discipline
3 10 1808	John McCool Sr.	Administering oaths
3 10 1808	Joel Ward	Married contrary to discipline
3 10 1808	Sarah Starr	Married contrary to discipline
7 11 1808	Thomas Smith	Held slaves
5 12 1808	Joseph Thomas	Married contrary to discipline
2 1 1809	Thomas Adams	
2 1 1809	Jacob Jenkins	Training in militia
6 2 1809	Isaac Davis	Married contrary to discipline
6 2 1809	Samuel Wickersham	
3 4 1809	Samuel Walton	Accepted an office in military service, purchased a slave, and administered oaths
7 8 1809	Isaac Adams	
7 8 1809	Robert Branson	Training in militia
7 8 1809	John Barrett	
4 9 1809	John McCool Jr.	Fighting and neglecting meetings
4 9 1809	Robert Painter	Attending a wedding accomplished contrary to discipline
4 9 1809	George Redd	Attending a wedding accomplished contrary to discipline
2 10 1809	Abraham Sinclair	Married contrary to discipline
6 11 1809	Jesse McKay	Neglected meetings and attended a wedding accomplished contrary to discipline
4 12 1809	Samuel Mendinhall	Married contrary to discipline
5 2 1810	Hannah, Elizabeth, Mary, and Phebe Mendinhall	Joined the Methodists
5 3 1810	Amos Mendinhall	Joined the Methodists
2 4 1810	Francis Shinn and Mary	Married contrary to discipline
7 5 1810	Phebe (Downing) Sharp	Married contrary to discipline
4 6 1810	Ellis Rees	
4 6 1810	Betty Mendinhall & d. Edith	Joined the Methodists
6 8 1810	Anna (Allen) Hawkins	Married contrary to discipline
3 12 1810	David Shinn Jr.	Married first cousin contrary to discipline
7 3 1811	Elijah Fawcett	Married contrary to discipline
7 3 1811	Rhoda Rogers	

From Book 4

Day Mo. Yr.	Person Disowned	Reason for Disownment
9 5 1811	Elizabeth (Mooney) Mendinhall	Married contrary to discipline
4 7 1811	Phebe Fawcett (formerly Holliway)	Married contrary to discipline (Reinstated 7-7-1825) (Of Center, Ohio)
8 8 1811	Lydia Humes (formerly Ross)	Married contrary to discipline
8 8 1811	Edith Lupton	
5 9 1811	Rachel Inskip	Joined the Methodists
7 10 1811	Mercy Lyles (formerly Horsman)	Married contrary to discipline
7 11 1811	David Barrett	Neglected paying of debts
7 11 1811	Jonas Chamberlin	Married contrary to discipline and moved away
5 12 1811	Mary Larry (formerly Dutton)	Married contrary to discipline
9 1 1812	William Neill	Married by hireling teacher
9 1 1812	Aquilla Coates	(Reinstated 5-9-1822) (Now at Uchland)
6 2 1812	Joel Rees	Attending muster and fighting
6 2 1812	Samuel Allen	
6 2 1812	Lydia Horsman (formerly Lupton)	Married contrary to discipline
6 2 1812	Olivia Wever (formerly McCool)	Married contrary to discipline
5 3 1812	William Adams	Trained in militia
5 3 1812	Ellis Pugh	Married contrary to discipline
5 3 1812	Joseph Horsman	Married contrary to discipline
5 3 1812	Stephen Brock	
5 3 1812	William Horsman	Married first cousin contrary to discipline
5 3 1812	Isaac Lupton	
5 3 1812	Ann Stroud	Joined the Methodists
9 4 1812	Enos Ross	
9 4 1812	Joshua Miller	Married contrary to discipline
14 5 1812	Mary Paton (formerly Morgan)	Married contrary to discipline (Reinstated 5-11-1818)
4 6 1812	Isaac Wickersham	Training in militia
4 6 1812	Lydia Antram	Testimony signed against and was reported to Women's Meeting

Day Mo. Yr.	Person Disowned	Reason for Disownment
4 6 1812	Samuel Hollingsworth	Married contrary to discipline
4 6 1812	Hannah Hansell (formerly Adams)	Married contrary to discipline
6 8 1812	Samuel Hurford	Married contrary to discipline, now living at Redstone
10 12 1812	Rachel Davis (formerly Gawthrop)	Married contrary to discipline
7 1 1813	Hannah Thornburg (formerly Lloyd)	Married contrary to discipline
7 1 1813	Martha Weaver (formerly McCool)	Married contrary to discipline
6 5 1813	Mercy Pickering (formerly Lupton)	Married contrary to discipline (Reinstated 7-11-1816)
10 6 1813	Benjamin Pickering (Reinstated 7-11-1816)	Married contrary to discipline
5 8 1813	John Painter	Training in militia
9 9 1813	Isaac Allen	Married contrary to discipline at Short Creek
9 9 1813	Phebe White (an elder)	Neglected meetings
4 10 1813	James Beeson	Neglected meetings; married contrary to discipline
4 10 1813	John Smith	Neglected meetings & failed to pay debts
4 10 1813	Abraham Neil	Married contrary to discipline
9 12 1813	Esther Busby (formerly Shin)	Married contrary to discipline
5 5 1814	Nathan Haines (s. of Robert)	Married contrary to discipline & trained in militia
5 5 1814	Jane Bruce (formerly McPherson)	Married contrary to discipline
9 6 1814	William Beall Jr.	Trained in the militia
7 7 1814	Rachel Haines (formerly McKay)	Married contrary to discipline
4 8 1814	Isaac Fawcett	Neglected meetings; trained in the militia; and married contrary to discipline
4 8 1814	David Fawcett	Neglected meetings & married contrary to discipline
4 8 1814	Mary Rees (formerly Shinn)	Married contrary to discipline and moved away
8 9 1814	Nathan Fawcett	Neglected meetings & married contrary to discipline

Day	Mo.	Yr.	Person Disowned	Reason for Disownment
8	9	1814	Miriam Devo (formerly Redd)	Married contrary to discipline
8	9	1814	Elizabeth Van Horn (formerly Holliway)	Married contrary to discipline
3	10	1814	Samuel Shinn	Trained in militia & married contrary to discipline
10	11	1814	Robert Fisher	Fighting
5	1	1815	David Lupton (son of Asa)	
6	4	1815	Jesse Fawcett	Attended a marriage accomplished contrary to discipline
8	6	1815	Sarah, Elizabeth, and Susannah Fawcett	Attended a marriage accomplished contrary to discipline
8	6	1815	Eliza Cowgill (formerly Coates)	Married contrary to discipline (Reinstated 10-8-1820)
8	6	1815	Joshua Pickering	Trained in militia & married contrary to discipline
8	6	1815	Sidney Mercer (formerly Wright)	Married contrary to discipline
6	7	1815	Hannah Probasco (formerly Wood)	Married contrary to discipline
6	7	1815	Hannah Lupton	
6	7	1815	Mary Craighill (formerly Griffith)	Married contrary to discipline
10	8	1815	John Antram	Hauled baggage in military service
7	9	1815	Elizabeth McKay	Joined the Baptists
9	11	1815	Nathan, George, and Jesse Holliway	Training in the militia—Nathan and George marrying contrary to discipline
7	12	1815	Mary Chamberlin (formerly Miller)	Married first cousin contrary to discipline
8	2	1816	Philadelphia Fawcett (formerly Holliway)	Married contrary to discipline
8	2	1816	Tacy Zigler (formerly Holliway)	Married contrary to discipline
4	4	1816	Robert McKay	Trained in the militia
4	4	1816	Barak Fisher	Hired a substitute in militia
8	8	1816	Joshua Pickering	
7	10	1816	Rebekah Yonley (formerly Lupton)	Married contrary to discipline
6	2	1817	Isaac Hurford	Neglected meetings; married contrary to discipline; and trained in militia

Day	Mo.	Yr.	Person Disowned	Reason for Disownment
6	2	1817	Mary Mason	Married contrary to discipline
7	8	1817	Isaac Wood	Married contrary to discipline
8	1	1818	John Fawcett	Married contrary to discipline
9	4	1818	Mary Cloud (formerly Smith)	Married contrary to discipline
9	7	1818	William Griffith	Joined the Methodists
4	2	1819	George Hiatt (s. of John)	Married contrary to discipline
6	5	1819	William Pidgeon	Married contrary to discipline & lives at South River
5	8	1819	Lydia Brown (formerly Fawcett)	Married contrary to discipline
9	12	1819	Rhesa Allen	Married contrary to discipline
6	4	1820	Susanna Glass	
7	9	1820	Richard Beason	Married contrary to discipline
7	9	1820	Ellis Lupton (of Back Creek)	Married contrary to discipline
9	11	1820	John White (of Middle Creek)	Joined the Methodists
8	2	1821	William Wood	Married contrary to discipline
8	2	1821	Hannah Kress (formerly Wright)	Married contrary to discipline
5	4	1821	Lydia Shinn	Married contrary to discipline
7	6	1821	Hannah White	Joined the Methodists
9	8	1821	Atlantic Ocean Miller (formerly Walton)	Married contrary to discipline
8	11	1821	John Haines	Married first cousin contrary to discipline
8	11	1821	Levi Shepherd	Married contrary to discipline
10	1	1822	Jesse Lupton Jr.	Married contrary to discipline
4	4	1822	Martha Shanks (formerly Cleaver)	Married contrary to discipline
9	5	1822	Lydia Tanquary (formerly Hackney)	Married contrary to discipline
6	6	1822	Ann Clendenning (formerly Wright)	Married contrary to discipline
8	8	1822	James Wright	Married contrary to discipline
5	9	1822	Thomas Fisher Jr. (from Back Creek)	Trained in the militia
5	9	1822	Susanna Cowarden (formerly Dutton)	Married contrary to discipline
10	10	1822	Nathan Wright	Married contrary to discipline
7	11	1822	Joseph Lukens	Married contrary to discipline
7	11	1822	Jonah Lupton Sr. (of Centre Meeting)	Married contrary to discipline

Day Mo. Yr.	Person Disowned	Reason for Disownment
5 12 1822	Rachel Shull (formerly Lukens)	Married contrary to discipline
5 12 1822	Hannah Dirk (formerly Pickering)	Married contrary to discipline
6 2 1823	John Rogers (of Back Creek)	
6 3 1823	Sarah Lupton (d. of Jesse)	Married contrary to discipline
8 5 1823	Jonathan Barrett	Attended a marriage accomplished contrary to discipline
7 8 1823	Ellis George	Married first cousin; lives at Fall Creek
7 8 1823	William Branson	Married contrary to discipline
4 12 1823	Samuel Downing	
10 6 1824	Lewis George	Married contrary to discipline
4 11 1824	Isaac Pidgeon Jr.	Married contrary to discipline; lives near Stilwater M. M., Ohio
6 1 1825	Hannah Thatcher (wife of Mark)	Joined the Methodists
10 2 1825	David Barret (Back Creek Meeting)	Training in militia
10 2 1825	Mark Thatcher	Training in militia and joined the Methodists.
5 5 1825	Silas George	Married contrary to discipline
9 6 1825	Hannah Rogers	
8 9 1825	William Dunn	Married contrary to discipline
6 10 1825	James Antrim	Married contrary to discipline
6 10 1825	John Adams	Moved away without settling his business affairs; lives at Centre, O.
6 10 1825	Jane Smith (formerly Rees)	Married contrary to discipline
5 1 1826	John G. Wood	Married contrary to discipline
9 2 1826	Julian Beeson (formerly Ridgway)	Married first cousin contrary to discipline
8 6 1826	Solomon Adams	Discontinued as a member by request
8 6 1826	Rhoda Shivers (formerly Barrett)	Married contrary to discipline
8 6 1826	Amy Griffith	Joined the Methodists
7 12 1826	William Haines	Joined the Methodists
7 6 1827	Jesse Lukens	Married contrary to discipline
6 9 1827	Bulah Lukens (formerly Painter)	Married contrary to discipline
8 11 1827	Elias Fisher	Married contrary to discipline & trained in the militia

Day Mo. Yr.	*Person Disowned*	*Reason for Disownment*
6 12 1827	Anthony Lee Jr.	Married contrary to discipline
8 5 1828	Sarah McCloy (formerly Hiatt)	Married contrary to discipline
5 6 1828	Samuel Haines	Joined the Methodists
5 6 1828	Eliza Babb	Joined the Methodists
9 10 1828	Juliet Beeson	
8 1 1829	Tacy Pope (formerly Ridgway)	Married contrary to discipline
5 3 1829	Susan Riding (formerly Painter)	Married contrary to discipline
7 5 1829	Mary Stone (formerly Pidgeon)	Married contrary to discipline
5 11 1829	Joseph W. Hackney	Married contrary to discipline
5 11 1829	Jonah Lupton (s. of Jesse)	Married first cousin contrary to discipline
5 11 1829	Deborah Hackney (formerly Morgan)	Married contrary to discipline
5 11 1829	Mariah Lupton (formerly George)	Married contrary to discipline
5 11 1829	Phebe Morgan (formerly Rees)	Married contrary to discipline
10 12 1829	Elenor Honacre (formerly Baniett)	Married contrary to discipline

The following persons were under dealing by Hopewell Meeting, but the minutes do not record how the cases were closed.

Nathan Rock	Ruth Faulkner	George Rubble
Lydia Rees	Enos Ellis	George Matloch
Thomas Loyd	Mordecai Ellis	Sarah Ellis
Jacob Branson	Mary Stean	Joseph Bonsel
John Lewis	Elizabeth Lewis Jenkins	

Evan Rees to be disowned.

Oddy and Jonathan Brock request certificates from Hopewell to Westland, 1-9-1795, but minutes for 11 month 1795 are missing and no further mention of them is seen.

Gideon Goodwin, from Uchlan Monthly Meeting, without a certificate.

Joseph Smith, Lydia his wife, and 7 children, Mordecai, Samuel, Elizabeth, Mary, Rebekah, William, and Edmund, desire to go to Miami, Ohio.

Thomas Halloway, married; is within the limits of Fairfax.

William Wickersham, attended muster.

Samuel Smith; date near 4-3-1793.

Isaac Woodrow left under care of committee 3-10-1808.

Jonathan Ross, at Alexandria; a certificate to be sent him. Date 3-10-1808.

Most of the foregoing items are from Hopewell Book 3, which covers the period 1791-1811.

REINSTATEMENTS
FROM BOOK FOUR

Day	Mo.	Yr.	Name
7	4	1814	Ann Antram
6	10	1817	Samuel Rees (now in Cincinnati, Ohio)
9	3	1820	Elizabeth Mahony
10	8	1820	Eliza Cowgill
10	8	1820	Mary Thompson
8	11	1821	Mary Steele
5	9	1822	Martha Murphy (now at Center)
5	2	1824	Mary Conoway (formerly Haines)
5	1	1826	Sarah McCardy—of Flushing M. M., Ohio
5	7	1827	Phebe Crispin (formerly Bonsell)—Lee's Creek, Ohio

(Cannot find where these were disowned or when)

FRIENDS UNDER CARE

Members of the several preparative meetings comprising
Hopewell Monthly Meeting

From records in Hopewell Books 3 and 4
(These gave satisfaction)

Day	Mo.	Year	Name
6	6	1796	James Coonrad (Attended wedding)
2	3	1801	Lewis Rees (Married contrary to discipline)
5	11	1804	Israel Jenkins
7	8	1809	Elizabeth McKay (Married contrary)
9	5	1811	Mary Sample
5	12	1811	Hannah McCarta (Married contrary)
4	6	1812	James McCool
10	9	1812	Isaac Nevitt (Strong Drink)
5	10	1812	Ebenezer Williams (Strong Drink)
7	1	1813	Joshua Cope
10	7	1817	Edith Adams
6	11	1817	Elizabeth (Lupton) Carter
5	8	1819	Rebekah (White) McDonald
9	12	1819	Jonathan Pickering Jr. (Married contrary)
8	6	1820	Jane Keefers
10	8	1820	Jonathan Barrett
7	2	1822	Joel and Mary Brown (Married contrary)
5	9	1822	Hannah (Thatcher) Wood
7	1	1823	Richard Lupton
7	8	1823	Rebecca (Rees) Simmonds
7	8	1823	William Brown
4	9	1823	Daniel Haines
5	2	1824	David Pickering
7	10	1824	Rachel (Adams) Hensell
6	1	1825	Richard Ridgway
5	1	1826	Elizabeth Himmelright
8	2	1827	James Allen
7	2	1828	Thomas White
7	8	1828	John Lupton
8	1	1829	Sarah (Lupton) Smith
8	1	1829	Sarah (Howell) Brown
5	11	1829	Israel Hoge

From records in Hopewell Book 3, but incomplete
(In these cases results not known)

Day	Mo.	Year	Name
5	1	1795	Jonathan Ross, wife & ch., Stephen, Phebe, David, Jonathan, Lydia, Ann, Martha, Levi, Rachel. Ask for certificate to Crooked Run.
1	9	1795	Mary (Hoge) Buckles. Went to Westland.
1	9	1795	Jonathan Ross, w. Martha, & 9 ch. Ask for certificate to Crooked Run.
?8	9	1795	Evan Rees (son of Thos.). Testimony against approved & signed.
28	9	1795	John Lewis (son of Sam'l). Certificate to Westland requested.
28	9	1795	Seth Smith. Paper from Seth Smith condemning his misconduct; also a recommendation from New Hope Prep. Mtg., which was read & rec'd for satisfaction.
28	9	1795	Rachel (Gordon) Ewen. Went over the Alleghanies to go to Ky.
4	1	1796	John Oldham. Married out—testimony against signed & approved; disowned.
4	1	1796	Amos Thornburg. Going to appeal—committee to report when ready.
4	7	1796	Jas. Gauthrop. Appealed; part of record missing.
1	8	1796	Peter Cleaver. Requests certificate to Crooked Run.
1	8	1796	Wm. Brown (son of Timothy). Requests certificate to Crooked Run.
2	1	1797	Job Jeffries, w. Rebecca, & ch. Darlington. Certificate to Redstone requested.
6	2	1797	Thos. Gauthrop. Hit a man—drinking—gave satisfaction.
7	8	1797	Beulah Ridgway. Testimony against signed & approved.
4	9	1797	Elizabeth (Ward) Butler. Married out—testimony against signed.
4	2	1799	Ruth Smith. Requests certificate to Fairfax.
4	2	1799	Wm. Barrett. Of Fairfield Mo. Mtg.—joined the Baptists—testimony against him signed.
6	10	1806	Susanna Faulkner. Asks for certificate to Miami—she is not found after this date.
6	10	1806	Eleanor Barrett. Same as Susanna Faulkner.
6	10	1806	Ch. of Philip Babb, Philip, Stephen, Mary, Eliz'h, Tamar. To be joined to New Garden Mo. Mtg., N. C.
2	1	1809	Sarah Russell. Asks to be reinstated.
3	4	1809	Martha Sheppard. Testimony signed against her & referred back to Women's Mtg.
1	5	1809	Patience Haines. Attended a marriage accomplished by a hireling teacher—testimony signed against her & referred back to Women's Mtg.

Day	Mo.	Year	Name
3	7	1809	Rachel (Redd) Painter. Married out—testimony signed against & referred back to Women's Mtg.
3	7	1809	Margaret (Jackson) Robinson. Testimony signed against & referred back to Women's Mtg.
2	10	1809	Elizabeth Mendinhall. Married contrary to discipline—at liberty to appeal & referred to Women's Mtg.
4	12	1809	Abigail (Painter) Tanquiry. Married—a testimony signed against & referred back to Women's Mtg.
4	12	1809	Sarah Downing. Testimony signed against & referred back to Women's Mtg.
4	12	1809	Isaac Redd. Cannot find what he did or what happened to him.
4	12	1809	Sam'l Shinn. Neglected meetings & trained in militia.
1	1	1810	Sarah Russell. Requests not granted.
5	2	1810	A marriage to first wife's first-cousin is considered not according to discipline; taken to meeting for discussion.
5	2	1810	Sarah (Pickering) Taylor. Married contrary to discipline—testimony signed against & referred to Women's Mtg.
5	3	1810	Mary (Wood) Vass. Testimony signed against her & referred to Women's Mtg.
5	3	1810	Ann Mendinhall. Testimony signed against her & referred to Women's Mtg.
2	7	1810	Esther (Mooney) Hough. Married contrary to discipline—testimony signed against & referred to Women's Mtg.
3	11	1810	Rees Branson, w. Ruth, & ch., Abraham & Mariah. Certificate to go to Plainfield Mo. Mtg. in Ohio, but decided not to go.
3	11	1810	Mary (Shinn) Dolby. Married contrary to discipline—testimony against & referred to Women's Mtg.
3	11	1810	Robt. Haines. Declined appealing—living at Miami.
3	11	1810	David Barrett. Continued into Book 4.
3	11	1810	Sam'l Rees. Testimony signed against—committee to report when ready.
3	11	1810	John Wright (son of John). Married & went to Miami.
3	11	1810	Nathan Conard. Of Fairfax Mo. Mtg.
3	11	1810	Mordecai Taylor. Moved to Chester—married.
3	11	1810	Miller Spencer. To join.
3	11	1810	Jonas McPherson. Business relations.
3	11	1810	Mary Milton. Goose Creek—married out.
3	11	1810	John Parkins, son of Jonathan & Jane. Married out—gone to Concord, O.; service not performed.
7	3	1811	Sol. Hollingsworth & w. Sarah. Married contrary to discipline; appealed; accepted.
7	3	1811	Francis Shinn. Certificate returned from Fairfax Mo. Mtg.
7	3	1812	Amos Haines. Asks for a certificate to Miami.
7	3	1812	Ann Haines. Received a certificate to Miami.

ELDERS AND MINISTERS

Robert Haines, for Crooked Run
Abel Walker, for Hopewell
Martha Rees, for Hopewell
Rachel Hollingsworth, for Center
Mary Ellis, for Hopewell
Esther Hains, minister, for Crooked
    Run
Eunice Walton, for Crooked Run
Charity Ridgway
James Mendinghall, for Middle Cr.
Anthony Lee, for Hopewell
James Mendinghall—minister
Jonathan Wright—minister
Sarah Brown—minister
Joseph Hackney and w. Martha
Jane Brock—minister
Abraham Branson
Sarah Lupton—elder
Jane Beeson—elder
James Mendinghall—minister
James Steer—elder
Rachel Neill—minister
Martha Mendinghall—minister,
    dec'd (a Memorial to be prepared)
Phebe Steer, elder, w. of Isaac
Isaac Smith—minister
Hannah Wright—elder
Edward Walker—elder
Sarah Neill—elder
Sarah Pickering, for Back Cr. (4-8-
    1760)
Richard Ridgway, for Hopewell
Abigail Steer, for Hopewell
Mordecai Ellis, for Hopewell
Enoch Ellis—minister
Joseph Allen, for Smith Cr.

Margaret Ridgeway
William Wilson, for Westland
Ellis Ellis, for Middle Cr.
Jacob McKay, for Hopewell
Mordecai Walker—minister
Ann Pugh—minister
William Wilson of Westland—elder
Hannah Pickering—minister
Edward Beeson
John McPherson—elder
Evan Hyatt—minister
Mordecai Walker—minister
Stephen McBride—elder of Back Cr.
Abram Branson—minister
Isaac Steer—elder
Sarah Brown—minister
Hannah McPherson—elder
Richard George—elder
Rebeckah Neill—elder
John McPherson
John Lee
Hannah Coats
Joshua Johnson
Ann Schofield
Margaret Swayne
Isaac Pidgeon
Mary George
Aaron Hibbert
Abraham Branson
Phebe Coburn
Sarah Branson
Martha Hibbert
Casandra Brown
Phebe White—minister from Back
    Cr.

CLERKS

The clerk was chairman of the business meeting, and wrote a minute of each item as it was being considered. The minute was then read by the clerk, approved, disapproved, or amended before the next item of business was taken up. At the next business meeting all the minutes of the preceding meeting were read, but for information only—they were not changed, though this meeting or a subsequent one might take different action.

Jesse Pugh
William Jolliffe
Robert Haines
Benjamin Thornburg
William Pickering
James Steer
Jonathan Lupton
Amos Hough

Jona Lupton
Nathaniel White Jr.
David Lupton
Joseph Steer
Goldsmith Chandlee
James Mendinghall
John McPherson
Lewis Walker

Joshua Lupton
Samuel Brown
William Jolliffe
Thomas Wright
Joseph Branson
Robert Bond
Amos Wright

12

CLERKS FOR WOMEN'S MEETING

Sarah Pickering
Ruth Jackson
Martha Dingee
Phebe White

Phebe Steer
Mary Rees
Mary Walker
Mary Wilson

Sinah Townsend
Ann Schofield
Rebekah Jolliffe

RECORDERS

The recorders entered into books provided for the purpose all births, marriages, accessions, removals, deaths, and burials.

Michael Shihon

James Mendinghall

Amos Jolliffe (certificates of removal)

David Lupton

Joseph Neill (certificate of marriages, births, and burials)

Joseph Rees (certificates of removal)

David Ridgway (certificates of removal)

Richard Wright (certificates of marriages, births, and burials) (in the place of Jos. Neill, dec'd)

Jonah Lupton (certificates of marriages, births, and deaths) (in the place of Richard Wright)

Lewis Lupton (certificates of removal)

Joseph G. Smith (certificates of births and burials)

TREASURERS

John Rees
Joseph Lupton

Joseph Branson
David Ridgway

OVERSEERS

1759-1851

Jonathan Parkins
Thomas Rees
John Painter
John Ridgway Sr.
Job Hastings, for Tuscarorah
Samuel Thatcher, for Tuscarorah
Evans Rodgers
Mordecai Walker
Rees Cadwallader
Rees Cadwallader, for Fawcett's Mtg.
George Fallice, for Stafford
Joseph Hackney, for Hopewell
Joseph Steer Jr., for Centre
William Wilson, for Monongahela
  River Mtg.
Jonathan Lupton, for Mt. Pleasant
John Brock, for Back Cr.
David Berry, for Back Cr.
Joseph Hackney
William McPherson, for Bullskin
Richard Barrett
Isaac Steer, for Hopewell
John Lupton
Richard Ridgway
John Painter Jr.
Samuel Pickering
Thomas McClun
Daniel Antram of Stafford
Abel Walker
Robert Ray, for Crkd. Run
Jackson Allen, for Smith Cr.
Levi Haines, for Crkd. Run
John Brock, for Stafford
Jacob Pickering, for Hopewell
John Jenkinson, for Monongahela
  River Mtg.
William Grub, for Hopewell
Jacob Ong, for Middle Cr.
William Wilson
David Ross

Evans Rodgers, for Back Cr.
David Shinn, for Hopewell
Joseph Bond, for Hopewell
John Branson, for Crkd. Run
Jacob McKay, for Crkd. Run
John Rees
Joseph Lupton
Josiah Jackson, for Back Cr.
James Steer
Anthony Lee, for Middle Cr.
Josiah Jackson, for "Senter"
James Steer, for Hopewell
Lewis Walker, for Middle Cr.
Isaac Parkins, for "Senter"
Edward Bond, for Smith Cr.
Josiah Rogers, for Back Cr.
Owen Rogers, for Bare (Bear) Garden
Lewis Walker, for Hopewell
John Cuzens
William Lupton
Stephen McBride
Josiah Jackson, for Hopewell
Enoch Ellis, for Middle Cr.
Lewis Walker, for Hopewell
Nathan Littler
John Fenton, for Back Cr.
Joseph Steer, for Ridge Mtg.
William McPherson, for Berkeley
John Wright
Jonathan Pickering, for Back Cr.
Richard George
Samuel Swayne
Samuel Brown
Joshua Fawcett
Nathan Haines
James Raley
William Hiett, for Hopewell
Samuel Lupton
Joseph Grubb, for Middle Cr.

Aaron Hibbert, for Middle Cr.
Charles Dingee, for Hopewell
David Barrett
Joshua Johnson
Elishia Fawcett
Anthony Lee
William Downing, for Middle Cr.
Richard Barrett, for Hopewell
Richard George, for Back Cr.

Joseph Bond, for Berkeley
Robert Coburn
Edward Walker
William Brown (son of Thos.)
John Griffith
John Bond
Mordecai Taylor
Isaac Smith Jr.

16

OVERSEERS FOR THE POOR

1759-1851

James Gawthrop
Thomas Wilson
Samuel Lupton
Levi Smith

Aaron Gregg (Meeting to furnish
20 pounds for one year to his under direction)
John Jolliffe Jr.

17

TRUSTEES

1759-1851

Abel Walker
Amos Jolliffe
John Bond, for Upper Ridge
David Lupton Jr., for Upper Ridge
Goldsmith Chandlee, for Biargarden
(Bear Garden)
Jonathan Wright, for Biargarden
(Bear Garden)

Edward Walker, for Biergarden
(Bear Garden)
Jonathan Pickering, for Back Cr.
Jonathan Barrett Jr., for Lower Ridge
Joseph Hackney, has care of Hope-
well Grave-Yard

COMMITTEE MEMBERS
In Hopewell Book 1
1759-1776

Joseph Lupton
William Dillon
Jonathan Parkins
William Pickering
Richard Ridgway Sr.
William Barritt
Morris Rees Jr.
John Painter
William Jolliffe
Phillip Babb
Henry Rees
John Ridgway
Robert Haines
Andrew McCoy
William Neall

Jonathan Taylor
Thomas Rees
Benjamin Thornbrough
Richard Ridgway
Edward Beeson
Abel Walker
Jesse Pugh
John Rees
James Steer
Thomas McClun
Andrew McKay
Jesse Faukner
Mordecai Walker
Anthony Moore

Evan Rogers
Jonathan Parkens
Enos Ellis
John Berry
Rees Cadwaller
Daniel Brown
Jacob McKay
John Garwood
George Shin
Lewis Walker
James Gauthrop
Samuel Pickering
John Lupton
Jobe Hastings

In Hopewell Book 2
1777-1791

Mordecai Ellis
Josiah Jackson
Anthony Lee
Joseph Hackney
David Ross
John Trimble
Joseph Allen
John Griffith
James Purvience
Jacob Pickering
Jonathan Wright
Jackson Allen
Joseph Wright
Rich'd Ridgway Jr.
Dan'l McPherson
Jonathan Lupton
Joseph Steer Jr.
Jacob Rambo
Lewis Neill
Meschach Sexon

Henry Cogill
Barak Fisher
Isaac Brown
Thomas McClun
Cuthbert Hayhurst
Joseph Allen
Nathaniel White
Thomas Fawcett
Richard Fawcett
David Rees
Abraham Branson
Isaac Parkins
Thomas Pugh Jr.
John McCool
Lewis Walker
Joseph Smith
William Grubb
Joshan Cope
John Fawcett Jr.
Sam'l Pickering Jr.

James Mendinhall
John Antrim
John Fallis
Michael Shion
William Branson
George Read
Jesse Halloway
John Hough
William Mathews
Joseph Elgar
Joseph Janney
John Bond
Nathan Pusey
Thomas Fallice
Daniel Antrim
John Paxton
Jonah Hollingsworth
Patience Berry
Martha Fanley
Isaac Smith

Joseph Lupton
Richard Barrett
Nath'l White Jr.

Ezekiel Cleaver
David Berry
Robert Rogers

Edward Morris
John McPherson
Owen Rogers

In Hopewell Book 3
1791-1811

William Hiett
Joseph Hackney
John Griffith
Lewis Neill
David Ross
Joseph Steer
James Raley
Evan Rogers
John Wright
John Antram
David Faulkner
Richard Barrett
Enoch Ellis
Anthony Lee
Jonathan Wright
Mordecai Walker
Abel Walker
Edward Beeson
James Mendinhall
Richard Ridgway
Lewis Walker
John McPherson
William McPherson
David Shinn
Stephen McBride

John Fenton
Nath'l White Jr.
William Downing
Joseph Bond
Abraham Branson
Robert Rogers
Walter Denny
Jonathan Ellis
Edward Ellis
Nathan Updegraff
William Grubb
Nathan Litler
Jonathan Pickering
Levi Smith
Daniel Brown
Nathan Haines
Moses Piggott
David Ridgway
David Lupton
Isaac Steer
Nathan Hayes
John Cowgill
Samuel Talbot
William Beall

Ambrose Taylor
Richard George
Abel Walker Jr.
Asa Lupton
Samuel Lupton
John Lee
Issac Brown
Thomas Wilson
Evan Hiett
William Lupton
Joseph Grubb
George Cop
Evan Rogers
Jonathan Lovett
Edward Walker
Lewis Neill
Richard George
Robert Coburn
Joshua Wood
Asa Hoge
Jesse Faulkner
George Hiett
Thomas Thatcher
Abel Janney

SPECIAL COMMITTEE MEMBERS
In Hopewell Book 3
1791-1811

To visit such Friends as were members and were disowned (1-5-1797): William Downing, Abel Walker, Richard Ridgway, Mordecai Walker.

To look after the "Education and Care of Our Youth" (7-12-1801): Abel Walker, James Steer, Abraham Branson, William McPherson, Joseph Steer, Stephen McBride.

To unite with overseers in a visit to such as are neglected in attendance to meetings (7-2-1803): Abraham Branson, James Mendinhall, James Steer, Joseph Grubb, Stephen McBride, William McPherson, Evan Hiett, John McPherson.

To take subscriptions for the use and benefit of the Indians—advised by last Quarterly Meeting: Richard Barrett, Edward Beeson, Abel Walker Jr., John Fenton, David Lupton, Samuel McPherson. The sum of $135.50 was subscribed for the benefit of Indians, 1-18-1803.

BUCKINGHAM RECORDS
Relating to Hopewell and Other Meetings in Virginia

Anna W. Smith of Bucks County, Pa., and Henry W. Scarborough of Philadelphia have supplied the following items taken chiefly from the records of Buckingham Monthly Meeting in Bucks Co., Pa.

1730, 6 mo. 4, Joseph Lupton and Mary Pickering, widow, declare their intention of marriage.

1735, 9 mo. 3, a certificate for Jacob Holcomb to visit Friends' meetings in Virginia.

1737, 5 mo. 4, John Scarborough requests certificate for his brother Robert to the monthly meeting at Opecking. Thos. Canby Jr. and Edmund Kinsey to make inquiry as to Robert.

1738, 7 mo. 4, Stephanus Haworth told the meeting that he and his brother Absalom had settled about 50 miles beyond Opeckon Monthly Meeting; requested certificates to the said meeting.

1738, 8 mo. 4, Cephas Child produced certificates for Stephanus and Absalom Haworth to Opeckon Monthly Meeting. They were approved and signed.

1739, 5 mo. 2, James Haworth requests certificate to Opeckon Monthly Meeting, whither he intends to remove. Joseph Brown and William Mitchener to make inquiry into his clearness in respect to marriage, conversation, and parents' consent.

1739, 6 mo. 6, report concerning James Haworth favorable, and he was granted a certificate; "as also something concerning his Brother John who is placed under the care of his Brother Absolom."

1741, 1 mo. 2, Thomas Brown requests certificates for himself, wife, and children, except his eldest daughter, to the monthly meeting at Hopewell in Orange Co., Va., in order to remove there. James Shaw and Cephas Child to make inquiry.

1741, 2 mo. 6, a favorable report on Thomas Brown. Joseph Lupton requests certificate for himself, wife, and family to move to Hopewell. John Dawson and Thos. Canby Jr. to inquire.

1741, 3 mo. 4, certificate for Thomas Brown to Hopewell. Report favorable to Joseph Lupton and his son Joseph; they also given a certificate.

1742, 6 mo. 7, certificates requested for Abel Knight and Solomon Knight to Friends in Orange Co., Va. Thomas Good and Nicholas Dillon to inquire into Abel's conversation and affairs; also into Solomon's conversation and clearness as to marriage and how he has settled his affairs.

1742, 7 mo. 6, certificate requested for William Lupton to Hopewell. Joshua Ely and John Schofield to inquire. Certificates signed for Abel Knight and Solomon Knight.

1742, 8 mo. 4, favorable report on William Lupton's conversation and clearness as to marriage and his affairs; a certificate to be drawn for him.

1742, 10 mo. 6, reported that William Lupton had a certificate signed at a weekday meeting.

1743, 4 mo. 6, William Lupton produced a certificate from Hopewell. It was accepted.

1744, 2 mo. 2, John Scarborough requests certificate to Friends in Maryland and Virginia to visit them in the concern of the ministry. John Hill to draw one.

1744, 5 mo. 2, John Scarborough made return of certificate granted him to visit Friends in Maryland and Virginia.

1744, 8 mo. 2, Jacob Holcomb and John Scarborough expressed a concern to again visit Friends in Maryland and Virginia and adjacent parts. The clerk to draw certificates.

1744/5, 1 mo. 4, John Scarborough made return of his certificate which was granted him to visit Friends in Maryland and adjacent parts.

1745, 4 mo. 3, Jacob Holcomb returns certificate granted him to visit Friends in Maryland and parts adjacent in the service of the ministry.

1745, 8 mo. 7, certificate requested for William Lupton for him and wife to Hopewell Monthly Meeting "in Orange Co. Va." Samuel Eastburn and John Schofield to inquire.

At this meeting was reported the marriage of William Lupton and Grace Pickering. They had made requests (1) 6 mo. 5, 1745; (2) 7 mo. 2, 1745.

1745, 9 mo. 2, favorable report on William Lupton. A certificate signed for him.

1746, 6 mo. 4, Anne Schofield, minister, made return of her certificate of 2 mo. 7, 1746, and also produced three certificates, one from Fairfax Monthly Meeting, one from Hopewell, and one from West River.

At the same meeting Pheby Smith, minister, returned her certificate of 2 mo. 7, 1746, and also produced three certificates, one from Fairfax, one from Hopewell, and one from West River.

1746, 8 mo. 6, certificate signed for John Scarborough, minister, to visit Friends in Maryland, Virginia, and North Carolina.

1746/7, 1 mo. 2, John Scarborough returned his certificate and produced three certificates, one from Pasquotank, one from Perquemons, and one from Nangemund (Nansemond?) in Virginia, date of 11 mo. 1, 1746. It is not stated that he was at Hopewell.

1750, 3 mo. 7, Daniel Jones requests certificate to Fairfax Monthly Meeting in Virginia. Thomas Gill and Benj. Fell to inquire. He changed his mind and did not go.

1750, 6 mo. 6, Thomas Ross reported as minded to visit Friends in Maryland and Virginia.

1750, 7 mo. 3, certificate signed for Thomas Ross, minister, to visit Friends in Maryland and parts adjacent.

1750, 8 mo. 2, Daniel Jones revived his request for a certificate to Fairfax. Thos. Gill and Benj. Fell to inquire into Daniel's conversation and clearness as to marriage, etc.

1750, 9 mo. 5, John Haworth produced a certificate from Hopewell in Virginia.

1751, 7 mo. 2, Joseph Borsun requests certificate for himself and 3 children, Absalom, Rachel, Deborah, to Fairfax. Wm. Michener and James Shaw to inquire. At the same meeting Joseph Burson Jr. requests a certificate to the same place.

1751, 10 mo. 2, certificate to Joseph Borsun (Burson?) and children, Rachel, Banjamin, Deborah, to Fairfax; also one to Joseph Borsun Jr. to the same place.

1754, 4 mo. 1, John Scarborough and Enoch Pearson, ministers, request a few lines to Friends in some parts of Maryland and Virginia.

1754, 7 mo. 1, John Scarborough and Enoch Pearson returned their certificate given them to travel "in the service of Youth" in Virginia and Maryland. The yearly meeting at West River and other meetings had written signifying unity and satisfaction with their services.

1757, 3 mo. 7, John Scarborough Jr. produced a certificate from Hopewell in Virginia.

1758, 12 mo. 4, Isaac Hollingsworth, minister, "on a religious visit to this Meeting produced a Certificate of concurrence & Unity of the Mo Meeting of Friends at Fairfax in Virginia to which he belongs."

CONCORD, GWYNEDD, AND SADSBURY

Removals to Hopewell

The following items of early date from the records of the several monthly meetings named have been supplied by Mr. Thomas H. Fawcett of Cheyney, Pa.

Concord Monthly Meeting

1736, 5 mo. 5, John Smith requests certificate; signed 6 mo. 2, 1736.

1737, 8 mo. 3, Friends appointed to prepare a certificate for Elizabeth Vestall to Hopewell, where she removed several years since; signed 9 mo. 7, 1737.

1746, 2 mo. 7, John Marshall and wife Ruth request certificate; signed 4 mo. 2, 1747.

1746, 5 mo. 7, Hannah Longacor requests certificate; signed 6 mo. 4, 1746. She was wife of Joseph Longacre.

Gwynedd Monthly Meeting

1736, 11 mo. 25, John Beson requests certificate; signed 2 mo. 26, 1737.

1741, 5 mo. 28, John and Joseph Morgan and wives request certificates; signed 12 mo. 1741.

1741, 6 mo. 24, Jesse Pugh and wife request certificate. On 7 mo. 29, 1741, reported to have gone to Hopewell—does not desire certificate until he sends for it. Signed for Jesse and wife Alice and sent to Hopewell 9 mo. 30, 1742.

1744, 6 mo. 28, John Roger, wife, and family request certificate; signed 7 mo. 25, 1744.

1746, 2 mo. 29, William Williams requests certificate to Hopewell. The Friends appointed to draw a certificate for William Williams to Collooden in Virginia have accordingly done so. Read, approved, and signed 3 mo. 27, 1746.

Sadsbury Monthly Meeting

1740, 2 mo. 7, Thomas Thornbrough and family request certificate; signed 3 mo. 5, 1740.

1742-43, 12 mo. 7, Robert Thornbrough, belonging to Hopewell Monthly Meeting, complained of; disowned 6 mo. 1, 1743, and copy of testimony to be sent to Hopewell. Robert presents certificate 2 mo. 1, 1751. Certificate refused 3 mo. 6, 1751—he to get another. On 8 mo. 7, 1751, he produced a certificate from Opeken Monthly Meeting, which was received. On 10 mo. 4, 1756, he requests a certificate to Carolina; signed for Robert, wife, and children to Wilmington Mo. Mtg. 4 mo. 2, 1759.

1758, 2 mo. 6, Thomas McClung requests certificate to Hopewell; signed 3 mo. 6, 1758, and to be sent to him.

1758, 6 mo. 5, certificate from Hopewell produced for Thomas Thornbrough. See minutes of Meeting for Sufferings.

RICHLAND ITEMS

Certificates from Richland Monthly Meeting

From "Old Richland Families," by Elwood Roberts, and records of Richland Monthly Meeting, Bucks County, Pa.

1748, 16th of 4th month, Wm. Hougue, wife, & sons William & Solomon.

1758, 16th of 11th month, Joseph Hoge to Virginia.

1759, 17th of 5th month, William Hoge to Virginia.

1760, 17th of 1st month, Samuel Iden to Fairfax, Va.

1781, 21st of 6th month, Ezekiel Green to Hopewell.

1782, 20th of 6th month, Mary Adamson and children, Thomas, James and Sarah, to Hopewell.

1782, 19th of 9th month, Solomon Hoge, wife Esther, and children to Fairfax, Va.

1791, 15th of 9th month, Jane Chilcot and husband to Goose Creek Monthly Meeting, in Virginia.

1792, 21st of 6th month, Ezra Kinsey to Fairfax, Va.

1796, 19th of 5th month, Abigail Walton, Nathan Walton, and wife Mary to Westland.

1798, 15th of 3d month, Job Strawhen to Redstone.

1799, 17th of 10th month, Diannah Walker and husband to Westland.

KINGWOOD ITEMS

Certificates from Kingwood Monthly Meeting

The following items are gleaned from the Kingwood Records, published by Mr. H. E. Deats of Flemington, N. J. Kingwood Monthly Meeting of Friends was located in Kingwood Township, Hunterdon County, N. J.

1762, 12th of 8th month, Samuel Smith, wife, and children moved to Fairfax, Va. [Evidently delayed.]

1763, 14th of 7th month, Samuel Smith, wife, and children moved to Fairfax, Va.

1770, 8th of 2d month, John Brock, wife, and 7 children moved to Hopewell, Va.

1770, 8th of 3d month, William Webster moved to Hopewell.

1774, 13th of 1st month, Mahlon Taylor moved from Fairfax, Va., to Kingwood, N. J.

1784, 13th of 5th month, Isaac Reeder moved from Fairfax to Kingwood.

NORTH CAROLINA RECORDS

The following marriages and certificates of membership and removal of Virginia Friends, prior to 1760, have been secured from the records of North Carolina Friends' meetings.

At New Garden, N. C., it was the custom to record the names of only twelve witnesses of a marriage, no matter how many names appeared on the certificate.

VIRGINIA MARRIAGES RECORDED AT NEW GARDEN

Thos. Thornbrug, s. of Thos., of Middle Creek on Opeckan in Frederick Co., Va., married *Abigail Brown*, dt. of James of same place, 18th of 1st mo., 1740/41, O. S., which is 29th of 3d mo., N. S. They had declared marriage intention at several monthly meetings held at Opeckan. Witnesses: Thos. Thornbrug, James Brown, James Brittain, John Gayham, Walter Thornbrug, Richard Beeson, Hannah Thornbrugh, Mary Wall, Ann Beeson, Charity Beeson, Sarah Wood, & Elizabeth Beeson.

John Hiatt, s. of John, of Opeckon, Frederick Co., Va., married *Mary Thomas*, dt. of Evan of same place, 12th of 2d mo., 1744, at Opeckan, Witnesses: James Wright, Wm. Hoge, Joseph Ballinger, James McGrew, Isaac Hollingsworth, Hur Mills, Mary Ballinger, Mary McGrew, Rachel Perkins, Rachel Mills, Ann Hoge, & Ann Taylor.

Richard Williams, s. of George, married *Prudence Beals*, dt. of John, of Monoquosy, Prince George Co., Md., 11th of 10th mo., 1746. They had declared marriage intention at Fairfax in Va., and Monoquosy. Witnesses: Wm. Kersey, John Wright, Anthony Chamness, Joseph Wells, Geo. Mathews, Matthias Pooley, Daniel Matthews, Thos. Hunt, Eleazer Hunt, Sarah Beals, Ann Hunt, Elizabeth Pooley.

Thomas Beales, Prince George Co., Md., married *Sarah Antram*, of same place, 12th of 9th mo., 1741. They had declared marriage intention in Va. Witnesses: Oliver Matthews, Thos. Matthews, Francis Henley, Amos Jenny, Evan Thomas, John Wright, Mary Matthews, Sarah Beales, Elizabeth Matthews, Hannah Ballinger, Susanna Moon, Mary Tannyhill.

Thomas Brown, s. of Thos., of Frederick Co., Va., married *Margaret Moon*, dt. of Simon, of same place, 10th of 6th mo., 1748. They had declared marriage intention at Hopewell. Witnesses: Abel Knight, Walter Thornbrugh, William Beeson, Joseph Britton, Samuel Brown, Wm. Brown, Deborah Brown, Ann Watson, Abigail Thornbrugh, Sarah MacIntire, Martha Beeson, Mary Brittan.

Robert Lamb, Roan (Rowan) Co., married *Rachel Taylor*, dt. of Simon, of Opeckan, Va., 29th of 9th mo., 1757. They had declared marriage at New Garden in Roan Co. Witnesses: Peter Dicks, Thos. Hunt, Zacharias Dicks, William Ozburn, Henry Walton, Wm. Hoggatt, Elizabeth Dicks, Mary Dicks, Martha Hiatt, Ruth Dicks, Rebeckah Ozburn, Mary Green.

Note. The last mentioned marriage was accomplished in North Carolina. It is included here because of the statement that Rachel Taylor was a daughter of Simon Taylor of Opeckan, Va.

CERTIFICATES OF MEMBERSHIP AND REMOVAL FROM HOPEWELL

Received by Meetings in North Carolina
Received at Cane Creek Monthly Meeting, Alamance County, North Carolina Men's Minutes

Date Received			Names	Date of Certificate		
Year	Mo.	Day		Year	Mo.	Day
1751	10	7	Martha Hiatt & children	1751	6	5
1751	10	7	John Hiatt	1751	6	5
1751	10	7	Aaron Jones	1751	6	5
1751	10	7	Elizabeth Vestal & sons, Wm. & Thos.	1751	2	1
1752	3	7	Benj. Beeson, wife, & children			
1752	3	7	Wm. Beeson, wife, & children	1751	3	6
1752	3	7	Mordecai Mendenhall, wife, & children	1751	3	6
1752	3	7	Elinor Edwards & children	1751	3	6
1752	5	2	Jonathan Harrold	1751	7	2
1752	5	2	William Baldwin	1749	8	2
1752	7	4	William Hiatt	1751	7	2
1752	8	1	John Mills	1752	6	1
1752	8	1	Able Knight	1752	6	1
1752	11	4	William Hunt	1752	6	1
1752	11	4	Thomas Thornbrugh	1752	7	6
1752	11	4	William Thornbrugh	1752	7	6
1753	1	6	Peter Dillon	1752	9	18
1753	1	6	Daniel Dillon	1752	9	18
1753	9	1	Thomas Hurr & Henry Mills	1753	5	7
1753	9	1	John Jones	1753	7	5
1753	10	6	Richard Jones	1753	6	4
1753	11	4	Ruth Brown & son Samuel	1753	8	6
1753	11	4	Thomas Brown	1753	8	6
1755	3	1	William Ellimore			

Received at Cane Creek Monthly Meeting, Women's Minutes

Date Received			Names	Date of Certificate		
Year	Mo.	Day		Year	Mo.	Day
1755	3	1	Abigail Elmore, with husband			
1756	7	3	Ann Moon			
1759	2	3	Mary Hiat, with husband			

Received at New Garden Monthly Meeting

1754	11	30	Richard Beeson & wife	1754	9	2
1755	3	29	Benjamin Britain	1754	12	2
1756	12	25	James Langley	1756	4	5
1757	6	25	Joseph Hiett	1756	6	5
1758	5	27	John Baels	1758	4	14
1758	6	24	Isaac Beeson Sr.	1758	6	5
1758	6	24	Nathel Beeson	1758	6	5
1759	7	28	Abraham Patten			
1764	7	28	Simon Taylor	1764	5	7
1765	8	31	James Wright, wife, & ch., Ralph Jeams, Ann, Susanna, Micaiah, Elijah, John	1765	3	4

Received at Pasquotank Monthly Meeting

1741	4	4	Samuel Pike & family			

Certificates issued by North Carolina Meetings

1752	5	2	Martha Hiatt, by Cane Creek
1737	6	4	Daniel Clancy, by Pasquotank
1737	6	4	Abigail Pike, d. of Sarah Martin, by Pasquotank
1737	10	1	Samuel Pike, by Pasquotank
1739	7	6	Sarah Martin, w. of Nathaniel, by Pasquotank

All the above certificates issued are addressed Opeckan or Opecking. Most of those received in North Carolina are recorded as from Hopewell. One is from Opecking, and two or three from Hopewell at Opeckan.

On the same date, 1759, 2,3, that Cane Creek women's minutes record the receipt of a certificate for "Mary Hiat, with husband," the men's minutes record one for John Hiatt, without giving the name of the meeting from which it came.

TABLE OF DATES

A CHRONOLOGY

1624, George Fox born in Leicestershire, England
1644, William Penn born in London
1647, George Fox begins preaching
1648, Robert Barclay born in Morayshire, Scotland
1656, First Friends in America—Ann Austin and Mary Fisher visit Massachusetts
1656-57, Elizabeth Harris visits Virginia
1672, First yearly meeting in Maryland held on West River
1675, Chester Meeting, Pa., established
1682, William Penn lays out Philadelphia
1682, Probable year of Alexander Ross's birth
1685, Bank Meeting House, Phila., erected
1690, Death of Robert Barclay
1691, Death of George Fox
1698, 9th of 9th month, first mo. mtg. in Cecil Co., Md.
1718, Death of William Penn
1725, Ballingers and others settle on the Monocacy
1726, Monocacy Meeting set up
1730, Nottingham Mo. Mtg. settled
1730, June 17, Isaac Vanmeter gets grant for 10,000 acres between Riverton and Millwood, Va.
1730, June 17, John Vanmeter gets grant for 10,000 acres in the forks of Shenando River and 20,000 acres on the south side of the Potomac
1730, Oct. 28, Alexander Ross and Morgan Bryan get grant of 100,000 acres on the Opequon
1731, Aug. 5, John Vanmeter sells his grant to Joist Hite
1731, Oct. 21, Robert McKay and Joist Hite get grant for 100,000 acres on the Shenando River
1732, Oct. 27, Alexander Ross and his partners petition for 20,000 acres more
1732, Nov. 23, "Abraham's Delight" surveyed
1733, Amos Janney and other Friends settle at Waterford

1734, Hopewell Meeting for Worship established

1734, Apr. 9, "The Forest," on the "Road to Opequon," surveyed

1734, Orange County, Va., organized

1734, Israel Friend, a Friend, settles near Harper's Ferry

1734, June 12, Patents issued to Hite and others for Vanmeter lands

1734, June 12, Robt. Brooke ordered to survey 10,000 acres for Wm. Russell, above the fork of Shen. River and NE of Robt. McKay

1734, Dec. 19, First marriage of Friends (George Hollingsworth and Hannah McKoy) in the Shenandoah Valley

1735, 10th of 9th month, Chester Quar. Mtg. grants a mo. mtg. for Opeckon and Monoquacy

1735, Nov. 12, Patents issued to Alexander Ross and 35 others of his colony

1736, Cold Spring (Md.) meeting house built

1736, John Fothergill at Hopewell

1736, 16th of 9th month, John Fothergill at home of Robt. McKay Jr.

1736, Lord Fairfax first comes to Virginia to have his lands surveyed

1736-37, A tentative survey made of Fairfax's lands—the Northern Neck

1737, June 17, Royal patents to Joist Hite and Robt. McKay suspended because of Fairfax claims

1737, after June 17, Lord Fairfax promises Hite and his assigns to sustain their titles

1737, Dec. 21, King George II directs how the bounds of the Northern Neck shall be fixed, guaranteeing his grants therein

1737-38, Presbyterians organize at Opequon (Kernstown)

1738, Providence Meeting (Va.) set up

1738, 21st of 5th month, Thomas Chalkley writes to Hopewell Friends about Indian lands

1738, Robt. Scarborough writes of a meeting on Smith Creek

1739, McKay, Hite, and others get grant for 7009 acres on Linville Creek

1739, Petition from the lower Valley for Frederick County
to be organized

1741, Providence (Va.) meeting house in use

1741, First Fairfax meeting house built at Waterford

1741, John Churchman at Hopewell

1742, May 10, Wm. Vestal and others take steps to build a
bloomery on Shen. River

1742, Edwin Peckover at Hopewell

1743, Courts first set up in Frederick County, Va.

1743, Oct. 9, Will of Benj. Borden probated in Frederick
Co., Va.

1743, Baptists organize on Mills's Creek

1744, Fairfax Mo. Mtg. established

1744, Death of John Fothergill

1745, "Great Case of Tythes" sent to Hopewell

1745, Jacob Janney settles near Goose Creek, now Loudoun
Co., Va.

1745, Augusta Co., Va., organized

1746, John Woolman at Hopewell

1746, 7th of 10th month, Robt. McKay Sr. makes his will

1747, Warrington Mo. Mtg. established

1747, Fairfax refuses deeds to McKay, Hite, and others

1748, October, Act passed by the Va. Gen. Assembly con-
firming royal grants in the Northern Neck

1748, Dec. 7, Will of Alexander Ross probated at Winchester

1749, Oct. 10, Joist Hite and Robt. McKay Sr. enter suit
against Fairfax

1752, 2d month, Winchester established by law as a town

1753, Death of Evan Thomas, minister

1753, Oct. 18, Moravians at Abram Hollingsworth's mill

1754, Woolman's treatise on slavery published

1754, Isaac Hollingsworth house built near Winchester

1754, September, Nine Friends imprisoned in Winchester

1754, Rev. John Hoge becomes pastor at Opequon Pres.
Church

1754, New Garden Meeting, Guilford Co., N. C., set up

1755, July 9, Braddock's army defeated near site of Pittsburgh

1756, Washington builds Fort Loudoun at Winchester

1756, Catoctin Baptist Church organized

1756, Baptists organize in McKay meeting house on Linville Creek

1757, 8th month, Letter to Quar. Mtg. about Hopewell Friends needing relief

1757, 5th of 9th month, Letter to Phila. about Hopewell Friends needing relief

1757, William Reckitt at Fairfax and Hopewell

1757, South River (Bedford Co., Va.) Mo. Mtg. set up

1758, Second letter to Phila. about Hopewell Friends needing relief

1758, 1st of 6th month, Thos. Branson leases 4 acres at Crooked Run to John Painter for 99 years for Friends' meeting

1758, 26th of 6th month, Meeting at Hopewell regarding Indian land claims

1758, 9th month, Stephensburg established by law as a town

1758, Nov. 25, English capture Fort Duquesne (Pittsburgh)

1758, Providence Particular Meeting (Va.) suspended

1758, Isaac Hollingsworth and others lay out additions to Winchester

1759, 26th of 3d month, Wm. Jolliffe Jr. made clerk at Hopewell

1759, Sept. 13, English take Quebec

1759, Friends' meeting on Mills's Creek

1759, Friends' meeting on Back Creek

1759, Upper Ridge Meeting already in existence

1759, Stone meeting house built at Hopewell

1759, Hopewell records burned

1760, Jonathan Parkins made recorder at Hopewell

1760, John Churchman at Hopewell

1760, Daniel Stanton at Fairfax, Goose Creek, and Hopewell

1760, Potts's Meeting (The Gap) visited by Daniel Stanton

1760, Friends' meeting on Middle Creek

1760, Crooked Run granted a preparative meeting

1760-61, Friends of Tuscarora, &c., to hold meetings in the "Old Meeting House of Providence"

1761, 1st of 2d month, A meeting for worship at the home of Morris Rees Sr. allowed

1762, Correspondence regarding Indian land claims

1765, John Griffith at Hopewell

1765, Stone meeting house built at Goose Creek (Lincoln), Va.

1765, British Stamp Act passed

1765, Aug. 23, John Fawcett wills 2 acres for Friends' meeting (later known as Mt. Pleasant)

1766, Stamp Act repealed

1767, Friends hold meeting at Bear Garden

1767, Isaac Zane Jr. acquires an interest in iron works in Frederick County, Va.

1768, McKays sell land on Linville Creek to John Lincoln, great-grandfather of the President

1768, 12th month, Rachel Wilson from Kendal, England, at Hopewell

1769, Stafford Friends ask liberty to hold a meeting

1769, Hopewell proposes a new quarterly meeting

1770, Robt. Hains appointed clerk at Hopewell to succeed Wm. Jolliffe Jr., dec'd

1770, July 3, Georgia Assembly grants 40,000 acres in Mc-Duffie County for use of Friends

1771, Fawcett's (Mt. Pleasant) Meeting set up

1771, 4th of 11th month, Steps taken at Hopewell to build a stable and repair the graveyard

1772, Berkeley County, Va., organized

1772, Dunmore (Shenandoah) County, Va., organized

1772, A meeting house to be built on Jackson Allen's land

1772, Rev. Hugh Vance installed at Tuscarora Pres. Church

1776, Warrington and Fairfax Quar. Mtg. established

1776, 18th of 3d month, First quarterly meeting held at Warrington

1776, May 28, Shen. Co., Va., court arraigns Jackson Allen for freeing slaves

1776, Meeting for worship near Isaac Parkins allowed

1776, Philip Fithian meets Isaac Zane at Stephensburg

1777, Sept. 29, Twenty exiles from Phila. reach Winchester

1777, 11th month, Decision reached to finish Center meeting house

1777, Back Creek meeting house built

1778, 6th of 1st month, Subscriptions at Hopewell to discharge Indian land claims

1778, 2d of 2d month, John Hunt speaks at Hopewell

1778, March, Thomas Gilpin buried at Hopewell

1778, April, John Hunt buried at Hopewell

1778, April, Rockingham Co., Va., organized

1778, Apr. 20, Exiled Friends leave Winchester for Phila.

1778, Apr. 30, Exiled Friends, returning, reach Phila.

1778, 2d of 11th month, John Garwood and others granted a meeting for worship

1779, 1st of 2d month, Steps taken to build a schoolhouse at Hopewell

1780, Nathan Updegraff establishes a hat factory in Winchester

1780, 150 people with right of membership at and near Redstone

1781, Preparative meeting settled at Center, near Winchester

1781, Crooked Run Mo. Mtg., including Center and Mt. Pleasant, set up

1781, Dec. 9, Death of Lord Fairfax

1782, or earlier, Westland Meeting set up

1782, or earlier, Redstone Meeting begun

1782, 2d month, Hugh Judge at Hopewell, Smith Creek, John Garwood's, and other places thereabouts

1782, 13th of 2d month, Hugh Judge finds Culpeper meeting house near John Garwood's

1782, Jonathan Bishop and family near Mt. Pony, Culpeper Co., Va.

1782, 29th of 5th month, First session of Crooked Run Mo. Mtg.

1784, Hugh Judge at Fairfax, Goose Creek, Crooked Run, etc.

1785, 5th month, Yearly meeting at Wayneoak (Weyanoke?), Va.

1785, Friends and others protest against a bill to "support religion" in Virginia

1785, Hugh Judge at Wainoke (Wayneoak)

1785, John Storer and Tho. Cally from England visit Hopewell

1785, A meeting house built at Westland to replace one burned

1785, 5th of 9th month, Friends east of the Monongahela and at Westland request a mo. mtg.

1786, Fairfax Quarterly Meeting set up

1787, 19th of 3d month, Last meeting of Warrington and Fairfax Quar. Mtg. held

1788, First-Day meeting granted to Friends near Mt. Pony (Southland)

1788, 3d of 5th month, Deed reported signed for Culpeper meeting-house lot

1788-89, Stone meeting house at Hopewell enlarged

1789, Meeting at Front Street, Phila., transferred to new house in Key's Alley

1789, Job Scott at Hopewell and Winchester

1789, Warrington and Fairfax quarterly meetings transferred from Phila. to Balto. Yrly. Mtg.

1791, Preparative meeting at Middle Creek

1791, Ridge (Upper Ridge) meeting house erected

1792, Hopewell Friends contribute towards the purchase of a pasture lot for the Balto. Yrly. Mtg.

1794, Name of Bullskin Meeting changed to Berkeley

1794, Death of Martha Mendenhall, minister

1795, Martha Routh, a minister from England, visits Friends' meetings west of the Alleghanies

1795, Friends near John Fallis request liberty to hold a meeting

1795, Death of Gen. Isaac Zane (Isaac Zane Jr.)

1796, or earlier, A meeting at Lower Ridge

1797, Southland (Mt. Pony) granted a mo. mtg. First mo. mtg. held 11th month 1797

1797, Quarterly mtg. established over the Alleghany Mountain, composed of Westland and Redstone

1798, 3d month, Fairfax Quar. Mtg. discontinues the "Youths Meetings"

1799, July, Henry Hull at Leesburg, Goose Creek, Hopewell, Winchester, etc.

1799, David Lupton builds Cedar Grove Mill

1800, Stephen Grillet at Hopewell

1800, A meeting for worship settled at the Ridge

1801, 19th of 12th month, Concord Mo. Mtg., Ohio, first held

1801, Fire at Center Meeting—"their meeting house took fire"

1802, 16th of 8th month, Alexandria granted a mo. mtg.

1803, 13th of 10th month, Miami Mo. Mtg., Ohio, opened

1804, 6th month, Southland Mo. Mtg. laid down—members returned to Crooked Run Mo. Mtg.

1805, 2d month, Southland Prep. Mtg. laid down

1805, or thereabouts, Susanna Horn of England visits Hopewell

1806, 2d of 6th month, Redstone Quar. Mtg. grants a quarter to Concord and Short Creek, Ohio

1807, 18th of 5th month, Crooked Run Mo. Mtg. laid down —members returned to Hopewell Mo. Mtg.

1807, 3d of 8th month, Stafford Meeting discontinued by Hopewell Mo. Mtg.

1808, John Brown purchases Conrad tanyard in Winchester

1809, 5th of 6th month, Mt. Pleasant Meeting discontinued

1809, 2d of 10th month, Bear Garden Meeting discontinued

1810, 5th of 3d month, Crooked Run Prep. Mtg. laid down

1810, 5th of 10th month, Report at Hopewell that Quar. Mtg. had approved laying down Crooked Run meeting for worship

1813, Ohio Yearly Meeting established

1814, Hugh Judge at Abel Walker's and Hopewell

1814, Tax paid on Isaac Pidgeon's wheeled "chair" (chaise)

1814-15, David Lupton in Europe with flour

1815, Beginning of Fair Hill Boarding School in Montgomery Co., Md.

1817, 30th of 4th month, Sarah Zane conveys lot in Winchester to Joshua Lupton, Samuel Brown, and Samuel Swayne for Center Meeting

1817, 6th of 10th month, Mary Naftel of England at Hopewell

1817, Steps taken to build meeting house in Winchester

1817, Brick meeting house built at Lincoln, Va.

1819, Sarah Zane makes her will

1821, Hugh Judge at Back Creek, Winchester, etc.

1821, Sarah Zane's will recorded in Phila.

1821, Sarah Zane leaves $1000 to Winchester for a fire engine, etc.

1822, Death of Goldsmith Chandlee

1827, Elizabeth Robson from Liverpool, England, visits Va. Friends

1827, Isaac Hollingsworth builds a fine mill on Abram's Creek

1827-28, The Separation

1828, Friendly Grove Factory established

1834, Hugh Judge at Winchester

1834, 21st of 12th month, Hugh Judge dies at Kennet Square, Pa.

1835, Brookland Woolen Mills established

1835, Railroad building from Harper's Ferry to Winchester

1838, Dr. John W. Marvin opens a boarding school in Winchester

1839, Smith Creek meeting house sold to John Neff

1848, 10th of 8th month, Hopewell Women's Meeting urges promotion of education

1850, 5th of 12th month, Death of Robt. Bond, teacher and overseer

1853, Yardley Taylor makes a detail map of Loudoun Co., Va.

1861, summer, Southern army uses Center meeting house in Winchester as a hospital

1862, Mar. 12, Stonewall Jackson carries off southward 21 Union men, including 6 Friends, and the Federals occupy Winchester

1862, Mar. 13, Federals take possession of Center Meeting House in Winchester

1863, Center Meeting House in Winchester destroyed

1863, June 15, Milroy driven out of Winchester by Lee's army, moving northward

1864, Sept. 19, Battle of Opequon—Sheridan occupies Winchester

1865, 9th of 8th month, Report made on Center Meeting House

1865, 7th of 9th month, Hopewell Mo. Mtg. acknowledges gift from Little Falls

1866, Daniel T. Wood builds Spout Spring Mill

1867, January, Rebecca Wright receives gold watch from Gen. Sheridan

1868, 6th of 4th month, Report made at Hopewell on the Library

1870, Stone wall around Hopewell graveyard constructed by "W. D. L." (W. D. Lee?)

1871, Center Meeting held in John W. Marvin's building

1871, 7th of 12th month, New meeting house in Winchester reported ready for use

1872, 8th of 2d month, First mo. mtg. held in the new Center meeting house in Winchester

1883, Death of Joel Lupton, inventor

1886, First-Day School organized at Hopewell

1890, Hollingsworth Spring purchased by the city of Winchester

1893, Jolliffe Family History published

1898, Young Friends Association advocated at Hopewell

1910, Hopewell meeting house repaired—the eastern (older) half rebuilt

1910, Hopewell Friends unite their meetings

1911, Hollingsworth mill burns, near site of old Center, Winchester

1920, Young Friends Movement recognized by Balto. Yrly. Mtg.

1933, Title bond to Friends' lot at Back Creek found

1935, Young Friends of Hopewell represented at Woodbrooke School, England

1935, Record of deed for Center graveyard found

1935, Hopewell Monument erected at Clearbrook

1935, Sept. 18, Philip Pendleton Nalle writes of Friends at Southland

PART THREE

INDEX

INDEX

(Including a Partial Thesaurus)

Brown, Joseph Jr. 417 (1781)
Brown, Joseph (3) 418 (s. of Eleazer 1781)
Brown, Joseph (4) 452 (s. of David 1833)
Brown, Joseph 281 305 412 458 503 533 (1739-1798)
Brown, Joshua 64 102
Brown, Josiah 359 449
Brown, Leah 417
Brown, Leon R. 467
Brown, Leslie R. 467
Brown, Levi K. 227
Brown, Lily M. 467
Brown, Lois R. 467
Brown, Louisa 355 449
Brown, Lucy S. 467
Brown, Lucy V. 467
Brown, Lydia 354 361 362 366
Brown, Lydia (Bull) 509
Brown, Lydia F. 353
Brown, Lydia (Fawcett) 519
Brown, Mahlon 417
Brown, Margaret (1) 418 (w. of Nathan 1781)
Brown, Margaret (2) 418 (d. of Eleazer 1781)
Brown, Margaret (3) 466 (b. 1787; d. of Isaac)
Brown, Margaret (4) 466 (b. 1803? d. of John)
Brown, Margaret 259 260 268 271 275 276 323 326 332 333 335 412 452 (1774-1833)
Brown, Margaret H. 332
Brown, Margaret (Moon) 539
Brown, Maria R. 331 332 340
Brown, Martha Sr. 413 467
Brown, Martha Jr. 413
Brown, Martha 359-361 367 369 370 444 449
Brown, Martha (Wilson) 339 468
Brown, Mary 55 (m. John Butterfill 1731)
Brown, Mary (1) 322 340 356 362 (1801-1826)
Brown, Mary (2) 322 340 356 362 (1801-1826)
Brown, Mary Sr. 347 (w. of Thos. 1813)
Brown, Mary Jr. 323 335 337 342 347 359 467 (b. 1791; d. of Thos.)
Brown, Mary 467 469 (b. 1780? w. of Wm.)
Brown, Mary 466 (1790-1794; d. of Isaac)
Brown, Mary 509 (m. Ducker 1794)
Brown, Mary 523 (w. of Joel 1822)
Brown, Mary 452 (d. of David 1833)

Brown, Mary 259 260 279 315 318 323 331 338 345 347-349 355 357 359 366 399 411 412 (1774-1827)
Brown, Mary E. 204 206 (m. Carter Louthan)
Brown, Mary E. Sr. 467 (w. of R. R. Brown Jr.)
Brown, Mary E. Jr. 467
Brown, Mary (Fries) 467
Brown, Mary J. 356 358 359
Brown, Mary (Jackson) 322
Brown, Mary L. 362
Brown, Mary M. 153 354 467
Brown, Mary R. 353 355
Brown, Mary (Robinson) 467
Brown, Mary (White) 259 467
Brown, Messer 62 240
Brown, Miriam Sr. 324 443
Brown, Miriam Jr. 324 443
Brown, Miriam 260 267 279 280 282 286 287 301 333 411 466 (1773-1807)
Brown, Mrs. (nurse) 24 32
Brown, M. W. 353
Brown, Nancy 354
Brown, Naomi 399 461
Brown, Naomi (Hurford) 398
Brown, Nathan 418
Brown, Oliver M. 354
Brown, O. M. 353
Brown, Pearl I. 467
Brown, Peggy 319 321
Brown, Phebe 381 384-387 391 397 415 466
Brown, Rachel 411 (w. of Timothy 1774)
Brown, Rachel 417 (d. of Joseph 1781)
Brown, Rachel 506 (m. Berry 1787)
Brown, Rachel 401 462 (w. of Joel 1797, 1806)
Brown, Rachel H. 340
Brown, Rachel (Inskeep) 399
Brown, Rachel N. 468
Brown, Rebecca 477 (m. Dr. Marvin)
Brown, Rebecca 340 362 369 437 449
Brown, Rebecca (Bonsall) 324
Brown, Rebecca M. 467
Brown, Rebecca R. 354 355
Brown, Rebecca W. 362 468
Brown, Richard 63 (1741)
Brown, Richard 177 340 (1811, 1837)
Brown, Richard B. 467
Brown, Richard R., Sr. 177 466 467
Brown, Richard R., Jr. 467
Brown, Russell E. 467
Brown, Ruth 540
Brown, Ruth A. 455
Brown, Ruth E. 467
Brown, S. A. E. 353
Brown, S. A. F. 153
Brown, Sally 373

Cupid active 133
Curative Treaty 122
Curl, Amy 425
Curl, Charles 425
Curl, Elizabeth 425
Curl, Hannah 425
Curl, Joseph 425
Curl, Maria N. 365
Curl, Rebecca Sr. 425
Curl, Rebecca Jr. 425
Curl, Susanna 425
"Curles" 226
Curles Neck 213 214
Curls Meeting 213 214
Curtis, Mary Sr. 18
Curtis, Mary Jr. 18
Curtis, Thomas 18
Custis, John 43 44

Daingerfield, Frances 335
Daingerfield, J. F. 363
Daingerfield, LeRoy 340
Daingerfield, Lucy 335
Daingerfield, Mary B. 342
Daingerfield, Richard 342
Daingerfield, Wm. 335
Dalby, Eliz'h (Smith) 511
Dancing 497 498 500 501 503 504 506 511
Dandridge, William 42
Danger from Indians 114 115
Daniel, Andrew 285 294 363 365 448 449
Daniel, Esther 371
Daniel, Hannah 266 285 288 294 416 431 449
Daniel, John 326
Daniel, Joseph H. 363 365 449
Daniel, Lydia E. 454
Daniel, Margaret 294 334 428 431 440 442
Daniel, Martha 340 352 363 449 454
Daniel, Martha J. 454
Daniel, Mary A. 363 365
Daniel, Maryann 449
Daniel (of color) 189
Daniel, Rachel 449
Daniel, Rebecca A. 454
Daniel, Rebekah (Ellis) 512
Daniel, Robert 340 352 448 449 454
Daniel, Robt. B. 454
Daniel, Robert (of Andrew) 363 365
Daniel, Ruth 453
Daniel, Ruth W. 451
Daniel, Sarah J. 451 453
Daniel, Sidney 447 451 453
Daniel, William 312 326
Daniel, Wm. F. 454
Daniel James Branch (small stream) 191
Darby, John 308

Darby Creek Mtg. 214 445 447 448
Dare, Lydia M. 453 454
Dare, Sarah J. 454
Darke, Joseph 184
Darke, Gen. Wm. 129 184
"Dark time" 101
Darlington, Anne 350
Darlington, Ann (McCool) 513
Darlington, Cath. (McCool) 513
Darlington, Eleanor 361
Darlington, Joseph 361
Darlington, Meredith 176 350
D'Aubigne 380
Davies, Charles 59
Davies, Hannah 59
Davies, Peter 338
Davis, Ann 318
Davis, Benj. F. 359
Davis, Charlotta 289
Davis, Edward 34 35 (See Devis)
Davis, Gabriel 311
Davis, Gabriel H. 350
Davis, Hannah 441
Davis, Isaac 306 431 441 515
Davis, Jacob 34
Davis, James Sr. 34 35 37
Davis, James Jr. 34
Davis, James 300 425 509
Davis, Jefferson 132
Davis, John 34 361 369
Davis, Joseph 425 511
Davis, Lydia 507
Davis, Margaret 361
Davis, Mary 318 404
Davis, Mary (Wickersham) 507
Davis, Rachel (Gawthrop) 517
Davis, Robert 34 37
Davis, Rodney 454
Davis, Sarah 34 350
Davis: from Chesterfield Mo. Mtg.: 1748, 9 mo. 3: Sarah Davis applied for cert. to Hopewell—reported clear; cert. for her reported prepared 10 mo. 1, 1748.
Davis, Sarah (Fenton) 512
Davis, Samuel H. 356
Davis, William 318
Davison, W. 208
Dawson, James 404
Dawson, John 533
Dawson, Thomas 28
Day, Catherine 253 469 (See K. Day)
Day, Evan 408 469 506
Day, George 469 505
Day, John 28
Day, Joseph Sr. 248 408 469
Day, Joseph Jr. 469 506
Day, Joseph 249 253 501
Day, Katherine 248 249 408 (See Cath. Day)

Fawcett, Hannah 492 (b. 1778; d. of Thos.)

Fawcett, Hannah 492 [b. 1784; d. of Richard (2)]

Fawcett, Hannah 274 393 395 397 400 403 460 (1781-1804)

Fawcett, Isaac 491 517

Fawcett, Jacob 460 492

Fawcett, Jesse 518

Fawcett, John Sr. 246 274 276 491 (b. 1716; d. 1786)

Fawcett, John Jr. 246 250 260 275 276 389 442 491 531 (b. 1749)

Fawcett, John (3) 470 492 [b. 1770; s. of Thos. (1)]

Fawcett, John (4) 492 [b. 1786; s. of Thos. (2)]

Fawcett, John (5) 442 (child of Mary 1809)

Fawcett, John 60 81 84 218 220 250 251 275 347 349 353 374 393 395 400 410 446 449 499 519 (1745-1819)

Fawcett, John, wills two acres 546

Fawcett, Jonah 348

Fawcett, Jonathan 403 441 460 492

Fawcett, Joseph (1) 492 [b. 1750; s. of Rich. (1)]

Fawcett, Joseph (a) 251 (1769)

Fawcett, Joseph (b) 251 (1769)

Fawcett, Joseph (2) 492 [b. 1778; s. of Rich. (2)]

Fawcett, Joseph (3) 470 492 [b. 1786; s. of Thos. (1)]

Fawcett, Joseph 93 250 347 390 403 404 460 464 484 (1768-1817)

Fawcett, Joseph J. 452

Fawcett, Joshua 442 529

Fawcett, Josiah 198 347 351 353 354 357 361 453 492

Fawcett, Levi 447

Fawcett, Louisa 452

Fawcett, Lydia (1) 491 [b. 1739; d. of John (1)]

Fawcett, Lydia (2) 492 [b. 1761; d. of Richard (1)]

Fawcett, Lydia (3) 492 [b. 1781; d. of Thos. (1)]

Fawcett, Lydia (4) 492 [b. 1787; d. of Thos. (2)]

Fawcett, Lydia 519 (m. Brown 1819)

Fawcett, Lydia 60 274 351 389 449 (1742-1819)

Fawcett, Lydia A. 452

Fawcett, Lydia T. 353

Fawcett, Mahlon 442

Fawcett, Mahlon T. 452

Fawcett, Margaret 491

Fawcett, Margaret (Brown) 276

Fawcett, Martha Sr. 470 492 [b. 1749; w. of Thos. (1)]

Fawcett, Martha Jr. 470 492 [b. 1773; d. of Thos. (1)]

Fawcett, Martha 252 257 272 274 310 347 376 379 382 386 388 393 395 397 400 401 403 446 501 504 (1770-1814)

Fawcett, Martha (Branson) 251 (m. 1769)

Fawcett, Martha H. 470

Fawcett, Mary (1) 492 [b. 1746?; w. of Richard (2)]

Fawcett, Mary (2) 492 [b. 1757; d. of Richard (1)]

Fawcett, Mary (a) 276 (1781)

Fawcett, Mary (b) 276 (1781)

Fawcett, Mary Jr. 275 (1781)

Fawcett, Mary (3) 492 [b. 1788; d. of Thos. (1)]

Fawcett, Mary (4) 347 464 470 484 (b. 1788; w. of Jos.)

Fawcett, Mary 275 347 390 400 401 403 404 422 442 446 460 (1764-1814)

Fawcett, Mary B. 347

Fawcett, Mary (Branson) 347 464 470 484 (m. Jos. 1813)

Fawcett, Mary (Painter) 393 (m. 1792)

Fawcett, Mary (Pickering) 250 (m. 1768)

Fawcett, Mary E. 453

Fawcett, Mary T. 452

Fawcett, Nancy 442

Fawcett, Nathan 517

Fawcett, Olivia G. 453

Fawcett, Phebe 403 460 462 492

Fawcett, Phebe (Holloway) 516

Fawcett, Phila. (Holloway) 518

Fawcett, Phineas A. 453

Fawcett, Rachel (1) 492 493 [b. 1725?; w. of Richard (1)]

Fawcett, Rachel (2) 491 [b. 1752; d. of John (1)]

Fawcett, Rachel (a) 246 275 (1764, 1781)

Fawcett, Rachel (b) 246 275 (1764, 1781)

Fawcett, Rachel (3) 492 [b. 1769; d. of Richard (2)]

Fawcett, Rachel (4) 470 492 [b. 1775; d. of Thos. (1)]

Fawcett, Rachel 60 250 251 274 389 390 393 395-397 401 403

Fawcett, Rebecca (1) 491 493 [b. 1717?; w. of John (1)]

Fawcett, Rebekah (2) 492 [b. 1774; d. of Rich. (2)]

Fawcett, Rebekah 60 246 274-276 374 390 452 (1745-1833)

Griffith, John 333 (s. of Wm. of Ohio 1807)
Griffith, John 123 196 271 281-284 287 294 296 297 300-302 304 306 307 310 318 320 336 340 343 345 347 352 357 364 376 384 393 414 441 530 531 532 (1777-1826)
Griffith, John 172 488 (b. 1853?; s. of A. H. Sr.)
Griffith, Jonah 457
Griffith, Joseph 171 172
Griffith, Joseph C. 488
Griffith, Joseph H. 366 368
Griffith, Lydia H. 489
Griffith, Martha (1) 285 (1786)
Griffith, Martha (2) 285 (1786)
Griffith, Martha 282 283 376 (1783, 1784)
Griffith, Martha 286 294 414 (d. of John & Mary; m. Morgan 1789)
Griffith, Martha 355 (1822)
Griffith, Martha 488 (1833-1839; d. of A. H. Sr.)
Griffith, Martha A. 354 359 361 363 365 367 368 (1819-1828)
Griffith, Mary Sr. 284 300 304 310 (1785-1796)
Griffith, Mary Jr. 284 296 302 313 (1785-1798)
Griffith, Mary (1) 286 294 297 316 318 321 414 471 (1747-1789; w. of John)
Griffith, Mary (2) 286 294 297 316 318 414 (d. of John?)
Griffith, Mary (3) 294 (1789)
Griffith, Mary 518 (m. Craighill 1815)
Griffith, Mary 283 296 301 302 304 306 310 313 315 330 333 336 340 343 345 347 352 354 355 357 419-421 441 (1782-1822)
Griffith, Mary A. 488
Griffith, Mary (Ellis) 376
Griffith, Mary (Hollingsworth) 488
Griffith, Mary (Smith) 333
Griffith, Polly 300 (1792; Mary?)
Griffith, Rachel 330 340 345 352 355 357 363 365 366
Griffith, Rachel (Hackney) 321
Griffith, Richard 286
Griffith, Richard E., Sr. 8 53 58 59 66 67 380
Griffith, Richard S. 172
Griffith, Robert D. 488
Griffith, Ruth (Butterfield) 301
Griffith, Samuel 286
Griffith, Sarah 344
Griffith, Sibbell 294 471 (Sybil)
Griffith, William (1) 301 333 457
Griffith, William (2) 519
Griffith, Du Pont & Co. 172

Griffith, Hance & Co. 172
Griffith, Hoge & Co. 171 172
Grillet, Stephen 107 548
Grim, Mrs. Hardy 25
Grimes, Rachel 349
Grimes, Tacy 349
Grimes, Tamar 349 446
Grimes, Thomas 349
Grisell, Ann 291
Grist mills 168 205
Grist, Ruth (Cowgill) 507 (Griest?)
Grizzet, Agnes 430 (Grisell?)
Gross, Ann 325
Grove, Mary 353
Grover, Ezra 312
Grover, mother of Benj. Borden Sr. 26
Grubb, Adam 290 298 302 319 336 415 511
Grubb, Beulah 322 329
Grubb, Curtis 290 302 319 328 329 415 513
Grubb, Elizabeth 319 371
Grubb, Hannah 290 302 415
Grubb, John 319 328 329 422 514
Grubb, Joseph 323-326 334 435 529 532
Grubb, Lydia 290 415
Grubb, Mary 415 (Grubbs)
Grubb, Phebe 329
Grubb, Rebecca 314 319 422
Grubb, Ruth 329
Grubb, Ruth (Haines) 328
Grubb, Sarah 290 302 328 415
Grubb, Susanna (1) 319
Grubb, Susanna (2) 319
Grubb, Susanna 259 283 290 302 324 328 329 422 443
Grubb, William Sr. 422
Grubb, William Jr. 290 422
Grubb, William (1) 302
Grubb, William (2) 302
Grubb, William 124 281-284 290 295 314 319 322 328 329 410 415 513 529 531 532
Grymes, John 42-44
Guernsey Co., Ohio 221
Guide wanted 134
Guilford Co., N. C. 212 214 220 225 544
Gunpowder Mtg. 216 419 420 425 427 432-434 445
"Guns Inside" 202
"Guns Outside" 111 201
Guthrey, Joseph 299
Guthrey, Mary 299
Gwynedd Mtg. 17 30 216 410 411 414 417 427 429 437 536

Haas, Catherine 354
Hack, Andrew 20

Lewis, Sarah 297 310 441
Lewis, Sarah (Antrim) 302
Lewis, Sudney 248 474 499 (Sidney?)
Lewis, Susanna 290 421 424 430
Lewis, Susanna (Hoge) 506
Lewis, Wm. 289 292 293 297 302 310
  429 430 441
"Liberty," church, etc. 199 200
Library at Hopewell 159-161 551
Library rules proposed 160
Lidner, V. 130
Life of Daniel Stanton 100
Light, Peter 333
Lightfoot, Edward 389
Lightfoot, Sam'l Jr. 121
Lightfoot, Thomas 121
Likens, Elizabeth 348
Likens, Henry 279 287 419 505
Likens, Jonas 255 260 261 279
Likens, Jonas Jr. 279
Likens, Mary 348
Likins, Phebe 278 279 419
Likins, Rebekah 255 279
Likins, William 296
Limestone sinks 190
Lincoln, Abraham 186 (militia captain)
Lincoln, Abraham 134 185 186 (President)
Lincoln, John 186 546 (pioneer)
Lincoln's great-grandfather 186 546
Lincoln, Va. 70 101 132 201 215 224
  473 546 549
Lincoln Cemetery 473
Lincoln mtg. house 546 549
Lindsey, Capt. John 116
Line between Frederick & Augusta 186
Lingbridge, England 184
Linseys made 172
Lisbon, Portugal 170
Litigation over titles 65
Linville Creek 168 186 543 546
Linville Creek Baptists 186 545
Linville Creek furnace 168
Linville Creek grant 186
Little, Chas. 354-356 449 451
Little, Hannah 356
Little, Isaac P. 451
Little, John 356
Little, Lydia 451 455
Little, Lydia (Parkins) 356
Little, Robert 356 (Little & Lytle)
Little, Wm. 451
Little Britain, Pa. 102
Little Britain Mtg. 217
Little Cacapon Mtg. 92 217
Little Creek Mtg. 214 217 418
Little Falls, Md. 104
Little Falls Mtg. 137 138 216 217 433
  455 550

Little Miami River 218 219
Little North Mtn. 18 76 92 145
Littlejohn, Ann 414 506
Littlejohn, Elizabeth 428
Littlejohn, James 414 509
Littlejohn, John Sr. 414
Littlejohn, John Jr. 414
Littlejohn, Martha 414 507
Littlejohn, Mary 428
Littlejohn, Sarah Sr. 414 428
Littlejohn, Sarah Jr. 428
Littlejohn, Thomas 414 506
Littlejohn, Wm. 414 506
Littler, Catherine 243 245 498 (m. Jones
  1765)
Littler, Catherine 298 420 (d. of Nathan; m. Wood 1791)
Littler, Chas. W. 345 354 356
Littler, David 420 514
Littler, Elijah 301 323
Littler, Elisha 306
Littler, Eliza 343 349
Littler, Eliza W. 354
Littler, Eliz'h 243 338 339 342 343
Littler, Isaiah 320 347 348 440
Littler, John Sr. 16 17 22 27-29 31-33
  56 168
Littler, John Jr. 32 243 249 298
Littler, John (1) 306 420 (1784-1794)
Littler, John (2) 306 420 (1784-1794)
Littler, John 298 320 339 356 451
  (1791-1828)
Littler, Lydia 310
Littler, Margaret 345
Littler, Maria 343 345
Littler, Mary (1) 16 56 241 243
Littler, Mary (2) 339 450
Littler, Mary (Ridgway) 356
Littler, Mary (Ross) 31 32
Littler, Nancy 356 357
Littler, Nathan Sr. 32 243 249 420 498
  (1748-1784)
Littler, Nathan Jr. 32 420 432 433 511
  (1784-1800)
Littler, Nathan 148 239 282-287 291
  293 294 296-298 300 306 312 315
  316 320 327 333 338 345 356 440
  529 532 (1783-1813)
Littler, Peggy 323
Littler, Rachel 32 282 306 420
Littler, Rachel A. 356 357
Littler, Rebecca (1) 249 282 297 298
  302 306 312 356 419 (1768-1798)
Littler, Rebecca (2) 342 356 357 (1812-
  1822)
Littler, Rebecca 320 327 338 339 342
  343 349 (1801-1815)
Littler, Sam'l (1) 32 298
Littler, Sam'l (2) 32

McClun, Mary 299 434 477 (1764-1798)
McClun, M. H. 337
McClun, Nathan 477
McClun, Rachel 313 332 337 338 340 344 346 348 351 477
McClun, Robert 351
McClun, Sarah 348 351
McClun, Thos. Sr. 32 123 147 149 243 245-250 252 256 259 262 263 313 477 529 531 (b. 1735)
McClun, Thos. Jr. 477 (b. 1771)
McClung, Thos. 536
McClure, Sarah 337
McConnell, Edward 494
McConnell, Eliz'h 382
McConnell, Hannah 337
McConnell, James 379 382 383 389 392 399 400 494
McConnell, Jesse 494
McConnell, Morris 382
McConnell, Rachel 494
McConnell, Rachel (Antrim) 382
McCool, Ann (1) 477 (b. 1715?; w. of Jas. Sr.)
McCool, Ann (2) 511 (m. Lewis 1800)
McCool, Ann (3) 513 (m. Darlington 1804)
McCool, Ann 27 240 251 302 305 311 312 315 420 (1749-1798)
McCool, Catherine 321 513
McCool, Charity 446 448
McCool, Deborah 280 290 305 414 420
McCool, Eleanor 254 264 267 289 514
McCool, Eleanor (Lewis) 253
McCool, Eliza 448
McCool, Gabriel 305 420 477 512
McCool, Grace 420 511 (1783)
McCool, Jas. Sr. 240 251 477 (b. 1709; d. 1751)
McCool, Jas. Jr. 251 253 289 302 311 420 448 477 500 509 523 (b. 1747)
McCool, John Sr. 477 515
McCool, John Jr. 515
McCool, John 124 248 250 251 253 254 264 267 289 315 352 531
McCool, Jonathan 297 (Jon.)
McCool, Katherine 315
McCool, Lewis 321 513
McCool, Martha (1) 248 251 477
McCool, Martha (2) 517
McCool, Mary 291 302 311 312 420 477
McCool, Olivia 516
McCool, Rachel 448
McCormack, Eliz'h 302
McCormack, James 301
McCormack, Jane 246
McCormack, Marcy 246 255 290

McCormack, Sarah 302 338 (See McCormick)
McCormick, Cyrus 173
McCormick, Dawson 344
McCormick, Eliz'h 385 386 388
McCormick, Jas. 256 385
McCormick, Jas. Jr. 386 388
McCormick, Marcy 265
McCormick, Mary L. 348 (See McCormack)
McCoy, Andrew 64 242 (McCay, McKay)
McCoy, Jane (Ridgway) 242
McCoy, Margaret 245
McCoy, Robert 242
McCoy, Robert Jr. 245
McCray, Samuel 247
McCumber, Caleb 107
McCurdy, Sarah (Rees) 505 (McKurdy)
McCurter, Ann 331
McCurty, Eleanor (McCool) 514 (McCurdy? McCarty?)
McDonald, Col. Angus 129
McDonald, Esther 258
McDonald, John 261 266
McDonald, Mary 313
McDonald, Rebekah (White) 523
McDonaugh, William 17
McDuffie Co., Ga. 97 228 546
McGill, Ann 304
McGill, Charles 287
McGill, Hannah 287
McGill, Hannah (Haston) 500 (Magill?)
McGill, James 248
McGin, James 28
McGrew, Alice 289 305
McGrew, Dinah Sr. 416
McGrew, Dinah Jr. 416 419
McGrew, Finley Sr. 270 272 416 419
McGrew, Finley Jr. 416 419
McGrew, Jacob 419
McGrew, Jas. (1) 51 61 237 238 240 539
McGrew, Jas. (2) 416 419 423
McGrew, Jane 423
McGrew, John 268 270 289 416 504
McGrew, Marg't 416 419
McGrew, Mary (1) 240 539
McGrew, Mary (2) 268 270 272 416 419
McGrew, Nathan 416 419
McGrew, Rebecca 416 419
McGruder, John 53
McGuire, Millicent 356
McIntire, Sarah 539
McKay, A. 241
McKay, Abigail 403 448 (McCoy)
McKay, Abigail (Shinn) 396
McKay, Abraham 499
McKay, Alice 388

McMunn, Ione 384
McMunn, Mary 384
McMunn, Robert 384 387
McNamee, Barnabas 281 417
McNamee, Elias 417
McNamee, Gideon 281 417
McNamee, Isaac 281 417
McNamee, Jacob 417
McNamee, Margaret 417
McNamee, Mary Sr. 281 417
McNamee, Mary Jr. 417
McNamee, Sarah 281 417
McNichols, Martha 441
McPherson, Ann (1) 508 (m. Moore 1792)
McPherson, Ann (2) 334 (m. Lupton 1809)
McPherson, Ann (3) 440 (child of Isaac 1806)
McPherson, Ann (4) 443 (child of Dan'l 1809)
McPherson, Ann 290 295 314 319 328-330 332 426 (1788-1807)
McPherson, Betty 328-330 440
McPherson, Dan'l (1) 410 (1771)
McPherson, Dan'l (2) 478 (b. 1775; s. of Wm. Sr.)
McPherson, Dan'l Sr. 295 (dec'd 1790)
McPherson, Dan'l Jr. 295 413 421 (1776-1790)
McPherson, Dan'l (a) 314 319 334 (1798-1809)
McPherson, Dan'l (b) 314 319 334 (1798-1809)
McPherson, Dan'l 123 283 284 290 315 316 321-323 326-330 341 371 443 511 531 (1778-1811)
McPherson, Eliz'h 328 438 443
McPherson, Eliz'h G. 330
McPherson, Hannah (1) 328 (1804)
McPherson, Hannah (2) 328 (1804)
McPherson, Hannah Sr. 337 (1810)
McPherson, Hannah Jr. 334 337 (1809, 1810)
McPherson, Hannah 290 301 314 319 321 329 330 334 336 339 414 448 526 (1776-1817)
McPherson, Isaac 321 322 326-329 353 440
McPherson, Jane 478 (b. 1752?; w. of Wm. Sr.)
McPherson, Jane (1) 290 (1788)
McPherson, Jane (2) 290 (1788)
McPherson, Jane Jr. 322 329 350 (1801-1816)
McPherson, Jane 517 (m. Bruce 1814)
McPherson, Jane 283 295 301-303 314 319 322 323 327-329 336-338 341 350 411 429 454 (1773-1840)

McPherson, Jane B. 326 329 332 334 335 338 340 342 345 346
McPherson, John 80 89 90 109 111 283 284 290 295 301 302 314 315 319 321 322 328 330 332 334 336-339 341 350 351 369 412 413 448 526 527 532 (1774-1830)
McPherson, John Jr. 328 334 337 350 351 448 (1804-1817)
McPherson, John A. 353
McPherson, Jonas 302 303 428 478 525
McPherson, Marg't 314
McPherson, Martha 303 427 429
McPherson, Martha (Beeson) 295
McPherson, Mary Jr. 322 (1801)
McPherson, Mary (m. Chamberlin 1802)
McPherson, Mary (1) 328 (1804)
McPherson, Mary (2) 328 (1804)
McPherson, Mary 446 (w. of Sam'l 1814)
McPherson, Mary 290 295 314 316 317 321-323 326 327 329 330 334 336 338 339 341 443 (1788-1810)
McPherson, Mary (Steer) 321 (m. 1801)
McPherson, Rebekah 295 314 319 322 328 329 332 334 337 339 426 443 448
McPherson, Ruth 283 421
McPherson, Sam'l 303 314-317 319 321 322 327 328 330 334 337 339 341 364 443 446 447 450 454 532
McPherson, Susan 353
McPherson, Susanna 319 327-329 341
McPherson, Tamzin 316 319 321-323 326 328-330
McPherson, Wm. Sr. 478 (b. 1751?)
McPherson, Wm. Jr. 478 (b. 1778; d. 1778)
McPherson, Wm. 94 148 283 284 290 295 296 314 321 322 327-330 334 336-339 341 345 353 370 447 529 532 (1772-1819)
Mead, John 272 379
Mead, Samuel 62
Mead, William 60
Meade, Benjamin 387
Meade, Bishop Wm. 178
Meade, Mary 379
Meat and bread 129
Meather, Margaret 392
Mechanical inventions 173 174
Medford Mtg. 218 226
Medlar apples 169
Meeting at Fawcett's, 1764 246
Meeting at Rogers's, 1771 253
Meeting at Strasburg, 1782 104
Meeting by indulgence 6 316 318
Meeting for Sufferings 6 27 39 117-120 122 140 158 180 182 536
Meeting held alternately 75

Moore, Jos. 265 269 378 380 390 456 500 502
Moore, Kames 376 (James?)
Moore, Lydia 265
Moore, Marg't 383 390
Moore, Mary (1) 378 383
Moore, Mary (2) 378 383
Moore, Mary 458 (d. of Anthony)
Moore, Mary 500 (w. of Jos.)
Moore, Mary 265 269 390 398
Moore, Miriam 272
Moore, Phebe 272 456
Moore, Rachel 391 458 478
Moore, Rebekah 272
Moore, Reuben 265 269 378 380 391 394 396 500
Moore, Robt. 376 378 387 458 478
Moore, Ruth 458
Moore, Sarah 478 (b. 1761; d. of Anthony)
Moore, Sarah (1) 265 (1777)
Moore, Sarah (2) 265 (1777)
Moore, Sarah 458 (w. of Robt. 1797)
Moore, Sarah 270 272 378 387 394 430 (1780-1793)
Moore, Sarah (Bond) 301 (m. 1793)
Moore, Thos. (1) 190 (1762)
Moore, Thos. (2) 456 (child of Jas. 1786)
Moore, Thos. 301 500
Moore, Wm. 378 429-431
Moore, Zilpha 241 272 378 380 387 458 478 (See Moor)
Moorstown, N. J. 214 223
Moorstown Mtg. 212 220
Moreland, Sarah 424
Morland, Stephen 215 216
Moravian Single Brethren 170 544
Morayshire, Scotland 542
Morgan, Ann 18
Morgan & Morgan 18 29 33
Morgan, Capt. Rich'd 116
Morgan, Cath. (Garretson) 33
Morgan, Col. Morgan 186
Morgan, Deborah (1) 509 (m. Lynn 1793)
Morgan, Deborah (2) 521 (m. Hackney 1829)
Morgan, Deborah 294 407 408 424 446 451
Morgan, Deb. L. 355 363 365-368
Morgan, Edward 244 497
Morgan, Gen. Dan'l 103 129
Morgan, Isaac 340 445
Morgan, John (1) 294
Morgan, John (2) 294
Morgan, John 310 341 424 442 536
Morgan, Jos. 244 294 426 498 512 536
Morgan, Martha 310 321 363 514

Morgan, Martha (Griffith) 294
Morgan, Mary 294 310 340 424 516
Morgan, Mordecai 244
Morgan, Morgan 363
Morgan, Morgan Jr. 243
Morgan, Morgan VIII 34
Morgan, Phebe (Rees) 521
Morgan, Rachel 244 497
Morgan, Richard 28 35
Morgan, Sarah 17 55
Morgan Mills 172
Morgan monument 33
Morgan's Chapel 33
Morgan's riflemen 145
Morris, David 423 436
Morris, Edward Sr. 436
Morris, Edward Jr. 436
Morris, Edward 292 300 313 316 318 423 532
Morris, Eliz'h 423 436
Morris, Hannah Sr. 423
Morris, Hannah Jr. 423
Morris, Hannah 292 300 306 436
Morris, Jane 436
Morris, Jonathan 313 318 321 (Jona.)
Morris, Joshua 121
Morris, Lydia 436
Morrison, Lucy 489
Moseley, Bethlehem 243
Moseley, James 302 431 440
Moseley, Jesse 307
Mother church of Hopewell 214
Mott, Rich'd 107 216 222
Mountjoy, Sally 377
Mt. Ery Furnace 167 168
Mt. Hebron Cemetery 463 465 467 472-475 477 481-484 488
Mt. Holly Mtg. 211 220 427
Mt. Jackson, Va. 74 100 224 378
Mt. Pleasant, Ohio 125 220
Mt. Pleasant (Va.) Friends 75
Mt. Pleasant graveyard 71 84 95 197
Mt. Pleasant Mtg. 66 82 84-86 93 150 212 215 218 220 274-276 389 390 403 470 529 546 547 549
Mt. Pleasant mtg. house 94
Mt. Pleasant school 156
Mt. Pony Mtg. 90 185 224 503 547 548 (Southland)
Moved to Carolina 499
Moved to Chester 525
Moved to Goose Creek 486
Moved to Kansas 472
Moved to Ohio 87 97 109 467 479 486
Moved to Waterford 486
Moving without advice 499 505 507 516 517 520
Moving without cert. 498 505 507
Mowing machines 173

Pusey, John 495
Pusey, Joshua 462 495
Pusey, Lydia 462 495
Pusey, Marg't 462 495
Pusey, Mary Sr. 260 462 495
Pusey, Mary Jr. 462
Pusey, Mary 274-276 376 379 381 382
  386 388 389 392 395 399-401
Pusey, Mary (Brown) 260 495
Pusey, Nathan Sr. 256 260 274-276 374
  376 379 381 382 386 388 389 392
  395 399-401 (b. 1748)
Pusey, Nathan Jr. 462 495 (b. 1790)
Pusey, Rachel 389 395 398-400 495
Pusey, Susanna 495
Pusey, William 462
Putnam Co., Ill. 213
Pyle, John 307 508 (Pyles)
Pyle, Jos. 290 509 (See Piles)

Quaintance, Ann 432 440
Quaintance, Eli 432 440
Quaintance, Fisher 432 440
Quaintance, Jos. 315 432 440
Quaintance, Sam'l 432 512
Quaintance, Susanna Sr. 432 440
Quaintance, Susanna Jr. 432 440
Quaintance, Susanna 315
Quaintance, Wm. 432 440
Quaker answers 134
Quaker center 218
Quaker colony 40
Quaker doctrines 140 141
"Quaker for the times" 167
"Quaker Graveyard" 214
Quaker historian 111
Quaker ideals 139 142 164 165
Quakerism in Ohio 218
Quaker ministers 113
Quaker of Nantucket 184
"Quaker of the Olden Time" 2
Quaker principles 114 115 229-233
"Quaker Road" 74
Quaker Rock 223
Quaker settlement 225
Quaker settlers 113
"Quaker's Faith" 229-233
"Quakers' Lawyer" 182
Quakers on Smith Creek 190 191
Quaker virtues 195 197
"Quaker Worship" 233 234
Quarreling 496 497 503 508 509
"Quarry Banks" 183
"Quarry Banks New Stile" 183
Quar. mtg. at Hopewell 107 111
Quar. mtg. at Redstone 110 548
Quar. mtg. granted in Ohio 109 110
Quar. mtg. in Winchester 162
Quar. mtg. proposed 82 83 546

Quar. mtgs. 201 532
Quebec captured 98 101 545
"Queen of Heaven" 107
Queens Co., N. Y. 217
Quicksburg, Va. 73 74 100
Quietism 141
Quietist mystics 141
Quinby, Daniel 198

Raccoon Ford, Va. 224 225
Race with wolves 202
Radford, Va. 222
Radford Mtg. 432
Radnor, Pa. 15
Radnor Mtg. 222 371 437 438 442 453
Ragan, Sarah 249
Rahway, N. J. 222
Rahway Mtg. 222
Railing against Friends 502
Railroad building 173 550
Rakestraw, Eliz'h 417 456
Rakestraw, Hannah 417 456
Rakestraw, Jos. Sr. 456
Rakestraw, Jos. Jr. 456
Rakestraw, Jos. 417
Rakestraw, Justinian 417 456
Rakestraw, Sarah 417 456
Raley, Abigail 436
Raley, Ann 281 384 386 417 419 436 437
Raley, Asa 436
Raley, David 437
Raley, Eli 110 384 386 388 422 437
Raley, Ellis 419
Raley, Frances 384 386 419
Raley, Francis 384
Raley, Hannah 436
Raley, James 110 280-283 290 296 298
  299 309 313 319 384-386 415 421
  436 529 532
Raley, Jane 419
Raley, John 417 437
Raley, Joseph 437
Raley, Joshua 436
Raley, Mary 319 322 388 437
Raley, Mary (Hutton) 281
Raley, Mary (Lupton) 386
Raley, Michael 419
Raley, Rachel 313 319 436
Raley, Rachel (Steer) 384 385
Raley, Robert 281 384 419
Raley, Robert Jr. 418
Raley, Sarah 437
Rambo, Deborah 378 379
Rambo, Isaac 414
Rambo, Jackson 380 390 394 414
Rambo, Jacob Sr. 414
Rambo, Jacob Jr. 414 457
Rambo, Jacob 124 265 269 378 379 381
  383 390 398 412 531

323 326 327 332 333 335 336 338
340 343 352 356 365 366 370 378
393 403 523 526 529 532 (1760-1827)
Ridgway, Sally (1) 301 510 (m. Rees
  1795)
Ridgway, Sally (2) 352 356 364-366
  (1818-1827)
Ridgway, Samuel 377
Ridgway, Sarah 303 304 306
Ridgway, Shedy 388
Ridgway, Tacy 521
Ridgway, Tacy B. 352 356 366
Ridgway family 172 177
Riding, Susan (Painter) 521
Rigg, Clement 281
Rigg, Sarah 419
Rightsborough 223
Rily, Patrick 20
Rinehart, Abraham 349
Rinehart, Mary 349
Rinker, Mary 289
Riple, William 130
Rippey, Mathew 351
Rippey, Nancy 345
Rippon, W. Va. 211
Riser, Catharine 266
Risler, Elizabeth 312
Ritenour, Annie 469
Ritenour, Edith M. 469
Ritenour, S. L. 469
Riverton, Va. 186 542
Roach, John 319 332
Roach, Mary 370
Roack, George 382
Road overseer 17
"Road to Opequon" 53 543
Road scraper 173
Roberds, Sarah 288 (Roberts?)
Roberts, Abraham 431 434
Roberts, Alfred 475
Roberts, Asenath 419 425
Roberts, Eliza 339 475
Roberts, Elwood 537
Roberts, Esther 287 419 430
Roberts, Griffith 308 431 434
Roberts, Hannah 431 434
Roberts, Jean (Harmon) 475
Roberts, John Sr. 425
Roberts, John Jr. 425
Roberts, John 382 419
Roberts, Joseph 187
Roberts, Lydia 419 425 431 434
Roberts, Marg't H. 475
Roberts, Mary 486
Roberts, Rachel 431 434
Roberts, Rebecca 239 419 425 431 434
Roberts, Sarah Sr. 419 425

Roberts, Sarah Jr. 419 425 430 (See
  Roberds)
Roberts, Susanna (Southwood) 496
Roberts, Thos. 357 419 425
Robertson, Wm. 103
Robeson Mtg. 210
Robins, Mary (Branson) 29
Robins, Zachariah 29
Robinson, Albert G. 8 489
Robinson, A. Alex. 481
Robinson, Andrew 361 481 482
Robinson, Andrew A. 350
Robinson, Ann 206
Robinson, Anna F. 482
Robinson, Annie 482
Robinson, Annie R. 481
Robinson, Arch. 160 481 482
Robinson, Arch. S. 482
Robinson, D. Arthur 8 92 482 489
Robinson, Austin 482
Robinson, Bertha P. 482
Robinson, Chas. G. 481
Robinson, Chas. H. 482
Robinson, Chas. W. 482
Robinson, Clara (Piggott) 482
Robinson, Clarence J. 482
Robinson, Cora M. 481
Robinson, David 481
Robinson, Edwin J. 481
Robinson, Effa S. 482
Robinson, Emeline (Wright) 481
Robinson, Esther S. 481
Robinson, Florence (Lauck) 482
Robinson, Geo. 21 185 206
Robinson, Geo. N. 481
Robinson, Hannah (Cather) 481
Robinson, Ida (Robinson) 482
Robinson, Jackson 481
Robinson, James 350
Robinson, Jas. J. 481
Robinson, Jas. K. 482
Robinson, Jas. L. 481 482
Robinson, Jas. W. 482
Robinson, John 42 43 44
Robinson, John F. 482
Robinson, Jonathan 138 482
Robinson, Jos. 467 477 482
Robinson, Jos. A. 455 481
Robinson, Jos. S. 481 482
Robinson, Josiah 482
Robinson, Kate (Pelter) 482
Robinson, Laura A. 482 489
Robinson, Leona I. 481
Robinson, Lewis A. 481
Robinson, Luther H. 482
Robinson, Lydia A. 453
Robinson, Lydia J. 481
Robinson, Lydia (Steer) 481 482
Robinson, Mabel 468 482

Rogers, Rhoda 436 515
Rogers, Robert (1) 483 (b. 1754; s. of
Evan Sr.; d. 1755)
Rogers, Robert (2) 483 (b. 1760; s. of
Owen Sr.)
Rogers, Rob't 253 266 267 289 298 302
311 313 315 511 532 (1778-1798)
Rogers, Sarah Sr. 27 240 246 248 308
483 (b. 1730?; w. of Evan Sr.)
Rogers, Sarah Jr. 292 308 483 (b. 1770;
d. of Evan Sr.; m. Ellis 1794)
Rogers, Sarah (3) 483 (b. 1775; d. of
Owen Sr.)
Rogers, Sarah (a) 266 292 (1778, 1788)
Rogers, Sarah (b) 266 292 (1778, 1788)
Rogers, Sarah 253 289 300 311 315
(1771-1798)
Rogers, Sarah (Ballinger) 240 483 (m.
Evan Sr. 1749)
Rogers, Sarah (Pugh) 501 (m. Evan Jr.
1777)
Rogers, Sidney (1) 240 (1749)
Rogers, Sidney (2) 483 (b. 1765)
Rogers, Sidney 289 292 293 308 311 312
404 513 (1787-1802)
Rogers, Thomas 26 326 338
Rogers, William 29
Rogers, Zadok 311
Rommins, Hannah 447
Ross, Albena 16 30
Ross, Alexander (1) 14 15 17 22 24
28-31 36 37 39 41 44 47 51 54-56
65-67 69 185 187 542 543 544
Gets grant of land 12 40 42 43
Proposes a meeting on Opeckon 45
Conveys land for Hopewell 146
Leader of Friends' colony 178 180
Surveys land 29
Makes his will 16
Ross, Alexander (2) 242 243 253 496
Ross, Alfred 354 363 367
Ross, Ann 524
Ross, Cath. Sr. 16 30 31 (See Kath. Ross)
Ross, Cath. Jr. 16
Ross, Cath. 241 280 284 285 287 306-
308 406 (1758-1794)
Ross, Cath. (Thomas) 253 483 (m. 1770)
Ross, David (1) 16 (b. 1705?; s. of
Alex.; d. 1750?)
Ross, David (2) 253 483 (b. 1742; s.
of John; d. 1763?) (prob. d. about
1803; see pages 253, 331)
Ross, David Jr. 307 316 323 331 [prob.
s. of David (2)]
Ross, David 124 193 239 243 247-250
254 260 273 276 277 279 282-288
291 293 294 296 300 302 304 306-
308 310 312 315 316 320 330 331-

333 371 442 524 529 531 532 (1761-
1809)
Ross, Enos 312 324 326 331 334 354
367 483 516
Ross, George 16 32 51 62 64 240-246
248 253 496 499
Ross, Hannah 361-363 367 448 450
Ross, John 16 51 56 182 253 483
Ross, Jonathan Sr. 524
Ross, Jonathan Jr. 524
Ross, Jonathan 243 307 312 324 331 332
370 408 414 521
Ross, Kath. 15 16 55 56 (w. of Alex.)
Ross, Kath. 253 483 [b. 1751?; w. of
David (2)]
Ross. Kath. 254 282 283 286 291 297
300 301 304 312 331 (1771-1806)
(See Cath. Ross)
Ross, Levi 524
Ross, Lydia 16 (d. of Alex.; m. Day
before 1748)
Ross, Lydia 182 483 (b. 1721?; w. of
John)
Ross, Lydia 354 367 (w. of Enos; dec'd
1819)
Ross, Lydia Jr. 307 (1794) (prob. d. of
Enos)
Ross, Lydia 524 (d. of Jonathan Sr.
1795)
Ross, Lydia (1) 331 354 367 (1806-
1827)
Ross, Lydia (2) 331 354 367 (1806-
1827)
Ross, Lydia 516 (m. Humes 1811)
Ross, Lydia 240 306 307 329 332-334
336 338 339 363 365 (1750-1826)
Ross, Lydia (Hollingsworth) 182 483
Ross, Lydia (Rees) 312 (m. Enos 1798)
Ross, Margaret 254
Ross, Martha Sr. 524 (w. of Jonathan
Sr.)
Ross, Martha Jr. 524 (d. of Jonathan
Sr.)
Ross, Martha (3) 354 (d. of Enos)
Ross, Martha 349
Ross, Mary (1) 16 31
Ross, Mary (2) 307
Ross, Phebe 307 312 331 524
Ross, Rachel (1) 307 (d. of David)
Ross, Rachel (2) 524 (d. of Jonathan
Sr.)
Ross, Rachel 293 294 296-298 300-302
304 306 312
Ross, Richard 261
Ross, Stephen (1) 62 253 407 498 (1758-
1770)
Ross, Stephen (2) 524 (minor in 1795)
Ross, Thomas 339 347 448 534 535
Ross and Bryan colony 14 37 39 40

Smith, Ann (2) 384 (1788)
Smith, Ann 440 (minor of Jacob 1807)
Smith, Ann 262 269 270 272 273 374
378 379 388 419 425 432 457 (1776-
1796)
Smith, Anna W. 11 533
Smith, Benjamin 418
Smith, Caleb 483
Smith, Capt. Jeremiah 116
Smith, C. Arthur 11
Smith, Christopher 394
Smith, Col. John 102 188
Smith, Copperthwaite 425 432
Smith, David 287 315 424-426 432 435
437
Smith, David R. 453
Smith, Deborah 292 298 425 432
Smith, Edith 273
Smith, Edmund 521
Smith, Edward 188
Smith, Eliz'h (1) 293 (1788)
Smith, Eliz'h (2) 293 (1788)
Smith, Eliz'h 255 294 419 432 511 521
(1772-1798)
Smith, Eliz. Peterson 259 (1774)
Smith, Enoch 511
Smith, Ezekiel 273
Smith, Frederick 294
Smith, George Sr. 459 (1798)
Smith, George Jr. 459 (1798)
Smith, George 281 287 308 331 333
338-340 343-346 396 418 419 427
(1781-1813)
Smith, Hannah (1) 409 (child of John
1770)
Smith, Hannah (2) 427 (child of Abra-
ham 1790)
Smith, Hannah (3) 354 367 432 (w. of
Wm. 1795)
Smith, Hannah (4) 440 (child of Jacob
1807)
Smith, Hannah (5) 453 (child of Isaac
1835)
Smith, Hannah 270 272 374 376 379
(1780-1786)
Smith, Hannah (Ross) 367 (m. 1827)
Smith, Hannah (Thompson) 296 (m.
1791)
Smith, Hannah W. 363
Smith, Henry Jr. 413 (1775)
Smith, Henry (2) 278 (s. of Sam'l 1782)
Smith, Henry (3) 419 (child of Sarah
1782)
Smith, Henry 262 265 268 277 281 287
315 (1776-1798)
Smith, Isaac (1) 265 (s. of Jos.; m.
1778)
Smith, Isaac (2) 432 (child of Wm.
1795)

Smith, Isaac (3) 440 (child of Jacob
1807)
Smith, Isaac (a) 354 (1819)
Smith, Isaac (b) 354 (1819)
Smith, Isaac Jr. 358 362 364 367 530
(1823-1826)
Smith, Isaac 89 90 199 264 291 294 296
298 299 301 304 306 310 312 315
316 321 327 333 336 338 339 343-345
347 349 358 361 363 367 394 423
427 448 453 526 531 (1776-1835)
Smith, Jacob 264 (s. of Jos.; m. 1776)
Smith, Jacob Sr. 440 (1807)
Smith, Jacob Jr. 440 (1807)
Smith, Jacob 239 263 265 276 282 294
296 308 311 (1776-1798)
Smith, James 255 340
Smith, Jane 59 375 412 (Jean)
Smith, Jane (Rees) 520
Smith, Jesse 446
Smith, John 59 (w. Jane 1736)
Smith, John 409 (w. Ann 1770)
Smith, John Jr. 253 403 (1770, 1799)
Smith, John (1) 379 (1786)
Smith, John (2) 379 (1786)
Smith, John 432 (child of Thos. 1796)
Smith, John 440 (minor of Jacob 1807)
Smith, John 453 (child of Isaac 1835)
Smith, John 18 30 63 253 270 272 287
374 376 383 384 388 393 502 517
536 (1736-1813)
Smith, John S. 446
Smith, Jonah 446
Smith, Jonathan 331 348
Smith, Jonathan G. 366
Smith, Jos. 483 (b. 1728; d. 1781)
Smith, Jos. (1) 273 282 294 (1780-
1789)
Smith, Jos. (2) 273 282 294 (1780-1789)
Smith, Jos. 521 (w. Lydia) (1795?)
Smith, Jos. 432 (child of Wm. 1795)
Smith, Jos. 432 (s. of Thos. 1796)
Smith, Jos. Jr. 315 (1798)
Smith, Jos. 43 264 265 277 278 287
293 296 299 302 318 333 343-345
363 413 447 510 531 (1730-1826)
Smith, Jos. G. 528
Smith, Jos. T. 354 363 367
Smith, Josiah 440
Smith, Jude 432
Smith, Levi 282 288 294 296 333 343-347
352 354 355 362-364 366-368 530
Smith, Lydia 299 302 318 325 425 432
440 521
Smith, Lydia A. 453
Smith, Lydia (Walker) 293
Smith, Mahlon 273 285 381 384 385
387 399 461
Smith, Marg't 270 272 409 432 493

Smith, Martha 277 278 281 294 363 365
418 424 427 453 (1781-1835)
Smith, Martha Jr. 291 (1788)
Smith, Martha (Payne) 282 (m. 1783)
Smith, Martha R. 357
Smith, Martha (Ridgway) 287 (m. 1786)
Smith, Martha (Ross) 354 (m. 1819)
Smith, Martha (Smith) 278 (m. 1782)
Smith, Mary 500 (m. Clevenger 1775)
Smith, Mary (1) 273 287 294 333 339
343 344 346 419 461 (1780-1813)
Smith, Mary (2) 273 287 294 333 339
343 344 346 361 419 (1780-1813)
Smith, Mary 423 (w. of Isaac 1786)
Smith, Mary Jr. 296 316 340 345
(1791-1813)
Smith, Mary 521 (minor of Jos.) (1795?)
Smith, Mary 459 (w. of Geo. Sr. 1798)
Smith, Mary 461 (w. of Mahlon 1805)
Smith, Mary 440 (minor of Jacob 1807)
Smith, Mary 519 (m. Cloud 1818)
Smith, Mary 473 (b. 1840? m. Jackson)
Smith, Mary 269 272 278 282 285 288
293 296 301 315 316 320 321 327
338 340 345 354 367 378 381 384 387
394 409 418 (1770-1827)
Smith, Mary (Allen) 265 (m. 1777)
Smith, Mary H. 368 (1828)
Smith, Mary (Hackney) 363 (m. 1826)
Smith, Mary J. 453 (1835)
Smith, Mary (Lupton) 133 483 (m.
1865?)
Smith, Mary R. (1) 349 352 354 355
357 (1815-1822)
Smith, Mary R. (2) 133 483 (b. 1833)
Smith, Mary (Rees) 345 (m. 1813)
Smith, Mary (White) 273 (m. 1780)
Smith, Mordecai 521
Smith, Naomi Sr. 281 418
Smith, Naomi Jr. 418
Smith, Nathan 483
Smith, Patience 288 507
Smith, Patience (Ballinger) 264
Smith, Patrick 389
Smith, Phebe 335 393 534
Smith, Phebe (White) 340 444 446
Smith, Rachel (1) 264 265 282 294 296
333 345 363 413 (1775-1813; w. of
Jos.)
Smith, Rachel (2) 427 (child of Abra-
ham 1790)
Smith, Rachel (3) 435 437 (d. of David
1802)
Smith, Rachel (4) 440 (minor of Jacob
1807)
Smith, Rachel (5) 343 (d. of Levi; m.
Wright 1812)
Smith, Rachel 339 342 363 449 (1810-
1826)

Smith, Rachel (Irish) 455 (1890)
Smith, Rebecca (1) 419 (child of Sarah
1782)
Smith, Rebecca (2) 379 409 (d. of John;
m. Swayne 1786)
Smith, Rebecca (3) 521 (d. of Jos.)
(1795?)
Smith, Rebecca (4) 482 (b. 1841?; m.
Robinson)
Smith, Rebecca 272 354 392 393 (1780-
1820)
Smith, Robert 28 414
Smith, Robt. H. 446
Smith, Ruth 417 435 524
Smith, Ruth (Wright) 315
Smith, Sally 345 356 359 362 366
Smith, Sally (Wright) 344
Smith, Sam'l (1) 278 (1782)
Smith, Sam'l (2) 278 (1782)
Smith, Sam'l 53 251 293 380 396 418
431 505 521 538 (1752-1794)
Smith, Sarah (1) 255 (d. of Jas.; m.
Lupton 1772)
Smith, Sarah (2) 419 (& children 1782)
Smith, Sarah (3) 440 (child of Jacob
1807)
Smith, Sarah 277 278 281 287 331 349
352 354 363 367 410 (1772-1827)
Smith, Sarah (Bishop) 505 (m. 1785)
Smith, Sarah (Lupton) 523 (m. 1829?)
Smith, Seth 282 440 507 524
Smith, Susanna 379 409
Smith, Tamar 459
Smith, Tamson 278
Smith, Thos. (1) 277 (1782)
Smith, Thos. (2) 277 (1782)
Smith, Thos. Sr. 278 (1782)
Smith, Thos. Jr. 278 (1782)
Smith, Thos. 272 287 291 335 340 344
379 391 393 401 409 424 425 432 446
515 (1770-1814)
Smith, Wm. (1) 273 (1780)
Smith, Wm. (2) 273 (1780)
Smith, Wm. 521 (ch. of Jos.) (1795?)
Smith, Wm. 450 (ch. of Isaac 1835)
Smith, Wm. 124 127 287 296 354 367
432 446 (1777-1827)
Smith, Wm. Drewet 127
Smith Creek, Va. 72 73 190 191 199
Smith Creek Friends 72 73 75
Smith Creek graveyard 73 94 199
Smith Creek Mtg. 66 72-74 80 85 104
106 108 224 265 269 341 378-381 383
390 394 398 404 415 417 529 543
547 550
Smith Creek Mtg. in 1738 72 100
Smith Creek Mtg. in 1757 99 100
Smith Creek mtg. houses 94 198 199
Smith Creek region 100 199

Stealing a young woman 496
Stean, Mary 521
Steel, Isabella J. 327
Steel, Jacob 392
Steel, John 305
Steele, Mary 522
Steer, Abigail (1) 296 (1790)
Steer, Abigail (2) 296 (1790)
Steer, Abigail (3) 296 (1790)
Steer, Abigail 239 247 252 255 256 268
273 276 277 279-281 284-287 289
290 294 300 302 304 306 310 314
315 322 323 331 334 339 384 408
526 (1767-1810)
Steer, Amos 438 484
Steer, Ann 313 317 319 321 323 326
328 437 484 (1786-1804)
Steer, Anna 325 (1802)
Steer, Anne 338 (dec'd 1810)
Steer, Ann L. 454
Steer, Benjamin 338
Steer, Beulah W. 454
Steer, David 299 313 321 322 325-327
425 438 484
Steer, Elizabeth 338
Steer, Grace Sr. 263 264 268 484 (b.
1717; w. of Jos. Sr.; d. 1794)
Steer, Grace Jr. 239 263 264 268 271
274 276 289 294 373 381 384-386
388 (1776-1790)
Steer, Grace (3) 263 425 438 484 (b.
1758; w. of Jos. Jr.)
Steer, Grace (Jr.?) 509 (m. Cope 1794)
Steer, Grace 248 249 252 255 257 259
260 262 279 287 291 296 299 304
317 319 321 323 327 339 384 391
398 408 (1767-1810)
Steer, Grace (Lupton) 263 425 438 484
(m. Jos. Steer Jr. 1776)
Steer, Hannah 239 247-249 268 289
296 304 384 385 408
Steer, Isaac Sr. 268 384 484 (b. 1757)
Steer, Isaac Jr. 239 289 299 384 484
(b. 1776)
Steer, Isaac (1) 385 (1788)
Steer, Isaac (2) 385 (1788)
Steer, Isaac 239 252 255 257 260 263
265 271 273 279 280 283 285 287-
289 294 296 299 308 313 317 319
321 338 339 355 388 419 425 437
443 526 529 532 (1769-1822)
Steer, Isaac E. 346
Steer, James Sr. 75 76 82 84 123 444
(1769-1812)
Steer, James Jr. 322 325 332 339 444
(1801-1812)
Steer, James 80 81 87 89 107 123 148
239 249 250 252 256 259 263 264
268 274 276-291 294 296-298 300-

302 304 306 307 312 314-316 319
322 323 327 329 330 332-334 338
339 343 384 408 526 527 529 (1767-
1812)
Steer, John (1) 252 (1769)
Steer, John (2) 484 (b. 1782; died
infant)
Steer, John Jr. 319 (1800)
Steer, Jonah 313 319 321 338 355 437
Steer, Jos. Sr. 263 484 (b. 1716?)
Steer, Jos. Jr. 123 239 249 252 257
262-265 268 269 271 273 274 276
278 289 294 299 306 313 314 316
317 321 326 381 384-386 388 391
398 529 531 (1768-1803)
Steer, Jos. 3d 239 289 384 (1787, 1788)
Steer, Jos. (1) 249 252 323 326 (1768,
1769, 1801)
Steer, Jos. (2) 249 252 323 (1768, 1769,
1801)
Steer, Jos. (3) 323 (1801)
Steer, Jos. 484 (b. 1783; s. of Isaac)
Steer, Jos. 444 (s. of Jas. Sr. 1812)
Steer, Jos. 80 110 197 248 250 255 257
268 291 296 307 309 313 316 317
319-321 327 339 342 373 425 437
438 527 529 532 (1767-1812)
Steer, Jos. E. 484 (b. 1754; prob. Jos.
Jr.)
Steer, Joshua 299 313 317 319 321-323
425 484
Steer, Leah 345 346
Steer, Leah (Lupton) 338 443
Steer, Louisa 356 450
Steer, Louisa (Brown) 355
Steer, Lydia 313 319 321 338 437
Steer, Lydia A. 481
Steer, Mary 247 249 (1767, 1768)
Steer, Mary (1) 252 (1769)
Steere, Mary (2) 252 (m. Isaac Parkins
Jr. 1769)
Steer, Mary 419 484 (b. 1780; d. of
Isaac)
Steer, Mary 299 313 315-317 319 321
323 338 339 430 444 454 (1792-1849)
Steer, Mary (Rees) 481 (b. 1869?)
Steer, Nathan 484
Steer, Phebe Sr. 437 484 526 (b. 1758;
w. of Isaac)
Steer, Phebe Jr. 437 (child of Isaac
1802)
Steer, Phebe 239 271 279 283 289 291
296 299 313 317 321 339 342 355
381 385 397 419 445 527 (1780-1822)
Steer, Phebe (Hollingsworth) 268 (m.
1779)
Steer, Rachel (1) 384 408 (d. of Jas.;
m. 1788)

Walker, Abel 72 75 76 80 82 93 104 108 123 148 149 182 194 239 242 243 248-250 253-257 260 263-265 273 274 276-288 291 293 294 296-298 300-302 304 306 307 310 312 316 318 322-325 327 330-332 334 338-343 345 347 349 350 352 358 362 364-369 452 526 529-532 549 (1759-1833)

Walker, Asahel 438 (Azel?)

Walker, Azel 302 304 318 320 322 325 327

Walker, Cornelia H. 454

Walker, Dan'l 138 151 200 352 358 362 367 486

Walker, Dan'l H. 364-366 368 369

Walker, Diana 537

Walker, Edw. 93 291 293 294 300 304 307 311 312 315 316 320 322 323 325 327-333 338 339 342 343 345 347 349 350 352 353 355-357 362-364 368 376 485 486 526 530 532

Walker, Eben. 244 248 249 370 485

Walker, Eliza 300 301 307

Walker, Eliz'h (1) 485 [b. 1732; d. of Abel (1)]

Walker, Eliz'h (2) 485 [b. 1773; d. of Abel (2)]

Walker, Eliz'h 509 (m. Babb 1793)

Walker, Eliz'h 479 (m. Isaac Pidgeon Sr. about 1812)

Walker, Eliz'h 182 242 294 299-301 304 310 320 322 323 327-329 331-333 338-340 342 343 345 (1760-1812)

Walker, Hannah 327 (1803)

Walker, Hannah (1) 438 (w. of Asahel 1804)

Walker, Hannah (2) 452 (w. of Abel 1833)

Walker, Hannah (Jackson) 325 (m. (1802)

Walker, Hannah (Lupton) 368 369 (m. 1828)

Walker, Isaac (Sr.?) 110 291 293 296 299 302 307 312 315 317 322 323 327 331-333 337 339 341 342 345 371 372 438 445 485 (1781-1812)

Walker, Isaac Jr. 312 316 318 322-327 329 330 342 (1798-1812)

Walker, Isaac (1) 320 (1801)

Walker, Isaac (2) 320 (1801)

Walker, Jane 438 454

Walker, Joseph 367 439 486

Walker, Joseph L. 452

Walker, Leah 322 325-327 330

Walker, Lewis (1) 485 [b. 1739; s. of Abel (1)]

Walker, Lewis (2) 485 [b. 1776; s. of Abel (2)]

Walker, Lewis Jr. 297 304 311 315 318 320 322-325 327 329 330-334 443 (1791-1810) [Lewis (2)?]

Walker, Lewis 75 79 84 85 124 239 242 244 248-250 258 261 271 276 278-289 291 293 294 296 297 300-302 304 306 307 310 312 315 316 320 322 323 326 327 329-333 335 339 342 347 349 527 529 531 532 (1761-1815)

Walker, Lewis B. 439 486

Walker, Lydia (1) 485 [b. 1778; d. of Abel (2)]

Walker, Lydia (2) 476 486 (b. 1804; d. of Edw.)

Walker, Lydia 110 291 293 318 320 322 323 325 349 352-356 358 362-364 366 368 369 (1788-1850)

Walker, Martha (1) 485 [b. 1762; d. of Abel (2)]

Walker, Martha (2) 486 [b. 1802; d. of Abel (3)]

Walker, Martha 239 265 279 280 282-284 287 291 293 436 439 (1777-1805)

Walker, Martha (Faulkner) 318 (m. 1800)

Walker, Mary (1) 485 [b. 1730; d. of Abel (1)]

Walker, Mary (2) 342 485 486 [b. 1744; w. of Abel (2)]

Walker, Mary (3) 342 485 [b. 1767; d. of Abel (2)]

Walker, Mary (4) 439 486 [b. 1770?; w. of Abel (3)]

Walker, Mary (5) 476 (b. 1781?; w. of Edw.)

Walker, Mary (a) 320 322 327 333 338 339 345 (1801-1812)

Walker, Mary (b) 320 322 327 333 338 339 345 (1801-1812)

Walker, Mary (c) 322 327 (1801-1803)

Walker, Mary (6) 438 (w. of Isaac 1803)

Walker, Mary (7) 452 [d. of Abel (4) 1833]

Walker, Mary 239 248 250 252 253 256 259-263 265 273 283 286 291 293 296 297 300 301 304 306 311 315 316 323 325 329-332 334 343 349 350 352-358 362-365 368 370 437 527 (1763-1828)

Walker, Mary (Beeson) 244 (m. 1761)

Walker, Mary (Branson) 320 (m. 1801)

Walker, Mary (Haines) 322 486 (m. 1801)

Walker, Mary R. 486 (b. 1849; d. of Dan'l)

Walker, Mary (Roberts) 486 (b. 1808?; w. of Dan'l)

Wright, David (2) 495 (b. 1788; s. of Jas.)

Wright, David 340 343 346 348 351 352 356 357 359 360 363 365 366 368 369 427 503 512 (1781-1828)

Wright, Edw. 262 264 408 431

Wright, Elijah 541

Wright, Eliz'h (1) 487 (b. 1714; d. of Jas. Sr.)

Wright, Eliz'h (2) 487 (b. 1747; d. of Jas. Jr.)

Wright, Eliz'h (3) 416 (child of Jos. 1780)

Wright, Eliz'h (4) 459 (child of Schooly 1799)

Wright, Eliz'h (5) 461 (child of Wm. 1806)

Wright, Eliz'h (6) 490 (b. 1860?; w. of Sam'l)

Wright, Eliz'h 269 (1779)

Wright, Emeline 481

Wright, Esther 280 487 (b. 1731; w. of Thos.)

Wright, Esther 108 240-243 245-247 304 313 317 319 321 326 354 356 357 362 363 (1749-1826)

Wright, Esther B. 343 344 346 (1812, 1813)

Wright, Esther (Brown) 340 (m. 1811)

Wright, Esther (Hiatt) 280 487

Wright, Eunice (1) 487 495 (b. 1761?; w. of Wm.)

Wright, Eunice (2) 461 (child of Wm. 1806)

Wright, Eunice 275 375 377 382 396 (1781-1793)

Wright, Eunice (Branson) 269 (m. 1779)

Wright, Frances 275 416

Wright, Frederick 490

Wright, Grace L. 465

Wright, Hannah (1) 24 487 (b. 1709; d. of Jas. Sr.)

Wright, Hannah (2) 487 (b. 1758; d. of Thos. Sr.)

Wright, Hannah (3) 499 (m. Isaac Painter 1770)

Wright, Hannah (4) 465 (b. 1781?; w. of Jonathan)

Wright, Hannah (5) 459 (d. of Schooly 1799)

Wright, Hannah (6) 438 (d. of Jas. & Phebe 1804)

Wright, Hannah (7) 135 472 (b. 1845?; d. of Amos)

Wright, Hannah 519 (m. Kress 1821)

Wright, Hannah 239 251 282 293 299 303 304 313 317 319 321 326 332 335 338 340 343 344 346 348 351

357 359-361 366 369 431 460 519 526 (1769-1830)

Wright, Hannah (Dillon) 503 (m. 1780)

Wright, Hannah (Pickering) 404 (m. 1800)

Wright, Hannah (Ridgway) 280 (m. 1783)

Wright, Hester 342

Wright, Isaac (1) 487 (b. 1723; s. of Jas. Sr.)

Wright, Isaac (2) 495 (b. 1786; s. of Jas. & Phebe)

Wright, Isaac 27 118-120 240 264 408 427 497 (1749-1790)

Wright, James Sr. 15 16 24 27 31 50 54 63 69 118-120 180 240 241 244 407 487 (b. 1671)

Wright, James Jr. 27 118 120 240 407 487 541 (b. 1718)

Wright, James (3) 438 487 495 (b. 1748; s. of Jas. Jr.)

Wright, James (4) 408 (minor of Isaac 1766)

Wright, James (5) 437 (s. of John 1802)

Wright, James (6) 438 (minor of Jas. & Phebe 1804)

Wright, James 261 264 268 273 298 311 315 371 373 404 406 412 427 519 539 541 (1744-1822)

Wright, Jane 308

Wright, Jesse (1) 315 316 365 (1798-1826)

Wright, Jesse (2) 487 489 (b. 1806; s. of John)

Wright, Jesse Jr. 363 (1826)

Wright, Jesse (4) 490 (b. 1880; s. of Sam'l)

Wright, John (1) 487 (b. 1716; s. of Jas. Sr.)

Wright, John (2) 541 (child of Jas. 1765)

Wright, John (2?) 487 (b. 1764?)

Wright, John (3) 461 495 (b. 1785; s. of Wm.)

Wright, John (4) 438 (s. of Jas. 1804)

Wright, John Sr. 525 (1810)

Wright, John Jr. 525 (1810)

Wright, John 27 93 94 248 256 264 266 267 270 280 289 292 308 310 316 318 321 330 337-340 342-345 349 351 352 374 376 404 405 433 434 436 437 439 441 512 529 532 539 (1746-1817)

Wright, John D. 488 490

Wright, Jona 304 313 315 319 (1793-1800) (Jonathan?)

Wright, Jonathan (1) 487 [b. 1750; s. of Thos. (1)]

LaVergne, TN USA
04 January 2010
168753LV00004B/16/P